THE ART OF MOVIEMAKING

ing their personal lives. This newfound independence would create the seeds of a social revolution that came to full flower in the 1960s.

Likewise, until the 1950s the genuine life experience of African Americans, Mexican Americans, Asian Americans, and contemporary Native Americans was almost completely ignored in the mirror that movies held up. Individuals from these groups were seldom seen except in token or demeaning ways. Ironically, however, the very omission of ethnic minorities from serious dramatic consideration on the screen reflected the sorry state of social and political inequality in those years.

Movies have the special ability to give magnitude to the events of everyday life. Rather than distorting them, a film can give insight into the dignity of ordinary lives and human activity. In 1955, Delbert Mann directed the Paddy Chayefsky script of *Marty,* the story of a shy, unattractive butcher from Brooklyn (Ernest Borgnine), who falls in love with a very plain young woman (Betsy Blair). He comes up against negative pressures from his family and friends when he expresses his desire for her. This Academy-Award-winning film touched its audience with its simple truths. Independent film director Victor Nuñez has spent most of his career pursuing similar commonplace realities in his movies. *Ulee's Gold* (1997) is about the life of a beekeeper (Peter Fonda) living in the swamps of Northern Florida. The story concerns the character's growing realization of the importance and strength of family, but the beauty of the film is in following the daily routine of beekeeping. About movies today, Nuñez laments, "What we are losing as a culture is an awareness of the miracle of everyday life. I concentrate on what's in front of the camera, not the camera itself." This mirroring of unadorned life can shock us with its vitality.

Some movies disfigure or exaggerate reality into dark fantasies—resembling the strange mirrors found in a carnival fun house. Ironically, many of these movies become very popular and spur imitations. *Friday the 13th* parts I-VIII (1980-89), *Terminator 2: Judgment Day* (1991), *Bram Stoker's Dracula* (1992), *Seven* (1995), *Halloween H20* (1998), and *Scream 3* (2000) reflect a terrible anxiety that races through our culture, splashing violence on the screen in predictable doses. They expose a fear of an unknown and terrible future, of science gone mad, of a brutal and faceless government, of crazy street gangs unleashed, of the havoc springing from dark mystical forces, or of the weird guy that just might be living next door.

These reflections may give insight into the angst of the times. After surveying the daily news reports of violence in the media, film may simply reflect a deep truth about personal and societal fears. It is hard to truly enlarge on some aspects of the culture's sense of desperation. But as film historian Neil Gabler states, "Taken as an aggregate, our films provide a continuing negotiation between the real and the ideal, between our lives and our dreams of transcendence, between our own shortcomings and aspirations, and the shortcomings and aspirations of the country."

Some contemporary critics reject the notion that movies simply mirror the culture. They suggest that modern mass media—with the enormous power of the movie industry creating cultural trends that lead the way—goes beyond simply *reflecting* human feelings and needs held in common to *actively molding* our personal and cultural expressions. In this sense, Hollywood has tended to cement its perception of our desires, some would claim, into **ideology.** Of course, all of the media—newspapers, magazines, books, radio, television, computer networking—participate in shaping our perception and taste, but motion pictures dominate with the sheer weight of its prestige as the elite popular entertainment. Because filmmakers are popular recorders of our cultural and social discourses—the national discussion we carry on concerning sexual differences, racial attitudes, fashion fads, acceptable speech patterns, taste in music—movies have a *normative* function. Through the years, movies have created, reinforced, and sometimes confronted the attitudes by which we live. Our definitions of what is "good," "bad," "beautiful," "sexy," "funny," "exciting" are constantly shaped by the outsized images of the movie screen. It is impossible to overestimate the capacity of motion pictures to transform ordinary activity into something seemingly extraordinary. Critic V.F. Perkins writes

> *In the fiction film, reality becomes malleable but remains (or continues to seem) solid. The world is shaped by the filmmaker to reveal an order beyond chronology, in a system of time and space which is both natural and synthetic. The movie offers its reality in a sequence of privileged moments during which actions achieve a clarity and intensity seldom found in everyday life.*

Life, as seen on the silver screen, is always magnified. Immersion in this imagined world remakes our perceptions of self and others.

MOVIES AS MYTH

"The point about movies as pure popular entertainment, directed by studio hacks, and starring stars playing the same roles over and over, is that they are unselfconscious, like primitive religious art. It is there, in genre films, and not in the artistic masterpieces, that cinema comes closest to myth."

Movie critic Ian Buruma

Motion pictures have become a powerful means for creating and passing on the myths of our modern culture. The meaning of **myth** is popularly misunderstood. Put simply, myths are the stories that a given society wants to hear and pass on about itself. Contrary to being an untruth, myths tap into basic cultural belief systems that are usually well understood and agreed upon at a deep level by that community. Often these assumptions are not articulated by the culture directly or literally. To do so would diminish their emotional force and mystery. Movies are like the parables of old, but with instant and massive impact. They explain culturally accepted values and practices in terms and with images that are easily understood by large numbers of people. The standard movie genres—horror, romantic comedy, science fiction, gangster, and many more—are cultural masks for our conflicts, consisting of adaptable sets of themes, actions, settings, and characters that play out the myths of our society.

The classic Hollywood image of the cowboy, for instance, is almost impossible to shake from one's mind when picturing the West in the latter part of the 1800s. The portrait may not been historically accurate, but generations of Americans grew up with this portrayal as their only vivid knowledge of that period. Contrary to firsthand accounts that described a land of brutal weather, endless boredom on horseback, and the struggle simply to survive, several generations of Western movies created a romantic and relatively comfortable frontier, peopled with dashing men continually on the dramatic verge of a shoot-out. The singular bravery, rugged individualism, and unrestrained personal freedom of men in these movies became the idealized cultural virtues. They resonated with twentieth-century American men caught up in the daily grind of urban life. Filmmakers (and cigarette companies) instinctually sensed this and exploited the imagery.

People want heroic fantasies. *Young Guns* confidently ride the West; *Rambo* fights our wars in the Middle and Far East; *Robo Cop* and *Batman* guard the city; *The Terminator* gives us an indomitable father no kid ever had, *Braveheart* inspires our imaginary heritage. *Superman* may be from Krypton, but he is surely an All-American guy. The bigger-than-life qualities of these characters, although outrageous on the surface, still reverberate with a great number of people. Even films about historical characters, such as *The Song of Bernadette* (1943), *Lawrence of Arabia* (1962), *A Man for All Seasons* (1966), *Butch Cassidy and the Sundance Kid* (1969), *Gandhi* (1982), *Elizabeth* (1998),and *Gladiator* (2000) **(1–4)**, when well told on the screen, appeal more by way of their emotional impact than their historical veracity. As film critic Parker Tyler points out, ". . . in short, *desires* may have the same power over the mind and behavior, indeed a much greater power, than *facts.*"

On the lighter side, motion pictures bring to life playful desires and sensuous dreams. Movies as different as *Rocky* (1976) and *Strictly Ballroom* (1992) show us the eternal hope of rising out of obscurity into a day in the sun. Just as *Always* (1989), *Ghost* (1990), and *To Gillian on Her 37th Birthday* (1996) give their audience solace with telling stories of earth-accessible spiritual immortality, so too did the light-hearted *Topper* (1937). Even the unrealistic portrait of a Hollywood hooker in *Pretty Woman* (1990) easily replaced the tough truths of real life on the streets with the whimsy of a girl suddenly swept up into a world of genuine male affection and fan-

1–4 *Gladiator* Movies have always had a way of giving us **outsized icons.** For a recent incarnation of a mythical superman, movie producers reincarnated a classic hero often used in old Hollywood films—the gladiator. With the odds stacked heavily against him, the once-supreme Roman general Maximus (Russell Crowe), after fortune turns against him, is sold into slavery before being thrust into the colliseum in Rome to fight for his life, to seek revenge, and to provide entertainment for the demented emperor Commodus, the boisterous arena spectators, and—well—us. In *Gladiator* (2000), director Ridley Scott triggered a fundamental audience desire to identify with the bruised honor and extravagant bravery of a hero at work.   (Dream-Works Pictures)

1–5 *Runaway Bride*   The world in movies can be a fairyland of romantic escape. For two hours, we can luxuriate in watching Julia Roberts and Richard Gere (and perhaps even merge with their screen characters) as they accidentally discover each other, then struggle with some annoying consequences, and finally realize what we, the audience, knew all along—they are perfect together. The **cherished myths** of movies such as those in *Runaway Bride* (1999) take on a reality of their own, so that the stars playing the parts seem indeed divine.   (Touchstone Pictures)

tastic material luxury. These films, and thousands like them, give graphic representation to those things for which we collectively yearn **(1–5).** Part of the joy in watching these films is the agreement we feel with the rest of the audience in our shared fantasies. Diane Keaton remarks of her childhood, "I remember that at the end of movies I liked—movies with happy endings—it thrilled me to think that life was reduced to a fixed, happy moment in time."

In creating the first *Star Wars* series, George Lucas sought out Joseph Campbell, the renowned scholar of mythology, for counsel in finding stories with deeply rooted universal themes. As exceptional as the production values are in those first three films, it is the strong mythical resonance of the stories that distinguish them from the pack of lesser science fantasy films. The popularity of these movies (the first *Star Wars* movie, 1977, is one of the five top grossing films of all time) should tell us that they were not just wild adventures in outer space loaded with great special effects, but something much weightier—a morality play dealing with the nature of loyalty and the search for the roots of one's identity. After viewing the film, many people left the theater sensing that they had witnessed something more than a simple space adventure. Parker Tyler notes, "The glamour actors and actresses of the movie realm are fulfilling an ancient need, unsatisfied by popular religions of contemporary times." The major characters in the film have taken on mythic significance, to the point that even the actors playing them shared in the glory. For a generation, Alec Guinness was idealized as a figure who embodied the virtues of noble warrior and gentle father. With the surprisingly successful twentieth anniversary re-release of the *Star Wars* trilogy in 1997 and the new series beginning with *Star Wars: Episode I-The Phantom Menace* (1999), it is clear that the force of the story is still strongly felt. Of course, claiming the status of mythic gravity in a film and delivering it are not the same. Many critics felt that the latest Lucas entry pushed too hard for the mythic meanings but, despite the media hype, the film had neither the requisite story substance nor depth to reverberate powerfully with moviegoers.

A TEAM ACT

"Nobody makes a film alone, not even the madness."

Director Nicholas Ray
(*Rebel Without a Cause*, 1955)

Moviemaking is a most eclectic art form, the ultimate team effort. Whatever machinations plague the business, the movie industry has always drawn to it the leading crafts-people, technicians, and artists from around the world, its films displaying the spectrum of allied arts. Throughout the twentieth century, artists in every medium traveled to the centers of film production—writers from New York City, actors from Dublin, dancers from Moscow, musicians from Detroit, art directors from Berlin, and hairdressers from San Francisco, Rome, or Omaha. If a costume designer, cinematographer, sound engineer, editor, or animator is at the top of his or her field, the lure of the movie lot is almost irresistible. How could it be otherwise? The motion picture industry offers the most money, the highest exposure, and that special celluloid magic. As far back as the 1920s, many of the most famous European directors, actors, and technicians immigrated to Hollywood to contribute their artistic expression to the film practices of this growing industry. Since then, artists with superior talent have joined with technical specialists to create communities of exceptional artistic know-how in every film capital—most especially, Hollywood.

The successful completion of a movie is a miracle of sorts. The process demands that a large number of independently artistic people come together with a single goal—the successful rendition of an idea to film, finished within a restricted time frame and budget **(1–6).** The same high level of cooperation is expected in every project, no matter how critically weak the movie may finally turn out to be. Not untypical of big budget features today, the credits that ran after *Volcano* (1997) listed 903 men, women, and organizations. Each was a top player in his or her respective field of expertise; many more than that worked on the project who were not named in the credits. Certainly the glamour is a big part of the initial lure, but the job of making movies soon focuses on the "can do" aspects of the work. And during the various phases of production, the special collaborative aspects of the industry demand an unusually high degree of focused communal purpose. In the clamor for a headline, a power player in the production may attempt to claim the glory for its success. When a movie finally arrives on the screen, however, no one person can legitimately claim to be the sole reason for its success.

In the simple swamp drama previously described, an array of arts come together

1–6 *Proof* The process of movie making calls on the talents of varied and expert crafts people, and therefore has always been seen as a **highly collaborative** art form. Each shot in a film demands the careful attention of the specialists on the set. The participation of every member of the film team is essential, regardless of the size of the budget or the film's national origin. In her debut film *Proof* (1991), Australian director Jocelyn Moorehouse engages her crew in the intricacies of a shot.   (Fine Line)

to form a seamless whole. A *writer* conceives of the idea and writes the script. Effective presentation of the cinematography depends on the combined talents of the *director* and the *director of photography.* The swamp and house are created on a sound stage, calling on the construction expertise and collaboration of the *production designer,* the *set decorator, art director, atmospheric effects specialist, carpenters,* and others. The *actor* is helped by the *hair stylist, costume designer, makeup artist,* and the *director.* A *composer, music editor, Foley artists,* and *recording engineers* work on the sound track. *Lab technicians, film editors,* and their *assistants* help finish it off. The *producers* are there from the beginning to the end. Who, then, can take credit for the film? Traditionally, the director has first claim. But the question cannot be fully answered without weighing the value of every contribution, and in the end, moviemaking is clearly a collective venture.

BUT IS IT ART?

"The old-time studio bosses followed their hunches. Today, these green-light decisions are very much a question of committees, focus groups, and rule by consensus. Not exactly a recipe for art."

Peter Bart, editor-in-chief of *Variety*

The Hollywood movie has certainly been roundly castigated by its detractors (and even some of its friends) through the years. The steady stream of motion pictures over the past 100 years has made these films, and the resulting culture, a ready target for wholesale critical abuse. Insiders, outsiders, reviewers, cultural commentators, self-appointed moral defenders, and just about everyone else have expressed their frustration when they feel that a motion picture has not measured up to their standards. And having been disappointed so often, many of us have developed a love/hate relationship with movies. Indeed, movie critic David Denby complains, "In so many Hollywood movies nothing much is at stake—no particular meaning, no powerfully articulated temper, no arrogantly singular sense of style, no fully achieved narrative."

Traditionally, the legitimacy of an art form is often measured by its acceptance in the respected educational institutions of the society. In this century the academic community was unhurried in acknowledging motion pictures as a legitimate subject for study in higher education. It was not until 1929 that the University of Southern California initiated a single course in film studies. Even by the 1960s, film studies had to fight to gain credibility on most college campuses. Presently, courses in the theory, history, aesthetics, and production techniques of cinema continue to find their way into the curricula of higher education, despite some resistance. It is true, however, that sophisticated film production classes are very expensive to start up and maintain, and relatively few universities have anything close to state-of-the-art facilities.

In today's pop culture, films are not judged purely on artistic merit. The media would rather report on the relative box office revenue figures of the latest smash release, or the problems between a director and actor on a shoot, or whether a poll of people leaving the theater thought that the ending of a hot romantic film made them feel upbeat and would they recommend the movie to a friend. The interest that a film generates is somehow determined by such incidental information. For a great number of people, such movie-hype holds more weight than what is actually presented on the screen. Because of the massive attention that movie promotion spawns, the central considerations of *art* in this grand medium have been slow to be isolated and appreciated.

The struggle of the film artist working in the Hollywood mainstream is legendary. In the 1930s, David O. Selznick, then a producer at Paramount, proclaimed in a memo questioning the financing of a film by the great Russian director Sergei Eisenstein, "The advancement of the art of cinema is not the business of this organization." Selznick was really speaking for almost every major studio power broker, then and now. Similar sentiments litter the folklore of "the movie industry." Despite the artistic genius of men like Irving Thalberg, a gifted MGM producer in the 1930s, the men who owned the movie studios were too busy overseeing the production of a film to pursue esoteric definitions of "cinema." No matter how much motion pictures were admired by the general public, they struggled to gain the level of respectability that other art forms came by traditionally. The sentiments of a few old studio bosses are even more heartily echoed in statements by the captains of the modern corporate movie world. When he was president of Paramount Pictures, Michael Eisner, now chairman of the Walt Disney Company, once wrote, "We have no obligation to make history, we have no obligation to make art, we have no obligation to make a statement. To make money is our only obligation." In response, it is little wonder that seriously concerned critics might say, "If you who create motion pictures do not seek artistic respect, why should we give it?"

Can movies stand with other traditionally recognized art forms **(1–7)**? The artist in every medium selects and organizes ideas and their material expression for purposes of beauty, insight, and pleasure. In this respect, the goal of film is no different. A film director, and those people heading the creative departments of a film pro-

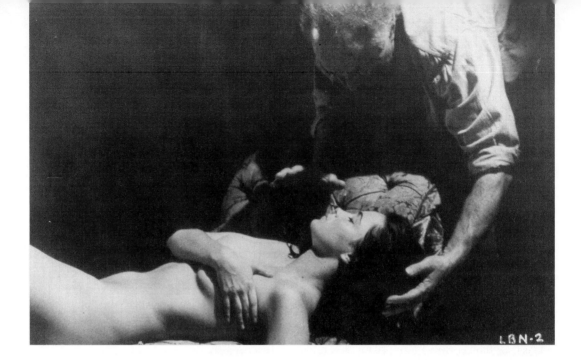

1–7 *La Belle Noiseuse* The dramatic presentation of other art forms—music, painting, dance—is often the content of movies. In Jacques Rivette's *La Belle Noiseuse* (1990), the story gradually explores a painter's delicate and growing obsession for his model, and her subtle participation in the relationship. The pace of the film taxes the viewer, demanding an almost similar fixation, as it incrementally explores the meticulous choices the painter considers in creating art with a woman he adores. What might be a rich subject for literature can become a challenge for a movie audience. However, for many viewers, their patience is rewarded, especially in this film, with a deeper understanding and enjoyment of an artist's sensibilities. (MK2 Productions)

duction, faces hundreds of choices, great and small, each day. Specific methods and principles have evolved in the art of moviemaking that govern their creative choices. Which color filter should be used and to what effect? Where and why are the cameras to be positioned in relation to the action? How long should a particular shot last? Will one more *take* bring out just the desired emotional weight in a scene? Which personal values are to be emphasized in the lead character? Ideally, after weighing the consequences of countless decisions, the movie will truly reflect the taste, abilities, and moral position of the director and other important artists working on the production.

Can movies aspire to high art, or because of commercial considerations, do they inherently pander to current popular taste? Some of the harshest critics are themselves filmmakers. Director F. Gary Gray (*The Negotiator*, 1998) comments, "Most action films that are released barely scrape the surface of human emotions besides thrills." But with the flood of films constantly pouring into theaters, video stores, and cable networks, what criteria can be used to pick through it all? Media critic Gene Youngblood, in his book *Expanded Cinema*, attempts to lay some ground rules for the definition of the art of film.

Art explains; entertainment exploits. . . . Entertainment gives us what we want; Art gives us what we don't know we want. To confront a work of art is to confront oneself—but aspects of oneself previously unrecognized. To a healthy mind, anything that is art is also immensely entertaining.

Norman Mailer, the chronicler of the American temperament and sometime filmmaker, echoes this when he writes, "Art serves us best precisely at that point where it can shift our sense of what is possible, when we now know more than we knew before, when we have—by some manner of leap—encountered the truth." This statement may sound a bit high-minded or even inapplicable when referring to movies, but on closer inspection, isn't this what distinguishes a memorable and affecting motion picture from one that is forgotten on the way home from the theater? Good movies force us not only to feel but to *think*. Sergei Eisenstein long ago wrote, "The film's job is to make the audience 'help itself,' not to 'entertain' it. To grip, not to amuse." A central role for film, or any art, is to surprise us by shaking up our familiar habits of perceptions, making us alive to the very process of seeing and knowing. The act of watching a film with awareness becomes a dimension of the aesthetic experience to be deeply enjoyed.

An obvious hazard for the filmmaker is the seemingly shallow thematic demands of the mass film audience. A persuasive tradition in mainstream Hollywood chides filmmakers to produce movies that neither challenge nor upset our basic cultural belief systems. The aesthetic theoretician Rudolf Arnheim long ago noted that the "preferences of the general public sweep everything before them. Some work of good quality can be smuggled in, but it does not compensate for the more fundamental defeats of film art." Because motion pictures, for hard financial reasons, strive to be so very popular, filmmakers with genuinely artistic intentions are always at high risk. The inherent economic pressures of moviemaking continually impose themselves on the choices of the person putting together his or her vision on film.

It is commonly accepted that in most movies that strive for large audiences, art usually bends to commerce. This can take shape in odd ways. *The Godfather III* (1990) went through twenty writers before a script was settled upon. The high-budget comedy *The Flintstones* (1994) was in development for six years, with innumerable script treatments and drafts submitted by thirty-five writers. The fear of not "getting it right" pushes studios to extremes. This is not the traditional image of a daring artist risking everything for a personal vision.

This is not to say that motion picture producers devise films that only soothe. Consider the many variations of stories telling of psycho killers, one category being "slasher" movies. It is significant that large audiences are attracted to movies whose whole intention is to entertain with the shock of extremely graphic violence. In the well-tested and familiar formula of the *Halloween* series (1978-1988), the filmmakers present a twisted world of pounding violence at every turn. But the clichés of sequels do not hold the promise of much real surprise, even when they exploit the prevailing fear of "Other" that seems to permeate the vulnerable public psyche. These dark films are outrageous, but predictably safe, cartoons.

On this point, it is interesting to note that when *Henry, Portrait of a Serial Killer* (1989), a story that gave genuine insight into the terrifying world of a psychopath, came out a few years ago, it could not find an audience until a few critics discovered it and word-of-mouth earned it "cult" status. The director, John McNaughton, showed relatively little explicit violence (by standards of the genre) to convey the terror of its story, relying on the realistic detailing of daily life in the grimy world of a psychopath. The film refused to treat violence as mere entertainment, instead uncompromisingly plunging into the heart of the matter. The film had the execution and integrity of great art, despite its cruel subject.

At its best, a movie should enliven the viewer to the splendid and unique ways that it tells its story. Despite the real limitations imposed on the artist working in film, the history of cinema is filled with great achievements that, by any measurement, must be considered high art. The French writer-philosopher Andre Gide may have answered the seeming dilemma when he wisely observed, "Art is born in restraint and dies in freedom." Movies have built-in financial pressures that can be thought of as restraints, and the best of filmmakers have used their struggle to arrive at their art.

BACKGROUND: THE OLD HOLLYWOOD

"Hollywood is in the middle of a barbarically provincial non-city, three thousand miles from our cultural capital."

**New York-based critic Dwight Mac Donald
writing in the 1930s**

The environment in which American movies are made has always provoked controversy. At the center of this controversy lies the richly complex history of the studio system in Hollywood. As always, the past informs the present. Whereas the early style and technique of movies were born long ago in France, England, and the Eastern seaboard of the United States, these filmic conventions were more fully developed and were firmly established in barnlike buildings put up on cheap real estate surrounding Los Angeles—in musty editing rooms, in the chemistry of film processing labs, and later in the art deco executive offices and frantic PR departments at studio headquarters. All manner of people drifted West— restless dreamers, hard-nosed businessmen, flamboyant showmen, technical wizards, and men and women with genuine artistic talent and inspiration.

One can be easily distracted when trying to find the essential elements of that past, of why and how Hollywood took shape in the odd ways that it did. Historians of American film must wend their way through an array of movieland fact and fiction, often to realize that the two are often indistinguishable. Early on, Hollywood found that the movies reflected the strange mix of the fantasy, glamour, and toughness of its town, and a huge audience out there was willing to pay to watch it. What goes on today in the movie business is built upon long practice and tradition.

The roots of motion pictures are clear. The nineteenth century was the Age of Invention and the industrial world was full of ingenious people in small laboratories creating new ways to run things mechanically and electrically. There are many excellent film texts that tell the detailed history of the determination to take the already discovered technique of still photography and make it move. Unlike the older arts, the evolution of movies as we have come to know them had to wait for the invention of two machines—the *motion picture camera* to take the pictures and the *projector* to show them. Simultaneously in the 1890s, inventors in France, United States, England, and Germany worked fervently to mechanically produce the illusion of motion.

In the United States, Thomas Edison applied for motion picture camera patents in 1891; with his wizard assistant, William Dickson, he opened the first movie studio—the *Black Maria*—in New Jersey in 1893. The first theatrical projection on a screen to a paying audience was in the basement of the Grand Cafe in Paris on December 28, 1895, by the French inventors and promoters Auguste and Louis Lumiere. The ten short films shown were simple visual recordings of common events—a railroad train arriving at a station, for example—but to those who had never seen motion reproduced, the experience was phenomenal. No one at the time could have ever imagined the colossus that would take shape in the next 100 years, but it can be argued that the movie business was started that night.

The first twenty years of filmmaking was a time of learning—not only how to *use* the camera, lights, and actors but for discovering what its *content* should be. Early on, the Frenchman Georges Melies made scores of short films with visual illusions, such as his famous *A Trip to the Moon* (1902), which immediately stretched the cinematic limits of the new medium. He found that people and objects could be made to suddenly appear and disappear on the screen with clever shooting and simple editing. American director Edwin S. Porter, with his earthbound tales of action, such as *The Great Train Robbery* (1903), showed that a unique feature of movies was the easy ability to manipulate the viewer's sense of time and space through editing, camera placement, and camera movement. By using the film's story to tie together contrasting scenes of separate actions, the audience would see *simultaneous action*, simply because one shot (bandits on horseback crossing a stream) cut to the next (the daughter of a telegraph operator untying him at the station). Porter trusted that the viewer would imagine separately filmed and edited actions as happening at the same time. Informally, early filmmakers learned these and a hundred storytelling techniques like them from each other. Every movie was (and still is) a potential textbook of photographic style, production design, editing technique, and performance strategies.

D.W. Griffith is recognized universally as the greatest and most serious filmmaker of his day. After having learned how movies worked by directing hundreds of short narratives, Griffith propelled the art of storytelling on the screen with his advanced camera and editing techniques. His hugely successful *The Birth of a Nation* (1915) could be called the first American blockbuster movie. Ironically, while it is still considered a landmark for the power of its imagery, uncanny pace, and the sheer size of its vision, the film's popularity at the time rested not only on the strength of its visual storytelling, but on the flagrant racism that was rampant at the time. Griffith's fanciful and biased interpretation of race history in America met with both frenzied enthusiasm and strong protest. He is said to have been shocked by the negative response, and followed it with *Intolerance* (1916), a spectacularly staged epic divided into four stories, which attempted to attack those people throughout history who imposed their ethical system on others. His contributions to the establishment of film as a serious medium of artistic expression are undeniable.

By 1915, Charlie Chaplin was a household name, and Mary Pickford was "America's Sweetheart." The readiness of the growing mass culture to choose its icons was astonishing. Chaplin, in his wonderful autobiography, tells of discovering the full impact of what the newly created label "movie star" meant, when in 1916 he traveled by train from Los Angeles to New York City and was greeted in the cities and towns by thousands of enamored fans.

I wanted to enjoy it all without reservation but I kept thinking that the world had gone crazy! If a few slapstick comedies could arouse such excitement, was not something bogus about all celebrity?

He hardly had time to ponder the question, for he arrived in New York City to ticker-tape parades and a new, unheard of $670,000 a year contract. Chaplin and a host of others soon to follow would establish a new elite social class in the American culture, with rules of entry as elusive as its benefits were attractive. Hollywood was quickly becoming a dazzling fulfillment of the American dream, the place where the rapid rise to fame and wealth was given marquee billing.

The Studios

"The heavenly gates swung open, and American motion pictures, so the chroniclers have universally declared, entered the golden age. Hollywood took center stage in the culture and consciousness of the United States, making movies with a power and élan never known before or seen again."

Film historian Robert Sklar

In the early years of the twentieth century, East Coast entrepreneurs began to promote movies by way of the storefront nickelodeons in the nation's increasingly crowded cities and awakening rural towns. These men—many newly arrived and struggling merchants from Eastern Europe—had streetwise instincts, accurately sensing how the emerging middle class wanted to spend their newfound leisure time and money. They soon started to produce their own short film programs for exhibition. Many small movie companies then headed West to southern California to avoid legal entanglements with the Motion Picture Patents Company (a conglomerate spearheaded by Thomas Edison), as well as to find an inexpensive light source to shoot movies. The sunshine was free.

With World War I over, by 1920 the economy was on the upswing, the middle class was discovering new freedoms in style and taste, and movie mania had swept the country. Small movie halls of the previous decade were replaced by grand theaters. Their glittering marquees invited patrons into luxurious lobbies displaying sweeping staircases and crystal chandeliers and into powder rooms lined with marble and mirrors before they entered the large, thickly carpeted auditoriums toned by recessed lighting and tiered with multiple balconies in front of movie screens hidden by rich velvet curtains. Smartly uniformed ushers with flashlights politely showed patrons to their thickly cushioned seats **(1–8).**

But what the industry needed most was a ready supply of superior product—a consistent parade of exciting movies that would bring audiences back week after week. As the rush for a greater quantity of movies escalated, however, their quality became more inconsistent. When costs of production rose throughout the 1920s and into the 1930s, the business eventually realized the need for the concentration and vertical integration of its resources. Tightly-run studio systems, staffed by the best talent in their evolving arts and crafts, were the key. Hollywood consolidated into

1–8 *Hollywood Revue* Generating **wide public attention** for the release of a major film by any outrageous means has long been the way Hollywood does the movie business. Live stage shows and musical entertainment preceding movies in the best theaters of major cites were common. When the 1928 film extravaganza *Hollywood Revue* (a film nominated for an Academy Award the following year) opened at the Astor Theater in New York City, MGM spent thousands on spectacular lighted signage, dangerously accented with live dancers. (Academy of Motion Picture Art and Sciences)

eight studios—five major, three minor. Sketched quickly here, each studio had its distinguishing operation, style, and personalities.

MGM. With "more stars than there are in the heavens," MGM was the classiest studio of the "golden era," having a host of famous directors and actors under contract, including George Cukor, King Vidor, Clark Gable, Spencer Tracy, Greta Garbo, James Stewart, Joan Crawford, Jean Harlow, Mickey Rooney, and Judy Garland. Well known for the glamour of its expensive productions, especially its musicals, MGM set a standard for the polish of its cinematography technique and set design. The studio was headed by the classically powerful and eccentric Louis B. Mayer, but was guided by the spirit of its creative producer, Irving Thalberg, until his untimely death in 1936.

1–9 Paramount Gate   The movie studio systems patterned themselves on the **business model** in the industrial world, most tellingly on the contemporary production facilities of the automobile companies. Studio lots resembled assembly line factories beyond their elaborate facades, but with a difference. The product was movies. For many young men and women aspiring to careers in movies, the ramparts enclosing Paramount Studios were a dividing line between fame and obscurity. The studios during their Golden Era were guarded fiefdoms, controlled by a select group of men who shaped the entertainment and cultural tastes of the nation. To be invited through the Bronson Gate into this realm of influence was a privilege reserved for the chosen few.   (Academy of Motion Picture Arts and Sciences)

Paramount.   This studio, founded by Adolph Zukor and controlled by him for the first forty years, benefited from a strong influx of European talent, especially as the specter of fascism spread through Germany in the 1930s. Films took on a continental look—dimly lit sets suggesting faintly decadent elegance—under the directorship of Ernest Lubitsch, Josef von Sternberg, Rouben Mamoulian, and the art direction of Hans Drier. But American director Cecil B. DeMille was the star director of Paramount's lavish movie spectacles, such as *The Sign of the Cross* (1932). The company had a varied group of actors under contract, including Marlene Dietrich, Fredric March, Cary Grant, Carole Lombard, Bing Crosby, Gary Cooper, the Marx Brothers, W.C. Fields, and Mae West **(1–9)**.

20th Century-Fox.   Darryl F. Zanuck headed up the production of this studio's solid output of films. Its conservative thematic range served the studio well, relying on the superior direction of John Ford and Henry King, and the fantastic box office appeal of child star Shirley Temple during the 1930s. The stability of the studio system encouraged teamwork within technical departments, and the special effects department at Fox was the industry leader. Henry Fonda, Tyrone Power, Loretta Young, Charles Boyer, and Don Ameche were among its stars under contract.

Warner Bros.   Like many studio heads, Jack Warner ("I don't want it good, I want it Tuesday") ran his company with an iron fist and an acute sense of what moviegoers wanted to see. The studio turned out a variety of films, but many reflected a no-nonsense urban toughness characteristic of the spirit of the times. The gritty look and quick pacing of films about gangsters and city newspaper staffs was partly due to the actual spare budgets of the productions. The studio had a solid base of polished actors under contract, including Humphrey Bogart, James Cagney, Edward G. Robinson, Barbara Stanwyck, Pat O'Brien, and Bette Davis.

RKO.   This studio struggled in competition with the larger ones, and although it owned a chain of theaters, the company was always on the verge of insolvency. But RKO was able to produce a series of outstanding films because of the relative freedom it allowed its talent. Fred Astaire and Ginger Rogers set the standard for dance musicals in movies like *Top Hat* (1935), and Katharine Hepburn was its most versatile star. Ironically, movies from this troubled studio turned out to be time-honored classics in every popular genre—the monster classic (*King Kong*, 1933), the dramatic historical (*Mary of Scotland*, 1936), and the "screwball" comedy (*Bringing Up Baby*, 1938). In 1941, RKO daringly produced the most controversial movie of the era, Orson Welles's *Citizen Kane*, a masterful film whose reputation continues to fascinate movie lovers.

Universal.   Because it didn't own an impressive chain of first-run theaters, Universal scrambled to gain attention by specializing in stylishly shocking horror films. The studio survived by knowing the market for low budget movies that dwelled in the fantastic. English director James Whale, Karl Freund, the German-trained cameraman who became an occasional director, Edgar G. lmer, Tod Browning, and others brought their vision to these now classic movies: *Dracula* (1931), *Frankenstein* (1931), *The Mummy* (1932), *The Invisible Man* (1933), *Black Cat* (1934), and *The Wolfman* (1941). Universal did produce lighter fare, most notably the musical comedies of Deanna Durbin and the slapstick movies of Abbott and Costello.

Columbia.   Although every studio had top-heavy organizational control, one man, Harry Cohn, dominated this low-budget production company with a classic Hollywood mixture of unsavory personal manipulation and crafty film sense. Throughout the era, Columbia made a steady diet of **B movies** (that is, films that filled the second spot in the common theater booking practice of programming double features, which were rented for a flat rate rather than on a percentage basis). Although the studio had few major stars and first-rate directors under contract, Cohn managed to temporarily hire talent from other studios. Harry Cohn and his Columbia Studios, with their uncanny insight into popular American taste, were able to patch together a number of blue ribbon hits by matching top quality directors such as Frank Capra, George Cukor, and Howard Hawks with quality stories such as *Lost Horizon* (1937), *Holiday* (1938), and *His Girl Friday* (1940), and contract actors Jean Arthur, Barbara Stanwyck, and Rita Hayworth.

United Artists.   Not actually a studio, this company distributed and exhibited films for a string of first-class independent producers, including David O. Selznick, Hal Roach, and Samuel Goldwyn. The company had been founded and owned in partnership by Charlie Chaplin, D.W. Griffith, Douglas Fairbanks, and Mary Pickford to circumvent the bureaucratic systems of traditional studios. The company is noted for having released some outstanding original work, including Howard Hawk's *Scarface* (1932), Charlie Chaplin's *City Lights* (1931) and *Modern Times* (1936), and William Wyler's *Wuthering Heights* (1939).

The names of these studios are central in the legendary history of Hollywood. Over the years, each has been transformed several times, many becoming the core entities of worldwide entertainment conglomerates. The experience gained from years of controlling movie production has benefited them in even larger arenas of worldwide communication enterprises.

The Typical Structure of a Studio

"The American cinema is a classical art, so why not then admire in it what is most admirable—i.e., not only the talent of this or that filmmaker, but the genius of the system."

Andre Bazin, French film critic

Thomas Schatz borrowed Bazin's phrase to title his book *The Genius of the System*, an exhaustive study of several Hollywood studios (Universal, MGM, Warner Bros., and Selznick International Pictures) during the heyday of the 1920s and 1930s. Chronicling the day-to-day conditions under which movies were made, the book makes clear that by the middle of this period the movie studios had begun to settle into a means of production that was thoughtfully established, efficiently uniform, and generally successful.

A truism in physics: **the structure determines the function.** That is, to understand fully how something *works*, one must first know its *configuration*, the relationship of its parts in forming the whole. Simply put, the internal design of something will predict how it performs. This is especially applicable to the classic motion picture studio. Understanding the unique structure of the studio system as it evolved is the key to comprehending the nature and quality of the movies it produced.

At the height of its Golden Era—from the mid-1920s into the 1940s—each major Hollywood studio not only produced about one film per week, but controlled the distribution and exhibition of the movie. To achieve this steady output, the studios became finely tuned creative film factories, simple in concept and design, but made hugely complex by the Machiavellian intrigue that often ruled life on the movie lots. On the one hand, the studios were the ultimate and best example of the capitalist system at work: each unit of production contributing and submerging itself to make a single thing of quality—the motion picture. At the same time, in the opinion of some uncharitable observers, a strenuous power game was continually and aggressively played out among self-worshipping studio heads, ambitious producers, insecure actors, increasingly aggressive unions, upstart agents, and clever movie accountants and lawyers.

For instance, today we delight in looking back at those tightly scripted, fast-paced Warner Bros. features of the 1930s about gangsters caught between the grim determinism of city life and their personal fatalistic visions. In the 1940s these films would evolve into a style designated **film noir,** shadowy stories filled with the tension of desperate people willing to do almost anything to survive. The themes are still broadly imitated by contemporary filmmakers. Warner Bros. films of this kind were notoriously low budget, and production of these films was helped partly because the methodology for making movies could be repeated. The same sets, costumes, and lighting arrangements were used time after time. The same production people worked on film after film made at the studio, hence the movies tended to have a similar look and feel. At many studios, what we sometimes now take to be brilliant artistic choices by a director may simply have been decisions necessitated by the economics and customs of the studio. In other words, the enticing world that big city newspaper dramas of Warner Bros. presented may have come into being simply because of the particular actors and technical staff under contract, the readily available production materials, and the prevailing aesthetic of that particular studio. The special style of these movies was no accident.

Many have condemned the studio system as autocratic and stifling. Certainly there were legendary abuses of power, and many lives were vindictively ruined for reasons now forgotten. The centralized hierarchy of the studios controlled the careers of everyone who worked for them. A relatively small handful of men at the top—all white males—defined a nation's cultural taste by determining what would and would not be seen on the movie screens of American towns and cities. In this sense, the films had many built-in cultural biases. But there were also many benefits to the system. Its efficiency cannot be denied. The closed production line methods meant that a score of films might be at various stages of production at any one time, each being attended to by extremely talented artisans trained in getting the job done on time. Somehow a great many movies produced under the old studio system in this era were of superior quality.

Perhaps the most lasting heritage left by the studio system is the bottom line "can do" mentality that still permeates the movie industry. Regardless of the disparate mix of creative artists and hardheaded businesspeople, the traditions of Hollywood film have always demanded that accommodations be made for both aesthetic values and box office numbers. The old Hollywood system, with its interweave of producers, lawyers, actors, accountants, agents, writers and the rest, laid the foundation for the movie industry that flourishes today. The original design of the industry established "a way of doing things," and although much has changed in terms of technology and financing, the basic structure of moviemaking—the phases of production, distribution, and exhibition—have stayed remarkably constant.

MOVIEMAKING IN THE 1930s

The assembly line process of moviemaking during the old studio system is illustrated here. Imagine this as an overly simplified floor plan of a large studio - Warner Bros. Because the professional staff was permanently employed by the studio, the flow of activity could be rather easily managed and controlled. The studio system made the difference. To a great extent, the daily working conditions and routine of a particular studio foretold it.

Take, for example, the process of a typical movie production as it moved through the old Warner Bros. studio. Once a story idea was introduced, the movie progressed through a series of incremental steps through production and toward theatrical release. If the project was a "gangster" film, the idea might be generated by Hal B. Wallis, Warner's Production Chief in the mid-1930s. During this **pre-production** phase, he would give the idea to the salaried team of writers, headed by Robert Lord, to be developed into a script. After it was written, a budget could be estimated dependent upon the production values, quality and size of the cast, and the length of the shooting schedule. The script would also have to be approved by the Production Code Administration, a censoring board established by pressure groups, especially the Catholic Church, and headed by Joe Breen. This private organization set strict boundaries for what the moviegoing

1-10   *The Old Studio System*

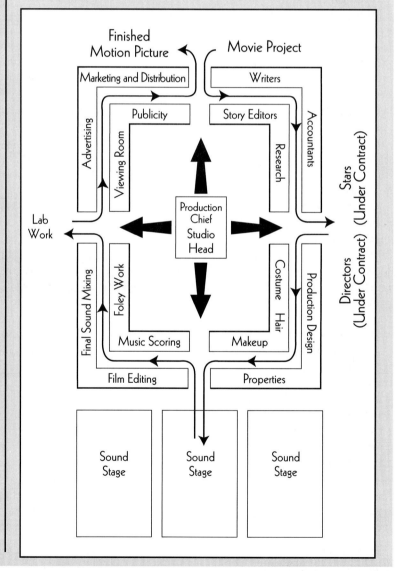

continued ▶

public could see and hear, especially in the 1930s and 1940s. In the meantime, Jack Warner, the ever-vigilant head of the studio, would oversee the movie project with varying interest and intensity, making sure that money was not being wasted. A director under contract, perhaps Ray Enright because of his predictable competency or an upgrade to Michael Curtiz for his visual style, was then assigned along with a cast that might include contract actors James Cagney, Barbara Stanwyck, Paul Muni, or Edward G. Robinson. The project then moved along to Max Parker or Anton Grot, art directors gifted in creating a hard urban look in the sets. The wardrobe and makeup departments could then get involved, performing their duties on yet another film on this familiar Warner story theme.

The **principal photography** phase would start when the film went to the backlot for shooting scenes on the outdoor "New York" sets. The interiors of the film were shot on the massive sound stages of the studio. After forty or so days of shooting, with the expertise of camera crews

headed by Sol Polito or Ernest Haller and other production technicians, the film was "in the can."

Now in the **postproduction** phase, the project moved into the editing rooms to be pieced together by an experienced team of editors. Music, perhaps by Max Steiner, and sound enhancement by the sound effects unit would be worked into the film, again by regularly employed staff at the studio. Wallis, Jack Warner, the film director, and the upper echelons at the studio would screen the completed movie, reserving the right to reshoot or reedit the work at any time. The West Coast production team, however, would always look to the East Coast office, which controlled financing and marketing, for final approval— brother Harry Warner being the ultimate broker of the company's funding. If the project was given the green light, the advertising, publicity, and distribution departments would then map out strategy for the movie release, and a flurry of media attention would surround the principals associated with the movie. A few weeks later, prints would be made; the movie would be

shown first at studio-owned Warner Theaters, and then ultimately released around the world.

Warner Bros. may have cranked out more than its share of gangster films, but surely this was not the only kind of film that the studio produced. It made some of the best biographical films of the era, including *The Story of Louis Pasteur* (1936) and *The Life of Emile Zola* (1937), as well as wonderfully extravagant Busby Berkeley musicals. But for Warner Bros., the tough, low-budget stories of city life were what it came back to repeatedly, and the narrative thrust of them later fostered the milestones *The Maltese Falcon* (1941), and *Casablanca* (1942). Every major studio of the time had its share of both ordinary and distinguished films. The system was efficient, a model for traditional capitalist production theory. At any one time, fifty separate movies might be at some position in the production pipeline. The studios continued these insular methods of movie development from the 1920s into the 1950s.

Hollywood: The Transition Years

Although a history of Hollywood filmmaking demands a much more detailed account than can be given here, it should be observed that the "Golden Era" of the studio system did come to an end in the 1950s. The smooth-running, self-contained production facilities found themselves burdened with previously ignored, inherent problems that now surfaced. For example, the high overhead costs of running these complex and very expensive film factories could be maintained only when the motion picture industry virtually monopolized the leisure time entertainment demands of the nation.

However, with the advent of television in the late 1940s, Americans suddenly found that they could get entertainment on a screen (granted, a very small one) free of charge. With this media eruption and other postwar sociological shifts, theater revenues tumbled. Compounding the troubles, in 1948 the Supreme Court, in a major antitrust suit (*U.S.* v. *Paramount Pictures Inc., et al.*), ruled that the studios must divest themselves of ownership of either their production facilities, their distribution control, or their theaters. The studios chose the last option. Henceforth, their movies could not automatically be assured of reaching an audience, but like most products, had to find a willing buyer/exhibitor. As a result, marketing costs for promoting a film escalated. In addition, the creative community was racked with both real fear and paranoia when hundreds of artists were "blacklisted" for rumored affiliation with the Communist party, or political activities even suspected of being on the political left.

This meant that many of the accused persons lost their jobs and never again worked in the movie industry. One result was a self-imposed censorship within the studios that limited the content of what could be written, shot, and seen. Filmmakers began to look toward Europe for lower production costs and fresh locations, while American movie audiences started going to "foreign films" **(1–11)** at idle theaters that became known as "art houses."

The movie industry fought back with attempts to make their product more attractive and accessible. In response to the very small dimensions of early television screens, movies in the 1950s began to offer

1–11 8½ The transition in the taste of American film audiences in the 1950s and 1960s was generated by an influx of unconventional movies from **Europe and Asia.** Many moviegoers wanted to see films with an aesthetic attitude that challenged its audience in the same manner that other great art forms routinely presented. Art movie houses sprung up in every major city. Although the foreign films presented no great financial threat to Hollywood, these movies did help shake filmmakers out of many staid approaches to both visual style and story content. Italian director Federico Fellini, in such films as 8½ (1963) shown here, shocked but delighted American audiences with timely visual metaphors that captured the chaos and shallowness of contemporary sexual politics. (Embassy Pictures) viewers enormous screens in the three-projector format of Cinerama or in Stereo-scopic 3-D (glasses included) with its convincing illusion of visual depth. The advent of a series of blockbuster films—*Around the World in 80 Days* (1956), *The Ten Commandments* (1956), *South Pacific* (1958), and others—shot in color and wide-screen formats such as CinemaScope, VistaVision, Panavision, and Todd-AO, gave movies a majestic aura that set it well above TV and established itself as the royalty of entertainment media. By contrast, a number of small independent producers began making tightly scripted films with strong, irreverent stories—*The Wild One* (1953), *The Man with the Golden Arm* (1955), *The Night of the Hunter* (1955)—ones that matched their foreign counterparts for claims of artistic merit.

The net effect on the traditional studios during this period was, first, a disintegration in the 1950s of the comfortable older system; then, in the 1960s through the 1980s, a gradual restructuring of the industry into massive international entertainment conglomerates. Often they retained the classic movie studio logos, but now had interests in not only motion pictures but in television, music recording, publishing, media equipment manufacturing, and theme parks. What we have today is something both very different from the Old Hollywood, yet strangely familiar.

THE BUSINESS OF MOVIEMAKING TODAY

"The pursuit of making money is the only reason to make movies. We have no obligation to make history. We have no obligation to make art. We have no obligation to make a statement. Our obligation is to make money."

Producer Don Simpson (*Top Gun,* 1986)

It is called the movie *industry*, not the movie *art*, and for good reason. The very expensive process of making a motion picture looks more like the complex manufacture of a commercial product that is packaged for sale than the artistic result of a personally inspired creative statement. The stakes are high in this business. Although to some people the subject of movie financing may seem peripheral to the subject of film art, money and the aesthetic choices made in movie production are so intricately bound together that it would be negligent not to give some attention to the business side of the industry. Every creative person seriously involved in motion pictures takes the monetary dimension of his or her decisions into account.

In the midst of the Watergate cover-up (the undoing of Nixon's presidency that was so well depicted in Alan Pakula's *All the President's Men* in 1976), the team of government investigators was totally confused by the misinformation and stonewalling being presented by the powers in Washington. To find the most direct path to the truth, Leon Jaworski, the chief federal prosecutor, counseled his investigators to simply *"Follow the money."* He suspected, rightly, that tracking the routes of canceled checks and bank account numbers would eventually turn up the major players in the scandal. Soon the operation became clear, and President Nixon resigned.

Follow the money is a useful motto when searching out how any enterprise works and where the power of decision making lies. This is especially true in the motion picture business. Daily, the widely-read trade publications *Variety* and *The Hollywood Reporter* give the news of the industry with an almost exclusive orientation toward how much *money* is being made—on which project and by whom. Articles on films in production detail what companies and individuals are working. Movies are reported upon primarily in terms of their box office successes and failures in every major city in the world. Kenneth Turan, film critic for the *Los Angeles Times,* explains the reality of the business, "Hollywood is a factory town, which at the more basic level means that a system is in place that simply has to turn out a product, good or bad, to fill quotas, keep employees busy, and ensure that the pipelines are operational."

Money is the key. Today, the money for filmmaking comes from a variety of sources. Certain major banks fund studios and production groups who they determine have a solid production record or a quality plan for future films; independent investment groups often come together to finance a particular movie; the traditional money resources of the distribution companies—Paramount, Columbia, Disney, and others—fund a set number of projects each year. A determined and hungry producer will tap anyone willing to risk capital for the tempting chance to strike it rich in the gamble of moviemaking. A leading movie industry executive complains, "It's a total jungle, a barroom brawl. A gentlemanly code used to exist, but that's gone. There's a whole new set of rules that says there are no rules. You do whatever you have to do." If there is some truth in this statement, how does a movie get made today in the midst of such chaos?

Planet Hollywood

"Many have learned the hard way that Hollywood is a world apart—a risky business where the uninitiated are routinely shorn. It is a fantasy factory where the insiders are often more skilled at creating illusions about themselves than they are at spinning magic for the screen."

Authors Nancy Griffin & Kim Masters

Unlike the old days, anyone can make a movie today if he or she has the financial assets to cover the production costs involved in planning, shooting, and completing a film. Smart businesspeople, however, rarely use their own capital. Therefore, the ability to connect and make terms with willing investors is an art unto itself. This newer way of doing things has brought in a very different breed of people becoming involved in movies— a less traditional, more maverick element. In old Hollywood, the movie production and distribution facilities were the private and guarded domains of a few legendary studio bosses; today, everything in the industry is *leased* to anyone willing to pay the price. Cameras, lights, soundstages, screening rooms, cranes, helicopters, and automobiles are for rent. What is more, actors, directors, cinematographers, costume designers, sound engineers, and other major artists in film production are **freelancers,** that is, they sell their services, commonly to the highest bidder. And almost everyone has an **agent.** People working on major films—the generator operator, the prop supervisor, the seamstress, the drivers, the secretaries—make top wages,

★ FOLLOW THE MONEY

Following the money can be a circuitous game when trying to track film costs and profits. When writer Art Buchwald sued Paramount for a percentage of the profits owed to him for disputed authorship of Eddie Murphy's movie *Coming to America* (1988), Paramount claimed that although the film took in over $125 million (Buchwald's lawyers said $160 million), there was a net loss of $18 million on the project. *Creative bookkeeping*, a practice of studio accounting that ensures the production and distribution costs of a film will always exceed its income, has long been an industry-condoned but secret and heavily guarded practice of Hollywood film-making. Many people in the industry make money on movies that never show a profit on paper. Buchwald's search of the Paramount's books may have temporarily upset the system, but little more than that.

Every level of moviemaking is expensive. Escalating production costs reveal the high-risk nature of the business. But this is also a very strange and imprecise industry. Investors bet heavily that the sometimes inspired, sometimes blind, choices of a select group of people working in the most desirable sections of Los Angeles will translate to the cultural tastes of the general public. In fact, every time a film is released, the financial wizards hold their collective breath. Although many movie people claim prophetic powers beforehand, who really knows what makes a "blockbuster"? Will it be *Howard the Duck* (1986) or *Who Framed Roger Rabbit?* (1988). One flopped, the other was hugely popular. In 1999, *The Blair Witch Project*, a small film produced independently for $35,000, defied the wisdom of Hollywood by breaking all of the accepted rules for success with its home-movie style, but fresh cinematic vision. The movie establishment watched in amazement as the film brought in over $150 million domestically, the most profitable film of all time based on a cost-to-gross ratio.

When a film fails, hard answers must be forthcoming to those people who borrowed the money. If a string of films does not live up to expectations, the studio heads and their teams find new jobs. A classic example is Michael Cimino's western *Heaven's Gate* (1981). The production went well over its huge original budget, and the movie opened to devastating reviews attacking its fractured continuity, overblown theme, and confused character development. The film died on opening night in New York City. The production not only ruined many individual careers, but also proved to be the death knell for United Artists studios as it was then configured. Several things had gone wrong, including a host of wretched business decisions and Cimino's self-indulgent management habits on the project. The artist's need for unbridled creative freedom cost many men and women their jobs and their incomes.

Still, the dream of financial and artistic triumph is realized often enough to rejuvenate even the most hardened skeptic. The economic impact of a highly successful movie will be felt throughout almost every sector of the film community and is reflected internationally on the stock markets of the world. When a studio can string together a series of moneymakers, euphoria sets in.

The Producer and the Package

"Is money everything? Is greed to be its master—its dictator? Are grosses to be the only measure of a film's excellence, of a director's visionary power?"

British director Michael Powell
(*Peeping Tom*, 1963)

Unfortunately, money *is* essential. Typically, the formative stage of a movie project looks something like this: A producer is looking for his or her opportunity to make a film. Producers come in all sizes, from giants with large permanent staffs, such as Castle Rock Productions, to small operations with just a desk, phone, and secretary. There are four times as many producers listed in *The Hollywood Creative Directory* than there were ten years ago. "Producers these days can range from Madonna's hairdresser to the guy who raises money in Chile for a film," muses producer Henry Winkler (*Goodfellas*, 1990). Large or small, they all must come up with a substantial amount of financing to develop and get a film into production.

With the crucial advantage of a high profile actor increasing the fan acceptance and popularity of a movie, film stars have won an inside position in the industry, as producers as well as performers. They regularly form companies that forge exclusive deals with studios to produce future films. These film projects may headline the star owning the production company, or may use other actors that satisfy the producer's financial goals and personal taste in film. This arrangement is not new. By 1916, Mary Pickford had formed her own production company. Years later, James Stewart, Bette Davis, and John Wayne started very successful film units. But today, a great number of actors, from Clint Eastwood to Alicia Silverstone, have established production companies in an attempt to control their artistic destinies.

Very often the process begins by acquiring a movie script on *option*—a contractual arrangement with the writer that allows the producer to shop the idea for a given period of time. With the screenplay in hand, the producer can approach selected actors in hope of interesting them in becoming a part of the project. If the right actor or actors agree, and especially if they are current high-profile players, they may well draw a good director to the project. With these three elements—**a viable script, attractive lead players,** and **an experienced director**—committed, the producer (or agency) can then claim to have a **package (1–13)**. According to the thinking of mainstream Hollywood, the best kind of project today is a "high concept" movie: one with unusually strong visual style, a story that keys into provocative issues or currently popular mythology, and stars who can deliver an audience. As one producer said recently, "The best way to get a movie going is to pitch the poster—*first!*" Of course, the best pitch one could have today is simply, *"Arnold loves it!"*

But there still may be no money to make a film. Therefore, the producer sets out to find financing. Funding can come from anywhere. Motion pictures are an attractive investment to some people, not for the glamour (although that can never be completely ruled out), but because certain films turn a very strong profit. Chase Securities, for example, is a leading moneylender in the industry; its managing director, John W. Miller, has stated that his company is not concerned about the artful quality of the films they finance, "We're bankers, not script readers." After going to

THE NEW PRODUCTION CONFIGURATION

In contrast to the predictably linear and efficient methods of movie production in the old studio system, moviemaking in the new Hollywood is a study in more circuitous interaction of elements. Today, independent forces within the industry must find a way to shape themselves toward an ilusive single goal: the completion of a commercially successful motion picture. Because of a host of potentially conflicting factors involved—the egos and reputations of the main players, the financial risks of the backers, contractual commitments to other projects, the integrity of the original movie idea, and much more—the movement from a movie's initial inspiration to its final completion is full of pitfalls. An illustration of the process is necessarily overlapping.

At the center of the action is the **producer**, the key player in getting the package together. Typically, this consists of enlisting a **workable script**, commitment from **lead performers**, and a respected **director. Money,** however, overrides everything else. Without the prospect of solid financing, movie projects never get beyond the "let's do lunch" stage of the business speculation. Financing can come from many sources, but normally the **established studios** and their traditional funding sources back mainline Hollywood films. For this service, the studios have commanding input regarding the style and content of the movie, as well as control its distribution. **Agents** have become key players in the crucial packaging negotiations, providing the know-how and energy to connect the various independent parties. The dynamic mix is never quite the same in any two film projects. In reality, the dominant power in a particular movie project may rest with any one of the players named in the game.

1–13   *The New Production Configuration*

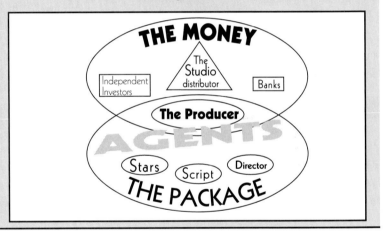

lending institutions, international financiers, and, of course, the film studios, the producer may get a joint venture going. Typically, a movie deal combines money from private sources and a deal with a major movie distribution company, such as Fox or Sony, which may take 50 percent of the gross receipts for their services. Because the ultimate control of any project will tend to follow the source money (the people paying the bills), the struggle of the original producer to stay in charge of the creative strategies and aesthetic considerations regarding the movie is in jeopardy.

Unlike the old days when the process of filmmaking could usually be safely predicted, today every movie has its own unique, and often hazardous, history. Movie deals have perverse ways of regularly falling apart. In the scenario just given, the producer might get stalled for many months in securing the money. Because of the delay, one of the stars may drop out to honor another movie schedule commitment, and upon learning of this, the director backs out because he doesn't like the story with any other lead player. On hearing of this, potential investors also back off the now shaky project. A year has now gone by, and the producer loses the option on the screenplay because it has not gone into production, and it reverts back to the writer who by this time has a better offer. A tremendous amount of energy was expended by the fledgling producer, and there is nothing to show for it.

The Agents

Agents connect people, then bargain. The value of what they have to offer can sometimes be clearly demonstrated. For instance, the worth of a star actor or director they represent is largely based on that person's perceived ability to draw moviegoers to the box office. This is obviously not an exact science and, therefore, an agent's talent at personal promotion is of great value. By knowing where in the industry the channels of power lead, a good agent can line up a client with just the right movie project, then fight for a good contract.

The agent has become the glue that binds the contemporary movie scene, bringing together the disconnected elements that must merge for a film to get started and be made. Agents are licensed and regulated by industry guilds, which prevent them from earning more than 10 percent from their clients for procuring work or negotiating contracts. The movie business has always been a power game, but with the vacuum created when the old studio system lost its supreme position, the major agencies have found themselves not only doing their old job of brokering talent, but active at every step in the successful evolution of a movie project. Ironically, the agent—by definition a middleman—has ended up arranging, and in some cases deciding, what movies with what stars the public will eventually get to see.

By the late 1940s and into the 1960s, MCA (Music Corporation of America) had a veritable stranglehold on the right to represent acting talent in movies. The giant agency had started out booking bands into dance halls in the 1930s and under the crafty manipulations of Jules Stein and, later, Lew Wasserman, had expanded their power into a near monopoly of the acting agency trade. Because of their expansion into movie and TV production (MCA eventually controlled Universal Pictures), pressure from federal antitrust investigators forced MCA to disperse its conflicting talent agency activity. In the 1970s, other super agencies—William Morris Agency, Creative Artists Agency (CAA), and International Creative Management (ICM)—were in a position to put together a network of movie talent from the large and varied client list under contract within their companies. Because they represented so many of the most recognized names in the business, these and other large Hollywood talent agencies have gained a dominant role in almost every aspect of moviemaking.

Each of these organizations has individual agents who specialize in the career choices of credited actors, the work of comedy screenwriters, in book and teleplay acquisition for clients, and the like. The agencies gain in stature as their client list becomes more impressive, and they then have the power to market these media personalities to major corporations for product identification and other advertising purposes. The competition is fierce.

During the 1980s and early 1990s, the most impressive show of dealing at the center of entertainment maneuvering and management was seen in the evolution of Creative Artists Agency under its former president, Michael Ovitz. The agency became an immensely powerful force for a time, not only in motion pictures but also in areas ranging from international entertainment acquisitions to the advertising industry. The major theatrical agencies, because they manage so much talent in the entertainment business, become involved in a wide range of negotiations. There are also scores of other agencies that deal in the entertainment business daily, many of them in highly specialized fields—child actors, art directors, music editors, etc. These midsize agencies, as well as the smaller "boutique" agencies, often wield strong influence, depending on the individual reputations of the agents and the talent they represent.

Most recently, management companies have risen to challenge traditional talent agencies. Many major actors have always paid personal managers to look after the financial planning and other details of their careers. Over the years, in the shifting power structure of Hollywood, managers have evolved to become, together with entertainment lawyers, a force that threatens the tight monopoly of talent negotiations by agents. The talent-savvy Ovitz has, in fact, launched Artists Management Group (AMG) to reshape this part of the industry. New management companies claim to handle their clients in a more personal, comprehensive, and effective manner. But because they are unlicensed, they can charge their clients up to 15 percent and, unlike agents, can produce and have financial interest in the movies of their clients. Many industry observers feel that the situation can lead to exploitation of the talent represented.

When the System Works

"What you need is a capitalist who believes in art or an artist who believes in commerce."

Brian Wilson
(WGA West executive director)

Of course many movies *are* successfully made. The more established production companies with long-standing ties to the industry, or red hot producers coming off a blockbuster movie, have relatively easy going in funding their next project. Their track records will carry them for awhile. However, many aspiring producers with exceptional movie scripts and connections, although meeting constant waves of resistance at every phase in the birth of the project, find ways to get them done. When they finally arrive on the screen, such films are usually a testament to the tenacity of the production group **(1–14).**

With the demise of the old studio structure, the system of movie production radically shifted. Certainly, the new CEO at Disney or Universal today wields tremendous corporate power over entire landscapes of leisure enterprises, but often the complex nature and sheer size of the organizations limit their daily involvement in movie production. Their studio production chiefs get that responsibility and are likely to live in some degree of fear and trembling. As one agent remarks about studio exec-

1–14 *The Player* The current Hollywood movie production milieu was brilliantly **satirized** in Robert Altman's *The Player* (1991). In this scene, Tim Robbins plays a studio production head being given a "story pitch" by two writers. Typically, these sessions are highly pressurized meetings that give story promoters a few precious but frantic moments to sell a movie idea to the person or group with enough power to set a project in motion. Whatever creativity and art might be contained in the story is reduced to catch phrases. The unspoken greed that motivates such encounters makes the Hollywood system of doing business ripe for humor.   (Spelling Films International)

utive's indecisiveness, "There is a tendency for everyone to have excuses why *not* to do something. Once you commit to doing it, you're risking money and your future." Approving an especially disastrous movie, or passing on a film that later became someone else's mega-hit, can signal a quick fall from grace.

The feverish drive of studio executives to solidify their positions often obscures the industry's better sense of artistic good taste. The eternal search for the blockbuster movie, and its sequels, is the truest path to windfall profits, while at the same time insuring one's personal job security. The pressures of the movie business force many film producers and studios, hedging their bets, to opt for the well-tested and safe formula pictures rather than chance the unknown.

Studio chiefs also run into a myriad of other intense players—superstars with their own production companies, agents with celebrity reputations, aggressive independent producers with a string of successes, entertainment lawyers with ties to huge money resources, and strong directors demanding absolute control. In the absence of the older fixed hierarchical system, the persons in the strongest *power positions*—real or imagined—are those who are perceived to have the ability to push movie projects through the perilous stages of production and release, and with that, to generate healthy financial rewards. The movie business today is a sophisticated and ever-fluctuating activity. Because of the extreme costs and time commitments involved, the artistic merits of a potential motion picture must be factored in with such things as the survivability of the studio head, mutations in a star's popularity, inconsistency in a director's work and personal life, and human factors concerning everyone associated with the film. It is a very fast, high stakes game, and fortunes can turn very suddenly.

Globalization

"Globalization in the release of motion pictures has increased the appetite for Hollywood cinema."

Cassian Elwes, agent at
William Morris Agency

Today, it is almost impossible to consider the movie business apart from that larger entity called "The Entertainment Industry." The giant conglomerates that comprise this select group started as the established motion picture companies that are now at the center of media power. The last decade has witnessed the global consolidation of communication industries, tightening the networks of manufacture and distribution. Because of the unique combination of historical circumstances in its history, the United States has developed the complex support systems necessary to produce, manage, and distribute to the rest of the world. This twentieth-century phenomenon, given the innocuous title "mass communications," produces and sends the same ideas and images to almost every part of the earth from sources that are becoming more and more concentrated in a few select media centers. The prizes are many, and the envisioned fiber-optic "superhighways" linking the nation and the world to a 500-channel universe are the key. Cable, network television, computer, and telephone companies; radio, music video, and the recording industry; movies studios, theme amusement parks, and the publishing business—all have become intertwined, feeding off one another to establish their position in the marketplace. Mass media delivery systems stayed economically sound at a time when other American industries (such as steel and autos) staggered. National boundaries have very little practical effect in this new information environment. Even cultures with insulated social and commercial values, such as mainland China and Iraq, find it hard to stay free from these outside influences.

It has become increasingly clear that broad economic, social, and cultural changes will be shaped by those forces that own and operate the largest hardware and software systems. As the *hardware* technology—from VCRs to satellite cable—has been able to deliver entertainment more easily and economically, enormous new markets

TABLE 1–1   THE TOP MEDIA COMPANIES HOLDING MOTION PICTURE STUDIOS

Moviemaking today is just one of the components of the increasingly concentrated power of a few media companies. Listed below are the complete or partial holdings of the six leading media conglomerates. A quick overview shows shows how the movie industry both feeds the interests of compatible media divisions within the companies and also can benefit from the exposure that those sectors provide. Media companies call it healthy **synergy**. Critics worry that centralization of the media limits the diversity of independent expressions of art and ideas.

MEDIA COMPANY	MOTION PICTURES	BROADCAST & CABLE	PRINT MEDIA	MUSIC	INTERNET	OTHER HOLDINGS
TIME WARNER	Warner Bros. Pictures; Castle Rock Entertainment; New Line Cinema	WB Network; CNN; HBO; Cartoon Network; TBS Superstation; Turner Network Television (TNT); Turner Classic Movies; Time Warner Cable; Warner Bros. TV	Time Inc.; Time; People; Life; Fortune; Money; Sunset; Sports Illustrated; Little Brown & Co.; Book-of-the-Month Club	Warner EMI Music: Atlantic, Electra-Asylum, Warner, Virgin, Capitol, Abbey Road, Angel, Blue Note	America OnLine; Road-Runner Online Service	Atlanta Braves; Atlanta Hawks; Atlanta Thrashers; World Championship Wrestling
VIACOM/CBS	Paramount Pictures; Paramount Classics	CBS Network; 50% of UPB; 35 TV Stations; 163 Radio Stations; CBS Television; Paramount TV; Spelling Television; King World Productions; MTV; VH1; Nickelodeon; Showtime; The Movie Channel; Country Music TV; Nashville	Simon & Schuster Publishers; Scribner; Pocketbooks		Medscape; Jobs.com; Big Entertainment	Paramount Parks; Blockbuster; Viacom Consumer Products; TDI Worldwide (Outdoor Advertising)
DISNEY	Buena Vista Motion Pictures Group; Walt Disney Feature-animation; Miramax	ABC Network; 10 TV Stations; ABC Radio; 44 Radio Stations; Buena Vista TV; ESPN; Disney Channel; Lifetime; A&E; E!; History Channel	Hyperion Books; Los Angeles Magazine; Discover Magazine	Buena Vista Music Group	Go Network; Infoseek	Theme Parks Disneyland Resort; Cruise Line; The Disney Store; Anaheim Angels; Mighty Ducks of Anaheim

continued ▶

TABLE 1–1 CONTINUED

Media Company	Motion Pictures	Broadcast & Cable	Print Media	Music	Internet	Other Holdings
NEWS CORP.	20th Century Fox Pictures; Fox Searchlight; Fox Animation Studios	Fox Network; 23 TV Stations; 20th Century Fox TV; Fox News Channel; Fox Sports Net; Fox Family Channel; Fox Health Channel; FX Networks	HarperCollins Books; William Morrow Books; Zondervan Publishing (Bibles); Avon Books; Regan Books; TV Guide; Times of London; Sun; NY Post; News of the World		Digital Publishing; News America	L.A. Dodgers; Echo Star British Sky Broadcasting; Star TV; Sky Latin America
VIVENDI/ UNIVERSAL	Universal Pictures; Canal +; October Films; Mandalay; Working Title Films; Spyglass Entertainment; Carolco Pictures; Sturio Canal	USA Network; Sci-Fi Channel; Studios USA; The Home Shopping Network; WAMI-TV (Miami); Europe's Leading Pay-Television Company	Groupe Havas Publishing	A&M Records; Island Def Jam; Interscope; Motown	Citysearch.com; Vizzavi [European Internet Portal); E.Medi@	Ticketmaster; Universal Studios Hollywood; Wet & Wild in Orlando; Spencer Gifts; United Cinemas International; Set-Top-Box Technology; Water, Energy, Transportation; Waste Management Companies; Real Estate Holdings
SONY	Columbia Pictures; Sony Pictures Classics	Columbia Tristar Television; Gameshow Network		Sony Music; Sony/ATV Music; Music Choice Europe		Sony Electronics; Loews Cineplex (jointly owned)

have opened up. In addition, because the movie companies own a huge backlog of films—the *software*—reflecting their production histories and subsequent film library acquisitions and because they have a wealth of practical experience in making and distributing packaged entertainment, these same companies have found themselves at the center of a global media revolution. The latest media revolution being ushered in is *interactive programming*—computerized systems that allow the viewer to participate as the programmer. It promises almost endless possibilities for the major communication companies. The financial investments involved are staggering, but then so will be the monetary benefits.

The result may be that "American culture is the only true mass worldwide culture," as communication consultant Sharon L. Patrick points out. People the world over seem to be especially enamored with the style and content of the big movies produced in the United States. A random weekly check of box office figures in England, Germany, Japan, Australia, France, and almost every other industrialized country will invariably list eight or nine of their top ten movies as ones produced in the United States. In 1998, the major American film studios brought in $6.821 billion in ticket sales in overseas markets alone, coming within a fraction of the amount—$6.877 billion—that those same companies made in the U.S. market for the year. The video sales of *Titanic* (1997) set domestic records of 25 million units sold, only to be superseded by the 30 million videos of that movie sold on the world market. Commercially, Hollywood seems to be doing the right thing.

Consolidation

The trend toward the interconnection of the communication and entertainment industries has created a new climate for filmmaking throughout the world. Each film project is now considered in its full impact on allied corporate interests.

In recent years, American motion picture companies have been the focus of the corporate buyouts. Time Inc., with strong traditions in the print media (*Time, People, Entertainment Weekly, Sports Illustrated, DC Comics*, Little Brown Books) and ownership of Home Box Office (HBO) and Cinemax cable television network, merged with Warner Communications (Warner Bros. movie studios, Atlantic, Electra-Asylum, Warner Records) to form Time/Warner. They added Lorimar, a giant in TV production, and created a model of a vertically integrated media organization. Later, Ted Turner merged his giant television and movie assets with Time/Warner. This megacorporation then merged with the leading Internet service provider, America OnLine, and with EMI, a leading music group (Capitol, Virgin, Abbey Road, Blue Note, Angel), to solidify its position as the largest media company in the world.

The possibilities for self-promotion are endless **(1–15).** For example, Warner Bros. studio can shoot a big budget film starring Madonna, record the sound track album for one of their labels, create her music video to promote the package, have her featured on the cover of *People* magazine, give her a two-hour HBO special or an interview with Larry King on Turner's CNN, review it in *Time* magazine, and push her image for an endless variety of product endorsements from soft drinks to lingerie. In a very real example of what is called *synergy* in the industry, the Warner Bros. movie *Father's Day* (1997) with Billy Crystal and Robin Williams had a wide release on a Friday. Conveniently, on the Thursday previous to the opening, both comedy stars showed up in cameo roles on the popular Warner Bros.-owned television series "Friends." The TV program reached about 25 million people, strongly composed of just the right young adult and teenage demographics of the primary moviegoing audience. It was an in-house job.

1–15 *Earthquake—The Big One* Today many movie studios have become the anchor for large **entertainment enterprises,** using both the mystique of movies and their practical experience in profiting from popular taste. The Walt Disney company established the model for amusement parks based on movie characters and fantasy themes during the past half century. Playing to pre-sold crowds, Universal Tours at Universal City Studios went on to exploit movie imagery by using special effect techniques that extend the movie experience into 3-dimensional entertainment spectaculars (including *Earthquake—The Big One* seen here). The ability to overwhelm the senses with sound and visual effects was born in moviemaking. (Universal City Studios)

Other companies making movies have found that mergers create different but equally intriguing possibilities. In the 1980s, Japan's Sony Corporation started a trend when they bought Columbia Pictures from Coca-Cola, wedding a leading manufacturer of communication hardware for home and industry to a film studio owning the rights to a huge movie library—as well as the facilities and know-how to produce many more. Similarly, in 1991 the massive Matsushita Electric Industrial Co. (Panasonic, Technics, Quasar) took over the most diversified entertainment conglomerate, MCA (Universal Pictures, MCA publishing, Geffen and MCA Records, USA Network, Odeon-Cineplex Theaters, Universal Studios Tours), only to sell it to Seagram, a Canadian corporation, then to the French controlled Vivendi conglomerate.

The trends toward globalization and consolidation have extended to other major American studios. Viacom, owner of Paramount Pictures, purchased CBS in the largest media merger to date. In a move that surprised some in the industry, the conservative Walt Disney Company tapped into Japanese capital for $600 million to fund new motion picture projects. The company then bought Capital Cities/ABC Inc. Twentieth-Century Fox is now owned by News Corporation, a group controlled by Australian Rupert Murdoch. MGM is managed by American Kirk Kerkorian and Seven Network, an Australian media company.

With some variation of High Definition Television (*HDTV*) about to become the industry standard, and with interactive-digital monitor systems being developed, the large communication and entertainment corporations are merging in various patterns. The Turner Broadcasting System acquired the previously independent New Line Cinema and Castle Rock Entertainment to become a serious member of the movie producing business. The company then merged with Time/Warner. Microsoft, Time/Warner, and Tele-Communications Inc. have joined forces to set the critical software standards for interactive TV in the future. Delivery systems for motion picture exhibition in the home will continue to change radically in the coming decade. The mergers go on relentlessly: Check today's paper for the latest configuration.

It has been noted that many businesspeople with no background in the movies are being recruited into the entertainment industry. In the past, Hollywood was more like a giant family affair, with sons and daughters, cousins and friends of a relatively limited group of industry people naturally gravitating into the business. There was always room for outsiders with talent and charisma, but they were not hired simply on the strength of a good-looking resumé. Nepotism has its insular side, but this inbred quality brought a certain stability to the movie business. Although the system was already changing before the acceleration of mergers, globalization of the industry has taken the business to a more removed level. What many fear about these mergers is a tighter and more restrictive control of the content of what is commercially released. Some critics fear that film stories may be offensive to the cultural sensitivities or obscure business interests of the new owners and will not get made. Others feel that the very size of these megacorporations will further emphasize the bottom-line financial numbers of a movie project, without consideration for its artistic or humanitarian values. The consolidation of global corporations signals a shift in the largest companies from being entertainment-based, in which top management reigns over their studios in the style of traditional, free-spirited "movie moguls," to becoming more dryly efficient cable and digital-oriented economic forces.

SUMMARY

"There is no way to completely understand the art of Flaherty, Renoir, Vigo, and especially Chaplin unless we try to discover beforehand what particular kind of tenderness, of sensual or sentimental affection, they reflect. In my opinion, the cinema more than any other art is particularly bound up with love."

Film critic Andre Bazin

This quotation of Andre Bazin in an essay on the uncompromisingly compassionate films of the great Italian director Vittorio De Sica may seem oddly sentimental. To define making films as an act of love may seem excessive to some, but what Bazin is getting at is that the best movies provide a unique entry for the expression of an artist's humanity. Whether in the form of science fiction, a detective story, or comedy, the content of the better movies is about the interaction of human beings. An honest and understanding description of spiritual and physical needs, desires, and behavior in film would seem to be an essential point of reference. This level of discussion, however, is rarely carried on in the popular media.

The wonder and beauty of film is this: In the end, budget bears little relation to the quality of art found in them. Through the years, many brilliant smaller movies did not win their acclaim on the strength of elaborate production values or media blitzes, but because of their fresh themes, originality of execution, and unity of purpose **(1–16).**

1–16   *The Limey*   Although big budget features get the most attention, **small independent films** have the luxury of artistic freedom. The disturbing and rapidly-cut images in Steven Soderberg's *The Limey* (1999) present a violent world of human isolation and societal corruption in contemporary Los Angeles. The film, with Terence Stamp as an ex-con and Peter Fonda as an elite drug baron, has an uncomfortable dark beauty, one that mass audiences may find puzzling. However independent film production, generated by more personal artistic visions, has enjoyed an emerging popularity, perhaps because of the public's weariness with films of formula.   (Artisan Entertainment)

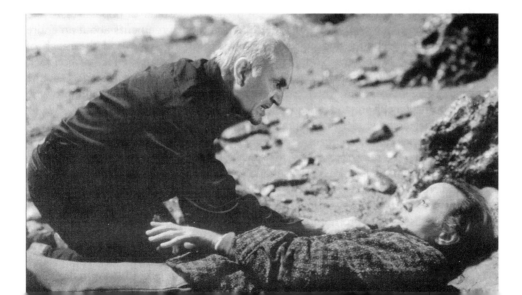

RP: How did Radiant Productions come about?

GK: Ultimately I met a director—Wolfgang Peterson—when I was working on a project. When I left the other company, we had a project that we were developing together. He decided to take it in "turn-around," and together we set it up at another company. I ended up being the co-producer of the project.

RP: You're just about to wrap *The Perfect Storm* with Wolfgang Peterson directing. Back in 1981 he directed *Das Boot*, generally recognized as the greatest submarine movie ever made, and some critics would say the best war film ever. Are most of your projects chosen with his special taste and talent in mind?

GK: We started Radiant Productions about ten years ago and, yes, we look for projects for him to direct. But we also look for films to develop with others in mind. Sometimes Wolfgang is not able or available to direct a certain film, or it may not be an appropriate project. We've had a number of films made that he didn't direct.

RP: From a movie producer's perspective, typically (if there is such a thing) how does a movie project get started?

GK: A movie can get started with just an idea from a producer, director, writer, or anybody. Often it comes from what we call a "spec script," or a play or book. Generally what I do is look for ideas from books and scripts that I can set up at a studio, whereby they can finance the buying of the script or the rewriting of it. Whatever it takes to get it into production.

RP: You're still shooting *The Perfect Storm*. As a producer, what does your typical day look like?

GK: Well, we start early and I'm on the set much of the time. I'm there for a lot of the shooting but I'm also constantly working on other projects, which are at various stages of development. I leave the set from time to time to attend meetings. I have a trailer right outside the set where I'm on the phone a great deal, working on current projects and trying to find new ones. I also have a staff of development people at Radiant who are working on other projects at all times. So it is really quite a varied day—from being on the set to going to studio meetings, meeting with writers, actors, and directors of future projects. We're also starting a television company, so we are also working on scripts in that area.

RP: What is the most difficult—the toughest—part of your job?

GK: I think that the toughest part, in some ways, is that the movie is the director's film, and the producer can be completely in charge of the project at various times, but at some point you're there to service the director, and you can have a lot of input or little input, depending on what your relationship allows. Depending on the circumstances, that can be difficult. Because as a producer, you nurture a project along, but have to give it up when the director takes command.

RP: Do you feel that you have any "artistic" input into the production of a movie? And if so, what is the nature of it?

GK: I feel that I have a lot of artistic input, in terms of the development of the script. I'm very involved in hiring the cast as well as the crew, in choosing the composer, in working with various post-production departments. I'm tightly connected to the film from beginning to end. This is certainly true when my partner Wolfgang is on the project. Sometimes when another person who is tied to another producer directs a movie, I may not be involved to the same degree. So my participation varies. But there's always a great deal of collaboration in the script.

RP: You have been the producer of many very high-budget movies—*Air Force One, Instinct, Mighty Joe Young, In the Line of Fire, Bicentennial Man,* others. Where are some of the places Radiant Productions looks for financial backing on such projects?

GK: These were pretty much financed by studios. In a couple of cases— *Instinct* and *Bicentennial Man*, for example—the movies were co-financed outside of the studio. But really, they are studio productions. There is some European financing that we are now using for television production, and possibly for feature films as well.

RP: Most of your movies are cast with so-called Hollywood superstars as leads – Clint Eastwood, Anthony Hopkins, Richard Gere, Kevin Spacey, Dustin Hoffman, Bill Paxton, Robin Williams, Sam Neil, George Clooney and others. How does having such major stars in your films affect the nature of your work, as opposed to a producer working more in "story-driven" films with a lesser-known cast?

GK: It certainly affects the movie's status. The project becomes a high-profile picture that everyone is monitoring and watching. Obviously, it also raises the price of the negative cost, so you have more interest from the studio in the picture. And in the marketing of the film there is a built-in public awareness. That's the positive. On the negative side, there is sometimes an unrealistic expectation put on it. There's also a certain amount of power or control that major stars have over script changes, the casting of co-stars. It's just a question of whether they abuse it. The situation can definitely change the balance of power in a film project. Everybody has heard that kind of story. But any problem is mitigated if you have a respected and successful director. Most actors are very respectful of a strong person directing. I don't have any unpleasant stories to tell.

RP: Do you ever personally initiate the idea for a film production?

GK: I have a couple things in development but nothing that has yet been shot. A lot of projects have many incarnations. They stop and start over five or ten years. Actually, although I wouldn't say that I initiated it because the short story was already sold, but *Bicentennial Man* was a project in which I hired the screenwriter to write a complete script, we developed it, and that script attracted Robin Williams and director Chris Columbus. It's not an idea from scratch, but the next thing to it.

RP: If my fact checking is right, Radiant Productions has several films in active development—*Conspiracy of Silence, Black Diamond, The Travel Agent,* and others. How far down the road does a company like yours plan?

GK: As far as we can. Hopefully the next film we'll be shooting is called *Endurance.* We've been working on it for six years. That's being rewritten right now by William Wittliff who wrote *The Perfect Storm. Endurance* and *The Travel Agent* are both at Columbia Pictures. Also script called *Labor of Love* at Fox and *That Others May Live* at Warner Bros. So we're working on various things all the time. You can't plan enough in advance because there are so many reasons for a project to fall apart and not happen. You've just got to keep going.

RP: How large is your permanent staff at Radiant Productions?

GK: It's very small. Radiant is really a development company. We oversee productions when we're involved. There are three other executives and a couple of assistants. So there's about seven or eight other people at any one time.

RP: Is there any particular genre that attracts you, one that you like working in?

GK: It seems like the movies that I make are generally thrillers or action/thrillers. But to be honest with you, I love romantic comedy. I want to make one, to have that instant gratification–laughter.

RP: You have been listed as a "producer" on some films and as an "executive producer" on others. What's the difference?

GK: It's hard to say what the distinction is. At first, I had to work my way up as "co-producer," then "executive producer," and finally "producer." It sometimes has to do with the pecking order or your ability to negotiate a title as well as a salary. At other times the title indicates the level of involvement. But I will tell you that I was listed as "executive producer" on *In the Line of Fire,* but in fact I produced it. In other movies, "executive producer" does say that I was not as "hands-on," not there working on it every minute. Right now, on *The Perfect Storm,* the "executive producer" is someone who is the "line producer." Because of his experience, he was able to negotiate that credit. On every movie you would need a history of just how it evolved.

RP: As you became more established in the Hollywood creative community, did the nature of your work change?

GK: It makes it easier to work with top writers, find better material, and connect with leading directors. The more established you are the easier it is to gain information about what's out there. Let's say we are interested in hiring a cinematographer, or even an actor, I can immediately call someone who is a friend, who worked with them on the last couple movies. So you're not just dealing with a credit but you're talking to someone who has worked with him or her first hand. That's a great advantage. It's a pretty small circle, and you keep coming across many of the same people.

RP: Is there any discernable advantage or disadvantage in being a high-profile female executive in Hollywood?

GK: The only advantage, it seems to me, is that we look out for one another. That I feel more connected to those with similar experiences.

RP: Have you seen any changes in the last ten years in this regard?

GK: There are more women at different levels of filmmaking. Other changes, of course, are that budgets have gone up very quickly, mainly starting with the cast The above-the-line costs have sky rocketed, more than the below-the-line-costs. It makes it harder to get some movies made.

RP: Is there a trend in filmmaking today that makes you feel uncomfortable?

GK: I think that star casting is valuable at times, but it too often has gotten out of control. Movies with good stories are still the key. There's a reason why those movies succeed. They touch people. For that reason, the most successful movies are word-of-mouth films.

RP: What are some of the satisfactions in your life as a producer?

GK: I definitely believe I have a fantastic job. I get to be involved with every aspect of making the film. I have the chance to work on the script—painful at times but very satisfying when it works. And certainly the different worlds I'm exposed to, the different subjects that the films are about, are enlightening. I get to learn about such a variety of things that I would never otherwise encounter if I were sitting in an office somewhere. In *The Perfect Storm*, for example, I became immersed in a world of swordfish and boats and the ocean and small-town blue-collar USA. And with people and families whose lives were affected by the men lost in the storm. It was a truly moving experience. On other films, I spent a lot of time working with the Secret Service, or with biologists at the CDC, or the whole world of robotics.

RP: If you were starting out now, with dreams of producing films, how would you go about it?

GK: I would start by reading scripts. Finding out which scripts work. And, of course, reading books and plays, articles, even the newspaper. Just watching great numbers of movies and analyzing why some work so well. My other advice is to try and get a job in the film industry. Obviously it's not an easy thing to do. I was lucky enough to move around and gain knowledge from the inside. But once you're in, you're in. At any level. And if you excel at what you are doing, people will notice. When I'm talking about the film business, I'm not just talking about a big studio. You could be at an agency or a small production company. Any job that exposes you to what really goes on in moviemaking.

RP: Is there anything that you would especially like to do in film production before your career is over – besides romantic comedy?

GK: If there were any chance, I would love to make a very small movie. The films I really admire are the group of directors following the "dogma 95 theory."

RP: From Denmark and Lars von Trier. It's the opposite end of the methods used in your current films.

GK: Right. I think that is just a fascinating way to make a film. If I had any opportunity, I'd love to do a movie with that simple, basic approach. ◀

FILMS TO CONSIDER

These fourteen films are all related to the **process of filmmaking** itself, each giving some special insight into the hardships and joys of the various movie production systems.

- *Sunset Boulevard* (1950): Billy Wilder's hard look at the end of a filmmaking era, and the careers that descend with it.
- *8½* (1963): Federico Fellini's self-portrait of a director in personal and artistic turmoil as he struggles to complete a movie.
- *Day for Night* (1973): A thoughtful consideration by Francois Truffaut of the interaction of characters and their craft on a movie set.
- *Day of the Locust* (1975): The adaptation of Nathaniel West's dark novel that uses the movie community of the 1930s as a visual metaphor for the bankruptcy of the culture of Los Angeles.
- *A Slave of Love* (1978): A visually stunning film by Nikita Mikalkov about moviemaking in its silent era at the start of the Bolshevik Revolution.
- *The Stunt Man* (1980): A convoluted story that explores the techniques and very nature of filmmaking, by producer/director Richard Rush.
- *Purple Rose of Cairo* (1985): Woody Allen's love affair with old movies plays with multiple levels of reality that the movies hypnotically encourage.

- *Cinema Paradiso* (1988): Guiseppe Tornatore shows us the wonder and rich heritage of movies as seen through the eyes of a youth living in a small Italian village.
- *Hearts of Darkness: A Filmmaker's Apocalypse* (1991): This documentary of Fracis Ford Coppola's Vietnam war film being shot in the Philippines is a plunge into the center of this director's artistic and organizational turmoil.

- *The Player* (1992): A humorous but deadly satire about how Hollywood really plays the game, with 65 star cameos, directed by Robert Altman.
- *It's All True* (1993): An intriguing documentary of the surviving Brazilian footage done by Orson Welles at the beginning of his decline as a power in Hollywood.

- *Ed Wood* (1994): This deadpan satire by Tim Burton, which has fun with the legendary 1950s director, shows the "B" side of the movie business.
- *Living in Oblivion* (1994): Although the film is a put-on, the real technical and interpersonal issues involved in shooting a film are laid out quite clearly.

- *Lumiere & Company* (1997): A well-told documentary about the beginnings of moviemaking.

THOUGHT QUESTIONS AND EXERCISES

Watch a film from this list, or another one suggested by the instructor.

1. What was the primary message of the film in terms of the experience of making a movie? Was the attitude of the filmmaker praising or critical of the world of cinema? Cite specific elements in the film that express its position.

2. Through which character or characters is the theme of the film revealed? Was that person an "insider" or "outsider" in relation to the motion picture business? How was that person changed by the events in the story?

3. In the film, how and in what ways does the movie experience and "real life" intermingle? What does the filmmaker want us to understand about movies by the end of the film?

4. Watch a second movie from the list. In terms of both filmmakers' viewpoints about the importance of movies in the life of the main character, in what ways are the two films similar or different?

5. Watch another movie, not on the list but by the same director. Do you find any similarities in his or her approach to the subject matter? Does a theme relating to moviemaking also recur in the other work? Are there other stylistic parallels?

FURTHER READING

Arnheim, Rudolf. *Film As Art* (Berkeley: University of California Press, 1957).

Berg, Scott A. *Goldwyn* (New York: Knopf, 1989).

Brouwer, Alexandra, and Thomas Lee Wright. *Working in Hollywood* (New York: Crown, 1990).

Brownlow, Kevin. *The Parade's Gone By* (London: Secker & Warburg, 1968).

Chaplin, Charles. *My Autobiography* (London: The Bodley Head, 1964).

Cleve, Bastian. *Film Production Management* (Newton, MA: Focal Press, 1994).

Cook, David A. *A History of Narrative Film*, 3rd ed. (New York: W.W. Norton, 1995).

Gabler, Neal. *An Empire of Their Own: How the Jews Invented Hollywood* (New York: Doubleday, 1988).

Gomery, Douglas. *The Hollywood Studio System* (New York: St Martin's Press, 1986).

Knight, Arthur. *The Liveliest Art: A Panoramic History of the Movies* (New York: New American Library, 1979).

Lees, David, and Stan Berkowitz. *The*

Movie Business (New York: Vintage Books, 1981).

Litwak, Mark. *Reel Power: The Struggle for Influence and Success in the New Hollywood* (Boston, MA: Silman-James Press, 1994).

McDougal, Dennis. *The Last Mogul: Lew Wasserman, MCA, and the Hidden History of Hollywood* (New York: Crown, 1998).

MacGowan, Kenneth. *Behind the Screen: The History and Techniques of the Motion Picture* (New York: Delacorte, 1965).

Miller, Mark Crispin, ed. *Seeing Through Movies* (New York: Pantheon, 1990).

Obst, Linda. *Hello, He Said: And Other Truths From Hollywood Trenches* (New York: Little Brown, 1997).

Powdermaker, Hortense. *Hollywood, The Dream Factory* (Boston, MA: Little Brown, 1960).

Schatz, Thomas. *The Genius of the System: Hollywood Filmmaking in the Studio Era* (New York: Pantheon, 1988).

Tyler, Parker. *Magic and Myth of the Movies* (Garden City, NY: Secker & Warburg, 1976).

Vasey, Ruth. *The World According to Hollywood, 1918-1939* (Madison: University of Wisconsin Press, 1997).

Youngblood, Gene. *Expanded Cinema* (New York: Dutton, 1970).

PART ONE

THE PREPRODUCTION PHASE

*"There are three unmistakable qualities of the best producers—
taste, passion, and tenacity."*
Fred Bernstein, president of Columbia TriStar studio

The **preproduction** phase is a time when the contribution of the movie producer oversees the entire movie project. The role of production teams varies from film to film, depending on the working style of the producers, the financial history of the project, and the creative dynamics of the entire production team. General observations, however, can be made.

A strong case can be made that the ultimate success of a movie is determined in the process of preproduction. This period is a time when the style, theme, and intention of a movie are decided. If the preproduction phase ends in serious misjudgment or in disarray, everything that follows will only multiply the blunders. For instance, if clear agreement cannot be won on the basic vision and execution of the project at the many meetings among the newly hired director, art director, screenwriter, leading actors, and anyone else with power to make decisions sitting in on the conferences, then the entire bewildered enterprise will simply wander into the phase of **principal photography**. The burden of redemption then becomes the job of the director, and the expectation is that he or she will perform some kind of miracle by suddenly discovering the essence of the film in the act of shooting it. It can happen, but it rarely does. The last chance, then, is that the **postproduction** work in editing and sound will untangle and recover the original flawed planning. That solution is even more rare.

On the other side, when the sure hand of a strong and knowledgeable **producer** guides a film project through the harrowing months preceding principal photography, chances are what follows will be on track. Screenwriter John Gregory Dunne (*True Confessions*, 1981) states, "What really good producers do is make you enthusiastic by the sheer force of their personalities about the most problematic ideas." The term *creative producer* is used to

describe men and women who bring a special kind of attention and input to a film project. These producers often have, first, their own extremely clear sense of the movie's vision, and second, the special ability to pull together the exact group of artists and crafts-people to realize that vision. Some element of the proposed project has stirred within them a commitment. An example might be a producer who acquired the rights to a favorite novel, and then is strongly focused on seeing that their vision of the work is faithfully reproduced for the screen. That kind of dedication is always infectious.

Other producers may take a more businesslike approach to a movie project—just as professional, but more detached. For these people, moviemaking is their regular and continuing profession, and when one film is finished another will start. Film production is purely a business. Movies, for them, are a serious financial investment with the possibility of very large monetary rewards. This is not to say that their movies will not be first-rate, but if so, the reasons will lie with the savvy choices the producers make in managing the project. Commitment to film as either art or a means of social enlightenment is a very secondary consideration.

Moviemaking, as has often been stated, is a collaborative art form involving great numbers of people. A movie will often succeed or fail on the quality of the production team's *synergy*—the interaction of elements that produces an effect greater than the sum of the individual parts. In practice, producers are involved daily with finding common ground in areas of artistic creativity, technical expertise, and sound business practices. Exactly how a movie is made is very difficult to predict and guarantee, or even to explain.

Movies in the shooting stage, for example, are often hindered by unresolved differences in preproduction between major members of the cast and crew. Sometimes these are simply personality problems, but often there are legitimate conflicts regarding the interpretation of the film. If these issues go unresolved, a film can end up with a disjointed dramatic structure, muddled character motivation, ineffectual production design, a misstated music score, an unfocused story conflict, and more. Conversely, experienced and careful planning by the producers during preproduction can set the stage for a movie project to be fully realized. The many separate and ego-laden talents that film production brings together can blend to create a movie with the chance of arriving on the screen in the form it was originally imagined, or better. The result will be greater than the sum of its parts.

The duration of preproduction may take as little as a few months, or stretch on for years while waiting for all the elements to come together. *The Godfather III* (1990) went through at least eight years of discarded scripts and participants before the shooting started. Other films have lingered for years in interrupted stages of preproduction. There is no "normal" preproduction scenario, but if things fall into place, 12 to 18 months work before shooting is not unusual.

Films that fall behind schedule become dangerous risks to investors. This is especially true for independent film productions because they do not have the deep fiscal resources of studio-backed films. To borrow money for their movies from banks or other financial sources, the independents must insure the delivery of their film against any possible disruption during the production. A specialized insurance and bonding industry has grown out of the need to cover for unforeseen complications. Some catastrophes, such as prolonged foul weather and political unrest, are beyond the producer's control. But of equal concern is the fear that a director, for whatever reason, might lose control of the shooting schedule, or the destructive lifestyle of a leading actor could seriously delay the production. A *completion bond guarantee* makes certain that a movie will be finished and delivered to the distributor. To compensate for this service, the bond company normally charges between 2.5 percent and 6 percent of the movie's budget. In addition, the insurer requires that the script, the director, the major cast mem-

bers, locations, the budget, and the shooting schedule be accepted and monitored by them. In extreme cases in which a project is seen to be financially out of control, the insuring company can take over the entire production.

After securing the financial backing for the film, the producer must put the money to work. The production strategy of films will vary, but certain elements are universal. Standard movie budgets are broken down into two categories: **above-the-line-costs** and **below-the-line-costs.**

- **Above-the-line-costs** are the contractual agreements that are negotiated between the producers and the agents for the rights to the story and for the salaries of screenwriter, director, performers, cinematographer, and possibly a few others. These costs are based on the competitive market at any given time. Some movie people are in heavy demand one year, less so the next. Some percentage of the expenses can be deferred if those involved are willing to agree to profit-participation agreements.

- **Below-the-line-costs** consist of the everyday work expenses involved in making a movie. These costs have to do with the mountain of details that consume much of the energy of the production team. Sound stages and mixing studios must be rented. Equipment and sup-

plies to shoot a movie are leased and purchased: lights, raw film stock, cameras, cranes, and dollies. Location shooting must be arranged with proper permits, transportation, housing accommodations, catering, portable dressing rooms, and toilets. Unions and guilds are notified regarding the makeup of the crews and their benefits. Wardrobe decides what it can afford, animal handlers are hired, tutors are arranged for child actors, music rights are obtained. The support services to the motion picture industry employ thousands, creating an entire network of economies in major film centers.

Production companies in this phase of a movie project are extremely active as they try to anticipate every need and prevent disasters when the shooting starts. This responsibility falls to the **production manager** or **line producer.** He or she takes charge of the production schedule, scouts locations, troubleshoots, and is the day-to-day link between the head producer and the director as principal photography begins.

Problems are a constant in the game in moviemaking, but much of this can be avoided when the preproduction phase is solidly grounded in common understanding and purpose by all the major creative figures signed onto the film. A tightly knit production team with unambiguous goals will shape the film in preproduction to maximize its chances of success during the following phases of filmmaking. The challenge in the preproduction phase is to clarify and hone the screenplay, envision and design the look of the production, and attractively cast the major and minor roles in a movie. The following three chapters investigate the nature of each interest area. What finally arrives in the theater is a surprisingly accurate reflection of the history of this phase of the project.

CHAPTER 2

THE SCRIPT

THE ROLE OF THE SCREENWRITER

"It starts with the writer—it's a familiar dictum, but somehow it keeps getting forgotten along the way. No filmmaker, irrespective of his electronic bag of tricks, can ever afford to forget his commitment to the written word."

Steven Spielberg, director/producer

The statement by Spielberg could be a motto emblazoned over the entrance of any movie production facility. Yes, movies start with the written word. Serious filmmakers do not proceed without the detailed blueprint of the story— **the screenplay**. A single fanciful

image might summarize the situation: It is as if the entire movie studio, with its thousands of experienced professionals, were geared for action, but must first wait for the screenwriter to arrive at the gates with a 120-page script. With the screenplay, accountants begin to formulate budgets, producers make more informed decisions about financing and management, casting agents determine the types and numbers of actors needed, performers begin to learn their lines, carpenters plan and build the sets, special effects groups study their challenges, and shooting locations are pinpointed. Writer Robert Towne (*Chinatown,* 1974) makes the point succinctly, "Until the screenwriter does his job, nobody else has a job." In other words, the myriad of details involved in filmmaking is first found in the words of a screenplay.

Does the script set the story in an Irish prison during the 1916 uprisings, is it a science-fantasy piece taking place in the next century at Aztec ruins, or is it about present-day ex-lovers living in the same upscale Manhattan apartment building? Whichever is the case, persons hired to help make the movie will be sent into flurries of activity, all of it triggered by the imagination of the screenwriter. Despite the fact that public recognition still may not be high, other privately satisfying rewards are considerable. Not the least of them is seeing one's written dreams come alive in pictures on the large screen, as writer Paul Ciotti (*Ted and Venus,* 1992) notes:

During one of the screenplay's many rewrites, the director suggested that we might put a horse in the story. So I wrote a scene in which our obsessed poet sees a virile young man riding a horse along a beach and then imagines himself riding the horse. And now, to my astonishment, here are 70 people, backed up by half a dozen support trailers, a lunch wagon, generators, lights, umbrellas, director's chairs, actors, extras, a stunt rider and a high-speed camera, all because late one night four years ago I wrote a few lines about a horse galloping through the surf.

A paradox of the art of screenwriting is that, while the movie being written may be seen by millions of people, the script is actually written for only a handful—the producers, studio executives, a few investors, a director, some major actors. If the script passes their judgment, it is used as a practical starting point for the enormous job of making a film. It is unlikely that more than a few film buffs will ever search out the original screenplay and read it as literature. In a very real sense, screenwriters play to a very limited, but important, audience—the industry people with the ability to set the film project in motion.

As one movie producer put it, "The most precious commodity in this town is a good script." But despite the acknowledged importance of the script as the source and initial inspiration for the movie, screenwriters themselves have seldom had the public recognition their contribution warrants, or even proper respect within the industry. Screenwriter John Gregory Dunne (*Up Close and Personal*, 1996) observes, "Beating up on screenwriters is a Hollywood blood sport; everybody in the business thinks he or she can write, if only time could be found." The Writers Guild of America West is in a running battle with directors who usurp sole authorship for movies by using vanity credits. Giving the example of *A Few Good Men* (1992), with a headline credit calling it a Rob Reiner film, screenwriter John Wells notes, "It's an award-winning play written by Aaron Sorkin, screenplay by Aaron Sorkin, directed wonderfully by Rob Reiner." Average moviegoers can list their favorite directors—David Lynch, James Cameron, Kathryn Bigelow, Gus Van Sant, Spike Lee, Quentin Tarantino, Steven Spielberg—and they can surely name great numbers of actors and actresses. How many can name a single screenwriter (who is not also a director)? Outside of the movie community, these women and men are likely to be names just sliding by on the credits.

Historically, this has been the case in Hollywood. With the advent of the commercially viable sound motion picture in 1927, hundreds of new and very talented fiction writers and newspapermen were drawn to the film capital for the substantial money that the industry offered. Movies have traditionally paid writers, with very few exceptions, much more money than they can earn in book publishing or newspaper reporting. In the 1930s and 1940s, for instance, established authors such as William Faulkner, Moss Hart, Lillian Hellman, Clifford Odets, and others came West to try their hand at the lucrative screenwriting trade. The extremely literate and witty films of the period were the result of scripts by former journalists: Ben Hecht (*Wuthering Heights*, 1939), Robert Riskin (*Lost Horizon*, 1937), Dudley Nichols (*Stagecoach*, 1939), and Herman Mankiewicz (*Citizen Kane*, 1941), Norman Krasna (*White Christmas*, 1944) to name a few.

Screenwriters can surely argue that without the script there would be no movie. Some directors have built reputations for wonderfully accomplished films, but unrecognized is that the brilliance of their movies was the result of lucid and inventive writ-

2–1 *Turtle Diary* Certain films bear the strong signature of the screenwriter. Harold Pinter wrote *Turtle Diary* (1986), a warm and intelligent story of friendship between a man (Ben Kingsley) and a woman (Glenda Jackson) which evolves from their common love of nature and a shared commitment to set a turtle free from its museum confinement. The unlikely story works wonderfully on the strength of its writing. Screenplays by Pinter are marked by their penetrating wit, paired-down dialogue, and convoluted plot structures. Pinter's varied work includes *The Servant* (1964), *Accident* (1967), *The French Lieutenant's Woman* (1981), *The Betrayal* (1983), and *The Comfort of Strangers* (1991).   (The Samuel Goldwyn Company)

ing **(2–1)**. Writer Gerard Brach has teamed with director Roman Polanski on many films, from *Repulsion* (1966) to *Bitter Moon* (1994); however, it is Polanski's reputation for unusual stories that soars. Brach has also written works for other directors as different and grand as *Quest for Fire* (1981) and *Manon of the Spring* (1987), but he will never gain the popular recognition of a director. Even purely visual action sequences are sometimes the inspiration of the writer. *The French Connection* (1971) pushed the excitement of "the car chase" to new limits. The scenes of narcotic cops dangerously racing after smugglers under the elevated tracks of Brooklyn were the signature visual sequence of the film. Writer Ernest Tidyman would argue later that the acclaim given to director William Friedkin for the conception of the scene was misplaced, and that the director was only following the extremely detailed shot suggestions of the script. Such rumblings from writers are not uncommon. But more common is a realistic acceptance of the contribution of scriptwriting to the final movie, "The writer on a movie is like someone running the first leg of a relay race," says screenwriter Frederic Raphael (*Eyes Wide Shut*, 1999).

An essential point of conflict for many screenwriters is one of creative control. When a novelist submits a book to a publishing house, not a phrase is changed by the editor without author consultation and permission. When a screenwriter sells a script, control of it rests solely with the production company. They can do with it as they wish. Characters can be dropped, dialogue rewritten, subplots introduced, endings changed. The writer lets go of any rights to the work. A unique feature of writing for the screen, one that has contributed to its lack of public recognition, is one hard fact: The industry recognizes movies to be a "director's medium." As brilliant and tightly written as a script may be, it is not a *movie* until that work is physically translated to the screen. In that act, the director claims the creative authorship for a completed work, and perhaps rightly so. The words and ideas of the script are fully realized in film when translated into images and sound, and that is the primary work of the director. Anna Hamilton Phelen (*Gorillas in the Mist*, 1988) voices a common and understandable lament of screenwriters :

> *To write a screenplay and not be admitted to the psychiatric ward at Cedars, it helps to be emotionally secure as a human being and have no attachment to the outcome. You get pregnant, gestate the baby, go through a live birth, cut the umbilical cord, and have to let everyone—including the wives, lovers, aunts, uncles—take the baby and do what they want with it.*

Sometimes, the original author is hired to revise the script in consultation with the director and the producers. In some cases, the director may invite the writer onto the set to work on last minute rewrites. Just as often the first writer is replaced and others are brought into the project to give a fresh perspective, to solve a problem in the storytelling, or to polish the dialogue. Final screen credit awards depend on how much of a writer's work ends up in the final draft. Points of contention are arbitrated by the Writers Guild of America, the organization that represents the vast majority of screenwriters in the industry.

Screenwriters from older literary traditions, such as novelists F. Scott Fitzgerald and Raymond Chandler, complained long ago that Hollywood corrupted the integrity and stifled the originality of the serious writer. Some have even refused screen credit on films that they felt were mutilated by the director or studio; others have left the business to return to writing that ensures more artistic control. But the fact is that the movie industry pays their writers very well. Today, some leading screenwriters

2–2 Ian Fleming   Successful movies start with good writing. The James Bond novels of Australian novelist Ian Fleming (pictured here) became the most popular movies series ever produced. Based on a single character, the written work of Fleming, with its flair for unapologetic story turns, proved a perfect vehicle for film adaptation. The extended sequence of films that the Bond character spawned, from *Dr. No* (1962) to *The World Is Not Enough* (1999), have never been equaled in terms of the financial success they generated.   (Photograph by Bradley Smith)

earn millions of dollars for their scripts, and a growing number of first scripts receive outrageous sums of money. In 1999, Columbia Pictures broke with an industry practice and offered top screenwriters 2 percent of the gross receipts of movies they've written. This shift in revenue sharing promises to affect the bargaining power and stature of screenwriters throughout the industry. Columbia Pictures president Amy Pascal states it bluntly, "Without writers, we'd have nothing. They're the foundation of the movie business." **(2–2)**

The role of screenwriters is clearly primary. Their creative contribution—the invention of a storied universe in which dramatic events will unfold—sets the process of filmmaking in motion. Producers will tamper with the vision, directors will shape it into cinematic form, actors will give it life, cine-

TABLE 2–1 SUCCESSFUL MOVIE FRANCHISES

A successful screenplay will invite repetition. The task of the screenwriter is creating a fresh story in each succeeding movie. Which film in each series listed below was the most satisfying. Which movie was the weakest?

Film Nucleus	First Produced	Number to Date
James Bond	1962	19
Star Trek	1979	9
Rocky	1976	5
Star Wars	1977	4
Superman	1980	4
Lethal Weapon	1987	4
Alien	1979	4
Batman	1989	4

matographers will find a visual mood, many more creative people will attempt to capture the spirit of the screenwriter's story and bring it to the screen. Ideally, this is what happens. The reality for the screenwriter, however, is often much more complex.

THE WORK OF THE SCREENWRITER

"A good story will survive bad photography; a bad story will not survive with good photography. There's not much you can do with a bad story."

Cinematographer Gordon Willis
(*The Godfather II*, 1975)

It is especially hard for the average moviegoer to analyze the work of the screenwriter and the relationship of the script to what finally becomes "the movie." Once the projector starts, the images flow ceaselessly on. Typically, a story is seductively introduced, characters arrive on the screen, action races ahead (exploding from time to time in moments of dramatic tension), and a climax of excitement is followed by a quick resolution. Things in movies just seem to *happen*.

The basic contribution of the screenwriter to the movie is *the story*. Good storytellers have very special gifts: confidence in knowing what subjects will resonate with an audience, a strong sense of dramatic time and rhythms, a solid grasp of human behavior and insight into the psychology that motivates it, and a lively ability to visualize. The screenwriter, however, must approach movie writing with the specific understanding of how screen stories work. It is not enough for the writer to be excited about the idea of a lost scientific mission at the South Pole or the drug problems of a suburban housewife. Gripping story ideas may be what starts a person writing, but it is in the appropriate written explication of the events that scripts come into being. The writer of an original script must not only invent the characters and the sequence of actions, but know the unique process involved in this special writing. Although great writing of any kind comes from one's creative depths, the mechanics of screenwriting can be described with some objectivity. As with all other art forms, screenplay writing employs particular techniques that can be learned.

THE MECHANICS OF SCRIPT WRITING: DESIGNING THE SCENE

The essential job of the screenwriter is to create engaging situations in which characters interact, revealing and modifying themselves, while pushing the dramatic action forward. For screenwriters, *scenes* are the building blocks of a film story. The **scene**—a unit of dramatic action, usually composed of a series of shots, taking place in a single location and within a limited period of screen time—is the basic unit with which the screenwriter works. When initially writing a script, writers are not normally concerned with the particular nature or the appearance of individual *shots*—whether the camera is focused on this actor or that one. An artful interlocking of the scenes shapes the flow of a movie and helps unify the style and content of the story. [See Appendix II for a detailed outline of the sequence of scenes in James Dearden's screenplay, *Fatal Attraction* (1986).]

Although every scene should move the story along, not all have equal weight. Writers typically use the opening scenes to provide important basic information about the main characters and their world. In the first scene of *Amadeus* (1984), we discover Salieri on the floor of his apartment with a self-inflicted wound. The next scene is a transition scene that shows him being carried through the snowy streets of Vienna to a hospital. It serves the purpose of introducing us to the look of the city in the early nineteenth century and links to the next, more significant scene: the first meeting of the hospital chaplain, Father Vogler, and faded court composer Antonio Salieri, who then begins his account of Mozart's life. Some scenes are short and blunt, giving a useful twist to the action or communicating just enough insight to intrigue us, then moving the story forward to the next scene. Other scenes are mood setters, visually poetic and used to establish characters in the context of their relationship with other characters or the environment they inhabit. Still other, shorter transitional scenes are used to link more important scenes, giving the story a sense of natural sequence.

The major scenes in a film will have an internal dramatic rhythm, with a discernible beginning, middle, and end. In writing such scenes, the screenwriter must isolate its specific dramatic intention and weight. Sometimes a single word or glance at the beginning of a scene can call up the desired emotions and begin on an interchange that builds to the emotional payoff—sometimes called the **dramatic arc**—desired in the scene. To illustrate, in David Lynch's *Blue Velvet* (1986), Jeffrey (Kyle Maclachlan) is a sincere lad with angelic sweetheart Sandy (Laura Dern), who gets in way over his head because of his overripe curiosity. In a crucial scene, Jeffrey has just witnessed the violent sex of drug-crazed Frank Booth (Dennis Hopper) and his oddly complacent victim Dorothy (Isabella Rossellini) through the louvers of a closed door. When

Booth finally leaves the apartment, Dorothy lies silently on the floor. Jeffrey emerges from the closet and startles her, but she accepts his aid to get to the couch. He is still mesmerized by what he has seen and wonders if she is all right. Recovering, Dorothy asks to be held. Jeffrey hesitantly complies, but when her fear turns quickly into warmth, then strangely becomes passion, the complexion of the scene changes. Dorothy now teases him with whispered erotic questions, then carries it full circle by demanding that Jeffrey physically hit her. Confused by what this strange encounter has awakened in him, Jeffrey backs away. With this reaction, Dorothy seems to dismiss him and goes into the bathroom, as a sobered Jeffrey says that he is leaving. But before doing so, he discovers a photo of Dorothy and her small child under the couch, a clue that becomes important in later scenes. In this single scene, Lynch introduces the action with an image of an abused woman, and gradually an entire spectrum of emotions evolve in the rise and fall of the scene's dramatic intensity. Such scenes retain their power even when taken out of context. The rise, peak, and fall of tension in this scene are considered by writers to be its *dramatic arc.*

It is important to distinguish the effort of the screenwriter from that of the director. A screenwriter, it must be remembered, cannot control how the film is actually photographed, that is, the number or kinds of shots that will be chosen to convey the action in a scene. That is the work of the director, cinematographer, and editor. In this sense, the screenwriter only creates the blueprint. A complex scene might be written with many shifts in the characters' interaction, but rather than being composed of several shots, a scene may entail just a *single* extended shot, depending on the pace and cinematic style of a particular director. For example, in Alan Rudolph's *Choose Me* (1984), Keith Carradine and Genevieve Bujold play out a complex seduction scene at a dining room table done with a single shot lasting almost 7 minutes. The style in which the scene was shot is an Alan Rudolph trademark. Normally, a screenwriter does not suggest to such a director how scenes actually might be shot. But screenwriters will often work with directors regarding the sequence of scenes. Speaking of the method he and director Roman Polanski used to structure the story of *Chinatown* (1974), screenwriter Robert Towne relates, "We took the script and broke it into one-sentence summations of each scene, then we took a scissors and cut those little scenes . . . and pasted them on the door of the study at the house we were working. And the game was to shift those things around until we got them in an order that worked." This creative process may seem mechanical to some, but the framework of screenplays lends itself to such approaches.

SCREENPLAY STRUCTURE

Theories concerning the essential nature of a screenplay have proliferated over the past few years as more apprentice writers seek an understanding of its methodology. A generally accepted way is to start with the examination of **story structure**. In a book on his screenwork, William Goldman emphatically announced "Screenplays Are Structure." His scripts for *Butch Cassidy and the Sundance Kid* (1969), *Misery* (1990), and many other movies are models for other writers. Structure is the operative word.

Recognizing and developing the structure of the story is key to screenwriting. Most people who deal with scripts professionally are inclined to agree with this perspective. Just as a building starts with steel girders that shape its ultimate design, the special screenplay structure gives the movie its underlying configuration. If the structure of a story is not carefully planned and executed, even well-written characters will seem lost in a string of aimless events and random action.

Narrative screenplays generally are conceived of as having a **three-act structure**—simply and logically, a beginning, middle, and end. This is a classic structure going back to Greek drama. But unlike the major segments of a stage play that are often delineated by intermissions, the passage from one act to the next usually slips by unnoticed in films. Although the designation of acts in movie writing is not strictly required, many writers work within this classic format and find it useful.

Act I: The Setup

Most screenwriters think of the first act in movies as taking roughly 30 minutes on the screen. In this initial act, the writer often introduces the main characters in their everyday lives. In the process, the script lays the groundwork for the entire story by establishing the time period, location, socioeconomic conditions, and the overall attitude toward its subject **(2–3)**. In what kind of apartment does the protagonist live? What is her taste in music? How does she react to her boyfriend over the phone? What's in her closet? Is she disturbed by something, and why? As viewers put together the information told and shown about the characters, we get to know them and become familiar with the ways they live and behave in their world. For a while, the audience may be satisfied with scenes that engagingly set up the story, but after the first 20 minutes or so, the audience will stir and unconsciously say to itself, "Good, that's very interesting. But what's this movie *about*?" In the language of the dramatist, the question is really an inquiry into the nature of *story conflict*.

A word about conflict. Conflicts permeate life. War, disease, lost love, threats from others, the temptation to despair, and yes, death, are obvious sources of conflict. We may wish it otherwise, but such things are a part of human existence. It could be argued that life does not have to be conceived as an eternal struggle between two rival forces, that conflict is a state of mind, and that nature is, at its core, harmonious. This may be true. But dramatists focus upon and intensify stories of troubled characters and fateful events, emphasizing the risk of a tragic outcome. This dramatization of life has the effect of giving human existence importance, excitement, and even dignity. How the central character of a story deals with the conflict presented is the stuff of drama.

The *protagonist* in a movie encounters conflict as a challenge. The struggle that follows often takes on a universal dimension. In this way, the viewer is invited to identify in some way with the dilemma of the lead character, even though the details of the story may be well beyond the average person's experience. Will the survivors of the airplane crash in the movie *Alive* (1993) make it out of the frozen mountains of South America, and at what human cost? Can Melanie Griffith in *Working Girl* (1988)

2–3 *The Rocky Horror Picture Show*   Most movies start out with an **inciting incident,** a plot device that sets the story in motion. The beginning of *The Rocky Horror Picture Show* (1975) is a classic parody of the horror genre, and audiences through the years have heartily entered into the rituals of its story structure. On their honeymoon, the car of Brad (Barry Bostwick) and Janet (Susan Sarandon) breaks down on a lonely road in a rainstorm— the inciting incident. The car trouble forces the pair to abandon the car and seek refuge at a nearby gothic mansion, setting the story in motion. By the end of Act I, at the terrifying mansion of Frank N. Furter (Tim Curry) and his troupe, the couple will begin to confront a series of unspeakable sexual challenges—the primary conflict of the movie. Almost all movies, regardless of their genre, use the same fundamental storytelling methods to engage the audience. In selected theaters, *Rocky Horror* has had a nonstop run at midnight screenings since its first release.   (Twentieth Century Fox)

overcome corporate forces, and her own self doubts, that stop her rise from the secretarial pool up the ladder into the echelons of power? Is it possible that Robin Williams in *Patch Adams* (1998) can find respect and acceptance for his unorthodox medical treatments? Will James Caan ever get free of Kathy Bates, his psychotic admirer in *Misery* (1990)? We may not have ever been in any of these situations, but a well-written movie absorbs us into their experiences.

As stated previously, the nature of the conflict is ultimately the central dramatic interest in a movie. This is usually introduced by the end of Act I and becomes the first major *turning point*. There will be more throughout the story. In many mainstream films, the turning points are very sharply defined for the audience, although the protagonist may or may not be totally aware of the dimensions of the challenge. For example, in *The Exorcist* (1973), by the end of the first act we have learned that ridding the young girl's body of evil spirits is going to be the harrowing job of two priests. The churchmen know this, but they do not realize the horrific degree of demonic rage they will stir up until it is revealed in stages throughout the other two acts in the movie.

Other films, such as *The Crying Game* (1992), may let the very nature of the conflict unfold in phases of revelation, so that the audience gradually becomes aware of the true scope of the conflict. In the case of this film, the conflict at the end of Act I seems to be the guilt an IRA fugitive (Stephen Rea) faces regarding his part in the death of a British soldier (Forest Whitaker), but a deeper conflict arises in later acts when the fugitive meets the soldier's lover (Jaye Davidson). The conflict calls for a resolution that involves a most critical personal definition of the nature of loyalty and love for another human being. In a few films, such as Mike Leigh's *Naked* (1993), the narrative is a slice-of-life set in the depressing, cruel world of England's underclass. The story follows the pressurized existence of a deeply depressed and brilliantly caustic young man played by David Thewlis. The first act in this movie relates one of many bleak episodes in the protagonist's life, but does not sharply lay out a single point of conflict or hope of resolution. The movie presents no single moment of a defining conflict, but sympathetically tells of the continuing disaster that the young man brings to his life.

The end of the Act I is the doorway through which the main character passes. Once that person enters the other side, whether by choice or by chance, there is no turning back—the door is now locked behind. New forces in the second act come into play that will generate unforeseen consequences. For example, if the story was about a man who decides to leave his family to seek out his private dreams, he may well come back to his home at the end of the film—but he will have been altered by the intervening events, becoming wiser. The situation to which he returns will also not be the same. Although the first act provides the necessary background for the rest of the movie, the screenwriter is well advised to hold back some important data. As Alfred Hitchcock once said, "A person who tells you everything right away is a bore."

Act II: Exploring the Conflict

After the conflict is planted at the end of Act I, the main body of action is set into motion in Act II, and for the next 60 minutes or so, ramifications of the conflict take over. For the screenwriter, this act is the hardest part of the film to sustain **(2–4)**. Scenes must be created that advance the story with action appropriate to the theme, creating peaks and valleys of emotional intensity. Filling the second act with enough gripping action, comedic situations, or engaging drama that logically grow out of the conflict introduced in Act I is not easy for the writer to sustain. In the genre of comedy, for example, the comic dilemma and characters are laid out in the first act and its exposition, if well done, gets laughs easily. The second act for the writer presents the more formidable challenge. Once the audience "gets" the primary joke of the film—that the Jim Carrey character is *dumb*—the filmmakers must create a continuous stream of scenes that humorously spin off of the comedic premise and still retain the freshness of its humorous premise—that he is *dumber*.

Some weakly written movies simply stretch out the second act with episodes of

2–4   *Once Were Warriors*   For the writer, the middle act is the longest and usually the hardest to write. The writer must find enough dramatic situations to build on the story and on the consequences of the conflict. *Once Were Warriors* (1994), from New Zealand by Lee Tamahori, details the life of Beth Heke (Rena Owen) as she attempts to find some sanity in a marriage ruled by her often violent, self-centered husband (Temuera Morrison). The compressed fury that too often happens within families explodes on the screen in Act II when repeated abuse is heaped on the wife and her daughter's rape by a friend of the father is introduced into the story. (Fine Line Features)

nonstop chases and explosives. But thoughtless action can burn out viewers quickly (except in those genres whose sole purpose is to exploit a manic pace). The natural rhythm of good storytelling calls for blending scenes of stinging power with other scenes that give the audience time to assimilate and regroup.

To develop and enhance Act II, one or more **subplots,** quietly sown in the first act, are explored in some detail. These second-level storylines give added dimension to a film, affording the writer alternative ways of create more texture and sidelights of interest. Typically, this might be done by adding a romantic relationship or sudden crisis that adds new dimensions to the story. The movie *Blue Sky* (1991) is about the tempestuous married relationship of Hank (Tommy Lee Jones), a tough Army officer/scientist, who is passionately in love with his volatile wife, Carly (Jessica Lange), a wild spirit constantly on the edge of emotional breakdowns. The nomadic life of this career military family brings them and their girls to yet another army housing project, this time in Alabama. Set in the 1960s, Carly is hypersensitive and sexually smoldering in her confrontations with conservative Army wives, and she soon draws the attention of Vince (Powers Boothe), the base commander quick to take advantage of Carly's need for male attention. The conflict of the film is the ever-deepening neurotic behavior of Carly and Hank's loving and frustrated attempts to reign in the frenzied behavior of the woman he knows so well.

To add depth to the plot in the second act, writer Rama Laurie Stagner, drawing from autobiographical sources, creates a *subplot* by having their teenage daughter Alex (Amy Locaine) discover sex with the base commander's son Glenn (Chris O'Donnell). This subplot takes us away from the chaotic intensity of Hank and Carly and lets us see the social life of others caught up in the garrison life of military families. It also will be used to trigger a *turning point* later in the second act. A second subplot has Hank being sent to Nevada to oversee underground nuclear testing that goes awry when two civilians are contaminated. While Hank is away, the two romantic youths are devastated to come upon Carly and Vince having sex. The ensuing scandal, as word goes around the social circles of the camp, damages everyone. But worse, the Army comes down on Hank for his independent behavior regarding the investigation of the civilian deaths. They imprison him in a military mental hospital to cover-up the facts of the case. At the end of Act II, this second subplot allows Carly to call up a much more grounded part of her personality and changes her into a fiercely loyal woman who fights the faceless bureaucracy to save the one man who ever loved and accepted her. In well-written scripts such as this, the characters must be interwoven so naturally throughout all of the story elements that the movie appears as a seamless piece of storytelling.

It is in the second act of a film that we see the protagonist begin to change and grow by virtue of the series of confrontational issues being played out. In the amusing action film *Romancing the Stone* (1984), Kathleen Turner plays an adventuring New Yorker, initially shown to be a dreamy author of cheap escapist novels. A desperate message from her sister sends her to Colombia, where her idle fantasies of the first act become life-threatening realities in the second act. In this part of the film, she meets an outrageous assortment of men, all determined to do her in for the sake of a treasure map. The job of the screenwriter, Diane Thomas, at this point is to propel the action forward in provocative ways. Luckily, Michael Douglas shows up in the jungle to guide the high-heeled heroine through a series of cliffhanging situations.

By the end of the second act, the protagonist should have fully explored the limits of whatever initial action was called for and be approaching a moment of deeper enlightenment and decision-making spinning out of the primary conflict.

Act III: Recomplication, Climax, and Resolution

Act III typically begins with a *recomplication* of the conflict. This turning point in the story can take several forms. In some action or suspense movies, it may simply mean greatly intensifying the pressure on the hero. Whatever danger existed is now doubled as the vise tightens. In more subtle dramatic works, recomplication may transform the original conflict into a deeper, more complex psychological or interpersonal challenge. As a more profound insight into the nature of the conflict is experienced in the third act, the demand for its resolution becomes more immediate and necessary **(2–5)**. These final 30 minutes of a movie are crucial. The pace of action accelerates in the compression of the third act. This part of the movie pulls together all of the elements of plot and subplot—all of the actions of major and minor characters—and presses the story toward its conclusion.

In the movie *Witness* (1985), Harrison Ford plays a Philadelphia detective, John Book, who must track down killers who eventually come after not only him, but an Amish widow (Kelly McGillis) and her son who witnessed a murder. It is a superior thriller filled with suspenseful events, the film's conflict having to do with the detective's ignorance of the involvement by the police department itself in a cover-up. As the second act progresses, the detective gains tremendous respect for the simple val-

2–5   *Dead Man Walking*   Act III converges, brings to a climax, and resolves the primary issues of the story. In the final act of *Dead Man Walking* (1995), the condemned inmate Matthew Poncelet (Sean Penn) breaks down and reveals the truth of his crime to Sister Helen Prejean (Susan Sarandon), his lone friend. The moment intensifies the story by raising the emotional stakes. With this shift to contrition, the first opportunity for empathy toward the killer is established. Although the ending is not meant to win over the viewer's full support to the prisoner's side, it does force the audience to ponder more seriously the moral consequences of the death penalty. Some movies fail when the filmmakers miscalculate and stress story points that are secondary to the film's central theme for the sake of a more commercial ending.   (Gramercy Pictures)

ues of the Amish people. The recomplication in the third act takes place when the Amish mother and the detective fully realize their tender love for each other, but also that the cultural gulf between them may be too great. The original cop-in-pursuit conflict is supplanted by a more personal, romantic one.

In *Life Is Beautiful* (1998), Roberto Benigni plays delightful Guido with the flair of a great silent comedian for an extended Act I that deludes the audience into imagining that life in pre–World War II Italy is simply surviving amidst a charade of blowhard right-wing politics. In Act II, however, he and his young son Giosue (Giorgio Cantarini) are suddenly rounded up and sent to a grim Nazi death camp because of their Jewish heritage. The second act radically shifts the tone by detailing the efforts of a father trying to spiritually protect his son from the daily horrors of the camp. He does this by portraying their experience as an elaborate childlike game. Act III raises the stakes, making it ever harder for Guido to shield and adequately deflect the imminent reality and danger of the gas chamber from Giosue. At the stunning climax of the film, this gently heroic father gives up his life to save his son.

The conflict for William Hurt, playing the homosexual Molina in *Kiss of the Spider Woman* (1985), is to survive the prison experience in a dictatorial South American country with his particular values and unusual sensitivities intact. He gradually develops a respectful relationship with his opposite, a politically persecuted cellmate, Valentin (Raul Julia). In the third act, Molina is released only to find that he has been changed by his loyalty to Valentin and that now he has a political conscience to wrestle with. When he commits to his new belief and consciously puts himself in physical danger, he is killed. This act is the **climax** of the movie and gives it a final and surprising bolt of energy. The climax is that point of the story at which all of the competing issues relating to the protagonist converge and call for understanding.

The **resolution** (or **denouement**) of the story follows the climax. In some films this means lingering moments to contemplate the message; in others it is a quick tying up of the action and giving a hint at what the future holds for the main character. In terms of screen time, it is usually very short. Yet this part of a film causes much aesthetic turmoil for filmmakers. Innumerable battles have been fought through the years between filmmakers and their producers over the endings of movies. The standard wisdom of very commercial film producers, based on exit polls after screenings, is that endings should be upbeat: Regardless of whatever tragedy and pain has been inflicted on the major characters, a silver lining should be uncovered in the last scenes. Audiences pay money to be entertained, not depressed—or so popular marketing thinking goes. Yet many very successful films have chosen endings that are tragic. *Bonnie and Clyde* (1967) would have been a much less satisfying film experience if the merry bandits had continued racing through Midwest towns robbing banks. The blunt finality of their death in a burst of police gunfire was a shocking but important statement—their star-crossed lives simply had no future in an era that closed the book on the idea of romantic outlaws. And certainly, *Titanic* (1997) may have dispelled that logic of happy endings forever.

Ideally, there should be both an inherent logic and an honesty to the ending of a film, based upon the motivations and theme of the story up to that point. This may vary, given the differences in cultural values in the country where the movie is produced. But that does not mean a filmmaker is without a whole range of legitimate choices. *Butch Cassidy and the Sundance Kid* (1969) ends with a **freeze frame** of the two gunmen breaking out of their hiding place and rushing toward their certain death. As the still image remains on the screen, the extended moment brings up a kaleidoscope of contradictory feelings: a fatalistic view of human existence, an admiration of their guts in playing out the game they had chosen for themselves, the emotional pain of their unavoidable deaths, the sweetness in this last flamboyant act of camaraderie, a sense of needless loss. This Western was adventurous and rather lighthearted for much of its story, but its ending turned the work into a much more thoughtful piece. *Falling Down* (1993) is a story about alienation of the everyman in modern urban society. In the end, the protagonist (Michael Douglas) finds his death in the water under an ocean pier. This resolution is much more fitting than if he had suddenly reconciled with his wife and the rest of the society that he felt plagued him.

The third act structure brings formal symmetry to a movie. Although different story elements, unique to each movie, may play favorably or cruelly upon the fate of the main characters, this standard structure allows filmmakers a common framework for their art to imitate life. When a viewer wants to praise or condemn a movie, the first consideration should invariably be the balanced writing and flow of its screenplay. A great script is the foundation for a great film.

Having outlined this Aristotelian three-act structure, it must be said that some young filmmakers either reject or ignore it. Many feel that the schematic promotes neatness at the expense of surprise—a tight formula that unduly restricts other cinematic possibilities. For years various popular screenwriting teachers have dominated Hollywood's aesthetic agenda, influencing agents and producers to accept only scripts that fit a rigid mold. Director Alexander Payne (*Election*, 1999) complains "The whole school of Act 1/Act 2/Act 3 is destructive to a striving, growing cinema."

2–6   *Before the Rain*   At times a filmmaker will take the three-act structure and invent new ways to intertwine the acts. In *Before the Rain* (1994), director Milcho Manchevski structures his movie into three very separate but cleverly related stories. The film explores the personal impact of the racial and religious wars in the Balkans. In the first act, entitled "Words," a young monk at first protects a frightened Muslim girl he has fallen in love with while she is hiding in his room, then witnesses her death at the hands of her vengeful family; in the second act, "Faces," a Macedonian war photographer (Rade Serbedzija) based in London goes through the turmoil of a love affair with a married woman; the last act, "Pictures," ties to the first, when the world-weary photographer returns to the homeland of his youth for a visit and learns  that the scars of war are too deep to be healed. The stories, though seemingly unrelated at first, tie together in the end to make at profound statement about the senselessness of ethnic conflict.   (Gramercy Pictures)

Movies such as *Being John Malcovich* (1999), *The Blair Witch Project* (1999), and *American Psycho* (2000) find their own unique rhythms of storytelling. Such movies as *Short Cuts* (1993), *Magnolia*, (1999) and *Things You Can Just Tell by Looking at Her* (2000) tell several stories that parallel and intertwine, with ensemble casts providing their dramatic force **(2–6)**. Mainline Hollywood will continue to ask for orthodoxy in story structure, but the financial success of iconoclastic independent movies has awakened even the most conservative filmmakers to alternative thinking.

THE NATURE OF STORY CONFLICT

The definition and expression of conflict in narrative films, alluded to while analyzing the three-act structure, needs further consideration. The nature of the conflict is the keystone of a movie, the reason for our sustained interest in a story. Every screen narrative presents the main character with a major spiritual and/or physical challenge, then tests the personal courage of that person to face and overcome that challenge. The courage to act on what one perceives to be the truth is, on some level, a heroic act. The nature of the conflict must be great enough for the audience to genuinely care about its resolution. Even violently antisocial characters can win our admiration for this struggle. In *Heat* (1995), Robert DeNiro plays a leader of a small gang of vicious high-tech thieves. A sympathetic side of him emerges when he meets a woman who, contrary to his code of noninvolvement, he learns to love. The question that plagues the character is whether he is able to change and quit his murderous life of crime. Whatever reservations we have about this strange man, we admire his gritty display of courage in attempting to resolve what appears to be an impossible dilemma. Not every protagonist will survive his or her conflict—DeNiro's character doesn't—but the screenwriter must make us invest concern in the fate of the character. Even in failure a lesson will be learned and some insight into the nature of being human is gained.

External Conflict

The simplest way to present conflict is to pit bad guys against good guys. Every culture and time period defines who these persons are. Action/adventure movies, for example, usually present the conflict of good against evil in absolute terms. The classic Western ran endless variations on this elementary situation, with the antagonists as evil ranchers, corrupt lawmen, or "savage" Indians. In the case of Native Americans, it is only recently that they have broken through cultural stereotypes and been portrayed as heroes in films of substance. Other ethnic groups are still maligned, in particular Middle Easterners who have been repeatedly portrayed as terrorists in Hollywood movies. An example is *The Siege* (1998), where generic Moslem terrorists hold New York City hostage and bring untold threats to this fragile democratic society as thousands of Arab Americans are put in concentration camps. Stereotypes give filmmakers a quick, if mindless, way to identify the cast of opposing players. **External conflicts** may come in the form of another special circumstance, an individual, a group, an institution, society, or the forces of nature.

An Extraordinary or Random Circumstance. Bad things happen. In drama especially, a sudden catastrophe is often introduced to create a reversal of fortune, upsetting and blocking the normal life of the protagonist. This event, or series of events, seems to conspire against the hero's good fortune. The shocking loss of a job, the announcement of a fatal illness, or a miscalculated scientific experiment can present a conflict that may appear to be insurmountable. In *Jumanji* (1995), a chance discovery of a mysterious board game pits two kids against a series of vengeful forces of nature. The key to survival rests in their sticking out the game to a successful ending. The circumstance that befalls the protagonist sometimes arrives innocently enough. When Mel Coplin (Ben Stiller) finds out of his biological parents' existence in the satire *Flirting with Disaster* (1996), he welcomes the chance discover his true parental roots. The episodes that follow that circumstance build to a hilarious (for us) series of disastrous encounters for Mel and his wife Nancy (Patricia Arquette), with mistaken families across America.

An Individual. The advantage of devising a conflict between individuals is that the story clearly becomes a confrontation of two wills, each having a differing and usually contrasting code of behavior. The movie *In the Line of Fire* (1993) sets a maverick Secret Service Agent (Clint Eastwood) against a treacherous genius (John

Malkovich) intent on not only murdering the president, but also haunting the psyche of the man with the mission to protect him. The high-stakes cat-and-mouse game between the two men is the central conflict of the film, and their verbal jousting provides the building blocks of action. Movies that starkly match one person against another can create intense dramatic pressure, and this stripped down one-on-one conflict gives such a film its dramatic charge **(2–7)**.

A Group.   A protagonist's problem takes on other dimensions when it involves a group of people. The confrontation of one person against a group usually requires more complex strategies to resolve the issues. The conflict will often present itself in the confrontation of the hero with antagonistic behavior of a group of people. In *Lean on Me* (1989), Morgan Freeman plays a school principal intent on cleaning up the scholastic and social failures of an inner-city high school. During the rocky course of his mission, he confronts various groups of out-of-control students, matching their street savvy and overcoming their hold on the daily attitudes of other school kids. Michelle Pfeiffer's portrayal of a high-school teacher in *Dangerous Minds* (1995) took on much the same challenge. In *The Rock* (1996), the protagonists are a crack team of anti-terrorists, including an amusing FBI biochemist weapons expert (Nicolas Cage) and a specially paroled political prisoner (Sean Connery) with firsthand knowledge of

2–7   *The Bodyguard*   The external conflict in *The Bodyguard* (1992) comes from the mad stalker of famous singer Rachael Marron (Whitney Houston). In this action/romance movie, the job of the singer's professional bodyguard, Frank Farmer (Kevin Costner), is to protect her from physical harm, despite her initial resistance to his confining protective measures. Actions of a single antagonist, in this case a crazed fan, create very clear and straightforward story conflicts, classically matching the strength and wit of two opposing and strong-willed persons.   (Warner Bros.)

the bowels of Alcatraz. They face off with a rough group of highly disciplined former Marines, headed by Brigadier General Hummel (Ed Harris), a fanatic, self-styled patriot, intent on wiping out San Francisco with deadly liquid gas rockets unless their political demands are met. As in many action/adventure thrillers, the logic of the conflict is secondary to the spectacular special effects that are set off as a result.

An Institution.   Organizations within a culture that have the power to control thought and behavior are often seen to be an enemy of the individual's ability to act freely or be fully human. The bureaucracies of the society—the CIA, hospitals, large corporations, prisons, Wall Street, schools, the military, the IRS, etc.—become antagonistic forces that challenge the hero with their relentless, confining force. In *Awakenings* (1990), Robin Williams attempts to cure patients with encephalitis, and does so for a time. Not only must he fight the disease, but he must also confront a depressingly bureaucratic hospital administration that discourages his innovative efforts at every turn. In *The Shawshank Redemption* (1994), Andy (Tim Robbins) is sent to prison for the murder of his wife and her lover. A former banker, he works the prison's financial books for a corrupt warden, who sees Andy's value to him and attempts to control his very existence. The oppressiveness of the prison system is unrelenting and without the friendship and guidance of another lifer, Red (Morgan Freeman), Andy's spirit might have been broken. Often the primary victory in such stories is a discovery of the protagonist's latent strength in the face of an authoritarian institution **(2–8)**.

2–8   *The Insider*   *The Insider* (1999) presents the complex economic politics of the television industry—relating a true story involving the Sunday night fixture "60 Minutes"—as the major external conflict facing a former tobacco company employee, Dr. Jeffrey Wigand (Russell Crowe), and a sympathetic producer of the show, Lowell Bergman (Al Pacino). This conspiracy film pits the powerful media institution and tobacco interests against these two men of integrity as they struggle with inner conflicts involving loyalty while at the same time attempting to rally public support to air their important message to the American public.   (Touchstone Pictures)

Society.   Sometimes the entire culture—"the system"—goes against the hero's most basic needs. This conflict is usually insidiously pervasive and must be discovered and identified by the protagonist, despite its obviousness to the viewer. In the German film *The Nasty Girl* (1990), a young female student sets out to find the truth about the complicity of her town in the racial atrocities that preceded World War II. For her tireless efforts, she faces being ostracized by her society. But she learns to stand up to enormous physical and emotional pressures, winning a personal victory. In the coming-of-age film *October Sky* (1999) set in the 1950s, young people in the West Virginia coal mining town where Homer Hickman (Jake Gyllenhaal) lives never expect to go to college. That sullen society of hardworking miners did not present higher education as an option. Inspired by a science teacher (Laura Dern) and his own inner vision, however, Homer breaks with the oppressive traditions of his surroundings and gains spiritual and physical freedom. A major conflict for the protagonist in science fiction is the human alienation often found in a future society, as portrayed in films as different as *Blade Runner* (1982), *Brazil* (1985), *The Running Man* (1987), *Closetland* (1992), and *The Matrix* (1999).

Forces of Nature.   The very titles of certain films give away the conflict. In *Never Cry Wolf* (1983), the outcome of a man's confrontation with the uncompromising natural solitude in Northern Canada is inspirational. *Alaska* (1996) does a similar thing in that state. The uncanny story twist in *Jaws* (1975) is that the writers gave "nature," in the terrifying image of a shark, a blind anger that seemed determined to feed on the innocents of a seaside resort. In *Backdraft* (1991), the filmmakers try to portray the element of fire in a similar antagonist position, as if the flames somehow consciously sought out its victims. Storms have also proven very popular. *The Wind* (1927), *Earthquake* (1974), *Hurricane* (1979), *Twister* (1996), *Hard Rain* (1998), and, most emphatically, *The Perfect Storm* (2000) present the protagonists with the raging and unleashed power of nature. With *Dante's Peak* (1997) and *Volcano* (1997) erupting, or *Deep Impact* (1998) and *Armageddon* (1998) raining down heavenly bodies, new catastrophes forever test earthlings' abilities to survive forces of nature that seem to have something personal against us.

Inner Conflict

An internal conflict within the main character is present to some degree in all stories. This struggle strengthens the dramatic purpose of any external conflict. No matter how physically threatened the hero may be by outside persons or events, the story will usually question the inner resolve of that person to survive and overcome the opposition. The primary conflict often will appear to be an external threat, but the tougher conflict has to do more with the hero's *internal* battle: the personal struggle against spiritual defeat and despair. *Philadelphia* (1994) is a story about Andrew Beckett (Tom Hanks) discovering that he has AIDS. The disease is obviously the external conflict, but the character's incredibly brave and honest internal response to the tragedy is what distinguishes the movie. The emotional vulnerability of the primary character, combined with the intertwining ethical questions in the story, gives us a deeper sense of his humanity. Some categories of **inner conflict** include self doubt, personal history, emotional problems, inexperience, and ethical values

Self Doubt.   The comedies of Woody Allen have been built on his character's battle with low sexual and social self-esteem. His conflict, which becomes the running joke throughout his films, is that his character gets stuck analyzing every question concerning his manhood to the point of absurdity. From *Bananas* (1971) to *Deconstructing Harry* (1997), his public never seems to tire of watching his struggles. In a movie with more sinister consequences, the problem for Jodie Foster as a raw FBI recruit in *Silence of the Lambs* (1991) was that she not only had to battle Dr. Lecter and a series of threatening physical trials, but she also had to face her own doubts concerning her abilities as an agent. Excessive self-questioning is the conflict in films ranging from a romantic comedy such as *When Harry Met Sally* (1989) to the classic presentation of the conflict in the many film versions of Shakespeare's *Hamlet*.

Personal History.   The entangled and sometimes tainted past of the main character often impacts the present, demanding that the protagonist either change his or her values and behavior, or face the consequences. In *The Grifters* (1990), the young con artist played by John Cusack is caught up in a struggle to survive in a hostile world in which cheating is the primary way he survives. We are led to believe that his strange upbringing under the influence of his scheming mother (Anjelica Huston) gave him few other choices. His normal life is most abnormal. Protagonists in such stories must reject the seemingly deterministic forces—whether it is a prison record, an alcoholic father, or a ghetto neighborhood—that claim control of their lives. The lead characters played by Laurence Fishburne, Cuba Gooding, Jr., and Ice Cube in *Boyz 'N the Hood* (1991) struggle with the mental pressure of dealing with their gang-related backgrounds and the turmoil of daily survival. Their dreams for the future are constantly being confronted by their grim ongoing backlog of problems. Stories will usually have tragic endings when the protagonist cannot break free from a damaging past.

Emotional Problems.   Anger, compulsive behavior, shyness, and a host of other personality flaws may block the lead character from achieving a goal. These emotional obstacles will block the protagonist from functioning until the problem is acknowledged and transformed. In *Klute* (1971), Jane Fonda plays a cynical prostitute being pursued by a deranged man. Based on the exploitive quality of her past experience with men, she distrusts the only person who seeks to help her, a detective played by Donald Sutherland. Until she is able to overcome her deep suspicions about his motives, her chances for survival are hampered. As an aging piano teacher in *Madame Sousatzka* (1988), Shirley MacLaine's fierce pride in demanding unusually high standards from her students is both the source of her attraction and a constant character flaw. We watch with fascination as she fights her inner prideful demons. Personal inner turmoil of the protagonist, from simmering to raging, is often the force that pushes the story forward **(2–9)**.

2-9   *The Waterdance*   In *The Waterdance* (1991), three young men (L to R: William Forsythe, Eric Stoltz, and Wesley Snipes) reside in a hospital facility and face intense emotional problems growing out of their confining injuries. Writer/director Neal Jimenez breaks through the formula writing that is often associated with the problems of the disabled to tell a story of young men plagued by personal anger and sexual frustration. Each young man learns to handle his individual internal conflicts by reaching out to the others with honesty and frank humor. The title refers to a dream of dancing on water, and the fear of drowning when one stops.

Inexperience.   The line between innocence and ignorance is sometimes finely drawn, and characters in film stories often walk the edge. It is a standard storytelling technique to have an uninformed protagonist introduced into a new and troublesome situation. Because of his inexperience, the central character runs into a series of dramatic walls set up by the plot. In *Blue Velvet* (1986), Kyle MacLachlan plays an innocent young man (Jeffrey Beaumont) who both seeks out and is repelled by a very dark underworld in his hometown of Lumberton. The conflict in the film grows out of his innocence, as he naively puts himself in the center of a violent pack of evil men, lead by Frank Booth (Dennis Hopper). An uninformed trust in his ability to independently save a young woman (Isabella Rossellini) leaves Jeffrey with some harrowing choices, maturing him quickly. Most **coming-of-age** movies base their stories on the inexperience of youth, using the problems caused by the main character's naiveté to propel the action.

Ethical Values. A common inner conflict is one that pits the moral code of the protagonist against persons or groups in opposition. There is often pressure on the hero to set aside or abandon his or her beliefs because of social pressure or the lure of materialistic reward. The consequence is that the hero will not be true to himself or herself. In the classic film *Mr. Smith Goes to Washington* (1939), Jimmy Stewart is slowly worn down by a political establishment that tempts him to abandon his ethically stable roots and give up his fight for political honesty. Miraculously, he hangs on, finds deeper courage, and triumphs over an intractable opposition. A more contemporary ethical dilemma is presented in *Return to Paradise* (1998). After three carefree buddies vacation in Thailand, Lewis (Joaquin Phoenix) decides to extend his stay. He is caught with a large quantity of cocaine inadvertently left behind, and, under strict Malaysian law, sentenced as a dealer to death. Two years later, Tony (David Conrad) and Sheriff (Vince Vaughn), safe in comfortable situations in New York City, are told of Lewis's fate by a lawyer (Anne Heche) and are confronted to accept their responsibility in the crime, return to Malaysia, and be sentenced to three years in a squalid prison. By doing this, they will save their friend's life. The film does not let the characters (or the audience) off the hook, as the story delves into the very tough moral decisions that each person cannot avoid. The movie is an intense series of investigations into personal ethics.

These and other conflicts set the story in motion and call for resolution. Several obstacles, external and internal, can be at work at the same time. But films with simply stated but profound central conflicts often resonate most deeply with audiences. The subtle and distinctive dramatic shadings of scripts depend on the interpretation given by the actors. The quality of performance helps us care about the nature and outcome of the conflict. But unless clearly stated dramatic conflicts are first written into the screenplay, any attempt to bring the story to life by the actors will fall short.

CHARACTERIZATION

Audiences come to movies to watch screen characters with whom they can identify or about whom they can fantasize. These characters may be bigger than life or as familiar as the person next door; perform outrageous feats or suffer heroically in silence. An overriding requirement of a movie is that the characters be *interesting*. The one thing held in common with Luke Skywalker *(Star Wars)*, Kevin *(Home Alone)*, Charles Foster Kane *(Citizen Kane)*, Nikita *(La Femme Nikita)*, Bijou *(Shanghai Triad)*, and Mrs. Doubtfire is that as we get to know them, we are willing to commit our attention to watching their dramas unfold, and we care about what happens to them.

From the writer's perspective, a well-developed story means creating compelling characters whose *motivations* are clear and credible. When the story conflict is presented, the protagonist must act in ways that would naturally result from what we are told or from what we sense in character. The lack of well-motivated behavior in the major characters is a common weakness in poorly written films. Equally essential for the audience is the recognition that the main character needs to *change* in some way to accomplish the indicated goal. The protagonist usually begins the story in a state of relative "ignorance" regarding the true nature of the obstacles to be faced. The person may be unenlightened, oblivious, unwarned, witless, unprepared, or simply blind to the problem. But during the course of the story, he or she will awaken to the nature of the dilemma, will act upon it, and as a result, will significantly change in some way. The unfolding process of *character change* in the story is what holds an audience. A movie may end in disaster for the main character, but this has less dramatic impact than the fact that the character has been transformed by some new awareness.

In *Silkwood* (1983), based on a true story, Karen (Meryl Streep) is unconscious at first of the dangers in her work, making plutonium fuel rods at the Kerr-McGee nuclear plant in Oklahoma. She is a feisty and self-indulgent worker, but hardly distinguishable from the rest of her crew. The audience witnesses with increasing interest the changes that take place in her character as she learns the horrible truth about what is happening at the plant. Safety regulations are being ignored, and workers are being put at risk for the sake of company policies. Spurred to action, she sheds the passive attitude that most of her fellow workers are encouraged to have in fear of the loss of their jobs. Karen grows to be a truly heroic union spokesperson and, for her activism, is finally killed in a suspicious car accident while delivering documents to a newspaper reporter that exposed the company. The effectiveness of the film rests with the audience's identification with Karen's development as an ordinary person with unusually stubborn integrity caught in the path of an angry industrial giant. The film would lack the needed depth of feeling, however, if the motivation of Karen were poorly established, or if she were the same person, in terms of self-awareness, at the time of her death.

Truly original character invention is not easily achieved in screenwriting. Apart from the intrinsic difficulties of fresh writing, the movie industry itself is ambivalent about inventing lead characters that are not quickly identifiable. Given the time constraints of movie length and a fear of viewer impatience, there is a tendency to rush the story points of a movie. Conventional wisdom has it that the audience needs to label characters quickly so that the story *action* can be pushed forward. Of course, the most memorable motion pictures are usually those in which the major characters are subtly detailed and singularly played.

DIALOGUE

Language characterizes our humanity. Good writers use it with purpose and beauty. Because dramatic writing hopes to convincingly distill life's essential experiences for the purposes of insight and pleasure, the invention of authentic dialogue is important. Dialogue externalizes the thoughts and feelings of the characters and generates the electricity between characters **(2–10)**. The beauty of a well-delivered line of dialogue is one of the joys of watching both stage plays and movies. Although the images of a movie are its most obvious feature, narrative films are about *people*. It is true that

2–10 *Casino* A crucial story element is characterization. The screenwriter creates believable characters by establishing their presence through dialogue that is on the mark. In Martin Scorcese's *Casino* (1995), the contentious verbal exchanges between "Ace" Rothstein (Robert DeNiro), a distracted casino manager, and his high-strung wife Ginger (Sharon Stone) lay the foundation for the theme of a self-destructing Las Vegas gambling empire during the 1970s. The close and accurate character observation and development of the main characters by writer Nicolas Pileggi gives the movie its heady reality. (Universal Studios)

silent films could convey the nuances of human relationships with the poetry of their visuals, but the spoken interchanges of sound films brought movies to life. Writing a strikingly good screenplay means writing effective dialogue.

Being close and accurate observers of human behavior, fiction writers are, in a sense, practicing psychologists. When creating a character for a movie, the writer will develop that person's personality through carefully constructed dialogue. If the lead character is male, questions arise: Is he to be macho, self-deprecating, curious, funny, ignorant, sly, despairing, phony, spiritual, laid-back, or just strange? If one or several of these descriptions apply, how does the writer convey this in **dialogue** on a page? That is, what words, language patterns, and undercurrents of emotion would give that impression? A writer of narratives must have an acute ear for the power of the spoken word and be a dynamic inventor of verbal exchange.

Having said that, however, the screenwriter must avoid the temptation to simply "tell" the story in dialogue. The primary mode of expression in film is through pictures. Experienced professional writers have learned this and write trusting the power of the camera. Screenwriter Anna Hamilton Phelan (*Mask*, 1985) observes, ". . . you want to stay away from getting all the information out in dialogue. And if you can find some creative way to do it—where people can *see* it rather than hear it— that always seems to feel better." Great dialogue in a movie finds its place within the synergy of the camera, the talents of the actors, and the internal narrative demands of the scene. Writers can create the narrative impact of the scene by writing great dialogue on paper, but they have small influence on how it is delivered by the actors, and no control of the camera recording it.

FINDING THE THEME

In the effort to distill a novel, a stage play, or an original movie idea, the screenwriter attempts to isolate the **theme** of the story. Early on and regularly thereafter, the writer must ask, "In essence, what is the story *about*?" Often, the complex structure of a long novel, for example, masks its basic statement. Finding it is the first step in shaping a script. Characters and events can be moved around to suit the demands of motion picture story structure, but if the theme of any story is obscure or misinterpreted, what comes out of it will merely compound the mistake. A good place to start is simply to reduce the story to one sentence:

> *This movie is about _____ [the subject] who _____ [the action].*

Sometimes even major movie projects struggle to find consensus with this simple exercise. The producers may envision one film story, the director another, the leading stars another still.

In some cases there is a legitimate choice. When screenwriter Frank Pierson adapted Scott Turow's novel *Presumed Innocent*, he found two equally strong themes: a "justice theme" and a "passion theme." One is about a district attorney falsely suspected of murder, the other about this man's inappropriate love affair with a fellow prosecutor. Pierson felt that one theme had to take the lead, the other becoming a subplot. By beginning the screenplay with a sex act that turns into a murder, he chose to emphasize the *love story*, but when a new director came on the project, the theme of *reverence for the law* became the primary focus, and Pierson rewrote the beginning scenes **(2–11)**. Therefore, the finished film opens with shots of the polished wood and brass of an empty courtroom, as Harrison Ford's voiceover solemnly tells what will soon happen there. The thematic implications of a movie can often be altered by redesigning a few scenes and character interactions.

2–11   *Presumed Innocent*   When searching for an overriding theme for the suspense/thriller *Presumed Innocent* (1990), screenwriter Frank Pierson chose to emphasize the concept of "reverence for the law" rather than stressing the possible romantic aspects of the

story. Harrison Ford plays a prosecuting attorney, married to an unforgiving wife (Bonnie Bedilia, center), but now accused and on trial for murdering a female colleague with whom he was having an affair. One way the screenwriter emphasized the theme of legal ethics in the story was strengthening the role of a brilliant and honorable defense lawyer (Raul Julia, left) for the accused.
(Warner Bros.)

FILM GENRES

To create some order in this puzzling business of storytelling-for-profit, the concept of genres has proved to be useful in movie production. As previously pointed out, the term **genre** is used to indicate a broad category of films, all sharing common story themes, conflicts, settings, character types, or visual styles. The concept of a story genre grows out of traditional literature. The plays of Shakespeare and the great novels of the eithteenth and nineteenth centuries established categories of narratives that connected with audiences of the time. In motion pictures, certain genres have been popular since the 1920s and 1930s, others emerged and disappeared as the cultural climate changed. A range of *comedy* categories, for example, has always been with us, but *karate* movies spun out of the more current interest in that fighting style and the dynamic of its photographic possibilities; and *pirate* movies, so common in earlier times, are rarely made today. On the other hand, *The Gladiator* (2000) is an attempt to revive extravagant Roman Empire epics (*Quo Vadis,* 1951; *Ben Hur,* 1959), a mainstay genre in the past for Hollywood studios. Genres are restyled to fit the changing tastes of each generation.

Finding a fresh angle for a standard genre is always a challenge for the writer. Because the demands of such writing seem so restrictive, in that the story has prescribed boundaries, some critics discount the creativity of mainstream film writers who must work within the audience expectations of a genre. Our taste as a film audience contains a paradox. On the one hand, we claim to want original stories with surprises at every turn. But perhaps more significantly, we love movies that replay the familiar situations—to the point of formula. Writer Steven E. de Souza (*Knock Off,* 1998) laments the current situation: "There is a list of things that currently go into action movies right now. Hostages, terrorists, car chases, fistfights, a scene in a bar with strippers and buddy cops—one black, one white." This tendency serves film producers very well. For this reason, previously popular movies and the **sequels** that are written from them are usually a relatively safe bet. The surprise hit *The Blair Witch Project* (1999), therefore, is quickly followed by *The Blair Witch Project 2* (2000). When audience taste and response can be accurately predicted, the expensive business of moviemaking becomes a little less hazardous to those studio executives who continually live on the edge of making a colossal career-threatening mistake.

The *western, science fiction,* or *coming-of-age* films each have a dominant or recurring dramatic attitude, called a **motif**. When the audience finds a special connection with such motifs and becomes conversant with them, they seek out other films with similar themes. For instance, when going to a western movie, we generally expect to see a man facing a rugged and unknown frontier, a land that has almost no formal rules of law. He must rely on whatever personal values and codes of conduct that hard experience has taught him. The traditional Hollywood cowboy—as played by John Wayne, Jimmy Stewart, or Gary Cooper—had well-defined and deeply held moral convictions. He was tough, fair, independent, and fearless when cornered. With scripts using variations of this character type, the classic western was refined. For years the studios have found huge audiences wanting to see the rite of frontier heroics repeated.

The exploration of a recognized genre by a writer can afford an exciting collision of present-day values with storytelling conventions from the past. As the film teacher Leo Braudy writes, "The joy in genre is to see what can be dared in the creation of a new form or the creative destruction and complication of an old one." The rapidly changing nature of society's taste in entertainment spawns continual shifts of emphasis in traditional genres and generates new definitions of audience interest. The various genres become story templates with which many screenwriter work. Following is a quick list, not at all exhaustive, of some popular movie categories within which screenwriters create.

Action/Adventure.   This genre has set the pace in the last decade. These films are **plot-driven,** the emphasis being less on exploring character than on filling the screen with fast action. They rely heavily on nonstop physical movement, spectacular special effects, extremely high sound volume, and frequent situations of graphic violence. Because these films—*Die Hard 2: Die Harder* (1990), *Speed 2* (1997), *The World Is Not Enough* (1999), *Mission: Impossible 2* (2000)—engage the viewer on a purely visual and visceral level, the story's action is easily understood by overseas moviegoers, a lucrative and important target audience. The car chases, explosions, and grizzly death scenes of *Face/Off* (1997) need little translation. This potential profit advantage normally justifies higher film budgets for this genre and insures its continuing dominance at Hollywood studios.

Science Fiction/Science Fantasy.   With the release of *2001: A Space Odyssey* (1968), based on a work by Arthur C. Clark, and with new developments in special-effects techniques, this genre was opened for writers and filmmakers to convincingly take the viewer into almost any reality without losing visual credibility. Screenwriters today need not restrict their imaginations for fear of the production team claiming that futuristic scenarios are unworkable. With the ever-changing *computer-generated special effects* technology, almost anything is possible. **Science Fantasy** expands the genre into limitless realms of the writer's imagination, sometimes combining futuristic and cyberpunk themes to paint dark and very challenging conflicts for their heroes **(2–12)**. Films such as *The Matrix* (1999) and *Existenz* (1999) envision a future in which alternate virtual worlds created by computers blur or substitute what we have known as reality, translating the spirit of writers such as William Gibson, Philip K. Dick, and Harlan Ellison to the screen.

War Movies.   The very nature of war is physical conflict created by opposing nationalistic or ideological rivalries, making the subject ripe for thrilling and tragic visual drama of every sort. There is hardly a war in history that has not been dramatized on film, from Greek expansionism in *Alexander the Great* (1955) to the Gulf War in *Courage under Fire* (1996). During and after World War II, for example, hundreds of films told stories of men in battle. One of the most realistic portrayals is Steven Spielberg's *Saving Private Ryan* (1998), a raw and shocking reenactment of the U.S. invasion of Normandy in 1944. This movie contrasts with Terrence Malick's *The Thin Red Line* (1998), a more visually meditative exploration into the psyches of the young

2-12 *Star Wars: Episode I—The Phantom Menace* Director/Producer George Lucas has always shown a strong interest in science/fantasy, beginning with *THX1138* (1971). He went on to give special and lasting definition to the genre with his extraordinarily successful series of Star Wars movies. With *Star Wars: Episode I—The Phantom Menace* (1999), reported to be a prequel to two subsequent movies, Lucas attempts to round out the mythology of space conflict that he created for the screen. In this frame, Jedi Master Qui-Gon Jinn (Liam Neeson) is surrounded by some of the imaginative characters that have given audiences a special affection for Lucas's elaborate tale. (20th Century Fox)

men fighting the same war in the South Pacific. But during the time of Vietnam, films about that conflict rarely were made because producers and writers, aware of the profound ambiguity the conflict held for the general public, shied away from facing the tough moral issues that split this country. It was not until after the war ended, with the films of writer/directors such as Francis Ford Coppola (*Apocalypse Now,* 1979) and Oliver Stone *(Platoon*, 1986), that deeper insights into the total spectrum of the Vietnam experience became the subject of films. Imbedded in the stories of many war films is an antiwar statement. The movie industry has an impressive list of films voicing strong opposition to military aggression, beginning with Lewis Milestone's *All Quiet on the Western Front* (1930), a film that shocked audiences at a time when realistic portrayals of war were rare.

Westerns. The mythology of the American West has always offered movies a dramatically rich subject matter. The sweeping landscapes of the old West were always a place of imagined adventure, especially for youths brought up in the cities of America and Europe. Classic themes of struggle lent themselves to the hot plains and dangerous mountain passes where cowboys might have faced multiple enemies: Indians, desperadoes, famine, the weather, loneliness. These repeated portraits of the Western hero as the popular model for rugged individualism were easily idolized by boys and men. The genre reached its height throughout the 1940s and 1950s. During the 1960s, television so inundated the public with every variation of the Western that the genre lost its wonder for the general public, and the subject became a routine exercise. But writers today still find the subject attractive because the stories are so ceremonial and visually rich. Each year another attempt is made to breathe new life into the genre. *Unforgiven* (1992) and *Tombstone* (1993) give credence to notion that the genre of the Western is far from exhausted.

Musicals.   The close relationship of film and music stems from the way they complement each other. The rhythms of musical sound enhance and transform the visual image. The classic musicals of directors Busby Berkeley *(Gold Diggers of 1935)*, Vincente Minnelli *(Meet Me in St. Louis*, 1944), and Stanley Donen *(Singin' in the Rain*, 1952) **(2–13)**, along with the performances of Fred Astaire and Ginger Rogers, Nelson Eddy and Jeanette McDonald, Judy Garland and Mickey Rooney, or Gene Kelly and Cyd Charisse, had stories in which everything suddenly stopped for a song and dance. The film narrative was usually constructed *around* the music, at its service. Variations proved highly successful, working well as *musical comedy*, the *musical biography*, etc. In the more recent past, just as recorded music began to permeate our daily lives, musicals reflected our new cultural environment, changing the way filmmakers envision the musical **(2–14)**. Just as rap music creates the cadence of street life in many places today, music in movies today does not so much interrupt the story as intertwine it into its fabric. Films as dramatically different as *Georgia* (1995), a

2–13   *Singin' in the Rain*   The genre of the musical is ever-changing as tastes in music evolve. The classic era of the song-and-dance movies of the 1940s and 1950s is past, but Gene Kelly's *Singin' in the Rain* (1952), written by Betty Comden and Adolph Green, remains a perfect example of the successful blend of sensational dance sequences and a clever story. The boundless optimistic energy of the performers comes through in every scene of this film.   (MGM)

2–14   *Selena*   In a more realistic modern vein, the musical *Selena* (1997) tells the story of a famous and genuinely admired singer, Selena (played by Jennifer Lopez), that ends in the true-to-life tragedy of her violent death in the prime of her career.   (Warner Bros.)

serious drama between a popular singer confronting her talented but strung-out sister, and *Still Crazy* (1998), a comical and touching reunion of a 1970s British rock group, show that musicians will continue to be appealing characters for writers to propel stories.

Romance.   As audiences, we are forever entranced with struggle of lovers to merge their lives in a bond of love. In many romantic films, that love can overwhelm almost every conflict, even death. **Romantic comedy** is the lighter side. Whether the reasoning is valid or not, in the niche market mentality of today's movie distribution system, these films are coded to appeal to women, the strategy being that the stories give box-office balance to the Action/Adventure thrillers directed toward male tastes. In contemporary times, some of these love stories are more reality-based, offering more profound and somewhat darker insights into male/female relationships. But the genre still appeals to that part of us that is eternally optimistic about finding a life-transforming relationship with the perfect stranger, in the manner of the classic nineteenth-century story by Jane Austen, *Sense and Sensibility* (1995), the modern Manhattan setting of *You've Got Mail* (1998), and the bohemian district *Notting Hill* (1999) of London.

Gangster Movies.   The public has always been fascinated with the clandestine life of the criminal. This world is mostly made up of men who live outside of the mores and activities of the ordinary person. It is a dangerous existence in which one's animal instincts for survival, basic street smarts, and quick verbal wit are primary virtues. The figure of the tough guy is inherently romantic, a loner in an uncaring city who makes his own rules even while accepting the code of fellow gang members. He is willing to suffer the consequences for his lifestyle; the chance of a violent death is always present. Women in these movies usually give the stories their moral compass and are used to offer some salvation to the lead character. The genre grew up in the 1930s with movies such as *Little Caesar* (1930) and *The Public Enemy* (1931), often with *good-guy-gone-bad* themes. But by the 1970s, with *The Godfather* (1972) and *The Godfather, Part 2* (1974), the form turned into historically accurate and very violent **mob** films, often showing the killing rituals of the Mafia in New York City and Las Vegas. In variations on this theme, the urban drug warlord has now become the chief antagonist in many of these films.

Horror.   The Germans and Scandinavians started making psychologically terrifying films in the 1920s, and Hollywood inherited the style, polished it, and made the genre its own. When these horror films slid into self-parody by the 1950s, directors Donald Siegel (*Invasion of the Body Snatchers*, 1956) and Alfred Hitchcock (*Psycho*, 1960) injected new levels of terror. In the past two decades, the degree of extreme graphic violence created a new kind of genre: the **slasher** movie. Theories abound as to why these films command such a large and loyal audience: Some say it is simply a reflection of the actual violence reported in daily media and, therefore, is reality based. But these dark movies ritualize our worst fears, establishing a formula that affords most of the audience with an emotional distance from the gruesome acts depicted **(2–15)**. Although the storytelling conventions of movies such as *Scream 3* (2000) confront us with the same fears that older films presented, the heightened nature of the extremely graphic violence is culturally disturbing to many critics of the genre.

2–15   *Night of the Living Dead*   George A. Romero rewrote *Night of the Living Dead* (1990) from his 1968 original. Writers working in the horror movie genre play on our unspoken primal fears to their advantage. Such stories conjure up our darkest nightmares, in this case the specter of being overwhelmed by an unknowable evil force. Once a particular storyline in the horror genre resonates strongly with the public, movie sequels are written and produced to plumb every angle of the original. Because many of these films often have few stars and can be shot quickly, the horror genre is attractive to moviemakers wanting cheap production costs and easy audience concept recognition.   (Columbia Pictures)

Comedy.   Although too inclusive to be strictly called a genre, the industry generally categorizes a varied group of films with the broad label *comedy.* Comedy has always been a top money-maker for the movie industry, dating back to the first films of producer Mack Sennett and the Keystone Kops. In its many variations—slapstick, romantic comedy, domestic comedy, dumb buddy films, satire, screwball comedy, parody, black comedy, and more—the best of these films find their way by being acutely sensitive to the manners and social climate of the day. Good comedy writers are highly prized in the trade, and many comedians—Charlie Chaplin, Woody Allen, Jacques Tati, Albert Brooks, Buster Keaton, Roberto Begnini, Mel Brooks—have regularly written, directed, and acted in their own films.

Epics.   This grand genre cuts across every subject, the only qualification being that the sweepingly spectacular visual qualities of the film are as expansive as the territory covered by the subject matter in the story. *Gone with the Wind* (1939) is still the classic model. Studios have always been tempted by the capacity of such movies to present an exceptionally broad scope drama and adventure on the screen, hence the many gaudy movies based on Biblical tales with casts of thousands. When an epic is very successful, as in the case of *Titanic* (1997), "going to the movie theater" becomes an extraordinary event in itself. The huge budgets of these films often present overwhelming logistical problems, but this fact is usually exploited in publicity and merely spurs more audience interest. Because of heightened expectations inherent in an epic, the screenplay is sometimes worked over to the point that its ideas are either too easily digested or any nuance in the story is lost in extravagant production values.

Many other genres appeal to the special interests of varying film audiences, combining elements of several genres. A sample of these includes **coming-of-age** films, which traditionally present young characters facing the desire for new freedoms and the fears of its responsibilities; **woman-in-jeopardy** stories, which often show a vulnerable woman who, during the course of fearfully heightened events, becomes physically isolated, in danger, and is saved by a man; and **inner-city** films, which have attempted to portray the realities of existence for African Americans and Latin Americans. A new generation of ethnic filmmakers has brought fresh dimensions of these conflicts to the screen. **Big city cop** movies usually tell of cynical law officers worn down by the redundancy of urban violence and have learned to play by their own rules **(2–16)**; and **road movies** are about the American urge to escape, get in a powerful car, head out (West, usually) and ramble, taking in everything as it comes. Film genres are always combining or changing their shadings to generate a new sense of discovery.

Some scripts shift from one genre to another in the rewriting of the drafts. James Brooks first wrote *I'll Do Anything* (1994) as a musical, then as he directed it, shifted the film into the genre of straight comedy, and finally in the editing removed the music. Robert Lawton's original script for *Pretty Woman* (1990) was based on the hard reality of a Hollywood Boulevard prostitute who, after having lived with a rich executive for a week, ends up back on the street. When Disney Studios brought in writer

2–16 *Bad Lieutenant* The turmoil of America's cities is distilled in the genre of "The Big City Cop." The *Bad Lieutenant* (1992) could be considered representative of the genre in its revisionist phase. The genre classically shows the excitement and heroics of police work on city streets. But in Abel Ferrara's movie, the degree of a cop's deterioration under pressure is a step beyond the usual cynicism found in this kind of movie. Early in the film, a detective (Harvey Keitel) is found in the depths of spiritual exhaustion, having lost any sense of basic codes of conduct. He becomes more corrupt than any criminal he might encounter. The unsparing vision of the film gives the audience a shocking portrait of a cop's life. (Aries Film Release)

Barbara Benedek, the script took on a fairy-tale aspect and director Garry Marshall, who had a background in comedy, lightened the film even further. The final movie turned out to be a slightly off-beat romantic comedy.

For the screenwriter and filmmakers, fitting a story into a genre often has practical consequences in the marketplace. If, for instance, a film script does not fall into a readily identifiable genre, the project may have a problem in gaining the confidence of financial backers and studio executives. The public will eventually ask the question, *"What's the film supposed to be about?"* and the promotional material must somehow answer it. For example, *Choose Me* (1984), a sly black comedy about a group of emotional wanderers in an urban landscape, could not be put into a category easily recognized by audiences, and therefore did not do well financially. Many excellent projects are never developed because they do not fit into conventional categories. The Catch 22 for screenwriters in Hollywood is that while the industry claims that it wants original stories, if a script does not fit into a mold of what has gone before, getting the movie produced is an uphill battle.

In seeking a simple solution, computer software for the scriptwriter can now be purchased that claims to develop stories designed to fit the genre formulas of the industry. One such program has a database of over 13,000 plots that can be blended in various ways. Some would say that this technological attempt at simplifying the creative process is yet another way that the industry commercializes art. The real problem for the screenwriter may be a much simpler one, starting at the very inception of the script acquisition process. As Steve White, a Hollywood agent for screenwriters, bluntly relates:

The hardest part of being an agent is getting people to read. And understand what they are reading. The attention of the buyer is so much in demand. The business is full of smart and talented people. But many don't have the strength of their own convictions. With movies, you are dealing with subjective taste and there are no rules for what's good and what's bad. And a lot of people out there buying material wouldn't know what's good if it hit them in the face.

★ GENRE CYCLES

Most genres can be said to pass through a **four-stage** life cycle.

Primitive. Each film genre has a formative stage, that is, a time when the ground rules and style are taking shape. When a film story first resonates with an audience, it happens as lightning striking. Successful filmmakers in any genre usually are working on instinct, and for this reason their movies have a sense of discovery that can be both seen and felt. For example, *Nosferatu* (1922), a great Count Dracula original, retains its eerie power as a horror movie, despite the technical limitations of the silent film era. But this period of development is marked with trial and error. The silent Westerns of William S. Hart and the first epics of Cecil B. DeMille show the struggle of the filmmakers to find the essential qualities of the genre. It is reported that DeMille, in particular, was well aware that his first effort at an epic, in the silent *Ten Commandments* (1923), was rough exploration. The musicals shot immediately after the introduction of sound are fascinating because of the fresh spirit with which they were made, rather than because of their high polish.

Classical. During this period, a genre is in full flower. Films representative of this stage have a confident dramatic flow, rich visual detail, and sure direction. Film historians may disagree about the time frame in which a particular genre first comes of age and which films best represent of this stage. For example, some critics feel that John Ford's *Stagecoach* (1939), shot in the grandeur of the Utah landscape and imbued with a sense of imminent danger and raw heroic action, created a classic model for the Westerns that followed in the next two decades. In a more recent genre, it could be said that the classical stage for science fiction began with *2001: A Space Odyssey* (1968) and gained vigor with *Star Wars* (1977) and *Alien* (1979). These films became the standard for excellence, not only because of the advanced special effects technology that was created for them, but because the theme, plot turns, characterization, and production design were so finely integrated with the story action. Science fiction films that have followed are often measured by their achievements. An interesting pursuit for the student of film is determining criteria of excellence for films representative of the classic period in a favorite genre.

Revisionist. When the formula of a popular genre is repeated endlessly, the stories become drained of their originality. Filmmakers then seek

continued ▶

ways to use the public's familiarity with a genre and twist its central theme in idiosyncratic ways. They can do this by retaining the familiar story structure, but adding elements that take the film into unexpected directions **(2–17)**. In *The Wild Bunch* (1969), Director Sam Peckinpah pushed the staid genre of the Western into a visually exciting mode with spectacular rapid editing of explicit violence. Later, such films as Arthur Penn's *The Missouri Breaks* (1976), with its unfamiliar Western locations and oddly drawn characters, gave the genre a modern sense of a moral wasteland. In both of these films, the filmmakers attempted to give characters an off-beat originality by deviating from the classical hero profiles. Many films in this revisionist phase combine motifs, blending one genre with another. This is especially true of musicals today. The style of classical musicals seems overly staged and dated by today's taste, and therefore such films are seldom attempted. But the musical now combines with romantic thrillers (*The Bodyguard*, 1992), personal tragedy (*What's Love Got To Do With It?*, 1993), racial conflict (*Mo' Better Blues*, 1990), realistic biographies (*The Doors*, 1991), societal tension (*The Commitments*, 1991), and other categories to crossbreed into new forms.

Parody.   One response to the clichés of a film genre is to make fun of them through parody. Some parodies are blatant slapstick films that expose the latent foolishness of the genre. Thus, *Blazing Saddles* (1974) ridiculed the macho posturing and racist assumptions of Westerns; *Airplane* (1980) wallowed in the melodrama of disaster films; *Hot Shots* (1991) spoofed the exaggerated high action of military theme movies like *Top Gun* (1986). Sometimes the parodies with have a lighter, more subtle touch. *The Freshman* (1990) and *Married To The Mob* (1988) take the heaviness of the modern gangster film and give the genre a dark quirky humor. The Star Trek television and movie series was wonderfully spoofed by the clever writing

2–17   *Three Kings*   War movies have traditionally drawn clear ethical lines between the good and bad sides. In the revisionist war drama *Three Kings* (1999) (story by John Ridley and screenplay by director David O. Russell), the movie begins as a dangerously zany heist movie set at the end of Gulf War. Four soldiers (George Clooney, Mark Wahlberg, Ice Cube, and Conrad Vig) set out to steal a stash of Kuwaiti gold bricks. But the movie soon turns into a morality tale in which the men must confront the complex social and political consequences of American military involvement in the Near East. The movie successfully shatters formulaic expectations of war movies, yet retains the tense visual and emotional excitement of the genre. (Warner Bros.)

continued   ▶

and superior production values of *Galaxy Quest* (1999). Throughout his career, Woody Allen has poked fun at the attitudes of various film styles, as in *Stardust Memories* (1980), a spoof of Fellini films, and *Zelig* (1983), a sustained imitation of an overly sincere documentary. *Shadows and Fog* (1991) imitates the classic expressionist movies, which were laden with actors staged profoundly on stark sets and photographed in high contrast black and white light.

Because of lightning-fast overexposure today, the entire cycle of genres can play itself out in a very short period of time. No sooner is a classic film made than a revisionist film or a parody of it will follow. Then, too, filmmakers continually desire to make one final "classic" in the genre. Hence, *Unforgiven* (1992), even though Clint Eastwood's revisionist character is an aging and reluctant ex-gunfighter, was promoted at the time as the last great Western.

STORY SOURCES: THE DIFFERING CODES OF CINEMA AND LITERATURE

"Movies and books are two autonomous art forms. Film is a director's medium . . . the camera is the narrator, instructing us where to look, and, with the help of music, lighting . . . whatever, how to feel. I was groping around finding a whole new vocabulary. A number of us have written fiction for years and won awards that are perceived as external signs of success. But to think that we can sit down and write a play or movie is a complete mistake. The tools are more limited. All exposition, except flashbacks and voice-overs, must be done in the present. Everything must be obvious or the audience won't 'get it' . . . they need to be cued."

Joyce Carol Oates, author of over twenty novels, adapted her story *You Must Remember This* to the screen.

Stories for movies come from two basic directions. The most common is the **original screenplay,** also called a *spec script*. Associated with this category are other stories generated directly from the movie industry sources, including *sequels*, *remakes*, and even *pitches*—the high-pressure ceremony carried out in a production executive's office in which a writer describes an original story idea with the hope of getting paid to write a full screenplay. The second source of screenplays is the **script adapted from another medium**—novels, stage plays, magazine and newspaper articles, TV series, comic books, and more rarely, short stories, songs, fairy tales, and even operas. Of the top fifty grossing film in 1998, for example, 30 percent were spec scripts; 28 percent were from published books; 20 percent were sequels, remakes, or TV spin-offs; and 10 percent were developed from pitches.

The Academy of Motion Picture Arts and Sciences, in fact, distinguishes between the two categories in its Oscar nominations. Whether the story begins as an original screenplay or as an adaptation, a mainstream movie must normally fit into a fairly well-defined genre. What all narrative writers have in common is the duty to be good storytellers. Marc Platt, head of production at Universal Studios, notes, "At the end of the day, it comes down to the story. Whether it's a script, a pitch, a book—if there's a story there, characters you care about, a concept you feel is a film, then you get involved." For the screenwriter, the origins of the story idea influence the nature of the job at hand. The issues involved in developing and presenting an original drama for the screen are significantly different from those involved in adapting a screenplay from either the stage or a book.

To faithfully translate *written* language to the *visual* imagery of movies presents many problems. Literature gives its information in a system of single units, ordered in linear patterns on a page. The process of reading is an exercise in which information is gained sequentially, in bits or small pieces, along a line. Words become sentences, then paragraphs, and chapters. When presenting a depiction of a physical space—the setting of a mining town in the Yukon, for example—a full description must be organized within the rigorous codes of written language. Capturing a complete experience in words may take pages of writing.

The "language" of motion pictures works quite differently. As the old saying goes, a picture *is* worth a thousand words. The information presented on the screen of the mining town is presented with virtual simultaneity, an *all-at-onceness*. A four-second shot may be enough to "say" what is described at great length in a book. In film, lighting, camera angles, the relationship of objects within the frame, shot duration, and other factors become aspects of its grammar. To work effectively, the screenwriter must not only be vitally aware of the essential differences between storytelling for books and for cinema, but have profound respect for what the camera does so well.

Films made from literature may come from short works, such as the novella by Cornell Woolrich for *Rear Window* (1954), or from a book of great length, such as the novel by Henry Fielding for *Tom Jones* (1963). But the time frame of standard commercial movies is fairly fixed. For most feature movies, a two-hour standard length rules. There may not be an inherent logic why movies should be mandated to be between 100–120 minutes in length, but over the years the vast majority of films fall within this range, and studios have come to demand it. Both producers and exhibitors want two shows a night at theaters. Directors are regularly bound by contract to bring in their film in less than a two-hour length. Therefore, most screenplays come in at about 120 pages, the rule of thumb being that one page of the script is roughly equal to one minute of screen time. Some epic films run three hours or more—*Children of Paradise* (1944; 188m); *Lawrence of Arabia* (1962; 221m); *War and Peace* (1968; 373m)— but these films have been relatively uncommon. Lately, however, studios have been releasing selected films, *The Green Mile* (1999) for example, at well over two hours. The conventions of the screenplay, however, are unusually tight, and the writer for narrative movies shares a variation of a restrictive format with the poet writing a sonnet.

TABLE 2–2 SCRIPTS THAT WIN

By 2000, 72 movies had won Oscars as Best Picture. The sources for the stories have varied.

- 42 percent originated from novels
- 28 percent were original screenplays
- 16 percent came from stage productions
- 10 percent came from nonfiction subjects
- 4 percent came from other sources

Adapting the Novel

"You make a big mistake by trying to be too faithful to the book. You're reinventing it in another medium entirely. Some novelists accept that idea, and some violently reject it. If I'm just a stenographer putting scene numbers on the chapters of a novel, that not screenwriting to me."

Screenwriter Frank Pierson
(*Presumed Innocent*, 1990)

The first attraction of a popular novel for filmmakers is that the story has a pre-sold constituency. Name recognition makes the release of a film based on a best-selling novel an anticipated event, even for those who have not read the work ("I really wanted to read the book but didn't have the time!"). Because of the demand by film producers to gain the rights to such novels, literary agents of popular fiction writers have become power brokers in the film story market. The writings of Stephen King have gained sure-fire attention from producers because of the wide media exposure of his work **(2–18)**.

Sometimes this works in reverse. The theatrical success in the United States of the Mexican movie *Like Water for Chocolate* (1993) called attention to the novel by Laura Esquivel, which had gained only small recognition here until the lush, romantic movie found its audience. As people discovered the movie, they then sought out the novel and sent it into top-ten book lists around the country. In yet another variation, aspiring screenwriter Michael Blake was driven by his research to write a movie about the

2–18   *Misery*   Novelist Stephen King continues to have almost everything that he has written adapted to the screen—with very mixed aesthetic results. The critical acclaim of the film *Misery* (1990) was greatly due to the well-written script of the veteran screenwriter William Goldman. This screenplay possessed a tight story structure readily translatable to the needs of the camera. The sharply defined characters were brought to life by the outstanding interpretations of James Caan (playing Paul Sheldon, a best-selling author) and Kathy Bates (a lonely mountain woman who claimed to be his "number one fan"). Other books by King have lacked the good fortune of such a talented screenwriter as Goldman in adapting their stories into a movie.
(Columbia Pictures)

Native American Indian experience, but first took the advice of Kevin Costner, "If you write a screenplay, it's going to go on a stack somewhere. It's got a much better chance to stand out as a book." Blake followed the advice and wrote the successful novel *Dances With Wolves*, then adapted it for the screen.

The most relevant issue to the screenwriter adapting any novel is that the basic story has already been tested with an audience and it must therefore come through in the film. A published novel is an already-known quantity, with fully developed characters and a defined and engaging conflict, structured with a beginning, middle, and end. The best traditions of novel writing *encourage* innovation in style and structure, and this freshness often captures the attention of first-rate filmmakers. Although these elements may seem fundamental, the poor quality of many scripts that circulate makes such basic writing virtues highly coveted. Alternatively, many producers are drawn to the safety of popular formula novels because they seem readily translatable to the film medium.

Having your favorite novel misinterpreted and then butchered by a filmmaker is not an uncommon experience. The problems of adaptation are many. Even with the best intentions, movies that come from literature face inherent problems. While the normal movie is experienced in one sitting, this is rarely the case with a novel. Getting through a good book can take weeks. Therefore cutting down the original story, and at the same time retaining its uniqueness, is the primary task of a writer adapting a novel. When director Alan Parker wrote the screenplay for *Angela's Ashes* (1999) from Frank McCourt's best-selling memoir, he had to condense the material. "The clues were all in the book," Parker notes. "Everything comes from Frank. There are about 4,000 scenes in the book. In the film there can be only a smattering." In many films, this may mean cutting down or eliminating complex subplots and even certain important characters of a lengthy novel. For example, if a significant character in a novel cannot be explored within the limited screen time of a movie, the question must be asked whether that person should be introduced into the film story. Generally, movies do not have time for more than two or three major character studies. This can be a maddening situation, because reducing or stripping away elements of the novel may fray or destroy the entire complex weave of a story. The alternative, however, may be watching a parade of one-dimensional characters moving on and off the screen.

Adapting the Stage Play

"Because one can make a movie 'of' a play but not a 'play' of a movie, cinema had an early but, I should argue, fortuitous connection with the stage."

Writer Susan Sontag

As with books, stage plays are attractive to film producers because they are tested dramatic presentations with name recognition **(2–19)**. Although relatively few people actually see a heralded Broadway play or even successful road shows that may follow, the publicity generated from the New York City theater critics and other entertainment media make the title

2–19   *Henry V*   William Shakespeare's plays have been a steady source of screen drama. Seen here in a 1989 version of *Henry V* is Kenneth Branagh as Henry and Emma Thompson as Princess Katherine of France. Many famous stage actors have successfully brought their interpretations of the playwright's characters to the expanded possibilities of motion pictures. Orson Welles, Laurence Olivier, Mel Gibson, Ian McKellan, Al Pacino, Paul Scofield, Laurence Fishburne, Leonardo DiCaprio, Kevin Kline, Ethan Hawke and many others have successfully translated Shakespeare's male lead characters to the screen. Bold experiments have been tried. Akira Kurosawa shifted *Macbeth* to medieval Japan in the spectacular *Throne of Blood* (1957) and even the science fiction classic *Forbidden Planet* (1956) borrowed its story from *The Tempest*.   (The Samuel Goldwyn Company)

of a quality stage play immediately identifiable. The movie industry also finds a special appeal because of the elements that film and stage have in common:

- The two forms of drama share common production elements and terminology, dealing with *actors, sets, costume, lighting, blocking,* etc. Both presentations are guided by a *director* who interprets and brings to life a playwright's work. Stage and movies both work *within* the physical confines of an auditorium proscenium *from* a script typically presented in a two- to three-hour time frame *to* a theater audience.

- The same conventions of story structure are at work, rooting themselves in the traditions of classic drama. Both movies and stage drama commonly present a protagonist with a *conflict,* which demands *action* and *resolution.* The process follows a protagonist through trials that demand personal courage and resolves the issues in a climax that offers insight into the human condition.

Early motion pictures drew heavily on the established talent pool of writers for the live stage, especially after the advent of sound. The stage has remained a training ground for movie writers, actors, dancers, directors, choreographers, lighting specialists, set designers, and even producers. However, almost all of these specialists report that when a person comes from a stage play background to a movie set dominated by the motion picture camera, he or she must adapt new methods for the new medium.

Some Essential Differences

Many film adaptations from the stage have failed to make the successful transition because either the writer, director, or producers, in an attempt to stay "faithful" to the play, failed to fully understand the nature of how the camera changes the storytelling process. The differences between narrative motion pictures and live stage productions are quite obvious, but it is important to realize even the subtle demands that adaptation from stage to screen will bring out **(2–20)**. The essential advantage of stage drama, of course, is that it is *live*. The charged dynamic tension that can develop between audience and performers in this setting directly affects the play. Moments of truth in the drama are simultaneously experienced by everyone present, and the connection—laughter, passion, sorrow—is immediate. An experienced actor knows just how well she is doing by the ongoing reaction from the audience. A blown line by a performer cannot be withdrawn; an especially brilliant rendition may never be exactly duplicated.

2–20   *Who's Afraid of Virginia Woolf*   In the 1960s, playwright Edward Albee was known for his incisive, uncompromising dialogue. His play *Who's Afraid of Virginia Woolf* (1966) presents the disorienting relationship of an emotionally brutal college professor (Richard Burton) and his hysterical wife (Elizabeth Taylor) during an overnight foray witnessed by a relatively naive younger couple (Sandy Dennis and George Segal). When it opened on Broadway, the stage play seemed especially unsuited for the screen, partly because of its raw dialogue and extremely harsh sexual undertone. But Ernest Lehman's heady script, Mike Nichols's superb direction, and career performances from all of the actors made the film one of the breakthrough movies of the 1960s. In this shot—a close perspective unavailable to a stage audience—Elizabeth Taylor lets out all the stops doing the "watusi" with George Segal.
(Warner Bros.)

In a stage play, the actors are physically before us for two hours, moving within the limitations of the stage dimensions. This fixed setting is further defined by the member of the audience sitting in row S, seat 15. That person's perspective—that physical relationship to the performers—does not change throughout the evening. If important details of the set design cannot be clearly seen from various distances, or if an actor's voice does not project loudly enough that essential expository information can be heard, the stage production fails to communicate its intended message. Stage producers are well aware of the nature and limitations of stage drama.

Movies continually shift the viewer's sense of *perspective*. Whereas the playgoer is "stuck" in a certain seat, the moviegoer travels anywhere the camera chooses to go, without threatening dramatic unity. Not limited to the confined area of a stage, a movie can take us to a mountaintop in the Sierras, then drop us on the streets of Philadelphia. Not only *can* the camera afford this physical range, we *expect* this to happen in many films. Although innovative set design and lighting can work miracles on a stage in terms of creating the illusion of location shifts, the physical limitations of the theater call on the production designer to create small miracles of illusion.

The physical relocation of the audience by means of the art of movie editing continuously reorients the relationship of the audience to the events before them. This ability of film to carefully control perception has a direct effect on every aspect of the adaptation of a stage play. Therefore, the first job of a screenwriter adapting a stage play is to *open up* the dramatic setting. Incorporating a strong understanding of the nature of storytelling with the camera, the screenwriter seeks out ways to expand the physical setting of the drama in ways that take advantage of its limitless visual choices. The screenwriter must be aware of the ability of film to use free, rapid, and complex shot and scene selection to advance the story. This can be achieved within the time constraints of a movie because of the speed with which it can shift locations and deliver information. One fleeting shot on film can speak volumes.

The screenwriter must know the unique ability of the camera to tell a story. For example, one camera shot—the **close-up**—especially distinguishes the motion picture, most importantly in relation to the stage play. With it, the filmmaker can direct the attention of an audience to important details: a revealing note by the telephone, a seductive hand sliding down a lover's back, the guilty flinch of an eye. The viewer has no choice but to take notice and react. On the stage, however, the eyes of an audience member can select any number of subjects to focus upon. A gun in an open suitcase, a relatively small but vitally dramatic object, may go unnoticed if an actor does not verbally or physically call attention to it.

Stage plays live or die on the strength of their dialogue. Great plays are noted for their verbal wit and the electrifying interaction of performers rendering the lines of the playwright. The stage play depends on the spoken word to introduce its characters, to express emotions, to carry the action forward, as the audience "overhears" the dialogue. When the highly successful Broadway playwright Neil Simon first began adapting his work for the screen, many critics complained that he was too verbose, that his work looked and sounded like stage plays recorded on film. Brilliant stage dialogue does not ensure movie greatness.

In movies, a close-up of an actor's face can say it all. Gary Cooper, among many others, built a successful career not by the content of brilliant dialogue but by his ability to project a quiet confidence interacting with the camera. When he was challenged to decide whether or not to face his enemy in a shoot-out, the camera would move in to study his face. Magnified on the screen, a close-up of his face is intended to capture the internal struggle between his deep-seated aversion to violence and the call to action. The full weight of his decision to act heroically could then be conveyed in the script by one simple word—"Yup."

These and other differences between stage and screen are important to the screenwriter adapting a play. It is not a matter of one medium being superior to the other; the delivery of information to the audience is substantially different. With reliance on the spoken word, stage plays tend to approach their audience through the intellect and the dynamic of live performance, whereas film internalizes the dramatic events sensually with images and sound, playing more resourcefully with subconscious responses.

Poetry and Cinema

Surprisingly, the actual writing style demanded of a screenwriter may have more affinity to poetry than to prose. Because movies deal in visual imagery, symbols, and metaphors so extensively, writers knowledgeable in film use these traditionally poetic devices with sharp intent. At the start of *Citizen Kane* (1941), a glass globe filled with swirling snowflakes drops from the hand of a dying Charles Foster Kane, shattering on the marble floor. His last word—"Rosebud"— sets the story in motion. The word and the image weave through a movie that reconstructs Kane's lust for power and his isolation in holding it. This simple imagery represents his buried need for the love and warmth that he lost in childhood. No matter how he filled his life with material possessions, the void was never satisfied.

Filmmakers often attempt to imbue their movies with overriding imagery or a singular symbol as a unifying visual element. *Chinatown* (1974), a story of power politics and personal corruption at a critical moment before the population explosion in Southern California, continually uses visual and literary references to dry aqueducts and the life-giving effects of *water* in an arid climate. The acquisition of water rights was essential for real estate development in that state, and the lust for control of this resource gives the film its very special sense of time and place. The *stars and stripes* on Peter Fonda's motorcycle in *Easy Rider* (1969) suggest young America of the late 1960s discovering itself and that youthful innocence is tragically destroyed by its trustful naiveté. The flag-shrouded *amusement park* with its deliriously exploding fireworks in *Avalon* (1990) represents the unlimited hope and excitement of newly arrived Jewish immigrants in this country at the start of the twentieth century. The *dark glasses* that Al Pacino wears in *The Godfather, Part III* (1990) may say that he is trying to retreat into himself after having betrayed his youthful ideals for a life that blindly continued the destructive path of his father as a Mafia boss.

Writing movie scripts calls for an economy of language normally associated with poetic works. Although scripts are usually not written for publication and are not often studied for their literary virtues, the quality of writing must be so high that its initial select audience—the studios, producers, director, and major performers—is convinced enough to invest the time, energy, and money necessary to make the films. For example, a strong poetic sensibility comes through in the following excerpt from the start of a draft of the *Jaws* (1975) script:

OVER BLACK

Sounds of the interspace rushing forward.

Then a splinter of blue light in the center of the picture. It breaks wide, showing the top and bottom of a silhouetted curtain of razor sharp teeth suggesting that we are inside a tremendous gullet, looking out at the onrushing undersea world at night. HEAR a symphony of underwater sounds: landslide, metabolic sounds, the rare and secret noises that certain undersea species share with each other.

CUT TO:

EXT. LIGHTHOUSE—NIGHT

Caught in its blinding flash, the light moves on, fingering the fog. A lone buoy dongs somewhere out at sea.

EXT. AMITY MAINSTREET—NIGHT

The quaint little resort town is quiet in the middle of the night. A ground fog rounds the corner and begins spreading toward us. It fills over the sidewalks and streets like a Biblical plague.

This concise, figurative writing and the 106 pages of the script that followed, by writers Peter Benchley and Carl Gottlieb, convinced producers David Brown and Richard Zanuck, director Steven Spielberg, and Universal Pictures to make the film that became one of the most popular in history. The poetic sensibility has its place in writing for the screen.

WRITING CONSIDERATIONS: FINDING THE VOICE

"For me, movies are irrevocably and richly rooted in kitsch, in childhood, in storytelling, in the rubbish of paperbacks, and sitting under streetlights. . . ."

Screenwriter Abraham Polonsky
(*Body and Soul,* 1947)

The very things that studio executives often discourage screenwriters from exploring are the same values that they seek out in the novelist. We expect the good novelist to have a singular and compelling style, to tell a story without literary compromise, to write with distinction that comes through on every page. The unique perspective and writing style that a person achieves is sometimes called his or her literary "voice." This term refers to the special way a writer approaches a subject and renders it on paper.

No two writers will tell a story in the same language, and the best writers will gain a following for the indelible recognition of their voice. Rather than seeking a neutral writing posture, serious writers develop confidence in their own ethical and aesthetic stances, and their literary expression of them. These elements set one book apart from another.

The process of script development, on the contrary, is an exercise in compromise for screenwriters. Commercial moviemakers find it hard to allow the same creative latitude for the screenwriter as book publishers give to their authors. Film producers sense that the general audience has a resistance to movies that are highly experimental or artistically innovative, even though such films may cause a momentary stir in the media. After having been battered by endless preproduction story conferences, script authors complain that movies coming out of Hollywood are more written by committee—called *roundtable writing*—than by an individual. Expensive films are seldom entrusted to the unfiltered aesthetic taste of a single screen author. The result is that the *voice* of many scripts comes across as the pallid echo of a groupthink team. The challenge in adapting a novel, for example, is for the screenwriter to recognize the voice that made the original work so special and transform its distinctiveness to the screen.

POINTS OF VIEW

"Now that I think of it, perhaps my imagination has always worked very much like a movie camera, at least in terms of visual framing. And like the camera, I do five or six "setups," as I now know them to be called, those camera angles that are required to capture each scene from all the various audience perspectives. In fiction, however, I am both the audience and the character. And I never see the back of my own head."

Amy Tan, author of the novel *The Joy Luck Club,* and co-writer of its screenplay

Every storyteller chooses a **point of view** in narrating a tale. Movie writers must deal with the question of how to adopt a point of view in storytelling that best suits the camera and screen. The ways in which a film narrative can present dramatic action have certain similarities with narrative literature, but the differences are significant. There are many choices.

The First Person.   Novelists often choose to write from the perspective of the *first person*. This very intimate style of novel writing places the reader inside the mind of the protagonist, and we experience the world within the physical limitations of that person's daily existence **(2–21)**. It allows the novel great leeway in giving expression to the interior thoughts and feelings of the person who is the "I" of the story. This subjective plunge allows the reader to identify with the detailed struggles of the main character.

In commercial movies, *first person* is very rarely tried, in a pure sense, for an entire film. It would mean looking out at the world through the camera lens, simulating the eyes of the protagonist, and this for two hours. The effect would be heavily stylized, an imprisoning situation for the viewer. (For *Lady in the Lake*, 1946, actor/director

2–21   *The Scent of Green Papaya*   The first person point of view is deeply explored, without resorting to extreme camera stylistics, in director Tran Anh Hung's *The Scent of Green Papaya* (1994). Actress Tran Nu Yen-Keh plays Mui, an innocent adolescent who has come from the countryside to work as a domestic in the household of a rich Vietnamese family in the 1950s. As the film very gradually exposes the intricate demands and social pressures of her new surroundings, the viewer discovers along with Mui—often from her exact point of view—the harsh limits of her new life. Pictured here, Mui is now 20 years old, beginning to explore her more personal desires and needs.   (First Look Releasing)

Robert Montgomery shot the entire film from a first person point of view, with a predictable claustrophobic effect.) Yet at times during a film, the director may want to drop into the singular reality of the protagonist and have us hear the thoughts and see the world from the inside of this person. A camera may be positioned to simulate the physical relationship of the primary character—called a **POV shot**—and very slowly **pan,** for example, a hospital room with the purpose of immersing the viewer in the helpless reality of a bed-ridden patient. Whereas the novelist tends to use it as a consistent point of view throughout, the filmmaker has more easy access to move in and out of the first person point of view.

An example of the selective use of first person is in *Rear Window* (1954) **(2–22)**. Throughout the movie, we are stuck in a small urban apartment with Jimmy Stewart, who has a broken leg. This story device ties down the audience in a single location, just as it does Stewart, forcing us to identify with his frustrations throughout the film. Screenwriter John Michael Hayes and director Alfred Hitchcock have Stewart's

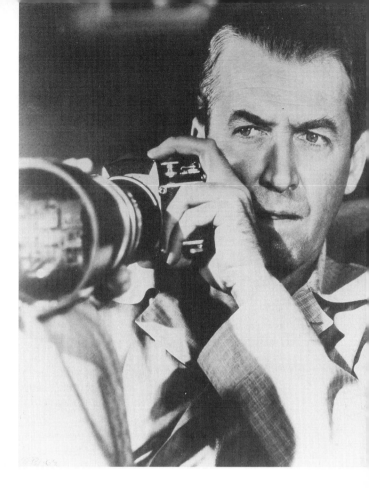

2–22 *Rear Window* An intriguing element of Alfred Hitchcock's *Rear Window* (1954) is that the movie uses several points of view so effectively. The overriding experience of the audience is the pleasure found in looking out at the confined apartment courtyard through the eyes of L.B. Jeffries (Jimmy Stewart), a photojournalist with a broken leg. The film works on at least two levels of cinematic voyeurism. The audience is caught up in watching the voyeuristic photographer as he satisfies his visual curiosity about the neighbors' secret lives, while at the same time sharing and enjoying his point of view. Although several films have attempted to convey the sly pleasures of spying on others, none has yet done it with as much humor and suspense as this classic. The outstanding movie script by John Michael Hayes from a novella by Cornell Woolrich is seldom acknowledged when the film is honored. After many years away from writing for the screen, Hayes returned to script *Iron Will* (1994).
(Paramount Pictures)

character first use binoculars and then a stronger telephoto lens to cleverly intrude on his neighbors across the apartment courtyard. By reading his facial reactions, we translate the importance of certain events happening before him. For periods of time, we literally are behind Stewart's eyes looking with his sensibilities at a magnified image—a *first person* point of view—discovering his neighbor's secrets as we peer into apartment windows. We suspect a murder has happened right along with him. Hitchcock uses this internal reality extensively, but also blends it with the more traditional objective observation of a *third person* narrative.

The narrative device in film of a **voiceover**—the expository method of having a voice, independent of the image of the person speaking, give explanation or comment on the events being seen on the screen—is discouraged by many filmmakers and story editors as being too facile. When used discretely, a *voiceover* can be an effective way to reveal first person thoughts. It was also used extensively to more easily present the complex backgrounds of the many lives portrayed in the screenplay by Amy Tan and Ron Bass for *The Joy Luck Club* (1993), quite successfully introducing all of the characters and their stories from that densely layered and intertwining novel. When used poorly, the practice of using a narrator has a self-conscious literary quality that may unnecessarily stylize and distance a story.

Limited Third Person.   Limited third person is a point of view most favored and most "natural" for storytelling in film. The camera seems to be *watching* the protagonist in an objective manner. The novelist most commonly uses a *limited third person* to put the reader in an objective position, writing about the protagonist as "he" or "she." This point of view can have many shadings. Some authors give the reader the interior monologue of the main character; others keep us outside and let us judge the protagonist by his or her actions. But the external reality of this person is the central focus of the story and almost no situation is told without that person being present. Yet because cinema, with its affection for the *close-up*, is such an intimate medium, we can read the thoughts in subtle facial responses. Films taking this narrative position will concentrate their focus on the hero, seldom letting the audience see or know more than the main character experiences. This filmic attitude places the viewer firmly in reality of the main character as we experience the unfolding events with that person. For example, in this mode we do not see what is behind the door until the protagonist opens it.

There are various shadings possible with this point of view, and the intensity achieved will depend on the artistic needs of the filmmaker. In *My Left Foot* (1989), director Jim Sheridan weds the viewer to the passion of Christy Brown, an Irish literary figure born with cerebral palsy. By focusing the camera so intensely on the details of his day-to-day survival, not only the external circumstances of Brown's growth come to light, but also his interior zest for life. By contrast, in *House of Games* (1987), when a female psychiatrist gets caught up in a series of unfolding deceptions, writer/director David Mamet coolly observes her primarily in long shots, at a physical distance and therefore emotional distance. Oddly, there is pleasure in the aloofness we feel toward her deepening problems. Maintaining a consistent point of view, whatever the subtleties involved, is proper concern of the writer and the director. Utilizing knowledge of point of view, a good filmmaker will know exactly how he or she wants the audience to relate and respond to the main character.

The Omniscient Point of View.   In literature, this writing angle allows the author maximum freedom and gives the reader a superior position to weigh the outcome of events. With this point of view, the *omniscient* author can "play God," moving around freely to tell in detail activities of any character, even when these are happening simultaneously. In our daily lives we may be restricted in what we know by the physical limitations of our senses, but the *omniscient* point of view in film gives the viewer the power to investigate graphic detail in any corner of reality. The audience can see all and know everything about the fictional world that has been created. Filmmakers are drawn to this point of view because the camera is not tied to the immediate activity of the protagonist and is free to roam, describing the story's fictional universe from any perspective. In *The Hunt for Red October* (1990), for example, we are underwater in the compressed world of a Russian submarine with Sean Connery, then in the frantic life of Alec Baldwin, U.S. Navy intelligence officer, as the story carries the viewer from Washington to the mid-Atlantic. At times the shots are of the confines of the boat's interior, but other times the sub, as it tries to evade danger, is observed from some neutral position through the luminescent blue water. The advantages of this overview position may be tempered somewhat if the reader feels manipulated by extensive plot dislocations and distanced by the coolness of the storytelling mode.

Movies with multiple points of view provide the viewer with a number of individual stories with varied perspectives relating to one central theme. The films usually have an episodic quality, the structure of the script giving each circumstance time to develop insight into the dramatic situation of selected characters. *Pulp Fiction* (1994) is such a film, a trilogy that tells the stories of several people living in edgy worlds of drug dealing, broken agreements, and menacing sexuality. An opening vignette shows two low-lifes, Pumpkin and Honey (Tim Roth and Amanda Plummer), debating the direction of their relationship; hitmen Vincent and Jules (John Travolta and Samuel L. Jackson) argue fine points of philosophy on the way to blowing away double-dealing drug clients, and then Vincent takes up with Mia (Uma Thurman) for a sexual dangerous liaison, and later acquires the services of Wolf (Harvey Keitel), a specialist in sanitizing murder, to dispose of a dead body. Butch (Bruce Willis) is a boxer who refused to take a dive; in escaping from the gamblers who lost their shirts on him, he lands by chance in an utterly perverse dilemma. The dark script by Quentin Tarantino is a stylishly updated parody of the hard-boiled fiction found in cheap magazines of an earlier era. The attraction of the story rests on the filmmaker's ability to deeply engage us in the separate lives of so many characters and then intertwine their stories into a satisfying whole. The *multiple points of view* quickly shift our focus, so that we enter into the lives of several characters in sketches designed to explore their subjective realities.

Finding the appropriate point of view is a major decision for filmmakers in approaching any story. It determines how a story will be told. The personal directing style of the director, in combination with the way the screenwriting has chosen to tell the story, will help determine the approach taken. As it turns out, many films oscillate among some or all of the storytelling attitudes just discussed, shifting between subjective and objective approaches. This freedom affords a director maximum leeway in presenting characters and actions. But whatever gains are made in the facility to easily move the film story along, movies that use all of the point of view options indiscriminately risk having little distinctive style or aesthetic impact. Ultimately, these decisions, however, are not the writers to make.

THE INFLUENCE OF THE DIRECTOR

"Ultimately there's no one author of a movie, there's an author of the screenplay but that's only one element in the making of that work and it's hard for a lot of writers to accept that."

Screenwriter Bruce Joel Rubin (*Ghost,* 1990)

The role of the screenwriter in filmmaking has been popularly undervalued. Every movie starts with a screenplay. But when a finished screenplay is acquired by the producers and the director, the story becomes theirs. At that point, the original writer is either totally separated from the script, or at the service of the film director. All control over the interpretation of the story is passed from the hands of the writer to the daily shooting schedule of the director. In this translation, the original vision of the writer may be enhanced, altered, or completely lost. The journey of a script to the screen can be torturous. There may be no one author of a movie, but in movie circles, the director surely is the first to be associated with the creation of a film.

This not uncommon situation can be illustrated by the in the case of *Cable Guy* (1996), which starred Jim Carrey. The film was a surprisingly dark movie, which midway through the second act turned mean-spirited. For many people expecting a typically lighthearted over-the-top performance by Carrey, the film was oddly disquieting. The original story by Lou Holtz Jr. was, in fact, a light comedy about a goofy cable guy who annoyingly hounds a subscriber (Matthew Broderick). When Columbia Pictures bought the script, they signed Jim Carrey to star and Ben Stiller to direct. Stiller and Carrey had other ideas, wanting to recast the film as a "satiric thriller." Although Holtz wrote four more drafts of the script in an effort to satisfy them, he was finally let go. Writer/producer Judd Apatow then took over and wrote drafts for the movie that transformed the story into a very dark comedy, one that would give viewers the eerie feeling that they were not watching a simple and likable loser but a borderline psychotic, ingeniously evil. Whatever the original intentions of the first screenwriter, the director took the core idea of the script, assigned a new writer to shape it to his taste, and—for better or worse—made it his own.

Screenwriters are free to create any stories their minds can conjure. Directors are free to remake them and fit them into film frames. With luck, a screenwriter will be able recognize his or her story when it reaches the screen. But whatever the process does in challenging the artistic patience of the writer, the rewards of having one's creative imagination made tangible on wide screens and in magnificent sound cannot be easily discounted.

SUMMARY

As a group, screenwriters have always felt a lack of recognition from the general public, and even within the industry, for their contribution. The truth of the matter is that the entire production process finally gets serious only after a script is turned in that everyone central to the project agrees is a movie. Although the inspiration for a movie may start in many quarters—from a true newspaper account of an incident, with an idea hammered out among producers over lunch, in the quiet of a writer's imagination—a viable screenplay must be written before almost every movie production begins. To call this a "blueprint" is to underestimate and reduce the intricacy and depth of the writing. Because a screenplay is literature, its job is to spur the reader's enjoyment and curiosity. It must, after all, convince its primary audience—the filmmakers with the power to bring it to the screen—of its value as a commercial project and as art. But a script must do more. A worthwhile script clearly presents to the director, actors, and all the artists and technical personnel a coherent story, credible characters, engaging dialogue, and opportunities for a visual exploration.

As with every art form, specific creative approaches and technical methods relating to presentation have evolved through time. The three-act structure, for example, is drawn from principles in classic Greek drama. However the movie script format is geared to the particular needs that directors face when translating words into pictures. The subject matter, of course, must be financially viable at some level. Therefore, scripts are written with the film audience in mind, even if the intention is to upset those popular expectations. The writer of movies must be a juggler of inspired ideas, fanciful images, and hard reality.

SPOTLIGHT

The Screenwriter: Buck Henry Interview

Aftr graduating from Dartmouth College, Buck Henry worked in New York as an actor with an off-Broadway improvisational theater group, and later wrote for television shows, including productions for Steve Allen and Mel Brooks. His screenwriting credits include *The Graduate* (1967); *Candy* (1968); *Catch 22* (1970); *The Day of the Dolphin* (1973); *What's Up Doc?* (1978); *First Family* (1980); *Protocol* (1984); *To Die For* (1994) and *Bathing Suits* (2000). Buck Henry directed *First Family* and co-directed *Heaven Can Wait* (1978). He also has been cast as an actor in nineteen films, from *The Troublemaker* (1964) to *Town And Country* (1999).

Richard Peacock: Scripts are only about 120 pages long with a lot of white space. What makes them so hard to write?

Buck Henry: I can't speak for anyone else, but the secret of a film script is compression. In a novel or in any narrative writing, you have all the time and space you need to develop the story. In a film, and therefore a film script, you've got about an hour and a half to tell an entire story with recognizable characters in a format with a so-called beginning, middle, and end. Scripts are generally not written to be read by the public. Film scripts are written for a target audience—producers, directors, and actors, the people who are going to make the film. It is basically a blueprint for a director to build what is normally a very fast narrative tale. The main difficulty, for me at least, is controlling the length of the script while developing its depth.

RP: You're saying that the screenwriter works in a kind of code, and some specific readers of the script understand the code?

BH: Absolutely true. It is a type of code. It isn't really narrative writing because there is very little description in it. Of course, there have been scripts with heavy description in them when there is very little dialogue. If the writer of the script and the director of the movie are two different people, there is a space between the composition of the script and the imagination of the director that is almost never filled in. The writer has to take on faith that the director will understand the ideas that are imbedded in a script and, in fact, add to them things of his or her own imagination that will not only reproduce what the writer intended but enhance its meaning. A lot of writers are amazed when they finally see their film because it was not at all what they had in mind. On the other hand, one can be nicely surprised. Movies are basically something to look at, they're not something to listen to. Heavy dialogue writers like myself always think we're in some kind of jeopardy.

RP: When you see your script on the screen, what is most surprising?

BH: It's a funny experience because what happens is the film takes over. And one forgets what one originally imagined. I know exactly what the houses look like when I write a scene. On the screen they don't look like that at all. But after a film is made, I think, "Yeah, that's the way I saw it." The new image supplants your imagination because movies are so powerful. It's very peculiar. The same with the voices. I hear all the voices of the actors in my head when I'm writing the script, but it comes out quite differently in the performance. In some cases, however, I've known the actors and have written with them in mind. In those cases, they've done almost what I imagined they would. But even then, it's probably not true. Afterwards I'm able to perceive it as my own invention.

RP: What do you think about screenwriting books that say the conflict of the story should be present on page 27 of the script, or some such thing?

BH: I think all the rules are horseshit. But they're good practice. And when one is stuck or confused by the inability to get at something, sometimes it's good to go back to the rules—whatever those are. But I never had a meeting with the rule makers that made any sense to me at all.

RP: Are you happy about the status of screenwriters in the whole mix of the film industry?

BH: Unlike a lot of my fellow screenwriters, I think that we get a pretty fair shake. More than a fair shake. We rarely take the blame when a film is bad, and sometimes get praise when a film is good. When a film is really good, the writer almost always comes in for the credit. More and more, the directors are their own writers. And that makes for a coherence of style. But there's also an incredible amount of junk out there.

RP: In *The Player*, you did a small skit at the beginning involving a writer giving a pitch on a new movie (actually a sequel to *The Graduate*) to a studio executive. Did the tone of that bit capture the flavor of studio encounters?

BH: I thought that sequence was very accurate. You know, the greatest and most legendary producers had those same meetings with writers. They seem silly from the outside because everyone is talking, 1) in a kind of code, and 2) in some desperation. In Robert Altman's film, of course, everything was reduced to its most banal. The conversations took on a formulaic thing— pitches that referred to *Pretty Woman* meets *King Kong* or whatever—that studios make writers indulge in. But wait, that's wrong too. Writers are happy to indulge in it. It shortcuts all the more difficult language that one would ordinarily use to discuss a literary project.

RP: *The Graduate* has been re-released. You cowrote the screenplay. It is commonly called the definitive movie of the era, the late 60s. If that's true, what makes it so?

BH: I have no idea.

RP: I remember seeing it when it first came out, and it was a rare situation. It was one of those films that, for me, spoke strongly about the discontent going on and personified the alienation of the time.

BH: I think it talks to a feeling that doesn't have any reference to a particular time, which is part of its success. I don't think it's locked in any time zone. It certainly doesn't talk about specifics of any decade. It is about a feeling that a lot of people have at a certain age. You know, it has clichés—grown-ups are the enemy. But it's a cliché that's been around for hundreds of years.

RP: When you were making the film, was there any sense that this movie was classic material?

BH: I don't think so.

RP: The film is from a novel by Charles Webb. Was the book your discovery or were you given the assignment?

BH: I brought it to [Mike] Nichols. We were given a great gift. The book is wonderful.

RP: Writing the screenplay for Joseph Heller's *Catch 22* must have been pretty intimidating. It was probably the greatest writing to come out of World War II. But it was a very long and complex story filled with interior monologues, an array of characters and locations. How did you approach it?

BH: With terror. And terror. My first draft was over 200 pages long because I wanted to put everything in. I wanted to put in all of the scenes in Joe's book that I loved. Consequently, the second draft was taking a hatchet and losing all these wonderful scenes and people, because I had to get down to the core of it. One of the problems in writing a script that is somewhat complicated is finding a style that mirrors the substance. Once I worked out that I wanted the structure to be circular in nature—having all the scenes come out of other scenes, not just straight narrative—it became both the gift of the story and the trap of the story. I knew how I wanted to put it together. I couldn't have just written it as a straightforward story.

RP: About your more recent film, *To Die For,* in an interview in *Scenario Magazine* you report that several key scenes were cut from the movie. As a screenwriter, do you ever get used to this aspect of the job?

BH: No, you never get used to it. And if you're smart you try to foresee it. But it's very hard to do. That goes back to your original question and my answer to it. Perhaps my greatest failing is the compression problem. I like to write a lot of dialogue, and I like to write a lot of scenes. I like to write scenes that seem on the surface to be about the same thing, but then I approach them from a slightly different direction. I find it very hard to drop material that I probably should. That was part of the problem with *To Die For*—I wrote a script that was just too long. There were too many monologues that I fell in love with. But I just didn't dump them in. I tried to attach everything to everything.

RP: How then do you approach writing a scene?

BH: You ask yourself the questions, "What does this scene do, and how does it relate to the scene that came before it and the scene that follows? Am I just playing a game here, or am I bringing the audience further in the intended direction, keeping the story in control?" When I'm working, I just sit and envy novelists—"Want to take 10 pages to develop a character's thought? O.K.!"

RP: Are there screenwriting styles that annoy you?

BH: A lot of films now that I find really irritating use a voiceover to advance the story. In some cases because, I think, the filmmakers aren't sure that audiences are going to understand what's going on. I think it's a really bad crutch. And it's used over and over these days. Unless a voiceover does something that makes a point which is *different* from what the audience is seeing—by either being ironic or making a solid dramatic statement—I think the voiceover is a terrible excuse for sloppy work.

RP: The voiceover, it seems to me, usually creates a distance in the film between what is being said and what you are seeing on the screen. I believe film should strive for just the opposite—movies should have a certain immediacy about them.

BH: That's true, unless the distance is the kind that Terry Malick created in the voiceover for the wonder film *Badlands*. In that film, the voiceover is at complete variance to what we are seeing. I think the words are from a diary that the girl is keeping. Part of the great irony of the film is the distinction between what she's saying and what she's doing. It's both funny and frightening. But I just don't get these dopey voiceovers that are telling you what you are already seeing in a less interesting way. I can't think of one great film where it's used successfully.

RP: How has acting in films affected the way you write them?

BH: I don't think it does. I don't *think* so, but I started as an actor and maybe it made me sharpen the voices a little.

RP: You have worked with Mike Nichols many times, but the last script, *To Die For*, was with a director from another generation—Gus Van Zant. From a writer's perspective, is there any difference, and does it matter?

BH: The relationship is different in every case. Sometimes there's an enormous line of communication between the writer and the director. In other cases, there is none. At other times, it's adversarial. They're like marriages, they're all different. Nichols and I were so close both in age and temperament and background. There was an unspoken ability to understand each other. I never had to worry that any line I ever wrote wasn't going to be said in a way that distorted it. It was usually the same way Mike imagined it.

RP: What part of screenwriting do you enjoy the most—shaping the concept, writing dialogue, character description?

BH: Dialogue is the easiest for me. It's just like good improvising. Shaping of the plot is a nightmare for me. I'm fine with character, I'm good with story, but plot is always hard. There are screenwriters who are particularly facile with plot. Some of them aren't even very good writers, but their particular ability with plot is to be envied.

RP: Are you hired to polish scripts, and if so, what's that like?

BH: I've done it a little, not much. The problem is that once I start, I've just changed everything, in a couple of cases, and wrote a completely different script. But if it's a short-term job it's nice, because I just worry about individual scenes and dialogue.

RP: Will the attention recently given to independent films have any affect on mainline Hollywood?

BH: A lot, I believe. All the new producers—that is, in the last fifteen years—are interested in putting their names on films that will be appreciated around the world, and that will have a secondary life on cassette. They are looking for stories that are original and voices that are different. They want to be associated with films that they can be proud of in a slightly different area than just box office. Obviously everyone wants a successful film and to make money, but if you look at the 1996 Academy Awards, only one—*Jerry Mcguire*—is a studio film in the old-fashioned sense. And even that film has built into it aspects that would not have been thought of as a traditional establishment film in the past. There's a dark side to the story, and it might not have been made without a superstar like Tom Cruise. But it could easily have been thought of as an independent film—a $5 million movie—without Tom or another superstar.

RP: Is there anything about film in the 1990s that's going to make it distinctive in the history of film?

BH: If there is, I'm not aware of it. ◄

FILMS TO CONSIDER

The twelve films listed have special **script** and **storytelling** characteristics that makes any one of them a worthy subject for deeper analysis and discussion.

- *Casablanca* (1943): The flawless script by Julius and Philip Epstein and Howard Koch is a model from which to start the discussion of the screenplay form.
- *Children of Paradise* (1944): This French epic love story by Marcel Carne is built upon the extremely literate and smoothly episodic screenplay by Jacques Prevert.
- *Lord of the Flies* (1963): The adaptation of William Golding's timeless novel by writer/director Peter Brook is a superior example of how a great book can be successfully brought to the screen.

- *Cabaret* (1972): This award-winning film fuses a story by Christopher Isherwood, a hit Broadway play by John Kander, a multilayered script by Jay Presson Allen, and the inspired direction of Bob Fosse.

- *Breaking Away* (1979): The theme of this coming-of-age movie still resonates strongly with people of all ages, primarily because of the deeply felt screenplay of writer Steve Tesich.

- *Tender Mercies* (1983): The exceptionally strong and subtly nuanced character, a former country western star played by Robert Duvall, grew out of the fine screenplay by Horton Foote.
- *The Nasty Girl* (1990): Writer/director Michael Verhoeven's movie has a nonlinear story structure that intensifies the hidden moral issues that a German community is made to face.
- *Blue Sky* (1991): The central conflicts of this Tony Richardson movie are easily defined, but rather than simplify the story, the drama that ensues gives the actors rich opportunities to dig deeper into the motivations of their characters.
- *Like Water for Chocolate* (1993): Novelist/screenwriter Laura Esquivel gives the story of a widow and three daughters a great metaphor—wonderful food—to show the depth of love within a Mexican family.
- *Flirting with Disaster* (1996): Humor is not easily sustained when the primary joke of the movie is laid out, but writer/director David O. Russell's episodic screwball comedy is on the mark from start to finish.
- *The English Patient* (1996): The enigmatic novel by Michael Ondaatje was thought to be untranslatable to the screen, but writer/director Anthony Minghella made a film that captures the unusual romance in this World War II saga.
- *The Cider House Rules* (1999): Novelist John Irving wrote a successful screenplay from his book about the bonding of a boy to an orphanage in which he grew up, and director Lasse Hallstrom brought it alive to the screen.

THOUGHT QUESTIONS AND EXERCISES RELATING TO SCREENWRITING

Watch one of the films listed.

1. Identify the central conflict of the movie and explain it in detail. Point out the **external conflict** of the story. Describe the **internal conflict** of the main character.
2. Focus on the **first act**—the opening 20 minutes or so—of the movie. Outline the action *scene by scene*. Comment on the screenwriter's strategy for introducing character, setting, and the film's conflict.
3. Choose a novel that you have read that was later turned into a movie. What specific problems do you think the screenwriter faced in adapting the novel?

Was the translation from the page to the screen a success or failure? How did the two experiences compare in terms of your satisfaction?

4. In what manner is the original conflict of the film **recomplicated** during Act III. Describe the new stakes that challenge the main character. Has the movie truly cast doubt on the resolution of the final conflict? Explain.

5. In what ways does the film fit into a standard **genre?** Is the film aesthetically satisfying in that regard? What elements, if any, help the story from sinking into a cliché? What stage of the genre life cycle does the film seem to reflect?

FURTHER READING

Blacker, Irwin R. *The Elements of Screenwriting* (New York: Collier, 1988).

Bluestone, George. *Novels into Film* (Berkeley: University of California Press, 1966).

Bordwell, David. *Narration in the Fiction Film* (Madison: University of Wisconsin Press, 1985).

Brady, John. *The Craft of the Screenwriter* (New York: Simon and Shuster, 1981).

Creative Screenwriting. 6404 Hollywood Blvd. Suite 415, Los Angeles, CA 90028.

Dunne, John Gregory. *Monster: Living Off the Big Screen* (New York: Random House, 1997).

Engel, Joel. *Screenwriters on Screenwriting* (New York: Hyperion, 1995).

Egri, Lajos. *The Art of Dramatic Writing* (New York: Simon and Shuster/Touchstone, 1960).

Elbert, Lorian Tamara, ed. *Why We Write: Personal Statements and Photographic Portraits of 25 Top Screenwriters* (Boston: Silman-James Press, 2000).

Fell, John L. *Film and the Narrative Tradition* (Berkeley: University of California Press, 1986).

Froug, William. *The New Screenwriter Looks at the New Screenwriter* (Boston: Silman-James, 1992).

Goldman, William. *Adventures in the Screen Trade* (New York: Warner, 1983).

———. *Which Lie Did I Tell: More Adventures in the Screen Trade* (New York: Pantheon, 2000).

Hauge, Michael. *Writing Screenplays That Sell* (New York: McGraw-Hill, 1988).

Horton, Andrew. *Writing the Character-Centered Screenplay* (Berkeley: Univ. of California, 1994).

Kaufman, Millard. *Plots and the Screenwriter: A Screenwriter on Screenwriting* (Los Angeles, CA: Really Great Books, 2000).

McGilligan, Pat. *Backstory: Interviews with Screenwriters of Hollywood's Golden Age* (Berkeley: University of California, 1986).

McKee, Robert. *Story: Substance, Structure, Style, and the Principles of Screenwriting* (New York: HarperCollins, 1998).

Scenario Magazine. 3200 Tower Oaks Blvd., Rockville, MD 20852.

Schanzer, Karl and Thomas Lee Wright. *American Screenwriters* (New York: Avon, 1993).

Schatz, Thomas. *Hollywood Genres* (New York: Random House, 1981).

Seger, Linda. *Making a Good Writer Great: Creativity Workbooks for Screenwriters* (Boston: Silman-James Press, 1999).

Vogler, Christopher. *The Writer's Journey: Mythic Structure for Storytellers &* *Screenwriters* (Michael Wiese Productions, 1992).

Wolitzer, Meg. *Fitzgerald Did It: The Writer's Guide to Mastering the Screenplay* (New York: Penguin Books, 2000).

Written By Magazine. Writers Guild West, 7000 W. Third St., Los Angeles, CA 90048.

CHAPTER 3

THE LOOK

THE WORLD OF THE MOVIE

"Production design concerns everything that is behind the actor."

Jim Bissell, Production Designer
(*E. T., The Extra Terrestrial*, 1982)

The wonder of movies is that we can so easily enter and live in the graphic setting of the filmmaker's imagination. Initially, we may assume that a movie creates its visceral impact because of its exceptional story or the distinctive character interpretation of the actors. However, it could be argued that the **look** of the film—the physical environment "behind the actor"—is equally important in that it establishes the world in which characters develop and the action reverberates. A good film matches its story theme with production design choices to provide a meaningful and engaging physical context for the action. Every aspect of the filmed environment must be given attention and thought, from the most massively constructed sets to the most minutely executed visual details. The design of a film should ground the audience in the desired reality of the story. "Like no other art form, film lives on reality," observes cinematographer Dante Spinotti (*Heat*, 1987). Unless a filmmaker consciously uses camera simply as a recording device, the visual atmosphere of the film should seduce us into the unquestioning belief that what we are seeing, within the varying fictional conceits of each story, is authentic.

But film reality is a fabricated world created by teams of artists. The look of a film is developed in the preproduction planning stage by the **film director,** the **director of photography,** and very importantly, the **production designer.** At the start of most movie projects, it is the production designer who often takes the lead by creating, with a staff of artists and craftspeople, the actual physical vision with sketches, blueprints, and storyboards. The choices made at this point by the production designer will profoundly determine the visual style of the movie. The movie is envisaged on this foundation.

The contribution of the production designer takes shape in the development of a distinct **visual syntax** for the film—the artful capturing of the story's essence in its visual images. The *production design group* must invent completely convincing settings in which the movie's fictional characters live so that the audience becomes immersed in whatever time frame, locations, set design, color choices, costumes, makeup, and myriad visual details are presented. This body of work should blend perfectly with the spirit of the movie's theme. The production designer creates an artistic base, and the patterns that emerge become the groundwork on which the story builds. The quality of this visual atmosphere strongly influences both the credibility and the enjoyment of a film.

Every movie presents a separate set of challenges. Early in preproduction, the filmmakers set out to establish a characteristic *look*. For example, *Dick Tracy* (1991) had a spectacular visual texture. Although it was a cleverly-written tongue-in-cheek movie, its uniqueness (and the element that led to its strong response at the box office) is found in its visual style. Created by production designer Richard Sylbert and his team, the comic strip world of Tracy was played out in bold colors—bright yellows, burnt oranges, electric blues, Kelly greens, scarlets, black, and white. The film is wildly exaggerated in every frame. The 1930s fashions, the bizarre makeup and hairstyling of the crooks, the empty streets of a city asleep, and the compression of these images within the frame—all imitate cartoonist Chester Gould's original art. Throughout the film, extensive *matte* work—those painted areas of a frame shot later used in composite images—drew the audience playfully into the sinister world of comic books and a more innocent time in this century when the portrayal of crime was more distant from the reality of everyday life.

Most big-budget fantasy and action/adventure movies display their costs upfront on the screen in the form of elaborate sets and the complexity of their other production values **(3–1)**. The enormous effort put into production design in high profile films—*Jurassic Park* (1993), *What Dreams May Come* (1998), *Star Wars: Episode I* (1999)—is very evident. In fact, the *look* of these films is by far their primary attraction. More than their stars or storyline, audiences are drawn to these films with a desire to enter into exotically concocted worlds promising strange and visually sensuous adventures. This is also true for directors and production designers. The subject of ancient Rome held no interest for director Ridley Scott when DreamWorks first approached him with the idea of making *The Gladiator* (2000). It had been reduced to a joke by the stiff and excessive epics of old Hollywood. But when he was shown a reproduction of an oil painting in shades of rich bronze and red by the French Romantic painter Jean-Leon Gerome displaying a gladiator heroically standing over a conquered foe before an adoring crowd in the Roman Colosseum, Scott was immediately captured by the image and drawn into the project, "I honestly hadn't thought about that world before, and it's a tricky one to address because of the 'toga/gladiator syndrome.' I thought it was a good pitch, a great story, and a great world to explore." He recruited production designer Arthur Max, a man trained in architecture with similar classic visions, and together they recreated Rome.

But films with even modest budgets can achieve this by masking their limits with creative planning and new technologies. For example, *The Lawnmower Man* (1992) was one of the first low-budget movies to exploit *computer-generated imagery*. Its creative team meticulously designed the sequences of virtual reality months before the film went into principal photography, and the result was a film that looked much more impressive than its relatively low $10 million cost would suggest. Since then, many

3–1 *The Fifth Element* Watching a motion picture is to move into the selected environment and graphic imagination of the production designer. In fact, entering that world maybe the primary attraction of particular movies. Designer Jean Moebus Giraud's visual creations for Luc Besson's science fiction fantasy *The Fifth Element* (1997), for example, were the highlight of an otherwise poorly realized movie. In conjunction with the special effects company Digital Domain, the production design team produced a highly stylized and haunting version of New York City in the mid-23rd century. (Columbia Pictures)

films with small budgets have found that the boundaries of visual style are greatly expanded with these new technologies.

Many films do not try to be visually overwhelming. A high degree of realism, in terms of design and location, has always been popular in films. After all, many engrossing stories are set in present time, in ordinary and familiar surroundings. But films shot in the spirit of realism present some of the most interesting design choices. Films as varied as *This Boy's Life* (1993), *The Full Monty* (1997), or *The Apostle* (1997)—would seem to be simple projects from a design perspective because they deal with environments that are common to many people. Yet the questions of art direction become simply more subtle, but no less easy to achieve. The job remains one of giving the audience significant visual information about the physical environment of the story. Production designer Bo Welsh (*Edward Scissorshands*, 1990) explains:

> *Sometimes it's easier if the script says "Interior: Castle," than when a realistic movie says "Interior: Hospital." What do you do with that? How do you set that apart from every other hospital scene? You really have to work hard to make that design as important as one that's huge and clear.*

Some movies are filled with sets that are designed to appear quite ordinary. But even the most stark settings, ones that would seem to be devoid of much alteration by a production designer, can be extremely potent. While appearing simple, such sets must establish a ring of singularity. In an extreme example, the French film *La Belle Noiseuse* (1991), the camera is primarily limited to one room—an artist's studio located in an old chateau—for most of the movie's four hours. But the qualities of the room—its capacity for light, the generous space created by its vaulting stone walls, a timeless silence that the room invites—allow the filmmaker to stay in one location with an artist and his model without a sense of being overly confined. Production designers must take into consideration the needs of the story, the film budget, the practical limits of the production facilities or location, the desires of the director, and the aesthetic effect on the audience.

BACKGROUND: THE SOPHISTICATION OF DESIGN

"I think many Academy Awards for the best cinematography were actually earned by good designers."

Cinematographer Don McAlpine
(*Romeo and Juliet*, 1996)

Early on, filmmakers realized the importance of impressive sets in giving weight to their stories and attracting the attention of moviegoers. In France just after the turn of the twentieth century, the studio sets of Georges Melies's early fantasies introduced patrons to magical worlds that film could so readily inspire. By 1912 with Enrico Guazzoni's *Quo Vadis?* the Italians were enthusiastically making spectacular historical films with three-dimensional outdoor sets that captured the imagination of world-wide audiences. Director Giovanni Pastrone followed with *Cabiria* (1914), a film with magnificent exterior sets built in North Africa, Turin, and the Alps to stage conquests of ancient Romans. With these films to inspire him, D.W. Griffith built a replica of an imaginary Babylon for his movie *Intolerance* (1916), with the incredibly massive set rising 300 feet and covering 10 acres. The film cost forty times as much as the average production in that year, and much of the money was spent on set construction. Cecil B. DeMille (*The Ten Commandments*, 1923), Allan Dwan (*Robin Hood*, 1922), Albert Parker (*The Black Pirate*, 1926), and others carried on the tradition of recreating history with lavish sets, while Erich von Stroheim, with art directors Richard Day and E.E. Sheeley (*Foolish Wives*, 1922), had replicas of the main square, casino, cafe, and hotel in Monte Carlo constructed for his contemporary story of sexual permissiveness. The German design work of **expressionist** artists such as Herman Warm, Walter Rohrig, and Walter Reimann for *The Cabinet of Dr. Caligari* (1920) influenced most films of that country through the 1920s and created the basis for the classic look of horror everywhere.

The special talents and aesthetic taste of the art department staff, assembled by the **art director,** became the studio's signature look in their films. MGM in the 1930s set the standard for what came to be labeled "production values." Under the older system, technicians in various crafts were permanently employed by the studios, forming highly skilled teams that moved from one production project to the next. MGM was commonly recognized as having the finest *below-the-line* talent in the industry. At its height, MGM had 3,200 artisans on the lot each day working on a variety of films. Carpenters, welders, seamstresses, molders, hydraulic engineers, animal trainers, painters, architects, and many other crafts all were at the service of movies in various stages of production. These crafts were ultimately at the service of the art director.

Heading the MGM art department was Cedric Gibbons. Starting in 1916 with Edison, Gibbons career spanned 40 years, in which he won 11 Academy Awards for art direction (he personally designed the Oscar statuette). In an array of films, from *Ben Hur* (1924) through *The Merry Widow* (1932) to *Lust for Life* (1956), Gibbons and his team created and developed the impeccably polished style that would become the trademark of MGM films. In the 1930s, his modern art-deco interiors, with their vivid black and white tile floors, sleek chrome lamps, and angular furniture, popularized these fashions both in movies and in the design culture. But his most ambitious achievement was undoubtedly the fantasy world of *The Wizard of Oz* (1939) **(3–2)**. Fully one-third of the studio craftspeople were assigned to this film. Gibbons, along with William Horning and Edwin Willis, designed and supervised the construction of over sixty sets, including the Emerald City, the Yellow Brick Road, the Haunted Forest, Munchkinland, and the Kansas sequences. Technicolor was still very new and erratic, and great care had to be taken with color selection so as not to have unwanted distortions when photographing the set. The details of the production were enormous, and the film was in active preproduction for nine months.

Although Gibbons established a new level of excellence in art direction with *The Wizard Of Oz*, his reputation was challenged by the work of several men, including

3–2   *The Wizard of Oz*   *The Wizard of Oz* (1939) was one of the most visually fanciful movies conceived to that time. As a response to Disney's successful *Snow White and the Seven Dwarfs* (1937), MGM commissioned its designers—art director Cedric Gibbons, set designer Edwin Willis, and costume designer Adrian—to make a film with even greater visual appeal. This group of men blended their talents in coordinating an extraordinary world of childhood fantasy and the result is still mesmerizing to contemporary audiences after all these years.   (Museum of Modern Art)

3–3 William Cameron Menzies   The groundbreaking production design work of William Cameron Menzies can be seen in films such as *The Thief of Baghdad* (1924) and *Around The World In 80 Days* (1956), but his work was truly immortalized in the epic *Gone With The Wind* (1939). Menzies brought a special talent for conceptualizing and sketching the visual possibilities of a movie. In the capacity of art director, he was most effective in coordinating and unifying the various design-related activities—wardrobe, set design and decoration, color selections—so that the artistic choices in his films created a visually coherent whole. His creativity showed through in the miniatures and effects shots during the difficult and spectacular fire scenes in the Atlanta sequence of *GWTW*. (Academy of Motion Picture Arts and Sciences)

Anton Grot at Warner Bros. and Van Nest Polgase at RKO. But the title of "Production designer" was coined by producer David O. Selznick for William Cameron Menzies's comprehensive art and design work in *Gone with the Wind* (1939) **(3–3)**. Menzies, who had shown his imaginative talent earlier in *The Thief of Baghdad* (1924) with Douglas Fairbanks and the visionary British production *Things to Come* (1936), was chosen by Selznick to visualize Margaret Mitchell's popular Civil War novel. This production designer did what had never been done before: He sketched out the entire script, which translated into a 220-minute movie. The process saved the production hundreds of thousands of dollars, laying out for the several directors of the film (he directed a portion of it himself) a clear sequence of graphic action. Selznick gave Menzies almost complete decision-making power in areas of design and color, and much of the ultimate quality of the film falls to his vision.

Many other early art directors contributed to the advancement of production design. More than a few were Europeans. Herman Warm, the German expressionist designer, later created the monastic starkness of *The Passion of Joan of Arc* (1928). Alfred Junge, another German, moved to Britain and gave *Black Narcissus* (1947), a story set in the Himalayas, an unworldly look. Lazare Meerson, a Russian who worked in France, gave the screen its first delightful example of how musical comedy should look in *Le Million* (1931). In the same vein, Hungarian Alexander Trauner created the realistic sets of Parisian boulevards for the massive French classic *Children of Paradise* (1944), then came to the United States to visually define the limited dramatic space in the award-winning *The Apartment* (1961). Russian-born Boris Levin worked in Hollywood from the 1930s, with his crowning art direction in *West Side Story*

(1961). American Richard Day's long career began with the exactingly realistic films of Erich von Strohiem of the 1920s, continued with *On the Waterfront* (1954), and finished with *Tora, Tora, Tora* (1971). He and other art directors had visual interpretations to their material that subsequent generations of production designers have used as texts.

The title of *production designer (P.D.)* has slowly become a popular designation in American films. Although the Motion Picture Academy still awards an Oscar for Best Art Direction, depending on the movie the person designated as *art director (A.D.)* now plays a more limited role: one of drawing up the plans for individual sets. Today, the title of *set designer* is also sometimes used to describe the latter job.

THE WORK OF THE PRODUCTION DESIGNER

"A painter organizes pigment and a musician organizes noise. A production designer organizes visual material."

Production Designer Richard Sylbert
(Reds, 1981)

A production designer comes to a film with a unique perspective. The great majority of production designers come from one of two backgrounds: *architecture* or *the stage*. Both backgrounds bring valuable skills to the job. Those persons from the stage often have art school training. Their work, therefore, tends to be more in touch with the effects of color, design, and aesthetic coordination in relation to the script. Architects, on the other hand, are usually stronger on the structural design and function of the sets. Most production designers will hire a staff that has worked together on previous films and complements each other's specialties. Although production designers need not know the technical complexities of every craft under their control, they must have a solid working knowledge of the specialized language and creative potential of every area.

A basic truth: *The budget of the film influences every production design decision.* With this in mind, the first thing a production designer must do is read the script thoroughly. In the process, some sense of production design cost takes shape. In the imagination of the production designer, the words on the page become tangible sets, locations, props, and visual moods. A below-the-line budget is then roughed out in discussions with the producers. The production designer now begins to envision the possibilities, given the money available. Large budget films allow for extravagant and highly imaginative planning; low budgets challenge the production designer to come up with creative alternatives.

The advantages of a large budget for production design are obvious. In 1995, production designer Joseph C. Nemec III, in the translating an impressionistic retro world of the 1930s radio drama "The Shadow" into a movie of the same name with the help of two art directors and their crews, was able to design and build over sixty sets on six soundstages at Universal Studios. The luxury of fully exploring the design possibilities suggested in a script is the dream of every person working in the field. With the time and material that a very large budget can afford, production design on a grand scale is possible.

Although the *production values* of a film will be greatly influenced by a film's budget, big budgets do not guarantee better-looking films. While it is true that more money can buy more elaborate sets and the time needed to fully strategize the look of each film segment, less costly and even unpolished production values can be adjusted to the theme and directorial intention of certain smaller movies. The original *Invasion of the Body Snatchers* (1956) by Don Siegel was an inexpensive offbeat science fiction film shot in black and white. The production values—from the unconvincing look of the "blanks" that emerge from extra-terrestrial pods to the unremarkable Northern California town—of art director Ted Haworth had a tawdry quality that, rather than diminishing the effect of the horror in the story, added a visual trashiness that gave the events an oddly realistic dimension. A later version, Philip Kaufman's *Invasion of the Body Snatchers* (1978), was also very effective, but was shot with a much higher budget. Its production values, created by art director Charles Rosen, were of a much "higher" scale, that is, the color design, special effects, constructed sets, San Francisco locations, and wardrobe were much more expensive and more carefully thought through. Abel Ferrara's *Body Snatchers: The Invasion Contin-*

3–4 *Rear Window* A prime example of the central importance of production design to the success of the movie is Alfred Hitchcock's *Rear Window* (1954). Hitchcock daringly chose a story in which one set dominated the visual impact of entire movie. Art directors Hal Pereira and Joseph MacMillan Johnson cleverly designed and constructed a set with thirty-one apartment units, twelve of which were completely furnished. This congested complex of apartments with a common courtyard is the stage laid out before the convalescing photojournalist played by Jimmy Stewart as he sits by his window. Absorbed with watching his neighbors in adjacent buildings, he begins to suspect foul play by a man in one of them. The nature of the controlled lighting of the set gives an intentional "doll-house" feel-

ing of having been shot on a soundstage, yet oddly, the apartments seem truly lived in. The set rivets our attention. Every minute architectural detail in the set relates to some facet of the visual suspense. For example, as the suspected murderer roams his apartment, he is temporarily "edited out" by the brick surfaces when not in view through the many window openings. Tension builds for the protagonist (and us) because of what the cleverly constructed set does *not* allow to be seen. The exceptional design of the set is a large part of the movie's pleasure. (Paramount Pictures) *ues* (1994) with production design by Peter Jamison, was shot on a much smaller budget than the 1978 film. It cut costs by placing much of the story in an atmosphere of bland government housing projects on a remote army base, giving the film a feeling of both eerie dislocation and nightmarish conformity. Its advanced special effects were restrained, never letting them overwhelm the enduring primal fear the story seems to generate. But judging among the three movies, one might well choose the first movie as the most successful because its cheaper look fit nicely with the exaggerated and creepy circumstances built into the plot. A degree of tackiness in its production values seems to highlight the deep sense of horror and deliciously dark humor that the original story suggests so well **(3–4)**.

STARTING OFF

Movies are well known for being a collaborative art form, and this is best shown in the scope of work and responsibility of the production designer. When a production designer is hired for a film, that man or woman will eventually oversee various department heads, who in turn manage the hundreds of specialized craftspeople working on the project. The supervising team will consist of the art director, sketch and storyboard artists, model makers, construction coordinator, set decorator, property master, location manager, costume designer, hairdresser, stunt coordinator, and visual effects coordinator (special effects supervisor). In addition, the personal staff of the production designer will often include several people from this list.

After reading the script and determining the parameters of the work involved, the production designer meets with the film director to exchange ideas about the vision of the films. A tight collaborative relationship between them will continue, especially throughout the preproduction stage of the project. Because the film should ultimately express the director's creative intentions, the production designer tries to make sure that they share a crystal clear understanding of the nature of the story, its characters, and the role of its visual environments. The amount of preparation time available before going into *principal photography* is crucial. A difficult project with only a few months for design development is at a real disadvantage. Only cutting corners or a great infusion of resources can make up the difference, neither option being desirable.

Every script contains within it possibilities for an array of visual interpretations. It becomes the job of the production designer to determine the story's **controlling images**—the dominant visual symbols that graphically embody the meaning, mood, and message of the story—giving them a physical shape and tone. Most movies have at least one controlling image, and usually several. The production designer, after studying the script, will attempt to distill the story into one or two visual metaphors to build upon. For example, in Hitchcock's *Psycho* (1960), the primary emblem was the gothic look of the Bates' house **(3–5)**. It provided a hovering specter that permeated the movie. The viewer immediately knew that some ultimate horror was housed there. Another *controlling image* that paralleled the house was the aging motel—an empty relic long ago by-passed and abandoned by freeway travelers. It may have represented a part of discarded middle-class America left to rot. Norman Bates moved

3–5 *Psycho* One of the most haunting images in all of motion pictures is the gothic house on the hill behind the Bates' Motel in *Psycho* (1960). The art direction team of Joseph Hurley, George Milo, and Robert Clatworthy gave the film a starkly simple yet classically haunted look. The Bates' house is the controlling image in the movie, and one not easily forgotten. Like a superior music score, effective design work triggers unconscious emotional responses from the audience, giving the filmmaker a powerful visual image upon which to build the movie.
(Paramount Pictures)

between these two worlds. These central images are interwoven into the film, gradually framing our emotional response patterns. The production designer's contribution to the drama is in discovering, then exploring, the visual power of these images.

After reading the script, the next task of the production designer is to get back to the film director and the producers with rough sketches. These graphic impressions represent the primary moments of action, major locations, or any stylistic features that give a movie its distinctive look. In many cases, the production designer may personally create some preliminary artwork, but normally *illustrator/sketch artists* are also on staff to render needed **concept art (3–6)**. This series of preliminary sketches becomes a valuable reference point at this stage in the production. In the planning stage, drawings are a relatively inexpensive way to present elaborate visual ideas for a movie. Good artwork can envision the exact visual mood needed to capture the tone of the story. If they do not work, the drawings can be easily modified or discarded.

During the conception of *Jurassic Park* (1993), Academy-Award-winning makeup-effects artist Stan Winston was given the job of creating the design of the prehistoric animals. "The approach was very simple, and it's what we do on every project," he said. "Artistically, everything starts on the drawing boards. We're certainly not going to throw two tons of clay at an armature and start sculpting a full size tyrannosaurus rex and hope that it looks great!" As agreement is reached on the increasingly detailed *look* of the film through these sketches, the entire project sets off on the same track. When real sets begin to be built, costs skyrocket.

Although collaboration with the film director is a primary responsibility, the production designer connects with a great number of other people at this time, both as an administrator and as a creative partner. If hired early enough, the director of photography will join in the planning discussions because the production designer, when constructing the sets, must take into account the needs of the camera in relation to various lighting possibilities. A major factor in the ultimate look of the movie will be the cinematographer's choice of *film stock* (see Chapter 7), and the designer should have as much detailed information as possible about this and other photographic preferences. Because of concerns regarding visual perspectives, for example, the director

3–6 *Phantom of the Opera*   At the very first stage of envisioning the physical look of a movie, **concept art** is created by a production Illustrator. These drawings give the production team their first graphic ideas and options for set construction as well as the visual style and dimensions of the world in which the story will live. Illustrator Joesph Musso began working with Alfred Hitchcock in the 1960s and since then has conceptualized scores of movies, including the proposed film rendition of Andrew Lloyd Webber's *Phantom of the Opera* for Warner Bros.   (Courtesy of Joseph Musso)

of photography will work with the production designer in determining how any *ambient background*—trees, a cloudy sky, the crest of a mountain—should be integrated into the primary sets.

THE DESIGN TEAM

" *It's like anything else: Good music is music that doesn't hit you over the head; good camera work is camera work that's really great but, again, you don't say, 'Oh my God, that's great camera work!' I think that's really true for just about anything to do with films: The best of it is where it's so subtle that you just don't know it's exerting such an influence on you.*"

Production designer Kristi Zea (*The Silence of the Lambs,* 1991)

The teamwork of filmmaking may be illustrated best in the work of the men and women who prepare the design of the movie. Each person's job touches into the design concepts of another. A constant flow of clearly understood information is necessary for getting the project into harmony.

The Art Director

Today, the man or woman with this designation puts the production designer's ideas to work by organizing and heading up the many artists—*draftsmen, storyboard artists, scenic artists, set decorators*—specifically responsible for creating the design of the film. This person also sees that the construction department is aware of how these

129

ideas will be rendered. To function well, the art director must be "married" to the same vision of the movie as the production designer. On the business end, the art director works closely with the production manager to function within the budget. The **assistant art director** builds scale models of the sets so that three-dimensional renditions can be studied for their aesthetic and practical worth.

Production Illustrator

This person performs a variety of useful and cost-saving functions. At the beginning of a project, a production illustrator will submit a few sketches simply to get a vivid feeling for what distinguishes this film from others of its kind. Later, more drawings will specifically show details of important sets or dramatic moments of physical action. These sketches, or **storyboards**, become handy instruments of communication for those involved in the early stages of the film project. As planning for shooting the film progresses, the production illustrator translates certain key narrative elements in the script into sketches. The storyboarding process is an essential part of preproduction decision making **(3–7a-k)**.

3–7   *Star Trek: First Contact*   Movies are made shot by shot. Many directors prefer to have their basic shot design laid out beforehand with the visual conceptualization of a storyboard. This technique gives a quick and inexpensive overview of how the camera might stage and shoot segments of the action. These cartoonlike pictures allow the director and cinematographer a vision of the film before committing time, equipment, and money to testing out complex action on film. These drawings for *Star Trek: First Contact* (1996) are typical of the process used in the preproduction stage of many high-concept movies. In this 11-frame excerpt by Illustrator Joseph Musso of a much longer storyboard, Hawk, "Enterprise E" Captain Picard, and Worf (Neal McDonough, Patrick Stewart, and Michael Dorn) set out to inspect their spaceship, invaded by the evil Borg during their battle to save the future. Each frame shows the progression of the action, taking into account the frame composition of actors as well as camera angles and distances. Good storyboarding gives a surprisingly accurate prediction of how the sequence will evolve.   (Courtesy of Joseph Musso)

a

168 (HB104) 3-Shot — WE SEE THAT HAWK, PICARD AND WORF ARE NOW RIGHT SIDE UP — PICARD ORDERS HAWK AND WORF TO MOVE OUT AS THEY START WALKING FORWARD —

Sc 169
(HB 105)

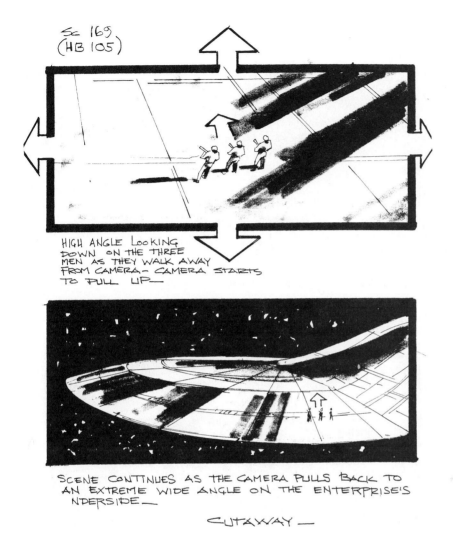

HIGH ANGLE LOOKING
DOWN ON THE THREE
MEN AS THEY WALK AWAY
FROM CAMERA - CAMERA STARTS
TO PULL UP —

SCENE CONTINUES AS THE CAMERA PULLS BACK TO
AN EXTREME WIDE ANGLE ON THE ENTERPRISE'S
UNDERSIDE —

CUTAWAY —

Sc 171
(HB 106) EXT: SPACE — THE DEFLECTOR ARRAY —

AN ANGLE FROM INSIDE THE "SPOON" LOOKING TOWARD
THE RIDGE

e

SCENE CONTINUES AS THREE HEADS RISE INTO VIEW—
HAWK, PICARD AND WORF PEER OVER THE LIP—

f   SC 172
   (HB 107)

THEIR POV — THE DEFLECTOR DISH — 6 BORG ARE WORKING
TO MODIFY THE GLOWING DISH — A LARGE MULTIFACETED
CRYSTALLINE STRUCTURE HAS BEEN ERECTED IN THE—
MIDDLE—

g   SC 173
   (HB 108)

CLOSE ON PICARD — STUDYING THE STRUCTURE—

Sc 174

h

CLOSER SHOT OF THE BORG TECHNOLOGY IN THE
CENTER OF THE DISH—

Sc 175
(HB 109)

i

RAKING THREE-SHOT — PICARD TURNS TO HAWK,
"IT LOOKS LIKE THEY'RE BUILDING A BEACON...."
HAWK, "IF WE TUNED OUR PHASERS TO FULL POWER..."
PICARD, "NO. WE CAN'T RISK HITTING THE DISH ITSEL
WORF, "THERE ARE SIX BORG..."
PICARD, "SOMETIMES...THE MOST EFFECTIVE..."

j

SCENE CONTINUES AS THE THREE MEN STAND UP
ANGLE WIDENS SLIGHTLY AND CAMERA TILTS UP.

k

SCENE CONTINUES AS THE THREE MEN START TO
WALK OVER THE HULL WIPING PAST FRAME —

CUTAWAY

Although film is a photographic medium, a series of well-drawn sketches can often best describe the mood, texture, and sequence of action in a movie. Curiously, the pictorial flow of images in a movie resembles more the art of a comic book than the literary construction of the novel from which it may derive. Storyboarding allows the director to graphically transmute words into pictures, predicting the look of important shots. This is especially important in two instances: *first*, when the sequence of shots contains high-budget production values due to the complexity of the action or the destruction of material; *second*, when sophisticated visual or mechanical special effects are used. Any trouble spots can be addressed beforehand, and solutions can be presented with relative ease, on an artist's sketch pad. Storyboarding lets the director and design team visualize complicated action in this step-by-step process.

Although storyboards are widely used, not every director uses them in the same way or with equal enthusiasm. After shooting *Sleepy Hollow* (1999), director Tim Burton observed, "Storyboards can sometimes confuse people instead of helping them. Generally, the people who want to see the storyboards tend to get too rigid in their adherence to them: they focus entirely on the boards and lose sight of the big picture. On *Sleepy Hollow* . . . we tried to use them as guidelines without relying too heavily on them."

Construction Coordinator

The execution of the set design of a movie falls on the construction coordinator. Working on the orders of the production designer, and at the same time supervising the *construction foreman*, the *paint foreman*, and the *labor foreman*, the construction coordinator sees that sets are built to match the vision of their creators. In money matters, the construction coordinator answers to the production manager. Here again, the budget is always a determining factor. The construction of an apartment interior can easily run into six figures, depending on its size, quality of the fixtures, etc. The construction coordinator must not only create authentic design and building materials but also put them together on location, sometimes in less than ideal work site and weather conditions. The period of preproduction is crucial for the construction coordinator, and the job of overseeing such a production can be monumental. Good construction work takes time, although film crews are used to working under the gun—a mild state of panic is normal on a film project. In building the sets for Steven Spielberg's *Hook* (1991), which included a full-size pirate ship and its wharf, 1 million board feet of lumber, 25,000 gallons of paint, 260 tons of plaster, and 10 miles of rope were used. Certain set construction needs extensive research—the exact representation, for example, of the familiar West Los Angeles area for *Volcano* (1997). The art deco architecture of a department store, the County Museum of Art, the La Brea Tar Pits, and other landmarks were built 80 percent to scale on an aircraft company parking lot by a crew numbering over 300. The buildings, cars, and palm trees were then set on fire so that when lava was added by computer-generated special effects, the result was surprisingly real. The work of this team of people was crucial to the success of the film.

Set Decorator, Property Master, and Set Dresser

The strict job separation in movie production is evident in the duties of these three positions. All of these people work with the production designer to furnish the set with the rich detail that makes movies visually pleasurable. But each person also functions independently. The **set decorator** researches, finds, and obtains all the items needed to dress a set—furniture, light fixtures, bathroom plumbing, wallpaper, what-

3–8   *The Craft*   The **set decorator** is responsible for acquiring the furnishings on the set. The rich detail of the occult candle shop in *The Craft* (1996) was supplied by set decorator Nancy Nye, adding to the spookiness of the film. The many lighted candles, the wooden cross, and the table covered with half-filled jars and bowls of mysterious herbs help create the fetish element in the scene. In this still photo, what does the set decoration tell us about the characters played by Nancy (Fairuza Balk), Rochelle (Rachel True), and the strange shop owner Lirio (Assumpta Serna)?   (Columbia Pictures)

ever is needed to physically establish the reality of the story **(3–8)**. Obviously, researching and finding decorative items for period films is a special challenge. The needs of the camera always come first. Close coordination with the director of photography and the production designer concerning color and placement of objects is important. Set decorators share Academy Award nominations with the production designers for films chosen in the category of Production Design. The **property master** is responsible for the hand props that an actor may use—a gun, book, wallet, telephone, etc. A thorough reading of the script is necessary to ferret out all the items needed before searching for suppliers.

The **set dresser** is a hands-on person who actually arranges the various decorations on the set. The work demands a close scrutiny of the set to make sure there is proper continuity from shot to shot. Although this work may seem routine, a good set dresser can make a scene more visually interesting with the critical placement of objects within the frame. The smallest detail in a frame can give a scene exceptional visual meaning. Eugene Lourie, the French art director for Jean Renoir's *Grand Illu-*

sion (1937), tells of an incident in the process of decorating the austere chapel/living quarters of German prison commander Von Rauffenstein (Erich von Stroheim),

> *When we were first scouting the Haut Koenigsburg location, I noticed a small pot of geraniums on the window sill of the janitor's lodging. I was impressed by this little speck of color amidst the grey stone surroundings. I asked Jean if he would not object to my placing a geranium in Stroheim's room. "By all means, put it there. I could use it." This little flower became a highly poetic symbol. Stroheim's cutting the geranium captured the emotional moment of the scene showing the death of Boieldieu.*

The Costume Designer

"Clothes make the man," the adage goes. The majority of us make judgments about another person by how he or she chooses to dress. We quickly define people by what they wear. It may be true that the face of a star is his or her paycheck, but the fact is that clothes usually cover the other 90 percent of that person's body. It is no wonder that many famous actors have their own personal wardrobe assistant.

Although, technically, most costume designers answer to the production designer, traditionally they work with a great deal of autonomy. In the glory days of the old studio system, wardrobe departments were usually proud fiefdoms, designing original fashions that the following year might well become the taste of the country. These designers could also authentically outfit an army of extras from the inventory of the studio. They became legends. For years, costume designer Adrian reigned at MGM. He designed the subtly suave clothes for Joan Crawford, Greta Garbo, and Katharine Hepburn, helping to establish a look that became the signature of 1930s fashion for women. From 1920 until 1981, the legendary Edith Head created costumes for over 1,000 films, winning eight Academy Awards **(3–9)**.

3–9   Edith Head   Costume design has established itself as a major factor in production design, widely heralded in the long and dominant career of Edith Head. From the 1930s through the 1960s, Ms. Head was sought out in the industry by movie stars as the premiere costume designer of her era, winning numerous Academy Awards, including *A Place in the Sun* (1951).   (Academy of Motion Pictures Art & Sciences)

Today, like everyone else in the film business, costume designers are independently contracted. Work starts with the reading of the script for every costume need. Many productions have a *costume illustrator* who works with the costume designer at the critical time when ideas are being presented to the film director and production designer. Costume designers will bring with them *wardrobe supervisors*, usually a male and a female, who are responsible for organizing and maintaining the clothing. *Key costumers* fit the actors.

Period movies with large casts demand extensive budgets for costume rental. The fantastic *Return of the Jedi* (1993) budgeted $800,000 for costumes alone. Large costume companies, such as Western Costume and Bermans International, stock thousands of items from every era and culture. Prestigious movies as varied as *Dr. Zhivago* (1965), *Glory* (1989), *Bram Stoker's Dracula* (1993), and *A Midsummer Night's Dream* (1999) require months of preproduction time for costume research and acquisition. The issues faced by costume designers are different for each film. For instance, "aging" the costumes becomes an issue for the costume designer to decide upon. Actors in a classic Western movie lose credibility if their clothes look as though they are brand new.

For films set in contemporary times, a particular problem is the lag period between the advent of a movie and its release. The costume designs must either be able to predict fashions 18 months in advance or choose so conservatively as to be safe. Whereas in the past most of the costumes for the principals were personally designed, today most of the clothing is acquired "off the rack" for films set in the present time. Part of the costume designer's job is checking out clothes at retail stores. "It's not like it used to be in the days of Edith Head," complains designer Monah Li (*Sugartown*, 1999), "What you do is become a shopper, more or less."

Because the costume designer dresses the principal actors, he or she must be vitally aware of what the costumes will *say* about these people **(3–10)**. The elegant men's clothing line of Georgio Armani worn by Richard Gere in *American Gigolo* (1980) was the key element in defining his fashion-conscious character. The image

3–10   *Hope and Glory*   Costume designer Shirley Russell developed the wardrobe for John Boorman's *Hope and Glory* (1986), a semiautobiographical World War II film about growing up in the wartime confusion of German bombing raids in England. The meticulously accurate clothing design not only captures the 1940s period, but tells us of the economic and social class in which they live as well as individual tastes of the characters.   (Columbia Pictures)

was so strong that the movie established a new awareness and market for designer clothes for men. For *Annie Hall* (1977), costume designer Ruth Morley gave Diane Keaton a loose floppy look that reflected the playfully ditzy personality of her character. Ellen Mirojnick chose the measured flamboyance of the wide suspenders, blue shirt with white collar, and brocade tie for Gordon Gekko, the unscrupulous mogul in *Wall Street* (1987). The clothing in *The Piano* (1993), designed by Janet Patterson for the character played by Holly Hunter, had to reflect the social, psychological, and sexual constraint of the late 1800s. But even in this situation, costumes should never overwhelm the actor.

Good costume design works best when it associates the clothing with the character so convincingly that the two cannot be thought of as separate. At times, however, costume designers take risks that work. Rita Ryack is a favorite costume designer of Martin Scorsese, having worked on many of his films, including *Cape Fear* (1991) and *Casino* (1995). The latter film was a major challenge because 7,000 extras had to be outfitted (at an average cost of $175) in 1970s "period" clothing, reflecting the garish Las Vegas style of casino mobsters and gamblers. In this physical setting where image is everything, their costumes defined both the period and the relative status of the various characters. As Rothstein (Robert DeNiro) gains power in the gaming world of Las Vegas, his clothing becomes more flamboyant, more tasteless, a risky choice in a story that Scorcese wanted to be taken very seriously. Ryack observed, "No one could pull off audacious clothing like that without appearing cartoonish. DeNiro still seemed sexy and dangerous."

Some costume designers become known for their expertise in specific kinds of movies. Anthony Powell is sought out for films with grandiose costuming because of his work in *Tess* (1980), *Pirates* (1986) , *Ishtar* (1987), two *Indiana Jones* (1984 and 1989) films, and *Hook* (1991). Dustin Hoffman, who played Captain Hook, attributed the definition of his role to Powell's costume work, "He gave me the character." Joseph Alushi has done three films with costume styles from the 1930s: *Brighton Beach Memoirs* (1986), *Ironweed* (1987), and *Billy Bathgate* (1991). The costumes of Richard Hornung seem to show up in movies with a *film noir* look, including *Patty Hearst* (1988), *Miller's Crossing* (1990), and *Sleeping with the Enemy* (1991). For *Barton Fink* (1991), Hornung dressed John Turturro in a thick, ill-fitting brown suit, which spoke volumes about an introverted New York City writer awash in the pizzazz of the 1940s Hollywood movie culture. Other costume designers find compatibility with a specific director. Ruth Carter has worked on four of Spike Lee's films; Gloria Gresham has done four with director Barry Levinson. Ms. Gresham notes, "It's a very close collaboration, and I don't think that a great film can be produced if the director is impervious to suggestion. You have to agree on things. If you don't, you shouldn't be working together."

Makeup

The illusion of movies is personalized in the realm of makeup. In truth, few actors are asked to play a part of someone who exactly parallels them in terms of facial characteristics, age, mental attitude, or general physical aura. The *makeup effects coordina-*

tor, working with the vision of the director and the talents of various *makeup artists*, and taking into account the *hair stylist* and *costume designer*, creates any transformations needed. There are three categories of makeup work:

- **Straight Makeup.**   Many women know quite well what small variations of facial makeup can do to their appearance. In realistic contemporary movies, the makeup artist may only be required to do the subtle things that many people do as part of a daily routine: change the line of an eyebrow, deeply shadow the eyes, bring back some youth with creams and cosmetics. But because in movies the *close-up* so magnifies the face, featured actors know that a slight variance in makeup can change the way an audience will feel about both the character being played and them personally. When the camera moves in, makeup choices become essential.

- **Character Makeup.**   A great number of films rely on creative makeup work to give the audience a quick read of the nature of the person on the screen. Many times, this will call for an exaggeration or unusual emphasis of some part of the face and hair. In *Nixon* (1996), Anthony Hopkins is transformed into the overwrought president whose face—the distinctive receding hairline, his slightly protruding teeth, the flared nostrils—was constantly being imprinted on media watchers during his various tenures in public office. Hopkins and others playing sharply defined characters needed very distinctive makeup to embody the physical and personality traits that were called for in the story. Playing a man with AIDS in *Philadelphia* (1993), the natural good looks of Tom Hanks grew progressively more pallid, blotched, and shadowy as the disease took over, but the makeup work of Carl Fullerton and Alan D'Angerio, so essential for creating credibility and empathy in the audience, could never make the man appear overwhelmingly grotesque. The job of the makeup effects coordinator in such movies is crucial to their success.

- **Special Effects Makeup.**   Makeup becomes fun for the audience when extreme change and illusion take place. The legendary master, Lon Chaney Sr., pushed his (and the audience's) imagination to the limits in movies such as *The Hunchback of Notre Dame* (1923) and *The Phantom of the Opera* (1925). In the excruciating process of altering his appearance over long periods of time, Chaney caused himself great bodily harm. In the early American studio system, the Props or Costume departments normally made actors into any monsters designated for a movie. In the 1930s, "regular" makeup artist Jack Pierce at Universal Studios worked his magic on Boris Karloff for *Frankenstein* (1931) and *The Mummy* (1932), and on Lon Chaney Jr. for *The Wolf Man* (1941). Pierce's singularly grotesque images are locked into horror film history. For *The Wizard of Oz* (1939), Jack Dawn set makeup standards for fantasy when he created the makeup for the Lion, Scarecrow, Tin Man, and the movie's other memorable characters.

Today, movies have stretched the imagination in every direction, especially into violent and surreal territory. As the themes of movies have become more bizarre and grotesque, the characters in them have taken on weird appearances. In the late 1970s, special effects makeup was established within the industry as a distinct category of artists, spearheaded by professionals such as Dick Smith (*The Exorcist*, 1973), Rob Bottin (*The Howling*, 1980), and Rick Baker (*An American Werewolf in London*, 1981). The art of aging characters was advanced in *Little Big Man* (1970) and again in *Amadeus* (1984) by Smith. He remade both Dustin Hoffman and F. Murray Abraham, respectively, into totally convincing old men.

Independent makeup laboratories now specialize in prosthetic masking, wound simulation, body parts, and general FX gore. New latex and urethane molding materials now allow makeup staffs to shape faces and bodies into every form imaginable. Movies such as the *A Nightmare on Elm Street* series (1984 et al.) would be at a loss without the curious technology of Freddy Krueger's special effects makeup. A crowning achievement for outrageous makeup was *Dick Tracy* (1990), when its cartoon figures came to life with the inspired work of John Caglione, Jr. and Doug Drexler. Rick Baker has continued his career, most notably transforming Eddie Murphy into the fat man, Sherman Klump, and five other characters in *The Nutty Professor* (1996) **(3–11)**. For Klump's body, silicone, foam, and liquid-filled bladders gave it the right bulk and

3–11   *The Nutty Professor*   Much of the comic success of *The Nutty Professor* (1996) was found in the bizarre but convincing appearances of Eddie Murphy that transformed him into, among other characters, an obese chemistry professor Sheman Klump. Special makeup effects artist Rick Baker created not only this visual identity for Murphy but also several other characters in the film. Rick Baker's other screen credits for makeup include *Star Wars* (1977), *Greystoke: The Legend of Tarzan* (1984), *Men in Black* (1997), and *Life* (1999).   (Universal Pictures)

jiggle. Pointing out the essential role of makeup in the success of the film, Baker stated ". . . if it didn't work, the movie wasn't going to work."

Successful makeup can be a deciding force in allowing an actor to shape the interpretation of a character. For *Kissinger and Nixon* (1995), actor Ron Silver had the formidable challenge of convincingly portraying the idiosyncratic character of Henry Kissinger, a face well known to the public. Makeup not only enhanced the look of the film, but aided the actor in his ability to submerge himself in the persona of Kissinger. Silver comments, " I leaned heavily on wardrobe and makeup. Having a mask like this gets you into a different type of acting. It's almost classical in terms of Greek theater. Once you put on the mask, it's amazing the amount of subtlety and exploration you can do because you have a mask."

Hairstylists

An actor's hairstyle is an instant comment on the character being played, as well as the time and location the story takes place **(3–12a-c)**. Hairstyles can make a character glamorous, frumpy, sharp, frazzled, mousey, and a hundred other personality shadings. In *Fatal Attraction* (1987), the wild locks of Glenn Close's character triggered threatening images of a modern Medusa, the Greek goddess with hair of

3–12a-c   *Used People*   Marcia Harden plays Norma, a character in *Used People* (1992), who is in the habit of displaying her fantasy sides. The actor's various hairstyles, designed by Ann Brodie, are constantly changing in the film, transforming her into the particular dream girl she wishes herself to be. The cut, length, and color of hair are a first signal for audiences in reading the personality of a character.   (20th Century Fox)

a

b

c

✦ THE STUNT COORDINATOR

Movies today visually thrive on daring physical exploits. "Action!" is more than a routine signal by the director to start shooting—it is the quintessence of film. Although stunt work is usually done with men and women performing in the place of trained dramatic actors, and might therefore be considered an inappropriate subject to be brought up in a chapter on production design, these people are a purely physical element in the films in which they appear. For some films, the exciting nature of what we see depends on the ability of stuntpeople to execute properly. For instance, the look of such popular action/ adventure movies as The Matrix (1999) depended, to a great extent, on the quality of its stuntwork. Because of the highly technical planning and coordination involved, the stunt performance by the leg-endary Wo Ping of Hong Kong kung fu movies with a wire harness during fight scenes was a visual and energetic highlight of this film.

Planning starts months before shooting. The stunt coordinator must be in touch with the director, special effects department, wardrobe department, the production designer, and the construction coordinator. Explosives must be tested, breakaway walls checked out, cables rigged, fights choreographed, and double cars ordered. Stunt-men and stuntwomen are assigned to work out details of precision driving, aerial exercises, horse riding, and skydiving. Loren Janes, founder of the Stuntmen's Association, draws the line between professional stuntwork and simple macho daring. "A good stunt-person is not only an athlete, but a very intelligent one. Not much is left to chance in this business. Too much depends on things going right the first time." The ultimate excitement and credibility of many films hinges on the effective work of the stunt teams.

Computerized effects are changing the way stuntwork is envisioned and played out. As the push to thrill the audience accelerates, writers and directors include shots that become more humanly dangerous. Each year stunt performers are regularly injured, and some even die, from errant calculations or bad luck. Hal Need-ham, a former stuntman turned director, foresees a change: "The stuntmen as we know them are going to be extinct. You will always need someone to go through a plate glass window, but the real big stuff, the hairy stuff, will be long gone." Computer-generated stunts hold the promise of unlimited visual possibilities.

snakes. Michelle Pfeiffer had a washed-out, greasy look throughout *Frankie and Johnny* (1991), telling us of her character's psychological depression as a waitress in a cheap diner. What would Garth (Dana Carvey) of *Wayne's World* (1992) look like with any other hairstyle?

Here, too, research is important, especially in period movies. Philip Kaufman's *Henry and June* (1990) takes place in 1930s Paris. With the shaved crown of Fred Ward, chief hairdresser Alain Bernard attempted to match Henry Miller's actual extreme hairline. The finger curls of Maria DeMedeiros, playing Anais Nin, and the straight pulled-back hair of Uma Thurman (June), with a single curl dropping over her forehead, are hairstyles that gave the film a pre-war Parisian look. A hairstylist will study every possible source to give the actor an unquestioned look of the time period in the story.

Hairstylists work most closely with the costume designer, director, and, naturally, the actor. Many actors either have their own hairdresser or they request one that they have liked on other productions. Beyond this, extensive use of wigs, in both period and contemporary films, broaden the hairstylist's responsibility beyond cutting and shaping. Almost an entire cast, in the case of *Hook*, had to be dressed in wigs from an imaginary pirate era, an enormous task for the hairdressers. The look of the film depended on it.

The Visual Effects Coordinator

A more complete discussion of **Special Effects (FX)** will be taken up in Chapter 6. However, during the preproduction phase, the production designer must have a clear idea of the proportion, complexity, and style of the special effects required by the movie **(3–13a)**. No two movies make the same demands. Detailed skill in the FX areas is beyond the range of most production designers, but it remains their responsibility to see that complete understanding with the **visual effects coordinator** is maintained regarding the look of the overall movie. A film relying strongly on visual effects must appear seamless. Combining the photographic work of various camera units is an exacting task.

In the old studio system, a single department employed a permanent staff to work out all the special effects. But the range of possibilities was limited by the technology current at the time. With Stanley Kubrick's movie *2001: A Space Odyssey* in 1968, it became clear that special effects had entered a state of exciting revolutionary change. As the motion picture industry has developed and multiplied its photographic technology, special effects has become a catch-all term used to cover several areas: physical special effects, optical special effects, and computer-generated special effects.

- **Physical Special Effects** include simple reality-enhancing elements—fog on a pond, a bombshell burst, a shed on fire—that are shot by the main production camera or second unit team to a complex series of car crashes and explosions demanding precision timing.

- **Optical Special Effects** take in the standard and proven photo/chemical techniques of matte work, blue screens, and optical printing, and as well as special camera work with miniatures, models, claymation, puppets, or remote control. Today, it also includes the integration of live-action photography with video technology—digital switchers to rapidly and economically create immediate results.

- **Computer-Generated Special Effects** refers to any image that is generated by a computer that bends screen reality. This *computer generated imagery (CGI)* creates highly technical composite photographic work that can become the stylistic basis of an entire movie or be seamlessly integrated into specific scenes to expand the limits of what is possible in standard live-action reality **(3–13b)**.

3–13a *Volcano*—Concept Art
Younger audiences especially
are drawn to movies with
extraordinary visual elements.
A blockbuster film, by current
definition, is one that should
dazzle the eye. To previsualize
a movie on the scale of *Volcano* (1997), the talents of the
illustrator are especially valuable. It is quite revealing how
the artist's vision of this cataclysmic scene so closely resembled the final screen image of
it.   (Courtesy of Joseph Musso)

3–13b *Volcano* The visual
effects of *Volcano* were the
film's outstanding feature.
Production designer Jackson
DeGovia coordinated a team of
digital artists headed by visual
effects supervisor Mat Beck
and his company, Light Matters Inc., to create the spectacular miniatures, digital lava,
and volcano effects that distinguished this fantasy. In such
movies, outstanding production design of the film sometimes covers whatever story
flaws the production may have
had.   (20th Century Fox)

Independent special effects companies that now specialize in inventive applications of this work are contracted to supply their unique visual magic. Companies such as Industrial Light & Magic, Pacific Ocean Post, Digital Domain, Boss Film Studios, Hollywood Digital, Apogee Productions, Dream Quest Images, Tippett Studios, and Pacific Data Images service the movie industry with the most advanced FX technologies. These companies tend to develop specialties that then become their trademarks. They can also provide a second unit with its own visual effects producer, art director, and director of photography to work on animated or special FX segments of the movie.

DESIGN ENVIRONMENTS

For the production designer, movies fall into three very general categories: contemporary films; period films; fantastic films.

Contemporary Flms

Movies set in present time strive to announce loudly that what you see is the way things look *right now*. Therefore, the production design of such films must very accurately depict life either as most people experience it or as they believe it is experienced by others. Audiences today are acutely alive to slight nuances in current taste, not only of recent clothing fashions and hairstyles, but also in the economic gradations of neighborhoods, the particular ambiance of a fast food chain or the contemporary feel of varying apartment interiors. All of it must look just right. New Yorkers, for example, are especially irked by movies with middle-income characters living in upscale apartments they could never reasonably afford.

Stories set in current times often use shifts of environment to comment subtly on the changing emotional and physical state of the main characters. In *Men Don't Leave* (1990), production designer Barbara Ling created a comfortable home in rural Maryland for the Jessica Lange character and her family, complete with a backyard playhouse for the young son. The setting clearly tells of their comfort and security together. But when her husband suddenly dies, the surviving family is quickly uprooted, moving into a small, downscale apartment in the middle of Baltimore. The change of location is literally at the core of the *conflict* in the film. The crowded urban location and drab decoration and interior design of their new place not only differs from their previous life, but it also visually parallels the growing depression of Lange's character in the story. When a male artist friend (Arliss Howard) who lives in a converted waterfront warehouse is introduced, his comfortably bohemian lifestyle presents an offbeat alternative and formidable challenge—a new start in life. The contrasting physical atmospheres in the film emotionally direct our sentiments toward wanting her to risk the change coming into her life. The dissimilar set designs reinforce the theme of struggle with life's transitions.

Many films take pleasure in showing off settings that reflect a contemporary look to strengthen the sense that the dramatic action is happening in the present time and at familiar locations. We take special enjoyment in seeing the common experience of our lives so glowingly mirrored.

Period Films

A very large number of films tell stories about the recent or distant past. The minimum requirement of these movies is that they look and feel authentic. Great effort is spent in researching and executing the details of production design. In movies, almost every period of history has been explored, in every genre, with heavy reliance on the production design team to fill the screen with detailed authenticity. Films such as *The Doors* (1991) and *JFK* (1991) delve into the changing music culture and political chaos of the 1960s; the late 1940s of *Bugsy* (1991) and *Tucker* (1988) is portrayed as a garish time of entrepreneurial optimism and corrupt men. Period films often rely on actual locations for veracity. The subject of variant sexuality in the first decades of the twentieth century is told in visual terms in films as different as *Carrington* (1995) in rural England, *Pretty Baby* (1978) in the plush salons of New Orleans, and *Days of Heaven* (1978) on the Western plains. Other centuries and countries have provided a rich source for film settings: *Persuasion* (1995) and *Angels and Insects* (1996) plunge into the rarefied world of nineteenth-century English architecture, dress, and manners; *Sleepy Hollow* (1999) pictures the eerie world of Washington Irving through the mind of Tim Burton; *Dangerous Liaisons* (1989) displays a sexual romp in the opulent chateaux of pre-Revolutionary France; *The Last of the Mohicans* (1992) captures a fierce portrait of the French and Indian War shot in the seldomly photographed Appalachian Mountains; *The Name of the Rose* (1986) envisions a monastic mystery in the late Italian Middle Ages, using crude realistic detail to portray the discomfort of the life; and *Satyricon* (1969) is Federico Fellini's unconventional and visually flamboyant speculation about the moral chaos of pre-Christian Rome.

For the production designer, these films have a common denominator—the need for historical accuracy. Without this virtue, period movies may be playful and perhaps well meaning, but they are fantasy. A great deal of careful research goes into serious productions of times past **(3–14)**. Studios have research staffs that can detail the evolution of clothing fashions, architecture, household furnishings, military uniforms, weaponry, and other details pertaining to the historical correctness of a given film. In *Pennies from Heaven* (1981), the dark comic musical set in the 1930s, production designers Bernie Cutler, Fred Tuch, and Ken Adam created sets and chose locations that reflected the depression-era realism of painter Edward Hopper. The visual interpretation of the period by Hopper inspired the configuration and lighting of many exterior shots. In the film, the city is a stark lonely place, its nearly vacant streets giving a message of urban isolation. Interiors have the drab coloring and design of an economically confined class. In the midst of this is the romantic dreamer, Steve Martin. In films such as this, every detail must fit perfectly, from the choice of automobiles to the light fixtures in a diner.

3–14 *Once upon a Time in America* The credibility of a period film depends on the authenticity of every detail within the frame. Here production designers Carlo Simi and James Singeles have recreated New York City's Lower East Side, a melting pot for new immigrants around 1900, for *Once upon a Time in America* (1984). The designers researched old photographs of the period to match them with similar buildings, signage, and street crowds in their frames. (Warner Bros.)

Fantasy Films

Films that stretch the limits of the art of storytelling also set a production designer's imagination free in ways that others do not. Even in film scripts with clear and exact prescriptions for where the action takes place, the design team usually has a wide array of approaches when executing the look of the film.

An obvious example is seen in *science fiction* films. In most cases, this genre attempts to wed accepted scientific attitudes and technological possibilities with a world of limitless imagination. This is often played out in graphic projections of a future in a very different environment. Whatever the inherent logic of the story dictates, it becomes the job of the production design team to give the writer's conceptions a physical existence in terms of constructed sets and special effects enhancement. These movies, naturally, rely heavily on the inventiveness of their production designer and the quality of the special effects units assigned to the project. These special effects units take on an enormous role in science fiction and fantasy films.

Special effects are, in fact, the co-stars of these films. Commonly, a special effects house is contracted independently to work on certain sequences. Their contribution is closely coordinated with all other aspects of filming and design, so the final film looks like one piece. However, the entire production design team has had a hand in bringing visual concepts alive, not only in the important space fantasies such as *2001: A Space Odyssey* (1968), *Solaris* (1971), *Zardoz* (1973), *Alien* (1979), and the *Star Trek* series, but also in a broad spectrum of other fantasy films, such as *Planet of the Apes* (1968), *Brazil* (1986), *Field of Dreams* (1989), *Total Recall* (1990), *Twelve Monkeys*

(1995), *The Indian in the Cupboard* (1995), *Dragonheart* (1996), *The Lost World: Jurassic Park* (1997), *X-Men* (2000)—and even a lower-budget thriller such as *Journey to the Center of the Earth* (1988). The nature of these projects encourages their designers to be freely creative—within the limits of their budgets.

A production designer may take a radically different approach from what is visually expected and come up with a brilliant new look. Ridley Scott's *Blade Runner* (1982) is recognized now as a trendsetter and genuine masterpiece of visual style. The story is set in the future, but it contradicts many of our expectations of such movies, establishing the location in a city—Los Angeles, 2019—that looks strangely familiar. Production designer Lawrence G. Paull set out to do something quite different: "It's not a film set in the future. We're doing a period piece. It just happens to be forty years from now as opposed to forty years ago." The set was designed to show a modern city and massive buildings covered with giant displays of advertising and aircraft smoothly maneuvering through, everything highlighted with buzzing neon. Below it all are rain-soaked streets in disrepair, congested with dreary crowds and violent intrigue. Along with art director David Snyder and special effects consultant Douglas Trumbull, the production designer created a movie in which there is not one scene that is less than spectacular in terms of its look. Although overlooked by general audiences when originally released, *Blade Runner* has built a loyal following since, influencing many subsequent filmmakers of futuristic movies. A "director's cut," reconstructed by Scott, was finally released and is now available.

SHOOTING SITES

Exactly *where* the movie will be shot is an important decision, with many ramifications for the production designer. Movies are made in two places: on a **soundstage** and **on location.** Most films use both sites. As a very general rule of thumb, exteriors are now shot *on location*, interiors on a *soundstage*. But the exceptions are numerous, depending on the intent of the director and production designer. Some realistic films are shot entirely on location; many others use studio soundstages and backlots that have been built to imitate real locations. The choice greatly affects not only the look of the film, but it also determines the environment in which actors, the director, and the camera crew will interrelate. In the last forty years, movies have regularly utilized every possible shooting location. This factor puts another level of decision making on the shoulders of the production designer. There is no right or wrong choice of where to shoot a film, but the final decision will predispose the movie toward a range of visual possibilities.

The Soundstage

At the height of the studio system in the 1930s and 1940s, the vast majority of films (excluding Westerns) were shot on studio soundstages. This accounts in part for a certain visual similarity among most the films of that era. Studio art directors under contract designed their films in the familiar confines of the soundstage, worked regularly with the same construction crews, and sometimes reused the same sets in later movies.

The modern production designer faces a particular kind of challenge with a soundstage. In its unadorned state, the soundstage is a cavernous, empty building. Here, the production crews create the physical environment of a movie from the ground up. Although designing, constructing, and decorating sets can be very expensive, in the long run the work is often more cost-effective than going to an actual location. This is true for many reasons. On soundstages, with the full services of the studio on call, film crews are working in welcome surroundings and can more easily coordinate their duties. For instance, sets on soundstages are usually designed with **wild walls**—walls of a room that can be easily removed to accommodate the large area needed for cameras and crew. This allows for faster, less complicated shooting that, in turn, saves production costs. A budget-conscious production designer must take this into account. But more important, this special construction allows the director and crew more access to a variety of camera positions for shooting a scene. Cinematographer Vilmos Zsigmond (*McCabe and Mrs. Miller*, 1971) says, "The sets have to give you plenty of opportunity for lighting—you know, light sources, windows, lamps, and all that. If I have to tell everything to the production designer, forget it: That picture is not going to succeed with photography."

Because no permits, location fees, or other clearances are required, soundstages are convenient. Unable to secure permission to shoot in the news offices of the *Washington Post*, production designer George Jenkins meticulously duplicated them for *All the President's Men* (1976) on the Warner Bros lot. In *Presumed Innocent* (1990), Jenkins couldn't find a suitably august courtroom that was available for the heart of the drama, so he built one on a soundstage inspired by a classic one in Cleveland. Albert Brenner, the production designer for *Pretty Woman* (1990), recreated the magnificent lobby and suite of the Beverly-Wilshire Hotel on a soundstage. If massive and empty, any interior of a building can be converted to a soundstage for set construction and shooting **(3–15)**. In Peter Greenaway's opulent *Prospero's Books* (1991), the audience was plunged into a sensuous Renaissance world of connecting rooms filled with candles, richly embroidered draperies, vibrantly colored walls, reflecting pools, and human bodies in movement. In reality, the movie was shot in an abandoned warehouse serving as a soundstage in Amsterdam.

Movies shot on a soundstage have the advantage of being in a completely controlled and predictable environment. Production designers can oversee the construction of sets and know that they will remain unaltered from one day's shooting to the next. The quality and volume of light are perfectly manipulated. It can be 7 A.M. all day long. For *Swing Shift* (1984), an entire block of classic California courtyard apartments, complete with a sprinkler system, was built on a soundstage by production designers Bo Welch and Peter Jamison. There was never a problem with extraneous sounds of street noise or jets overhead.

Transforming the interior of a soundstage into a credible *exterior* is not an easy matter. Although shooting on a soundstage has many advantages for the production designer, the look of the film will probably be affected. Movies shot on soundstages often tend to have a "hot house" quality about them. For some films, this artful visual

3–15   *Nixon*   The work of the production designer can demand painstaking research and accuracy when the set represents a place well known to the public. The Oval Office in the White House is a frequently photographed location. For Oliver Stone's *Nixon* (1995), it was essential that the details of the room be an authentic recreation. Luckily, *The American President* (1995), with Lilly Kilvert as the production designer, had just finished shooting and the set was available. PD Victor Kempster modified the set slightly, making it accessible for the special techniques of cinematographer Robert Richardson, but the convenience of having the elaborate room saved both time and money. In this shot President Nixon (Anthony Hopkins) accuses his Secretary of State, Henry Kissinger (Paul Sorvino), for his failures as the rest of his staff look on.   (Buena Vista)

style may give the movie an intentional "storybook" element, for example, the sets built on the soundstages of Warner Bros. for Gotham City in *Batman Returns* (1992). The production designer must determine if the texture of the visuals matches the content of the story. For the movie *Hook* (1991), Steven Spielberg and production designer Norman Garwood had originally planned to shoot the exteriors with the pirate ships in the Caribbean, but for aesthetic reasons decided to build the sets on a soundstage. "As Steven got further into the story, he decided the Caribbean would be too realistic. He wanted to keep a theatrical, fantasy feel about this film," observes Dean Cundey, the director of photography on the movie. The pirate ship and wharf took up an entire soundstage at Columbia Studios. Some critics complained that the look was *too* enclosed, resembling an airless exhibit at an amusement park.

While planning the film *Naked Lunch* (1991), director David Cronenberg and production designer Carol Spiers had to make a crucial choice—whether to shoot the film in Tangier, the actual site of the drama in the book, or recreate the city on a soundstage in Toronto. Tangier was the original choice because Burroughs had written his book there, but an ongoing war and the fact that the city had changed since the 1950s upset the plans. The decision to shoot on a soundstage and build the sets not only changed the look of the film but the focus of the story. Cronenberg states:

> *I honestly was on the wrong track, thinking* **Tangier** *when we should have been thinking* **Interzone**, *which is another matter entirely—a kind of weird, eternal limbo land. Having to cancel my trip to Morocco forced us to come to terms with that. Because my conception was that the writer, William Lee, never really leaves New York. My screenplay is very concerned with writing and the molding, or education, of a writer in a way the book is not. I was particularly interested in writing as a creative act in which we create our own realities and felt that Interzone was one of those realities. Canceling the trip to Tangier brought this into focus.*

However, a controlled environment can work against some films, giving them an unwanted "stagey" look, but a good production designer can usually create sets that are indistinguishable from the real thing. To simulate the outdoors, *scenic painters* give movies backdrops of mountain ranges or seacoast sunsets. For *The Old Man and the Sea* (1958), all of the scenes with Spencer Tracy adrift in a small boat on the Caribbean were actually shot in an enormous soundstage in Burbank, California. The painted backdrops of art directors Art Loeb and Edward Carrere gave the film its natural credibility. Another option is blown-up *photo backgrounds*, mounted and merged with live foregrounds to give a seamless total image of a desert or city street.

If outdoor scenes must be shot, many directors and production designers prefer to do it on the open air *backlots* of the studios. The logistics of moving, housing, crowd control, unwanted noise, and even feeding a large film crew at a location away from a movie production center are considerable. Most studios today still have areas with permanent facades of buildings on their property—New York brownstone apartment fronts, a traditional midwestern neighborhood, an old Western frontier town—built to substitute for the real thing. These can be dressed to suit any number of purposes. The *set decorator* can alter the look by painting new storefront signs, by covering the streets with water, snow, or gravel, remaking its appearance. The same backlot setting at Warner Bros. studios was used to represent New Orleans in *Saratoga Trunk* (1943) and the Midwestern city in *Back to the Future* (1985).

A more advanced process for creating any backgrounds needed is a technology called **subtle effects**. In this process, traditional special effects and computer-age technology—*blue screen photography, optical composites, animation, matte paintings, motion-control photography of models*—are blended by special effects companies to breathe life into sequences shot on film stages. Special effects producer Keith Shartle takes note of some distinctions: "With a special effect we want to wow people. But with a *subtle effect*, you want to create an ambiance." This allows the background in any scene to come alive—trees sway, clouds move, and shadows shift.

On Location

"I was against location shooting when I first started in the business. But now I've come to realize that the sets on a soundstage can be rather cold aesthetically. There's intrinsic stuff on location sets. Something you can't put your finger on."

Production designer Gary Frutkoff
(Out of Sight, 1998)

Good locations speak with an undeniable authenticity that production designers often want. Audiences can usually sense when a movie is indeed at the location it claims to be. Photographing the "real world" allows the production designer a vast array of choices, and a scope of vista selections that is not limited to what might be specifically created on a soundstage. German director Wim Wenders incorporates very personal photographic tastes into his location choices. "For my films I often choose locations or buildings because I know that they're soon to be permanently altered or demolished." His film *Paris, Texas* (1984), for example, shows an older America of dried up and dying small rural towns. Taking advantage of the unique ability of movies to transport their audiences anywhere, production designers, teaming with *location managers* and *scouts*, look for sites that arouse visual curiosity and capture our interest.

A film location is not simply a passive background for the story, but an integral part of its fabric **(3–16)**. Alan Parker struggled with politicians to shoot much of *Evita* (1996) in the streets of Buenos Aires and the countryside of Argentina and give the story its natural setting. "I've spent most of my career on streets, as most directors of my generation have. I've always said that you have to smell it for it to be real," claims Parker. In Hitchcock's *The Birds* (1963), the lonely hills and primal seascapes of Bodega Bay in California were a central image, seducing the viewer at first with its

3–16 *Limbo* The authenticity of location is especially essential to certain films in which the genuineness of site is especially stressed. For *Limbo* (1999), writer/ director John Sayles and his crew searched out remote Alaskan sites to shoot his film. Choosing such locations adds realism to what is shot, but sometimes at a cost. "It rained on us almost every day," said cinematographer Haskell Wexler, "John likes to feel some physical adversity if it's supposed to be there; that approach may help the actors, but I don't think it necessarily helps the crew!" (Screen Gems)

raw beauty but eventually becoming a place of horrible isolation. Genuine locations in the icy wastelands of Northern Canada in *The White Dawn* (1974) made the frozen danger of its characters real. The rotting majesty of Leningrad in *The Russia House* (1990), the mean streets of south central Los Angeles in *Boyz 'N the Hood* (1991), the rugged isolation of Silver Creek Colorado in *Misery* (1990), the indelibly imprinted overview of Dealey Square in *JFK* (1991), the glittery interior of the Riviera Hotel in Las Vegas in *Casino* (1995), the grungy streets of Elvis Presley's Memphis in *Mystery Train* (1989), or the one and only Punxatawny, Pennsylvania in *Groundhog Day* (1993) all convince their audiences that these fictional films take place in the real world. For unmatchable authenticity, important scenes depicting legal research were shot in the reading room of Boston's historic Athenium Library for the lawyer's tale *A Civil Action* (1998). Even in the cerebral film *Mindwalk* (1991), the imposing French monastery of Mont-San-Michel—a unique work of architecture built upon the values of the Middle Ages—is a vital and constant visual statement on the theme of this probing movie. As the actors (Liv Ullmann, Sam Waterston, and John Heard) move through the medieval passageways, they argue timeless questions about our present-day systems of logic, science, and aesthetics.

The production designer and director research locations with the particular needs of the script in mind. A scene may call for an old bridge, farmhouse, or weathered barn, and countrysides will be scoured to find the right one, such as those found for *The Bridges of Madison County* (1995). The Pennsylvania Dutch countryside, so important in *Witness* (1985), was searched out by Stan Jolley for fitting pastoral locations. To stay true to the original book, designer Paul Silvestri found remote locations in Algeria that no one had filmed before to shoot *The Sheltering Sky* (1990). Bo Welch discovered a perfect subdivision in the Tampa Bay area for the pastel look of *Edward Scissorshands* (1990), and then went on to enhance the comic symmetry of the neighborhood with carved shrubbery, lawn paraphernalia, and brightly painted house trim. For *Chinatown* (1974), a film saturated with the look of an expanding but still untarnished Los Angeles of the 1930s, production designer Richard Sylbert found twelve basic locations in the city that accurately suggested the era. Using the detailed script by Robert Towne for inspiration, Sylbert chose a reservoir in the Santa Monica Mountains, a lake in urban Echo Park, the legendary Brown Derby restaurant, a small bungalow apartment with an enclosed courtyard, and other more gracious homes that reflected the Spanish/Moorish faux design that was a trademark of the period. Director Roman Polanski gave credit to the production design for the film's reputation as a classic: "Without that, you would just have another detective thing."

Sometimes locations are chosen with the performance of the actors in mind. For *Awakenings* (1990), much of the film was shot in an industrial building in Brooklyn. Designer Anton Furst commented, "It was very important to all of us to do it in New York, because it's a New York story and we knew that the actors involved would respond more if they were there. I don't think that Robert DeNiro would ever have done that performance if he'd been on stage in Toronto." The excruciatingly tough jungle locations in South America for Werner Herzog's *Aguirre, the Wrath of God* (1972) and *Fitzgeraldo* (1982) pushed both the cast and director to their emotional limits, and the result can be easily seen in those movies. Not only the rich visuals but also the level of truthful performances in the movies could probably never have been duplicated on a soundstage.

For very low budget films, shooting on location near the home city of the crew can reduce cost by reducing travel time for cast, crew, and equipment. By using existing buildings, parks, and streets for rapid camera set-ups, valuable hours can be saved. Balancing this with the needs of the story, the production designer must weigh these factors. This issue was present in Wayne Wang's small film *Smoke* (1995), set in a neighborhood cigar store. Its low budget and dramatic style was determined because it used a real location in Brooklyn.

DELINEATING CHARACTERS

Exploring the characters of the men and women who people a movie script is not just the work of the actors and director. The production designer must also know the characters intimately. Visual definition of a character gives information to the audience much faster than can be achieved in dialogue **(3–17)**. Motion pictures enable audiences to *read* the screen swiftly and to assimilate its information instantly. A five-second shot of a private detective's office can give us a wealth of detail about the person who works there. Good design choices provide a shorthand interpretation of the characters, saving valuable time in the film's exposition. Many of these choices, for

3–17 *Clueless*   Director/writer Amy Heckerling, in *Clueless* (1995), was able to quickly establish the characters and setting of the story with the comically elite clothing of the main actors. An affluent Los Angeles high school is background for the undisguised manipulation and sincere shallowness of Cher (Alicia Silverstone) and her friend Dionne (Stacey Dash), the latest movie edition of benign machinations by two "Valley Girls." Effective production design choices silently define characters.   (Paramount Pictures)

better or worse, rely on cultural codes, stereotypes, and traditional storytelling conventions for movies. A checklist of important considerations for the production designer about each character would include

- **Economic condition.**   The style of people's lives is greatly determined by how much money they have. An audience gets a quick read on a character's situation when the designer shows the level of material affluence surrounding that person. If the main character is a big city cop, what kind of house and neighborhood could he reasonably afford? If we first encounter him in his very swank uptown apartment, what might that tell us about him?

- **Social milieu.**   The production designer must recognize and present subtle social nuances, such as those that distinguish the living situation of an upscale San Francisco *stockbroker* from that of a successful San Francisco *artist*. Both houses may be nicely furnished, but their separate social circles and personal tastes should be reflected in design of the floor plans, color choices, furniture, and art. Which person would you expect takes greater fashion risks? In reality, it might be impossible to say, but in movies, filmmakers speak in visual codes that communicate clearly to audiences.

- **Geographic location.**   The accurate rendering of a particular location establishes a visual base for the credibility of characters. The external world in which the main characters move says much about who they are. Do they hang out on the streets of Miami's Little Havana, or in West Palm Beach nightspots (or both)? If the home interiors of these characters are to be constructed on a soundstage, they must also faithfully mirror the special South Florida ambiance of rooms we might expect in that geographic location.

- **Time period.**   For a production designer, a story set in the *early* 1960s may vary greatly from one set in the *late* 1960s. The difference of even a few years can be important. Visually defining the dorm room of a young college student in either period would require a very different combination of hairstyles, room furnishings, clothes, record titles placed by a stereo, wall decorations, and books on the shelf. As production designer, what specific design choices could distinguish these two periods?

- **Ethnic background.**   Is the protagonist a New York Italian restaurateur, a Georgia Baptist housewife, a Syrian grocery store owner in Detroit, a Jewish entertainment lawyer from Los Angeles, an Asian student in Berkeley, or an African-American musician from New Orleans? Their homes, cars, and personal choices in art and clothing will be significantly different. Creating a character's ethnicity always risks falling into stereotyping, but (fortunately or not) coding of nationalities is widely understood by audiences and therefore used.

- **Sex.**   Obviously, the gender of characters influences the choices of a production designer. How would a small studio apartment of a female character differ from that of her male counterpart? Would one more likely have drapes and the other have blinds? Their closets—stuffed with the latest fashions? Orderly or messy? What would each alternative choice "say" about a man or woman?

The design team of a film explores these and other questions. The images created by the production designer should not just be engagingly interesting but also make the film more concretely believable.

DESIGNING WITH COLOR

"It took one film to show everybody about control of color, Bertolucci's **The Conformist.** *We looked at it—costume designers, the people in charge of props, set designers, everyone—to see how the designer had approached the use of muted color in a very brilliant way, with lots of blacks and dark purples and dark greens. We went along with that kind of palette in both* **Day of the Locust** *and, to some extent, in all of my films."*

Director John Schlesinger
(*Pacific Heights*, 1990)

The choice of the *color palette* for a movie can be crucial in suggesting how its story is presented at any moment. Upon first reading the script, the production designer usually attempts to visually define the *mood* of the story. The psychological impact of color has long been a subject of study, and we know that it strongly influences emotional responses in dramatic situations. For example, a movie that plays on the audience's sense of nostalgia might have warm autumn colors and familiar set designs that tend to soothe the viewer. Horror films gain their terror from large areas of the screen that are shrouded in cold hues and deep shadows. For musicals and comedy, designers normally select brilliant primary colors. Science fiction and hi-tech thrillers may go for an electric blue and silver metallic set of images. The cinematographer's job is to capture these colors on film with creative lighting and lensing, but the basic color choices inherent in the sets and costumes must first be decided upon in collaboration with the production designer.

Production designers, with their directors, can tightly color coordinate a movie to establish complete visual harmony. Colors are selected to visually comment on certain important scenes, but very often stream through an entire movie to emphasize a thematic viewpoint. In *Dead Ringers* (1988) production designer Carol Spier consistently used subdued grays and blues for the interiors of the doctor offices of the two strange drug-addicted twin brothers (both played by Jeremy Irons). At first, the texture and color of the film reflects a cool medical professionalism, but as our uneasiness turns into dread due to the erratic behavior of these two gynecologists, the operating room gowns introduce a surprising red color for the first time. The bright splash of red color—as if signifying the blood lust of a matador—is a visual shock, and signifies a dramatic escalation in the degree of cruelty in the lives of the two doctors. The color choices greatly add to the film's story of a secret sickness amidst high-tech medicine.

A very different color situation existed for production designer Patrizia Von Brandenstein, who wanted very warm colors for the comfortably insulated interiors of a very upscale New York City apartment in *Six Degrees of Separation* (1993). The intention is to establish the background for the self-satisfied life of a wealthy art dealer

(Donald Sutherland) and his wife (Stockard Channing), whose world becomes suddenly disrupted by an intruder (Will Smith) from another racial and social class. The dense rich colors, many in the paintings that graced the wall, seem to add to the cultural and physical separation of the art dealer's life with the world as seen through the window of their Manhattan high-rise apartment.

Patterns of color are sometimes used to visually juxtapose conflicting elements in the story. Akira Kurosawa staged a massive battle with three opposing armies—their battle array separately outfitted in brilliant blues, yellows, and reds—in his epic *Ran* (1985). Their dazzling uniforms and banners give the huge and deadly battle scenes a glorious flair, but also logistically allow the viewer to easily keep track of the changing configurations of the warring horsemen and foot soldiers.

Films that want us to revere the past often use yellow or other rich warm tints, calling up nostalgic feelings for a seemingly more comfortable time. These shades immediately signal to the viewer that certain dramatic attitudes are being conveyed by the storytelling filmmaker, the meaning of which should be registered. They color our feelings.

A CASE STUDY: The Rocketeer

Every movie can be analyzed in terms of its production design decisions and execution. *The Rocketeer* (1991) is a typical example of a big-budget period film. It is worth a closer examination in light of its production design. Touchstone Pictures put a great deal of attention on the project, hoping that the film would generate not only strong income from its box office success, but enough magical charm to translate its mock hero and the iconography of an optimistic America of earlier times into a merchandising bonanza for Disney World and its product lines. The movie's effectiveness would depend largely on its visual style—a very real challenge for the production designer, James Bissell.

The Rocketeer, first off, was a tongue-in-cheek science-fantasy nostalgia movie. Based on the graphic novels of Dave Stevens, the story depicts the adventures of an idealistic young man growing up in sun-filled Los Angeles of the 1930s. In the story, this city, with its self-indulgent movie community and its newly arrived solid Midwest working class, has also become the center for international political intrigue, bringing together the many disparate influences of those pre-war days. The thrust of the designer's research was not to recreate strict

historical truth, but to convey a popular notion of the spirit and flavor of the period in the imagery of the film. The antagonists in *The Rocketeer* are stereotypical Nazi agents set loose in Southern California, evil buffoons intent on stealing America's most advanced technology.

The *Rocket Pack* is the central image of the movie **(3–18)**. This primitive personal jet device had to visually blend with the rest of the gear worn by the Rocketeer. A team of designers, including director Joe Johnston, illustrator Ed Eyth, John Bell from visual effects company of Industrial Light & Magic, Ron Cobb, and Bissell worked on the outfit. Getting the look just right was essential to the overall design of the movie because it represented not only the style of the main character, a whiz-kid maverick, but also an entire age when science still seemed to trailblaze into a future of technological hope. The gear went through many design refinements. Getting the Rocket Pack to appear to ride easily and naturally on Cliff's back was a challenge. The twin silver rockets were precisely designed to look streamlined and functional at whatever angle they were photographed, and not simply comical. There is an edgy sense that this whole thing is an

3-18   Rocket Pack   Young inventor Cliff Secord (Bill Campbell) inspects his newly discovered Rocket Pack, the controlling image for *The Rocketeer* (1990). The concept for the prop went through numerous drafts by the design artist Ron Cobb. He wanted to create the imaginative technology to look feasible and stylishly 1930s state-of-the-art. Very practically, it also had to be worn during the movie and not fit awkwardly. The Rocket Pack is intended to represent the most advanced design styles of the period, the dream technology of a young mechanic. (Touchstone Pictures)

accident waiting to happen. On the other hand, this breakthrough invention had to look as though it could actually fly. After all, the Rocketeer is not a harebrained clod, but a young man with old-fashioned ingenuity who invented a spectacular personalized propulsion system. The final image was that of a leather jacketed World War I aviator fitted with a newly minted rocket technology.

When reading the script, Bissell determined that there were two major areas of controlling images. The major action of the story would take shape in these environments. The following are the production designer's cornerstones.

Youthful American Optimism and 1930s Industrial Design Revolution

The story is imbued with the innocent trust in progress that so filled the dreams of the American middle class in the 1930s. A "can-do" attitude takes

its physical shape in three settings: the airstrip, the Bulldog Cafe, and the Howard Hughes office. Cliff, the Rocketeer, and other mechanics hang out at the airstrip, tinkering on the streamlined racing planes that thrill crowds at rural air shows. Bissell and crew built an airstrip set in Santa Maria, California that allowed for shooting in a 270 degree circumference and gave the illusion of a free-spirited center of invention solidly set in the 1930s. Low tan mountains and orange groves filled the background. Before constructing the actual hangers, viewing stands, and other buildings, however, Carl Stensil designed a table-top model of the airport to analyze the relative location of the buildings to one another, and for photographic purposes—how the sun at various times of the day would play with shadows. The tower and hangers have a lean, honest look, cavernous workshops where men toil in grease, shaded from the warm California sun. In popular mythology, American industrial innovation takes root in such frank and inelegant surroundings.

The *Bulldog Cafe set* is where the mechanics and their girlfriends come together to eat and socialize after work. The bizarre exterior is a classic monument to movie make-believe in this land of outrageous architecture **(3–19)**. The giant Bull Dog exterior was modeled by set designer John Burger from an actual Los Angeles eatery. In contrast, the richly detailed interior of the cafe was designed in efficient ceramic tile and comfortable wooden booths—a workingman's luncheonette. The blue-collar familiarity it affords reassures us of the communal rewards of a good day's work. Their after-hours camaraderie established a warm emotional base, and the compact design of the cafe enhanced this atmosphere. Filmmakers can fall in love with their designs and want to keep them undisturbed. Although this special set was built with an elaborate set of wild walls, because film director Joe Johnston did not want to disrupt the special ambiance of the cafe during the shooting, they were not used. Both the airport and the Bulldog Cafe, along with Cliff's snug home in a classic bungalow of the time, were well-conceived designs that made important comments about the social milieu the Rocketeer moved in.

Taking the imagery further, the *Howard Hughes set* represents the high-tech end of modern industrialization that was beginning to be realized in the 1930s. Although the country was still stuck in the depression, technology and design were racing ahead, giving expression and reward to the brightest of those with blueprints for the future. The designers of the film tried to find the right imagery to crystallize these circumstances. Sleekly designed aerodynamic airplanes symbolized the vision; Howard Hughes was its personification **(3–20)**. The Hughes set was a large, symmetrically designed office with royal red walls, leather and chrome furniture, a retractable movie scene, a cleanly sculpted fireplace, and a masterful desk. The impeccably

3–19 The Bulldog Cafe   Research into the bizarre architectural facades of Los Angeles of the 1920s and 1930s was an important first step for the designers of *The Rocketeer*. As playful as the design may seem in the film, the actual streets of the "movie capital" during this period were even more fanciful. This cafe in *The Rocketeer* is the after-work hangout of Cliff Secord and his airplane mechanic buddies. That such a bizarre building should be such a normal part of their environment tells us that these bluecollar workers may be touched with fantasies not common to most people. (Touchstone Pictures)

3-20 The Howard Hughes Set   The clean lines of the architecture inside the "Howard Hughes hanger" represent the streamlined efficiency of this legendary inventor. For Cliff Secord in *The Rocketeer*, the offices of Hughes are the Mecca of the industrial future, and the sleek airplanes are the most marvelous icons of the age. (Touchstone Pictures)

tasteful office looks down through a grated partition onto a huge black and white hanger space, complete with a suspended model of the Spruce Goose, an autogyro, and other experimental planes. These are not the chambers of a detached captain of industry, but rather the elegant workplace of an immensely successful Super-Inventor. The set symbolizes an age of industrial optimism and represents everything that Cliff could ever personally aspire to. The Bulldog Cafe group, working with old-fashioned determination and raw talent, could only fantasize about the technological luxuries that Hughes had literally at his fingertips. The offices of Hughes provide a contrast to the world of the Rocketeer and his buddies.

The Merging of Hollywood Kitsch Art and Architecture with the Decadence and Inflated Drama of Nazi Taste

This odd mixture of controlling imagery speaks to the collision of cultures so common in the movie industry. The story is about a young aviator's desire to fly and how his dreams come true in the city of make-believe. This situation allows the production designer to introduce images that run counter to many of the inherent values of the straightarrow Rocketeer. The conflict of the film is graphically presented in the contrasting styles of these sets and the values we associate with them. Popular notions of star-crazed Hollywood venerating opulence and self-indulgence are realized in the Movie Studio Set, the South Seas Nightclub, the Zeppelin Set, and Neville Sinclair's Estate. Neville Sinclair is both a swashbuckling movie star and a secret Nazi agent. The film story puts Cliff's girlfriend, an aspiring starlet, at risk of being seduced by Neville and his enchanting surroundings.

The Movie Studio set—a castle interior thinly constructed on an actual soundstage—is a handy metaphor for the artificial and delusionary ways of the movie business. When Cliff visits his girlfriend on the set, his garage-inventor values run up against the effete self-aggrandizing attitudes of pampered Hollywood. The visual irony, of course, is that Cliff looks as though he just stepped out of a Buck Rogers film himself.

The South Seas Club set is the jewel of the film (3-21). Inspired by the classic MGM nightclub sets of Cedric Gibbons in the 1930s, Bissell and designer Paul Sonski created a room of hypnotic swirling floor patterns, a marbled staircase, Greek columns supporting an overhang, tables that elegantly displayed the patrons, and a giant shell, pool, and waterfall surrounding an orchestra. The set is a visual summation of every element of the fantasized "high life" of Hollywood movies. To add a touch of the sinister because this is the playground of the duplicitous Sinclair, the designers used the color green very liberally on the set.

161

Neville Sinclair's House set combines the two controlling images. On the one hand, it is the place of his decadent movie colony seductions, but worse, it is the headquarters for the Nazi espionage ring. The house design was based on a Frank Lloyd Wright structure, a starkly modern place of shaped slab concrete. The cold look of Sinclair's rooms are reminiscent of the severely overpowering architecture so popular in the Third Reich.

The Zeppelin set showed off what was then the state-of-the-art flight technology of the Germans. A replica of the craft provides the final setting for the last explosive action of the film. Besides building a scale model of the Zeppelin, two major sets had to be constructed—the gondola that housed the crew and captives at the film's climax, and the huge tail section where the Rocketeer demolishes his enemies. This lumbering airship contrasts nicely with the Rocketeer's zippy Rocket Pack invention.

By identifying the controlling images in the script, production designer James Bissell and his associates were then able to convert their visual themes. Although some of the images of the time period were juxtaposed, the movie had an overall unity of design. The very special look of *The Rocketeer* was its outstanding feature.

SUMMARY

"I did good movies when I had good production designers, and I did bad photography when I had bad production designers. If the production designer doesn't do his job right, you have an immense effort to try to do something good."

Cinematographer Vilmos Zsigmond
(*Sliver*, 1993)

As a film moves from the preproduction stage into production, with its unrelenting daily shooting schedule, a noticeable shift takes place in the relationship between the film director and the production designer. Initially, the director was in constant contact with the production designer regarding plans for the construction of the set and the hundred details that must be ready for the first day's shoot. At this time, the director's energy begins to turn toward the actors and the camera. The bulk part of the work completed in the preproduction stage, the production designer must now vie with others for the attention of the director.

But if the production design team has done its job well, the movie has established a solid basis for the visual style and atmosphere of the movie. It is the production designer's job to create a world. Actors will play in it; cinematographers will capture it on film. Movies have the wonderful power to transport the audience to remote realities. The design team has worked to make that journey either as subtly natural or dazzling to the eye as possible. When it works well at this level, audiences both see and feel the inexplicable realness or graphic dream that is so unique to the movie experience.

SPOTLIGHT

The Production Designer: Patricia Norris Interview

Patricia Norris has worked steadily in the film industry since 1972, first as a costume designer, later as a production designer, often in both capacities on the same film. A partial list of her credits includes costume design credit for *The Candidate* (1972), *The Missouri Breaks* (1976), *Silent Movie* (1976), *California Suite* (1978), *Francis* (1982), *Scarface* (1983); with Oscar nominations for *Days of Heaven* (1978), *Elephant Man* (1980), *Victor/Victoria* (1982), and *2010* (1984); as well as an Emmy for the television series *Twin Peaks*. Although she continued to work in costume design throughout the 1980s and 1990s, beginning with David Lynch's *Blue Velvet* (1986), Ms. Norris took on the expanded responsibilities of a production designer. Since then she has often worked in the dual capacity of production designer and costume designer, in such notable films as *Tap* (1989), *Wild at Heart* (1990), *Twin Peaks: Fire Walk with Me* (1992), *Leaving Normal* (1992), *The Journey of August King* (1993), *Lost Highway* (1997), *The End of Violence* (1997), *Hi-Lo Country* (1998), and *The Straight Story* (1999).

Richard Peacock: To stay on top of the business, do you live in Los Angeles?

Patricia Norris: No, I live in Boulder. I work out of town most of the time anyway, so there's no real point in living there. It works out fine. It's two hours to L.A. If I have to meet someone there I can be back on the same day.

RP: How did you initially get into the industry?

PN: I studied archeology and paleontology at Stanford. I married, had children, and divorced. I got my first job as a stock girl in the wardrobe department at MGM studios. It was quite good in a strange way because I learned an awful lot.

RP: Did you have any thought at the time that you would like to get into costume design?

PN: After a while, yes. I didn't really like being a stock girl. It was a little limiting. [laughter]

RP: You worked for many years as a costume designer in films. Was it a natural progression into the broader field of production design?

PN: It's that old thing, an opportunity comes along, like when David [Lynch] asked me to do *Blue Velvet*. I don't think he asked me because he thought I was terribly talented, probably they didn't want to pay a lot of money. [laughter] I hadn't thought about production design too much, but I had some. At the time, in 1986, it was a very male-oriented area of work. Now there are a lot more women doing this. I remember that when I first got into it, someone asked me, "But how will you talk to construction men?"

RP: How do you?

PN: "Please" and "thank you" seems good enough. [laughter]

RP: Right. But now you most often have the dual credit of production designer and costume designer.

PN: Yes, I still do the clothes. It's all about character. Where they live and what they wear all seems to go together.

RP: You've been connected to an enormous variety of films. In some ways it's easy for a screenwriter to put in a script "The year is 1815 in the rural south" as in *The Journey of August King*, or "It's present-day Miami in the Cuban community" as in *Scarface*, or "It's 2010" as in *2010*. But as a costume designer or production designer, you have to make that written line a visual reality. Doesn't each project seem like you have to literally start from scratch again?

PN: Oh yes, very much so. And you also don't want to re-create what you've done before. I get excited doing research. I'd almost rather do that than do the work, do the set. I love discovering things about the subject. The way I try to work is to find the reality of story situation, and then close all the books and go on my imagination from then on. I loved doing *The Journey of August King* because the only research is reading and letting your imagination go. I had to think about who were the immigrants, where did they come from, and what did they bring with them? That's what makes it so interesting. You learn a lot.

RP: How much time do you normally spend in researching a movie—if there is such a thing as normal?

PN: It depends on how long a lead time you have. And I never really stop the process until the shoot is over. There is always the opportunity to do something else.

RP: Where do you look for help in researching the design of a film?

PN: I just really like bookstores. I have a huge number of books. I love books, I love reading. There are also things that you learned a long time ago. You try to make things not look like things you see all the time in films. That it's familiar, but a little bent. And depending on the area that I'm working in, I usually can find a lot of information. When I was doing *August King*, I physically went to look at the Appalachian Trail to see how it came out of the mountains. You find out all kinds of stuff—the inns they had in those days were nine miles apart because that's how far they could drive a pig. Stuff like that gives you a whole feeling about the time period.

RP: As both a costume designer and production designer, do you study films from the past for inspiration with current problems?

PN: Never. I don't want to copy anyone. Of course you may end up copying them anyway, but at least you don't know it.

RP: But as a costume designer, weren't there some figures in the field who you admired and perhaps have drawn inspiration from?

PN: No, not really, because it's always constantly changing. Thinking about period movies, for example, it was very odd being a stock girl at MGM, and also at Warner. You find these wonderful 1860 dresses made in the 1940s with shoulder pads! The whole concept of actors looking authentic is relatively recent. You look at the old John Wayne movies and they just look silly. Everything is so clean and the women have pointy bras on.

RP: You and David Lynch have connected on many films, from *Elephant Man* to *Straight Story*. Do your aesthetic sensibilities naturally line up with his, or do you simply read his visual needs very well?

PN: I don't know. We seem to have the same definition of ugly. And he gives me a great bit of freedom too. We have a good time working together. We eat grilled cheese sandwiches in diners, dutch I might add. Yes, sometimes you hook up with someone and they're just real easy to work with. And I've worked with others that are really so difficult that it's not worth it.

RP: You also worked with Mel Brooks on quite a few films.

PN: He's good. I learned about what was funny from him. That clothes aren't funny, the people wearing them are funny, if that makes any sense. It's like you're doing a parody of Tippy Hedren in *The Birds* in the birdcage always holding her clutch bag. If you look at some of the old films that Brooks did take-offs on, there's always something bizarre—you know, people are in a high wind and every hair is in place. But that's the style of 50s–60s kind of movies.

RP: It's interesting that you bring up humor because in David Lynch's films humor underlies almost everything. The production design speaks to it all the time.

PN: Perhaps. Half the time you don't know what you're doing, it just seems right. You really don't have a reason for your choices. When people ask, "Why did you do that?" Well, it just seemed right to me.

RP: *Blue Velvet* is a classic film in most ways, in no small part for its production design. For example, the interior color scheme and design of Dorothy Valiens' apartment is one of the strongest elements in the film. What was your approach to that set?

PN: It was like a womb. But it was odd and weird and mysterious. They said, "Nobody has ever painted a room in this color. Are you sure that you want this?" "Yezz, and I want black molding." When we finished, David liked it because it was different. You know, if you look in your wardrobe, we all have colors. Basically most people always look the same—if you have a lot of black you're not going to suddenly be wearing bright orange. So if you can give each character a look that matches with their environment, then you've got it. Particularly with David's movies, some of the characters don't go all the way through the story. You don't get to know them too much, but by color and such. You can know who they are, without being hit over the head with it.

RP: Visual mood for Lynch seems almost more important than character or story sequence.

PN: That's very true.

RP: Doesn't this put an unusual amount of pressure on you to come up with production concepts that can dominate the look of the film?

PN: No. [laughter] David is a hoot; he's really a nice man. I won't say he's ordinary, but he's a really nice person. He's not a mean person. And there are some directors who are really mean and those are the ones you don't want to work with. I've had my share of them. It's not worth it.

RP: You don't seem to be a person who is highly pressured.

PN: I can't be. I learned that a long time ago. If I get upset, it just doesn't work. So much of our work is brain work. You can't even be trained for it. Maybe the thing is not to be trained for it. I know some colleagues who do everything by the numbers, and their work is never really interesting because they don't take a chance. I think you need to take chances.

RP: But in production design, although there is an immense amount of creativity, isn't there also a need for solid organization?

PN: A tremendous amount. There's a crew of forty or fifty people. But it's still, "Please and thank you" or maybe, "I'd like to see that by this evening," then finally "Do it *now!*" But you try to get people of good cheer around you. Those who like working and are eye-to-eye with your attitudes. No whiny people.

RP: When you come on a project, do you first read the script to define the characters and your thoughts about them?

PN: I read the script then totally break it down to every element in it. And then I get together with the director. I come on anywhere from 5 to 12 weeks before the shoot. Sometimes it doesn't make any difference. Then again, it depends on the size of the movie. It's lovely to have more time, but then again, so much can happen at the last moment that turns out very good.

RP: How hard is it to get everyone on the same page in terms of the look of the film?

PN: I don't think it's hard at all. Especially when the director's behind you, "O.K., you don't like it? Let me go tell David. Better yet, go tell him yourself." [laughter] No, it's not hard. You really have the advantage because you've thought about the film a lot longer and done the research.

RP: Do you have a lot of conversations with the director of photography?

PN: Yes and no. It's odd. The DP usually comes on later, and if you know the person, you chat and discuss colors and mood. A lot depends on whether you've worked together before. Camera people don't look at movies the same way. I have to make things come alive. The people have to look real, their houses have to be real. That's not what a cinematographer has to do. They photograph it after I've done that.

RP: Do you do sketch work in preparation of your design concepts?

PN: I draw out most everything. But in terms of costumes, a lot of times I don't do much until I meet the actors. I really need to talk and get to know them so that I can get a feel for how to work it out. You can't force actors to be who you think they should be. It may be too foreign to their look.

RP: So then are you saying that many actors have a fair amount of input into the wardrobe they wear in a film?

PN: You try to let them think so. [laughter] "Don't you think that. . . ." Actually, you always talk to the director first to see what he or she wants, then to the actors, and then get some of your own wishes in there. Movies are such a group participation that it is best to find harmony.

RP: To get specific for a moment, in *The Missouri Breaks*, Marlon Brando's fringed white buckskin jacket is memorable, but rather an outrageous departure for a traditional Western desperado. You were the costume designer on the film. Did you come up with that concept?

PN: It was both of us. The dress was his idea.

RP: What was your idea for the clothing in *Days of Heaven*? Although his was the impoverished rural West, the simple design of the wardrobe for Richard Gere and the cast was almost fashionable, creating a clothing style in itself.

PN: There is a style in that period and you just take advantage of it. Nestor [Almendros] was great to work with. He almost never used lights. In the fields of the open prairie, depending on the light of the day, I would change colors on all the costumes. It was magic.

RP: As a costume designer, one of the bigger projects you worked on was *2010*, for which you received an Oscar nomination. Are space movies something you would ever want to go back to?

PN: No. I've done a couple of them and they're very hard to do. If you go back in the space program, you realize there are few changes in the way astronauts look. It's not like spacesuits went from thirteen layers to six layers. And the changes aren't visual. Also it's hell to make those things work—the endless details. I hate those things! No, you couldn't make me do that again.

RP: Obviously a production designer's job is never easy, but would it make any difference to you to take on a very high budget project—*Batman and Robin,* for example? In other words, is the nature of the work essentially the same, or does the increase in the *degree* of complexity result in a different *kind* of activity?

PN: I tend not to do those kinds of movies, I'm really not comfortable with them. And never will be. I know people who work on them and you hear these horror stories. I just don't see how you can create anything with that many people around. I'm not drawn to it. They hire art directors, sketch artists, blah blah blah. I just wouldn't feel I had really created anything in the end. To do the third or fourth sequel of something doesn't excite me.

RP: Is there any kind of film that as a production designer you haven't done that you would like to tackle?

PN: Any film in a period that I haven't done . . . I don't particularly like contemporary films. I like David's because they are odd, but most modern movies I just turn down. ◄

FILMS TO CONSIDER

The fourteen films listed presented special challenges for their **production designers**, ranging from building fantasy worlds to capturing the raw reality of everyday life. Watching them from a design perspective is enlightening.

- *Frankenstein* (1931): This Gothic horror movie by James Whale set a high standard, not only for expressionistic art direction but also for its remarkable makeup by Jack P. Pierce, influencing the visual style of later films in the genre.

- *The Wizard of Oz* (1939): The fantastic and delightful world of Oz was the work of a very large design team, headed by Cedric Gibbons, with costumes by Adrian and makeup by Jack Dawn.

- *Invasion of the Bodysnatchers* (1956): The collaboration of the director, Don Siegel, and the production designer, Joseph Kish, in the clever choice of location and props transformed this low-budget feature into a classic horror film.

- *Psycho* (1961): Alfred Hitchcock's attention to physical detail was his hallmark, executed in this film by set designer George Milo, whose shabby motel and cursed Bates' house established just the right specter of gloom.

- *Satyricon* (1969): Federico Fellini and production designer Danilo Donati created outrageous images of pagan Rome that were at the same time visually captivating and morally unsettling.

- *Alien* (1979): The physical look of this landmark movie is one of the great examples of a production design team's contribution to a challenging project, including the limitless vision of P.D. Michael Seymour, design concepts by Ron Cobb, and H.R Giger's costumes.

- *Stalker* (1979):   Director Andrei Tarkovsky, working as his own production designer, used drab wasteland landscapes and wet underground chambers to create the territory that had to be traveled to get to the forbidden "zone."
- *Fitzgeraldo* (1982): There have been few more genuinely hellish locations than the ones chosen by Werner Herzog, as he drove some of his crew and cast to madness on the Amazon River.
- *Blade Runner* (1982): The award-winning art direction of Lawrence G. Paul in his rendition of futuristic Los Angeles as a wet neon nightmare is the most permanent memory of the film for most people.
- *Brazil* (1985): Production designer Norman Garwood combined expressionistic romantic dream sequences with a visually torturous reality to both delight and depress the viewer.
- *Ju Dou* (1990): A traditional Chinese cloth dying factory, filled with material streams of flowing color, dominates the life of each person in this tragic love story by Zhang Yimou.
- *Dick Tracy* (1991): The fantastic comic book look of this film was intentionally achieved with the help of production designer Richard Sylbert and makeup artists Cheri Minns and Kevin Haney.
- *Richard III* (1995): Placing this Shakespeare play in the 1930s was successfully realized because of the imaginative risks taken by production designer Tony Burrough and costume designer Shuna Harwood in creating a retro-fascist look.
- *Angela's Ashes* (1999): The stark reality of this film, set in the deepest poverty of Limerick, Ireland, was given credence by the harsh and confining set designs of Geoffrey Kirkland.

THOUGHT QUESTIONS AND EXERCISES RELATING TO PRODUCTION DESIGN

Watch one of the films listed.

1. Looking at the movie as a whole, describe and define the visual ambiance that was created through its production design. What are the key sets chosen for the story? Explain in detail how they contributed to the effectiveness of the movie.

2. After watching one of the films, imagine the story taking place in another location or time period. Describe how this might be realized in other areas of the production, including the story line, casting, wardrobe, and shooting style.

3. Select the central controlling images of the original film and determine how they could be changed and redesigned. How might the production design be altered to accommodate the story, yet give the film a fresh look? Project the effect such alterations might have on the movie.

4. Choose a major scene that takes place in the living environment of the main character. Analyze the set decoration. What do the details of it "say" about that person? Could some elements be added or detracted to the benefit of the film's message about the character?

5. Wardrobe and hair design are key elements in the relationship between the audience and the actor. Consider the main character and define what you feel the director and the design specialists wished to achieve in their selections of clothes and hairstyles. Did it work?

FURTHER READING

Affron, Charles and Mirella Jona Affron. *Sets in Motion: Art Direction and Film Narrative* (New Brunswick, NJ: Rutgers University Press, 1995).

Albrecht, Donald. *Designing Dreams: Modern Architecture in the Movies* (New York: Harper & Row/M.O.M.A., 1986).

Baygan, Lee. *Makeup for Theatre, Film, and Television* (New York: Drama Publishers, 1993).

Ettedgui, Peter. *Production Design and Art Direction* (Storeham, MA: Focal Press, 2000).

LoBrutto, Vincent. *By Design: Interviews with Film Production Designers* (New York: Prager, 1992).

Location Update Magazine. 7021 Hayvenhurst Ave., #205, Van Nuys, CA 91406.

Olson, Robert. *Art Direction for Film and Video* (Newton, MA: Focal Press, 1993).

Preston, Ward. *What an Art Director Does: An Introduction to Motion Picture Production Design* (Los Angeles: Silman-James Press, 1994).

Sennett, Robert S. *Setting the Scene: The Great Hollywood Art Directors* (New York: Harry N. Abrams, 1994).

Simon, Mark. *Art Direction for Film and TV: The Craft and Your Career* (New York: Drama Publishers, 1997).

———. *Storyboards: Motion in Art* (Storeham, MA: Focal Press, 2000).

Surowiec, Catherine A. *Accent on Design: Four European Art Directors* (London: British Film Institute, 1992).

TCI Magazine: The Business of Entertainment Technology and Design. P.O.Box 470, Mount Morris, IL 61054.

Vacche, Angela Dalle. *Cinema and Painting: How Art Is Used in Film* (Austin: University of Texas Press, 1996).

Woodbridge, Patricia. *Scenic Drafting for Theatre, Film, and Television: Principles and Professional Examples* (New York: Drama Publishers, 1997).

Yarwood, Doreen. *Fashion in the Western World: 1500 to the Present Day* (New York: Drama Publishers, 1996).

CHAPTER 4

CASTING THE PERFORMERS

THE CRITERIA

"An actor is like a canvas without paint: He needs the colors of somebody else."

Actor Marcello Mastroianni

A central concern of the producers during the preproduction stage is how best to assign the major and minor acting roles in the film. Because a film will only be as good as the performers who interpret its story, movies depend on unerring casting. No two actors will interpret a character in exactly the same way. As a consequence, the choice of actors, based on the best-informed guesses of the producers and the director before any shooting takes place, will decide its fate. Great casting decisions may not insure a superior film, but they give the movie an excellent chance of achieving its dramatic goals. In this chapter, we will consider not only the casting of actors but also the nature of acting for the camera.

When casting a film, a great number of factors, both artistic and practical, determine which actors are cast in the major roles.

The Pure Box Office Appeal of a Select Group of Actors.   Every film era has its stars. The surest way to create interest in a film is to cast the brightest of these in a major role. This has been true for as long as Hollywood has been in business. Today, however, with foreign box office accounting for more than 50 percent of revenues, the international appeal of an actor will be needed to generate overseas presales for movie funding. The reasons for the general public's attraction to a particular actor are debatable and ultimately may be a cultural mystery, but the box office receipts are proof enough for most film producers. Some have larger followings, with different demographic profiles, than others. For example, Cameron Diaz, Ben Affleck, Drew Barrymore, Jackie Chan, Hugh Grant, Eddie Murphy, Anthony Hopkins, Jim Carrey, Sandra Bullock, Antonio Banderas, Kate Winslet, Wesley Snipes, and Jean-Claude Van Damme have their diverse and loyal fans. In casting a movie, the filmmakers must guess whether the story and character of the proposed movie will tap into continued popular appeal for the chosen actor.

171

The Ability of an Actor to Fit the Role.   Some actors seem to be born for certain roles; other actors must shape themselves to the part by the strength of sheer talent. When Dustin Hoffman was cast in *The Graduate* (1967), the character and the actor seemed as one—it is hard to imagine another actor playing the part with the same winning combination of boyish charm and driven integrity. For the Tina Turner role in *What's Love Got to Do with It?* (1993), Angela Bassett had the exact physical attributes and acting range necessary for the role of an abused and well-known singing star. In a very different movie role, Daniel Day-Lewis faced an acting challenge that very few actors could have realized so astonishingly when he took on the demanding character of Christy Brown, an Irish writer with cerebral palsy, in *My Left Foot* (1989). The part called for him to evolve from dependent boy to a man confidently moving in sophisticated literary circles outside the reassurances of his home. One tends to assume that good professional actors can play any role until seeing a movie in which one is very badly cast. A wooden Charlton Heston playing a Mexican bigwig in *Touch Of Evil* (1958) is a classic example of putting the wrong actor in an important role. The result is that, to fully appreciate the classic *film noir* movie, one has to look past his performance to enjoy the many striking cinematic moments and the acting skills of others in the film. For *In Love and War* (1997), the hard-boiled public image of Ernest Hemingway is transformed by cherub-faced Chris O'Donnell. Film critic Anthony Lane felt that "The casting is so wrong that it's very nearly inspired . . . ."

The Interpersonal Chemistry among the Performers.   The excitement generated by the pleasure of seeing great or famous performers interact is a key element in the box office success of a movie **(4–1)**. A great deal of negotiation within offices of talent agencies involves finding the right combination of actor and studio to create magical marquee appeal. The casting of Clark Gable and Marilyn Monroe in *The Misfits* (1961), Barbra Streisand and Robert Redford in *The Way We Were* (1973), or Clint

4–1 *Leaving Las Vegas* Actors are paired in movies because of the special energy that might be discovered between them and that the camera will then capture. In some films, the rightness of the casting is undeniable. The chemistry between Nicolas Cage, playing a self-destructive drunk, and Elisabeth Shue, a caring prostitute, in *Leaving Las Vegas* (1995) is the central force that transforms an otherwise thoroughly depressing story into a film of heartbreaking romance. The intense emotion displayed between the actors is some of the most poignant ever filmed. (MGM/United Artists)

Eastwood and Meryl Streep in *The Bridges of Madison County* (1995) almost guaranteed the curious attention of filmgoers. Great actors help one another, but it is not always easy. Acting involves intimate sharing and psychological risk-taking among the cast, especially the lead players. It is clear, when watching the desperate survival tactics going on at a real-estate office in *Glengarry Glen Ross* (1992) that the cast of Jack Lemmon, Al Pacino, Ed Harris, Alan Arkin, Kevin Spacey, Alec Baldwin, and Jonathan Pryce challenged one another to perform at truly inspired levels. Director John Cassevetes had an unusual ability to create situations that triggered unpredictable and intense energy among actors, as in the explosive chemistry between Peter Falk and Gena Rowlands in *Woman under the Influence* (1974). The bond between Fernanda Montenergro, playing a worn-down older woman, and young street waif Vinicus de Oliveira in the Brazilian film *Central Station* (1998) was in reality genuine; their chemistry generated the core emotion of pure caring in the story. On the other hand, casting entails some guesswork, and history is replete with examples of off-screen incompatibility and on-screen flatness of the major actors. Julia Roberts and Nick Nolte, as competing but romantically involved newspaper reporters, for example, never find the sexy dynamic tension between them that is necessary to make *I Love Trouble* (1994) worth watching.

Budget Issues and Availability.   An actor's salary will sometimes determine who is finally cast. Obviously, a film with a moderate budget cannot afford a major star unless that person feels compensated in some other way by doing the project. Occasionally, a popular actor will sign on to a small film because of a challenging and unconventional script or to work with a favorite director known for unorthodox filmmaking or simply to get involved with an appealing film project at a less pressurized level. Meg Ryan, Sean Penn, and Kevin Spacey, all at the height of their star power, chose to join in the small-budget film *Hurlyburly* (1998) based on a stage play about coke-crazed minor movie executives living in the Hollywood Hills. Ryan played a drugged-out party girl, quite unlike the sweeter roles that have won her a large following. The movie quickly disappeared.

Gathering the talent to fill the many parts in a typical movie is a task that falls to the **casting director.** At the outset of a project, the producers usually hire a casting agency to work with the director to give faces to those characters that are roughly sketched in the script. Casting a film involves the collective judgments and taste of the filmmaking team. After reading the screenplay and comparing notes with the movie director, the casting director contacts various **talent agencies** with a description of the type of role available and the particular needs of the story. The budget of the film, again, is always the prime factor. Complicating matters, many actors have scheduled movie commitments that run many months into the future, and although they may want to work in a particular film, they are simply not available during the shooting period.

As in all lines of business, *networking* is the unofficial mode of communication. It is based on familiarity, common interest, and trust—major factors at the casting director's level of activity. The job calls for the interlocking of many potentially disparate interests: production companies, accounting departments, movie directors, and actor's agents. The system is working well when all parties realize that they will be doing business long after any single project is completed, and therefore some degree of honor must be maintained.

A computerized *breakdown service* has been developed in the movie industry that immediately sends out to all the talent agencies the complete casting needs of every film going into production. A flood of responses, in the form of photographs and biographies, results. The casting director will also have a backlog of personal experience by way of having scouted actors in live theater, television, and other public forums. From these sources, actors will be called in to the casting directors' offices to read for the parts. Some better-known actors may send in a short video of a significant piece of work. Out of these actors, five or ten may be chosen to be interviewed by the movie director for the part. Casting directors find special satisfaction in discovering a new actor who goes on to a solid film career.

Consider one of the strengths of *The Godfather* (1972), that is, its superior casting. In this grand mosaic of characters, each member of the cast was an inspired, if somewhat unorthodox, choice. The director had to fight an internecine war to win approval for the cast that now is recognized as having brought the film so much of its distinction. During preproduction, executives at Paramount Pictures resisted the casting choices of Francis Ford Coppola, many of whom they considered either unconventional or risky. This is especially true for Marlon Brando, an actor who had fallen from favor in Hollywood, but Coppola's choice as the central figure in the story. Brando went on to create the definitive movie archetype of an underworld boss—the aging but still powerful and vigilant Mafia chieftain, Don Vito Corleone. Other actors were equally well cast. Al Pacino, James Caan, and John Cazale, as three competing sons caught in the family traditions of the Mafia, gave the film both its compelling sense of family loyalty and its cold sibling conflict. Robert Duvall played Tom Hagen, an Irish lawyer deeply loyal to his adopted family, with restrained intensity. Diane Keaton was the non-Italian wife of Pacino, convincing as a woman spiritually and physically outside this inner circle of clannish men. Sterling Hayden, John Marley, Richard Conte, Al Martino, and others were impeccably cast in important minor roles, each actor contributing distinctively to the cultural authenticity of this sweeping drama. The masterful casting by Coppola in this film was central to its effectiveness.

BACKGROUND: THE STAR SYSTEM

"With the studio system in the old days, the studios themselves created the stars. Now we wait for a star to happen. It's more a free-for-all."

Casting director Heidi Levitt

For most of us the motion picture business immediately conjures up images of its stars. The very concept of a star—a woman or man who is a lead actor and, because of fortunate casting and personal charisma, captures the collective attention of an entire society—is very much a twentieth-century phenomenon. Until about 1910, actors in movies were anonymous figures, at best identified by a title card announcing the character's name—"Little Mary," or some such simple identification. Fledgling movie companies had little idea of how to reach the potentially large audience at a time when they seemed so ready for quick, inexpensive recreation. Without name recognition, the actors could not easily demand higher wages. Carl Laemmle, an innovative producer, first recognized that people wanted to know more about the actors with whom they had been so emotionally involved in the darkness of the theater. He rightly figured that higher salaries for leading actors was well worth it. Florence Lawrence, the first "Biograph Girl" (identified only by the production company), was making only $5 a week until Laemmle signed her to work at IMP productions; he then launched a series of publicity stunts, including false reports of her death, that were emblazoned in headlines. Fame and fortune came quickly after, and the fledgling industry learned lessons it never forgot. A host of "stars" followed in the next ten years: Mary Pickford ("Little Mary"), Lillian Gish, Charlie Chaplin, Mae Murray, William S. Hart, Fatty Arbuckle, Nazimova, Douglas Fairbanks Sr., Mabel Normand, Buster Keaton, Gloria Swanson, Clara Bow, and many others.

In 1915, William Fox changed the course of Hollywood forever when he invented and exploited a star for what he perceived to be the public's appetite—Thedeodosia Goodman became Theda Bara, "The Vamp." Already by 1911, fan magazines had gained wide circulation, but Fox was one of the first to promote his star by planting stories (now an accepted practice) about Theda Bara's shadowy erotic background. Her contract, for instance, stated that she could only travel by limousine and that she always appears in public heavily veiled. By the time her first film (*A Fool There Was*, 1914) appeared, the press and public could not get enough. In the next four years she made thirty-nine movies, most of which created the screen life of a woman who openly used men and sex, and didn't care. For a short time the character intrigued audiences, and Fox's PR men continued to control her public image. By 1919, Theda Bara was making $4,000 a week; by the next year fans grew tired of her overexposed guise and her acting career quickly burned out. The fast rise and fall of stars was a common pattern that many women and men sorrowfully learned in Hollywood **(4–2)**. Such stories became part of the lore of movies.

The evolution of the *star system* has continued through each decade, increasing in scope and momentum. The movie industry came to realize that its success depended on the love and loyalty of the public to chosen actors. The film stories might be intriguing, the production values first rate, but it was the lure of a male or female star (and teasingly pairing them) that sold the most tickets. Each studio had its publicity department geared to promoting the careers of its stars through a web of contacts with the media. Today, an entire mass media industry—public relations—is now at the service of the motion picture business. Every movie actor with aspirations to stardom will employ a public relations company to generate attention from the hundreds of publicity opportunities: introductions on TV special award shows, hosting of charity banquets, endorsing a product, personality profiles in magazines, guesting television and radio talk shows, the rumor planted in a newspaper column—any means of presenting an attention-getting and intriguing image to the public. Anthropologist and marketing theorist Grant McCracken makes the point, "Celebrities own their mean-

4–2   Louise Brooks   Because this culture worships youth, stardom can be fleeting, especially for women. Louise Brooks was a rising star in the 1920s both in Hollywood and German productions. Seen here in G. W. Pabst's *Diary of a Lost Girl* (1929), she presented a screen persona that was at once a perfect reflection of the new freedom women of the period enjoyed and a timeless beauty whose screen style seems surprisingly current. Off screen, Ms. Brooks was a very realistic and witty woman who quit movies in the 1930s to find literary satisfactions in relative obscurity.   (Kino International)

4–3   Gong Li   The universal popularity of a movie performer is tied to exposure, and that can be affected by the limitations of his or her culture. In China, Gong Li was by far the most recognized star of the 1990s, garnering wide press attention in that country for her beauty and performances in many exquisitely photographed films with director Zhang Yimou. Her reputation has spread quickly however as her films, such as *Ju Dou* (1991) and *Shanghai Triad* (1995), gained a more international audience.   (Miramax Films)

ings because they have created them on the public stage by dint of intense and repeated performance." Actors aspiring to stardom must establish a readily recognizable screen persona that becomes part of a larger network of psychological and cultural associations **(4–3)**.

All stars are actors, but not all actors are stars, or even working. The Screen Actors Guild represents about 73,000 professional actors and performing artists. Begun in 1933 and finally recognized in 1937 after threatening a strike, its primary responsibility has been to negotiate and enforce contracts with the entertainment industry, establishing working conditions and a minimum wage scale. At present, nearly 80 percent of the Guild membership earns less than $5,000 a year, less than 5 percent earn over $50,000. For many, being a movie actor means being unemployed.

STORY-DRIVEN VS. STAR-DRIVEN MOVIES

Movie scripts are categorized by producers and by casting agencies in two general ways: story-driven and star-driven films.

Story-driven scripts will become movies whose main attraction is their unique and especially well-told narrative. Often, the script is from a well-constructed novel, with such inherent dramatic weight that its story overshadows the contribution that any one actor might bring to the project. With certain scripts, there may be no single overpowering role, but, rather, the focus is on the inner workings of a group of characters. Barry Levinson's *Avalon* (1990), a fond study of Jewish immigrants to the United States, was such a story. It traced the changing values of a family through the earlier part of the twentieth century in Baltimore. The film had no star billing, but needed none. An earlier Levinson film, *Diner* (1982), was also a story-driven film, this time about young men at various stages of maturity. At the time, it was cast with relatively unknown actors because the issues within the story carried the weight of the movie. Since that movie, however, Mickey Rourke, Kevin Bacon, Daniel Stern, Steve Guttenburg, Paul Reiser, Michael Tucker, and Ellen Barkin have all been individually successful in later work. A fine story-driven movie often brings out the skills of a good actor. But movies with strong dramatic material are often best told without a highly popular actor to draw away the attention.

Story-driven movies face an uphill fight in the industry to get made. Plots that take on controversial political or social issues and give them precedence over the highlighting of any stars in the film are often seen as having a narrow audience base and therefore questionable credentials. Writer/director John Sayles (*Lone Star*, 1996) has made many provocative films over the years about the social and personal dramas of this country's past, and although some of them were cast with well-known actors, the thrust of his movies emphasized the genuine ethical questions rising out of the conflicts. Studios rarely back these films with the money and media concentration allotted to less thoughtful themes. This industry attitude translates into limited release patterns and small audiences. Writer/director Phil Alden Robinson (*Field of Dreams*, 1989) tried for many years to get his script about the civil rights movement financed, but its rejection by the studios had nothing to do with the inherent quality

4–4   *The Crying Game*   Story-driven movies face problems getting the public's attention. Certain of these movies, however, succeed famously. *The Crying Game* (1992) about an I.R.A. gunman, Fergus (Stephen Rea), escaping arrest after having been ordered to kill a British soldier (Forest Whitaker) featured no high-profile stars. But the unconventional story held a great surprise, widening the dimensions of Fergus' conflict. What was at first a challenge in terms of a traditional sense of universal human justice becomes a personal confrontation with the definition of Fergus' manhood, and more importantly, his humanity. In a culture that worships movie celebrities, films that emphasize the strength of story over stars must struggle to find their audience.   (Miramax)

of the story. "Every studio said the same thing. There's no foreign sales for a film like this. The stuff that translates the best is big action films and star-driven movies." Reaching a wide audience with a story-driven film usually entails issues beyond the quality of work by the actors, director, and producers **(4–4)**.

   Star-driven scripts fall into two categories: (1) those with characterization specifically written to show off the particular skills or charismatic persona of a leading actor (or actors), or (2) those written with such provocative characters or *high-concept* formats that they are perceived as vehicles for stars to further their careers. The major roles in these films are written to showcase the personalities and acting styles of the selected stars, sometimes tailored with a "bankable" actor in mind. Producers of these movies attempt to cast high-profile actors in principal parts to bring what may be an interesting story to a greater level of audience attention. Increasingly, the funding of movies hinges on the casting of the lead roles. By casting Julia Roberts in *Erin Brokovich* (2000), the studio transformed a worthy story about the human tragedies that follow government neglect and the abdication of industry responsibility—themes that do not usually electrify the mass movie public—into a battle between a glamorously litigious female and a devious gang of frowning corporate heads. Her character proved enormously popular ,and the movie went on to be highly successful.

Jere Hausfater, a senior VP at Buena Vista International, observes, " Star power in today's market is critical. And it has increased in the past few years in certain areas of the world—the Far East, Latin America, certain parts of Europe. Star power is key to getting these films booked and opened around the world." In any one season, ten to fifteen actors, mostly male, will form an unofficial "A+" list. The defining measure in reaching this position is an actor's power to guarantee financing for his or her film project and the ability to "open a picture" (in the jargon of the trade), that is, to insure that a film will get maximum distribution with a large base of fan support. These actors, on the strength of their recent track record, will be able to draw enough investors to make almost any reasonable movie they wish. Some of these current actors—Tom Hanks, Leonardo DiCaprio, Tom Cruise, Harrison Ford, Nicolas Cage, Mel Gibson, Will Smith, Jim Carrey, Jodie Foster, Kevin Costner, Julia Roberts, Jack Nicholson, Meg Ryan, Arnold Schwarzenegger, Bruce Willis, Brad Pitt, George Clooney, John Travolta, Robin Williams, among others—have enough clout to establish their own production companies for finding material and financial backing. This subjective but trusted list of stars will then link with studios with a guarantee of production control over future films they develop. The power position of a star can be a fleeting moment of grace, dependent on the fickle taste of film audiences. But while on top, the strength of an actor's name can carry a project through from the initial conversations between producers and studio executives to the final edited film. Agents like to label them "fireproof," in that they can guarantee a movie's financial backing regardless of genre, script, producer, director, or co-stars. In terms of business, producers realize that if a particular star or stars—even those not listed at the very top—would commit to doing their film, the entire project would have the momentum needed to attract solid financial backing, the right ancillary creative support, enthusiastic distribution, and wide media attention.

WHAT MAKES A STAR?

"The reality is that the camera does not lie— if only because it arbitrarily flatters certain faces and postures, and not others."

Daphne Merkin, *The New Yorker* film critic

Despite the exaggerated attention that certain actors achieve, no amount of publicity can automatically transform an actor into that most illusive designation: a **movie star (4–5).** At first glance, one requirement would seem to demand that an actor be either extremely handsome or beautiful. However, an evaluation of leading actors past and present suggests that there is no single standard, or even broad guideline, for predicting what mix of physical characteristics will elevate an actor to *star* status.

4–5   Sean Connery   Movie stars have always been bigger than life. It is hard to measure their influence on a culture, but the brightest of them become icons we hold in wonderment. Although Sean Connery was the quintessential male star of his era, his good looks and charisma are timeless. From the 1960s through the 1990s, he presented a male figure that was both thoughtful and decisive—a sleeping tiger. On location in the Caribbean for the first James Bond film, *Doctor No (1962)*, *Life* magazine photographer Bradley Smith caught Connery napping between setups. For most of the time since, he has been on the elite A+ list of stars. (Photograph by Bradley Smith)

Women crowned queen at beauty pageants and men fresh out of *GQ* magazine seem to have no great advantage. Otherwise, how does one explain the very successful careers of Whoopi Goldberg, James Woods, Gerard Depardieu, Ben Stiller, Geoffrey Rush, Dustin Hoffman, John Lithgow, Frances McDormand, Gary Oldman, Danny DeVito, Kathy Bates, Gene Hackman, and others as stars who do not fit those standards?

The obvious reward for the most fortunate movie actors is that not only are they paid extremely well for their film work, but in our current media-controlled culture, many reach unbelievable heights of fame and corresponding financial success in spin-off activities—in advertising, endorsements, and entrepreneurial investments. The exposure of actors has escalated exponentially with the sophistication of the mass media and its diverse "delivery" systems. When the machinery of the modern press is fed by multinational entertainment conglomerates, a whirlwind of media attention is generated not only about the final film, but any related issue in the production that can be deemed eye-catching or provocative. The release of a major motion picture becomes a fleeting but enthused public relations event, and intense public interest in the major performers usually follows. For 24 hours a day, cable TV channels pour out a continuous stream of new movies and old releases. The electronic media competes with the print media for coverage of actors who are reigning and those who might. A string of TV entertainment shows and magazine articles that expose "inside" information about the lives of actors service the expanding publicity needs of the movie industry. Strong audience loyalties are formed that make little distinction between an actor's on-screen and off-screen existence. The result is that the public is exposed to huge doses of detailed information about the careers and personal habits of a large number of actors, and after a while, the audience believes it cares. Somewhere in this process, *stars* are born.

The rise to stardom of Matthew McConaughey is instructive. Studying for a law degree at the University of Texas, he was cast for a small part in *Dazed and Confused* (1993), a small independent movie by Austin filmmaker Richard Linklater. Within the year he was signed by the Morris Agency, but by 1995 had only two small movie roles. He was then the surprise choice for the lead in *A Time to Kill* (1996), a major Warner Bros. project from a John Grisham novel. Set for a July release, the publicity machinery moved into place, first to push the movie, then honing in on McConaughey. Over a nine-month period preceding the film's release, McConaughery became a star. First "48 Hours" did a TV feature, followed by a mention by columnist Liz Smith, then articles in *The New York Times* and *US* magazine. "Hard Copy" called McConaughey one of the "sexiest men alive." While he went on a press junket promoting the film, and himself, on TV shows such as "Entertainment Tonight," McConaughey made the covers of *Entertainment Weekly*, *Interview*, and *Vanity Fair* magazines in rapid-fire succession. During the process, he became such a hot item that he was signed immediately to a series of other movies, including Robert Zemeckis's *Contact* (1997).

Certain actors obviously possess special acting abilities and physical gifts that give them a hold over film audiences. Throughout the years, studio executives, agents, casting directors, and movie critics have tried, with very mixed results, to recognize and predict the things that lift one actor above the rest. Producer Richard Zanuck (*Jaws*, 1976) has said, "Star quality is one of the most difficult things to describe. When someone who possesses this quality walks into a room, everyone else responds automatically, though no one can really define what they're responding to." The following personal dimensions do not give a complete explanation of stardom. But all popular actors known as *stars* have some of the features described here:

Talent.   Nothing in an actor can replace raw acting abilities. Great actors seduce audiences by making the craft look natural, even easy, but their talents have been finely tuned from years of training and experience in the profession. The fantasy of a person being discovered in a drugstore and suddenly rocketed to top billing is the hope of those unwilling to face the hard reality of an actor's life. For example, Morgan Freeman was over 50 years old, with a solid background on the Broadway stage, when he got a great part in *Street Smart* (1987), then a breakthrough opportunity in *Driving Miss Daisy* (1989). Gene Hackman, by no means classically handsome or physically imposing, for over twenty years has remained a lead actor on the earned reputation of his pure talent. It is not by chance that Hackman and other actors of his cut remain so interesting to watch. Skill in the craft of acting is best realized by performing continuously. Even actors in their teens, with seemingly meteoric rises to fame, on closer examination have solid credentials in either live or filmed performances. Jodie Foster began making movies when she was 10 years old. Whitney Huston has performed musically in front of critical audiences throughout her life. Until an actor can sustain consistently high performances, he or she cannot hope to reach the rarefied status of star. Talent shows through **(4–6)**.

Reflective of the Times.   Critic Louis Menand writes, "Stardom is the intersection of personality with history, a perfect congruence of the way the world happens to be and the way the star is." Every era has actors who accurately embody the cultural taste of the times in which they reached popularity. In the 1930s, the feisty and independent Jean Arthur or the robustly confident Clark Gable were models for an age that dreamed of better times. June Allyson and Van Johnson were eternally teary-eyed in the 1940s as the longing for separated lovers reflected the mood of the war years. By the end of the 1950s, Rock Hudson and Doris Day probably summed up, as well as any two stars, the image of goodness and sincerity that the decade promoted. It is always more difficult to gain perspective on one's own era, but somewhere in the acting styles of Lisa Kudrow, Parker Posey, Ewan McGregor, Angelina Jolie, Joesph Fiennes, Mary Louise Parker, Ice Cube, Ashley Judd, Leonardo DiCaprio, Juliette Lewis, Matt Damon, Sarah Polley, Freddie Prinze Jr., Renee Zellweger, Michael Rapaport, Drew Barrymore, Heather Graham, and others are per-

4–6   Gena Rowlands and Gene Hackman   Gena Rowlands and Gene Hackman, seen here in Woody Allen's *Another Woman* (1988), are two of the most respected and talented actors in movies. Each actor is known for the ability for discovering the most sublime undercurrents of the character they are playing, a quality that sets them apart as actors. Although both are capable of explosive performances, the intensity of their acting can be as easily witnessed in roles that call for sustained restraint.   (Orion Pictures)

sonified clues to the mix of the values we hold. However, some acting styles and familiar personas go out of season. Although they still retain the aura of stars, by the year 2000, actors such as Paul Newman, Sylvester Stallone, and Barbra Streisand have become icons of an earlier time.

Intelligence.   All great actors possess a quick wit and an uncommon insight into whatever character they are playing. Such actors are alive to all of the possibilities that the role might present, and their acting choices have the stamp of originality. For example, Jeremy Irons in *Reversal of Fortune* (1990) made brilliant decisions in his characterization of socialite Claus von Bulow. Irons combined a distantly cold and pompous interpretation with an almost boyish naiveté, with the result that the rogue character turned out to be oddly sympathetic. Robert DeNiro, as the ravaged boxer in *Raging Bull* (1980), went far beyond the stock manner that this kind of tragic character is normally played and infused the part with both penetrating primal intelligence and unexpected grace. Great actors reveal a sure confidence in their work. This intelligence can most often be detected in an actor's eyes—yes, the windows to the soul. Major actors such as Meryl Streep, Robert Downey Jr., Judy Davis, Anthony Hopkins, Gena Rowlands, John Malkovich, Kathy Bates, Kenneth Branagh, Nicole Kidman, Sam Neill, Lawrence Fishburne, Edward Norton, among others, approach their characters with unusual intelligence.

Strength of Personality.   The sum total of an actor's mental, physical, and emotional characteristics comes across in any major role in a film **(4–7)**. Although the art of acting seems to imply pretending to be someone you are not, in fact the better actors invite the camera to discover and reveal the deepest aspects of them. Audiences perceive the force of an actor's personality, and respond with attention and respect, even in roles that the character being played is weak or morally ambiguous. One senses this strength in actors such as Jessica Lange, William Hurt, Kate Winslet,

4–7   Wesley Snipes   The screen image of the heroes of action/adventure films is often a direct reflection of the strength of personality of the actor. They must not only have the charisma to carry a lead role but must often display real physical gifts. Wesley Snipes has shown both exceptional acting skills and a memorable physical presence in such films as *Jungle Fever (1991); White Men Don't Jump (1992); Passenger 57 (1992)* (pictured here); and *Murder at 1600 (1997).*   (Warner Bros.)

James Earl Jones, Sigourney Weaver, Harrison Ford, Kathleen Turner, Jeff Bridges, Angelica Huston, Harvey Keitel, or actors from earlier times, such as Bette Davis, Spencer Tracy, Ingrid Bergman, Henry Fonda, or Barbara Stanwyck. Screenwriter Robert Towne (*Mission Impossible*, 1996) may have come closest to it with his observation of a star's zen-like simplicity and strength, "They do it by being photographed . . . Great actors have features that are ruthlessly efficient . . . a fine actor on the screen conveys a staggering amount of information before he ever opens his mouth." The camera exposes not only the physical body but the inner spirit of an actor, and the general audience has a ready desire to identify with these empowering qualities.

Vulnerability.　Although this trait may seem to contrast with the *strength* of personality, vulnerability gives the movie actor a more accessible and attractive human dimension. Perhaps it simply inspires a viewer to "care for" those actors that he or she feels strongly about, but the actors who reach the top usually have a sensitive child-like side to themselves. Both tragedy and comedy demand that actors be open, in touch with their emotional confusion and hurt. The great actor Gerard Depardieu says, "I am not afraid to show my feminine side—that's part of what makes me a man. Our society wants us to be men with guts. But the greatest thing you have as a man is to have the guts—and the vulnerability too." In the past, James Dean, Montgomery Clift, Marilyn Monroe, Judy Garland, River Phoenix, and, currently, Robin Williams, Jennifer Jason Leigh, James Spader, Julia Ormond, Matthew Broderick, Andie Mac-Dowell, Matthew Modine, Winona Ryder, and John Cusack are among those who have shown an innocence and softness that invites viewer empathy on various levels. In certain actors, their degree of expressed vulnerability will hint at some past damaging experience, which they then use in the interpretation of their role. This distinctive acting trait marks their style. For instance, although Dustin Hoffman and Tom Cruise have contrasting screen personas, in *Rainman* (1988) both presented unprotected and accessible parts of themselves that endeared audiences. In *The Bridges of Madison County* (1995) the glimmer of a lost little boy is present even in the rocklike persona of Clint Eastwood.

Association with Mythic Character Roles.　One way an actor can rise to the majestic position of super star in the motion picture industry is to be cast in a role that indelibly associates him or her with a larger-than-life character in a popular film. John Wayne in *Fort Apache* (1948) and scores of other Westerns defined the cowboy for all time; Charlton Heston *became* Moses in *The Ten Commandments* (1956); Peter O'Toole is forever associated with the exotic hero *Lawrence of Arabia* (1962); and Arnold Schwarzenegger personifies the *The Terminator* (1984) character. Sylvester Stallone, with the five portraits in the *Rocky* series, built his stardom on the triumphs of that glamorous fighter. Tom Cruise has done many roles, but the relentless young Navy pilot in *Top Gun* (1986) defined his screen persona. Steven Seagal will always be the super-hero in high-action thrillers such as *Under Siege* (1992), and, possibly, Cate Blanchett may never free herself entirely from the image of Queen in *Elizabeth* (1998). Marilyn Monroe was the "Blonde Bombshell" in most of her films and built a career playing variations of that character. If the connection is both written and por-

4–8   John Travolta and Rene Russo   John Travolta is a prime example of the power of that most inscrutable star quality—charisma. From the start, movie makers have searched for actors who have it. Beginning with *Saturday Night Fever* (1977), Travolta has displayed an electric screen presence that combines boyish innocence with streetwise savvy. On the other hand, in many ways *Get Shorty* (1995) is typical of what many women actors confront in the film business. Rene Russo, a very accomplished actor, plays Karin, the romantic love interest in Chili's (Travolta) life. The role is a solid supporting part, but she is overpowered in the film by the character played by Travolta.   (MGM)

trayed vividly, and if the movie character resonates with the public in ways that set off its collective imagination and devotion, the combination will generate the special dynamic to set an actor apart.

Charisma.   This most elusive factor necessary for an actor to have is charisma. This star quality seems to be a gift given to some and not to others **(4–8)**. Essayist John Lahr defines the quality best when he writes, "Glamour agitates as it ravishes. It creates a climate of want." *Charisma* is that special magnetism that draws audiences to adore actors as diverse as Sean Connery, Bette Davis, Marlon Brando, Liv Ullman, Antonio Banderas, Jane Fonda, Paul Newman, Vanessa Redgrave, Cary Grant, Greta Garbo, Marcello Mastroianni, Liz Taylor, Warren Beatty, Grace Kelly, Jimmy Smits, George Clooney, Susan Sarandon, Mel Gibson, Gwyneth Paltrow, Al Pacino, Val Kilmer, and so many others over the years. When Jack Nicholson is on the screen, his figure will dominate the audience's attention in each shot, and his presence in the movie will inspire the entire project. The exact nature of movie *charisma* has baffled Hollywood from the beginning. Author Garry Wills defines John Wayne's charisma in physical terms, "His body spoke a highly specific language of 'manliness,' of self-reliant authority. It was a body impervious to outside force, expressing a mind narrow but focused, fixed on the task, impatient with complexity." Certainly, charisma has to do with an actor exuding some inherently sexual aspect of his or her nature—smoldering, bold, sweet, bawdy, natural, sly, confident, steamy, charming, naive, or some combination of them all.

Luck.   Good fortune is not exactly a quality of stardom, but some of it is necessary for an actor to reach the top. To "make it" as a leading actor, the pursuit goes beyond acting skills and the logic of good planning. As in every aspect of life, being there at the right time often determines the sequence of events that follows, and "the right time" is anybody's guess. The movie industry, for actors, is a grand catalog of spectacular successes and disappointing near misses. Many actors can perhaps rightly claim that if they had gotten "a break"—a top agent, the patronage of an influential production head, the right part in a movie—their personality and abilities could have taken them into the inner circle of stars. The veteran Italian actor Marcello Mastroianni, near the end of his successful career, reported, "Very important, luck. An encounter can change your life, like in the old-style Hollywood movies. I had other friends, perhaps better than I, who didn't have this chance." Despite the qualities previously outlined, there is some sentiment in the industry that contends that simple chance is the deciding factor.

While all of these elements are present in some manner in those men and women we recognize as stars, a complete definition goes beyond tidy categorization. Critic Daphne Merkin may say it best, "In the end, of course, star power is unfathomable—which is one of the reasons we're so affected by it."

CASTING AGAINST TYPE

In an effort to discover fresh dimensions in a character, a filmmaker will sometimes cast an actor in a part that goes against the grain of audience expectations. Often a director senses that an actor's range has been limited, and that unusual casting will infuse unexpected energy into the project. In other cases, although an actor may seem initially unsuited, casting a person whose screen persona runs counter to the scripted character will sometimes bring out unexpected possibilities in the story **(4–9)**. The desire may also be prompted by the actor who is tired of the sameness of roles being offered and who is looking for new challenges.

A classic example was the casting of Jimmy Cagney in the song and dance musical *Yankee Doodle Dandy* (1942). For years, Warner Bros. had shaped Cagney's image as that of a tough, no-nonsense streetfighter. But Cagney chafed at the severe limitations of such typecasting and wanted to express his considerable "song-and-dance" talents in this story. The studio at first resisted the idea, then went on to make a surprisingly well-executed biography of songwriter George M. Cohan. Cagney's playfully brilliant performance was the key. There are many examples of successful *casting*

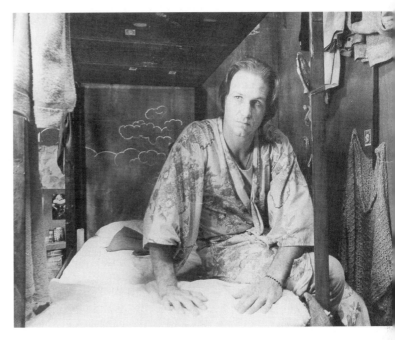

4–9   *Kiss of the Spider Woman*   One of the two leading roles in *Kiss of the Spider Woman* (1985), a prison picture set in South America, called for one of the actors to play a transvestite. William Hurt was successfully cast in the part, despite the fact that his then-current screen image as a thoughtful and brooding star would never have suggested his fitness for the role. Hurt was also physically "wrong" for the part, with a bulky body and heavy features. But by casting against type, director Hector Barbenco achieved a visual surprise, and challenged the audience to give the character special attention. (Island Alive)

against type, among them Humphrey Bogart as the bumbling, soft-hearted river captain in *The African Queen* (1951), the previously gentile and glamorous Liz Taylor as the brawling spouse in *Who's Afraid of Virginia Woolf?* (1966), or a humorless Jerry Lewis in *The King of Comedy* (1983). Comic actor Bill Murray risked taking the role of a cruel loan shark in *Mad Dog and Glory* (1993). Matthew Broderick had been best known at the time for his comic flair in such movies as *Ferris Bueller's Day Off* (1986), so casting him in the pivotal role of a young Union Army colonel in *Glory* (1989) demanded that he create a portrait of a young officer thrust into a critical leadership position. The character is most convincing, as he emerges heroic in the most cruel and morally challenging conditions. The remarkable casting drew out a subtly modulated performance from Broderick.

Frequently casting against type fails miserably. When the film audience has gotten to know and strongly identify certain actors with specific types of characters, they sometimes refuse to accept any other type of casting. Throughout the 1980s, Sylvester Stallone was a megastar in the roles of a colorfully raw boxer or the over-the-top war hero, but he was rejected as a dapper comic figure in *Oscar* (1991). The artistic and financial disaster of *Bonfire of the Vanities* (1990) was widely attributed to bad casting, especially the choice of Bruce Willis as a fey British journalist who is intended to give the film a warped perspective from a drunken outsider. Having been associated with harder edged roles, the choice of Willis confused most people. After a series of successful films playing savvy, if shaddy, urbane characters, John Travolta was roundly ridiculed for his acting in the grim *Battlefield Earth* (2000) as an arrogant and wretched green-eyed "psycho." Audiences do not always react well to movies when their expectations going into a film are not realized.

⋆ CASTING WOMEN AND ETHNIC MINORITIES

In the 1930s, five of the top ten box office moneymakers were women. Joan Crawford, Greta Garbo, Claudette Colbert, Marlene Dietrich, Mae West, and others matched their male counterparts in credits and salary. In recent years, there have been very few women who could so consistently claim such power in the industry. Depending on who one interviews, various reasons are given for the small number of dominant female leads:

- The lack of good scripts for women.
- Audience indifference to stories about women.
- The stress on the high-grossing "blockbuster" movie, giving male-oriented, high-action adventure films, with strong international appeal, the priority.

Whatever the "Catch 22" reasoning, the result is that female actors, from the top to bottom, are working less in film. In 1998, the Screen Actors Guild (SAG) reported that of the 13,025 roles assigned in feature films for that year, only 37 percent went to women. Furthermore, by the time women are

over forty years old, only 8 percent of the movie roles are available to them. SAG figures show that male actors made 72 percent of the total earnings made under the contracts for theatrical releases. For years female actors have complained that the reality—or even fantasy—of our society is not being adequately reflected from a woman's perspective. Casting director Carrie Frazier claims, "It's much more difficult to cast female characters than male ones. The leading guy can be kind of ugly, he can have funny legs, he can be appealing or sassy or a lot of different things. Your female character has to envelope everyone's idea of a woman. She has to be smart. She has to be pretty. She has to be a safe harbor, but you can't think of your woman character who could possibly hurt anyone in any way." While exceptions could be pointed out, the essence of the statement holds true. The distinguishing feature of Linda Fiorentino's character in *The Last Seduction* (1994), now a cult classic, is that she plays a heartless woman who wins, not an uncommon part for popular male heroes in movies.

Until the 1990s, much the same situation existed for eth-

nic minorities. In past years, Black, Asian/Pacific, Latino/Hispanic, and Native American Indian actors have been able to get very few roles in which they were not broadly stereotyped. In 1998, SAG reports that African Americans were cast in 13.4 percent of the total number of roles (down almost a full percentage point from the previous year). Latino/Hispanics (about 11 percent of the U.S. population) held only 3.5 percent of jobs as actors. Again, the standard reasons given for denying minorities are the same as those just listed for discouraging women. The subject of cultural discrimination has a complex history tied to every aspect of American life in this century and before. It is true that in the 1970s, for example, a series of well-made low-budget action movies such as *Shaft* (1971) and *Superfly* (1972) gave African-American actors heroic roles. But apart from a small number of thoughtful dramas like *Sounder* (1972), these movies sank into a formula labeled "Blaxploitation," and soon lost their impact on the movie industry. Put very directly and simply, the Hollywood movie business has always been dominated by affluent white males who have

continued ▶

tended to promote film stories that reflect their own values, experiences, or fantasies. Such entrenched socioeconomic systems are slow to change.

The positive side of the movie business indicates that Hollywood is very sensitive to the dictates of the box office. One very weak financial year in the movie industry, or a single popular film about an ethnic minority, can suddenly trigger a series of films about situations with more open and imaginative casting opportunities. The demands for movies with different cultural issues, styles, and stories change, and ethnic awareness has proved to be profitable. Today, more starring roles are being cast with racial minorities. For example, African-American actors have fared better with the rash of films featuring aspects of Black history (*Amistad*, 1997), contemporary experiences (*Waiting to Exhale*, 1995), action features (*Shaft*, 2000), or pairing with a white star in a buddy movie (*The Negotiator*, 1998). The film work of Spike Lee (*He Got Game*, 1998) has forged the way. Asian-American actors were given a boost with the success of *The Joy Luck Club* (1993), *The Corruptor* (1999), *Three Seasons* (1999), and *Shanghai Noon* (2000); Latinos in *El Mariachi* (1993), *My Family* (1994), and *Selena* (1996); and Native Americans, first with *Dances with Wolves* (1990) and more recently with *Smoke Signals* (1998). As producers and studios continue to discover the commercial rewards in making movies with ethnic diversity, opportunities for minorities will move beyond the tokenism of the past.

CASTING SUPPORT ROLES

Although a major star may be the primary draw for a film, a script will not work well unless the entire project is creatively cast with actors carefully selected to fill the many other roles. The supporting cast fills out the fabric of interaction and dramatic background for the story. The selection of these actors, and the subsequent manner in which they weave together, will determine much of the quality of the film. One of the pleasures of watching a good film is witnessing the way in which all of the actors mesh into a seamless total performance.

At times, supporting actors can bring to life an otherwise ordinary movie. As viewers, we scan the screen for bits and pieces of original performances in smaller roles. Often these minor parts stand out long after much else in the film has been forgotten: Sean Penn's portrait of a stoned surfer in *Fast Times at Ridgemont High* (1982); Morgan Freeman as the attractive but lethal drug dealer in *Street Smart* (1987); John Turturro in *Do the Right Thing* (1989) as the violently angry son of a pizza shop owner; M. Emmet Walsh as the greasy private detective in *Blood Simple* (1989); Max Perlich's quirky performance as the kid-next-door in *Drugstore Cowboy* (1989); Jaye Davidson in *The Crying Game* (1992) as the surprise love interest; Mira Sorvino as the ditzy porno star in *Mighty Aphrodite* (1995); William H. Macy playing the frazzled, murdering car dealer in *Fargo* (1996). Great performances in smaller, well-written roles are often scene-stealers and add unexpected fire to a movie.

When casting a film, the supporting roles to be filled follow a host of patterns that are surprisingly common. Apart from the lead actor as the **protagonist**, no matter how freshly they are conceived, most films need to cast a series of stock parts.

4–10 *The Hit* During this scene from Stephen Frears *The Hit* (1984), the arc of the dramatic action would seem to be ripe for interpretation. In the supporting role of a loutish crook, Tim Roth is an antagonist in the film, turning the tables on his equally evil boss and fellow kidnapper (John Hurt). They have taken two hostages (Laura Del Sol and Terence Stamp), but now a mutiny has arisen. Tim Roth has made a career out of playing stylized antagonist roles in movies. (Island Alive)

The **antagonist** is that person who personifies the conflict in the film—the bad guy **(4–10)**. A classic example is the Wicked Witch of the West (Margaret Hamilton), in *The Wizard of Oz* (1939), as she terrifies the good gang of misfits lead by Dorothy. The antagonist usually can be played very colorfully, because the part is usually so open to rich and eccentric interpretation. For example, Alan Rickman, in both *Die Hard* (1988) and *Robin Hood* (1991), gave memorable performances as a malevolent force intent on doing in the protagonist. We relish his range of acting mannerisms that signify an evil intelligence at work and that, in turn, rivets our attention. Movie lore is replete with many great male and female actors who have played scene-stealing antagonists.

The **reflector** is a staple in movies because this character allows the protagonist the chance to externalize ideas. Because he or she is a "buddy," a reflective character is nearby the protagonist in times of trial, allowing the lead character to bounce ideas and secret concerns off that person. In the simplest situation, the trusted "sidekick" in old Westerns filled this role. In other films, the character was something like a good-luck charm, a lighthearted confidante chosen to share in the fate of the hero. In *Pulp Fiction* (1994), Samuel L. Jackson presented a strong independent character, but to a great extent cued his role to the lead character played by John Travolta, drawing him with provocative commentary and helping to define the portrait of Travolta as a bizarre and unconventional hitman. These roles are at the service of the leading actors.

The **romantic** character affords the movie its love story, often the subplot in any genre of film. Popularly accepted cultural views—accepted, perhaps, only by the Hollywood entertainment community—are filtered through movies, and because of this, most stories are still written with a man as the central character; most *romantic* roles fall to women. The romantic character can be interesting, but it is also limiting in the sense that the performance of the actor is not intended to seriously challenge the lead character for attention. In *Mission: Impossible* (1996), for example, Emmanuelle Beart's character, Claire, provides the romantic possibilities in the story, but the screen clearly belongs to Ethan Hunt (Tom Cruise). The romantic role is sometimes almost equal to that of the protagonist, depending on the nature of the movie. Often, however, this part is played to simply to give us a chance to see either the softer, more vulnerable side of the lead character, or his more passionate qualities.

Movie stories are also peopled with bit parts—housemaids, bartenders, secretaries, therapists, cops, clerks, streetwalkers, and teachers. These parts help create the detailed background of credibility for the story, but also frequently can provide attention-getting moments in the hands of clever actors. These smaller roles, performed with twists of fancy or absolute truthfulness, give a film its color and texture.

There is a danger for some actors in being **type cast**. Certain actors—because of distinct facial, body, or personality characteristics—get slotted by casting directors as a "chubby best pal," "neurotic girlfriend," "silent suffering housewife," "Italian-American police detective," etc. Once an actor is strongly identified with certain roles for a period of time, it is often hard to break out, and narrow supporting roles become their fate. The actor J.T. Walsh was regularly cast as a "corrupt bureaucrat" in movies, and audiences came to mentally label his dramatic position in a movie by his parts in previous films. Of course, some actors realize the narrow range of their work and accept their limited, but often very steady and financially rewarding, smaller roles.

THE DEMANDS OF ACTING

All the world's a stage
And all the men and women merely players.

                    William Shakespeare

All of us put on our daily performance—as serious students, irate customers, reliable mechanics, experienced lovers, playful zanies, or whatever. Growing up, we learn a wide variety of communication skills and behavior. We try out a range of roles, adjusting them to social circumstances. Throughout our life, our everyday techniques are sharpened. At times we put on performances quite consciously, as when we interview for a new job or search for the appropriate attitude when arriving at a party. Language, dress, level of energy, personal grooming, posture, and a host of other intangibles all come into play. If it all works well, we feel successful.

Actors behave similarly. Of course, the circumstances in which professional movie actors work are quite different. First, these performers do it for a living, and second, they must perform on call, regularly playing characters that may be quite alien to their temperament and experience. In fact, to be successful, the performance of actors should unfailingly convince the audience in three essential ways. It is the responsibility of an actor to make the audience

- **believe** in the motivations of the character.
- **become emotionally involved** in the activities of the character.
- **care** deeply about the character's fate.

Acting of any kind is hard and exacting work. It asks that an actor be an acute observer of human behavior, exploring the deep undercurrents of emotional confusion and suppressed desires, as well as expressing the most minute and subtle physical manifestations of them. An actor must be able to reflect the most ordinary and predictable habits of the common man or woman, yet also understand how that same person would react physically and emotionally in a moment of great crisis. The capacity to take in, synthesize, and reproduce this information is at the core of the actor's art.

It is in the *execution* of a role—physically found in an actor's carriage, voice, facial expressions—that the quality of a performance is realized. For example, in the delivery of a line, how does an actor distinguish between the vocal shadings of a character described as feeling one of the following emotions: "excited"; "aroused"; "impassioned"; "enthused"; "possessed"; "animated"; "feverish"; "hot"; "burning"; "ablaze"; "aflutter"; "blowzy"; "vivacious"; "cheerful"; "buoyant"; "jaunty"? Each attitude has its own slightly distinct motivation and impact. The good actor must know how to play the subtleties of each one. Acting teacher Lee Strasberg gave a very simple definition of acting: "The ability to create complete reality while on stage." With this ability, the actor can both convince the audience of the "truth" of the performance, and move them with personal acting skills.

Stage Acting

Acting for the stage and the screen calls for a profoundly different preparation, approach, and delivery. Some of the differences were listed in the chapter on screenwriting, but from the perspective of an actor, additional points need to be made. Although films are a visual experience lasting approximately the same length of time as a stage play, unlike the live performance on the stage, the domain of movies is not a "real time" presentation. This is very evident in the performance demands of the actors. The stage actor must sustain a level of intensity for the duration of an evening's presentation, then must repeat it again night after night. Of course, **stage acting** has a tradition that goes back for centuries. Over the years, acting styles for the stage have come and gone, but some things have not changed.

- Because stage acting is *live*, there is an **on-going relationship** with the audience. An actor's performance can be immediately adjusted in response to their reaction in the theater, and momentum can be built.
- **Strong voice projection** and articulation are essential to the stage actor. Actors must play to every part of the theater, therefore their emotional and physical style must be great enough to fill it **(4–11)**.

4–11 *The Immigrant* Distinctive acting styles of a stage play are evident in this photo from *"The Immigrant—A Hamilton County Album,"* with Ann Gilbert, Mark Harelick, and Guy Raymond. A certain exaggeration of posture and gesture are needed on the live stage to convey emotional attitudes to the far reaches of the theater. Actors must physically present a readily apparent sense of the character in order that the audience can easily identify their thoughts and feelings. If a play were shot as a movie without any adjustment in a stage actor's approach, the performance would appear on the screen as badly overacted. (Courtesy of Hereford/MTF Press)

- Actors must **commit to memory** their lines and blocking of their performance for an extended span of time. Acting for the stage gives the sense of an organic whole, a constant emotional movement forward.

- Once the nightly play begins, actors are "on their own," with little possible input from the director. Because of this, the actor has freedom to explore a variety of character nuances during each performance.

The live theater has always provided a steady and rich source of actors for motion pictures. After the coming of sound in the late 1920s, an influx of actors from dramatic Broadway shows, vaudeville, local theater, the British Isles, and elsewhere came West to establish the core of acting talent in Hollywood. The interchange between stage and screen is still lively today. But one thing invariably takes place: *Stage actors must relearn their craft for the camera.*

Acting for the Camera

"The camera allows no deceit. Either you are truthful or you are not."

Acting coach Tony Barr

Movie acting happens in an unnatural and self-conscious environment. Instead of a receptive audience waiting anxiously in a theater, the movie actor is faced with the cold intrusion of the camera and crew. Every action is played for the sake of one factor: the lens of the camera. Beyond it, the setting is often chaotic—a cavernous soundstage dominated by shifting lighting systems, cables covering the floor, a busy technical crew scurrying to get everything in order, other crew just standing around. A two-hour movie commonly may take sixty disconnected and confusing days to make. Movies are almost always shot out of sequence, in bits and pieces—moments of suspended time recorded on filmstrips and later assembled into a new time frame in an editing room. For an actor, this means that highly charged or important moments are performed isolated from the flow and emotional context of scenes that in the completed film will come earlier. In the extreme, a story may demand that a movie performer take those sixty days of shooting to portray a single night in the life of the character. Screen actors find sustaining the necessary rhythms of intensity in the delayed pacing of a movie production to be very challenging.

The situation can put great strain on actors. Ideally, part of the job of the movie director is to ease the tension, facilitate unhampered performances, and generally inspire the actors. Of course, some directors have been known to compound the inherent problems with personality conflicts and disorganization. That aside, an actor is faced each day with arriving very early in the morning for *make-up* and *wardrobe fitting*. Depending on the film, this can take hours. *Rehearsals* are at the discretion of the director, but *blocking* for the camera must be established. Most of the day is not spent acting, but rather waiting to be called to the set. This in itself can be highly distracting and exhausting.

The demands of the camera rule an actor's life. Any number of *takes* will be shot in an attempt to match exactly the performances during the previous *set-ups*. Typically, the director may use three basic set-ups for the many takes of a dramatic encounter: a **long shot**, inclusive of all the elements; a **medium shot**, drawing attention to the main player's body; and a **close shot** or **close-up**, detailing whatever facial expression is to be emphasized (see Chapter 6 for further term definitions). This problem is compounded because every shortening of the camera distance demands that the actor respond with slightly scaled down and subtler acting methods.

When the actor is finally called, he or she must pull every bit of concentration to create the appropriate action, emotion, or response in the scene, take after take. Given the start/stop nature of filmmaking, this is obviously one of the hardest tasks of the actor. Sustaining the tonal continuity of an acting performance within a scene—which on the screen covers perhaps two minutes, but which in reality might be shot over a three-day period—is the test of an actor's skills in this medium.

The Close-up and the Actor

In the movie *A Dream of Passion* (1978), the camera focuses on an aging and still ravishingly beautiful Melina Mercouri framing her face with her hands and looking directly at the camera, as she boldly quotes Tennessee Williams:

> *There is a thing called the "close-up." The camera advances and you stand still. In your head, your face is caught with the light blazing on it, and all your history screams when you smile.*

4–12   Catherine Deneuve   Unlike the stage actor, the **close-up** is a fact of life for the screen actor. Every lead actor must deal with the challenge of performing at this camera distance. The shot can be uncompromising in its recording of facial detail. Unfortunately, for many actors this means a career-long struggle with cosmetic surgery. However the physical appearance of a few stars seems almost untouched by consequences of getting older. In Andre Techine's *The Scene of the Crime* (1986), the great French actress Catherine Deneuve (43 years old at the time) is photographed with light and lensing that compliments her natural beauty.   (Kino International)

One unique factor, above all others, has made motion pictures a medium that celebrates glamour: the **close-up.** Because of the movie's ability to put a huge image of an actor's face in *close-up* on screen to be studied and held in wonder, audiences became intimately involved in the nuances of expressions and secret personal meanings that might wait behind them **(4–12)**. The face of a movie star is as familiar as the face of one's lover. An effective close-up framing the face seems to penetrate the very soul of the actor. The camera in close-up not only photographs the obvious, it seems to have a special power—a virtual x-ray machine of the spirit—to record every nuance of feeling below the surface. In his book *Acting in Film,* Michael Caine observes:

> *The close-up is the shot on which film relies most when it comes to transmitting the subtleties of emotion and thought. It can give an actor tremendous power, but that potential energy requires enormous energy to be realized.*

It exposes parts of actors' personalities that suggest that we the audience might know the persons better than they know themselves.

The camera loves an interesting face. Because of the dramatic power of the close-up, the screen actor must use minutely refined skills to meet its demands. A close-up shot of a mundane conversation can carry great dramatic weight when the camera and the actor work their magic together. A simple *reaction shot* of a face in close-up can become a most telling exploration of a human personality. The close-up, then, has the potential to be both worshipping and, paradoxically, unforgivingly harsh. The contour of the hairline, the alertness of the eyes, the angle of the nose, the shape of the lips and mouth, the texture, color tones, and light reflection off the skin—these are the physical aspects of the actor that are studied by audiences in the grand exaggeration of the close-up.

Acting for the camera in close-up becomes an exercise in minimalism, calling for the man or woman to know every shade of one's inner feelings and how those might be translated into physical expression. For the screen actor, the job requires not only reducing the scale of a performance to play to the needs of the camera, it means shaping an attitude toward the art of acting itself. There is no room for misinterpretation. The camera will catch the smallest wave of feeling, truthful or not. For instance, in the offbeat comedy *The Ref* (1993), when Kevin Spacey is listening and reacting to the over-the-top antics of Judy Davis, he is *actually engaged* in that activity, his face reflecting a mind alive to every turn of conversation. But if in a shot the director wants the audience to witness the emotion of "pure pleasure" in an actor's face, and instead there is any hint of "doubt" reflected in the eyes or mouth, the intended impact of the shot and its larger dramatic context will be slightly distorted. Referring to the unusual depth of acting the probing camera requires, Michael Caine points out that "screen acting today is much more a matter of *being* than *performing*."

The exaggerated size of the image has made actors into popular icons, embodiments of idealized or errant human traits—"the girl next door," "the mob boss," "the femme fatale." As much spectacular action that a film might have, the real emotional power of a movie can usually be found in a seemingly simple dramatic moment of an actor shot in close-up.

The Actor's Voice

When sound first arrived in film in the late 1920s, the studios discovered that the voices of some silent actors were inadequate. Many had never been trained on the live stage and not only their tonal qualities but the tempos of their delivery were off. With Broadway-trained stage actors waiting, however, there was no lack of talented replacements. Since that time, the quality of an actor's voice in movies has been a major part of his or her strength on the screen.

Great actors of the past are often remembered as much for their voice as their looks. Some have a throaty fogginess, crisp enunciation, or a languid softness. Regional and national accents can compel attention—a slow Midwestern drawl, a clipped English phrasing, a classic Brooklyn accent. The unique vocal qualities of Edward G. Robinson, Kirk Douglas, James Cagney, Cary Grant, Orson Welles, Jimmy Stewart, Claude Rains, Bette Davis, Judy Holliday, Jean Arthur, Ingrid Bergman, and Katharine Hepburn, to name a few, did as much to shape their screen personas as their other acting skills. The same could be said of Debra Winger, Clint Eastwood, Woody Allen, Helena Bonham Carter, Samuel L. Jackson, Richard Dreyfuss, Whoopi Goldberg, Arnold Schwarzenegger, Dustin Hoffman, Jack Nicholson,

Holly Hunter, Sean Connery, Rosie Perez, Robin Williams, James Earl Jones, and other distinguished actors making films today.

Because more major actors today seek out roles dealing with characters of different ethnic backgrounds and social strata, much weight has been given to developing a range of accents. Meryl Streep has consistently sought out difficult ethnic roles and mastered dialects throughout her career, most impressively, perhaps, in *Sophie's Choice* (1982) with a flawless Polish accent or *Dancing at Lughnasa* (1998) as an Irish matron. One of the pleasures of *Fargo* (1996) was listening to a Minnesota accent, not often replicated in mainstream films, developed by Frances McDormand and others in the cast. On the negative side, there was considerable criticism of Kevin Costner's voice in *Robin Hood* (1991), that his bland American accent seemed unusually weak and too modern given the classic story of Sherwood Forest and the vocally rich band of actors who surrounded him. Writer Anne Rice complained mightily about the casting of Tom Cruise for the role of Lestat in *Interview with the Vampire* (1994) because she did not think his voice had the "roughened velvet" sound she had imagined for her character. Rice makes the point shared by many, "I don't think I've ever fallen under the spell of an actor when the voice hasn't been a big component."

In terms of the volume needed in an actor's voice when working in film, *less* is better than *more*. Today's highly sensitive microphones can pick up the faintest breathy whisper. Therefore, the delivery of lines has nothing to do with "reaching" the audience in the stage acting sense, but rather finding the perfect tone, texture, and tempo to convey the right level of verbal interchange for the scene. If, by chance, the audio quality is not up to standards, or simply was impossible to get down due to interference of background sound, it is redone in *post-synching* sessions with the actors in a more controlled sound studio environment (explained further in Chapter 9).

TYPES OF ACTING STYLES

Technique in all of the arts—painting, architecture, clothing design, music—has evolved over time. The manner of performing drama has also changed over the years. The evolution of acting styles has been affected by the revolutions in culture and taste during the twentieth century. Although any individual actor's practices may have grown out of his or her personal history, that actor has also inherited the cumulative experience of other past performers. Many influences in this century have come into play: deeper insights into the layers of the human personality; the hard lessons of economic depression and poverty; the shocking cultural effects of major wars and political oppression. On the practical side, actors have responded to the general development of changing motion picture techniques, and, more specifically, to the experiences of communal and experimental groups in the performing arts.

Emerging from the thousands of individual approaches to the art of performance, several distinct "schools" of acting in this century can be identified. As with any attempt to cleanly categorize a subject, there is overlap and contradiction. But historically, some general observations can be safely made. Acting styles can be grouped into four types: *personality, technical, method,* and *integrated.*

Personality Actors

"There's something charismatic about American actors like John Wayne and Clint Eastwood. Bogart, Monroe, Sinatra. We don't produce anything in Britain near that dimension of personality. People like John Wayne may not have the ability to play King Lear and neither does Eastwood, but they are so much more watchable."

British-born actor Anthony Hopkins

Movie fans have always seemed to idolize not only the "actor," but the *person* who is that actor. Because of this, from the early days, actors were encouraged to project a distinctly *personal* image of themselves that could be admired, imitated, desired, packaged, and gossiped about. Movie actors were selected and promoted because the studios hoped that the public would embrace them as captivating stereotypes of their collective fantasies. Therefore, female actors were tested to fit into certain categories: "the loyal wife"; "the gal with a past"; "the sprightly ingenue"; "the continental seductress"; "his girl Friday"; "the dizzy socialite"; "the sexy blonde"; "the career woman"; and endless other variations. Male actors were designated to be "the Latin lover"; "the disturbed loner"; "the Irish street kid"; "the debonair escort"; "the maverick"; "the big-hearted jerk"; "the other guy," etc. The studios designed the roles and actors were needed to fill them.

Certain actors fit the parts perfectly. For some, their "natural" personality traits, acting ability, and physical looks matched nicely with the characters that they were chosen to play. These parts primarily called for an actor to "be yourself." When some of these actors became recognized as *stars*, movie scripts were written specifically for them, reinforcing the bond between the screen image and the actor's actual persona. John Wayne was essentially John Wayne, on or off screen. This is not to say that his private life was filled with heroic deeds, but that the manner in which he played his screen characters was a direct extension of his perceived personality bent. Added to this, Wayne's imposing size, body control and rhythms, restrained on-screen emotions, and rugged good looks made him an ideal Western star.

Other personality actors had to "play" the part to which they seemed so well fitted. Because of their physical attributes and acting skills, these men and women could create a screen personality that was so impressive that audiences came to believe that there was no separation between the actor and the person. Judy Holliday was cast in *Born Yesterday* (1951) as a dizzy, buxom blonde gifted in the art of quick retorts, when in reality she was a very bright woman with committed political positions. She obviously must have felt some strong affection to her characters, however, to play them with such gusto. In any case, the screen character was repeated and honed enough times in movies that Judy Holliday was indelibly associated with the type.

To define personality actors as being limited by their roles and by audience expectations is not to disparage their acting abilities. A great many personality actors were, and are, exceptional performers. Their presence on the screen discloses a natural physical and spiritual attraction, and the major task of the directors seems to be finding ways of simply letting the actor's qualities shine through. Much of the focus is on recognizing what these actors do best, knowing their limits, refining the singular virtues they possess.

4–13   Clint Eastwood   Many major actors in the old Hollywood could be classified as **personality actors,** that is, their actual physical and emotional characteristics invited movie roles that reflected their off-screen personas. Even today, some actors carry on that acting style. For years, Clint Eastwood has played a hard-boiled loner, quite often in Westerns such as *Unforgiven* (1992). His tough exterior usually only hints at the suppressed motivations and emotions that might be going on inside. Eastwood helped defined "manliness" for a generation.   (Warner Bros.)

Personality actors were not just a phenomenon of the old studio system. More recently, there are a number of actors who are perceived by the public as playing *themselves* in almost every film they are in **(4–13)**. For years, movie audiences went to "Charles Bronson films." The same can be said of Robert Redford, Arnold Schwarzenegger, Hugh Grant, Clint Eastwood, Bette Midler, Sylvester Stalone, Steven Seagal, Barbra Streisand, or Michael J. Fox, among others. These actors have either self-imposed or industry-shaped parameters on the range of characters they play, usually aiming to enhance their reputations by repeating similar movie roles that established them. The application of this term to an actor is a two-edged sword. On the one hand, to be designated as a personality actor means that the person has reached a point in films where he or she is sought out by the audience to repeat and sink into a favorite movie character. Yet such a label can be limiting to an actor who wants to test out a wide range of performance skills.

Technical Actors

"Shakespeare, like God, is an Englishman. Therefore, the English believe, all theater began in England."

Writer John Heilpern

Great technical actors are often associated with the British school of performers. England and Ireland have long and proud traditions of live theater. The sheer number of active theater production groups creates unofficial national academies for training in the performing arts. An integral part of their training invariably is found in the works of

Shakespeare and the classics. The stress on traditional as well as respected contemporary stage works gives actors a full appreciation for the richness and suggestion of the spoken word. A key to their professionalism is found in their dedication to rehearsing scenes for much greater lengths of time than is customary for American actors.

Perhaps the term *technical actor* is too dry and mechanical for describing the high standards of performance that great actors given this label regularly achieve. Drama teacher Eva Mekler objects, "The American notion that British actors are totally external is very false. They are very much in touch with their feelings, and use them to find authentic moments. They are economical with their emotions, and not technical at all." But it is *regularity*—the ability of the professional actor to be counted upon to deliver a solid, thoughtful, well-executed performance in a variety of roles— that has become a distinguishing attribute of the *technical actor.*

This school of acting has been associated with actors trained in traditional live stage productions. Night after night, the stage actor must be awake in the moment, perfecting each performance through ever more exacting repetition. He or she must be alert to the manner in which a gesture is made, to the way a line is delivered, to how a word is emphasized, so that the desired effect is projected correctly. Typically, stage actors are eventually asked to play a wide variety of roles, from lovers to villains, from leading roles to minor parts. This continuous training sharpens an actor's craft, giving the person a facility with the "tricks of the trade." When these persons move into film acting, their technical skills have been well tested.

The work of Alec Guinness is instructive. In many ways he was the consummate technical actor **(4–14)**. From his first significant screen work in Dickens's *Great Expectations* (1946), his series of sly comedies in the 1950s, the commanding roles in *Bridge on the River Kwai* (1957), *The Horse's Mouth* (1958), *Tunes of Glory* (1960), *Lawrence of Arabia* (1962), *Star Wars* (1977), *Little Dorrit* (1987), and others, Guinness has given a range of challenging and vastly different performances that both thoroughly explored and beautifully delivered the characters. There is a graceful economy in his

4–14   Alec Guinness   Throughout a long and extremely productive career, Alec Guinness gave definition to a school of acting that could be categorized as technical acting. His performances (pictured here in Chistine Edzard's *Little Dorrit,* 1988, from a book by Charles Dickens) have been invariably marked by quick wit and thoughtful dramatic control. Dating from his first major film, *Great Expectations* (1946), Guinness had absolute correctness in character definition, marked by a brilliant delivery of his lines.   (Cannon Releasing)

THE ROYAL HERITAGE

The British Isles may no longer have a reputation for exporting automobiles, but throughout this century their actors have gone to other countries and raised the level of performance on stages and in movies. A partial roster of British/Irish stage-trained actors who have excelled in film includes: Charles Laughton, John Gielgud, Laurence Olivier, Joan Plowright, Richard Burton, John Mills, Vanessa Redgrave, Hugh Grant, Richard Harris, Helen Mirren, Robert Shaw, Paul Scofield, Brenda Fricker, Ben Kingsley, Maggie Smith, Bob Hoskins, Oliver Reed, Tom Conti, Patrick Stewart, Sarah Miles, Peter O'Toole, Jeremy Irons, Gary Oldman, Albert Finney, Vanessa Redgrave, Bob Hoskins, Nigel Hawthorne, Gabriel Byrne, Michael Caine, Susannah York, John Cleese, Sean Connery, Ian Holm, Natasha Richardson, Ian McKellen, Jonathan Pryce, Glenda Jackson, Kenneth Branagh, Julia Ormand, Ralph Fiennes, Derek Jacobi, Miranda Richardson, Daniel Day-Lewis, Juliet Stevenson, Stephen Rea, Emily Watson, Alan Rickman, Emma Thompson, Liam Neeson, Fiona Shaw, Anthony Hopkins, Brenda Blethyn, Robert Carlyle, and many more. The quality of movies here and abroad would be sorely diminished without their acting talents.

style that comes from knowing exactly what a subtle shift in expression, slight variance of intonation, or silent knowing pause can do to carry the dramatic moment. A single scene performed by Guinness—as when at the end of *Tunes of Glory* he plays a proud and haughty commanding officer whose life suddenly disintegrates before a room full of subordinates—could be for a student of acting an entire course on the subject. Great technical actors are known for such moments.

Method Acting

"You'd be surprised how much you can do, doing nothing."

Lee Strasberg, co-founder
of the Actor's Studio

When Marlon Brando appeared on the screen for the first time, as a hospitalized, paraplegic World War II veteran in *The Men* (1950), and then as a crude husband in *A Streetcar Named Desire* (1951), movie audiences immediately recognized that they were watching a very different kind of acting **(4–15)**. Little before had prepared us for Brando. Unlike other actors, he seemed to struggle to be articulate and appeared aggressively spiteful of the viewer, almost throwing away lines, not caring if his words were heard or fully understood. He moved like a sensuous and wary cat, eyes distrustful of anything outside himself. Audiences could not stop watching him. We could only guess what was going on inside his head, but couldn't wait until he gave some clue with each half-formulated sentence. Brando seethed with an energy that seemed barely under control. We did

4–15 *A Streetcar Named Desire*   Marlon Brando played Stanley Kowalski with Vivian Leigh as Blanche DuBose in Tennessee Williams' *A Streetcar Named Desire* (1951), directed by Elia Kazan, and both actors gave compelling performances. But their acting styles had very different roots, and it is evident in the film. Leigh was trained in the classical British school of finely honed acting, whereas Brando gave the first definitive model for method acting on the screen with his unpredictably steamy performance as her rough-edged working class brother-in-law.   (Warner Bros Pictures)

not know what could set it off, or what electrifying direction it might take, and he teased audiences with his moody restraint. Brando was a very gifted actor—the most classic example of a school of actors who would broaden and deepen the art.

In fact, Marlon Brando had come to the screen with very special training as an actor. In 1947, The Actors Studio was opened in New York City—the center for radically ideological theater since the 1930s—by movie director Elia Kazan, Robert Lewis and Cheryl Crawford, soon to be joined by Lee Strasberg. Taught by master acting instructors, the studio afforded actors deeply shared experiences and a unique attitude in approaching their craft. The teachings were derived from the ideas of the great Russian stage director and acting teacher Constantin Stanislavski. The Actors Studio would make a strong impact on the actors associated with the school and influence almost every actor in following generations in one way or another. A partial roster of names that attended classes at the studio is still impressive: Julie Harris, Lee J. Cobb, Montgomery Clift, Maureen Stapleton, Patricia Neal, E.G. Marshall, June Havoc, John Forsythe, James Dean, Kim Hunter, Karl Malden, Martin Balsam, Eva

Marie Saint, Lee Grant, Shelly Winters, Marilyn Monroe, Rod Steiger, and Brando. These men and women formed a core group of actors whose style—**method acting**—would revolutionize the way in which performers approached their work.

Stanislavski had presented many of his ideas about acting in a book, *An Actor Prepares* (1926). During his life as a stage director, he had reacted against the stiff, declarative style of acting that was still prevalent on stage, in which actors took turns competing with one another with exaggerated profundity. The "Stanislavski System" demanded that the actor take a radically different method in playing the character. Freudian and Jungian insights into human psychology, still fresh at the time, had shown that a person was influenced as much by subconscious forces—the dark side being *compulsion*; the light side *intuition*—as by the rational self. With training, an actor could find ways to tap into and unblock subconscious emotions to fuel his art, while at the same time becoming disciplined in traditional acting skills. In discovering how a character was to be played, Stanislavski taught that the actor must find new methods to enter into and *be* the character.

> *If you take all these internal processes and adapt them to the spiritual and physical life of the person you are representing, we call that living the part. This is of supreme significance in creative work. Aside from the fact that it opens up avenues for inspiration, living the part helps the artist to carry out one of his main objectives. His job is not to present merely the external life of his character. He must fit his own human qualities to the life of this other person, and pour into it all of his own soul. The fundamental aim of our art is the creation of this inner life of the human spirit, and its expression in an artistic form.*

Richard Boleslavsky, who developed the ideas at his American Laboratory Theater, brought the theories and practices to the United States. In the politically radical 1930s, Stella Adler and Lee Strasberg pushed the teaching approach further when they started the Group Theater, a company of actors, writers, and intellectuals committed to reversing the direction of the staid drama of the establishment by plunging into the realistic and often tragic world of the common man. The nature of the plays that were staged—many by avant-garde playwrights Clifford Odets and Eugene O'Neill—and the experimental style of the acting matched well. The communal spirit and shared goals of the repertory theater promoted a dynamic of free expression, which in turn encouraged more extemporaneous acting styles. This ran counter to the prevailing values in the "star" oriented camp of Hollywood actors of the 1930s. Indeed, members of the Group Theater held them in contempt. When one of their own, John Garfield, went West into movies and became a leading man, he was accused by some of "selling out." Garfield, however, brought a smoldering intelligence to the screen that foreshadowed the work of Montgomery Clift and Marlon Brando.

There was no uniform agreement among interpreters of Stanislavski and teachers of *the method*, and varying degrees of emphasis were given to some of his ideas. But the following three issues set the *method actor* apart.

- **Acting as an extension of real experience.** Elia Kazan had noted, "The only way to understand any character is through yourself." Instead of seeing the actor as being engaged in something extraordinary and removed from normal experience, this approach encourages an actor to share in the physical and emotional life of the character being played—especially at the most common levels of daily life. According to this approach, life is first experienced sensually, that is, through the five senses: touch, sight, sound, taste, and smell. The actor must therefore get in touch with "sense memory," the remembrance of how anything was physically experienced when it first happened. For example, when in a drama a hesitant lover first touches the arm of her boyfriend, it is essential for the female actor to experience that moment with absolute newness, in the physical expectation and excitement that is generated by such an action. Therefore, preparation for any part means that the actor must *be there physically*, as if for the first time. The use of sense memory tended to give a natural texture to the performances, rather than an aura of artificiality. Paradoxically, this process sometimes had the reverse effect when poorly done. By making the search for "real" moments into a "sacred" mission, one layer of affectation was replaced with yet another.

- **The memory of emotion**. Because each person is a reservoir of past emotional experiences, and because the essence of every emotion—fear, anger, joy—is common to all persons, the actor can call upon an *equivalent* personal emotion trigger from a personal memory bank to match the circumstances of the character being played. Boleslavsky had stated, "After having decided what is the feeling necessary for a certain part of his role, the actor tries to find in his affective memory a recollection similar to that particular feeling." Achieving this is not easy. It demanded of the method actor a continuing inner quest, enhanced by exercises for "unblocking" the personality. Lee Strasberg strongly recommended psychoanalysis for his students in order to dig deeper into the self. Even director Ingmar Bergman, a man not known for being associated with method acting, claims that, "Actors who don't have a direct contact with their childhood are not good actors." The intensity of such an approach showed up on the screen when these actors came into film. Method actors attempted to reach more deeply into themselves than ordinary actors of the day.

- **Improvisational style of delivery**. Although teachers of method acting did not encourage disrespect for the author's lines (Stanislavski was quite clear about actors accurately learning scripted dialogue), the actors used improvisational acting exercises to break into deeper levels of playing a character. As a result, they broke out of the "taking turns" routine when rendering traditional dialogue. Method actors chose off-beat rhythms to deliver lines, sometimes with unexpected hesitations, at other times by overlapping dialogue when following through with the emotion of a character. As the actor seemed to search for the language to express a feeling, a tension was allowed to grow, giving the lines a sense of immediacy and spontaneity. Method actors gave the audience this extra level of excitement by playing their parts in ways that seemed unpredictable to even the actors themselves.

Struggling actors tend to carry the method to an extreme, missing its subtlety. Because they focused so much on themselves, lesser actors tended to bore audiences with their endless search for their "real self" in role after role. When they went into themselves to discover the recesses of deep feeling, either they brought up a flood of overheated, inappropriate emotions, or they brooded inwardly and never returned. Good acting has always been realized in the cogent delivery of lines. Critics can easily find fault with such self-indulgence and ridicule the entire approach. But, in fact, the great method actors rarely fell into that trap, and their professional record is one of original and inspired performances.

Integrated

"There are basic internal and external skills that every actor should have, there is intelligence and taste and honesty, and there is knowledge that comes from exposure to experience of those who have preceded us. But rules? No."

Actor and acting coach John Crowther

Surely the teachers and early actors trained in the method have influenced the subsequent styles of acting that have since evolved. No serious actor today could ignore the work of the men and women involved in the movement, the record of their substantial performances on film for all to watch. But tracing the lineage of influences on the modern film actor is similar to following musical heritages. The original blues musicians certainly created the framework for much of today's popular rock music, but numerous other influences have also contributed to it. Who can neatly define and relegate to a "school" the style of Sean Penn, Christian Slater, Andie MacDowell, Nicholas Cage, Annette Bening, Woody Harrelson, Tim Robbins, Uma Thurman, Kiefer Sutherland, Robert Downey Jr., Ellen Barkin, Matt Dillon, and other contemporary actors? It may be as simple as how Wesley Snipes sees it, "There ain't no formula, it's the groove."

The movie actor today inherits the rich experience of those actors who have gone before **(4–16)**. Many superior acting workshops and formal academies incorporate a spectrum of approaches and exercises to acting. Further insights into the psychology of human behavior give today's actor an even wider base from which to study the motivations of characters, the dynamics of human communication, and an actor's own personal blocks. Depending on the philosophy and experience of the individual instructors, the teaching ranges from more formal methodology to the highly innovative practices. On the West Coast, UCLA together with Nina Foch and Jeff Corey have had highly respected acting schools; Herbert Berghof/Uta Hagen, the Juilliard School, Northwestern, Carnegie-Mellon, the Yale Drama School, and Sanford Meisner at The Neighborhood Playhouse are well known in the East. The Royal Academy of Dramatic Arts in London, Bristol Old Vic Acting School, and the Abbey Theatre Company in Dublin have outstanding reputations overseas.

Acting students and professionals coming from these or other fine acting schools may have received very specialized training, which emphasized one style of acting over another; a great amount of cross fertilization has occurred in the past, and it is

4–16 Morgan Freeman and Tim Robbins   Actors learn their trade from the cumulative acting experiences of performers who have gone before. Most contemporary schools of acting have borrowed from a variety of acting traditions, so that it is difficult today to handily categorize performance styles. For example, Morgan Freeman and Tim Robbins (seen here in *The Shawshank Redemption,* 1994) would be hard to neatly classify, beyond saying that their work represents an integrated style. Today it is more common for each actor, with the help of an acting teacher, to weigh his or her natural bent as an actor, and develop skills within that framework, refining the talent found there.   (Columbia Pictures)

still happening. Theater director Anne Bogart of the Saratoga International Theater Institute developed an approach to acting called "Viewpoints" that goes against the grain of the method's absorption with inner motivation and instead concentrates on the spatial relationships of the actor to the performance environment, along with rigorous training that emphasizes quick improvisational responses among actors. In fact, for some actors the approach to a role has come full circle, away from deeply analyzing the motivations of the character being played to simply following the common sense of the script. Morgan Freeman says that acting is "nothing more complicated than learning the lines and putting on the costume. Because you're not any different in a tie and vest than you are in a top hat and gold-tipped cane. You may want to be careful with your diction and your accent, but really there's no mystery to the process beyond saying the lines and letting them define who you are."

Acting is always an experiment, but one that takes place in full view of the public. The emerging styles of most actors show a partial **integration** of every acting theory and practice. Everyone borrows a bit of anything to find something that works.

FINDING THE CHARACTER

In researching a new role, actors not only carefully read the script as lines to be interpreted and put to memory, but they must fully understand the character at every level possible. Fictional characters do not arrive in the first act of a movie without a history. As we in the audience study the lead characters at the start of a film, their physical appearance, dress, speech patterns, and attitudes give clues to what they are like. Often the screenwriter indicates something about the character's past, but it falls upon the actor to make the part come alive. This happens not only in the words of the scripted dialogue, but in the depth of insight and feeling that the actor brings to the character **(4–17)**. The actor must clearly understand and convey the character's **motivation.** People do things for a reason. The impetus for an action may be forced on them from the outside, or stem from conscious choice or emotional need. But unless the actor can find the source of the character's actions, the portrayal will lack energy and direction.

One of the valuable lessons learned by method actors was in finding the character's *motivation* by plunging into the **back story**—the cumulative personal history of the character before the point of physically entering the story. There are various ways to get to know a character's back story. A method actor would typically prepare for a part by constructing specific personal histories, asking herself such things as, "What was this person doing the day before the events in the movie are told? What did she eat for breakfast? Was she a cheerleader in high school? Why not? What or who stopped her?" These and similar basic questions help get the actor inside the character. Many actors actually attempt to live the life of the person—Jon Voight stayed at

4–17   *Richard III*   Every role demands that the actor first *discover the character*, then find a way to freshly play the part. The inspired interpretation of Shakespeare's villainous king in *Richard III* (1995) by Ian McKellan is one of the screen's classic renditions. Rarely has the obscene malevolence of this famous character been so richly portrayed. McKellan has a chameleon-like ability of wonderously transforming himself in difficult roles.   (United Artists Inc.)

a veterans' hospital for months researching his part in *Coming Home* (1978) as a paralyzed Vietnam vet. Other actors have gone to prisons, visited NASA, or hung out in the slums of cities to learn how the particular environment affects a character. A few directors push actors to the limits. English director Mike Leigh, for his film *Naked* (1993), not only encouraged his actors to go out into the real world and interact with it in character, but intentionally went into production without set dialogue in hopes of letting the actors discover the characters as the scenes evolved. Leigh comments, "Things get swapped around. So the process of shooting is actually an investigation, a discovery of what the film is." Because rehearsals were so volatile, the film took 12-1/2 weeks to shoot.

The choices the actor makes in discovering the motivation of a character are based in some general areas of investigation **(4–18).**

- **Psychological Motivations.** Insight into the deep unspoken desires, hurts, pleasures, and misunderstandings of a character gives every action of the character a base of *motivation*. Often, the actor will have to invent the sources of these feelings, then infuse them into the actions and thought process of the character. The indicated psychological back story of Annie Savoy (Susan

4–18 *Ironweed* In *Ironweed* (1987), Meryl Streep and Jack Nicholson play two people down on their luck during the depression years. For inspiration to find such characters, actors must be able to immerse themselves in the cultural psychology and social tenor of the period. Actors are helped considerably by such things as authentic wardrobes and hairstyles. Throughout their careers, both Streep and Nicholson have shown an uncanny ability to merge themselves into the characters they are playing.   (TriStar Pictures)

Sarandon) in *Bull Durham* (1988) was a complex combination of needs for recognition, sex, companionship, and outrageousness in a small Southern town with not much going on except baseball. As an actor, Sarandon had to convey an entire psychological history within the limits of the character, as written. Achieving psychological credibility for the character is usually the greatest challenge to the actor.

- **Ethical Values**. All relevant drama has a moral dimension. It may be masked in comedy or cynicism, but the audience ultimately judges characters on some aspect of their moral values. Actors must discover and fill out the personal codes by which their characters act. Even though little of the ethical back story is explicitly presented about tycoon Gordon Gekko (Michael Douglas) in *Wall Street* (1987), the thought and care that Douglas put into playing the character is quite evident. We may not know exactly how ruthlessly Gekko has behaved in similar situations in the past, but when Douglas plays him with such practiced arrogance, we can surely guess. The cold, aggressive thought process that Douglas brings to Gekko's character and business dealings speaks to his values in other areas. The job of actors includes showing what their characters believe in.

- **Sociological Background.** Each of us is molded by our social environment— family, friends, religion, profession, the part of the country in which we live. Often, this implied back story sets the tone for the entire film. In *Drugstore Cowboy* (1989), the addicted husband and wife team of Bob and Diane Hughes (Matt Dillon and Kelly Lynch) seems to come out of nowhere. They arrive on the screen robbing drugstores to support their habit. But in their powerful portrayals of stoned losers on the road to nowhere, we sense their social backgrounds as young drifters and dropouts in their mercurial behavior, the twisted delivery of lines, their spiritual inertia. The strength of their performances reflects a secure knowledge by the actors of where the characters fit in the larger society.

- **Physical Attributes**. Naturally, the age and size of the person are important. Actors are often called upon to play both older and younger parts. This may not mean simply working with makeup, but also that the actor take on a very different physical carriage and gestures. The beauty of the characterizations of Joanne Woodward and Paul Newman in *Mr. and Mrs. Bridge* (1990) lay greatly in their accurate physical translation of the parts. Their older, conservative Midwest ways are reflected in their worn looks, stiff posture, and hesitant movements. If an actor is not convincing physically, the entire effect of the performance breaks down. Both actors *became* their characters.

With a strong grasp of the back story of the fictionalized individual, the actor "knows" how the character would act and react in the story situations. An actor's thorough preparation expands the range of available dramatic choices. Certain movies present special challenges. Robert Altman's *Short Cuts* (1993), based on the short stories of Raymond Carver, is a movie that cuts through the lives of at least twenty major characters, intertwining them in various states of frustration, manipulation, and tragedy. Even though the film runs over three hours in length, each actor had only a little screen time to create an extensive persona for his or her character. Altman comments on his approach: "The format is really telling stories that didn't happen, showing the empty spaces, the blanks, and letting the audience make up their own assumptions, their own story." But this interesting directorial attitude toward the narrative only works if the individual actors have a solid grip on their characters. Given the sketchy and abrupt manner in which they were introduced, the actors had to have their own sense of the character's back story to fill the "empty spaces" with richly nuanced and skillfully detailed performances. Because of their mastery as actors, the audience felt that they knew the characters quite intimately by the end of the movie.

PLAYING THE SCENE

"It got to the point where I couldn't remember the voices I originally heard in my head when I wrote it. When you have two great actors playing a scene, something wonderful happens—their voices totally replace what you first heard in your imagination."

Writer/director Steven Zaillian speaking about a pivotal courtroom corridor scene with Robert Duvall and John Travolta in *A Civil Action* (1998).

Just as screenwriters work with the basic element of the scene, actors also use this as their dramatic base. An actor sees a scene as a coherent unit of continuous dramatic interchange. Within this framework, actors trigger and play out whatever action, movement, and dialogue are called for in the script.

Each scene has a dramatic intent, envisioned as an arc. The **dramatic arc** consists of the scene's rising action, climax, and resolution. Because these elements create a dramatic arc of emotional intensity within a scene, it is important for the actors to be able to identify the exact points of conflict and have agreement on how to play off of them. This is not always easy. Because scenes come in all shapes and sizes, where the central emotional moments should land or what actions should be emphasized, and to what degree, is often open to question. The writer in creating the script and the director in visualizing the scene may have very clear ideas about the shape of the arc—the high point to which the scene builds. But while the curve of dramatic energy is immediately clear to all in some scenes, in others it is discovered by the actors while rehearsing or performing before the camera, often with unexpected interpretations. To simply illustrate the possibilities: in a scene in which a young man declares that he's joining the Foreign Legion, does the scene peak with his announcement of the decision? With his girlfriend's tearful reaction? At the moment of his lonely departure from the room? Much of the time, the arc will hinge on less eventful moments: an actor's subtle phrasing of a statement, the sudden raising of a voice, or a prolonged gaze. The decision on where to place the emotional emphasis will determine the performance choices of the actors, and ultimately the audience's response to the scene.

Some scenes take on a life of their own, beyond the ideas of the scriptwriter or the control of the director. In *Last Tango in Paris* (1973), Marlon Brando enters a room to confront the dead body of his suicidal wife laid out in a coffin. Their history together has been one of magnetic desire and utter frustration. He speaks to her at first as if in normal restrained conversation, pausing for her unuttered replies. Then his memory is triggered and he angrily accuses her of a history of conscious neglect and disloyalty. Hovering over the coffin, Brando's emotions explode in deep rage at having been abandoned by her self-inflicted death. This outburst suddenly turns into the deeper revelation of his immense sense of loss. He then breaks down sobbing—the *dramatic arc*—and starts to retract his cruel words. In extreme distress, he now confesses his unconditional love, physically rearranging the flowers on her body with childlike care and attention. Finally a voice calling from another room brings him back to the present, and he leaves the room. This scene is composed of just six shots. Not only does the scene give information about his relationship with his dead wife that was previously unclear, but it also reveals other levels in Brando's character that were obscured by the armor of a damaged life. It contains a rise and fall of dramatic confrontation and resolution in a masterful series of rhythmic transitions, created by Brando's unerring instincts.

Much could be said about the electricity produced between actors in a scene that is going well. Exploring the possible character dynamics with others in the scene is essential to the actor. The way that each actor plays a scene will also depend on which other actors are in it. The dramatic choices of any actor not only define his or her own character, but also shape those of the others involved in a scene. If the scene is to be effective, an actor must be able reasonably to anticipate the degree of response from other actors and work at that level.

Each scene is strung together with a series of beats, as the two or more actors play off one another other. A **beat** is a single measure of interchange between actors in the form of an action, statement, or silence that shifts the dramatic energy of the moment. It is in the rhythm and flow of the beats that actors find their connection and inspire the scene. A beat can punctuate a previous dramatic moment or give impulse to the next. Each beat creates and continues the linkage that shapes and binds the scene.

Not every scene is dramatically powerful. Some scenes simply pass on useful detail for the story to move the action along. But even in these relatively sparse scenes, there will be minimal exchanges and subtle shifts of emotional focus using beats. Actors might well interpret the emphasis of a scene in very different ways. Whether the scene is a climactic turning point in a film, or a simple situation designed to be a transitional few moments, actors must translate the essence of the dramatic issue at the basic level of the action/reaction phraseology and be in perfect agreement as to the tone, tempo, and meaning of the exchanges. The actors and director must find the special rhythm of the dramatic moment **(4–19).**

Along with this, the actor must consider the *where*, *when*, and *with whom* of each scene. It makes a difference if the scene takes place in an *exterior or interior* location—on a green hillside in West Virginia at dawn or inside a Chicago slaughterhouse at night. Part of an actor's focus will be on finding the appropriate mental and physical

4–19 *Oleanna Oleanna* (1994), written and directed by David Mamet about the claim of sexual harassment on a college campus by a student against a teacher, is built upon a series of confrontational scenes. To successfully convey the anger and frustration of the opposing characters, actors Debra Eisenstadt and William H. Macy had to continually find the high point of emotional release—the **dramatic arc**—in each of their many encounters.   (The Samuel Goldwyn Company)

attitude of the character being played in relation to the selected location for the scene. Exceptional environments can influence actors in profound ways that may alter their performances in very real ways. Actors, like any ordinary person, emotionally respond to the ambiance in which they find themselves, and the reaction often unintentionally comes through on film. Because of the prolonged chaos of the situation during the shooting of *Apocalypse Now* (1979) on location in the jungles of the Philippines, one actor (Martin Sheen) had a heart attack and other members of the cast were pushed to stages close to madness. When the film's principal photography was complicated by a series of disasters and shooting went on endlessly, the very real stress of the cast in this remote and uncompromising location was a prime reason for the disquieting intensity of the acting in this movie.

TEXT AND SUBTEXT

We don't always say what we mean. This piece of folk wisdom is a cornerstone for the actor when working with dialogue. The richness of dialogue is found in the shadings that words and phrases generate in the shifting underground contexts of a drama. A good actor is aware of the nuances of meaning that a line of dialogue will suggest. Proper delivery of dialogue will work on different levels, sometimes with purely literal meaning, at others with veiled intent. What we *literally* say when we speak is called the *text* of a statement. The buried meaning and interpretation of a statement is the *subtext*.

Consider this familiar situation: A man asks a woman: "What are you doing tonight?" The *text* of the question could be easily interpreted as simply his call for seemingly neutral information concerning her activities. But the *subtext* might well be translated: "Will you go out with me tonight?" If the woman were to read this subtext into the question, she might suddenly answer, "Are you kidding me? I'm busy!" Reacting defensively, the man might then answer back in any number of ways, depending on whether he felt hurt, amused, humiliated, angry, or just bewildered. In life, we are continually scanning the texts of what people say to us and probing the possible subtexts in hopes of finding out what the other person "really" means.

Actors play with subtexts. A scriptwriter typically generates sharpened verbal exchanges by having one character say things with witty, profound, or ambiguous subtexts. The other character then misreads the meaning, thereby triggering some turn of emotion. The job of an actor in such an exchange is to suggest in the delivery the intended levels of meaning and draw out a fitting response. The following excerpt is a fine example of such dialogue.

CASE STUDY: Fatal Attraction—"The Restaurant Scene"

The restaurant scene from the 1986 movie *Fatal Attraction* is crucial to the story. After being caught in the rain, Dan (Michael Douglas) has spontaneously invited new business acquaintance Alex (Glenn Close) for a drink at a nearby intimate restaurant. The two characters approach this potentially seductive situation with feigned innocence and charged expectation. Alex is a woman with an intentionally obscure back story. We sense that she is a professionally talented person, but she seems to have been damaged by past relationships in her life, the result being an unexpected aggressiveness toward Dan that comes across at first as intense interest. We suspect that she is a volatile and neurotic woman, but sharing Dan's curiosity, we want to know more about her. Dan is the urban everyman. He genuinely loves his wife and child, but cannot resist going to the edge of his moral boundaries to see what else is available. It is important to the story for Douglas to keep the sympathy of the audience on Dan's side, even when they may not approve of his actions. By emphasizing his shy and boyish side, he seems to be more naive than cunning in compounding the difficulties in the story, hence he is more forgivable. By the end of this short scene, Alex will control the fate of the evening, and Dan will coyly give in to his sexual attraction.

As the restaurant scene starts, Dan tells a personal anecdote about his mother wanting to hire him in her divorce with his father. It is one of those stories that simply lets the person telling it appear urbane and humorous to a new acquaintance. He tries unsuccessfully to hail a waiter, making fun of his lack of status at this place. The conversation then turns more directly personal:

Dan: It's funny being a lawyer. It's like being a doctor. Everyone is telling you their innermost secrets. (*he lights a match for her cigarette.*)

Alex: You have to be discreet. (*she leans forward toward the match.*)

Dan: Oh God yes.

Alex: *(looking directly at him)* Are you?

Dan: Am I what?

Alex: Discreet . . . *(she confidently bends to light the cigarette.)*

Dan: Yes I'm discreet.

Alex: *(settling back, smiling)* Me too.

Dan: *(after a beat, suddenly personal)* Can I ask you something?

Alex: What?

Dan: Why don't you have a date tonight, it's Saturday night. . . .

Alex: *(insidious and haughty)* I did have a date. I stood him up, that was the phone call I made. *(girlishly)* Does that make you feel good?

Dan: *(blushing)* Doesn't make me feel bad.

Alex: *(smiling in triumph, then speaking flatly)* So where's your wife?

Dan: *(taken back)* Where's my wife? . . . My wife is in the country with her parents visiting for the weekend.

Alex: *(seductively)* And you're here with a strange girl being a naughty boy.

Dan: *(blushing)* I don't think that having dinner with anybody is a crime.

Alex: Not yet. . . .

Dan: Will it be?

Alex: *(feigning coyness)* I don't know, what do you think?

Dan: Oh, I definitely think it's going to be up to you.

Alex: *(playing at disinterest)* I can't say yet. I haven't made up my mind.

Dan: At least you're very honest.

Alex: *(intimately factual)* We were attracted to each other at the party, that was obvious . . . you're on your own for the night, that's also obvious . . . we're two adults . . .

Dan: *(swallowing hard)* I'll get the check.

CUT TO:

####

Many features of the actor's trade are evident in this scene. First, a cursory look over the dialogue on the printed page shows an economy of language. Even though the flow of conversation sounds natural, the lines play in a very spare manner, each word loaded for maximum emotional impact. The writer knows that each actor will bring to the camera a repertoire of performance skills and will give the scene unique interpretations beyond the written words. When Alex leans forward to get a light for her cigarette and intentionally waits a beat to engage Dan with her eyes, no words of dialogue could tell the moment more clearly. She has asked if he is "discreet." He pauses as his mind whirs with the possibilities of it all, then answers "yes."

Staying with this dramatic moment, the scene also is a fine example of the text/subtext issue. In the midst of their conversation about lawyers, Alex interjects, "You have to be discreet"; on the face of it, the phrase implies an endorsement of grace and tact. In the context of conversation in which it was spoken, the statement could be taken simply as a casual observation. However, given the general sexual undercurrent of the scene and the way in which both of them play with its meaning, the word "discreet" becomes a code for much more, such as, "We have both been around and have the good sense to know the dangers of quick erotic dalliances. But don't worry, I'm cool." Of course, this core mistake was not a misreading of the subtext—they both rightly understood each other at that moment. But shortly after, Alex is shown to be frantically clinging to this weekend lover, to the point that Dan consumes her every action. Alex becomes most *indiscreet* and that becomes the crux of the film's conflict.

SUMMARY

Every art has its instruments. The body is the actor's only means of expression. With his or her body, the actor creates illusions. By using its voice, movement, intelligence, and intuition, written drama takes on a fully human dimension. We watch in the dark with fixed attention to every nuance of appearance and emotion.

Each scene of every movie presents actors with a new challenge. When *The Color of Money* (1986) opens with Paul Newman playing Eddie, an aging pool hustler turned liquor wholesaler, he is talking softly to his girlfriend Janelle (Helen Shaver) with a voice textured by years of whiskey drinking. Expounding on the special quality of the brand in the shot glass between them, he physically savors the smell, color, and taste of the liquor with the relish of a collector of fine art. He's excited by his own eloquent descriptions to Janelle of subtle but substantial variations in whiskey and builds sensual intimacy between them by lovingly caressing the shot glass, tasting the amber liquid, and whispering its satisfactions. Newman fills the start of this scene with so much hushed intensity that he establishes the manner and aesthetic of Eddie for the rest of the movie.

Great actors take deftly written dialogue and complex character descriptions and give them an unforgettable screen presence. Their techniques are drawn from the accumulated wisdom of past performers and their innate interpretive skills. Acting is a continuous process of discovery for them and pleasure for us.

SPOTLIGHT

The Casting Director: Pam Dixon Mickelson Interview

Pam Dixon Mickelson has been the casting agent for a variety of major Hollywood productions, including: *Made in Heaven* (1987), *The Moderns* (1988), *The Music Box* (1989), *City Slickers* (1991), *The Waterdance* (1992), *Mr. Saturday Night* (1992), *Equinox* (1993), *Much Ado about Nothing* (1993), *Angels in The Outfield* (1994), *Goldeneye* (1995), *Forget Paris* (1995), *The Craft* (1996), *The Mask of Zorro* (1997), *Prefontaine* (1997), *Cookie's Fortune* (1999), *Vertical Limit* (2000), and *Dr. T and the Women* (2000).

Richard Peacock:	As a casting agent, at what point do you get involved in the project?
Pam Dixon Mickelson:	At the very beginning. Basically I am sent a script and break it down in terms of its characters—who is in it.
RP:	Do you get any help from anyone in the description of those characters?

PDM: I first use the writer's description in the script, and then I talk to the director to see if he or she concurs. That person might have a different idea than the writer had in mind. And then, based on that, I begin to think of actors. I start at the leading roles first.

RP: So you're involved in casting the leading roles—the principal stars—of the film, or are they already on board?

PDM: Well, it depends. If I'm doing a film, for instance, that Billy Crystal is directing, then of course he's on board. But normally nobody is set.

RP: Is it by chance that you have worked on so many Billy Crystal films—*City Slickers, Mr. Saturday Night, Forget Paris*, and others?

PDM: Once a casting director has worked for a director, you usually repeat. Looking at my credits, for example, I've probably done eight or nine movies with Gale Anne Hurd [a producer]. The same with Ron Underwood. If it's been a good relationship, they want to reuse me.

RP: Do you use a breakdown service in contacting the agents?

PDM: Yes. In film, there's a breakdown service. It's a place that delivers scripts to all the agents that are franchised in Los Angeles. Basically, it gives the details of the film: who's directing it, the producers, the distribution studio, the shooting dates—everything we're looking for.

RP: Would you describe the actual casting process, what physically happens?

PDM: How you approach the leading parts is totally different than how the supporting parts are done. For the leading roles—for both high budgeted films and even low budgeted movies—you're thinking about people who are recognizable, who have a track record, those actors who are considered, in one way or another, stars. Then you call their agents to see if they are available for the time period that you're going to be shooting the film. That's called "checking their availability." After that happens, you sit down with the director and discuss who best fits with what he or she wants to do. You might also have to get the producer's opinion. And then in conjunction with the people who are financing the film—usually in my case a studio—you have to get their approval for the offer to the person the director wants. Sometimes the studio agrees, sometimes they say no, and we continue to seek out some other star. Everybody has to agree.

RP: What about the lesser parts?

PDM: The supporting roles are those you're going to audition. Typically, the actors are not as well known, they may have done some films or television. For the audition process, you again call the agents, find their availability. Then you give them a "side." A side is a scene from the script in which they will appear. They look at the side—not memorize it—and come in and audition in front of myself, the director, and possibly the producer.

RP: On an average, how many actors would audition for the supporting role?

PDM: It depends. I just finished casting *The Mask of Zorro*. There are over a hundred actors who speak in the film. In the auditions we probably saw a thousand actors for the supporting roles.

RP: From your point-of-view, what is the most important thing that an actor should bring to an audition?

PDM: Two things simply. First, they must be thoroughly prepared. And next, they have to bring a reality to the part they are reading. It has to be believable.

RP: What is the most stressful part of being a casting agent?

PDM: Probably the pressure to get the job done within a limited period of time. Sometimes I'll get a script just three weeks before shooting, which means I won't know who is in it until I read it. Or I'll start with one script and they will tell me they want to rewrite it. Sometimes, over a ten-week period the script will be reworked by several writers. They might eliminate characters or create new ones.

RP: How much is the budget a factor?

PDM: Certainly the budget is an essential consideration. We may want Tom Cruise for a part but may not have the luxury of going to him. So we will have to look for a lead who will fit within the budget.

RP: You have cast some very large budget films—*Goldeneye* and *The Mask of Zorro*—but you have also done some smaller budgeted independent films, such as *Waterdance* and *Equinox*. Is the budget the only difference between the two types of film?

PDM: I think there are two differences. When you're doing an independent film the budget is one thing, but it also gives you more freedom because there are fewer people involved. Usually when you are doing a small film, the people financing it—whether its New Line or an independent guy somewhere—usually care about the main lead, but after that, it's mainly up to you and the director to decide who goes in the movie. So you have a lot of freedom.

RP: But big stars do show up in small films. How does that work?

PDM: I just did a Robert Altman/Alan Rudolf film called *Afterglow* that was under ten million, so we knew there were limitations. But by the same token, we have some famous people in it. We went to them and said that this was a work that we really care about. And they liked it enough to say, "You know what? We like it a lot too. We want to do it." So we were able to get Nick Nolte, Julie Christie, and other fine actors. But if the movie were made by a studio, the stars would not have agreed to it.

RP: *Goldeneye* had a huge cast. Were you involved in all of the casting decisions?

PDM: I was hired originally to find James Bond. When they called me, there had been other casting directors on it but they were not successful in choosing somebody. When they hired Martin Campbell as director—he had worked with me previously—the first thing he did was bring me on board. My job was to tell the producers and Martin who I felt should be the lead. I always loved the idea of Pierce Brosnan.

RP: What triggered that choice for you?

PDM: Number one: *Goldeneye* was a movie who's main audience—teenagers—had never heard of. I have a son who, when I mentioned James Bond or Golden-eye, didn't know what I was talking about. I recognized that he had no pre-conception of who should play James Bond. The other thing I realized was that the humor in the film was actually a kind of English humor. You had to have a guy that you didn't laugh at. He had to have finesse so that the audi-ence was rooting *for* him rather than laughing *at* him. My feeling was that Bond was handsome and humorous. But he also had to fall between a cer-tain age range so that you would believe that he was agile enough to perform all those stunts. I thought of all the Americans who might play the part, but they really didn't seem to work. I made list after list of possibilities, and finally came to the conclusion that the best person would be Pierce. The producers had thought about him from time to time but also thought that there might be someone out there they had missed. They ended up agreeing and we made an offer to Pierce.

RP: Characters in films, it seems to me, tend toward stereotypes—the ruthless Mafia boss or the sweet girl next door. Do you cast actors who obviously fit those stereotypes?

PDM: I think that in casting you try *not* to do that. You call it stereotyping; I call it casting "on the nose." When I was doing *The Craft,* there was only one boy in it. I took a kid named Skeet Ulrich who was not the stereotypical leading guy—he was offbeat, he was pretty not handsome, he was untried. But we decided in *The Craft* that we wanted a really interesting guy—someone who you never knew what he was thinking. So we went against the type. The part was written for a Melrose Place-kind-of-guy, and we absolutely didn't want to do that. What I think makes good casting direc-tors is the ability take a role and not do it as expected. It's much more inter-esting when you see a film not to be able to see an actor and immediately say "Oh, he's the killer."

RP: What then do you think is the most creative part of your work?

PDM: What I just mentioned. Coming up with people who are not "on the nose"—what is expected. Like when I was doing *Angels in the Outfield*. The lead role in the script was a warm likable catcher. But he was never ever written as an African American. I thought the guy should really look like a catcher because it was a kids' movie and I don't think you can fool kids. He also had to be warm and likable. At a meeting with the director Bill Dear and the producers I suggested Danny Glover. They thought it was a great idea and we made him an offer.

RP: Casting "against type" must hold some risks. Are there other films that you are proud of in this regard?

PDM: When I did *The Moderns* and cast John Lone, I thought that was an interesting choice. That was totally against all typecasting in terms of his looks. Another time, when I was production vice president on *Officer and a Gentleman*, the director, Taylor Hackford, wanted an actor who I wasn't real crazy about. I got him to look at a number of his films and he came back willing to listen to me. I suggested Lou Gossett—I'm not even sure why—and Taylor looked at me and said, "You know, that's a really interesting idea." We got on the phone and called William Morris, brought Lou Gossett in the next day to read with Richard Gere. Not only was it interesting but the actor absolutely changed the entire movie. I can't imagine the movie without him. I have to give credit to Taylor Hackford for being open. The hardest part of my job was standing up to him and saying, "I really don't like your idea. Do you think that you can look at somebody else?"

RP: Did that experience with Taylor Hackford get you into casting?

PDM: I was production vice president at Paramount but I had already started in casting even though I didn't do it on the line. I have always loved actors and so when I left Paramount—basically because I had children and wanted to have a job that wasn't as crazy—casting was perfect.

RP: I've noticed that there is a high proportion of women in casting as compared to other parts of the industry. Is there anything that a woman brings to the work that is especially different?

PDM: Casting is a very detailed job, and I think that women tend to do this kind of work very well. But right now there are as many men in casting as women. I don't think it is very one-sided anymore. Also casting doesn't have a union, so people can go into it without the credential of, let's say, a director of photography. Anyone can hang out a sign and say that they are a casting director.

RP: When you are not actually casting a film, are you and your associates continually scouting for new talent? And where do you find the actors?

PDM: We find more people from the New York theater than almost anywhere. But we do go to theater in Los Angeles. We also stay aware of the different ends of businesses, like the music business, modeling, sports to a degree. It's just being aware of everything that's going on in the culture. We like to pick someone who is big in one element and bring him or her into our element. Like from the music world. I put Reba McEntire in a cameo role in *Tremors*—she had never acted before but she was certainly a big country western star.

RP: How should a young person in the movie business measure success?

PDM: Beginning actors always say to me "Do you think I'll make it? Do you think I'll be a star?" I tell them that success is whatever you want to make it. I think that the most important thing, especially for actors, is to believe in themselves and persevere. There's a lot of rejection in the business. In the end, the really good actors do win out. ◀

FILMS TO CONSIDER

These fifteen films have one thing in common—outstanding performances by their actors. The movies selected cover the last half of the last century and are, admittedly, personal choices.

- *Red River* (1948): The Howard Hawks' Western is a clear contrast in acting styles, the controlled swagger of John Wayne challenging and finally finding compromise with the more sensitive but surprisingly determined Montgomery Clift.

- *All about Eve* (1950): Bette Davis gave a daring performance as an aging actress confronted with threats from an ambitious younger actress (Anne Baxter). The supporting roles by George Sanders and Thelma Ritter were especially strong.

- *On the Waterfront* (1954): The method acting of Marlon Brando is perhaps best featured in this hard-edged New York movie about the fate of dock workers, complemented by equally strong acting by Karl Malden, Lee J. Cobb, and Eva Marie Saint.

- *Tunes of Glory* (1960): The technical expertise of British acting is never better displayed than by Alec Guinness as a washed-up flamboyant colonial in a Scottish regiment replaced by a by-the-book soldier, played by John Mills.

- *The Entertainer* (1960): The legendary acting reputation of Laurence Olivier can be readily observed in his portrayal of a worn-out vaudevillian bent on staying center stage, even if it ruins the lives of everyone around him.

- *Red Beard* (1965): The many levels of Toshiro Mifune's acting intensity are shown in his ability to play a doctor who is fatherly, soft-spoken, and wise, yet quick to strike out physically when a moral issue demands it.

- *Who's Afraid of Virginia Woolf?* (1966): The Mike Nichols' film is a showcase for the electrifying performances of Elizabeth Taylor and Richard Burton, supported by the outstanding work of Sandy Dennis and George Segal.

- *Midnight Cowboy* (1960): In an odd prototype of buddy movies to follow, Dustin Hoffman and Jon Voight give their characters totally original interpretations, and in doing so transform a good script into a great movie.

- *Opening Night* (1977): The development of an actor's character is explored in the exchanges between Gena Rowlands and John Cassavetes (partners in creating movies as well as in marriage) as they struggle to find themselves in the rehearsals for a play.

- *A Dream of Passion* (1978): The story, based on traditional Greek tragedy involving a grimly aberrant act, gives Ellen Burstyn and Melina Mercouri the stage to stretch their considerable talents to the limit.

- *Fatal Attraction* (1986): Michael Douglas, Anne Archer, and Glenn Close form a triangle of opposing sensitivities, motivations, and agendas that drive the story to its provocative and disturbing conclusion.

- *Glory* (1989): Good dialogue can bring out the best in actors, as this Civil War movie did for Matthew Broderick, playing an untested Union officer, and Denzel Washington and Morgan Freeman as brave foot soldiers

- *Glengarry Glen Ross* (1992): Star-studded casts rarely work so well, but the dynamic tension created by Al Pacino, Jack Lemmon, Kevin Spacey, Ed Harris, Jonathan Pryce, Alan Arkin, and Alec Baldwin makes David Mamet's screenplay of male aggression and panic vibrate.

- *Secrets and Lies* (1996): The open directorial style of Mike Leigh gave Brenda Blethyn the chance to sink into the emotional depths of her character as a dysfunctional woman who finds a new life when her adopted daughter shows up.

- *Music of the Heart* (1999): To watch Meryl Streep over the years is to attend an acting workshop, and her smooth, seemingly effortless, performance as a music teacher in Harlem is another in a long series of acting wonders.

THOUGHT QUESTIONS AND EXERCISES

Watch a film from those listed.

1. Watch the performance of the lead actor in a film. As clearly as you can, define the nature of his or her special appeal as a screen presence. What makes him or her a star? Use a specific example of the person's acting style from the film to demonstrate your thinking.

2. In the first scene of the movie in which the main character is introduced, how does the actor convey the temperament of the character and back story of that character, other than using dialogue? Specifically detail the physical techniques the actor develops during the scene.

3. In your mind's eye, cast another actor in the lead role of one of the movies listed. In what ways do you think that actor would have reshaped the character? What differences in interpretation might you predict? Give an example in reference to a particularly important scene.

4. Choose a film and an actor in it. What special factors and problems do you think that the actor faced in "finding the character"? What choices did the actor appear to make in translating the character to the screen? Cite some specific examples.

5. Analyze a central scene in a film. Determine what you think is the dramatic arc of the scene. Detail how the actors chose in their verbal and physical choreography to build to the arc. What was their method and style of playing it out?

match well with those of the primary director.

The Task at Hand

One of the most difficult and important tasks of this stage is getting a clear idea of what is actually being shot. The **dailies (or rushes)**—the filmed takes of the previous day's shooting—are usually viewed at the end of each evening to give some sense of how things are going. This immediate feedback gives the filmmakers some perspective. But the movie, at this point, is being seen only in fragments. Even the practiced eyes of veteran filmmakers have some degree of uncertainty about what they are seeing. Even when the last day of shooting is done and the footage is "in the can," the ultimate quality of the work is often still largely a mystery. An unedited film may hold moments of perceived brilliance, but it is not yet a *movie*. That

will evolve and come into being in the final stage of postproduction. Director Richard Attenborough (*Chaplin*, 1993) sums up the issue:

> Obviously, the most important talent that a director acquires is his ability during the shooting of the picture to be able to contain and maintain in his mind, in his eye, the entity, the whole, the shape, the tempo, the graph, the thrust forward.

The pressures during the stage of principal photography are very real: The producers closely scrutinize its progress; peers watch with critical interest; the creative work of the director and other professionals is tested. It is a time that combines personal aesthetic and practical compromise; good sense and risk taking; conviction and angst; skill and luck. This phase of filmmaking is clearly consumed with the *art* of moviemaking.

CHAPTER 5

THE DIRECTOR

THE ART OF STORYTELLING ON FILM

"Movies aren't for me a piece of life. It isn't a job, it's everything. You can't make them unless you are obsessed. They tend to take you over. They guide your dreams as much as they guide your waking. There's no escaping movies."

Director Phillip Noyce
(*The Bone Collector*, 1999)

The words of Phillip Noyce carry the passion of many film directors. Screenplays may be both conceived and written by another, but on the first day of shooting the movie belongs to the director. The director is in charge of bringing the screenwriter's idea to life, playing at being a god who is in charge of creating a tangible world. During the process, the written language of the script is transformed into the physical realities of sets, performance, light, and movement. In the process, the vision and execution of the original idea by the director usually overwhelms any claim by the writer of principal authorship of the final film. It is therefore generally agreed that movies are a "director's medium." There is no other job on earth quite like it.

A director works at both the *macro* sphere of thematic vision and at the *micro* level of detailed and practical daily management—an agile juggler at both ends. On the micro scale of things, the director must be vigilant regarding very specific details that inevitably arise each day. There are hundreds of people attached to the production waiting for orders. Much of the responsibility is rightfully delegated to others—matters having to do with specialized technical choices, location availability, work assignments, labor problems, personal compatibility, or equipment procurement. But a director should be generally aware of even small decisions that may affect the final film.

On the macro level, the conceptual issues of the film must be given shape and substance. Is the story envisioned in the script and agreed upon in preproduction planning actually the one being shot? Though the film is being shot in tiny and seemingly disconnected increments, are deeper connecting themes of the story being planted and nurtured? Good cinematic storytelling does not happen by chance. In the massively complex *Lawrence of Arabia* (1962), for example, film director David Lean was somehow able to correctly intuit the consequences of a thousand specific choices, yet keep

227

5–1   David Lean   Director David Lean (left), seen here in a moment of contemplation on location during the shooting of *Doctor Zhivago* (1965), was one of a rare breed of directors who could consistently produce quality films of epic size. With grandiose budgets available for his films, Lean had the special ability to never lose sight of the importance of nuance in stories with monumental themes. He began as an editor in England, and his filmography includes works spanning from *Great Expectations* (1947) to *A Passage to India* (1984).   (Photograph by Bradley Smith)

his comprehensive vision of the larger story in the confusion of distant film locations **(5–1)**. With an eye cocked toward the next phase of editing, and with an instinct for sensing the relationship of images and movement in creating visual rhythms, Lean could step back from the wealth of detail to gain and maintain some perspective. Lean's uncanny ability to oversee sprawling film projects and stay on course was a quality that set him apart and put him in demand as a director of epics, a genre so often mishandled by incompetent filmmakers.

"An epic vision isn't worth much if you can't tell a story," critic David Ansen has noted regarding the job of film directing. But there is no easy formula for making good movies of any size. There are many methods of visual storytelling: Some directors are straightforward and strive for graphic punch; some directors emphasize the poetic blending of image, color, and sound; some directors are gifted at drawing out stellar acting performances; others are technical wizards. Films may be action-packed and heavily episodic, or may lead us through the story of one person that unfolds in quiet revelations. The primary responsibility of the director is to *engage* the audience. Whatever distinctive personal style and adroit technical skills used are worthwhile only if that task is achieved.

BACKGROUND: THE RISE OF THE AUTEUR

"I can make any film I want to make. Any subject—comic, serious. I can cast who I want to cast. I can reshoot anything I want as long as I stay in the budget. I control the ads, the trailers, the music."

> Director Woody Allen
> (*Deconstructing Harry,* 1997)

Woody Allen is the rare exception among directors, past or present. Directors dream of having complete control of their work, but most are restricted on all sides. Orson Welles had such freedom for one movie. Welles is a classic example of an exceptional young man who was given the rare chance to direct a movie with almost no previous film experience. At 24 years old, he came to RKO with a successful stage and radio reputation and was presented with the unheard of privilege of controlling his own film production. The result was the mature and profoundly innovative *Citizen Kane* (1941). But the hard realities of the industry soon wore him down. After directing the movie *Touch of Evil* (1958), he reflected:

> *A typewriter needs only paper; a camera needs film, requires subsidiary equipment by the truck-load, and several hundreds of technicians. That is always the central fact about the filmmaker as opposed to any other artist: He can never afford his own tools. The minimum kit is incredibly expensive; and one's opportunities to work with it are rather less numerous than might be supposed. In my case, I've been given the use of my tools exactly eight times in 20 years. Just once my editing of the film has been the final version put into release.*

Despite his recognized brilliance, Welles spent a lifetime struggling for opportunities to direct film with unfettered personal vision **(5–2)**. Even for the best, there are no guarantees.

The use of the French word *auteur,* as it relates to film directors, should hold no mystery. It translates to "author," and as applied to film, the term identifies the important role of the director. Today, there would seem to be little controversy about the idea: Just as a novel has an author, so too does a movie. But when Francois Truffaut, as a young film critic for *Cahiers du Cinema,* wrote about this in the 1950s, and as American critic Andrew Sarris popularized the "theory" in the 1960s, many people were awakened to what today may seem obvious: For a select group of directors, their films greatly embody their own aesthetic taste, personal values, and unique personal history. Furthermore, the entire output of a director's career can be analyzed and judged as it evolves out of those elements. Producer/writer Steven Bach observes, "Personality—or personal style—has been invoked to enshrine all kinds of meretricious trash, but try to think of a great picture without it." We can talk seri-

5–2 *Orson Welles* Attempting to pursue his personal taste in moviemaking after the sensational release of *Citizen Kane* (1941), in 1942 Orson Welles set out to film *It's All True* in Brazil for RKO (in cooperation with the State Department). It was one of many career disappointments for Welles. He fell in love with the people, especially a group of workers whose basic human rights were being denied. Pictured here with a leader of the jangadeiros, Welles's movie was never allowed to be completed. Despite his recognized brilliance in all phases of filmmaking, Welles had enormous problems finding funding for his projects throughout his career. Serious production complications seemed to hound him. His films continually ran out of money, often stretching out their completion for years. *It's All True*—what exists of the stunning footage shot on his stay there—was finally released in 1993.   (Paramount Pictures)

ously, therefore, about threads of thematic or stylistic continuity in the films of directors Stanley Kubrick, Eric Rohmer, Vittorio DeSica, or even John Hughes.

Historically, there is some justification for downplaying the role of the director. The old studio system was notorious for submerging the distinct contributions of individual directors under the commanding studio logo of the company producing the films. In many cases, directors were treated more like glorified stage managers—important to be sure—but still hired hands and very replaceable. It was not uncommon that a film would have a number of directors, if during production the original director was assigned to start on another project or there was some uncertainty about how well things were going on the set. Even *Gone with the Wind* (1939) had a sequence of four directors, although Victor Fleming's name is the only one credited. The reputations of many directors were undervalued.

Before the 1950s, few directors had any conscious popular following. Early on, D. W. Griffith's *Birth of a Nation* (1915) swept the country, and his strikingly photographed movies, many of them idealized romantic stories, made his films a marquee draw until the mid-1920s. Charlie Chaplin and Buster Keaton were outstanding directors, but most of the public identified them first as comedians. Cecile B. DeMille's reputation for epics (*The Ten Commandments*, 1923 & 1956) made him a heralded director: Film titles with his name over them ensured wide attention. Busby Berkeley musicals and John Ford Westerns stood out from other filmmakers' movies in their respective genres. The media scandal surrounding story references to the life of

William Randolph Hearst in *Citizen Kane* (1941) gave Orson Welles name recognition as an infamous director, although the great percentage of the moviegoing public never went to his films. And although the quality of John Huston's work was evident even in his first film (*The Maltese Falcon*) in 1941, it was not until much later that his name became legendary with movie audiences.

Despite these conditions, many directors working in the United States survived the system with their integrity intact and their art wonderfully expressed. Looking back, Hollywood has a long list of directors with superior talents. American movie fans who possessed more acute taste recognized and sought out the fine films of some outstanding directors. Although this text is not a formal history, a greater appreciation of film can be gained by watching the movies of the following American directors: King Vidor (*The Crowd*, 1928), Tod Browning *(Dracula*, 1931), Ernest Lubitsch (*Design for Living*, 1933), Merian C. Cooper (*King Kong*, 1933), Rouben Mamoulian (*Becky Sharp*, 1934), Frank Capra (*It Happened One Night*, 1934), Clarence Brown (*Anna Karenina*, 1935), Howard Hawks (*Bringing Up Baby*, 1938), William Wellman (*Beau Geste*, 1939), Alan Dwan (*The Three Musketeers*, 1939), George Stevens (*Gunga Din*, 1939), Raoul Walsh (*High Sierra*, 1940), John Ford (*Stagecoach*, 1940), Michael Curtiz (*Casablanca*, 1943), Henry King (*The Song of Bernadette*, 1943), and William Wyler (*The Best Years of Our Lives*, 1946), among others. Wyler biographer Jan Herman writes of his career in terms that could be applied to many American directors of this period, that "eclecticism tended to hurt his reputation with purists who preferred to think of artists as people obsessed by a lifelong subject or two. . . . Anyone whose body of work does not conform to that pattern may be regarded as deficient: lacking in depth or purpose or—the ultimate deficiency—a true calling." The studio system, with its frequent arbitrary directing assignments, tended to reinforce the situation.

Each of these American directors had stylistic strengths that added to the base of filmmaking skills and understanding for those who followed. As important as these directors were to their art, however, they were not names quickly recognized and sought out by the general public. It was not until later that large audiences gained perspective on the artistic and cultural impact of the Hollywood studio system and the contributions of directors who labored in it. But every active director paid attention. Director John Badham (*Saturday Night Fever*, 1977) admits, "Anyone who tells you they're not influenced by the past or current directors is probably fibbing. It's almost impossible not to be influenced. Me, I take the attitude that if it's a good shot and I can use it, I'll steal it. I have no shame. My goal is to make the best film possible."

With the help of film scholars and media writers—and the focused exposure of older movies on television to new audiences—individual film directors from past eras have become recognized for their often outstanding body of work. For example, although most of George Cukor's films, from *What Price Hollywood?* (1932) through *Love among the Ruins* (1975), were quite brilliantly composed and executed, the average fan at the time did not intentionally go to his movies because he directed them. "Movie stars" were the ones who filled theaters: The public went to see Spencer Tracy, Katharine Hepburn, Robert Taylor, Greta Garbo, Audrey Hepburn, Rex Harrison, Cary Grant, or Jack Lemmon, rather than Cukor's direction of them.

Alfred Hitchcock was one of the grand exceptions **(5–3)**. By the late 1930s and for the next three decades, films that he directed stood apart in the minds of film audiences. They paid money to see a "Hitchcock film." Yet when he first arrived in Hollywood in 1939, even he suffered under the same system that many directors of the day endured.

A producer used to take a finished film, rewrite it, reedit it, and so on. I first experienced this when I started **Rebecca.** *I'd rehearse a scene, but before I could get ready to shoot it, the script girl would come up and whisper, "I have to phone Mr. Selznick now." He had to okay the final rehearsal before I could shoot! That's how heavy the hand of the producer was in those days. Another example is retakes. When I used to complain of a technical defect and ask to reshoot a scene, he'd say, "No retakes!" "Why not?" I'd ask. He replied, "It may not be in the picture." The producer used to assemble the film, arrange the credits, even outfit it with a temporary score taken from a music library. Within three weeks of the last day of shooting, you'd have a sneak preview.*

As Hitchcock's reputation grew, so did his control over his productions. He became recognized as a master storyteller. His movie audiences began to anticipate films with intelligent suspense and surprising plot turns, in which the actors were of less interest than the mind of the director behind the camera. A theme is repeated throughout his films: An innocent man is falsely accused or mistakenly involved in a crime, yet a generalized guilt haunts him as he seeks redemption. From *Rebecca*

5–3 Alfred Hitchcock Alfred Hitchcock could be called the first superstar director. His film style was always visually distinctive and his subject matter was equally intriguing. The process of moviemaking calls on the talents of varied and expert crafts people, and therefore has always been a highly collaborative art form. But in his maturing years Hitchcock was always firmly in command of his films. Each shot demanded his careful attention. Here Hitchcock directs Edmund Gwen and Mildred Natwick in *The Trouble With Harry* (1955). (Universal Studios)

5–4   Ingmar Bergman   Few directors have had more influence on their peers than Ingmar Bergman. When his films first gained international recognition in the 1950s, they introduced audiences to deeper and more introspective levels of the film experience. Rather than merely entertaining with familiar themes, Bergman invited his public to explore the mysteries of the human spirit and heart in the struggle for deeper human relationships. Seen here on the set coaching Ingrid Bergman in *Autumn Sonata* (1978), he was renowned for the courageous performances that he drew out of a small group of actors who appeared again and again in his movies.   (New World Pictures)

(1940) through *Notorious* (1946), *Strangers on a Train* (1951), *Rear Window* (1954), *Vertigo* (1958), *Psycho* (1960), and *The Birds* (1963) and into the 1970s, the public treated his signature on a project as the guarantee of a finely crafted movie. For the first time, American audiences became sharply aware of the director's hand in manipulating their emotions and found special enjoyment in Hitchcock's black humor. To achieve this he paid close attention to every aspect of a director's duties: fine-tuning the script, devising innovative photographic techniques, demanding disciplined performances, giving special emphasis to the sound quality, and closely supervising the editing. Hitchcock taught his audience the delights found in the cinematic craft.

Some critics today discount the *auteur* approach to understanding filmmaking as a fervent but overreaching search for thematic interconnection, and therefore profound meaning, in the work of a director. The progression of a directorial career may happen quite by chance, as Alan Parker (*Angela's Ashes,* 1999) explains, "When I choose a new project, it's usually a reaction against the film I just finished—or whatever else is being made. . . . I like to do different things each time, and not plow the same furrow." In addition, it is hard to ignore the current emphasis on filmmaking as an intensely collaborative effort—the cumulative result of the work of many specially trained and talented people.

But it cannot be denied that many directors do return again and again to story themes and visual aesthetics that have a recognizable pattern. John Cassevettes (*Opening Night,* 1977) spent his directorial career in a bond with a small group of actors who repeatedly attempted to break down the barriers of acting and real experience. Ingmar Bergman (*Hour of the Wolf,* 1968) made films that somehow always presented the human condition as struggling to find an answer to the spiritual isolation that seems so inherent **(5–4).** Michelangelo Antonioni (*L'Avventura,* 1960) presents that isolation primarily in visual terms of human figures in stark landscapes. Independent filmmaker Hal Hartley (*Trust,* 1991) gives another variation of modern alienation in the vacant eyes and dry responses of his characters in film after film. Screenwriter Frederic

Raphael tells the story of submitting a draft to the reclusive director Stanley Kubrick for the movie *Eyes Wide Shut* (1999), "Kubrick did not seem interested in words. He might admire the sharpness of my dialogue, but it was not something he wanted to film, and film alone was his art." Considering the total body of work by a director is bound to say something—possibly even something about triviality—regarding special skills, artistic taste, and the private life of that man or woman.

THE WORK OF DIRECTING

"The word itself—The Director—is difficult for people to comprehend because it means different things to different people. But at the very least it means working with a group of others and putting your finger right into the place that's most serious to them. Which is the middle of their art. That's what you're touching all the time, and that makes for all the complications."

Director Stanley Donen
(*Singin' in the Rain*, 1952)

There is no tidy handbook to read that can make a person a film director. As with many jobs, one learns by observing and doing. To facilitate the complex process, smart directors surround themselves with a talented production crew and clear chains of delegated authority. During the stage of principal photography, the director should be free to concentrate on three subjects:

- **The director of photography:** Organizing the daily shooting schedule and conferring about the aesthetic choices for photographing the action.
- **The actors:** Counseling about character interpretation and the nature of their performances in achieving it.
- **The director's own personal vision:** Keeping sight of the essential theme and thrust of the movie, while at the same time shooting and reevaluating daily.

It is hard to predict and quantify the exact mix of talents that need to come together in a given man or woman aspiring to be a director. A good director is an inspirational leader, an efficient manager, an intuitive teacher, a knowledgeable technician, and an inventive visual artist. Because the financial gamble is so high in film, successful directors—those with some tangible record of artistic or commercial achievement—are highly valued.

Organization

"You have to be strong—and strong willed—or everyone starts making his own little movie. It's chaos—and I've seen it a lot. Nearly 600 people need to be told what to do."

Director Jan De Bont (*Twister*, 1996)

Solid organizational skills are a most valued asset in a director. Thorough preparation is a key to effectiveness on the set. Each day the director should have a clearly outlined plan. The shooting day, from the director's perspective, can almost be defined as a series of *setups*—the arrangement of camera, setting, props, lighting, and actors for a shot. This process of organizing the complex needs of each technical aspect of cinematography can be very time consuming. Moving filmmaking equipment, for example, in a major production presents real logistical problems and although film crews are trained to work quickly and efficiently, any number of factors can conspire to delay things. Directors are regularly stymied by the physical complexity of the shot planned **(5–5a-d),** the unusual nature of the location, the inability of actors to satisfy the dramatic intention of the script, technical glitches, the weather, extraneous production problems, etc. Four to five *setups* are considered satisfactory progress for an average day's shooting. Fewer camera setups save valuable time. Movies are very rarely shot in the natural sequence in which the story is told on the screen. If a scene early in the script takes place at a rural gas station, and the climactic scenes at the end of the film also take place there, it only makes economic and logistical sense to shoot everything possible while at that location.

In the face of a multitude of logistical and aesthetic decisions, directors have to be adept managers of time, material, and people. By cutting down confusion on the set and laying down clearly understood rules of procedure, the day-to-day rhythm of a movie project can become reasonably businesslike. Directors strive to maintain a pace that keeps the set active with a sense of tangible accomplishment. Director Bernardo Bertolucci finds inspiration on a movie set in the energetic scramble of cast and crew, but for other directors its disorder can seem overwhelming. In *L.A. Story* (1992) director Mick Jackson used eighty-seven different locations and innumerable setups in fifty-seven days of shooting. The movement of the film team, and the attendant procedures for setting up equipment, was monumental. Somehow both he and the movie survived.

When, as in the well-documented case of Michael Cimino's $44 million *Heaven's Gate* (1980) fiasco (a huge budget at the time), the director poorly plans and mismanages a very expensive production, the project self-destructs. Cimino's excessive takes and costly retakes, to list one problem, resulted in the director shooting over two hours of film footage each day to produce, on average, about one and a half minutes of useable material. Editors could not make the storyline comprehensible, despite (or because of) the overflow of choices available. The film came in well over-schedule and far overbudget. In a film review representative of most, *The New York Times* critic Vincent Canby wrote, "Nothing in the movie works properly. For all the time and money that went into it, it's jerry-built, a ship the slides straight to the bottom at its christening." The few audiences that saw the film in its first release agreed, and the movie died.

On the other end of the spectrum, some directors find value in working with a lean crew and smaller budgets. Director Victor Nuñez (*Ruby in Paradise*, 1993), a successful independent filmmaker, both operates his own cameras and edits his own films. In mainline Hollywood filmmaking, this situation is almost unheard of. Nuñez prefers "a small crew with everyone getting involved. I really believe the process, the way a film is made, is incredibly important and I want to control that." The consistent quality of his work is the best testament to his simplified approach.

An individual director's work habits determine how production shooting is set in

a

b

5–5a-d *Hud* The modern Western, *Hud* (1963), was directed by Martin Ritt and shot by James Wong Howe. In this scene, Hud (Paul Newman) attempts to seduce the housekeeper (Patricia Neal) in her cabin. In testing out possible ways to shoot the scene, Ritt considered these four possibilities of camera placement to present the action. Study the alternatives closely. If you were going to select one perspective, which camera placement would you use: a, b, c, or d? Why? What subtle emphasis is created with each choice? What happens when the location of actors shifts within the frame? Which frame has the most dramatic power? Every director is presented with hundreds of similar choices in each movie. (Photographs by Bradley Smith)

c

d

motion. The organization and mechanics of directing a film vary greatly. No two directors are alike, as evidenced in the way different directors approach their work each day. One director will insist that each shot is carefully preplanned, with storyboards, diagrams of the camera setups, and a fixed schedule for rehearsals; another director may be more spontaneous, waiting to see how the dynamics of the actors, the script, and the set suggest the day's shooting to be handled. Alfred Hitchcock was a leading example of a director with a specific plan, "To me, a picture must be planned on paper. People are always asking me why I don't improvise on the set, and I always answer, 'What for? I'd rather improvise in a room with a writer.' My method is very simple." Because he knew the precise intention of his stories, he could rely heavily on storyboarding to guide him. Time spent on the shooting set was minimal. This prudent style obviously worked well for him. Of course, Hitchcock's imposing stature and reputation also ensured the rapt attention of production crew and actors on the set.

Other directors need and invite more creative interaction from those around them. "Moviemaking is a process. You end with something different; that's what gives it life," says director Bernardo Bertolucci (*Besieged*, 1999). "I cannot plan a film as a script or as a storyboard. I need a camera; I need actors. I can't do it on a desk. I need the reality to whisper to me." Such directors rely on the electricity that shooting a scene often generates. What happens on these sets cannot be predicted, so that the best of these directors will follow their intuitive sense, combining the finest moments of performance with the right camera work. A few directors deliberately *encourage* a very loosely disciplined set. As director Gus Van Sant (*My Own Private Idaho*, 1991) says,

> *Part of the way I direct films is that I put things in a state of confusion. I like it when there's chaos on the set and you say 'roll it' and no one knows what's supposed to happen. . . . Working this way, people learn to think for themselves, because nobody else is going to do it for them. In order to survive during the take, they have to come up with something, and that allows an element of reality to enter into it.*

These directors want to record the illusion of an unstaged atmosphere to give their movies a sense of naturalness. To do this, some directors feel they must, in a sense, subvert the system to faithfully capture the way people actually behave away from any cameras. Traditional producers tend to become very uneasy when directors heavily rely on improvisational methods on the shooting set, seeing the style as unpredictable and therefore potentially more costly.

Working with Actors

"Good actors put everything on the line; good directors help them do it."

Director Lee Grant (*Staying Together*, 1989)

Actors on stage get immediate feedback from an audience of strangers on the effectiveness of their performance and adjust accordingly. On a movie set, actors play to a single critic: the director. A director must evaluate whether an actor has reached deeply enough into the character, and explored all the dramatic

5–6　Krzysztof Kieslowski　Many observers feel that the primary contribution of a director is the ability to draw out top performances from actors, thereby bringing the characters and story to life. The work can involve intense and direct confrontations with actors, often triggering its own drama. Here Polish director Krzysztof Kieslowski gives instruction to Irene Jacob, the star of *The Double Life of Veronique* (1991).　(Miramax)

choices available in playing the part **(5–6)**. When judging a particular *take*, the director determines if the actor has made the appropriate interpretation of a line, congruent body posture, correct pitch of voice, honest facial reaction, subtlety of hand gesture. The degree of control that directors wield over actors is potentially enormous. This power rests in the right of the director to dictate whether a take is to be reshot.

There is no all-inclusive explanation of how the process works best. But when the shooting starts, the director's most precarious relationship is with the actor. Most directors and actors know that they are interdependent, that a movie will not work for either of them unless the acting is inspired. The involvement with the actors in rehearsals, in personal conferences, and before the camera is a prolonged test of director's judgment, patience, and skill. Methods for workings with actors vary greatly. Autocratic and removed directors have commanded great performances from actors; compassionate directors have done the same.

Because their record of movie accomplishments may demand unquestioned respect, certain directors carry enough weight to be plainly authoritarian. Some film directors foster an exaggerated dictatorial mystique. Authoritarian directors can be very effective if their instincts are unerring, and if they have the trust of the actors.

These directors may be sensitive to actors, but they expect them to come to the set well prepared and rehearsed. Under these conditions, shooting the film is often a swifter exercise, with less interchange about alternate readings of a role. Director David Lean could be adamant.

> *I can't bear some actors, the rambunctious type who think they know every-thing. You've got to knock them down and make them realize that they don't know everything. If you've really done your homework on the script, you, the director, know the part better than any damned actor, because you've been at it for months. I've had lots of actors who want to change dialogue. I stop them from doing it. I won't have it. They took on the script, and they should stick to it.*

Other directors of this tradition will use actors only as material to be pho-tographed. Federico Fellini was known to keep the script away from his actors so that they didn't know what they were to do, apart from taking instructions about where to move or what to look at. Actors in his films are often best remembered for their striking visual appearance. Traditionally, such classic movie directors present actors with the image of a strong "father figure," and they in turn rely on the director's crit-ical approval. A dominant authority figure works effectively with actors who submit to this rather special relationship. For years, one implied excuse used by the studios to resist women directors was they could not fit this paternal role. Now with the grow-ing success of women directors, some producers may have come to realize that a "mother figure" can work just as well.

Most major directors want a more balanced relationship with their actors. They have developed the project with a strong sense of the roles and how to play them. For example, if a male actor has a background in successfully playing characters with deeply scarred histories, a director does well to find out his thoughts about the way a similar character should be played. New and deeper layers of a character can be found in prolonged discussions and tough rehearsals involving the actors and the director. Because a significant number of directors have themselves been actors, the dynamics triggered in the process can be a most exciting part of filmmaking.

Certain persons have reputations for being "actors' directors," that is, directors who not only respect the concerns of actors, but who have ways to generate new lev-els of excellence from them. This is not always achieved simply with camaraderie on the set. "I have as few searching conversations as possible," John Huston once said about his relationship with actors. However, he was also well known for giving his actors the freedom and space to test out their interpretation of the characters. Steven Soderbergh (*Erin Brokovich*, 2000) takes a most antiauthoritarian stance.

> *I think it's important, when you are directing your own script, to have a healthy disrespect for your own material. . . . I believe that actors have to sound nat-ural. And if you are objective about it, if you have good actors and can tell them, 'Look, if you're having trouble with the lines, just make up your own,' then they will. It's idiotic not to take advantage of actors who have really good ideas.*

Good communication is a key. It is not surprising that directors choose the same actors for a series of films (or that superstars choose *directors* they have liked in the past). Director Ingmar Bergman (*Face to Face*, 1976) worked so closely with Liv Ullmann that his camera seemed to anticipate her every move and emotion, capturing intense emotional sequences rarely seen on the screen. "I come out with words in a way I never knew I would," says Ullmann about the penetrating directing style of Bergman. The intimacy created in his films with her and others found its source in the extremely high level of communication—not always verbal—that evolved between them. Irvin Kershner (*The Luck of Ginger Coffey*, 1964) says, "It is very simple. You give them love, and you give them confidence. You give an actor that self-assurance by giving him confidence in himself and in yourself. You take away fears. That is what it amounts to." The bond between the director and actor can be deeply symbiotic.

Finding the Image

"Whatever you say, film is an image. It's a way by which one can become a painter."

Director Jacques Demy
(*The Umbrellas of Cherbourg*, 1964)

Much of a film director's time on the set is spent working out shooting strategies with the director of photography. Shot composition preoccupies much of their time on the set. Actors' positioning must be blocked, camera movements planned, and lensing chosen. Moreover, individual shots should not be perceived in isolation from one another. Editing will eventually connect them, and the director must have an active sense of how shots will match. The director must anticipate the progression of shots and calculate their relationship in their edited form. In addition, the director will keep in mind even larger patterns, that is, whatever overriding motif is desired for the film.

A director has an infinite number of ways to stage and photograph action. For example, the relationship of the camera to the subject is a paramount decision. If the subject of a film is a romance in Edwardian times, a director might choose to shoot the characters primarily in medium and long shots, maintaining a formal distance reflective of the manners of the period. In *Shanghai Triad* (1995), director Zhang Yimou continually shot the action from the perspective of a young servant boy observing with wonder the household rituals of a Chinese gangster warlord. As these camera placements were carried through the film, either low angle shots or viewpoints from the likely positions of a curious young eavesdropper established the slightly removed but ever-present relationship of the boy to the events in the story.

Good photographic technique alone, however, does not necessarily make a good movie. An entire *visual style* of the film must be found. The director's guiding artistic purpose should be felt in the design of each film image. Some directors are astute masters of the camera, either by previous training or through years of experience. Director Roman Polanski, for example, was thoroughly schooled in all aspects of cinema at the Lodz [Poland] Film School and is widely known to have highly refined camera skills. His best movies are visually adventurous and flawlessly lensed.

5–7 *Paris, Texas* German film director Wim Wenders and cinematographer Robby Muller joined their visual artistry in *Paris, Texas* (1984). The filmmakers effectively used the lonely landscapes and half abandoned towns of Texas as a metaphor for the mental state of Travis (Harry Dean Stanton), a man lost in the depression of a failed marriage. Still haunted by his love of Jane (Nastassia Kinski) who has been reduced to the depressing world of cheap sex clubs, the filmmakers found powerful images that conveyed their barriers. Coming from another culture, Wenders and Muller seemed to see the American Southwest with a different gaze. (20th Century Fox)

But most directors leave the details of camera execution to the director of photography (DP). Although some directors may be first-rate storytellers and acting coaches, their relationship to their cinematographers is one of communicating what they want visually, and leaving it to that person to execute the details of the shot **(5–7)**. James Bridges (*The China Syndrome*, 1979) sums up the attitude of many directors: "I still don't know that much about the camera. I hire the best people, and I work with them and tell them what I want." Of course, a director must know and be clear about just what he or she wants in a shot or from a scene. A director with this approach is free to give other areas of the shooting process more attention. Movies are judged in many ways, none more important than the quality of the cinematography.

STYLES OF DIRECTING

"I am not just a director with a personal style; I am cinema."

Director Michael Powell
(*Black Narcissus*, 1946)

Few directors would speak in such a mystical way about their work, but many would know what Michael Powell is getting at. Most directors yearn to fuse their personal vision with the traditional techniques of the filmmaking medium, so that what arrives on the screen has artistic unity. In the act, distinctive styles of directing evolve over the course of a career and can be described. That is, in approaching and executing film material, a director's taste and technique will emerge in discernible patterns. Part of a director's art is quite consciously chosen, but family and cultural roots of that person also undoubtedly influence it. The particular film style of a director becomes his or her signature.

Although each director's work is to some degree unique, a few generalities can be made about the myriad of directing styles. For example, a defining attitude toward film direction will result when a director is drawn toward one of the two following aesthetic orientations:

- **Realism.** A director can *objectively* approach a subject with the intention of recording unadorned physical reality on film.
- **Expressionism.** A director can *subjectively* explore and enhance the psychological, spiritual, or artful aspects of a subject on film.

In oversimplified pop terminology, a director can either "tell it like it *is*" or "tell it like it *feels*." In truth, the filmmaker's choices are much more varied and complex than this, but it is useful to look more closely at these options.

Realism

"For me, filmmaking is combining images and sound of real things in an order that makes them effective. What I disapprove of is photographing with that extraordinary instrument—the camera—things that are not real. Sets and actors are not real."

Director Robert Bresson
(*Diary of a Country Priest*, 1950)

A definition of *realism* leads to a discussion of the very nature of the film medium. Motion pictures share with still photography the remarkable ability to record and reproduce the nearly exact look of physical reality. This unusual quality—the capacity of the camera to mirror the world before it—is what draws us to it. Of course, movies go beyond still photography into more complex arenas of time, movement, and continuity. But some theorists—best articulated by critic André Bazin in his collection of essays *What Is Cinema?*—believe that the medium of film has a natural propensity for capturing reality simply, and that it is most effective when it functions in that manner. Jean Cocteau (*Beauty and the Beast*, 1946), a filmmaker not noted for his realistic images, felt that "the more you touch on mystery, the more important it is to be realistic."

By the middle of the twentieth century, the films of Italian "NeoRealist" and French "New Wave" directors were gaining a worldwide audience **(5–8)**. Among others things, these directors believed that the filmmaking of the day was weighted down in stale filmic conventions and artifice. Movies seemed to be removed from life as it was actually experienced by most people. Although some directors approached realism in films from early in the twentieth century—as seen in the work of Erich von Stroheim (*Greed*, 1923) and Jean Vigo (*L'Atalante*, 1934)—the hackneyed ways of some conventional directors who ruled Hollywood filmmaking were challenged by a

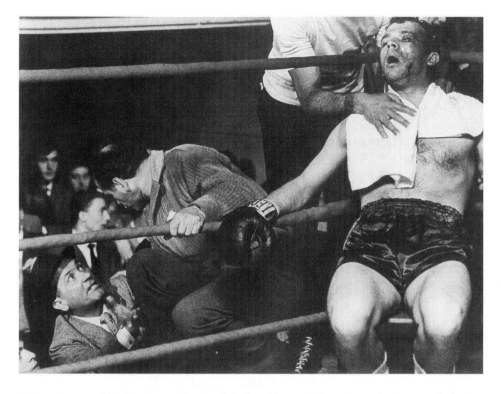

5–8   *Rocco and His Brothers*   The classic Italian Neorealistic style was losing popularity by the time Luchino Visconti's *Rocco and His Brothers* was made in 1960, but the film remains one of the finest examples of this filmmaking attitude. The story sets two brothers, one a boxer (Renato Salvaroti) and the other a sensitive lad (Alain Delon), both in love with a prostitute (Annie Girardot). The cultural and family traditions limit choices, as the human dilemma implodes in their lives. The director seems to rip scenes out of life and put a frame around them.   (Museum of Modern Art)

new breed wanting to test out more natural cinematic styles and politically relevant themes. After the human tragedies of two world wars, moviemaking was ready to turn its attention and address the tougher truths of life. The critically neglected French director Georges Franju (*Eyes without a Face*, 1959) saw a paradox, "What is artificial ages badly and quickly. Dream, poetry, the unknown must all emerge out of reality itself. "

Since the time of movie realism's most concentrated influence—from the mid-1940s into the 1960s—many directors have incorporated various degrees of that style into their films. Many of the film stories today are presented as true-to-life experiences, and directors favor visual and dramatic elements—use of available light, unpolished delivery of dialogue, seemingly accidental framing of the subject, rapid pans—that promote a sense of authenticity. Some directors are driven to realism by their minimal budgets; others want to awaken and shock audiences by giving them a strong dose of the hard-boiled reality of the street. Realism in films encompasses a director's orientation toward all of the production values, including the following:

- Directors working in a realistic mode tend to want the picture quality of the film to have an intentionally rough texture. This effect is caused by the film stock used when filmmakers shoot their subject with *available light*. What may be lost in terms of high picture definition is replaced by images that suggest what we are seeing is the unadorned truth randomly caught on film. The realist director will tone down high color contrasts so that the eye is not dazzled and distracted from the content of what is dramatically taking place. For example, *Angela's Ashes* (1999) is director Alan Parker's adaptation of Frank McCourt's grimly poetic autobiography, set in the gray wet slums of Limerick, Ireland. To honor the spirit of the book, Parker and cinematographer Michael Seresin, BSC strove for visual realism, created by using shafts of daylight to illuminate the small rooms where the poverty-stricken family lives, and the simple glow of a few lights at night to fight the dark. "The temptation is always to round the light off and make it look like a canvas by Rembrant or Vermeer," Seresin says. "In my opinion, that approach would have looked too cosmetic, and it wouldn't have worked for this picture. I think we had fair success in resisting the beautification of the light." Filmmakers seeking realism in their movies resist the lure of enhancing a set with excessive light sources.

- Realist directors tend to *frame* their shots in ways that often appear almost *inadvertently caught* by the camera. This seemingly unstudied camera placement promotes the feeling that *anything* might suddenly happen before it. The action captured in the frame has a randomness about it, as if spontaneously photographed. For this reason, the hand-held camera is a favorite with these directors. Oliver Stone's *Salvador* (1986), set in wartorn Central America, used the style extensively to give his story a constant feeling of nervous tension. At other times, to help achieve an unaffected look, realistic films are often shot with the cameras at the normal positions at which we sit or stand, that is, the shots approximate the eye level at which a person usually experiences the world, avoiding extreme angles that might give an unwanted "arty" look to the movie.

- Realist directors tend to prefer shooting on locations saturated with *authentic visual elements*, rather than in the make-believe world of a movie studio set. Locations consistent with the actual nature of the action are not used simply as background but as essential environments that become part of the message in the story. A director doing a drama of coal miners in Kentucky, a gang film in Liverpool, or a story shot in the Amazon jungle will choose a realistic film style that emphasizes the genuineness of the place through its graphic details. Typical of the realist aesthetic, English director Ken Loach sets *Riff Raff* (1992) in the dirty gray working districts of London as he gives voice to the tragicomic stories of a construction gang. The uninteresting streets, modest interiors of houses, the dreary construction sites give the movie an air of legitimacy that permeates the powerful human drama being told. For the low budget *The Blair*

Witch Project (1999), the directors Dan Myrick and Eduardo Sanchez shot their film in Maryland's Black Hills Forest, as their actors searched out the mystery of a haunting local legend. The story's immersion into the eerie location produces a terrifying effect as the characters become genuinely disoriented and frightened by a series of nightly harassments staged without the knowledge of the actors. The result is a shockingly realistic film experience for the audience.

- Story events in the realist style are often structured and presented to appear as matter-of-fact moments in *everyday life,* witnessed by the camera in ways that we normally seem to experience them **(5–9)**. The action may appear somewhat ragged and not neatly scripted, giving the feeling that we are accidentally observing a random *slice-of-life*. To support this, some directors may encourage spontaneous dialogue and natural, offhand performances by actors. *Non-professional actors* are often used to reinforce this sense of plainspeaking. In *Straight Out Of Brooklyn* (1991), 19-year-old director Matty Rich told a story of life in the projects with a cast primarily made up of people from the neigh-

5–9   *The Match Factory Girl*   Often directors are drawn to realism by the existential nature of their subject. Aki Kaurismaki's *The Match Factory Girl* (1992) from Finland, tells the story of the extreme emotional isolation of a young woman (Kati Outinen, center) as we follow her through her daily life—at hopelessly routine job, at home with her cold parents, in a depressing night spot waiting for a partner to ask her to dance. Her conflict is locked within herself, unable to find adequate expression for terrible loneliness. We watch her move steadily toward a tragic conclusion.   (Kino International)

5–10   *Black and White* Writer/director James Toback pushes his filmmaking style into deeper levels of contemporary reality that sometimes shake the viewer awake from the traditionally controlled storytelling method. Shockingly blunt confrontations happen in *Black and White* (2000) when a group of affluent white amateur filmmakers (led by Brooke Shields) attempt to record the cultural and ethnic mix of the New York music scene. (Screen Gems)

borhood. The interchanges ring true, as if we are overhearing parts of spontaneous conversations. But often even professional performances are captured that appear more loosely written and acted than, in fact, is the case. Robby Muller, the cinematographer for Lars Von Trier's realistic *Breaking The Waves* (1996), points out the effect of experiencing raw performances was not for lack of a plan, "Everything is scripted, but Lars doesn't want much rehearsal. He often used the first take, after that, he felt the performances could become artificial." The dramatic effect, for this movie, pushed the viewer into a more intensely realistic relationship with the characters in the story **(5–10)**.

Mainstream directors often mix this realistic style with older narrative movie conventions—stories set in the mean streets of a real city but with clearly fictional heroes who perform bigger-than-life exploits, nicely surviving every explosive turn in the plot. But some directors are strongly committed to strict styles of movie realism. In the extreme, their narrative films attempt to imitate the authenticity of subject matter and the visual textures of the documentary filmmaker. A classic example is Gillo

DOGMA 95

In 1995, a group of Danish filmmakers published the *Dogma 95* manifesto, which outlined a list of ten rules called "The Vow of Chastity." This statement was a call by directors Lars von Trier, Thomas Vinterberg, and others to rediscover the basics of film realism and make films within certain aesthetic guidelines.

1. Shooting must be done on location. Props and sets must not be brought in (if a particular prop is necessary for the story, a location must be chosen where the prop is to be found).

2. The sound must never be produced apart from the images, or vice versa. (Music must not be used unless it occurs where the scene is being shot.)

3. The camera must be hand-held. Any movement or mobility attainable in the hand is permitted. (The film must not take place where the camera is standing; shooting must take place where the film takes place.)

4. The film must be in color. Special lighting is not acceptable. (If there is too little light for exposure, the scene must be cut or a single lamp must be attached to the camera.)

5. Optical work and filters are forbidden.

6. The film must not contain superficial action. (Murders, weapons, etc. must not occur.)

7. Temporal and geographical alienation are forbidden. (That is to say that the film takes place in the here and now.)

8. Genre movies are not acceptable.

9. The film format must be Academy 35mm.

10. The director must not be credited. Furthermore, I swear as a director to refrain from personal taste! I am no longer an artist. I swear to refrain from creating a "work," as I regard the instant as more important than the whole. My supreme goal is to force the truth out of my character and settings. I swear to do so by all the means available, and at the cost of any good taste and any other aesthetic considerations.

These realist ideals have been followed, with some glaring lapses, in several films, among them Vinterberg's *The Celebration* (1998), von Triere's *The Idiots* (1999), Soren Kragh-Jacobsen's *Mifune* (1999), Kristian Levring's *The King Is Alive* (2000), and Paul Morrissey's *The House of Klang* (2000). Kragh-Jacobsen claims, "It's fun to stick to the rules and find liberation in them."

Pontecorvo's *The Battle of Algiers* (1967), a hard-hitting reenactment of the Algerian struggle for independence from the French. Although the film was a scripted, fictionalized story, it was based on the actual events of the revolt. The people and streets of Algiers were photographed in a way that convinced the viewer that events of the story were being caught in the rush of the unfolding moments. The documentary-like camerawork—black and white film stock, frequent use of the zoom lens, hand-held cameras—reinforced this feeling. Pier Paolo Pasolini's *The Gospel According to St. Matthew* (1964), a radically envisioned life of Christ using non-professional actors, took much the same approach. In a different vein of realism, the films of Henry Jaglom (*Always*, 1985) are a good example of autobiographical stories that appear to be spontaneously put to film. During such films, the director seems to invite us to eavesdrop on private conversations meant only for those engaged in them.

It is important to note that realism is a consciously chosen film style of a director, *an aesthetic attitude toward its subject*. Even though the style seems uncontrived and natural, the director has made deliberate selections to convey the *look* of realism: film stock, locations, lighting, actors, and certainly many conscious choices in the editing process. Confusion can arise about the concept of realism because certain film subjects may seem to be more "real" than others. War—a very real situation—could be shot in any stylistic manner, including a highly subjective one, stressing the interior mood of a young man through techniques of visual exaggeration by the camera. The subject matter of a film does not determine a stylistic approach, the director does.

Expressionism

"My cinema is deliberately artificial, and it's always self reflective. Every time you watch a Greenaway movie, you know you are definitely and absolutely only watching a film. It's not a slice of life, not a window on the world. It's by no means an example of anything "natural" or "real." I do not think that the naturalism and realism is even valid in cinema. Pursuit of realism seems to me a dead end."

Director Peter Greenaway
(*8 1/2 Women*, 2000)

Historically, *expressionism* was a movement in literary and visual arts that acknowledged the artist's subjective rendering of "reality." German dramatists in the early twentieth century inspired playwrights for both the stage and for motion pictures. The basic ideas were not new. The value of any artistic work had long ago been judged on how deeply it reflected the soul of the person who created it. But in the early years of this century, the growing popularity of psychology gave artists new tools for gaining insight into the human spirit and its corresponding behavior. Artists were encouraged to explore and visually describe the subconscious, shaping their work from that fluid and provocative level. A shadowy and free-form pictorial style developed that depicted the newly discovered psychological territory, and the expressionistic movement was born.

For filmmakers, expressionism was a natural ally. The dreamlike qualities of their medium seemed to embody perfectly the thrust of the new interest in hidden emotions. In the 1920s, German directors heartily took to exploring ways to express in screen images the deeper, and often darker, feelings that were masked by the conventional mores of society **(5–11)**. Their startling imagery spoke to subconscious levels of the self, and in doing so, had an almost hypnotic power to stir buried feelings in an audience. Expressionism encouraged personal interpretation of material, believing that at some subterranean level of life, a common language of symbols exists. Critics would claim that these filmmakers were simply obscure and self-indulgent.

5–11   *The Cabinet of Dr. Caligari*   The cinematic look that German directors brought to the screen in the 1920s influenced every later generation of fantasy film stylists. The horror film, as we came to know it, was first born in the dark dreams of such films as *The Cabinet of Dr. Caligari* (1919). Werner Krauss (Dr. Caligari) holds a strange power over Conrad Veidt, a twilight monster who carries out the doctor's evil desires. The haunting aspect of expressionism was seen in some later American movies such as Hitchcock's *Psycho* (1960) and evolved to the point of becoming a parody in some contemporary movies and music videos.   (Academy of Motion Pictures Art & Sciences)

Theorists such as Rudolf Arnhiem, in his book *Film As Art,* challenged the tenets of realism by simply expanding the definition of reality to include the subconscious. Interior representations of the human experience, they would argue, are just as valid as the surface "objectivity" that realists prize. For example, F.W. Murnau's *The Last Laugh* (1924) is a silent German film about an older man (Emil Jannings) who has two lives. He works as a doorman at a swank hotel, proudly wearing a pompous uniform that symbolizes authority in his limited world of influence. At the beginning of the film, the filmmaker directly translates the doorman's inner world to us. After showing off the splendid entrance of the hotel—the small but luxurious space that the doorman controls—a frantic camera then gives a subjective sense of his exhausting work as he struggles to unload two huge steamer trunks from a cab. The hotel manager coldly observes the doorman's troubles. By contrast, the doorman's living quarters are pictured as a drab apartment in a large dreary tenement building. The set of the tenement exterior (by art directors Robert Herlth and Walter Roehrig) is artfully distorted, infusing the frame with a nightmarish sense of being overpowered by gray prison walls. As the doorman comes and goes through its enclosed court, the ominous specter of the somber building conveys his spiritual dread. Later, when he is demoted at work to being a lowly custodian of the lavatory, it is a devastating scene. The doorman's private humiliation is underlined by Murnau as the camera frames the beaten man sitting hunched at the end of a row of sinks, two bare light bulbs casting the only light in the empty room. The exaggerated visual drama of the shot not only presents the doorman's external situation but it also reflects his emotional desolation, giving the audience a strong sense of his rejected inner state. The director, it could be said, has distorted reality to blatantly manipulate the audience's emotions, but the sensual excess of the film moment might come closer to the truth of a broken man's life than a more realistic film rendition.

Some degree of expressionist style infuses most films today. Long ago, filmmakers discovered the emotional power of the medium and realized that latent feelings could be explored visually by the skillful techniques of a director. Directors drawn to an expressionist approach would readily admit that movies depend on a manipulation of sensual experience, but also claim that every art form is involved with selecting and shaping its private images. Federico Fellini *(Fellini's Roma*, 1972) reverses the argument of realists:

> For me, the only real realist is the visionary because he bears witness to his own reality. A visionary—Van Gogh, for instance—is a profound realist. That wheat field with the black sun is his; only he saw it. There can't be greater realism.

Expressionist directors would admit that the mirror they hold up to the viewer sometimes grotesquely distorts, or idealistically makes greater, the "normal" way we see the world. But they would claim, the nature of cinema invites this. Some common elements of expressionism on film follow:

- The expressionist director sees the movie screen with much the same *spirit of invention* as the painter approaching a canvas **(5–12)**. The challenge is not only to communicate by using the limited space available, but to use that space to present not only the objective reality of the subject matter but also its emotional or logically contradictory underpinnings. Directors in the expressionistic mode build their movies with studied camera work that connects characters and their environments to reveal more than just sensible representations of surface reality. These directors often focus on the *connotative power of images* as a more effective way to convey deeper meaning. Director Peter Greenaway admits, "I would rather spend more time with my cinematographer and my art department than with my actors. The personal origins of this are to do with my discipline as a painter." It is not that Greenaway disdains the contribution of actors, but he feels the essence of his films is best revealed in the visual messages of its graphic presentation.
- Aware that the quality of light is the central issue of photography, expressionist tastes in lighting freely accentuate any features of the set or a human figure that might *manipulate and intensify* the desired mood of the shot. Either

5–12 *Prospero's Books*   Director Peter Greenaway used his artful imagination in his *Propero's Books* (1991), a fanciful interpretation of Shakespeare's *The Tempest*. Consistent with his expressionistic approach to film, Greenaway carefully exaggerates everything seen on the screen—the lighting, costumes, color choice, placement of characters within the frame, dance movement—so that every element is designed to serve his aesthetic interpretation. Each shot can stand alone as a composition to be studied. Prospero (John Gielgud) is majestically positioned in the center of the picture, but with critical lighting choices, Greenaway also calls attention to the dancers and the rest of the room. Greenaway is not as concerned with the literal impact of his images, but more with the dreams they induce. Expressionism can be unabashedly and wonderfully self-indulgent.   (Miramax Films)

strongly accented artificial lighting that moodily casts sharp contrasts of shadow and light or highly illuminated bright colors that startle our visual common sense might be used to underline dreamlike inner feelings. For the glam-rock period film *Velvet Goldmine* (1998), director Todd Haynes and cinematographer Maryse Alberti conspired to translate and even heighten the futuristic shocks of color and lighting that so identified this outrageous music world of the early 1970s.

- Sound effects and music speak directly to the emotions. Unlike films made in the spirit of realism, expressionist directors freely use *suggestive film music* and *heightened sound effects* to trigger and enhance sensory responses in the audience. A typical example occurs during the passionate union of Shakespeare (Joseph Fiennes) and Lady Viola DeLessep (Gwyneth Paltrow) by a river's edge in John Madden's *Shakespeare in Love* (1998)—the musical score of composer Stephen Warbeck underlines the tenderness and wanting of the two desperate lovers. By generously adding sound and color elements to magnify screen images, expressionist movies emotionally inform the viewer of intended meanings and also open new avenues of interpretation.

- One goal of expressionism is to fully engage and align the viewer with the *subliminal intentions* of the director's visual style. Again, for *Velvet Goldmine*, the filmmakers attempted to capture the visual style of an earlier period. Director Todd Haynes explains, "The camera of the late 60s and early 70s seemed to really hold back—it didn't physically enter space, it would instead *zoom, pan,* or *swish* through the space. It would then rack-focus suddenly, identifying one part of the frame. The difference is that you really got a sense of surface, this beautiful, almost caressing of the surface of the screen." For other directors, the techniques of camera placement and movement are often tightly choreographed, with little left to chance. Uncommon camera positioning, extensive camera movement suggestive of inner realities, the use of slow motion, or superimposed images might be used if it explicates an interior feeling, gives an artful perspective on the action, or is simply visually spellbinding.

- *Certain subject matter* readily lends itself to the expressionistic style. *Horror, suspense, musical, and romantic films* usually attempt to touch deeply into subjectively emotional issues of fear, joy, and sensuality and are natural subjects for the expressionist to play upon. For *What Dreams May Come* (1998), a film fancifully depicting life after death, director Vincent Ward was challenged to graphically portray a world beyond: "I wanted to evoke a sense of a nineteenth-century painting, because at that time most people still believed in the after life and the notion of Paradise, so that's what we mainly referred to." The result came in some spectacular scenes that vividly brought to mind the work of the French Impressionists. The later movies of the Italian director Federico Fellini, such movies as *Juliet of the Spirits* (1965), *Roma* (1971), and *City of Women* (1981), are exercises in the deliberate exaggeration of image, acting, and story, conveying a perspective on human folly that had never before been shown in such delicious visual manner **(5–13)**.

A category of expressionist filmmaking—*film noir*—has been influential from the early years of moviemaking. This dark thematic and visual style grew out of the German tradition and then the low-budget films of old Hollywood. Visually, these movies featured high contrast black-and-white film stock to outline the hard edges of their often fatalistic subject matter. The genre became especially popular in the 1940s and 1950s, a time when cynicism and hard-boiled attitudes were the underside of Hollywood's more idealized renditions of American life. Wet empty streets of a city's waterfront at night were more than just atmosphere, but the visual environment representing the oppressive and threatening world of the hero. The genre lives on in films such as *L.A. Confidential* (1997), with stories of people caught in the hell of mean streets of large cities, although a carefully selected palette of subdued color usually replaces black-and-white film stock.

Of course, any subject can be powerfully captured in either a realistic or expressionistic mode. In fact, excitement is usually ignited when a director will do the unexpected and go "against the rules" of either expressionism or realism. For example, in the investigative documentary about a falsely convicted police killer, we would normally expect a flatly realistic style to tell the facts. But when Errol Morris made *Thin Blue Line* (1989), he chose a dramatically expressionistic style. The theatrical lighting, re-created events, moody red and blue filters, camera angles that slightly disoriented normal ways of watching factual stories—all were very effective in giving the issue of

5–13 *The Navigator* Because of the nature of the film's subject, New Zealand director Vincent Ward chose to shoot *The Navigator* (1988) in an expressionistic manner. The story involves a fourteenth-century boy living in a medieval English village who has the super-natural power to help his people escape the plague by burrowing through the earth's core and finding refuge in the twentieth century. This inventive time-travel movie could best be realized by adopting a visual style in the disorienting dreamlike imagery, playing on the viewer's fascination for dark fantasies.   (Circle Films)

mistaken justice a powerful impact. On the other hand, instead of shooting in the exaggerated expressionism that has become a hallmark of horror films, John McNaughton directed *Henry: Portrait of a Serial Killer* (1986) in a realistic mode, choosing a grainy look, with the camera recording actions rather than interpreting emotions. The choice gave this honest film its brutal force—and its X rating. In general, when expectations about not only the content of a film but even its visual style are not satisfied, audiences often show their discontent by staying away.

The Middle Way

"The trick is to conceal the magician's hand. When you go to hear a great musician play an instrument, if you feel him working hard, it's not right. It should feel like breathing. To get the movie to feel like it's as easy as we breathe, that's the trick."

Director Stanley Donen
(*Singin' in the Rain*, 1952)

Many directors have no pronounced stylistic commitment. Traditionally, mainstream movies from Hollywood have been most concerned with putting the story first and subduing more radical or flamboyant directing styles **(5–14)**. The product that the movie industry sells, the prevailing wisdom asserts, must be one that the customer wants to buy. Despite radical visual styles that continually show up, most people still go to the movies to see a good story with their favorite actors, not a

5–14 *love jones* Most commercial Hollywood films with contemporary stories call for a visual film style that is neither starkly graphic nor excessively flamboyant, thereby drawing attention away from interest in the storyline and its characters. This is especially true in romantic comedy. For *love jones* (1997) with Nia Long and Larenz Tate, director/writer Theodore Witcher shot his story in an unobtrusive visual mode that properly focused on the ups and downs of a love relationship. (New Line Cinema)

director showing off technique. Therefore, the basic tenet of traditional studio fare has been for the director's hand to be invisible on the screen.

Traditionally, *clarity of story through image* is the first directorial goal. Rather than delivering a personal artistic statement, much of mainstream moviemaking has always seen the director's role as, first and last, a good storyteller. Over the years, standard procedures have evolved and been established by the artists, technicians, and craftpersons in the movie industry. Industry handbooks describe the orthodox way to produce the needed visual results. These practices have shaped the taste in movies of the general audience. The director's work, in this credo, is to keep the forward motion of the story as primary, submerging the possible temptation for either extremely gaudy or overly realistic camerawork, offbeat acting, disjointed editing, or a highly experimental sound track. But even a self-effacing directing attitude is not easily realized. The intent of the photography and the story action must blend into an easily comprehensible whole.

Even the directors recognized as most stylistically distinctive have benefited from the straightforward methods hammered out through years of practice in the industry. Akira Kurosawa (*Hidden Fortress,* 1958), the Japanese director whose brilliantly photographed movies went on to influence moviemaking around the world, conceded that he used the solid cinematic standards of mainline Hollywood as a training ground:

> *Western dramas have been filmed over and over again for a long time, have been kneaded, pounded and polished, and in the process have evolved a kind of "grammar" of cinema. And I have learned that grammar.*

In the recent past, however, the orthodox grammar and accepted style of Hollywood studio films has mutated in countless ways. A rising trend has been toward more flamboyant visual styles that take precedence over traditional emphasis on story coherence and clarity. Many reasons could be cited for this change—the influence of MTV's flashy camera and editing techniques that put style over substance, the thoughtlessness of video games, advertising's bombardment of kinetic images to sell products. Whatever the case, the directors most in demand today are not necessarily those who clearly lay out a narrative with intelligence and flair, but those who can overwhelm their audience with any style that sends them from theaters dazed by visual and audio input. The visual assault of *Mortal Kombat* (1995) is being imitated by directors with little talent for creating and sustaining a coherent storyline. *Tomb Raider* (2000) and *Final Fantasy* (2001) are designed with the hope that superior animation can make up for a lack of storyline. That style goes beyond the aesthetic considerations of realism or expressionism and into the realm of pure sense stimulation.

The combination of expressionism and realism can often produce a singularly sensitive and accomplished film. In the Italian film *Lamerica* (1996), director Gianni Amelio went to Albania to shoot on location in a country so economically and spiritually ruined by decades of cruel dictatorship that the land and people photographed seem from another world. The director tells the story of two Italians who go to Albania to take economic advantage of the plight of a people set loose after years of absolute control, fighting for survival in a ravished land. One of the Italians (Enrico Lo Verso) is drawn into the barren countryside where he is progressively stripped of his small wealth, his arrogant values, and even his identity. Although shot in stark locations that shock the viewer with the grim reality of people who have never before been in front of a movie camera (reminiscent of earlier Italian neo-realist filmmakers), the movie is elegantly photographed in sharply defined color and smoothly choreographed camera movement. The final scenes are especially striking as an overloaded refugee ship sets sail for Italy with the once arrogant protagonist aboard, jammed together with a thousand other stunned bodies. The final images are delicate and sensitive portraits of men, women, and children who have known nothing but hardship, yet retain a resonance of dignity. Amelio's method of taking on his subject blends realism and expressionism, but it is hard to label it the middle ground, if that implies mediocrity. The director uses elements of both attitudes to create this small masterpiece.

RESUMES OF CURRENT DIRECTORS

"I know I shouldn't say this, but if you surround a first-time director with a great director of photography, editor, production designer, and first a.d., almost anyone can make a film."

Dale Pollack, head of A&M Films

There is no uniform preparation for becoming a motion picture director. The ranks of the profession are comprised of people from many backgrounds. The odd variety of personal and acquired talents demanded of a director assures that there is no single training ground. Director Joel Schumacher (*8 mm*, 1999), for example, began working in film as a costume designer. What directors have in common is an overwhelming desire to make films.

- Although formal training programs for a few select apprenticeships are available through the Director's Guild and the American Film Institute, the numbers coming out of the organizations qualified as second assistant directors are small. Furthermore, the road up through the ranks to full directorship is by no means then guaranteed. The middle echelons of film production demand nuts and bolts logistical skills; however, this hands-on expertise can be seen as a drawback by those with the power to hire directors. There is a tendency to label some people as only competent technicians, and therefore not capable of the artistic creativity needed to direct. The road to becoming a film director is filled with overcoming obstacles such as this.

- *University film programs* have been a starting point for some directors **(5–15)**. Typically, these persons have gained reputations for directing after having entered small festivals with short movies made at film school. This initial success can sometimes lead to opportunities to direct feature-length, low-budget movies that are independently financed. With these credentials—and if the body of one's work looks smart and thoroughly professional—some producers are inclined to give the new director a chance. Francis Ford Coppola took a Master of Fine Arts at UCLA film school and then worked for the king of low-budget features: Roger Corman. Martin Scorsese went to NYU film school,

5–15   Francis Ford Coppola   Francis Ford Coppola (*Apocalypse Now*, 1979) was one of the first of a new breed of directors whose background was shaped in the cinema studies programs of American universities in the 1960s and 1970s. They infused a new energy into what was becoming an inbred profession. Ironically, this photo still of Coppola and Dennis Hopper comes from a film made by Elinore Coppola, his wife, for the documentary *Hearts of Darkness: A Filmmaker's Apocalypse* (1991), a fascinating chronicle of the production team filming in the Philippines.   (Triton Pictures)

stayed on as an instructor, and scraped together enough money to shoot his first movie before also hooking up with Corman. George Lucas attended film school at USC, then gained praise for a short science fiction film: *Electronic Labyrinth: THX 1138:4EB* (1967). John Carpenter (*Halloween*, 1978), Steven Soderberg (*sex, lies, and videotape*, 1989), John Singleton (*Boyz 'n the Hood*, 1991), and others have had similar backgrounds, either gaining experience in film school or working first in small independent movie productions.

- *Television* is a ready source of training for feature films. The amount of work available in TV affords continuous opportunities to refine directing skills. Edward Zwick (*Glory*, 1989) was a regular director on the TV series "thirtysomething," and Terry Hughes (*The Butcher's Wife*, 1991) did episodes of "The Golden Girls." Many directors have graduated from TV commercials: Tony Scott (*Top Gun*, 1986); Ridley Scott (*Thelma and Louise*, 1991); Alan Parker (*Evita*, 1996); Adrian Lyne (*Flashdance*, 1983); Hugh Hudson (*I Dreamed of Africa*, 2000), and others. Howard Zieff (*The Dream Team*, 1989) says of his strategy in this work, "I never wanted to do commercials where people pointed at a product, my goal was to do little movies." Music-video has become an increasingly rich training ground for movie directors. Rap-video director Tamera Davis made her first feature with *Gun Crazy* (1992) before going on to make *Billy Madison* (1995). Other directors with music video backgrounds include Michael Bay (*The Rock*, 1996), F. Gary Gray (*Set It Off*, 1996), and David Fincher (*The Game*, 1997).

- *Actors* often make the transition to directing quite naturally. By profession, every actor is alert to nuances of story interpretation, a basic groundwork of directing. In addition, major actors often have enough clout in the industry to get what they want from producers and studios. Famous actors have always been drawn to directing, from Charlie Chaplin, Eric von Stroheim, and Buster Keaton in the 1920s to the present. The list of actors who have directed significant films is long, including: Bob Fosse (*Lenny*, 1974), John Cassavetes (*Woman under the Influence*, 1974); Woody Allen (*Husbands and Wives*, 1992); Barbra Striesand (*The Prince of Tides*, 1991); Clint Eastwood (*The Bridges of Madison County*, 1995); Robert Redford (*The Legend of Bagger Vance*, 2000); Rob Reiner (*Misery*, 1990); Danny DeVito (*Hoffa*, 1992); Richard Attenborough (*Shadowlands*, 1993); Albert Brooks (*Mother*, 1996); Sean Penn (*The Crossing Guard*, 1995); Penny Marshall (*Awakenings*, 1990); Gary Oldman (*Nil by Mouth*, 1998); Kenneth Branagh (*Hamlet*, 1996); Tim Robbins (*Dead Man Walking*, 1995); Robert DeNiro (*A Bronx Tale*, 1993); Forest Whitaker (*Waiting to Exhale*, 1995); Tom Hanks (*That Thing You Do*, 1996); Anthony Hopkins (*August*, 1996); Steve Buscemi (*Trees Lounge*, 1996); Robert Duvall (*The Apostle*, 1997); Tim Roth (*The War Zone*, 1999); Diane Keaton (*Hanging Up*, 1999); Anjelica Huston (*Agnes Brown*, 1999); Edward Norton (*Keeping the Faith*, 2000); and, of course, Orson Welles.

- Some *editors* and *cinematographers* have been tempted to try directing. Their critical involvement with artistic decision making in film gives them rare insight. The close communication of both professions with the director can make the transition tempting. George Lucas' first work in film was as an editor's assistant. Robert Wise (*West Side Story,* 1961), David Lean (*Doctor Zhivago,* 1965), and Hal Ashby (*Coming Home,* 1978) were established editors before becoming very successful directors. Unlike editors whose talents depend on their ability to make a coherent story out of raw visual material, a cinematographer's strength seems to be in capturing image and mood. Although a few directors of photography, such as Jan DeBont (*Speed 2,* 1997), have had great commercial success as movie directors, major cinematographers such as Haskell Wexler (*Medium Cool,* 1969), William Fraker (*Monte Walsh,* 1970), John Alonzo (*FM,* 1978), Freddie Francis (*Trog,* 1970), Mikael Saloman (*A Far Off Place,* 1993), Philippe Rousselot (*The Serpent's Kiss,* 1997), and Januz Kaminski (*Lost Souls,* 2000) have not had consistent good fortune as directors.

- *Writing professionals* with other specialties within the film community have moved into directing. Writers often feel qualified to either translate other literary work to the screen or to best bring their own. In the past, Preston Sturges (*Sullivan's Travels,* 1941), John Huston (*The Maltese Falcon,* 1941), and Robert Rossen (*The Hustler,* 1961) had worked for years in the studio system as writers. More recently, Buck Henry (*Heaven Can Wait,* 1978), Lewis John Carlino (*The Great Santini,* 1979), Lawrence Kasdan (*The Accidental Tourist,* 1988), Mary Agnes Donoghue (*Paradise,* 1991), Robert Towne (*Pre,* 1996), Nora Ephron (*You've Got Mail,* 1998), and Hampton Fancher (*Minus Man,* 1999) have made the transition from writing to directing.

THE IMPACT OF INTERNATIONAL DIRECTORS

Most moviegoers in the United States see "American" movies exclusively. Movies from foreign countries with language in subtitles represented less than 1 percent of U.S. box office revenue in the last decade. For many people, films from non-English-speaking countries are outside of their experience, or even interest. As modern mass media becomes more "Americanized," narrow ethnocentric attitudes in this country may seem normal for a majority of the audience. Because of its increasing control of media content by entertainment producers, the United States rightfully has been accused of cultural imperialism as it saturates the world with images mirroring itself. In terms of all-time worldwide revenues, the first non-English speaking film (*Life Is Beautiful,* 1998) comes in at 70 on the list. Given the universal acceptance of American movies, however, it is easy to see why the average U.S. moviegoer might have little interest in films from other places. Many people cannot keep up with the overabundance of titles that Hollywood produces, so why bother studying the seemingly obscure work of directors from unfamiliar places?

Many arguments can be given, and some are obvious. We live increasingly in a global society. The neatly dotted lines and colors that separate countries on maps no longer work, if they ever did. By passing up films from other countries, we cut ourselves off from the opportunity to enjoy the great artistic heritage of very rich and diverse cultures. Few people want to be labeled as insular: Not many would shun as "foreign" Paris clothes fashions, Italian shoes, Brazilian music, Danish furniture, Mexican, Chinese, or Greek food. Yet many American moviegoers show themselves as closed-minded and culturally exclusive in their aversion to films from other countries. It is true that language differences pose a problem—but only until one gets used to reading subtitles, a surprisingly easy transition. But motion pictures is a medium that communicates so strongly in images that the value and pleasures of a movie often need no translation. Whatever language hurdle that must be made is a small price for the many rewards that wait in the best films from international directors.

Consideration of the work of directors from countries other than the United States is a complex journey. The Hollywood movie industry, unlike the general public, has had a high degree of interest in international directors. In addition, American film directors themselves have closely watched and admired leading directors regardless of national origin. The nature of moviemaking is truly international. Indeed, given the fluidity of cultural exchanges today, it is often impossible to clearly label the national origin of any individual movie. Just as Nike shoes might be called an American company residing in Eugene, Oregon, it is hard to identify their product so confidently when it is manufactured in China or Indonesia, with material from places unknown. So, too, with the movie industry today. The film business draws its resources—financing, technical equipment, skilled working professionals, support industries—from many countries. Leading the list are directors.

The situation of American directors has been described in other parts of this book. Generally speaking, these men and women fall into two categories: 1) those directors working in the mainstream of the studio production system with the financial benefits that come with it, and 2) directors making independent movies of various descriptions that generally allow them more personal freedom and artistic expression.

International directors are inheritors of their special national backgrounds. Movies are so intertwined with the cultures in which they are inspired and made that it is important to consider the artistic and economic environments in which they are made. The term "international" director—an appropriate label given the current negative connotation of the word "foreign"—may be difficult to define in the present-day scheme of things. Two points help explain the situation:

- Many *international directors* make films primarily financed and filmed in their native lands, outside the United States. Every industrial country has motion picture production capabilities and almost all of them have actively made films—*Variety International Film Guide* describes the year's film production in sixty-one countries. Although American film production and distribution since the 1920s has tended to dominate most world markets, movie industries in other countries have flourished at various times. For a multitude of reasons, a few countries have not had strong traditions in motion picture production, but directors from almost every culture have contributed to the wealth of films that make up the body of cinematic art. The movies reflect both the cultural tastes of the countries in which they are produced and the personal aesthetics of the directors. These filmmakers are necessarily influenced by the practical limitations of their modest budgets—by Hollywood standards—and limited distribution possibilities. A Swedish film has to "win" recognition; an American film can buy it. Some of these directors—Federico Fellini and Vittorio DeSica (Italy), Satyajit Ray (India), Claude Chabrol (France), Akira Kurosawa (Japan), among others—did gain worldwide reputations despite the fact that they made movies without the full clout of Hollywood film marketing. Other filmmakers of lesser reputation find satisfaction simply in the privilege of directing films in their native lands.

- Some international directors move with great freedom between two systems: Hollywood and their native country **(5–16)**. It was once easy to label directors as "foreign" or American. But with the merging of worldwide talent, crosscultural tastes, and transoceanic financing, such boundaries get blurred. In the past, many of the fine international directors worked in Hollywood movies for various lengths of time—Germany's Fritz Lang, England's David Lean, Austria's Billy Wilder, France's Rene Clair, Hungary's Michael Curtiz, Italy's Michelangelo Antonioni, and many others. In more recent times, many international directors first learned and practiced their trade at home, then moved to Hollywood, working in studio filmmaking exclusively. Other directors feel free to work on various kinds of movie projects, both in their native land and through the American system, as the film opportunities present themselves. Among these are Milos Foreman (Czechoslovakia); Peter Weir, Baz Lurhmann, and Bruce Beresford (Australia); Lasse Hallstrom (Sweden); Paul Verhoeven (Holland); John Boorman, Ridley Scott, and Michael Apted (England); Hector Barbenco (Brazil); Peter Jackson and Lee Tamahori (New Zealand); Roman Polanski (Poland); Andrei Konchlovsky (Russia); Wim Wenders and Volker Schlondorff (Germany); Jackie Chan (Hong Kong); Constantin Costa-Gavras (France); Alphonso Arua (Mexico); Norman Jewison, Arthur Hiller, and David Cronenberg (Canada); and others too numerous to list. As the world shrinks culturally and electronically, crossing borders to work in film becomes less relevant.

5–16 Roman Polanski Few directors have had such success making movies in both the USA and Europe as Roman Polanski (seen here on the set of *Death And The Maiden*, 1994). Trained at the Polish Film School in the very early years of the cold war, his formal cinema education in directing, camerawork, acting, and lighting proved helpful in every aspect of his subsequent film work. After gaining recognition as a cutting-edge director in Europe, Polanski hit his stride in Hollywood with such films as *Chinatown* (1974). Legal problems sent him back to France in the 1970s where he has continued to make provocative films. (Fine Line Features)

Some Distinguishing Qualities of Foreign Directors

"Before Ingmar Bergman, film was mostly about what could be seen and depicted in the external world. Very little of important cinema was psychological: It was wars, chases, situation comedy. Bergman was the first filmmaker to build a whole oeuvre through the exploration of the internal world—to make visible the invisible drama of self."

Film critic John Lahr

It is difficult to generalize about international directors; simply put, they come from such different geographic locations with immensely varying ethical values, sexual customs, religions, political systems, and national histories. One way to approach the subject is by way of a negative definition. The one common thing that all have shared, at least at the start of their careers, is that they worked *outside* of the Hollywood studio system. Despite the well-known benefits of fame and fortune that are associated with mainstream American productions, the limitations of the industry on a director are considerable. The demands of the accepted Hollywood aesthetic can be inhibiting. The overriding consideration that the Hollywood-produced movie be commercially successful usually translates to mean catering to the demanding tastes of the widest possible audience. By the time they reach theaters, many Hollywood movies are often not so much the artistic statement of a single director, but the composite judgment of a large circle of corporate decision makers. In contrast, the work of the better international directors has been distinguished by its freedom from the sometimes subtle, but always firmly understood, commercial pressures and expectations quite common in the American film industry. Many international directors would claim that they have made films with one great advantage: They have been free to make movies outside of the Hollywood system.

The following points are areas that distinguish international directors for American audiences. Some of the most unorthodox aspects of their work in films is what attracts audiences who are excited about originality and innovation in movies. Not all of these characteristics are exclusive to foreign directors. Independent American directors take many of the same approaches to cinema because they too work outside of the mainstream. But working in movies outside of the United States, it must be conceded, is a category apart. Naturally, these are very general observations about the work of international directors. When speaking of worldwide film production, the range of films is enormous, and there is a tremendous amount of cross-cultural influence. But some differences are noteworthy.

Unusual Filmmaking Conditions.   Each director's vision is shaped by the economic and social system under which he or she is working. International directors are no different in this way. Because very large budgets are relatively rare in other countries, the positive side of the situation is that more personal, smaller budget films can be made, relatively free from the demand of returning huge profits. This working atmosphere broadens the aesthetic choices at every level, from thematic emphasis to shot selection. As a result, a great number of directors have had a chance to pursue their art in more experimental or individual styles.

To compete with the overwhelming advantage of the American film industry, in the past many other governments subsidized a portion of the production costs in some form of a *national film institute*. These formal schools of filmmaking proved to be a rich source of talent in some countries. National film schools in Sweden, Poland, Russia, Hungary, the Netherlands, and elsewhere were a ready training base for aspiring filmmakers. With government sponsorship, however, comes a certain bureaucracy, not commonly thought of as friendly to the artistic spirit. But, ironically, even the clumsiest systems sometimes worked to the advantage of its budding directors. When a young director could wend his or her way through the system, the chance to make a well-produced small movie was quite possible. Even directors from repressive Eastern European countries during the Cold War years found that, although they could not shoot movies directly critical of the system, they were quite free to use very innovative structural and photographic approaches to their work. In doing so, they often gained world recognition as skilled filmmakers and were admired by American directors working in a seemingly freer, yet in some ways, artistically more limiting system.

But times have changed. An instructive model can be seen in the Czech Republic. During the years of Communist rule in Czechoslovakia, the state-subsidized film industry was very active—with its large Barrandov Studio complex in Prague employing thousands and producing scores of small films each year, many of which gained international reputations for their special sensitivity. The state film school, FAMU, was the center for a group of daring directors whose politically subversive films in the 1960s were christened the "Czech New Wave." Vera Chytilova (*Daisies*, 1966); Jaromil Jires (*The Joke*, 1968); Elmar Klos and Jan Kadar (*The Shop on Main Street*, 1965); Milos Forman (*Fireman's Ball*, 1967); and Jiri Menzel (*Closely Watched Trains*, 1966) are some of the Czech directors who gained international attention before the Soviet crackdown in 1968. In the 1990s, with the radical changes in the political and economic system, Barrandov Studio must now compete with big-budget American films that flood the Eastern European theatrical market. The result is that today, without government sponsorship, a once-vibrant studio makes fewer than ten locally produced films a year and is leased to foreign studios wanting to shoot in the country. The studio facilities have begun to flourish from this activity, with films such as Luc Besson's *Joan of Arc* (1999), but young Czech directors there have much less opportunity to work independently in the film medium despite the liberation from a politically oppressive regime.

Other European production facilities have found new life as a site for shooting well-budgeted Hollywood movies. These studios include Pinewood, Shepperton, Ealing, and Leavesden (Britain); Ardmore (Ireland); Cinecitta (Italy); Eclair (France); and Bavarian (Germany). The influx of American capital has reestablished the financial stability of these studios and allowed for the relative health of international film production. It is in the face of this reality that international directors must find their place.

Diverse and Unexpected Storylines.   Films from other cultures have different ways of interpreting life and the events that fill it. Even though the United States prides itself on its cultural diversity, at the same time there is an unwarranted assump-

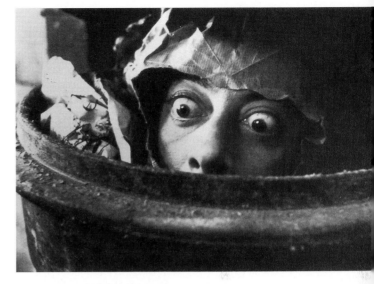

5–17 *Delicatessen*   Movies with surreal themes have a history in European films dating back to Luis Bunuel's *Un Chien Andalou* (1928). In *Delicatessen* (1991), co-directed by Jean-Marie Jeunet and Marc Caro, the story is told of the bizarre people living in rooms above a butcher shop stocked with meat derived from the tenants in the building. This black comedy achieves humor by the extreme insanity of its premise and its unique application of film sound.   (Miramax Films)

tion that Americans have shared values and common tastes. When one encounters cultural mores that are unsettling for film audiences, a kind of unspoken agreement seems to have been broken. International directors are not locked into the same story proscriptions that often define Hollywood directors' work **(5–17)**. For example, an unusual insight into traditional Japanese folklore is presented in *The Ballad of Narayama* (1983) by Shohei Imamura. The story, set in the nineteenth century, deals with the strange customs surrounding community, family life, and death in an isolated mountain village. Although their world is alien by today's standard, the basic human issues of sex, survival, loyalty, and cultural continuity are presented in such an unfamiliar setting that the film is able to give rare and shocking insight into the subjects. A more current film of the director, *The Eel* (1997), takes on another equally unpopular subject in a skillfully told story—that of a man trying to start a new life after serving a prison term for murdering his wife, presenting the issues with compassion and even some humor.

Quite naturally, foreign directors give an expanded perspective of the human experience and one that can offend American sensibilities. They sometimes present an inside picture of the culture that does not welcome the viewer but rather challenges, an attitude not normally experienced through the prism of Hollywood's camera. In the Israeli movie *Kadosh* (2000), director Amos Gitai explores the world of Jerusalem's ultra orthodox Jewish quarter through the experience of a husband and wife who are deeply in love but are pressured to separate by a rabbi when he concludes that they cannot have a child. The movie is meticulously developed both in its lingering visual style and its close attention to cultural detail. Contemporary American taste in movies immediately limits the commercial horizons of this revealing film about women's rights. In a seemingly more popular vein, English director Danny Boyle's *Trainspotting* (1996) shows the violent lives of young heroin addicts in Edinburgh. At first, the film seems to take a neutral and even dark stance toward what is generally treated as socially condemned behavior. The cumulative effect of the film certainly presents the grim reality of this desperate drug culture, but along the way there are many moments of vibrant humor and genuine empathy. The film message is not noticeably underlined. It is telling that for the U.S. release, the American censors cut out a scene of a young girl enjoying having sex, but let pass the young boy's shooting up drugs. The screen treatment of some subjects by international directors allows for more freedom to experiment.

Autobiographical and Other Personal Themes. Films that present a deeply subjective vision of the director's world are recurrent in international cinema. Although American directors at times clearly use events from their past for dramatic purpose, the work of foreign directors is often very plainly autobiographical, in the tradition of prose works. Just as many novelists are free to delve into very personal histories, many film directors working outside the mainstream of Hollywood have used cinema to convey their innermost feelings. Because quite often the international director is also the writer of the film, a tightly coherent vision is more easily maintained. There is no gap between the writer's imagination on paper and the director's execution on the screen. For instance, Ingmar Bergman in *Through a Glass Darkly* (1961), *Winter Light* (1961), and *The Silence* (1963) tells of the futile struggle to find answers in religion and even in human relationships. A sense of alienation permeates the thinking of Bergman himself, which is dramatized again and again in his films at this stage of his career. One cannot see Bergman's films without entering into his personal striving for meaning in life. After having directed several more starkly powerful but abstract films on the subject, Bergman turned more frankly autobiographical in *Fanny and Alexander* (1983), a film that details the experience of two children in a tempestuous Swedish family life that roughly parallels his own experience with his religiously strict father, a clergyman. Many of Bergman's films have a level of visual intimacy and intellectual argument that limits their mass appeal, but that once experienced cannot be easily forgotten.

The autobiographical movie was given a most audacious boost with Federico Fellini's *8 1/2* (1963), a surrealistic plunge into the real and imagined life of a film director torn by the pressures of a demanding wife, capricious mistress, vicious critics, incompetent doctors, fickle public, and a clownish protagonist, Guido. "I am Guido," Fellini has said, and the image of him at the end of the film holding hands with all of its characters in a circle dance sums up Fellini's comic and poignant view of life. Such movies display a playful self-indulgence not readily available to American directors working in the studio system.

Experimental Visual Technique. Traditionally, international directors have been relatively free to play with a variety of cinematic styles, thereby giving fresh insight into the nature of the art. Because movies, in Europe especially, grew up in a tradition that emphasized film as an experimentally beguiling extension of the other visual and plastic arts, testing out the kinetic possibilities of the new medium was to be expected. In the 1920s, Russian Dziga Vertov (*The Man with a Movie Camera*, 1929) explored the camera's power to take hold of an audience and reshape the limits of their visual reality through the use of split screen effects, different camera speeds, superimposed images, prismatic lensing, and shock editing styles. In Germany, Fritz Lang's *Metropolis* (1927) overpowered audiences with futuristic images of an industrial hell and premonitions of the Nazi state to come, as his cameras followed the intricate choreography of hundreds of faceless workers.

Today, the tradition of experimentation is carried on by others. Danish director Lars von Trier designed *Zentropa* (1991), a fantasy of a young man's train journey after the defeat of the Nazis in which allusions are made about the collective guilt of all on the train as it moves into the night. A subconscious reality is suggested by the use of extensive traveling matte shots that enhanced a dream-like state, and its black-and-white photography splits its image at times with selected color effects. Von Trier continually indulges in experimental film techniques in *The Kingdom* (1994), *Breaking the Waves* (1996), and *Dancer in the Dark* (2000) with tinted pictures to indicate varying sections of the story and 360 degree traveling shots to create a sense of the world set free from it moorings. International directors, not limited by exaggerated commercial demands, often take artistic chances that are not practically available to others. Mainstream directors are sometimes quick to integrate styles that are effective, but it is important to acknowledge the original sources.

Unorthodox Pacing and Rhythms.   The visual and emotional experience that many international directors achieve in their movies is often disconcerting to American audiences because of the *tempo* at which a story is presented. Their rhythms have unfamiliar beats. The photography and editing often create an unexpected flow of images, resulting in the viewer being caught up in an unusual way of *experiencing* films. For example, Soviet Sergei Eisenstein's *The Battleship Potemkin* (1925) is a mesmerizing film that gains its strong beauty from the staccato pace of its cutting. The viewer is swept along in an unrelenting and spectacular series of shots. At the time—and even today—the film was visually breathtaking. On the other hand, Hungarian Miklos Jancso, in *Winter Wind* (1969) and his other movies, uses very few cuts, so that his films are consistently strung together with three- to four-minute shots of amazing fluidity and tempo. His movies often dealt with revolution, and the camera itself put the world in a constant state of flux. French director Alain Cavalier's *Therese* (1986) created a slow contemplative pace in keeping with its subject matter—the saintly life of a cloistered nun. The viewer, by means of minimal camera movement and extended shot duration, is naturally drawn into the unfamiliar and remarkable life of a woman who silently gives each moment to her belief in Christ.

Variety in editing styles creates numerous interesting ways in which a story can be told. Jaco van Dormael's *Toto Le Heros* (1991) tells its story of an old man's depressing life in a stream of *crosscuts* that go beyond how the storytelling device of the flashback is normally used. The film weaves past to present so tightly that we gain tremendous insight into the mind and heart of a man who has continually lived with and never forgotten the dreams and tragedies of his childhood; their emotional consequences are played out in his adult years. One reward of seeing the film is that it opens the student of film to new dimensions for creative editing.

Radical Political and Social Perspectives. Ingrained in the American heritage have been restrictive attitudes regarding what was acceptable politically and socially in Hollywood films. The fear struck into the hearts of Hollywood filmmakers during the House Un-American Activities Committee investigations in the 1940s and the resulting Blacklisting in the 1950s inhibited studios from seriously questioning the accepted doctrine of established political beliefs. But what was controversial in the United States became quite legitimate fare in some other countries. Gillo Pontecorvo directed the starkly authentic looking *The Battle Of Algiers* (1965), giving the untold and unpopular native Algerian side of the struggle to free itself from France. The movie became a rallying call for oppressed groups wherever it was seen. When French director Constantin Costa-Gavras dramatized the rightwing take over (backed by American foreign policy) by the generals in Greece in the movie *Z* (1968), the bold revelations of the crimes detailed in that true story were very instrumental in gaining the worldwide support that brought back democracy within a decade. Greek director Theodor Angelopoulos (*Landscape in the Mist*, 1985) has consistently incorporated sympathetic Marxist attitudes into stories of the alienated and dispossessed.

Hollywood movies about social issues that are not geared to have sentimental resolutions are rarely produced for mass consumption. For example, it may not be until we encounter the story of a boy buried in the relentless poverty of the cruel and intricately structured underclass of India in director Mira Nair's *Salaam Bombay* (1988) that we fully realize the narrow perspective of other cultures normally portrayed in Hollywood movies. Her handling of the material gives the audience a profound understanding of the daily human tragedies, and very small pleasures, in the lives of street orphans. New Zealand's Lee Tamahori in *Once Were Warriors* (1994) took on the under-publicized social problem of domestic violence in a fiercely graphic and uncompromised manner that is rarely seen in films here. One cannot go away from the film unaffected.

An Expansive View of Sexuality. A more natural openness toward sexual matters marks the films of many international directors, especially those from Europe **(5–18)**. Free from the inhibiting strains in the United States that tend to both heat up and inhibit any objective discussion of sexuality, Europe's frank acceptance of sexual relations as a normal human experience allows for its dramatic possibilities to be more easily integrated into films. Examples are too numerous to mention, but Vilgot Sjoman's *I Am Curious Yellow* (1968) was a landmark film in that it brought an end to court-condoned censorship in the United States. Italian Bernardo Bertolucci directed *Last Tango in Paris* (1973), a mature exploration about the unforgiving sexual distance between a middle-aged man and a young woman. In a more outrageous vein, the confrontational movies of Pier Paolo Pasolini (*Salo*, 1975) introduced darker images of sexual fantasies. Since then, American filmmakers and their studios have struggled with their historically unresolved social, personal, and commercial attitudes concerning sex. Bertrand Blier (*Get out Your Handkerchiefs*, 1978) has made a series of films that deal with the tragicomic sides of sexual relationships. *In the Realm of the Senses* (1976) by Nagisa Oshima was first seized by U.S. customs for its graphic depiction of

5–18   *Ma Vie en Rose*   The subject of sex has always thrown up a distinctive set of contradictory reactions in the United States, from titillation to denial. In contrast, many Europeans see themselves having a more balanced and mature attitude. In Alain Berliner's *Ma Vie en Rose* (1997), a 7-year-old boy, Ludovic (Georges du Fresne), tells his parents that he wants to be a girl. Instead of dealing with the subject as comedy, the director shows how this innocent desire brings down anger then hostility from those around him. The serious and sympathetic story of childhood sexual conflict would be difficult to produce here.
(Sony Pictures Classics)

a man and woman fatally transfixed by their passion for each other. Neil Jordan's sensational film *The Crying Game* (1992) from England surprised audiences with a plausible love relationship between two men. *The Lover* (1992), from the semiautobiographical novel by Marguerite Duras and beautifully shot by French director Jean-Jacques Annaud, tells of a young girl's affair with an older Chinese man in Indochina. The English movie *Damage* (1992) by French director Louis Malle takes up a similar situation; however, a triangle develops that tragically pits father against son. More recently, French filmmaker Catherine Breillat's *Romance* (1999) tells of a young woman discovering herself through increasingly exotic forms of sex. The director comments, "When you elevate sexuality above the bestial plain to a truly human plain, then it's magnificent." Many American films certainly include sexual themes and graphic scenes. However, the subtle sexual differences in attitude based on cultural traditions, although hard to define absolutely, are often evident when you see them on the screen.

The Introduction of Talent Not Otherwise Exposed.   Part of the joy of movies is the discovery of great performances of actors from other cultures. With the range of the entire world to draw upon, international directors have introduced hundreds of outstanding actors that have made motion pictures incredibly richer. A very partial list of now familiar actors introduced to American audiences in the past forty years includes Gerard Depardieu, Isabelle Huppert, Klaus Maria Brandauer, Dominque Sanda, Giancarlo Giannini, Jeanne Moreau, Max von Sydow, Liv Ullman, Yves Montand, Sonia Braga, Toshiro Mifune, Melina Mercouri, Marcello Mastroianni, Sophia Loren, Bruno Ganz, Hanna Schygulla, Philippe Noiret, Anna Parillaud, Lothaire Bluteau, Catherine Deneuve, Gong Li, and Juliette Binoche. Most of these actors have played in English-language films, but a large body of their best work has been done with directors in their native language.

Great film direction knows no nationality. A director brings to the job both a personal aesthetic and a heritage of values absorbed from his or her culture. But directors also work within the economic realities of the motion picture system in the country that they are making films. The opportunity to direct films, and the very methods of making them, can fluctuate depending on the particular climate of the political system and the dynamics of the country's movie production industry. No two nations have the same conditions. Directors working in the United States have some well-recognized advantages, not the least of which is the potentially huge audience available to them. Directors making films at major Hollywood studios have the luxury of budgets adequate to meet all their needs. But directors from other countries often have a most envied situation: the freedom to make their own films. Through the years, the results often have been astonishing.

AUTEURS WORKING IN AMERICAN MOVIES TODAY

With the demise of the old studio companies, successful directors have not only exercised more artistic freedom but have risen to fill leadership roles left by the tightly controlled production system. Much of the power of directors stems from the fact that when the shooting starts, the money and the reputations of many people in both high and low positions must ride on their judgments. With very rare exceptions, there is no turning back. For this reason, many directors have become important players in every aspect of a film's production, stars in their own right.

In the old days there was a tendency to pigeonhole the talents of directors—some being labeled as having a special sense for visual gags of comedy or the camera flow of a musical. This is also true, to some extent, today. Directors often gain deserved reputations for being especially accomplished with a particular film genre, visual style, or unique storytelling ability. They are then sought out by producers to repeat and build upon their previous films **(5–19)**. In the process, a director will establish a body of work that becomes his or her artistic identity. Naturally, some directors will at times intentionally choose a project that will be very unlike what he or she is known for. Therefore, when Martin Scorsese decided to direct *The Age of Innocence* (1993), an Edith Wharton story of nineteenth-century manners and morals, the subject seemed very out of keeping with the tough contemporary stories of urban males that had been his specialty.

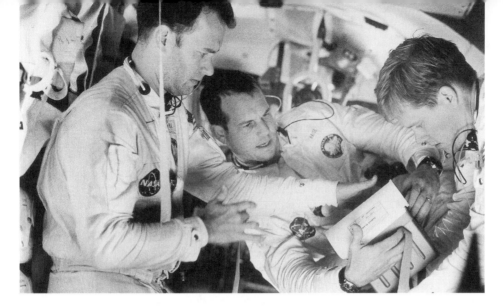

5-19 *Apollo 13* Although many directors specialize in certain film genres, others follow in the path of classic Hollywood directors who were often harder to pigeonhole. Ron Howard is not easy to label because each outing seems to bring a different genre: *Night Shift* (1980) and *Parenthood* (1989), both comedies; *Cocoon* (1985), a nostalgia/fantasy; *Backdraft* (1991), a fiery disaster film; *Willow* (1988), a children's fantasy; *Far and Away* (1992), an epic immigrant/Western; *Apollo 13* (1995), a hi-tech tale of astronauts, and *EDTV* (1999), a satire of our communication age. (Universal Pictures)

It is useful to see how directors are associated with major categories of film. Certainly producers, agents, and other decision makers in the motion picture industry judge and hire directors on their technical strengths and their history of accomplishments with given subjects or in special film styles. Although almost every director could be classified in several ways, the following descriptions offer a way to reference the work of some directors who regularly make movies in Hollywood:

The Hi-Tech/Action Adventurers. No one is valued more today in Hollywood that the director who can take command of an action film loaded with special effects and not only envision the final look of the film on the screen but also wend through the mass of technological production problems inherent to such movies. This category is broad because, today, some degree of special effects can be found in almost every genre, and every director is challenged to have some facility with working with them. But, clearly, certain directors have mastered this craft and become very successful in this often high budget and always complex work. Once directors become known for proficiency in this high-risk filmmaking—by making a total-action film that registers huge box office receipts—the studios go back to them again and again. Extensive experience with special effects is fundamental to their work. Director James Cameron is almost legendary for his knowledge of FX technology and his facility with using it (in college, he majored in Physics). His film projects—*The Terminator* (1984), *Aliens* (1986), *The Abyss* (1989), *Terminator 2: Judgment Day* (1991), *True Lies* (1994), *Titanic* (1997)—have consistently demanded an extremely high ability to integrate developing technology with the traditional rapid and coherent storytelling that marks the best of action/adventure films. He continued his leading edge work with the innovative 12-minute long *Terminator 2 3-D* (1996), a series of action sequences with the original actors that takes the old 3-D technology and upgrades its amazing capacity to put the viewer right inside the screen action. "I make murals, not paintings," says Cameron in defense of his massively budgeted movies. Tony Scott (*Top Gun*, 1986); Ridley Scott (*Alien*, 1979); John McTiernan (*The Last Action Hero*, 1993); Richard Donner (*Lethal Weapon*, 1987); Renny Harlin (*Die Hard 2*, 1990); Andrew Davis (*Under Siege*, 1992); Jan De Bont (*Twister*, 1996); Chuck Russell (*Eraser*, 1996); Martin Campbell (*Goldeneye*, 1996); Jonathan Frakes (*Star Trek: Insurrection*, 1998); Roland Emmerick (*The Patriot*, 2000); Joe Johnston (*Jurassic Park 3*, 2001); and others are directors chosen for their considerable abilities to handle massive high-tech projects. Perhaps Renny Harlin speaks only for himself but the spirit of his mentality sums up how much of the movie industry approaches these films: "I don't want accidents, I want disasters. I don't want dirt, I want filth. I don't want a storm, I want a hurricane. . . . I don't want suspense, I want terror. . . . I don't want humor, I want hysteria. . . ." The stakes are very high for directors of hi-tech/action films. Their budgets are increasingly larger and Hollywood increasingly relies on them to produce the blockbusters of each season. Harlin's expensive *Cutthroat Island* (1996), for example, was a critical and box office disaster. It is much easier to forgive, even oneself, when failures happen on a much smaller scale.

The Social Critics.   A strong line of social criticism is evident throughout the work of some directors. The industry has resisted using movies as a platform for radical social debate, sometimes to avoid the attention of media-hawking politicians, others times with the claim that movies work best as entertainment, not forum for advocacy. But many individual directors through the years have chosen to emphasize the need for change in the pursuit of social fairness and justice. Mervyn LeRoy did this in *I Am a Fugitive from a Chain Gang* (1932) regarding prison conditions. Frank Capra's *Mr. Smith Goes to Washington* (1939) was a patriotic call for governmental integrity and reform, and, later, Stanley Kramer was a strong advocate for racial equality and ethnic justice in *The Defiant One* (1958), *Judgment at Nuremburg* (1961), and *Guess Who's Coming to Dinner* (1967). Sydney Pollack, in such varied films as *They Shoot Horses, Don't They?* (1969), *Three Days of the Condor* (1975), *Absence of Malice* (1981), and *Random Hearts* (1999), sounded various warnings about the power of society, government, and the media to subvert human interchange. Although filmmakers who have made individual films with strong social messages are too numerous to list, the work of Gregory Nava (*El Norte*, 1983), Edward James Olmos (*American Me*, 1992), John Singleton (*Boyz 'n the Hood*, 1991), and Allen and Albert Hughes (*Menace II Society*, 1993) are noteworthy for the moral reactions they have provoked.

Two current directors—Oliver Stone and Spike Lee—have consistently made films that challenge staid societal notions regarding race, militarism, and politics. The powerful work of these directors has challenged the conscience of politicians and the public. The passion of Oliver Stone centers on what he sees as the hypocrisy of the governmental establishment, specifically regarding the catastrophic events of the past

5–20   *Malcom X*   For *Malcom X* (1992), director Spike Lee had to capture the many seemingly contradictory sides of that militant spokesman for a new African-American identity in the 1960s. Lee was greatly aided by Denzel Washington who was convincing as Malcom X, a thoughtful critic of social injustice and a passionate organizer of his people. Spike Lee has consistently made films that deal with this society's most ingrained racial and cultural problems.   (Warner Bros. Pictures)

forty years. *Salvador* (1986); *Platoon* (1986); *Born on the Fourth of July* (1989); *JFK* (1991); *Heaven and Earth* (1993); *Nixon* (1995); and *Any Given Sunday* (1999) all speak loudly of his concern. Spike Lee, in *Do the Right Thing* (1989); *Mo' Better Blues* (1990); *Jungle Fever* (1991); *Malcom X* (1992); *Crooklyn* (1994), *Get on the Bus* (1996); *He Got Game* (1998); and *Summer of Sam* (1999), has shown a passionate interest in telling the urban African-American experience in his uncompromising yet engrossing terms **(5–20)**.

The Masters of Fantasy.   Hollywood has developed a moviemaking strategy that not only creates blockbuster films, but also creates an accompanying merchandising industry that makes millions of dollars. Fantasy movies most easily mold themselves to these ends because of their appeal to young and old. "I love dreams, even when they are nightmares, which is usually the case," said the iconoclastic Luis Bunuel (*Viridiana*, 1961), a most independent Spanish director who spent most of his career outside of the commercial mainstream but whose words might be a credo for directors who test the imagination of audiences. Movies have always drawn a group of directors whose work ranges from the offbeat to the surreal.

Because film can convincingly create any physical location or mental state, the temptation toward the bizarre is inherently present. Directors have often freely used the film medium to express their innermost artistic visions, and the results have seduced audiences into worlds of the wildly inventive and, when done poorly, to places needlessly incomprehensible.

Directors with an affinity for blending childhood dreams, adult nostalgia, robust action, and a bold visual imagination are highly prized. Steven Spielberg (*Close Encounters of the Third Kind*, 1977) and George Lucas (*Star Wars*, 1977) set the trend in motion in the 1970s with their mastery of the technical and business ends of such productions. Their continuing appeal to the child in everyone is undeniable. Today, these directors have moved into commanding positions, with Spielberg and Lucas heading up film entertainment empires. For many years Spielberg has been in a position of drawing a following by attaching his name to films that he produces but does not direct. The immediate attention that his new studio, DreamWorks, gained in both the media and the movie industry grows out of his uncanny sense for making films that stir the childhood fantasies in all of us.

Tim Burton has also built an unfaltering reputation since his first whimsical direction in *Pee Wee's Big Adventure* (1985). Burton has an uncanny knack of taking an absurd story idea, as in *Beetlejuice* (1988), *Edward Scissorshands* (1990), *Mars Attacks* (1996), or even the classic story *Sleepy Hollow* (1999), and drawing the audience into caring about the strangely ridiculous characters that populate his films. Robert Zemeckis (*What Lies Beneath*, 2000) has similar talent, but with a somewhat more traditional observation of narrative story structure. Darker images sometimes imbue Terry Gilliam's highly imaginative work, as seen in *Brazil* (1985) and *The Fisher King* (1991), yet in *Adventures of Baron Munchaussen* (1989) and *Time Bandits* (1981) he can indulge in very light children's fantasies.

The Humorists.   When done well in movies, comedy is a valuable resource to the movie industry and directors of it are in high demand. The genre calls for special skills of not only working with the rarefied consciousness of comics, but it also demands that the director have an acute sense of humor, or at least the ready ability to recognize the possibilities for laughter in a shot or scene. It is an accepted truth that all comedy has to do with timing. Comic rhythms in film come not only from the actors in the spoken word or gesture, but from the director's sense of the dynamic of the scene, especially as it is constructed later in the editing of the film. The director of comedy must both see and foresee the opportunities for a laugh.

The great comedy directors certainly include Mack Sennett's Keystone Kops movies from the silent era, Buster Keaton (*The General*, 1927), and Charlie Chaplin (*The Gold Rush*, 1925). In the golden era of studio production when movie assignments came from the top, many directors tried their hand at comedy with success. George Cukor, for example, found a special affinity for working in comedy, directing Katharine Hepburn in a series of winning comedies such as *Philadelphia Story*, (1949); *Adam's Rib* (1949); and *Pat and Mike* (1952). Humor, like most things, is a matter of taste, and although his movies were juvenile, Jerry Lewis (*The Nutty Professor*, 1963) directed a number of films that were favorites in the 1950s and early 1960s.

Today, the comedy director whose work most typifies the kind of movies Hollywood covets is Ivan Reitman. Some of the movies he has directed include *Meatballs* (1979), *Ghostbusters* (1984), *Twins* (1988), *Kindergarten Cop* (1990), and *Dave* (1993). The high profile cast and liberal use of special effects have established Reitman as a highly prized director and producer. In a longer and more varied comic career, Blake Edwards has ranged from the formula of the six films of the *Pink Panther* series to the playful *Victor/Victoria* (1982). Danny DeVito has proven to be a first-rate director in the dark comedy *The War of the Roses* (1989); John Hughes (*Ferris Bueller's Day Off,* 1986) has often used what he perceives to be adolescent consciousness to frame comic situations; Albert Brooks (*Mother,* 1996) shapes his films to match his odd brand of delayed humor. But even though Michael Ritchie has never been without work as a director, his comic flair can be as cutting as *Smile* (1976), a biting spoof of beauty contests, or as flat as the Chevy Chase movie *Cops and Robbersons* (1994). The work of directors Peter and Bobby Farrelly in *There's Something about Mary* (1998) seems to have found just the right edge of sexual humor for the end of the decade. Director Frank Oz (*Bowfinger,* 1999) has shown the uncanny ability of creating shaping scenes with lunatic behavior into tightly crafted visual jokes.

New talent continually emerges. But Woody Allen has gone on as the neurotic godfather of film humor for the past thirty years. His output matches, on a microscopic scale, the consistency of the large studios in their heyday. Rarely does a year go by without a new Woody Allen offering, each with a slightly different twist on the previous one. In no other genre but comedy could an individual director today make so many films with the assurance of a loyal audience.

The Male Perspective.   For the first eighty years of filmmaking, directors were almost always exclusively men. Movies were filtered through the private tastes and social conditioning of male sensibilities. The Western movie is the classic monument to the definition of maleness. Whereas some men directors did show deep interest in the perspectives of both sexes, many others showed neither understanding of women's issues nor an interest in realistically dramatizing them on the screen. Women were always very useful, however, as sex symbols. Then, too, the reality of the American box office revenues shows that males 14–24 still dominate movie attendance. Hollywood pays attention to their tastes in movie subjects.

In the 1960s and 1970s, director Sam Peckinpah (*The Wild Bunch*, 1969) gave heightened definition to movies of male orientation. His films were shamelessly macho, spilling over with fast action and blunt violence. Peckinpah's camp took no prisoners. The popularity of his films encouraged a more intense focus on visual excitement generated by blatant male aggression and combat. Less accomplished directors added their versions. Two of America's preeminent directors—Francis Ford Coppola (*The Godfather,* 1972) and Martin Scorsese (*Raging Bull,* 1980)—have devoted much of their work to exploring the world of men. They describe the tough societal codes that prevail in male subcultures. In his series of films on the subject, Coppola has shown the Mafia to be deadly but intriguing families that play out male initiation and control rituals. He studied the minds and hearts of other male warriors in *Apocalypse Now* (1979). Scorsese has plunged into similar themes, but has been less

5–21 *Pulp Fiction* Many directors begin making films independently before crossing over into more mainstream filmmaking. Quentin Tarantino gained attention with *Reservoir Dogs* (1992) and solidified his standing in the industry directing the surprising hit movie *Pulp Fiction* (1994). Here over breakfast, two petty criminals (Amanda Plummer and Tim Roth) share their seriously distorted realities and misapplied logic. Two distinguishing features of Tarantino's films are his strong male story perspectives as well as the clever and engrossing dialogue between reckless men and women adrift in violent urban landscapes. (Miramax Films)

operatic than Coppola, basing his characters in grimier, somewhat more realistic settings. The films of Scorcese have a raw male brazenness. The brilliant and exacting direction of both Coppola and Scorsese has made their films fascinating studies of men locked into games of pride, conquest, and revenge.

Clint Eastwood has perhaps given the most true-to-type portrait of the ideal American male in the many movies he has directed and starred in. In movies starting with *High Plains Drifter* (1973) through *Space Cowboys* (2000), Eastwood has presented the screen image of a man, who when put under pressure, has no self-doubts. Sylvester Stallone, in directing his series of *Rocky* movies and many other action films, has managed to successfully create live action cartoons that become catalogs of self-aggrandizing male fantasies. Abel Ferrara (*Bad Lieutenant*, 1992); Quentin Tarantino (*Reservoir Dogs*, 1992); Walter Hill (*Last Man Standing*, 1996); and others have also given audiences experiences of driven and desperate men **(5–21)**. Other softer aspects of the maleness are done in film, but it is the heroically overblown or more brutal side that seems to consistently attract large audiences.

The Female Perspective. Of the 7,332 movie features produced by American studios between 1950 and 1980, fourteen were directed by women. Before 1960, Lois Weber (*Chapter In Her Life*, 1923), in silent films, Dorothy Arzner (*The Bride Wore Red*, 1938), and Ida Lupino (*The Hitch Hiker*, 1953) were almost alone as recognized female Hollywood directors. The question arises—Why?

Apart from the built-in structural bias of the Hollywood system that has already been discussed, many women have felt that their way of approaching and translating the world has been largely ignored in the direction of movies. It could be pointed out that a male director looks out at the world with the only eyes he has. Men view the conflicts of life from their real or imagined experience of them, and they naturally infuse movies with the socialization process growing out of their maleness. No matter how open and aware male directors might be toward women's concerns, some would claim that it ultimately becomes impossible to completely take on the sexual consciousness of the other gender. The internal and external experiences of the two sexes may be too much at variance. What value does a woman director, as opposed to a male director, place on the complex concerns of childbirth and motherhood, emotional openness between two people, the daily details of nurturing a family, awareness of monthly cycles in the female body, the pressures of surviving in a sexually competitive business world, the economic fears of survival, or the concepts of pleasure and pain? This is not to say one sex or the other works at a more insightfully profound level, only that a female film director may well give a different interpretation to a character or scene because of her sexual perspective.

The difference in the choices that a female director makes is subtle, but they can be very real. Martha Coolidge, while directing *Ramblin' Rose* (1991), faced the issues of her feminine experience in bringing out the main characters of the film. The movie deals with an emotionally volatile young Southern girl growing up in 1935. She is exploring her sexuality, going against the commonly held mores of her society that denied women's honest needs. The movie put demands on the director to interpret the action with female sensitivity. Coolidge made this observation about translating the script while directing the film: "On the page, Rose does not have a full and complete life of her own. The male characters go through the greatest changes because this story was written by a man (Calder Willingham). I think the greatest risk had this been directed by some men was that Rose might have been shallow—a symbol of sexuality—and a mother one-note, bizarre lady." Directors naturally fall back upon personal experience when bringing a movie to life. "Maybe that's why I did a good job with teen comedies for so many years. I remember how the blood rushed to your head when someone looks at you," says Coolidge. In one key scene when Rose (Laura Dern) is in bed with a younger boy (Lukas Haas), the sensuous moment hangs on the director's timing and awareness of the hidden dynamics of the situation.

Women directors in Hollywood have made great inroads for the last fifteen years **(5–22)**. Women from other countries initially led the way, with the acclaimed work of Agnes Varda (*Le Bonheur,* 1965) and Diane Kurys (*Peppermint Soda,* 1979) from France; Mai Zetterling (*The Girls,* 1966) from Sweden; Lina Wertmuller (*Swept Away,* 1972) from Italy; Gillian Armstrong (*My Brilliant Career,* 1979) from Australia; and others. Apart from the experimental cinema of Maya Deren (*Meshes in the Afternoon,* 1943) and the landmark documentary work of Shirley Clarke (*Bridges-Go-Round,* 1959), the movies of Elaine May (*The Heartbreak Kid,* 1972) and Joan Micklin Silver (*Hester Street,* 1974) were the first of a new generation of women to awaken producers to the value of their special directing sensibilities.

Some current female directors show a more distinctly feminine perspective in their films than others. The work of the following have chosen material that invites a female director's hand: Joyce Chopra (*Smooth Talk,* 1985); Susan Seidleman (*Desper-*

5–22 Beeban Kidron Seen here directing actors Shirley MacLaine and Marcello Mastroanni in *Used People* (1993), youthful director Beeban Kidron faced the common situation at the start of a filmmaking career, that is, taking command of a film as a director with a cast seasoned veterans. The temperament and communication skills of the director will affect everybody on the set. Some directors are relaxed, encouraging easy relationships between themselves and the actors. More women are finding that their talents are best expressed in the directing profession. (Columbia Pictures)

ately Seeking Susan, 1985); Lizzie Borden (*Working Girls*, 1987); Patricia Rozema (*I Heard the Mermaids Singing*, 1987); Nancy Kelly *(Thousand Pieces of Gold*, 1990); Julie Dash *(Daughters of the Dust*, 1990); Jodie Foster (*Little Man Tate*, 1991); Tamra Davis (*Guncrazy*, 1992); Nancy Savoca (*Household Saints*, 1993); Amy Heckerling *(Clueless*, 1995); Allison Anders (*Grace of My Heart*, 1996); Lisa Krueger *(Manny & Lo*, 1996); Jocelyn Moorhouse (*A Thousand Acres*, 1997); Nora Ephron (*You've Got Mail*, 1998); Audrey Wells (*Guinevere*, 1999); Karyn Kusama (*Girlfight*, 2000); and Joan Chen (*Autumn in New York*, 2000).

Other women have directed films that are not easily classified as "women's subjects," but have certainly brought their unique experience in the world into their work: Euzhan Palcy (*A Dry White Season*, 1989); Barbra Streisand (*The Prince of Tides*, 1991); Sondra Locke (*Impulse*, 1990); Mira Nair (*The Perez Family*, 1994); Lili Fini Zanuck (*Rush*, 1991); Randa Haines (*Wrestling Ernest Hemingway*, 1993); Rachel Talalay (*Ghost In The Machine*, 1993); Penelope Spheeris (*Wayne's World*, 1991); Penny Marshall (Awakenings,1990); Rachel Talalay (*Tank Girl*, 1995); Kathryn Bigelow (*Strange Days*, 1995); Betty Thomas (*Doctor Doolittle*, 1998); Beeban Kidron (*Swept from the Sea*, 1998); Mimi Leder (*Deep Impact*, 1998); Julie Taymor (*Titus*, 1999); and Mary Herron (*American Psycho*, 2000).

The future is quite bright for female directors. Lucy Fisher, vice chairman at Columbia TriStar, comments:

It is both better and not good enough for women. There are more female directors and producers and executives, and women make up a larger part of the audience than they did before. But the power dynamics still lean in the other direction. The biggest directors and stars are still men. Gradually, gradually . . .

Although movie directing still has the aura of "men's club" about it, women are bringing their talent for organization and leadership, as well as a fresh perspective that is overdue. Audiences have responded well to many of the films that women have directed, and the business of movies is always alert to what is succeeding.

The Independents.   If the word *auteur*, as applied to filmmaking, is meant to define a director who presents a personal point-of-view in terms of theme, technique, and style while breaking away from mechanical approaches to subject matter, the one group of filmmakers who could most truthfully claim this label are those directors in the United States called *independents*. The term independent covers a wide range of directors, but complex artistic activity resists easy classification. The label gained currency in the 1960s when there was a renewed interest in film that used the medium without the traditional constraints of the Hollywood moviemaking system. Any person with the charisma to win the loyalty of a few dedicated and talented people, and with access to a camera and minimal filmmaking equipment, could make a movie.

John Cassavetes was one of the first independent filmmakers. Although he had a budding career as an actor in commercial films, Cassavetes' first love was directing; he made *Shadows* (1960), an unscripted film about the New York jazz scene that caught the cadence of real speech. In later films, he experimented with variations of this semidocumentary look and a generation of young filmmakers, including NYU student Martin Scorsese, got excited. About the same time, Kenneth Anger's short classic *Scorpio Rising* (1963) shocked even the avant-garde with its bold poetic images of sex and violence in a clandestine world of bikers. Andy Warhol was not only a leading figure in the art world at the time, but he also lent his vision and talents to movies, encouraging a string of experimental films—some directed by Paul Morrissey (*Trash*, 1970)—that became emblematic of the underground culture growing out of the 1960s. Melvin Van Peeples, an African-American poet, jolted those audiences who saw *Sweet Sweetback's Baadasssss Song* (1971) with the uncensored ghetto reality of it. Paul Bartel (*Private Parts*, 1972) introduced his brand of bad taste for the sake of entertainment, and the concept caught on for others to practice. A later breakthrough was made by first-time director Steven Soderbergh in *sex, lies, and videotape* (1988), a highly polished film dealing with outer-edge sexual behavior in middle-class lives. The film won first prize at Cannes, and independent filmmakers were given new life. Easier economic survival became a possibility as distributors took a second look at the impact of these films on a new generation of film lovers.

Typically, young filmmakers just out of school and in the first stages of a career by necessity make small-budget movies, often wanting to express in them contemporary attitudes or radical film styles that are not common in mainline productions. Many of Hollywood's top directors—Steven Spielberg, Spike Lee, Penelope Spheeris, and others—began with experimental films that showed elements of brilliance. Kevin Smith followed this path in making *Clerks* (1994), a fast-talking story film about two guys working in a dumpy strip mall grocery and video store, and the random bunch of customers and friends that show up. The film cost exactly $26,685 to make and that, in a sense, was the beauty of it. The action on the screen feels like unfiltered real life in any-city USA. Miramax Films, alert to the new market for such films, distributed the film with much media attention and relative financial success. Before that, Richard Linklater had taken his camera to the streets of Austin, Texas, and recorded a rambling first account of Generation X in *Slacker* (1991). In the very low budget *El Mariachi* (1993), Robert Rodriquez told a story of violence laced with humor set in a border town. Columbia Pictures took the film, even though it was shot with Spanish dialogue, upgraded its weak technical elements, and distributed the film with its studio marketing advantages. Nick Gomez made *Laws of Gravity* (1992), an authentic tale of the mean streets of New York City in the 1990s, and shot it with all the uncompromising language, rough sexual relationships, and pervasive despair that happens in the lives of some young people. The film was one of many in the past ten years that showed off how clearly independent directors can see when they are not looking at the world through the tinted glasses of filmmakers on palm-lined studio lots **(5–23).**

Some more experienced directors see independent film as an opportunity for unique artistic expression, and they choose to make an entire body of films outside of the studio system, which they see as restrictive to their cinematic vision. NYU film student Jim Jarmusch, with some financial help from German director Wim Wenders, made *Stranger than Paradise* in 1984. The unusual pace of the film—an episodic series of isolated moments that gain meaning in their cumulative force—became a

5–23   *Pi*   Director Darren Aronofsky with his first feature *Pi* (1998) won the directing award at the Sundance festival. Its challenging plot deals with a reclusive mathematical genius (Sean Gullette) who is hounded by a Wall Street company and a Hasidic group for mystical keys that unlock answers to the universe. The film was shot in 16mm at a cost of $300,000 but returned over $4 million in box office revenue, a 13.3 profit ratio. All independent filmmakers dream of such initial financial success.   (Artisan Entertainment)

trademark of the Jarmusch style of filmmaking. Although his low-key visual style and languid editing rhythms are fascinating, the effect on the screen is not highly commercial. Though he could adjust to a more popular mode of storytelling, to this point he has gone his own way with films that emphasize the anticlimactic, such as *Down by Law* (1986), *Mystery Train* (1989), *Night on Earth* (1991), and *Dead Man* (1996). Hal Hartley, in *Trust* (1991), *Henry Fool* (1997), and other films, seems equally committed to making a coherent philosophical statement in his film work, but with a peculiar alienated humor that infuses them not with lightness but depression. Jan Jost (*Uncommon Senses*, 1987), in over ten films, travels the country to portray lives of isolation and confusion. His approach is a blend of intellectual perceptions and felt spaces, and the effectiveness of his work is realized best in the total experience of them. Todd Haynes (*Safe*, 1995) takes a visually formal approach to subject matter that makes borderline neurotic behavior seem acceptable. Henry Jaglom (*Always*, 1986) has spent most of his filmmaking career putting himself, his family, and his friends on film in a kind of extended stream of consciousness. His direct intrusion of the camera into the personal details of his life and others around him draws the viewer into his world, like it or not. This kind of director is not using his film as a stepping stone to glossy Hollywood productions and the budgets that come along with them. Often, their movies are so obviously personal and removed from the taste of even large art house audiences that no invitation to Hollywood is offered. Many times, their films are not the standard narrative length commercially proscribed, and their films are distributed in specialized catalogs to educational institutions or other special markets.

A group of independent directors has been active in the mainstream and while not adverse to making movies that can "crossover" into wide commercial markets, has found that by dropping out, at least for periods of time, they can make movies that satisfy their aesthetic needs. Many of these directors walk the fine border between major studio movie budgets and less surely financed projects released by first-line independent distributors. Throughout his career, Robert Altman has been a model for a high-profile filmmaker who has retained his independence. From *That Cold Day in the Park* (1969) through *The Gingerman* (1997), Altman has directed films that have bridged almost every shape and style of filmmaking, moving freely between productions from stage material (*Come Back to the Five & Dime Jimmy Dean, Jimmy Dean,* 1982), to nine James Carver short stories (*Short Cuts,* 1993); psuedodocumentaries for television (*Tanner '88,* 1988); a biography (*Vincent and Theo,* 1990); a musical comedy (*Popeye,* 1980); a revisionist Western (*McCabe & Mrs. Miller,* 1971); a black comedy set in an army field hospital in Korea (*M*A*S*H*,* 1970); and many more. Altman's more than thirty films have been distributed by companies ranging from 20th Century Fox (*3 Women,* 1977) to Sandcastle 5 (*Secret Honor,* 1985), and his approach is proof to many others that directors do not have to spend entire careers compromising to make films of interest to themselves.

Many other directors have successfully retained the artistic control that independent directors so dearly cherish: John Waters (*Hairspray,* 1988); David Lynch (*Wild at Heart,* 1990); John Sayles (*Passion Fish,* 1992); Tim Robbins (*Bob Roberts,* 1992); John Dahl (*The Last Seduction,* 1994); Nancy Savoca (*Household Saints,* 1993); Alan

Rudolph (*Trixie,* 2000); Whit Stillman (*Barcelona,* 1994); Ethan and Joel Coen (*Fargo,* 1996); Gus Van Zant (*Good Will Hunting,* 1997); and Paul Schrader (*Affliction,* 1998) to list a few. Independent directors working in the United States have few things in common, except that all have struggled to find the financing necessary to make movies. For most, it has only whetted their desire. The treasures found in their films are well worth the effort in seeking them out.

SUMMARY

The work of directors—the *auteurs* of film—can be classified in any number of ways, certainly within commercial filmmaking communities. Some are associated with action-oriented films, others are renowned for drawing out peak performances from actors, still others are trusted for their no-nonsense efficiency. Ultimately, the labels are only useful if they provide some insight into the contributions of an individual director. As with all other artists, directors function within the framework of their backgrounds, the necessities of the moment, and their dreams. These men and women work under intense pressure—from the financiers, from the media, from their peers, and from their own expectations.

Sometimes directors are just as confused about the value of what is being shot as the stagehand watching it. Director Irvin Kerschner wonders, "Isn't it funny that the results are only shadows on a piece of celluloid? You look at it, everybody looks at it, and yet you have no idea what you have until the audience sees it." This uncertainty comes with being an artist. He or she works at the edge of failure. Still, most people close to the movie business, and many outside, would fulfill their wildest personal fantasy by having a chance to actually direct a motion picture.

SPOTLIGHT

The Director: Vondie Curtis-Hall Interview

Vondie Curtis-Hall grew up in Detroit, trained as an actor at Detroit Repertory Theater, and later studied at Juilliard in New York City. He has been a featured actor in the TV series "Chicago Hope" and has also done the theatrical films *Passion Fish* and *Falling Down.* He has now turned to directing. His first film, *Gridlock'd* (1997), received strongly positive critical reviews.

Richard Peacock:	You have acted in movies and on television; how did your acting experience influence your approach to directing?
Vondie Curtis-Hall:	It really started with me writing the script because I wanted to write dialogue that actors could speak. I think it's a terrible thing to get a script that's not the way people actually talk. It doesn't connect. So although the story was important, from an

actor's point-of-view I wanted to do something that really flowed—stuff that the actors would be comfortable saying and that would be fun. And then I wanted to set up an environment where the actors could take risks.

RP: Did it work out that way?

VCH: Yah. When Tupac [Shakur] and Tim [Roth] sat around getting to know each other, we had two weeks of rehearsal before we started shooting. At that point we went through the script and anything the guys didn't feel comfortable with, I changed. Tim was doing an American accent, and there were some things he really couldn't say, or weren't true for him. I let them both have as much input as they wanted. I also gave them a lot of background because the story was semiautobiographical. They wanted to know more about Detroit and the character of these guys they were playing. Then we brought in some of the supporting players and let all of them bounce off one another. So that by the time we started filming, we were all pretty much in sync. I really tried to have it that there were no surprises. With that security, the actors were then free to try different things. The script wasn't precious to me. It wasn't Shakespeare.

RP: When you wrote *Gridlock'd*, did you have the clear intention of directing it?

VCH: Yes, I wrote it specifically with the idea of directing it. It was one of those things where I thought I'd do it for about a hundred thousand dollars or so, and that I'd star in it with my best friend and my wife. We'd shoot it in guerrilla-style like so many of my other friends had done at film schools—You know, get Panavision to donate a camera kit and contact Kodak and that sort of thing. I wrote it at AFI [American Film Institute]. It was a very specific script with all the camera movements. The movie was literally what was on the page.

RP: It must be very satisfying to have that kind of control.

VCH: Yeh, it really is. I have to say that for my first film, I'm really happy with the way it came out. As an actor, I read many scripts. Then you see the movie and say, "I loved that script but whatever happened to the movie?" Sometimes it's just not translated. But I have to say that God smiled on us with this one. It really is what I wrote and intended.

RP: Your film obviously cost a lot more than the amount you mentioned. Who ultimately financed it?

VCH: Polygram Film Entertainment. I sent the script to a friend, Jim Stark, the producer of Jim Jarmusch's movies. I had worked with Jarmusch on *Mystery Train*. I gave it to Stark with the hope that he might produce it or at least give me some guidance. He called back and said, "Do you really want people to see this movie?" I said yes. He said, "First, don't use your own money. Second, try to attach a star to it. What actors do you like?" I mentioned Tim Roth or Gary Oldman. So I proceeded to get the script to Tim. He was doing *Rob Roy* at the time and didn't read it for about three months. Then he read it on the day he finished shooting and called up and said, "I want to do this movie." When we met, I promised that I wouldn't make him look stupid, even though I was a first-time director. It was all right there in the script.

RP: When the actors took over, did you discover anything about the characters that you hadn't envisioned?

VCH: I did. It was a completely different thing when Tim and Shakur came on board because it was really their movie. My preconceptions all changed. It became a story about the truth of these two guys. But we all made the discovery together. Once we started filming, the movie took on its own life. The chemistry between Tupac and Tim just showed up on the screen. It was amazing. Because you never know what's going to happen. We had done a read-through sitting around a room and it was funny and fast, but you never know until you actually see the dailies how these guys actually come off together.

RP: What qualities attracted you to cast Tupac Shakur as Spoon?

VCH: His incredible passion to do the movie. And then his take on Spoon—he really saw this character. Before I first met him, I didn't want him. At that point the studio wouldn't do the movie without a star. We could either not afford or didn't want the other Black stars available. So when Tupac said he had to meet me, and when we actually sat down, he had a great take on the Spoon character as well as a sense of the movie. In fact, the character was much like he himself. He very much wanted to prove some things: 1) that he was a responsible actor at a point when nobody in Hollywood wanted to touch him because they thought he was bad news; 2) he wanted to show that he was a good actor; 3) he wanted to play someone he had never done on the screen before. We then did a screen test and he was great. Now I can't imagine anyone else having done that role.

RP: What was it like on the first day on the set as a first-time director? What did it feel like when you walked on the sound stage?

VCH: I was terrified. I had been up the entire night before. It was kinda like the character in *Living in Oblivion*. I couldn't sleep because I was trying to figure out the first shot. I had storyboarded the whole movie, but there was this one shot that I just couldn't make up my mind about. There were a couple of ways I wanted to do it. I wanted to show some nice movement, I wanted to show the studio some virtuosity without being too flashy. I wanted to be organic—and flashy.

RP: What shot was that?

VCH: [laughter] It's not in the movie. It's the only scene I left out. When I finally got on the set, I still had two options for the shot. O.K., I'm going to do one or the other. So I chose one, but the geography on it didn't let it make sense for what I had planned cutting to. So I changed the shot. Then with 150 people standing around looking at me, I changed it again. So they had to take the camera up to another level to get the angle, and then I changed the shot again! That was the most difficult moment. But after that everything

Director Vondie Curtis Hall (center) on the set of *Gridlock'd* (1997) discusses the script with Thandie Newton, Tupac Shakur, and Tim Roth. (Gramercy Pictures)

smoothed out. By the end of the first few days we were actually ahead of schedule and the studio really liked what we were shooting, and we never saw them again. They just left us alone.

RP: As a first-time director, how much did you rely on the judgment of your cinematographer, Bill Pope?

VCH: Bill was invaluable to me. I'm dyslexic. So my left and right get confused— he's looking left; I'm looking right; camera left, camera right. So Bill helped me an awful lot with eye lines. I didn't worry too much about crossing the line [action axis], I don't think it showed up, but you never know. [laughter] But he and I had worked a lot of the stuff out on paper. We did the location scouting, so most of the planning came early on with Bill—can we shoot in this place, can we light it? Actually, we didn't do too much lighting at all in this movie. We used a lot of natural sunlight. So Bill, myself, and the production designer Dan Bishop just came together and set up this whole world and how we were going to shoot it. So, for the most part, we shot the storyboard.

RP: There is a real confidence you can feel in the film. It seems that the movie knows exactly where it's going. That doesn't happen with all films.

VCH: That's very true. I really feel lucky and blessed. As a first-time director you want to surround yourself with really good people, and I had great support. You know, we didn't get a chance to loop in postproduction because Tupac was dead. So that the actor's voices recorded under freeways, for example, was all we had. The sound guys saved my butt. Everybody did, nobody dropped the ball. And the studio left me alone to make my own movie.

RP: Although the movie deals with a story of drug dependency and the struggle to find help, the film still manages to be a comedy of sorts. How did you achieve that?

VCH: First and foremost, I wanted it to be a *real* story. But you can't be didactic and hammer the audience over the head. It had to be a movie that they would both buy and enjoy. I never knew what was going to be funny to the viewer—you know, I'm sitting at my computer writing it in a little vacuum. My wife read it and liked it. She even suggested that dark part where Cookie [Thandie Newton] is dead and the two guys are still shooting up. She said, "She should just be lying there." It combines irony with my own weird sensibility. But I really felt that the humor came out of the choices the guys made. They might not be the choices the general public would make, but given those characters with their backgrounds, they were very real. At each juncture—whether it's reverting to getting high or choosing to be stabbed so that they could get help in a rehab program—the actors had to believe that at the moment it was the best choice the character could make. And, oddly, that's what makes it funny. I told them in rehearsal, "If we *play* this for a joke, we're gonna be dead. You have to *believe* every moment is real."

RP: Did you have any other film in mind that you used as a pattern?

VCH: *Midnight Cowboy*, in terms of their relationship. The fact that the two guys in the film—Ratzo and Joe Buck—needed each other to just make it through this day. I wanted to make *Midnight Cowboy* for the 90s—the urban setting, even some of the color palette. At meetings, the studio would ask how we saw it, and we'd say sorta like *Midnight Cowboy* and *Drugstore Cowboy*.

RP: I assume that the story is somewhat autobiographical. What was it about your life experience that you wanted to express in the film?

VCH: We have this image of all dope fiends being these indigent guys lying in the gutter. Heroin addicts don't just wear dirty clothes and hang out on the corner with their hand out. But heroin has always been the drug of the outcast—the jazz musician and later the heavy metal rock performer. It's cool until its not cool. I wanted to do a couple guys who were not in the gutter yet. They obviously have had to change their lives to have a life.

RP: The central conflict of the film seems to focus on the depersonalized bureaucracy of the health and welfare system. Was that your experience of it?

VCH: Yes, my own experience was that of a musician in Detroit. I played in a punk band. The whole idea was how to play faster guitar and write better songs because it was a heavily competitive band town. And everybody was into drugs. Then one day the bass player and myself were sitting around and came up with the idea that maybe we could play better and could write better songs if we weren't stoned all the time. At the time we were doing everything. But I was still only 17 and still living with my parents. To get into rehab I'd have to give my home address, and I didn't want them to send a letter there saying "Your son's a dope fiend." So we just went around just like these guys, from place to place, getting put off all the time because we didn't have a social security card or something. So I always remembered that. It's the film.

RP: What was the hardest thing for you about directing?

VCH: Holding on to what I knew was right. I heard that one of the teachers at AFI came up with the figure that typically a director is asked about 700 questions a day. I don't know how they got that number but it's probably true. Because the studio has an idea, the cameraman will have an idea, the script supervisor will have thoughts and questions about something, and, of course, the actors are going to have opinions. But at the end of the day, it's got to be your movie.

RP: Did you second-guess yourself?

VCH: It's not that. It's the little things, the details, that I think I somehow overlooked. I wish I had done this or that. Had I paid more attention to one thing, then what followed may have been different.

RP: Almost everybody in the business wants to take a crack at directing. You get to create this private universe. Is it everything you imagined it would be?

VCH: It is. It is everything and more. And that's good and bad. As a frustrated actor, all the power you ever wanted to have, you now have. But it's an incredibly tough job. You end up being a therapist and a driver.

RP: Is there a director, past or present, whose films you watch with special attention?

VCH: I have four. My awareness of film history is not very long or deep, even though I went to film schools. I'm in the process of learning more. My interest really started with Spike Lee's *She's Gotta Have It*. I saw it and decided "I can do this." Then Jim Jarmusch, John Sayles, and Martin Scorcese. They were all New York independent filmmakers at one time. They had done movies of the size that I could aspire to make. In fact, I did my first paper in film school on *Strangers in Paradise*.

RP: How do you evaluate the situation of the African-American artist in Hollywood today? I know that is a very broad question. Are the opportunities as open as you would like?

VCH: I certainly think it's moving in a positive direction. Of course, this is America and Hollywood is a microcosm of it, so there's always more work to be done. But I think since Spike Lee and the new Black Wave, we've got more Black actors in dramatic roles; Black writers and Black producers are telling their own stories. I think that's very important because during the Black exploitation period back in the 1970s, we didn't have that much. Some of those stories didn't ring as true to the Black experience as movies being done today. For myself, I'm getting offered scripts that are not just Black scripts but normal big budget films with white characters like anybody else. I read somewhere that paying attention to the particulars makes things universal. But we've got to tell different stories. We can't continue just doing stories of the hood or wacky comedies. So now it's got to be about other African-American experiences. ◀

FILMS TO CONSIDER

The following fourteen movies are generally older films by outstanding directors, each one adding to the evolving language and style of filmmaking.

- *The Passion of Joan of Arc* (1928): Carl Dreyer's command of every filmic nuance, especially his fanatical control in shaping Renee Maria Falconetti"s historic performance as Joan, firmly established the dominant artistic role of the director.

- *La Bete Humaine* (1938): The precision of Jean Renoir's directorial skill and vision comes through in this haunting film of a seemingly moral man (Jean Gabin) driven by inner dark forces beyond his control.

- *Bicycle Thief* (1948): Vittorio DeSica's film about a terrible mistake by an out-of-work laborer, devastating his young son, is an example of how the Italian Neorealism movement could find profound meaning in a simple human failing.

- *Rashomon* (1951): This virtuoso directing work by Akira Kurosawa of four versions of a rape and murder was not only a study in meticulous storytelling, but the film gained the attention of the world for Japanese filmmaking in general.

- *The 400 Blows* (1959): This frankly grim autobiographical movie of the most personal aspects of director Francois Truffaut's stern schooling became a model for other filmmakers to risk honestly telling of the pain of youth.

- *La Dolce Vita* (1960): The sly irony in every frame of Federico Fellini's film of the Italian postwar economic and cultural boom created a directorial attitude that silently criticized cool modernity with its ironic observation.

- *Viridiana* (1961): The director as iconoclast was the legacy of Luis Bunuel, a filmmaker who challenged the hypocrisy of the church, the brutality of the state, and economic systems that turn men into things of greed.

- *Lawrence of Arabia* (1962): This perfectly realized epic of the English adventurer T.E. Lawrence is the work of David Lean, a master director of stories with frighteningly large casts and crews and theater screens to fill.

- *McCabe and Mrs. Miller* (1972): In this unusual western, the sense of seemingly spontaneous freedom of both the actors' deliveries and the photographic choices is the trademark of Robert Altman's directorial style.

- *The Godfather* (1972): Francis Ford Coppola's visualization of Mario Puzo's book and script brought in a refreshingly serious reinterpretation of the gangster genre, presenting the story as a multilayered history of the dark side of America's culture.

- *The Marriage of Maria Braun* (1979): The extremely prolific German director Rainer Werner Fassbinder shot this film, and others, with a headlong passion that mixed sex, money, and decay, awakening the audience to a bolder style of storytelling .

- *Raging Bull* (1980): Boxing films have had an uncommonly consistent popularity, but Martin Scorsese's imposing movie, based on the mutilated life of Jake LaMotta, gave the genre its most visually eloquent and dramatically profound expression.

- *The Cook, the Thief, His Wife, and Her Lover* (1990): Extreme expressionism is a style that can artfully envelop the viewer, as Peter Greenaway's imagery shows in this film that tests the limits of accepted values with its visual and thematic provocations.

- *Leaving Las Vegas* (1996): Mike Figgis achieved what many independent directors aspire to, that is, he created an idiosyncratic story that follows the fate of a completely original character, yet makes a universal statement about the human spirit.

THOUGHT QUESTIONS AND EXERCISES

Watch a film from those listed:

1. Choose a film. How is the director's personal aesthetic reflected by the visual choices made in the film? In terms of its images, what is particularly distinctive about his or her work? Give some examples from the film.

2. Does the film you have chosen tend to exhibit attitudes of *realism* or ones of *expressionism*? Point out scenes in the film that make your case. In your opinion, what was the rationale for this approach to the film subject?

3. A director often announces a system of values in his or her expression of a movie's theme. In one of the films listed, discover and write about the director's moral code as manifested in his or her special approach toward the subject matter. Does the director take an unambiguous position? What sequence in the film best sums up his or her attitude?

4. Working with actors is a core activity for a director. What, do you believe, were the essential qualities of performance that the director chose to draw out of the main actors? Can you imagine how the characters could have had a different nuance and been more effective? Choose a key scene to demonstrate how the director generated its dramatic impact.

5. In your opinion, is the message of the film you are watching primarily conveyed through the information provided by the actor's lines and character

portrayals, or does the director capture the theme basically through image and visual style? Give examples to make your point.

FURTHER READING

Arheim, Rudolf. *Visual Thinking* (Berkeley: University of California Press, 1969).

Bazin, Andre. *What Is Cinema?* Vol I (Berkeley: University of California Press, 1967).

———. *What Is Cinema?* Vol II (Berkeley: University of California Press, 1971).

Bogdanovich, Peter. *The Cinema of Alfred Hitchcock* (New York: Museum of Modern Art Film Library, 1963).

———. *Who the Devil Made It* (New York: Alfred A. Knopf, 1997).

Clurman, Harold. *On Directing* (New York: Fireside, 1997).

Cowie, Peter. *Ingmar Bergman: A Critical Biography*, 2nd ed. (London: Andre Deutsch, 1992).

Eisenstein, Sergei. *Film Form and the Film Sense* (New York: Meridian, 1968).

Fairweather, Rod. *Basic Studio Directing* (Boston, MA: Focal Press, 1998).

Figgis, Mike, ed. *Projections 10* (New York: Faber & Faber, 2000).

Geduld, Harry. *Film Makers on Film Making* (Bloomington: Indiana University Press, 1981).

Kawin, Bruce F. *Mindscreen: Bergman, Godard and First-Person Film* (Princeton, NJ: Princeton University Press, 1978).

Katz, Stephen D. *Film Directing Shot by Shot: Visualizing from Concept to Screen* (Boston, MA: Focal Press, 1991).

Kozarski, Richard. *Hollywood Directors, 1914–1940* (New York: Oxford, 1976).

Mamet, David. *On Directing Film* (New York: Viking Penguin, 1992).

Pintoff, Ernest. *Directing 101* (Studio City, CA: Michael Wiese Productions, 1998).

Pye, Michael and Lynda Myles. *The Movie Brats: How the Film Generation Took over Hollywood* (New York: Holt, Rinehart, Winston, 1978).

Sherman, Eric. *Directing the Film* (Los Angeles: Acrobat Books, 1988).

Singer, Michael. *A Cut Above: 50 Film Directors Talk About Their Craft* (Los Angeles: Lone Eagle, 1998).

Stevens, Jon. *Actors Turned Directors* (Los Angeles, CA: Silman-James Press, 1997).

Thompson, Kristin, and David Thompson. *Film History: An Introduction* (New York: McGraw-Hill, 1994).

CHAPTER 6

THE ART OF TECHNIQUE

ON THE SET

"A clear vision is a wonderful attribute. Pre-visualization, *as Ansel Adams defined it, is the basis for the creation of any worthwhile art."*

Roy Wagner, ASC (*Nick of Time*, 1996)

Preproduction film planning and arranging culminates on the first day of principal photography when the director, the camera crew, and the actors come together to shoot the film. The months of preparation finally arrive at this moment of truth. At this point the director takes full control.

For an expectant onlooker on a movie set, watching a film being shot can be a disappointment. Unlike the rapid evolution of story movement seen on the screen, there seems to be very little going on that can be recognized as "action." Actors wait restlessly in mobile units or on folding chairs off the set. The members of the production crew are caught up in the details of their specific jobs. Unless part of a scene is actually being photographed, which is often not the case, the director, cinematographer, and camera crew appear to be standing around in idle conversation. In reality, the director and crew are probably working out time-consuming technical details for the next shot, or perhaps planning for the next setup—a new camera position with its requisite lighting needs.

THE NATURE OF A SHOT

Whereas a book is written sentence by sentence, a movie is made shot by shot. Just as a writer thinks through each sentence going onto the page, so, too, the director and cinematographer must lay out the strategy of each shot. The selected shots that survive the editing process are the building blocks that make up the movie. When watching a movie, it is almost impossible to be conscious of individual shots as they pass by on the screen. To do so would spoil the pleasure of going to a film. It would also defeat the purpose of the filmmaker, which is to win the audience to the illusion that the film's seamless shifts in perspective and space are within the natural and inevitable flow of reality. Yet, it is important to know that without encountering film at the basic level of the *shot*, one cannot understand the nature of cinema.

Reduced to its barest essentials, moviemaking is the execution of the shot within the situation of a setup. The *setup* entails positioning the camera and arranging light sources to shoot an actor or other subject. A successful shooting day is usually measured, for the most part, by the number of separate setups and the quality of the footage that is shot. This stage of preparation involves considerable logistical planning. Cameras and lighting equipment are complex, and the work crew is large. Because of the time required in arranging proper conditions for shots, directors usually take full advantage of the situation by shooting everything possible from established setups, regardless of when the scene will show up in the final version of the film. For example, a camera may be mounted on a small crane to photograph a pilot climbing into a cockpit of a jet fighter before taking off. If appropriate, the director will usually shoot, using the same placement of the camera, lighting, and prop placements, any other shots in the script that call for the same basic visual perspective—for example, the pilot getting out of the jet after the flight. Similar procedures are repeated again and again throughout the long days allotted to principal photography.

At the outset, a semantic problem arises because the film terms *shot* and *take* are often used interchangeably. Strictly speaking, the definition of a shot is simple enough: A shot is the exposed film that passes through the camera from when it is first triggered until it is turned off. The duration of a shot can last for as little as a second or for as long as several minutes. The term *take* normally refers to a provisional shot that may or may not be repeated, depending on the judgment of the director. The director or actors may be displeased with any number of things in any single *take*—misapplied lighting, poor blocking, a faulty performance. Normally several takes (shots) are made of a given subject or action so that the director can find the exact one that works best in the larger context of the scene. As the physical details of a *shot* become more complex, the chances for some small error increase. Each *take* is sequentially numbered on a *clapper board*. With a comfortable budget, a filmmaker will always shoot excess film footage, making it possible for the editor to have ample material from which to cut.

The most fundamental element of a shot (or take) is its *duration*—the time needed to continuously record a subject on film. The final *edited shot*—the picture that arrives on the screen in the completed film—will have been timed, trimmed, and judged in relation to the other shots that precede and follow it. The majority of exposed film footage is discarded at some time in the editing process. What started out at the time of shooting as a 45-second *take* may well end up as a 5-second *shot* in the final edited version. The dramatic intention of the director will determine the ultimate duration of each shot. But as the director actually shoots the film, the immediate concern is recording as many high-quality shots of varying lengths to fully cover all the dramatic action of the story.

SHOT CHARACTERISTICS

You sit on a park bench. You may turn your head to take in the panorama of the landscape. Or you could walk to the water fountain, and in doing so the details of the fountain would be brought into sharper focus. You might also choose to lie face down on the grass to study the microscopic world of insects or possibly climb a tree to gain an unusual and adventurous overview of the park. Camera shots imitate these and other human movements and perspectives.

Movies do even more. The most powerful and distinguishing feature of motion pictures is its ability to put the audience in almost any physical location the filmmaker chooses, and do it *immediately*. Released from the normal limitations of our physical bodies, the camera—aided by the editing process—can range around, through, and over a familiar world to show us a variety of points-of-view in quick succession. The viewer is able to experience, almost simultaneously, the landscape of the park from any number of angles.

Every director and camera operator has an array of shot possibilities from which to choose. Whether the subject is two lovers lying in bed or crowds on a congested Chicago street, filmmakers will choose the shots that best convey the information they want to have drawn out of the moment. This process of *shot selection* is their daily work. There are few rules for shooting a movie, and none that cannot be broken. Over the years, however, a range of conventional shot selections have emerged, and filmmakers have used them effectively in narrative movies to visually orient the audience. What follows are some of those choices.

Camera Distances

The physical relationship of the camera to the subject is crucial. The audience has no alternative but to live in the environment—seen through the camera lens—of the filmmaker's creation. We, in a sense, *are* the camera. Whether the camera is surveying a Western landscape or in the face of Madonna, we are right *there*.

The decision of the director and the cinematographer as to where to place the camera is both elemental and profoundly important. *Camera distance*—the space between the lens and the subject to be photographed—always tells us something about how we are to regard the subject. Filmmakers know that every change in the proximity of the camera to the subject will alter not only one's physical perception but also the values and meanings applied to what is seen. Is the audience to be a cool remote observer of an action, or does the camera insist we be intimately involved? The Japanese director Yasujiro Ozu (*Floating Weeds*, 1959) preferred the studied and elegant *long shot*, which gave his films a quiet, formal tone. American director John Cassavetes (*Faces*, 1968) was at the other end of the spectrum, in love with the probing and confrontive use of the *close-up*.

The choice of camera distance by the director and cinematographer will strongly influence—and usually determine—our reactions to what we are seeing. The seeming distance of camera to subject may be an illusion, however, because certain lenses—wide angle and telephoto—can distort the viewer's perceptions **(6–1a-g)**. The following are a standard selection of possible shots:

Extreme Long Shot (ELS).   The **ELS** is commonly used as an *establishing shot*, that is, a shot that orients the audience to the larger physical context in which the action will take place. The shot distance gives the viewer a panoramic overview of an entire location or set. To provide initial information succinctly about the time period and location of the story, a movie might start by presenting vistas of a pristine mountain range or several city blocks of brownstone apartments with automobiles of the 1930s parked by the curbs. At one moment in *Black Robe* (1990), an ELS is very effectively used to show the canoes of a doomed missionary party moving down the steel gray St. Lawrence River. The shot from a mountain above the small crafts in the expanse of wildness visually convinces the audience of the dangerous isolation the group is entering. This single shot tells it all.

Long Shot (LS).   For a more limited range of camera-to-subject, this shot often focuses on a human figure or object in relation to an ample view of its larger environment. For example, a car racing through city streets in a long shot is effective and exciting. Because the background gives clear context for the action, space and motion relationships are clearly perceived and understood at this distance. Typically, when Tom Cruise playing a Navy lawyer in *A Few Good Men* (1992) wins his controversial case, a final lingering *long shot* in the courtroom shows him as a man now distanced and isolated from the military system to which he belongs.

Full Shot (FS).   A **full shot** is used when the intention of the filmmaker is to present a sufficiently complete view of the body of a character and yet still provide some sense of the immediate physical environment. It allows the director to show the body carriage of the actor, thereby creating a total screen presence. Although the human figure is usually dominant in the shot, there is still enough defined background to put the character in a recognizable visual context. Movies that emphasize the beauty or physical dexterity of the human body, for instance, would be inclined to use the *full shot* as an effective way to capture its shape and flow.

Medium Shot (MS).   This distance usually covers the actor from the waist to the head, while providing good detail of facial characteristics. When watching a movie, note how often the *medium shot* is used in narrative films. The shot is popular because it can be used to convey many things about a person so well. With the MS, expressions of the eyes and lips can clearly enhance the dialogue, and yet the upper body and hands can also be used to complement a dramatic effect. The distance to the character photographed is comfortable, resembling the normal spatial proximity at which we encounter most people in conversation in Western cultures.

6–1a *Extreme Long Shot*

6–1b *Long Shot*

6–1c *Full Shot*

6–1d *Medium Shot*

6–1e *Close Shot*

6–1f *Close Up*

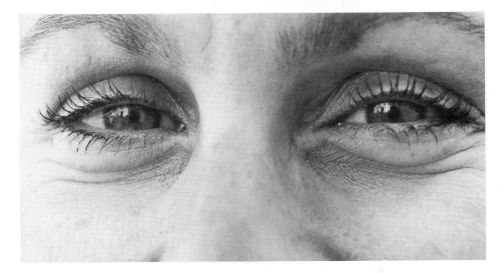

6–1g   *Extreme Close-Up*   (Photographs by Beck Peacock)

Close Shot (CS).   Intimacy in movies is felt as the camera is placed closer to its subject, or its lens makes it appear so. The **close shot** includes the shoulders and face of the actor, allowing the audience to study the range of facial expressions in reaction to the dramatic moment. The central focus of attention becomes the actor's physical and emotional response, reflected by the tilt of a head, the squint in an eye, shape of the lips as words are spoken. The CS can be very complimentary to actors, the purely visual impact being comparable to a still portrait photo.

Close-Up (CU).   The **close-up** shot, when focused on the human form, usually concentrates on a face, enclosing it from the chin to the hairline or crown. At this distance, visual information becomes even more refined because the visual impact of the shot becomes increasingly more personal. The shot emphasizes whatever subtle facial expressions the actor has chosen to express. Most actors desire the close-up shot for its complete command of the screen. Close-ups also have the effect of excluding all background, thereby limiting our visual choices. For example, a director intentionally will come in tight on a person so that he or she dominates the frame. This, in turn, can create dramatic tension, as the audience cannot see what is happening just beyond the boundaries of the frame.

Extreme Close Up (ECU).   This shot maximizes a single detail, a significant part of an object or feature of a person. The exaggerated impact of this close range shot is used primarily for several purposes. It may unequivocally point out a piece of visual information important to the story: the serial number on a pistol, for example. The shot may also show us a magnified portion of a familiar object, which in the *extreme* *close-up* may appear strange or provocative. The trigger of a gun, when filling an entire screen in ECU, can look like a half moon of steel waiting to be pressed. Human features can take on a grotesque aspect. The opening credits of *The Rocky Horror Picture Show* (1975) give us an ECU of white teeth and painted red lips in a black background singing introductory music. The shot, as it goes on, is bizarrely disorienting, a perfect start to a movie that flaunts its unconventionality.

All of these shots are on a continuum of possible camera distances and image framing, and other gradations of distance may be used by individual cinematographers. Certain camera operators make the finer distinctions, such as *medium long shot* or *medium close shot*.

Camera Angles

"Angles tell us emotional things in ways that are very mysterious. And emotional things that I'm not very aware of. I think a particular angle is going to do one thing and it does something quite different sometimes. I no longer have any sure sense that I have a grasp of it. Angles are the most mysterious thing about movies to me."

Michael Chapman, ASC (*Raging Bull*, 1980

Just as the director decides on the distance that a subject should be from the camera, so too the **angle** from which it is shot must be chosen. Unlike stage directors, moviemakers have the choice of putting a camera, hence the viewer, at any angle in relation to what is being given dramatic attention. Psychologically, the nature and the degree of the angle will help shape our attitude to the subject. The chosen angle literally gives the viewer a *point-of-view*, and with it, a clue to how the visual information is to be interpreted. For example, if the situation is one in which a worker is about to be fired by his boss from his job after 25 years with the company, various angles could be chosen to present this action: a high angle shot toward the worker to emphasize his oppressed position; a low angle shot of the boss emphasizing a position of authority; a mid-range shot of either person giving the viewer an eye-level "confrontational" or at least neutral perspective.

- **High Angle**. High angles can have a "god-like" feel about them, a gracious quality when done well. In the extreme, the filmmaker may choose to take a bird's eye view of a location, or a person within it **(6–2)**. When filming the crowded lobby of an office building, the high angle shot might be chosen to not only show off its architecture but to watch the pattern of movement as a significant character rushes through it. But when used more subtly, this angle is often used to simply indicate the difference in height between two people, as when a man and a boy walk along a road. The high angle sight lines of the camera suggest a taller man's perspective of the shorter lad. In some contexts, shooting from an angle that looks down is used to intentionally put its subject in the subservient position. When a prisoner is first put into a jail cell, the camera might capture the man with a high angle shot to visually emphasize his

6–2 *Black Rain* In Yashiko Tanaka's *Black Rain* (1988), the high angle shot of a group of people on a small ferry attempting to flee Hiroshima after the atomic bomb was dropped is especially effective. The people seem helpless, having no choice but to accept the grim fate that is befalling them from the heavens. The overhead camera angle accentuates their victimhood. (Angelika Films)

trapped space. This dramatic shot is a direct statement of attitude toward the man's claustrophobia.

- **Low Angle.** The **low angle** shot sometimes visually defines a challenge or an obstacle. For instance, as a knight rides through the forest to the castle, a shot might capture the hero from a low angle with the massive height of the stone walls that separate him from his maiden. One such well-positioned shot can clearly show the obstacle he faces. Directors use low angle shots to stress the physical or psychological dominance of a character—to "valorize" the person— whether it be a triumphant boxer in the ring, or a cruel headmaster on the first day of school **(6–3)**. It is not surprising that film posters have shots of Rocky (Sylvester Stallone) taken from a low angle. We then must literally "look up" to him, a position of superiority that the fictional boxer has supposedly earned. The angle itself predisposes the audience to form various attitudes toward the subject photographed in this manner. Low angle shots can also be used for reasons of style. In *Citizen Kane* (1941), Orson Welles constructed some sets so that the camera could be placed at floor level. This allowed him to shoot entire scenes from this odd but dramatically imposing angle. In one scene at the newspaper office, Welles and Joseph Cotten look like forlorn giants as they circle each other pondering Kane's political defeat. Because of the angle, the ceiling becomes part of the exposed set and seems to oppressively confine the men within the room.

- **Mid-Range.** This is the most common angle from which to shoot because it is the most natural **(6–4)**. Directors, especially those who stress the tenets of realism in their visuals, find themselves visually drawn to a consistent use of the *mid-range* perspective. These filmmakers will broadly limit themselves to camera angles that reflect normal ways most people see and experience their world. The style resulting from shooting in the mid-range imbues a movie in any genre with a naturalistic sense. The mid-range angle can be very dynamic

6–3 *Mona Lisa* The low angle shot is inherently dramatic. The figure seems to hover over the viewer, giving him a certain magnitude. or solemnity. In this shot of Bob Hoskins in *Mona Lisa* (1986), the angle also provides a view of the majestic ceiling of a great hall, the bright shafts of light adding to the solemn effect. (Island Pictures)

6–4 *The Comfort of Strangers* The mid-range shot is commonly chosen because it places the viewer at eye-level with the actors. In *The Comfort of Strangers* (1990), this neutral angle presents each member of the interesting group (played by Natasha Richardson, Chistopher Walken, and Rupert Everett) as one would see them passing naturally on the street. (Skouras Pictures)

and involving, placing the viewer at eye-level and on a par with the characters in the drama. This range recognizes that most of us live life from a point about four feet from the ground (when sitting in a chair) to five, six, or seven feet high (depending on how tall we are). In addition, it might be argued, we rarely lie on the floor to observe others or perch in high corners of rooms. However, even the most realistic films will, at times, choose angles of vision that are not limited by strictly realistic perspectives. At times, an odd angle can awaken the viewer to the message in a scene. The art of storytelling with the camera demands that the filmmaker consider every shot possibility suggested by the dramatic action at hand.

FRAME COMPOSITION

"The major criterion of a good composition is whether it supports emotionally the scene and the dramatics. The composition has to serve that purpose. You can achieve that with a balanced or unbalanced composition, a symmetrical or an asymmetrical composition; it's proper if it emotionally supports the dramatics. Again, the play's the thing."

Laszlo Kovacs, ASC (*Easy Rider,* 1969)

Anyone who ever took a snapshot of four friends knows that the first moment of decision comes in arranging them into an interesting configuration, taking into account the nature of the location and background. The first inclination may be to line up the group in a row facing the camera and filling the frame. But a more inventive arrangement might put one sitting in the foreground, two standing behind, and the fourth off to the side. If the group were at the rim of the Grand Canyon, the person photographing would want to include areas in the shot for an impressive view of the geography in the background. Backpacks and climbing equipment might be placed on the ground closer to the camera. The picture now takes advantage of the special surroundings and creates a pattern of positioning that is visually more involving.

In somewhat the same way, the director and cinematographer plan out each composition to take advantage of whatever elements within the shot may have to offer. The major difference, of course, is that the movie camera does not simply capture a single instant in time, but records its subject in a series of frames that allow for movement. The director and cinematographer take into account their size, shape, and color values, and then determine which factors hold the strongest intrinsic interest, given the larger visual and thematic intention of the scene. The filmmakers repeat this discussion shot after shot.

Frame Size

The director and cinematographer confront the information seen through the lens in much the same way a painter approaches a canvas. The question for painters is how to fill the two-dimensional surface in front of them. The problem for filmmakers is similar. But unlike the painter, movie directors must take into account that the results of their work will be exposed on film stock of a specific gauge that have fixed and proscribed ratios.

The standard film frame size in America is described in terms of its **aspect ratio**, that is, the ratio of width to height. Before the 1950s, the ratio was a somewhat squarish 1.33: 1, but as movies began to compete with television, the industry felt the need to have not just a larger screen, but one specifically intended to stretch wide the viewing surface. After experimenting with Cinerama (4: 1), Cinemascope (2.35: 1), and Todd-AO (2.2: 1), the *American widescreen* in 35mm camera stock has become the standard at 1.85: 1, although the European ratio is smaller at 1.66: 1. For the majority of films shot here, the canvas onto which directors in the United States paint uses the American widescreen format. However, a turning point, according to many in the industry, was the success of *Dances with Wolves* (1990), shot with Panavision's wider lens in 65mm camera stock and projected on 70mm print stock creating again a format of 2.35: 1. Since its release, a sharply increasing number of American films have chosen this more panoramic screen image.

One reason audiences are drawn to movie theaters is simply that the picture size is so excessive. We want to be overwhelmed by the images. A perfect example is the film history of *Star Wars* (1997). When first released, the movie was a huge financial success, but like all films, ultimately settled over the years into becoming a popular videocassette package and cable feature seen on small television screens. When the movie was rereleased in 1997, its creator, George Lucas, and others in the business expected a modestly profitable interest from the public. It was assumed that most people were familiar with the film because of its ample media exposure. Instead, the movie recaptured massive audiences, primarily because of the presentation of an enhanced edition on the big screen. "The best part is that it has become a celebration of the theatrical experience," said Lucas after. For many media observers, it reconfirmed ongoing domination of viewing films on screens of very large-scale dimensions.

The dimensions of a frame influence what is shown within it. Because the ratios favor the horizontal over the vertical (the picture is nearly twice as wide as it is high), the director has more space to fill at the left and right portions of the frame. For example, an *extreme long shot* of street with a small figure of a man in the center of the frame brings into question how to fill the "empty" space on either side. If the figure on a street is enclosed at the boarders of the frame by tall buildings defined by their deep shadows, the impact of the shot "boxes" the person in and may feel confining. However, if the 1.85: 1 aspect ratio were reduced to the old motion picture ratio of 1.33: 1 (now the standard of the common television set), the effect of such a shot would change. The shot just described would have to be cropped at its horizontal boarders, the result being that the figure, no longer hemmed in by any buildings at the edges of the frame, would be seen in a very different context—a more neutral one. The person would not seem so much "confined," but rather "alone."

The key to understanding how motion pictures work—often repeated in this study in a variety of contexts—is that *each shot*, no matter how short and seemingly inconsequential, is carefully and singularly constructed for visual effectiveness. The predetermined size ratio of the frame becomes the compressed world in which the filmmaker must function. It is a limited space. The job of most filmmakers working in the narrative form is to make the frame appear to be as inclusive as the reality that we normally experience. What is included in a shot, and excluded from it, becomes the informational and aesthetic choice for the director.

Mise-en-scène

The term **mise-en-scène** is borrowed from live French theater has to do with the placement of elements on a stage. Cinema practitioners have translated the concept into a filmic context. As already stated, the movie screen has height and width, but no third dimension: *depth*. The task of the filmmaker, therefore, is to make the viewer sitting in a darkened theater believe that the screen before them has the same dimensions of space that one regularly perceives and experiences in real life.

Very practically, for the movie director, mise-en-scène refers to the arrangement of all the varied elements which make up the composition of each frame: the actors, objects, and natural surrounding, each with a visual mass weight. These factors will influence the camera positioning and lensing, as well as the quality of light and shadow created. With the thoughtful and often painstaking mix of these factors, the director sets up each shot to create the illusion of frame depth **(6–5)**.

A movie screen has three general areas, or *planes,* and the cumulative effect of

6–5   *Que Viva Mexico*   Mise-en-scène can be illustrated simply in this shot. The arrangement of figures has human skulls in the foreground, monks in the middle ground, and young religious boys with a cross in the background. The very placement of each grouping creates a visual statement about the cultural dominance of religion. The Soviet director Sergei Eisenstein and his famous cameraman Eduard Tisse in 1931 traveled to Mexico to make an epic film of an unsuccessful uprising of peons at the turn of the century. *Que Viva Mexico* was reconstructed in 1979 by a surviving collaborator, Grigori Alexandrov.   (Kino International)

them enhances depth perception. By manipulating physical elements at various spots on the planes of photographed space—the *foreground, middle ground,* and *background*—their relationships are designed into the frame. In approximate terms, those actors or objects placed closest to the camera are in the *foreground,* those in the area farthest away make up the *background,* and the heart of the shot is normally the *middle ground.* In desiring to create a truer sense of depth, the filmmaker will compose shots with an awareness of what plane each component is found in in relation to the camera. Elements on each plane also visually link to one another, creating within the shot various patterns that shape the viewer's perception. At times the director will arrange objects precisely balanced within the shot; at other times a seemingly random imbalance works best to produce to desired asymmetrical effect. Not every shot is an obvious study of planes. For example, by its nature, a facial close-up can entirely fill the screen and negate the issue of the planes. However, longer shots necessitate dealing with the visual possibilities using all three planes.

- The **foreground** can be a dominating plane simply because those objects in it, if they are in focus, are closest to us and are the first to demand our attention **(6–6)**. By placing something in the *foreground*—a telephone on the desk in a bedroom—the director is telling us of its importance. The phone may or may not ring, but it will be a controlling image for the time being. Normally, objects in the foreground will take up the entire lower third of the screen, but not necessarily so. For example, the face of a worried cop, may be closest to the camera, but fill only the left side of the frame. To the right of it, the middle ground with the flashing red lights of a police car, and the background, a Boston warehouse district, are distinguished by their relative size or unusual visual attraction, rather that their physical position on the screen. As viewers,

6–6 *Camille Claudel* In *Camille Claudel* (1989), her passion for both Auguste Rodin and his art controlled the life of Camille Claudel (Isabelle Adjani), and the frustration of having to submerge her own creative talent ultimately drove her mad. By placing the sculpture by Rodin in the foreground of the shot, the filmmaker (Bruno Nuytten) quietly suggests the commanding position his work holds in her life. (Orion Classics)

we sort through this visual information, from the foreground to elements deep into the picture.

- The **middle ground** is commonly where the primary action of a shot takes place. Working in the middle ground centers the actors and allows them an ample space in which to move and yet still command attention. When positioned in the center plane of the frame, characters can be captured in a *long shot* or *full shot*, in the midst of the foreground and background. In the scenario just described, if elements within the shot were rearranged, the effect would be quite different. For example, the police car might be in the foreground with its red lights flashing. After first registering this visual announcement of an emergency, the primary focus of attention of the viewer might move to the physical actions of a cop as he roams in the middle ground, with the warehouses providing atmosphere in the background. Such an arrangement positions the main character in this scene for a greater range of activity in the middle of a dangerous environment.

- The **background** is important not only in setting up an atmospheric context for the shot, but because it also promotes a genuine sense of depth in the frame. When photographed with a wide-angle lens (together with the appropriate aperture setting and light level), clearly defined details in the background give the viewer an acute awareness of relative distances. The viewer can select any number of features in the background to focus upon **(6–7)**. In the previous shot description, the warehouse in the background could hold special

6–7   *The Bridges of Madison County*   The background of a covered bridge was natural inclusion in shots from *The Bridges of Madison County* (1995). Although the primary interest in the scene concerns the romantically hesitant exchange of Francesca (Meryl Streep) and Robert (Clint Eastwood), the bridge in the background is a constant reminder of the conservative environment in which their daring relationship struggles. The very popular fiction novel by Robert Waller, firmly set in the Midwest, needed the genuine look of an Iowa farming community described in the book.   (Warner Bros.)

interest, beyond simply establishing atmosphere, if human movement were seen on an upper floor and a rifle barrel slowly slipped through a broken window. Our eyes would pick out the primary interest in the frame, even though it is in the background. It is also true that the background, if not in focus, may simply provide a blurred image or a wash of color, so that it does not draw attention away from the other planes.

Depending on the dramatic intentions of the director, the three planes are given varying emphasis in each shot. **Deep focus** lensing enables all the planes to be in focus, and in this way is less controlling, giving the viewer a choice of what to watch. The eye can wander from some detail in the foreground to something else far in the background. With deep focus photography, a director will regularly use concentrated lighting on an object or movement of a key player as elements in the frame to lead the audience's attention to a desired center of dramatic interest. One common method is to intentionally focus on only one plane—a woman smiling wickedly in the background—rendering the other planes unwatchable. Some motion picture critics resent this controlling style, seeing it as overly manipulative in that it forces specific visual attention. Others see such tactics as simply the prerogative of any artist.

The Connotation of Lines

From the viewpoint of the visual artist, one way the world is seen and can be explained is by its **lines**—*horizontal, vertical, diagonal, curved, straight, jagged,* etc. Mountains, furniture, buildings, the human body—everything around us—can be visually defined and appreciated in terms of its *lines*. The content of any film frame can be said to have an internal design created by its *dominant lines*. Most cinematographers are aware of these linear values, especially in specific shots that emphasize images of large or juxtaposed graphic mass, and many compose their shots to subtly build on their shape. For example, cinematographers are very aware of the visual impact of shadow lines in a shot. Such strong linear definition can add a powerful dramatic statement to a moment in film **(6–8)**.

6–8   *Reservoir Dogs*   The linear energy within a frame may be gained simply by the posture of bodies. In Quentin Tarantino's *Reservoir Dogs* (1992), the visual interest in this shot is, in part, the effect of the lines formed by their extended arms that appear to almost physically connect these two characters (Steve Buscemi and Harvey Keitel) in a deadly face-off. This terrifying symmetry creates the visual tension of this shot.   (Miramax Films)

Although the following definitions are generalities and are affected by spatial contexts, it seems to hold that certain line directions suggest particular emotional meanings for people in this culture.

- **Horizontal lines** can give a feeling of serenity, harmony, and stability. The ultimate horizontal line is, not surprisingly, the horizon. When we picture an unbroken stretch of the horizon, whether it is from an ocean shore or the endless fields of the prairie states, a common reaction might be one of calm. Generally, filmmakers will emphasize such lines in their frames when striving for tranquil responses. Paradoxically, depending on the intent of the filmmaker, horizontal lines sometimes suggest boredom and tedious uniformity, or even an uncomfortable expectation of some ominous arrival. In *North by Northwest* (1959), a dull fear begins to grow in the hunted Cary Grant character (and the audience) when he is left off in the silent, flat, and seemingly endless Indiana farmland. It presented a physical dimension with seemingly no escape. Hitchcock achieved the emotional force of this scene by purely visual means.

- **Vertical lines** demand to be noticed because they interrupt the sweep of our eyes across the screen. Vertical lines may suggest potency and vigor, and perhaps even a challenge **(6–9)**. A lone horseman on the plains is easily spotted, as is the only boy with his hand raised in a full classroom. Shots that stress the perpendicular lines of buildings or the sharp rise of walls in a room call attention to themselves with their opposite visual energy. For *Matilda* (1996), in

6–9   *Thirty Two Short Films about Glenn Gould*   **Vertical lines** can suggest opposition, conflict, confinement. In Francois Girard's biographical film *Thirty Two Short Films about Glenn Gould* (1994), a movie about the eccentric and extremely talented Canadian pianist, the director shot Gould (Colm Feore) behind metal stands in a recording studio. The visual effect is one of imprisonment, an apt comment on the pianist's emotional state. Alert filmmakers visually design their shots to reinforce the dramatic purpose of a scene.   (The Samuel Goldwyn Company)

6–10 *Shallow Grave* The **diagonal lines** created by shafts of light caused by gunshots into an attic reflect the demented mental state that David (Christopher Eccleston) has sunken in Shallow Grave (1994). Having found his roommate dead from a drug overdose, he and two others cut up the body and stolen a suitcase of cash. This leads to a string of paranoid betrayals. The film effectively conveys the resulting madness best in purely visual terms. (Gramercy Pictures)

shots set up in the UCLA library, director Danny DeVito and cinematographer Stefan Czapsky emphasized the impressive vertical lines of the book stacks in order to give the room the majestic thrust of a cathedral, a visual tribute to the world of literature and imagination that captures the spirit of Roald Dahl's book. A theme of this film is expressed by these imposing lines that enclose and overwhelm the viewer, suggesting a sense of intellectual security that literacy can bring.

- **Diagonal lines** tend to imply movement, striving, urgency, or simply confusion **(6–10)**. In a shot featuring track and field athletes, the linear image of a sprinter on the blocks, all angles forward, gives a sense of the power of the diagonal line. These lines, especially when used at random, can indicate confusion. The many diagonal lines used in the nightmarish set design throughout the classic silent film *The Cabinet of Dr. Caligari* (1919) creates an off-kilter world, effectively disorienting the viewer. The images are meant to reflect the emotionally disturbed inner reality of a madman, and the effect is memorably achieved.

- **Straight lines** bring up uniformity, exactness, agreement, or, at times, monotony. A filmmaker will sometimes deliberately fill the screen with images displaying undeviating line patterns to give a visual sense of order and dependability.

- **Curved lines,** it has been observed, hold more intrinsic interest than straight lines. Perhaps it is human nature for the eye to be attracted to lines that create fluent and varied shapes. Consistently, a fascinating subject for both photographers and painters has been the curving lines of the nude human body.

Linear considerations will not be a factor in the composition of every shot, and some filmmakers give little notice to their effect. But it would be careless not to weigh the impact of lines when very important shots that establish the visual environment of a film are being planned. In *Alien* (1979), the details of the interior and exterior of the spacecraft have rounded lines rather than sharp angles. The nature of the threat—a vicious alien lifeform—is foreshadowed in the many organic-looking shapes designed into the movie. By means of the careful manipulation of line patterns and the resulting spatial relationships within the shot, the director silently determines our emotional expectations and response.

The Illusion of Depth: Linear Perspective

As we become engrossed in a movie, it is difficult to imagine the movie screen as having only a two-dimensional surface. The movie camera, after all, is actually recording a three-dimensional space in which people walk, cars race, and the wind blows onto two-dimensional film stock. In a theater, the movie screen then feeds us with continuous information about the relative size, shape, and speed of each element photographed. We become absorbed into the filmed world presented to us, convinced on a visual level that the event is actually "happening" in three-dimensional space.

When considering the placement of images within a two-dimensional frame, filmmakers must weigh a host of factors when preparing to shoot. The director composes a special world within each shot composition, taking into account the placement of the elements. Working on a sound stage, this calls for physically manipulating the arrangement of objects, human and otherwise. But when on location, the task becomes one of sharply observing the existing environment and positioning the camera, if desired, so that the full dimensions of it are completely explored. The director can do many things to enhance the illusion of depth, facilitating our unquestioned involvement and credence.

One talent necessary to cinematographers is an acute sense of **linear perspective.** In our daily lives, we mentally balance the varying degrees of size and shape of things, forming a natural and delicate sense of depth perception from our cumulative experience of motion and space. For the filmmaker, every potential shot has physical elements within it that are situated at various distances from the camera lens **(6–11)**. For example, when an automobile waiting at an intersection suddenly drives off toward the distant horizon, becoming progressively smaller until it almost disappears, we match our perception of the event on the screen with what we commonly know about physical movement and our experience in three-dimensional space. We see objects at various distances—objects farther away from us naturally appear smaller in size—and project a linear connection to their relative shapes and sizes, depending on where they are in relation to the horizon. With the gradation in relative size of the objects becoming smaller within the frame as they recede in space, we project imaginary lines drawn along referent points of objects in the *foreground*, *middle ground*, and *background*. When a camera lens is placed parallel to the ground, the "lines" will seemingly converge at what is properly called the *vanishing point* on the horizon. The

6–11 *Let Him Have It* Artful linear perspective is designed into this shot to enclose a killer (Paul Reynolds) in its shapes and light. In this climactic scene from Peter Medak's *Let Him Have It* (1991), a killer (Craig Reynolds) is trapped by police on a rooftop, and by placing the character at the center of converging lines, the message appears to be that there is no way out. (Fine Line Features)

filmmaker uses our linear common sense to achieve an illusion of depth on a two-dimensional screen **(6–12)**.

Directors traditionally favor the movement of objects and people *toward* and *away* from the camera at various angles. By exploring movement that travels *into* rather than *across* the screen, the viewer sees that action without reminders of its very real frame dimensions. The director uses the limited dimensions of the screen well when people and objects pass directly or diagonally *into* or *out of* the depth of the shot. It is in that direction in which *infinity* lies, whereas the actual physical width of the screen may be only, let us say, 30 feet. To illustrate simply: A fixed movie camera films a security guard passing from left to right at a normal pace. On the screen, we would first see a blank screen, then the sudden introduction of the guard on the left, her stride as she crosses the screen, her disappearance, and again a blank screen. Lateral movement that takes a person literally in and out of the frame at the borders can have the effect of heightening audience awareness of the finite dimensions of the screen, and therefore the momentary recognition that what they are watching is "only a movie." Smallest elements that work against the "suspension of disbelief" are avoided when possible by most filmmakers.

6–12   *The Trial*   This shot from Orson Welles' *The Trial* (1962), photographed by Edmond Richard, illustrates how the linear perspective of an image aids the filmmaker in transforming the screen's two-dimensional borders to appear as three-dimensional space. Joseph K. (Anthony Perkins), the white collar worker from Franz Kafka's novel, is caught in the nightmare experience of being permanently under suspicion for unspecified crimes. The seemingly endless rows of lights, beams, and desks of an office interior give a visual sense that the lines converge toward infinity, registering for the viewer as the perception of depth on an otherwise flat surface.   (Museum of Modern Art)

READING THE FRAME

Directors, cinematographers, and editors generally agree on certain principles of how the movie screen is "read." Although watching a film seems to be an activity that is happening *to* us, in fact, we are vigorously involved in putting together the many visual details and relate them to our base of understanding. Filmmakers have discovered that most viewers see and interpret what is on the screen in a similar manner.

It is helpful, for example, to refer to the movie screen in terms of the *division of thirds*. Just as it is instructive to explain the screen in terms of foreground, middle ground, and background, when reading the frame laterally it is useful to define its space as the *left third*, the *center third*, and the *right third*. Visual emphasis will not often be equally distributed to each section of the screen. This holds true especially for films shot for the wide screen ratios.

It is widely believed as people in cultures of *western* orientation, we "read" the movie screen as we do words on a page—with left to right eye movement. Thus, we normally scan the images starting with those on the *left* section of the frame (as we face it) and move through the other two thirds of the screen. With each new shot, we quickly reregister at the *left* and absorb its information in a sweep to the *right* (modified somewhat if the following shot puts the dominant action in the same area where the previous shot had focused our attention). If this is true—many filmmakers shoot movies assuming this—it is still not clear which third of the screen naturally *dominates* our attention, and in what manner. To the casual viewer, the question may seem to be idle speculation. For the purpose of illustration, imagine this simple scenario:

> *In a whitewashed "Mediterranean Villa," a woman confronts a man about his unfaithfulness. Moving about the room, they argue. They reach a stalemate— she leaves; he reflects upon what just happened.*

For the director shooting the action, at some point a decision must be made where actors are to be seen on the screen. These choices become the refinements of directing. The implications of this positioning have special consequences, and how the director chooses to develop the action of the actors in the frame depends on several factors. In staging this scene, suppose the outraged woman in the living room of the villa is positioned in *left* portion of the screen, a small empty space takes up the center, with an astonished but defiant man on the *right*. Something can be said for the dramatic impact of each position.

- The *left third* of the screen has the first and therefore seemingly the most important impact **(6–13)**. For example, in our scenario, the woman on the left immediately takes our attention. We start with her before our eyes travel to

6–13 *Mister Johnson* The left third of the screen is often reserved, as it were, for the "subject" of the shot. Reading the frame from left to right, our eyes first pick up objects at this point which we register as the first object of interest, and often, therefore, of primary importance. In *Mister Johnson* (1990), the lead actor (Maynard Eziashi) controls the frame from his left corner position.

(Avenue Entertainment)

6–14 *Prisoner of the Mountains* In *Prisoner of the Mountains* (1996) director Sergei Bodrov uses the center third of the screen as negative space. Here we see two Russian prisoners (Sergei Bodrov Jr. and Oleg Menshikov), alienated from each other for reasons established in the plot, being held hostage in a Chechen village. The white space of the wall in the center represents both the personal chasm they feel between them and the hopelessness of their situation.   (Orion Classics)

the right of the screen where the man stands. A figure in the left area can be considered the "subject" of the shot, comparable to its traditional grammatical sense in the description of language.

- The *center third* of the screen is the natural focal point of attention. In the balance between the outer thirds of the screen, it is the area of greatest *intrinsic interest*. In the shot previously described, the center of the screen between the man and woman is a *negative space*, representing the "chasm" between them **(6–14)**. The impact of this empty section is as important as if it were the center of a physical activity.

- The *right third* is thought to be the *heaviest* part of the screen, the "direct object" as we read the screen grammatically **(6–15)**. We tend to drift to the right in the frame and momentarily settle there. In the example, we move from interpreting the woman on the left to discovering the reaction of the man on

6–15 *The Year My Voice Broke* The right third of the screen is often the area where the "object" of the dramatic action in the shot is positioned. In this still photo from the film *The Year My Voice Broke* (1988), the obvious focus of attention for both the girls in the story and the audience watching is the boy standing (Noah Taylor). Our eyes run from left to right (following the interest of the girls) coming to rest on the boy who is receiving hesitant scrutiny.
(Avenue Entertainment)

the right. As our eyes settle on the *right third* of the screen, we look for his response to her anger.

If, in fact, we do tend to read the movie screen from left to right, certain practical and aesthetic considerations for the director in designing movement within the shot will follow. Because the right third of the screen is believed to have more weight, its density is thought to draw our eyes to this location. Therefore, the direction of the movement of objects within the frame presents some interesting practical questions. For example, in a film about two young people who hop into a car and hit the open road to finally escape the confining life of their small town, the favored screen movement of the car would be from *left to right*. The direction of the car matches the natural sweep of the eyes across the screen, and their flight from their restrictive past has an easy and visually free sense to it.

Conversely, if the filmmaker wishes to subtly emphasize the struggle and pressure that the two young people may be feeling, a *right to left* direction for the car would have it moving "against the grain," as it were, of the flow of vision. The shot of a person or object moving toward the left border of the screen is often used to give the feeling of struggle against an opposing force inhibiting the movement in that direction. If, in a horror movie, an unknowing and innocent victim walks in a darkened hallway of a haunted house, having him go from *right to left* seems to take him in a direction that *physically* opposes him. The resistance is felt by the audience, which silently roots for him to turn back.

These "rules," however, are not always observed. Indeed, in other situations a filmmaker may consciously choose to go against the accepted practices to create a slightly off-balance, eccentric feeling in a movie. The director of a horror film may have the potential victim in the hallway move in the opposite direction, from *left to right,* to create a seductive attitude of lightness, so that when a grim surprise at the final door comes, it will have greater shock value. In another circumstance, if the two people (Thelma and Louise, for example) leaving town in the car are escaping West, the director most likely shows their car moving toward the *left* border of the frame no matter what their psychological orientation, because in the visual logic of map reading, west is left; east is right.

There are also positions of **emotional dominance**. Every movie has scores of situations between two characters in which one of them, for the moment, is in the more assertive dramatic position. Positioning these figures in the frame is an interesting puzzle. A boy is asking a girl for a date. Commonly, the boy would be in the *left third* of the frame because the dramatic energy is being initiated by him. The girl would be positioned in the *right third* of the shot, normally the "receiving" end of the screen. In that spot, the audience tends to focus on evaluating the girl's *reaction* to the advances being sent her way. Her facial and body language would be the object of attention, the position becoming one of *emotional dominance*. On the other hand, the director might put the girl on the *left*; as a result the *emotional dominance* would tend to fall on the boy to the right, calling attention less to his assertive request than to his verbal or nonverbal reaction to her response. The two shots have a slightly different dramatic energy. Movie directors play with many such visual nuances.

Graphic Weight

Reading the frame, however, has even more complexities. In the "Mediterranean Villa" scenario, the shot could be filled with physical details—furniture of unusual design, the enclosing lines of the room, the posture of the man, the color of the woman's dress, a striking view sail boats at sea out a window on the back wall—all of which have varying linear designs and visual strengths. Every object in a frame carries a **graphic weight.** It is as if the screen were a sensitive scale that can be tipped one way or the other, depending on the mass of graphic weight in any one area **(6–16)**. For example, sometimes the pure *size* of the actor—a John Candy—assures the visual command of the screen. But *weight* does not only refer to absolute size. Anything placed close to the camera will take up a great percentage of screen space, hence, its *graphic weight* is exaggerated. Then too, if in the frame a man were wearing a neon red shirt, our eyes would be pulled by the *weight* of color. Or if the woman was standing by a door inlaid with intricate patterns of rosewood, our eyes might be drawn to the left. Larger, more strikingly designed elements in the picture will demand our attention. Because of the eye's attraction to elements with strong graphic mass, the alert filmmaker will compose each shot predicting where visual interest will rest.

It is useful to consider Michael Snow's 45-minute experimental film *Wavelength* (1967). It is a wonderfully extreme exercise in the slow evolution of graphic weight

6–16   *The Wages of Fear*   *The Wages of Fear* (1953), a highly suspenseful thriller by Henri Georges Clouzot, is about two men attempting to escape from a rural South American mountain village in a truck loaded with nitroglycerin. The constant sight of this dangerous vehicle is a the primary source of the film's unrelieved tension. The graphic weight within the frame is established by the massiveness of the truck, dominating three-fourths of the screen in this shot.   (Kino International)

⋆ A TOUCH OF EVIL

A famous 200-second shot opens Orson Welles' *Touch of EviL* (1958), which demonstrates power of a screen alive with shifting graphic weights, created by inventive camera work and intricately choreographed body movements within the frame. During the shot, an array of *fluctuating graphic weights* develop due to the confluence of a camera almost always in motion and figures in the frame continually changing their physical relationship to one another. An outline of the movement follows:

It's nighttime. The shot begins with a close-up of a timer being set for an explosive, swings wide to show a darkened street with a man and woman, then the camera follows the bomber as he puts the device into the trunk of a white convertible. The shot rapidly swoops up (the camera is on a crane mounted to a vehicle) as the couple get in the car and drive, our viewpoint sweep-

ing the rooftops of shabby buildings before catching up with the car and moving ahead of it as the car turns a corner and cruises toward a retreating camera, now lowered to near street level. The camera by now has revealed a street corner at night in what appears to be a sleazy downtown area. When the car stops for cross traffic, the camera picks up another man (Charlton Heston) and woman (Janet Leigh), and they walk briskly down the street. The screen at this point is alive with a flux of visual information—the varying distance of the camera from the couple, the changing background of buildings as they walk in front of them, the convertible now showing up again, other street people coming into the frame and passing by as the camera continues on. As the couple reaches what turns out to be a border crossing, they are stopped at the U.S. Customs shack by a gate guard, where they announce

to him that they are newly married. At the same time the white convertible, an older man and young woman in it, pulls up next to them. When Heston and Leigh circle behind the car, the camera at first stays with the car passengers and the guard, then refocuses on the couple as they continue to walk and talk. The single shot ends with the two lovers kissing, then suddenly cuts to the convertible blowing up!

This exceptional shot is a classic example of sustained visual energy on the screen. As the camera defines what is framed and as objects converge, the complex surges of movement propel the viewer both forward and in conflicting directions. Such extended shots take much planning and exacting choreography. At any moment, the relative graphic weights of the images are being altered. With it, our emotional reactions also change.

within a frame. The piece consists of just one slow *zoom shot*, starting with a wide shot in a New York loft and finally bringing a photograph on the far wall into *extreme close-up*. During the shot, several dramatic events happen in and out of the range of the camera, but the zoom is unrelenting as it "closes" space. The experience of watching this film is excruciating, and one could claim that little is happening. On the other hand, the film's images and mass weights are constantly shifting and being displaced, so that viewers are intermittently awakened by the gradual but complete reshaping of visual elements and the values that we then attach to them. *Wavelength* seems to tell the viewer that spatial investigation itself is a proper and fundamental subject for film.

In more limited and less exhausting ways, many commercial movies use the technique of the focus a camera closing in on a subject as other elements in the shot are eliminated. For example, a crucial shot in Francis Ford Coppola's *The Conversation* (1974), a film about electronic eavesdropping and paranoia, is one from high above a crowded downtown plaza. The shot is so inclusive that at first we don't know what we are looking for. As the shot very slowing zooms in, we gradually discover, by the exclusion of alternatives, that we are focused on and following a young unaware couple. Much of the film's technique has to do with the selection of reality by a highly driven and neurotic wiretapper (Gene Hackman).

A FUNDAMENTAL SHOT SERIES

Much of shooting narrative film involves simply recording exchanged dialogue with certain standard cinematic practices. For example, despite his many innovative experiments with the camera, a close study of the films of Alfred Hitchcock shows that his basic style was very deliberate and lean, repeating variations of the shot selections similar to those described here. Setting up a simple scene and selecting the shots that convey natural verbal interchanges is not as easy as it may appear. This situation must be planned in exact detail if the flow of the conversation is to maintain its visual interest and naturalness. To illustrate, consider this common scene involving two persons: a young man and woman sit at a table in a coffeehouse having a conversation. Quite typically, a filmmaker could approach shooting this scene from the following basic seven-shot repertoire, illustrated in figures **6–17a–g**.

6–17a   *Master Shot*   This inclusive master shot establishes a couple sitting at a table in a cafe drinking coffee and conversing. Commonly, a scene will evolve by breaking down the action into smaller components, such as those that follow.

6–17b   *Over-the-shoulder (favoring the woman)*   The camera uses a medium shot of the woman talking or listening from a point of view of the man. The view comes from behind his shoulder and includes a small portion of his head.

6–17c   *Over-the-shoulder (favoring the man)*   This shot is a reverse of the previous one. Over-the-shoulder shots can be repeated many times as the conversation continues. The sight lines—the direction of the eyes of either person as they appear to look at each other's face—are established in the shot and are usually maintained in the shots following.

6–17d   *"Cheat" shot (on woman)*   The camera distance in relation to the woman is basically the same with this shot, but now the man is removed from the frame. In film grammar, once the visual relationship between the man and woman is established, the camera can take the liberty (that is, *cheat*) to concentrate on a single figure.

6–17e   *"Cheat" shot (on man)*   A reverse of the previous shot from the opposite side of the table. These shots may repeated, be interchanged with over-the-shoulder shots, or go on to the next more intimate shots. The sight lines, however, should remain relatively fixed, with the assumption that another person is present across the table and interacting.

6–17f   *Close Shot (on woman)*   This shot creates a more intense focus on the participants, and is used to raise the level of intimacy. Although the person's opposite has moved no closer, the viewer now lets go of realistic space relationships and enters into dramatic alliance with the character.

6–17g   *Close Shot (on man)*   To balance the concentration of the scene, the filmmaker might match close shots of the two lovers with repeated cuts, or retreat to a less intimate distance. The director can keep the sight lines intact, or may chose to have the actor look directly into the camera lens.

Some directors, especially those with an aesthetic grounded in realism, tend not to take this shot making approach. Director Mike Leigh (*Secrets and Lies,* 1996) remarks, "I never shoot part of a scene. I shoot the whole scene to get the action." This filmic attitude would want the critical drama of a scene to grow organically in real time, as it were, from the interaction of a continuing performance by the actors.

The Axis of Action

One of the subtle but real problems of telling a story in edited shots is that confusion for the audience arises if there is no coherent sense of spatial relationships. The position of each character in relation to the others must be clearly understood by the viewer. For example, if two people are supposed to be engaged in a face-to-face discussion, yet as one shot cuts to the other, they seem to be looking in the same direction, with the exact background detail in each frame, a viewer would be properly confused.

The problem is solved for filmmakers by a method of shooting using the **axis of action** (also called the **line of action**). This is an imaginary zone of 180 degrees within which the camera (or cameras) must stay when recording a set piece of action. When shooting, the director must always be aware of the boundaries of the axis of action. In the seven-frame sequence just illustrated, note the position of the camera as it covers the action. Placed to the right of the man, he is always looking toward the left edge of the frame that at first includes the woman. The woman looks in the opposite direction, that is, from right to left. In order for the rest of the scene to make visual sense, the camera's relationship to them must stay somewhere in this same zone, the boundary of which is an imaginary line dissecting their bodies. As long as the camera stays a few degrees on one side of the established axis of action, a visual logic of the conversation can be maintained. If the camera, in the middle of their discussion, were to be suddenly placed outside of the designated line of action to the opposite side of the table (by the window), the positions of the two people would appear to be looking in the same direction (in other words, sitting on the same side of the table.) The problem is explicitly realized when putting together the shots during editing. The flow of action would become visually confusing **(6–18)**.

CAMERA MOVEMENT

A special phenomenon of motion pictures is that not only does the camera record movement before it, *the camera itself* can move while continuously taking its pictures. This important feature gives the filmmaker almost unlimited possibilities when photographing a subject. The camera is free to approach the dramatic action of a story in a variety of ways—the camera, in fact, can *become* the action. The mobility of the camera allows the viewer to experience either an incremental gain or loss of visual information, and the *sensation of movement*. A simple experience of movement happens when a camera is mounted on the lead car of a roller coaster: as the viewer experiences the rapidly evolving inclining and curving tracks with the same excite-

6–18   *Mindwalk*   When shooting three people, a triangular arrangement is often used to make plain the visual flow of conversation. In *Mindwalk* (1991), a movie that repeatedly confronts philosophic issues, John Heard (center) is positioned in the center as the *arbiter of attention,* that is, his eye direction guides the audience about where to focus their judgment. The next shot would logically be a reaction shot favoring Sam Waterson (left), rather than a close shot of Liv Ullmann (right).   (Triton Pictures)

ment as rider. Nothing in movies is ordained to be static. The pure sensual stimulation of the person sitting safely in a theater seat is exhilarating. The mobility of the camera *generates* the changing patterns and shifting relationships within the shot.

Certain film genres announce their preoccupation with movement. It is one of their primary attractions. Movies with themes developed in hi-tech action/adventures, dance/musicals, sport, and war movies advertise their visual excitement, and studios bet on this appeal. Adam Greenberg, the cinematographer of the blockbuster *Terminator 2* (1992), was acutely aware of the power of the moving camera in this film. "There's not one static shot. Even in the closet, the camera moves; inside the car, the camera moves!" A greater degree of camera movement in narrative movies over the past decades is evident. Audiences have become accustomed to the dynamic uses of camera. The reasons for this are many, including the extraordinary advances made in the equipment that carries cameras. Director Robert Altman (*Short Cuts,* 1993) favors extreme camera movement as a method of discovery.

It's all very, very challenging for the cinematographer, but I like to keep the camera in motion, nearly at all times. We set up an event and document it. We don't compose pictures. I've often said that all good things in a film are a series of accidents, and this technique enables us to capture those accidents as they happen.

But increased camera movement may also be of deeper cultural significance. Whereas the stationary camera plants itself and records a world from a fixed position with secure precision, this style of camera work may be more reflective of a time past, when life seemed more rooted and when events seemed more predictable and certain, less ambivalent. Today, the constantly moving camera suggests—imitates, actually—the continuous change and evolution that we see almost daily in politics, behavior, values, style, and taste. The camera slides through space, giving endless changes of perspective. Nothing is fixed. The very subject of certain films is movement. The primary intention of the Jerry Bruckheimer-produced movie *Gone in Sixty Seconds* (2000) is the film's capacity for visual exploitation of nonstop movement, whether by the cameras or the streaking cars and frenzied people they record. Certainly the content of movie scripts has changed over the years, but the very method in which the films are shot also reflects a culture overwhelmed with motion and change. Movies, even in technique, can be said to mirror life.

The Russian/Cuban production *I Am Cuba* (1964) is a spectacular example of how camera movement can both energize and comment upon the theme of a film. Made as a tribute to the Cuban revolution, Soviet director Mikhail Kalatozov and cinematographer Sergei Urusevsky roamed through the city of Havana and the lush mountainous countryside, continually exploring and surrounding the sensuous environments and varied action with the camera. An unsurpassed showcase for the extensive use of hand-held (and later body-mounted) cameras, the filmmakers immerse the audience in a visual adventure of movement that takes us seamlessly in and out of contrasting environments. One continuous shot begins with a beauty contest on the rooftop of a luxury hotel set in corrupt pre-Revolutionary times. The camera wanders through a crowd of bikini-clad women and leering men, moves to a lower terrace to another large group of partygoers congregated around a swimming pool, peers over the edge of the building to the beaches far below, then follows a woman in a bikini into the pool, the camera sinking blow the surface to record the revelry from that angle. In this one extended shot, with a camera moving through space, the filmmakers capture the hectic and lavish reality of a pampered class. Camera movement in most movies is much more subtle, but the sense of visual freedom that a moving camera brings is an attractive option for every director.

The art of shooting a film is not easily codified. Much is learned as the film is being shot. The director must weigh the aesthetic implications of each shot. In the end, the prime consideration of any shot selection is how well it advances the story. If the cumulative progression of shots does not build coherent scenes, and if the scenes do not become the structure and rhythm of filmic storytelling, the director has not done the job.

There are a number of standard camera movements, however, that have developed through the years, some very basic. As equipment has become ever more innovative, camera movement has become increasingly sophisticated. What follows is a descriptive list of shots created by moving cameras:

Pan Shot.   When a camera turns and records horizontally on a fixed axis, usually mounted on a fluid head tripod, the movement is called a **pan**. Simply put, the camera movement resembles tracing an action by turning one's head. There are three primary uses of the pan shot.

- First, because the *pan shot* mimics head movement, it is often a *subjective* shot intended to give us the interior experience of the person watching an action. At an outdoor cafe, from a fixed position (supposedly the seat of the character observing), the camera follows a woman as she walks by from left to right, slows to light a cigarette, and then passes on. During this pan shot, the woman is centered in the frame so that we are watching *her*, rather than being concerned with the passing background. Although she is moving, she is always in the same area of the frame, and therefore there is a constant source of focus.

- Second, the pan shot is used to *discover* new bits of information or *reveal* backgrounds in a gradual and visually digestible manner. For example, such a shot might pan a young man's bedroom, letting us first see an old model airplane tucked away on a shelf, then move to his dresser with socks hanging out, a college pennant on the wall, photos of several different girls in bathing suits, a traffic ticket on a messy desk, and finally to the character sleeping in a disheveled bed. The shot demands our alertness to discover what will be visually disclosed moment by moment. If it is a left to right pan, for instance, our eyes search out the right edge of the frame, as it brings to light new information. By the end, we have learned something about this young man.

- Third, the pan can be used as a tool of storytelling to indicate a *relationship*. If a shot were to first focus on a man with a briefcase sitting in an airline terminal, then pan left across a row a waiting travelers, and finally settle on a suspicious-looking man glancing to his right, we would know, without a word spoken, that either some kind of a relationship exists between the two men or one would soon become evident. Pan shots create visual bridges between their beginning and end points.

A **cross pan** describes a shot that picks up and follows the movement of one subject, but when it intersects with another, the camera then locks on the second subject to trace the direction of its movement. A **swish pan**—a very fast camera swing that blurs the intervening images—is used stylishly to either shock the viewer into attention upon the final resting point of the shot or as an editing device to take the viewer from one scene and zip to the next.

Tilt Shot.   Like the pan shot, the **tilt shot** is usually done with a camera fixed on a tripod, but now it scans a subject *vertically*. Again, this shot lends itself to the subjective reality of an observer. For example, when a young woman gets out of a cab at the high-rise office building of her new job, a tilt shot moving up the building might be intended to capture the awesomeness of the moment. Or when Mr. Right arrives at her apartment door in his brief jogging outfit, the camera starts at his sneakers and slowly tilts up his body. Tilt shots can make humorous commentary: the movement from garish tie to the homely face of the person wearing it or a subtle revelation when a shot *tilts down* from a character's eyes to a notepad she is writing on.

Dolly Shot. This is a most versatile and inventive camera movement. With a camera mounted on a platform cushioned with rubber wheels and designed for maximum maneuverability, the effect of the shot is a smooth, gliding movement through space. Because the camera lens becomes the eyes of the viewer, use of this shot gives the sensation of real passage through whatever environment is being shown. In this sense, it is a discovery shot **(6–19)**.

   Dolly shots are regularly used to create a slight but telling *intensity*. A seated man, in a medium shot, is being interrogated about a murder by a detective. The camera very gradually dollies forward, now evolving into a close shot of the accused man. His expression is unchanged. However, the dimensions of the images within the frame have gradually been redefined by the compressing dolly movement as we are drawn closer to him. We now have been silently "told" by the camera to study this face for a clue to his guilt or innocence. Depending on the nature of the story, the effect may confirm the accusation for the audience. The movement creates an almost tangible

6–19 *Prick Up Your Ears* By fixing the camera to a dolly—a platform on cushioned wheels—film photography becomes very mobile. The mechanism allows the cinematographer a great latitude of flexibility, as it smoothly moves the camera through space. Here, director Stephen Frears (seated) plans his next dolly shot for *Prick Up Your Ears* (1987). (The Samuel Goldwyn Company)

sense of expectation and pressure. Contrary to this, a camera movement away from the subject often decreases tension and signals the end of a scene.

Like the pan shot, a dolly shot also may be used to indicate a subjective point of view, but instead of imitating the human head turning, it puts us into someone's body as that person moves forward. In doing so, we see that world unfolding. For example, in a suspenseful film, the dolly shot might start in the hallway of a house, pass through the arch of the living room, approach a coffee table to take note of a broken vase, swing around to look at a dreary landscape through the window, then continue on to a darkened kitchen. The flow of things past the camera as it moves in the rooms gives the viewer a sense of not being just a cool observer of the place, but being a part of it.

Elaborate and intricately planned dolly shots are expensive to shoot because so many things can go wrong, calling for repeated takes. For example, the dollying camera must always maintain perfect depths of field and be always on target. Lighting the set for a camera in motion is also very complex because the quality of luminosity has to be predicted with every shift of position. In addition, dolly shots often entail not only the movement of a camera, but also actors changing their positions in relation to one another and the camera. Because such shots are frequently of a longer duration, to achieve a flawless take, the actors must pick up their cues perfectly. Sometimes a greater number of takes are needed than with a fixed camera placement and with that, precious time is spent on the set. (It is understandable, therefore, that camera work for most television drama is usually kept simple and straightforward, avoiding costly extended use of the dolly shot.)

Some directors simply like the gracefulness of the shot. The dolly shot has gained popularity with many directors, giving them endless opportunities for a more lavish look. Don McAlpine was the cinematographer in Philip Noyce's *Patriot Games* (1992), and *dolly shots* were an integral part of the film's effectiveness; as McAlpine notes, "I'd say that the camera's moving in 80 percent of the shots in *Patriot Games*. Sometimes I'd do what I eventually dubbed the 'Noyce creep,' where on a single close-up we'd just be imperceptibly creeping in; the audience will never notice, but it adds a little tension." When used well, the design of this shot should complement the inherent complexity of the subject matter.

Tracking shot. This method is another way to move the camera through space. For convenience and to insure a smooth glide of the camera, *tracks* are actually laid down so that the camera platform can traverse some distance with sure and steady ease. Commonly, this has been used outdoors where uneven ground is a problem, so that a steady, parallel, and regular camera distance can be maintained. Two people in conversation walking through a field may have the camera either in front of them tracking back, or alongside them, shooting at three-quarters or in profile. This allows the actors to remain centered in a frame that is not jiggling. Some directors prefer to use tracks on sets to provide focal accuracy and precise control of the camera.

Zoom Shot. Sometimes the zoom shot is confused with a dolly shot in that both shots bring the primary subject of the shot either closer to, or farther from, the viewer. But the two shots work in very different ways. A *zoom-in* or *zoom-out* shot is less complicated (and therefore less expensive) than a dolly shot because it simply calls for lens adjustment. The **zoom shot** relies on the particular qualities of the camera lens—a good zoom lens has focal length between 20mm and 200mm—and when the lens is adjusted, it either pulls in or pushes away the central image and the background equally. With the *zoom-in shot*, it is as if one were to hold a photograph at arm's length, then gradually brings it much closer to the eyes. The entire picture would be brought forward with its relative dimensions within the photo unchanged. A constant distance between the subject and the camera is maintained as the main figure is brought closer, even though elements on all sides are increasingly lost. Again, the reverse is true if it's a *zoom-out shot*. A dolly shot, on the other hand, physically moves the camera (hence the viewer) *into* the set, and as the movement carried on, the frame progressively increases the size of objects in the foreground at a faster rate as objects move past the camera. The reverse is true if the dolly shot moves backward.

The zoom shot is effective when the purpose of the shot, for example, is to draw attention to a specific figure by drawing it closer, at the same time giving the viewer the comfort of a distant bystander. Documentary filmmakers first found this shot very useful when photographing situations from safer or less intrusive shooting venues. After having seen the zoom shot in countless documentaries, audiences have tended to associate the technique with a more realistic style of filmmaking. The technique was overdone in the 1960s and now has a slightly dated look when it shows up with great frequency in a movie.

Body Assisted Shots

When a camera operator holds the camera, the chances for capturing a spontaneous moment on film are greatly increased. **Hand-held** camera work allows for flexibility and quick judgment of the person using the camera—both desirable qualities. But motion picture cameras are heavy, and the result is that the pictures are, at best, mildly unsteady, and, at worst, downright jerky: Its effects may be hard to watch. This look goes against orthodox standards of classic Hollywood studio camera work. Such irregular movement continually calls attention to the edges of the frame, therefore reminding the viewer of the fact that "a movie" is being watched. Paradoxically, much of the success of the low budget *The Blair Witch Project* (1999) was due to the filmmaker's choice to shoot the film with hand-held cameras. The amateurish effect of the jerky camera work gave the pseudodocumentary film a realistic look, allowing the viewer to easily believe that the trio of young filmmakers was actually lost and terrified in the forest. A narrative movie, however, normally works best when the viewer is not distracted by an awareness of the boundaries of the frame, but is caught up with the drama *within* it.

Ernest Francis Moy and Percy Henry Bastie invented the first hand-held movie camera in 1908, to be used for aerial photography by the British navy. Since then, hand-held cameras were absolutely necessary for documentarians, especially during the frontline battles of World War II and the wars since. Because hand-held 16mm cameras were capturing the raw images of battle, or in more recent times, street scenes of urban turmoil, people came to associate this rough style of camera work with "uncensored truth." The film style—later labeled **cinéma vérité**—became a way to present a visual shock of reality-as-it-happens. The strength of the technique and style was also its limitation. The commercial movie industry prefers the 35mm camera, but its weight made the hand-held option virtually impossible. At times, major productions have used a hand-held 16mm camera to create a stylized effect within a story—for some shots of the chaotic prison riot sequence in *Natural Born Killers* (1994)—but the visual impact of the shot is a temporary contrast with the primary look of the movie.

The *Steadicam®* system has resolved the problems of shot smoothness, and allowed the camera operator even more mobility and freedom **(6–20)**. A camera operator is fitted with a vest designed to support a camera by means of a mechanical support arm, spring supports, and counterbalances. The innovative workings of the system render the camera almost weightless, as the burden is distributed throughout the torso rather than just the arms and shoulders. The camera floats alongside the operator's body, the shock caused by walking dissipated by a series of springs, and the recorded picture is presented without the hated wiggling edges of the frame.

The net effect of the Steadicam® system when shooting a movie has been rev-

6–20   *Steadicam®*   Through an intricate series of counterweights incorporated in the *Steadicam®* system, a trained operator can move a camera through space with seemingly effortless grace. Shots that call for rapid, continuous movement are recorded smoothly, with none of the jiggle associated with hand-held camerawork. The *Steadicam®* process has opened up the photographic choices available to the director in approaching a scene. The ready maneuverability of the camera is shown during the filming of *Terminator 2*.   (Courtesy of Steadicam®)

olutionary. This camera-carrying mechanism has made shooting situations involving intricate or random movement a faster, and therefore less expensive, operation. With it, a single experienced operator can follow an actor through an office building, run down steps with an escaping crook, circle boxers inside a ring, or capture the spontaneous play of children in a yard—all with the smooth result of a dolly or tracking shot, but with the added dimension of having free movement for photographing unexpected opportunities. Operating Steadicam® equipment is a special skill in itself. Garrett Brown, the inventor of the technology, observes that of all the active Steadicam® operators, "only several dozen are absolutely top-rate masters."

One such operator is Australian Brad Shields, who worked with director of photography John Toll on the visually engrossing Terry Malick war film, *The Thin Red Line* (1998). The advantages of the Steadicam® became clear immediately, affecting not only the look of the film but also the very nature of actors' performances. Toll relates,

> *Terry and I talked extensively about creating a sense of movement throughout the whole picture. . . . On the first couple days of the schedule, we shot some scenes with a moving camera on a dolly, some with stationary cameras incorporating conventional coverage and angles. It was all technically correct, and there was nothing wrong with the scenes, but when we viewed the footage it sometimes felt very "staged' and overly structured. We knew we wanted something more, so we decided to loosen up our approach a bit.*

The team began using a Steadicam® to explore and drift through the space, which in turn, because of the relatively unpredictable camera coverage, encouraged the actors to play the scenes with more spontaneity.

There are many other fine examples of interesting Steadicam® work, but one of the best is in Martin Scorsese's *Goodfellas* (1990), a continuous shot that starts outside of a nightclub and follows a young gangster, Henry Hill (Ray Liotta), through a dark maze of passageways, into a crowded steaming kitchen, finally opening into a stylishly impressive showroom where a ringside table awaits. Along with Hill, we experience the contrasting shift of environments in the club. Although the shots may not have the extreme precision possible with a dolly shot, especially on a controlled soundstage, this camera mount is very effective in natural locations or tight situations, which often prove cumbersome for a dolly. In John Badham's *Nick of Time* (1996), his desire was to create a stylish documentary look for a ticking-clock story that occurs within screen time of the film. Almost the entire film was shot with either Steadicam® or hand-held cameras to enhance the feeling of urgency.

Vehicle-Assisted Shots

The **crane shot** is one of the most traditional shots in filmmaking. The idea is simple enough: Put the camera, operator, and (sometimes) the director on the arm of a crane so that anything can be shot from varying heights with fluid ease. The perspective from an extreme overview—for example, being above a crowded glittering carnival—is an important option in visual storytelling. It places the viewer in a privileged and objective position to observe the action. A more recent technology is the Louma® demountable camera crane. It has a boom arm that encases a rotating rod, which allows a camera to tilt and pan at the direction of a cameraperson using a video-assist screen to monitor the subject. The crane could be used, for example, on location to bring the camera to the top of a building to photograph the action through a window by means of flexible hydraulic arms. As the cameras roll, the very smooth movement of the crane arm gives the director a great number of choices in deciding how to approach the subject. The Akela® crane, with its long 72-foot arm, gets the camera into places otherwise inaccessible. In *The Thin Red Line* (1998), this crane was used at a very low angle in sweeping motions over tall jungle grass to simulate the rushed troop movement up a hill in the South Pacific toward a hidden enemy fortification.

Camera cars, specifically designed with platform extensions for mounting a camera, are an essential mode of filmmaking. The cameras may be secured in a fixed position, or often a Steadicam® operator will take up a position on the platform. Companies specializing in this service also have trucks with a crane, so that the camera can travel not only down a street, but also vary its height during the shot. More and more, high action films make new demands on the director of photography to capture the thrill of a car chase, while movies in almost every genre use shots of moving automobiles with greater frequency.

Helicopter shots were at one time used only in high-action films, and then only when flight scenes were incorporated in the script. Today this point-of-view is a common and desired one for any number of purposes: to give an extended establishing shot of a secluded estate, to race behind cars escaping along desert highways, to wrap around a high-rise building on fire at any height. The first shot of *The Birdcage* (1996) whizzes the viewer just over the sea toward a Miami Beach hotel, a spectacular opening to an intentionally gaudy film. With cameras either fixed to the nose of the helicopter with remote tilt control or mounted to exterior platforms and operated manually, the extreme maneuverability of the aircraft has opened a wide range of alternatives when shooting from the air. The same companies that have designed sophisticated camera mounts for aircraft—Spacecam®—have developed similar mounts for boats, with stabilizing controls to reduce the effects of wave action.

The entire camera accessory industry is highly inventive, continually developing and refining equipment to give the filmmaker the slightest advantage in photographing the subject. New products are continually becoming available. A whole range of ever more sophisticated designs for dollies and tripods are being marketed, some with digital controlled or counterweighted jib-arms that allow the camera even more freedom of movement. For example, Steadicam® has developed the Skyman®, consisting of an ultralight cable car in which an operator, with 360-degree rotation, rides on a cable over previously inaccessible terrain or rivers. Again, the intent of this and every camera-mounting device is to eliminate unwanted shakiness of the camera while giving it more mobility.

SPECIAL EFFECTS

"I never write something for the sole purpose of taking advantage of the technology because the film will seem like a demo reel for a special effect company. It won't have its own internal logic, and the audience will sense something is wrong."

Director James Cameron (*Titanic*, 1997)

Because movies inherently are the art of illusion, the cinematographer is forever challenged to play with its possibilities. In the past forty years, the traditional set of visual tricks has become more sophisticated; in the last ten years, the technology for creating magic on the screen has raced in several directions. All categories of special effects have gained such a prominent position in moviemaking that it is not uncommon for work to start on them in the preproduction stage at various specialty companies that service the industry. Live action is then built *around* the special effects footage during principal photography. This was true for cinematographer Mark Irwin on *Robocop 2* (1990): "Quite a lot of the film is rear projection with multiple added elements with blue screen pieces to add to rear stop-motion foreground—four or five layers in a single shot. To see it all six months in advance is quite a challenge." Whatever kinds of special effects are employed, a great amount of preplanning is required. As a rule, although audiences are drawn to certain movies that advertise their heavy use of special effects, one standard should be kept: The viewer should *never* sense that "something isn't right" with the effects.

As touched upon in Chapter 3, much of the responsibility falls to a visual effects coordinator. As outlined, the categories include: 1) physical special effects; 2) optical special effects; and 3) computer-generated imagery.

Physical Special Effects

The department of special effects in the old studio system was founded as a *physical effects* group. Many films had spectacular moments—car crashes, explosions, fires, rain storms, etc.—that required the technology of a trained crew to create those realistic elements. Although the technology of physical special effects may seem, when compared with newer electronic systems, rather commonplace, in fact the work remains an essential part of the moviemaking process and when done well is still visually convincing.

To illustrate, the mechanical effects in *The Fugitive* (1993) were the centerpiece of its visual attraction. Early in the film, the convicted man (played by Harrison Ford) escapes from custody when a prison bus is hit by a freight train. Rather than attempting to fabricate the sequence by means of advanced optical or digital effects, the producers chose to capture the reality of an actual crash staged to happen. Warner Bros. budgeted $1.5 million to film this single scene set in North Carolina on the existing tracks of the Smoky Mountain Railroad. A seventy-person second-unit film crew with the help of special effects expert Ray Arbogast set up cameras in sixteen locations to photograph the one-time event. After the crash, a 65 mm camera, which was shooting the locomotive at eye level, was buried in 25 feet of dirt, but the film was intact and provided spectacular footage. Although other less chanceful approaches could have been taken to create the sequence, it is doubtful that any other than the basic techniques of *physical special effects* would have brought such a rousing response from film audiences to the crash.

At times, the classic look of traditional physical special effects is still preferred. For *Bram Stoker's Dracula* (1992), Francis Ford Coppola deliberately chose very basic physical and optical effects. Visual effects coordinator Alison Savitch notes,

> *Francis didn't want to go for the high-tech look. What he wanted, aside from creating unusual effects, was to draw from many of the old-style effects that have been used throughout the history of film—and he made no bones about it. He drew ideas from everywhere—old horror movies and German Expressionistic films—and ended up creating something very stylized and artistic. Francis wanted the effects to convey a feeling of drama, rather than a sense of realism.*

Despite the advances in the field of digital special effects technologies, many directors stay with physical special effects, convinced that nothing quite replaces photographing a cataclysmic event on a set or on location. For the shockingly graphic Normandy Beach scenes in *Saving Private Ryan* (1998), physical effects supervisor Neil Corbould depended upon both standard and improvised effects to simulate the horror of that battle. Over 17,000 *squibs* (faked bullet explosions) were used almost non-stop giving reality to the overwhelming firepower the soldiers faced. A large grid of air pipes was put just under the water surface and in the sandy beach to give the illusion of machine gun hits as actors moved through. Air cannons blew large holes in the battlefield at points close to the actors while high explosives were set off in the background. The relatively harmless air cannons were especially effective visually when the crew filmed some of the amputee stuntmen as their prosthetic limbs were blown off. Visual effects supervisor Roger Guyett praised director Steven Spielberg's decision to rely so heavily on traditional physical effects in this definitive war movie. "I think Steven had the right idea, which was basically to film everything in-camera if possible."

Director James Cameron, an authority on CGI, built a replica of the ship in *Titanic* (1997) at a time when miniatures and computers might have done the job. Jan DeBont, in *Speed II: Cruise Control* (1997), chose to photograph a full-scale mock-up of the bow of a cruise ship plowing into the dock of a colonial village. But as production designer Dan Weil (*The Fifth Element*, 1997) observes, "With models and digital effects, you have to be very, very precise. On a real set you can play with the camera and staging. It gives you much more freedom." For *Sleepy Hollow* (1999), a gothic horror tale shot in cold blue-gray colors, director Tim Burton felt that the murky atmosphere of the lonely rural setting was more important to the story than advanced special effects, "We wanted to rely as little as possible on postproduction special effects. The village is like a character. When the images are strong, they tap into your subconscious." Physical special effects will continue to be

6–21 *Anaconda*   The use of mechanical special effects is as old as movies themselves. Creating the physical facsimile of the monster snake in *Anaconda* (1997), with complex mechanical techniques by special effects supervisor Walt Conti called "animatronics," added a reality for the actors and director to the otherwise preposterous story. Although when poorly done, some physical special effects can look simplistic and phony, when done with expert care, the results are visually gripping. Here, Terri (Jennifer Lopez) lends a brave hand to panicked Danny (Ice Cube) during their ill-conceived journey down the Amazon. (Columbia Pictures)

used because of the familiarity that filmmakers have with the techniques used to photograph them **(6–21)**.

Optical Special Effects

From the start, filmmakers invented a large variety of ways to create fantastic illusions that would either 1) be impossible to shoot live, or 2) be very expensive to execute otherwise. Through the years, cinematographers and special effects technicians have developed an array of production tricks that became shortcuts through visual difficulties. In Terry Gilliam's film *The Adventures of Baron Munchausen* (1989), for instance, the filmmakers used 275 **optical effects**—blue screens, mechanical effects, miniatures, etc. Even at that number, the movie broke no new ground in its special effects, but those well-tested techniques employed in the movie worked wonders. Some of the more standard ones are listed here.

Matte Work.   Although traditional methods of matte technology have rapidly changed in the electronic revolution, it is useful when studying older films to understand the standard ways in which it was done. When staging a ten-second establishing shot of knights approaching a castle on horseback, for example, a production team had the choice of arranging the complex details of the shot at some European location, or shooting it as a *matte shot* in a much more convenient and inexpensive manner. Several procedures were followed:

- The simplest method was to mount a painting or photographed transparency of the castle and the surrounding area on glass or a stiff board between the camera and the knights (the knights being shot at a different time and separate location). The area of matte in the frame that the knights were to be seen was then carefully removed so that they showed up as being near the castle.

- Another method used to shoot the knights live, then project that image on a matte board, at which time a matte artist precisely outlined the small area that their image fills. The shot was then rephotographed with the castle matte in place.

- A bipack system of matting and printing was often used. In a complex procedure with a process camera, two pieces of film—one live action, the other artwork or a photograph—were superimposed on a single film to form a *composite* image.

The major problem of this older effect technique was matching the two areas. In poorly crafted productions, the *matte line* was often misaligned causing *matte bleed*, the light qualities differ between the two elements, or the artwork looks false, thereby making the shot incredible. When done well, the results can create believable action in any context. Although matte painting was employed with impressive results in such recent films as *What Dreams May Come* (1998) and *Star Wars: Episode I—The Phantom Menace* (1999), digital effects have superseded and generally are eliminating the usefulness of traditional matte work. The industry's fascination with the computer has led some traditional matte artists to paint by hand and then scan their work electronically simply to satisfy the demands for the look of a more high-tech digital image.

Rear Projection.   Traditionally this process was used for interior shots of a scene staged for a "moving" automobile. In the studio, an actor sits in a car as the background of the countryside races quickly past. In fact, a projector casts that background onto a translucent screen seen through the car window as the camera records the entire action. In some situations in which movement is not an issue, a single slide is used as background **(6–22)**.

Front Projection.   Although somewhat more complex, this is a more commonly favored process. With this, the projector providing background is actually *in front* of the actor, at a 45-degree angle to the camera. A special mirror is placed so that the images are reflected off of it to a screen behind the actor. The major problem with this method is that actors have to align perfectly with the camera and cannot be very

6–22   *The Nasty Girl*   Rear screen projection, as used in *The Nasty Girl* (1990), is done for surreal purposes. Rather than using rear screen projection, as is usual, to convince the audience of the visual truth of the moment, director Michael Verhoeven presents the library as an obviously staged background. The effect gives this otherwise reality-based film about a girl's investigation (Lena Stolze) into the complicity of her hometown with the demonic Nazi agenda a sudden timelessness. Notice the intentional bending of the image at the left and right.   (Miramax Films)

mobile because the camera will pick up the shadow on the back screen. But the background is much brighter on a glass-beaded screen from this projection than with a translucent one used in rear projection. The procedure has lost favor recently because of advanced computer technology, and it is rarely used today.

Introvision.   Although the process for creating the train crash in *The Fugitive* relied on *mechanical effects*, the scene also used *optical effects* to complete its action. As the out-of-control train comes roaring off the track, Harrison Ford is seen frantically trying to escape from its path. The frightening scene is memorable. Actually, Ford was shot on a soundstage with dual screen techniques developed by the Introvision System®. The real time background train footage was projected onto two screens, one next to the camera, the other screen behind the actor and set props. A projector transmits images at a 45-degree angle through a **beam-splitter** (a half-silvered mirror) in front of the camera lens, which then records the action as three-dimensional space. The simple advantage of this process is that the director and cinematographer, viewing through the camera, can physically see just how the interaction of the actor and the background is taking place, without waiting for lab processing work, as required with the bluescreen techniques. The background footage can be replayed immediately until the director is satisfied.

Miniatures.   Although digital artistry has opened almost unlimited possibilities for creating objects that need not have a physical reality beyond a computer screen, small-scale replicas built by *model makers* are more popular than ever **(6–23)**. The camera, when freed of any referent points, can make any size object seem normal. Therefore, it is artistically liberating as well as cost-effective to build everything small, from exotic animals to futuristic cities. The quality of the images, naturally, is directly related to the painstaking care that model makers take, and how naturally they are lit by the director of photography. Although some production people feel that the art of model making is being usurped by computer art, miniatures can still hold their own against the latest computer technologies. Even for the computer-enhanced *Titanic* (1997), a huge 45-foot "miniature" of the ship supplemented the scale model replica built especially for the production, the smaller ship model used when it was seen from long distance at sea.

The legendary English model maker Derek Meddings created totally authentic small-scale objects and environments in films for thirty years, including his final work on the James Bond feature *Goldeneye* (1995). His crew built, among other things, a

6–23   *Total Recall Miniatures* Model designers Alex Funke (left) and Eric Brevig (right) give perspective on the set for 20th Century Fox's *Total Recall* (1990). The exotic landscapes of science fiction films can be inventively simulated in the exacting detail in a well-constructed and photographed miniature layout. Vast landscapes are visually suggested with clever design and camera work. (DreamQuest Studios)

poison gas factory, a 1/7 scale radar dish, which is hit by a Russian MIG-29, and an entire Swiss Alps landscape. Meddings complained about the lack of respect given to traditional special effects, "We've been making films here and in America for years without computers, and they've looked fantastic." Often miniatures are used in combination with digital effects, however, as in the movie *Con Air* (1997). An 18-foot faux sign of the Hard Rock Hotel in Las Vegas was used as the movie's signature image. A 1/5 scale model C-123 with a 22-foot wing span smashed into the famous logo. Apart from computer enhanced exhaust smoke from the airplane, digital wire removal techniques had to be used to eliminate the cables attached to two construction cranes that helped suspend the model airplane as it was powered forward toward the sign with rigging attached to a Ford Bronco.

A great boost has been given to photography of miniatures and models with special lenses, mini-jib arms, and fiber optic lighting systems developed by such camera technology as Innovision®. Tabletop miniatures are photographed with precise motion control systems at extremely close range, so that a complex of small-scale streets and buildings can be smoothly traversed most realistically. The ability to move within miniature constructions gives the cinematographer a flexible instrument for exploring limited visual environments. Mike Shea, visual effects supervisor at Dream Quest, says, "Digital can enhance what model photography lacks, like showing atmospheric perspective. It's a great sweetener." Rather than being displaced by new technologies, models have been given a boost by computers.

Blue Screen/Green Screen.   This process has certain advantages over both rear and front screen projection because it permits more movement, and in that sense is considered a *traveling matte* **(6–24)**. Eric Brevig, visual effects supervisor at ILM, explains,

> *By doing a blue or green screen shot, you're trying to make something look as if it is someplace else. This may be for safety reasons: Filmmakers often don't want to place an actor or stuntman into an environment that would be too hazardous to actually execute. In other cases, they have to put talent in an environment that is too expensive or impractical to build, or in a place that is impossible to shoot, such as outer space or a planet surface.*

An actor is photographed in movement in front of a plain blue or green background. The key to the process is capturing the contrast between the actor's skin tones and the blue or green screen behind. The human flesh is primarily a red tone. The clear separation of the foreground from the background allows technicians to successfully transfer objects and persons by means of photography or computers to any desired environment. In the complex printing process in the laboratory, for example, a series of color negatives is made with the result that the background is opaque and the actor is clear—a moving empty space. With a bipack optical printer, the original color image of the actor is restored and combined with a very different background. In the *Star Wars* trilogy, amazing blue screen effects were achieved, opening the door for films such as *Superman* (1978), *Top Gun* (1986), *The Ghost and the Darkness* (1996), *Batman and Robin* (1997), and many others to create their sophisticated effects.

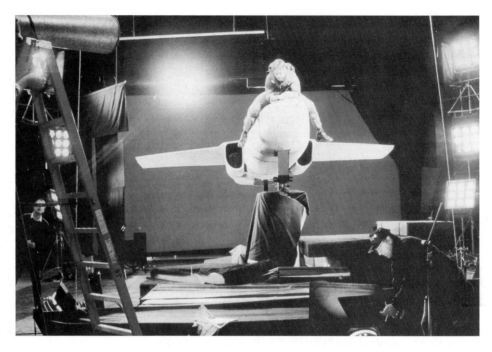

6–24   *Hot Shots!*   Blue screen techniques have been a standard visual effects technique for many years. The blue screen process by DreamQuest studio for the 20th Century Fox parody *Hot Shots!* (1991) is typical of the work. Essentially, a figure is photographed in front of a blue screen, and later various backgrounds can be optically introduced to achieve the total image desired. Here, the actor mounts a missile and seems to be hurtling through space. This process works for rear screen or front-screen projection, because the moving camera is free to shoot the primary object from any angle. Other elements—animation, other settings, or additional action—also can be composited with an optical printer. (DreamQuest Studio)

Optical Printer.   Some special effects are so common that we hardly notice. However, such standard techniques as fade out/fade in, dissolve, and the freeze frame do not naturally occur and obviously must be created with filmmaking technology. The *optical printer* is the basic machine that puts exposed film onto raw stock and reworks the effects in any number of ways. Essentially, this massive equipment combines a camera and projector precisely aligned and facing each other, with the ability to move on tracks closer or farther apart. The projector sends the image directly into the lens of the camera. A variety of different techniques and devices allow the original film to be altered in significant ways.

For instance, rather than being done in the original camera, frame sequences can be optically blown up or zoomed into by means of the optical printer. The frame size also may be *cropped* to eliminate unwanted objects or space; a daylight sequence can be rephotographed by the printer with filters and process camera adjustments to appear as night; slow motion and fast motion are sometimes done with the printer rather than in the original camera. The director of photography is well aware of the possibilities of changing and fine tuning the film with the optical printer away from the set. For *Avalon* (1990), a movie that lovingly recalls the history of an immigrant family in Baltimore during the first half of the twentieth century, Allen Daviau, ASC wanted to indicate the changing stylist tones of earlier time periods by using various photographic techniques. For one scene of a waterfront fireworks display in which director Barry Levinson wanted to affect either an odd psychological distancing or a dream-state, Daviau shot at 16 fps, then the dailies were stretched to 24fps with an optical printer.

Optical special effects remain a most important resource for creating illusion on film, especially the blue screen/green screen process and miniatures. But nothing is changing faster in the movie industry than the technologies that generate movie magic.

Computer-Generated Imagery

"Digital technology has reached a point where virtually anything can be done, so producers are no longer in a position where they can't solve a problem."

Producer Rick McCallum (*Star Wars: Episode I—The Phantom Menace*, 1999)

The digital world of computers has been around for many years, but while filmmakers have been fascinated from the beginning, they were also confused about how the technology could practically apply to standard moviemaking. Now, after featuring the new methods in a series of box office mega-hits such as *Men in Black* (1997) and *Mission: Impossible 2* (2000) and scores of films whose use of the technology is less obvious, digital effects specialty studios that service the industry with **computer-generated imagery (CGI)** are firmly established. Many older systems used for special effects are becoming dated, and with them, the jobs of specialists who were master illusionists in certain techniques. Unthinkable even a few years ago, The Cinematographer's Guild now offers its members classes in computer imaging and digital design.

CGI has redefined the way movies are made. Ed Jones, director of postproduction at Industrial Light & Magic, observes: "Digital technology opens up a whole new world of illusion. The stories of our fantasy world can now come to the screen exactly as we've dreamed them. It will take time to fully define the idiom, but the possibilities are infinite. Scriptwriters and directors will translate ideas into images in ways that haven't been practical or possible before." Digital technology has created radically new attitudes in film production, starting at the point when a director first reads a script. A technique called **previsualization** has been developed using design models created on a computer to not only envision the set design but also to simulate the camera movements within each shot. If this imagery is satisfactory to the director, actual physical models can be built to the relative proportions and scale of those on the computer. The effect is that directors see the film before shooting it, one long step beyond storyboards.

CGI can do almost any special effect seamlessly and more quickly than traditional optical effects techniques can. Stunts involving explosives can safely be presented, or actors can embrace in a heavy rainstorm, with perfect digital matting. Because of the computer, **optical compositing**—an image combining two or more separate shots achieved in an optical printer—has become obsolete over the past few years. For the beach scenes of an invading army in *Saving Private Ryan* (1998), computer-generated ships at sea, landing craft, barrage balloons, trucks, and jeeps were created to fill in the imposing background. Director Steven Spielberg offers, "My film cost $65 million. Had I really gotten that many ships to anchor off Omaha Beach, it would have cost $85 million. With a few digital effects, I was able to save millions."

Forrest Gump (1993) was an early example of the effectiveness of computer-generated imagery. The CGI teams were commissioned to create an authentic look—a "docu-fable," as it were—for a man's life covering forty years of historical highlights. They merged original archival footage with studio shots, blended 16mm and 35mm film stock of various grains, refined "mouth morphing" to reinvent historical moments, used footage of explosions, then scanned and married them to computer images of Phantom F4 fighters hitting their targets. The cost of such effects is a fraction of what it would have been to do these scenes by any other means.

Cinematographers working on high action thrillers must now project how the footage to be shot will incorporate the technology and art of the digital special effects unit **(6–25)**. *Twister* (1996), a movie about "stormchasers" caught in the ravaging path of a Midwest tornado, relied on strong visuals for its impact. Digital special effects experts from Industrial Light & Magic (ILM) worked closely with the director Jan DeBont and cinematographer Jack Green when shooting the picture. Both men knew that when filming the story under the cloudless summer skies of Iowa, extensive computer graphics would be added to each frame to achieve the ominous threat and destructive results of nature's rampage. In setting up the shots on location, ILM was

6–25   *Lawnmower Man*   The low-budget *Lawnmower Man (1991)* was one of the first films to create sophisticated digital imagery that could be incorporated into an otherwise visually ordinary movie and boost the look of its production values beyond the actual cost. Computer-generated imagery (CGI) has become an exciting and seemingly unlimited mainstay in world of special effects.   (Fine Line Features)

consulted regarding how framing of essential shots would be structured to allow the digital artists to do their job later. Green explained that although ILM was extremely flexible in their needs for the quality of film footage, "whenever we set up a shot that was going to include CG, we'd get together and talk. We'd arrange the composition to allow room for the tornado or for the trucks tumbling through the sky or for houses blowing apart. We were never 'alone'—there were always the as-yet unseen digital effects to be taken into account."

Background: The Evolution of CGI

An outline of the history of computer-generated imagery is a study in bits and pieces. In terms of raw screen time before 1990, CGI was used in only a fraction of even the most experimental films in this area. The highlights of its development, then, are those parts of certain films that worked especially well in riveting the viewer to their eye-catching artificial realities. Some films that used computer-generated imagery as key elements are mentioned here.

George Lucas's *Star Wars* (1977) is the grandfather of the new technology. A computer model of the space trench used lines of light as the pathway. The movie became the launching pad for new directions in special effects and established its computer team as the leaders in the field. *Tron* (1982) was a very ambitious film digitally, with about 20 minutes featuring a Light Cycle race and a Solar Sailer. The effects were brilliantly executed, but paradoxically, because the film was a box office failure, producers became more cautious for a time about using the technology extensively. *The Last Starfighter* (1984) produced spectacular starship battles that were completely computer-generated. The stained glass window that came to life in *Young Sherlock Holmes* (1985) as "the glassman" was the most effective use of digital work not in a futuristic vein. CGI truly impressed audiences with the "liquid tendril"—a glowing and slippery underwater alien—in *The Abyss* (1989). The creators at ILM were not only able to visually surprise viewers with the quality of the imaging, but also somehow infused it with emotion, as a character (Mary Elizabeth Mastrantonio) relates to the water-born stuff as "friendly." In this turning-point film, director James Cameron incorporated 290 special effects shots into a 21-minute segment.

The convincing visual effects opened new possibilities in digital assisted cinematography. Movies that relied on special effects would never quite be the same. The same group recreated the technique even more effectively in *Terminator 2* (1991) with the character T-1000. Other films made notable breakthroughs: *Star Trek II* (1982), *2010* (1984), *The Flight of the Navigator* (1986), *Labyrinth* (1986), *Total Recall* (1990), *Batman Returns* (1992), *Hocus Pocus* (1993), *The Mask* (1995), *Casper* (1995), *Twister*, (1996), *Titanic* (1997), *What Dreams May Come* (1998), among others.

Toy Story (1995) deserves special mention. The Disney-Pixar 78-minute production was the first fully computer-animated feature film. Whereas the admirable *Jurassic Park* had about 60 computer-generated images, *Toy Story* created over 1,500 CGI shots done by twenty-seven computer animators. The whimsical children's movie set a new standard of technical focus and achievement in the area of CGI. *A Bug's Life* (1998), directed by animator John Lasseter for the same company, carried the process even further. This movie had nearly 50 animators and over 600 models, nearly double the number used in *Toy Story*. Scott Ross of Digital Domain predicts continuing challenges. The techniques being used for animation are blending into live action in the form of computer-generated characters and digital effects of every kind. Today, animation rarely uses just one technique. To create a visual complexity that looked natural in the 3-D shots for *The Prince of Egypt* (1998), its animators added bits and pieces of 3-D and 2-D CGI to the hand-drawn scenes throughout the film. Of the 1,180 shots in the film, all but eight have some kind of 3-D images. "We're in a new revolution with the use of electronic imaging, but we're at the tip of the iceberg, and we need 10 to 15 years of fleshing out and developing the technology."

Industrial Light & Magic is the oldest and most established effects house, its heritage running back to the men who made *Star Wars*—Dennis Muren, John Dykstra, and Richard Edlund. This production team went on to found the independent companies Industrial Light & Magic, Apogee Films, and Boss Films, respectively. In the past few years, several vibrant companies have become major players servicing the film industry in the field of CGI. Writer/director James Cameron, special effects experts Scott Ross and Stan Winston, and IBM joined together to form Digital Domain, a company that has the technical range to challenge ILM.

Scores of other CGI companies specialize in different areas of image creation: Pacific Data Images (PDI) is known for its expertise in wire removal; Pacific Title has a growing reputation for image compositing; Pixar created the spectacular style of computer animation using its proprietary rendering software for Disney's *Toy Story* and *A Bug's Life*. Certain major studios have formed their own in-house digital effects units—the best known being Buena Vista Visual Effects for their creation of the environment in *Mortal Kombat* (1995). These and other effects companies have formed a core group of computer technology applied to film, and many others have followed **(6–26a-b)**. They have drawn their talent from very diverse and unrelated backgrounds—computer whizzes, video post production editors, digital artists, photo retouchers, painters, and others with traditional film experience.

The Mechanics of Digital

"This type of work is a craft that uses technology to achieve its artistic premise. But no effect is totally created by a machine. It always starts with an idea, and the more tools you have, the more you can create."

Stuart Robinson,
Head of Digital Effects, ILM

Before the application of computers to the field of special effects, as Richard Edlund of Boss Studios states, "We had taken regular special effects as far as it could go." But interfacing the film and digital technology creates neverending possibilities. The value of all computers is their ability to store and move information. Film also receives, stores, and transmits information, but in a much different way. Film is slow; computers are fast. Film records sequentially on tangible material; computers work electronically.

6–26a *The Matrix* For shooting sequences in *The Matrix* (1999), visual effects supervisor John Gaeta at Manex Visual Effects devised a circular array rig of as many as 120 Canon still cameras mounted on adjustable vertical rods fixed to a flexible steel track. The system, which can trigger frame rates up to 600 fps simulates a movie camera recording at very high rates, was dubbed FLO-MO. The action of actors within the circle was then photographed with extremely high shutter speeds, which when projected at the normal 24fps presents images in hyper-slow motion without the blurring effect that would come with ordinary motion pictures. Ironically, this very high-tech process mirrors somewhat the basic still-frame photographic experiments of Eadweard Muybridge in his classic studies of motion during the 1880s. (Manex Visual Effects)

a

b

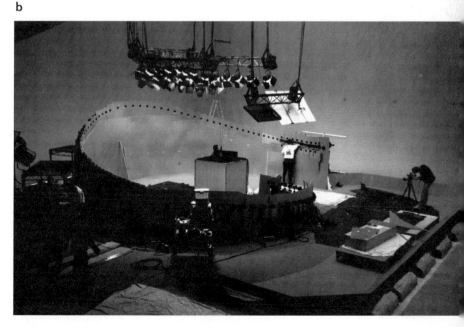

6–26b *The Matrix* After the still cameras are precisely set up to focus on the exact being predicted motion of the subject, the FLO-MO array is covered with a special green screen designed with small holes for the many camera lenses to matte out the rig. The technique allowed for the eventual digital compositing the photographed subjects into realistic virtual environments in computers before being transferred back to film. (Manex Visual Effects)

A common problem: In film, getting rid of unwanted visual elements in a frame is a technological hassle. For example, when anyone "flies" through space in a movie, the wires attached to the body are a problem. When Arnold Schwarzenegger sails over a culvert on a motorcycle in *Terminator 2,* it is done with wires. Traditionally, artful manipulating of lighting helps, or meticulous frame-by-frame lab work can eliminate the telltale mechanical assists. There are also easier ways to create clouds, rain, rainbows, snow, and almost any physical enhancement. With computers, answers can be found digitally.

The beauty of effective CGI is that a moderate film budget can be masked by the clever use of technology. *The Lawnmower Man* (1992) was an early successful advance in the field of computer graphics. The story deals with "virtual reality," the ability to immerse oneself into the simulated world of computer reality. Because the film was budgeted for a fraction of major sci/fi feature movies, the work was primarily done by small companies specializing in computer-generated imaging for TV commercials. The digital process freed the filmmaker from the physical limitations of creating physical special effects. The computer's unlimited ability to easily transform characters and landscapes provided a versatile new way to create the fantasy. The quality of the computer imagery was very advanced for the time, recreating the central character Jobe (Jeff Fahey) into a three-dimensional figure that could enter into an artificial but sometimes threatening universe.

Entire environments and even characters within them can be created digitally **(6–27)**. In the past, the viewer has usually been able to sense a special effect on the screen; now it is almost impossible unless the director wants to let you in on it. With digital, directors can see what they have at any time and, because of their new-found interactivity with digital effects technicians, can change whatever they choose with

6–27   *Independence Day*   In *Independence Day* (1996), rolling and luminescent cloud movement foreshadows the destructive arrival of a massive space vehicle. By filling the upper half of the screen with these threatening shapes created by computers, the filmmakers effectively create a sense of physical oppression, suggesting a world about to be enclosed and attacked. Special effects supervisor Douglas Smith and his staff won an Oscar for their computer-generated imagery and other effects in the movie.   (Warner Bros. and Universal Pictures)

relative ease. But Stephen Burum, ASC (*Mission Impossible,* 1996) makes the point that the process of shooting, from the cinematographer's point of view, is not really new: "Everyone makes it out to be very complicated, but it's not. CGI is a simple matting process that happens to be done in a computer instead of an optical printer. For the cinematographer, the technique is basically the same. Figure out the areas that you want to cut out, and place other footage in the hole you've cut."

- **Digital Image Processing**. At Kodak, a CCD scanner can convert the standard 35mm film into the digital format. From there, unwanted parts of the image can be eliminated, or digital alteration of color, sharpness, and shape can be created. For example, if an airplane is accidentally captured in the film frames of a story set in medieval times, as happened when a 747 flew into the background during a very long dialogue sequence in *Braveheart* (1995), it can be eliminated easily. Working in the digital mode, elements can be moved around or electronically painted over. The color of a person's hair could be changed independent of the rest of the information on the frame. In *Apollo 13* (1995), Digital Domain used computers to create the ice fragments and whirling dust that made the rocket liftoff look so realistic. The original film footage of the event was used as a model, but the computer designers had to not only match but also enhance this powerful visual effect on the large screen. James Cameron remarks: "Now the line between filming and editing is getting blurred. We cannot only edit from image to image, but we can edit *within* the image—taking things out and putting things in to improve the flow or tell the story better or even cover mistakes."

- **Compositing** from the digital format overrides the need for the conventional and artistically hazardous *blue sceening,* and it is much faster. What sometimes took six weeks to achieve photo chemically can now be done in a matter of days digitally. Actors can move *within* the background instead of simply in front of it. In the interactive environment of digital image processing, the director, DP, and production designer can add to the images when the composites are being made. For instance, when images are scanned into the digital format, scenes can be integrated with matte work by using the computer as a paintbox, much like an airbrush painter. In the end, the digital format is translated back into 35mm film. Ironically, the process somewhat insures the continued use of film (the preferred vehicle of most people in the industry) rather than High Definition Video (the technology that threatens to take over). Another level of **compositing** involves providing a three-dimensional space in which synthetic characters and other objects are created. These can then be blended with actual filmed material **(6–28)**. The effect is that almost any creature can be made to look as if natural when placed in a real three-dimensional environment. The technique is a blend of art and technology. In *Alien 3,* shots of the gruesome creature moving were very effective. The key was being able to digitally shadow the images to give them a valid physical dimension. CGI can invent worlds that combine fantasy and reality. As Dennis Muren, visual effects supervisor at ILM, says, "We can create characters who don't have to follow the laws of physics. We can assemble and mold shapes like electronic

6-28 *Starship Troopers* Many action films today rely so heavily on special effects that within the industry they are called just that—special effect films. *Starship Troopers* (1997) used a combination of live-action location shooting in Hell's Half Acre, Wyoming, and computer-generated images to achieve its futuristic look. Shooting the film was a massive undertaking requiring over 500 visual effects and 300 artists and technicians led by the Tippett Studio and four other effects studios. (TriStar Pictures)

clay." For *Waterworld* (1995), hundreds of composite shots were produced by various special effect studios, including those of *The Deez*, the corroding super-tanker. The ship was actually constructed and shot in the Mojave Desert. Digital artists at computer work stations composited the three-dimensional illusion of the fog and ocean that surrounded the evil vessel.

• **Morphing** (short for "metamorphosis") uses CGI to create the fluid transformation of images. The possibilities seem almost endless in this area. Some people have speculated that with CGI, even the need for live actors could be eliminated. But those closest to the technology point out that there are real limits. Computers can create images with which we are not acutely familiar—the dinosaurs in *Jurassic Park* (1993) or the penguins in *Batman Returns* (1992), but the realistic image of a human face in close-up is beyond the scope of computer work if we are to believe that it is an actual living person. Unlike prehistoric animals, we know faces too well. In fact, any human movement is a problem. James Cameron has had more experience than most directors in this field: "As human beings, we've spent literally thousands of hours watching other human beings. The movement is encoded so deeply in our cerebral cortex that we inherently know when it isn't accurate."

- **Go-motion** is the digital step beyond stop-motion special effects. **Stop-motion** was a standard effect used for many years in fantastic films, from *King Kong* (1933) to *The Empire Strikes Back* (1980), involving building articulated puppets with flexible limbs. These miniature figures were photographed one frame at a time, with incremental changes made to imitate movement. The process was pioneered by Willis O'Brien in *King Kong* and Ray Harryhaussen in *Mighty Joe Young* (1949), and later highly refined by Academy-Award–winning Phil Tippett and other animators. But the advent of computer-graphic animation has overtaken this older technology. A technique called **go-motion,** developed by Industrial Light & Magic, reached a new level of refinement. Computers are used to animate the stop-motion figures by using the single frames to build computerized sequences of movement. When played back, effects such as *secondary animation* (the reactive movement of weight on a body following, for instance, a footstep) or *motion blur* (the natural blur in an image during exposure as an object moves through a frame) can lend to its realism.

- **Computer Animation.** With the spectacular dinosaur creations in *Jurassic Park* (1993), an entirely new era of animation began. Although the film was first conceived using older techniques of *stop-* and *go-motion*, it soon became clear that these methods would be inadequate for the task. For this movie to work as it was envisioned, a new level of believability had to be reached, one with no room for visual incredulity. An entire team at ILM and the Tippett Studio had to reinvent the process of animation using computer-generated images exclusively. The work first demanded that its creators thoroughly understand the physics of animal movement. To some degree, this was also necessary for stop-motion animation, but with computers the animators had to literally see objects from the inside out and create dinosaurs and other animals that appear totally real in every regard. A system—*Digital Input Device (DID)*®—was developed that replicated a dinosaur skeleton in hinged metal. Sensors then translated various movements directly into computer images. From there, various complex stages of refinements were carried out by three-dimensional animators, working interactively in the digital world of computers. Phil Tippett notes

    I think that history will show that **Jurassic Park** *succeeded in the cross-pollination between two different disciplines, from the old craft to a brand new one, and vice versa.* **King Kong** *and* **Star Wars** *also made great technological leaps. . . . Technology becomes obsolete. Evocation does not.*

For many major films, an entire array of traditional and computer-generated effects will be utilized. No one source will supply all of them. In the past, names of individual technical innovators were the most significant in the final credits of a film. They are still important, but now *teams* of digital experts better represent the work done in a film. In *Batman Forever* (1995), for example, *computer graphics* were created by Warner Bros. Imaging Technologies, Pacific Data Images, Rhythms & Hues, and

Metro Light; *matte paintings* were made by Illusion Arts and Buena Vista Visual Effects; *compositing* was handled by Compositing Image systems; *scanning* was done by Efilm; and *underwater miniature photography* by Video Image. These and many other specialized companies servicing the needs of filmmaking have become an essential and invaluable part of the movie industry.

A major problem is that the parameters of digital special effects technologies are still not clear, even to experts in the field. The technical language of CGI as applied to film is still evolving, and there is some confusion and inaccuracy because each effects house has tended to developed a customized jargon relating to their specialty. Apart from learning new techniques, the industry is continually flooded with new hardware and software so that language applied to the technology is in a rapid state of flux.

Also, accepted job descriptions get blurred and must be reevaluated. When a computer operator adjusts the lighting of an image that will be printed, is that person usurping the role of a gaffer? The question may seem inconsequential, but not to a guild member. In addition, some directors have felt that once the imagery of a movie enters a computer, it is out of their control, at least in previously defined terms. But with the enormous success of high-profile films using extensive CGI, the industry has become converted. Money that would have previously gone into building expensive and elaborate sets for a big-budget film is now directed toward computer technology that can get the job done more efficiently and imaginatively.

As a new breed of filmmaker emerges, the technological landscape of the industry is changed forever. Douglas Trumbull, a pioneer in advanced special effects, heads the Imax theaters, which now seamlessly blends computer graphics, miniatures, and live action into the imagery of a compact simulator, three of which can create a 3-D effect in specially designed environments. The technology promises to radically alter the possibilities for the visual entertainment. Trumbull, the effects genius behind *2001: A Space Odyssey* (1968), speculates

> *I think that what we are now seeing as a result of the integration of computer graphics, live action, and miniatures is the ability to realize the fundamental goal of the entertainment industry from its inception: to stay inside the studio and create any world we can possibly imagine, and do it absolutely seamlessly and photo-realistically in a way that's far superior to any old techniques.*

Given the speed at which computers have transformed the landscape of almost every medium of communication, such ideas are within reach **(6–29)**.

SUMMARY

Envisioning and shooting a film call for an extremely acute visual and artistic sense. The work enlists the talents of the director, the lighting crew, and image specialists in every area. The director of photography has an essential role. The complex process of shooting a movie spans every phase of the project, from the *preproduction* planning to the multitude of choices made by the director and cinematographer during *principal photography*, into the *postproduction* lab and computer refinements.

6–29 *Twister* Jan DeBont's *Twister* (1996) is a prime example of the convincing reality that computer-generated imaging can accomplish. To achieve the effect pictured here, the director and cinematographer (Jack Green, ASC) had to shoot actors Bill Paxton and Helen Hunt running along a picket fence being blown by wind machines, while at the same time the filmmakers needed to allow for the special effects of Industrial Light & Magic's digital compositing teams (including Sandra Karpman) to later add splintering wood and debris-filled air. The exact coordination of live shooting and computer imaging is the shared responsibility of both the director and the effects studio. (Universal Studios)

In addition, when extensive use of *special effects technology* is called for, the coordination problems between what is shot on the set and what is created and integrated elsewhere can be enormous. Simultaneously envisioning and executing the thematic and artistic goals of a movie while it is being shot in small increments is a huge challenge. John Gaeta, visual effects supervisor at Manex Visual Effects for *The Matrix* (1999), comments, "We break ground with every job—camera control, virtual control, synthetic photography. Each film is an exponential leap forward."

But, as always seems to be the case in moviemaking, the most complex procedures are ultimately reduced to rather simple logic. Ed Jones, president of the special effects studio Cinesite whose work on *Space Jam* (1996) advanced CGI methods at the time, says, "It's still about telling stories with moving images, only now we have a bigger tool kit that gives us more flexibility. It's up to us to use them in appropriate ways. Digital technology doesn't make you creative. It gives you more opportunity to express your vision."

SPOTLIGHT

Special Effects: Sandra Ford Karpman Interview

Sandra Ford Karpman has been with Industrial Light & Magic since 1984, becoming a part of the computer-graphics department that grew from five people to almost 300 today. A partial list of her credits includes being a computer-graphics supervisor on *Die Hard 2* (1990), *The Rocketeer* (1991), *The Nutcracker* (1993), *Manhattan Murder Mystery* (1993), *Last Action Hero* (1993), *The Mask* (1994), *Radioland Murders* (1994), and *Congo* (1995). For *Twister* (1996), Karpman was the Lightning & Debris Effects Supervisor.

Richard Peacock: Industrial Light & Magic is rather legendary in the world of special effects today. When did you join the group?

Sandra Ford Karpman: I joined ILM in 1984. Of all the great stories of how people eventually ended up at ILM, mine is rather unique. During a PE class at the local junior college, I commented to one of my gym mates that I needed a new job. She said that she currently worked night shifts at ILM as a janitor. She said that being a janitor was like being paid to work out. I had never even heard of ILM. She told me that they made *Star Wars*. I thought "cool." I interviewed the next week and got a janitorial job.

RP: What classes were you taking in school?

SFK: I was a math major. Math has always come easier for me, or maybe it's that English was just so hard. I was also taking some Unix-based computer classes, but I had never taken a film or art class.

RP: Did you have any thoughts about a career at ILM?

SFK: At that point in my life I didn't really know what I wanted to do for a career. But about eight months later, ILM was screening all the FX work that they had just completed for the movie *Cocoon*. I walked in the room just as it started. Everyone was sitting in that room, looking at their work, but they were taking such great pride in each other's work. It wasn't so much that they were just enjoying their own contribution—the stage guys were appreciating the opticals stuff and the editors liked what the roto artists had done. There was a real magic feeling in that screening room. I could just feel the pride in the whole room in the fact that all of these people were responsible as a team in putting these images on the screen. At that moment I knew what I wanted to do. I wanted to be part of this team. I psyched up for two months and applied in the animation department as a production assistant. I took the chance and I got it!

RP: What was your first work like?

SFK: I was the basic department "gofer." I ordered supplies, I made sure that if a particular animator liked soft lead pencils, that we had soft lead pencils. But eventually the job grew into shooting their art work on the cameras—a process called "cel flopping." If an FX shot is 3 seconds long, that means it's 72 frames. That means I would shoot 72 pieces of artwork with the camera for the 3-second shot. The animators were happy to have someone else take care of the cameras and shoot their work, and my math background came in handy.

RP: What was the next step up?

SFK: After shooting the animators artwork on static animation stands, I learned to operate the computer-driven Motion Control Animation Cameras. These cameras work when an operator programs a "move." The move is then stored by the computer and recalled later. By 1988, I joined the Computer Graphics Department. At the time, we only had about six people in it; now there are over 400 men and women.

RP: I don't suppose that today it's possible to go the route you did at most special effects companies.

SFK: Oh no. I would never be hired at ILM today with what I had to offer when I started. But there are still a few backdoor routes. We have a couple of computer artists who came in through the mailroom and security. And we have a few coordinators and production assistants who used to work in reception. But the best way in is by getting schooling in art classes, film classes, and lots and lots of computer-graphics classes.

RP: Take us through a typical day at ILM, if there is such a thing.

SFK: There are typical days for different jobs. The job that I'm doing right now is called an *effects director* or *visual effects supervisor*. The first thing I do is hack a little script together. I'll get a *hero frame* from each of the shots that were rendered overnight. For example, if there is a movie in which we are doing twelve shots in a row, I want to make sure that they all look good—not a situation of one yellow, one blue, one light, one dark. They have to all follow together, because not only are you working on a shot, but also that shot has to fit into a sequence. So the first thing I do is check everyone's shot, making sure that I have previewed them before we go into watching the dailies. In this way I can go to Joe and say that his foreground element is a little blue here, or he's going to have to yellow it up, or it's a little bright there and it's going to have to be brought down. So in the dailies I go over each shot with the individual who is running that shot—and I tell him or her what is needed for that day. I may give them a list of things to create or correct and tell them to call me and I'll make another correction on the fly while I'm there.

RP: Do you supervise stage work as well?

SFK: Yes. We do a lot of things both on computers and on the stage. I watch film from the previous day and I make lighting or compositional adjustments on the stage shoot. Then in the computer I review what we have. We polish the final product but we may also created elements for the final product. Most of the day is reviewing shots or preparing to do stage work that day. In short, in the mornings I am observing everything, and in the afternoon I make sure everything is progressing.

RP: What, then, are your hours?

SFK: It's like an 8:30 A.M. to 7:00 P.M. schedule. That's five days a week unless we are pushed and then it's six days.

RP: *Twister* is a film that is well known to most people attuned to special effects. It must have presented ILM with a great many problems. What challenges did it have for you in particular?

SFK: Personally, it was not seeing my kids for about six months. But professionally, it was tricky. We were doing a lot of sky manipulation. With *Twister*, there were some things you could get away with, and some things you couldn't. They shot the movie over many months, and the skies were always changing. The problem is, when played back, some scenes are edited back to back but they've been shot weeks apart. We had to make it all look continuous. That's the really hard part. Remember, we were creating tornadoes. It's a very large part of the frame, and the connection point is a large border. When you have a small border point you can "cheat" things really well. But with a large border there's no place to hide your errors. Visual effects is nothing but cheat, that's what it's all about. How can I make this look real without having a camera there in the middle of a tornado? The question is always, "What's the simplest way I can get this to look right?"

RP: You were special effects supervisor for "lightning and debris." I just saw *Twister* again and paid special attention to those effects. The volume of those effects is quite overwhelming. In fact, the debris effects is what makes those tornadoes visually credible. What did your work entail?

SFK: One of the most important things is that the debris be at a consistent speed from scene to scene. And then we're adding a ton of dust. With debris and dust you have to take a dynamic path, you can't have things flying on the same path. You need your dust beads to correlate with the debris speed, and you need them both to be consistent over the entire sequence—in color-tone as well. The problem is that you can put only so much debris in with the actors because some of it was real, it was originally shot that way—but most of the material was CG [computer generated]. A further problem was that in the live action from scene to scene, there were extremely different volumes of dust and debris. The original plates were very inconsistent. So I had to make this perfectly consistent in color, volume, and density. When you see the final, it was our goal that nothing struck you as out of place. For example with the "crossovers"—the debris that goes in front of and behind the actors—you want to make sure that's just right. I think that you can't assume that the average viewer would *not* notice these things. The public is getting very sophisticated, especially with more computer tools out there like Photoshop, people are saying, "Oh, I see what they're doing."

RP: How many shots did your team work on, do you have any number?

SFK: My team worked on 120 of the 360 shots in *Twister*. It was really fun. I called our team the twister annex. We had a very small team and a very short time, so that each person had to get one shot out every week. That was incredible.

RP: Did you have any actual contact with the director of the film, Jan DeBont?

SFK: Twice a week we had what's called a *vivex* session. We would talk with Jan on a TV monitor, and we would show a shot for discussion. He would want to O.K. certain things before they were final. For example, in one shot Helen Hunt was ducking her head. Now you have to put something in there to motivate her sudden movement. So we put a pitchfork flying right at her. But Jan said, "Oh no, honey, we can't do that. It's too much danger for Helen and Bill."

RP: Each film project presents unique problems and, I suppose, you're learning all the time. What did you learn during *Twister*?

SFK: What really saved me on *Twister* was that old adage : "A stitch in time saves nine." That works. I'm very organized and coming in everyday to stay right on top was essential. There's a temptation to say "Oh, that's not so important. I'll fix it on the fly." Well, forget it. It doesn't work.

RP: When you are working on your corner of the film, do you have a clear idea of the total context of where and how this all fits into the story?

SFK: Yes, we could really see the flow of the sequence. And Jan was great. He was extremely clear on what he wanted. He made life very friendly for such a tight deadline. If he said he wanted A on Tuesday and he got it on Thursday, he accepted it. He didn't suddenly say he wanted B.

RP: What is the biggest change in your field of work in the last five years?

SFK: For the effects business in general, it's the onslaught of digital. The traditional ways of doing things have been complemented by the digital side. Traditional opticals have been replaced. We still make clay models so that we can get a better feel for what to do in digital. The digital influx is unbelievable.

RP: How has that affected the structure of the special effects business?

SFK: When everything was traditional, small companies could not afford $100,000 optical printers. Now everybody can afford a PC and some software. So today it doesn't take much money for a start-up company. And now there's an incredible pool of talent out there—working in what I call "garage shops." That's wonderful, and there are so many effects movies being made because of these garage shops. The downside for them is that companies like ILM who could afford that optical printer can also afford to stay on top of the digital technology. Because the small company that bought a computer a year ago now finds it outdated. The start-up company can make money right away, but two years down the road their equipment is old, and they can't afford to spend millions each year to keep their machines on the cutting edge. Sadly, I think in five years most of these garage shops won't be around. It's just too darn expensive in the long run.

RP: Do you see a time when every film will be using digitally enhanced imagery?

SFK: Oh, yes! The effects don't have to be in your face. It's the subtle things. Look at the *Forrest Gump* effects. When you see the film you say "Where's the effect?" Well all those people in the background never existed at once. They shot a hundred people and kept rubber-stamping them. Remember, every square foot on a sound stage equates to big money. The same for every set you build. Every wall limits your D.P. and lighting guys. So the more simple it is, the less money is spent on principal photography. People may get tired of the *Jurassic Park* movies, but producers will never get tired of spending less money to shoot films. And believe me, a week of a technical director's time on a computer costs less than an hour on a shooting stage. In other words, if you can fix something two days on a computer to save a company an hour of shooting, then the producer will say, "Great, move on!"

RP: What personal qualities must a person have to be successful in your field?

SFK: As in any profession that works long hours; you have to love what you're doing. If you do it for the money, it's a horrible job. With any business, there can be people in power who have no talent. But if you love the work, you just take it as part of the job. A good attitude gets you a long way.

RP: Is there a high burnout rate in the field? Is that an important factor?

SFK: Quite a bit. There are some companies that when the show is over, there's an exodus, like rats deserting a sinking ship. But at ILM, a very high percentage stay. The morale is very high here. Some of our people are offered incredible promotions from companies in Los Angeles, and we lose some that way rather than from burnout. Because you put so much into your work, you tend to take things personally when it may be only business. Let's say you work four weeks on a shot, but then it is cut in the final edit. You must realize that they're not cutting it to get to you. The shot might have been great but the movie played better without it.

RP: Do you have a sense that you are in the motion picture business, or does your work seem to be a self-enclosed activity?

SFK: It's weird. I see most movies at home on my satellite TV. I know what is going on in the outside world but what I'm not aware of is how excited people are about the movie I'm currently working on. I'm so close to it that I lose touch with the audience's passion for these films. Like for *Jurassic Park*, I had no idea how much people were jazzed about it beforehand.

RP: What would you like to be doing five years from now?

SFK: I'd like to direct a movie. [laughter] Actually, I give myself five years to write a screenplay. If it never gets made, that's O.K. But I really want to get some thoughts down on paper. ◀

FILMS TO CONSIDER

Knowledge and command of the emerging technology and methodology in the act of shooting a movie is a primary challenge for directors and their crews. The following films provide useful and varied examples of how some filmmakers achieved their goals:

- *Metropolis* (1926): This classic German futuristic film by Fritz Lang and cinematographer Karl Freund is striking in every aspect of its frame composition, throughout the movie weighted with massive and threatening elements that overwhelm the viewer.

- *King Kong* (1933): The still awesome special effects created by a team headed by Willis H. O'Brien were light years ahead of their time; even today, the big ape can send out shudders.

- *Citizen Kane* (1941): Orson Welles and D.P Greg Toland have been praised for every aspect of their filming techniques. However, one might appreciate this film simply for the employment of its subtly shifting mise-en-scène.

- *Floating Weeds* (1953): The contemplative visual yet dramatically edged attitude of Japanese director Yasujiro Ozu is evident in each frame of this story about a reunion of a leader of a traveling acting group with his former lover and their son.

- *North by Northwest* (1959): Alfred Hitchcock was a master of the incremental progression of suspenseful photographic detail, as witnessed, for example, in his climactic scene on Mount Rushmore.

- *L'Avventura* (1960): Michelangelo Antonioni's use of empty space in the frame reinforces his statement about the boredom and alienation of his characters, lovers denying the passion for life around them.

- *I Am Cuba* (1964): This vision of Cuba in the 1960s, pictured at times with a restless camera and at others with the magical lens of Russian director Mikhail Kalatazov, is an ode to the beauty of the island and the tenacity of its people.

- *The Red and the White* (1968): The story, by Hungarian Miklos Jancso, of the shifting fates of two armies is captured by presenting the military confusion on both sides with very few takes but incessantly smooth camera movement.

- *Faces* (1968): The camera close-up was never so effectively used as in this overheated story, by John Casavettes and his friends, of a few men and women drifting in the chaos of changing moral values during a night in Los Angeles.

- *Star Wars* (1978): The breakthrough special effects created by George Lucas and his Industrial Light & Magic group laid the groundwork for every science fantasy film that followed.

- *Goodfellas* (1990): The Steadicam, as employed by Martin Scorsese's team in this gangster film, clearly shows why this method of camera movement is now an essential tool in the technology of filmmaking.

- *Babe* (1995): Computer-generated effects are insinuated into almost every movie made today, but when used as wonderfully as they are in this well-conceived fantasy, it's clear that a new age of animated story possibilities is here.
- *Titus* (1999): Former theatrical director Julie Taymor created a visually overwhelming movie of Skakespeare's most violent play, each frame worthy of study in terms of its composition of weight, line, angles, and depth.

THOUGHT QUESTIONS AND EXERCISES

Watch a film from those listed.

1. The camera's distance from and angle toward the subject of the shot is telling. In the final climactic scene of the film, what is the primary relationship of the camera to the main character? What emotional or thematic effect is achieved by the director's choice?

2. On your VCR or DVD, freeze on a frame from an important scene in a film in which there is relatively little camera movement. Analyze its composition. List the elements in the foreground, middle ground, and background. What are the reasons for their location within the frame? What effect does the configuration have on the meaning of the scene?

3. Choose a shot from a movie with significant camera movement. Study and outline the movement of the camera and the shifting relationships between the lens and the subjects photographed. What dramatic effects are realized by the rendition of the shot in this manner?

4. Select a scene in which the major characters of the movie come together. Physically, in what part of the screen does the director position them? Can you find in the dramatic context of the movie any reason for their particular placement within the frame? Is one of them on the "receiving end" of the dramatic moment?

5. Choose a film with extensive special effects. How would you classify them: primarily mechanical, visual, or computer-generated? Is the intention of the filmmaker to draw your attention to them, or do they become the ambient background of the movie? How convincing are the special effects? Were the special effects overdone in relationship to the "straight" cinematography in the film?

FURTHER READING

Arijon, Daniel. *Grammar of the Film Language* (Boston: Silman-James Press,1976).

Carrington, Robert L. *The Making of Citizen Kane* (Berkeley: University of California Press, 1985).

Catine, John, Susan Howard, and Brady Lewis. *Shot by Shot: A Practical Guide to Filmmaking,* 2nd ed. (Pittsburgh: Pittsburgh Filmmakers, 1995).

CGW: Computer Graphics World. 10 Tara Boulevard 5th Floor, Nashua, NH 03062.

DGA Magazine. 7920 Sunset Boulevard, Los Angeles CA 90052.

Filmcrew Magazine. 244 Madison Ave., #263, New York, NY 10016.

Filmmaker: The Magazine of Independent Film. 5858 Wilshire Boulevard, Los Angeles, CA 90036.

Garvey, Helen. *Before You Shoot: A Guide to Low Budget Film Production* (Santa Cruz, CA: Shire Press, 1988).

Katz, Steven D. *Film Directing Shot by Shot: Visualizing from Concept to Screen* (Stoneham, MA: Focal Press, 1991).

Lawson, Bill. *Filmmaking: A Project-Based Approach* (Stoneham, MA: Focal Press, 2000).

McCarthy, Robert E., *Secrets of Hollywood Special Effects* (Woburn, MA: Butterworth-Heinemann, 1992).

Millimeter. 5 Penn Plaza, 13th Floor, New York, NY 10001.

Perisic, Zoran. *Visual Effects Cinematography* (Woburn, MA: Butterworth-Heinemann, 1999).

Rogers, Pauline B. *Art of Visual Effects: Interviews on the Tools of the Trade* (Woburn, MA: Butterworth-Heinemann, 1999).

Zettl, Herbert. *Sight, Sound, Motion: Applied Media Aesthetics,* 2nd ed. (Belmont, CA: Wadsworth, 1990).

CHAPTER 7

The Cinematographer

MAKING PICTURES

"Up until the time that the camera exposes the film, the movie is just an abstraction. It's the dream of a lot of people. Then it reaches the form in which the public is going to see it, and the cameraman is the chemist."

Haskell Wexler, ASC
(*The Secret of Roan Inish*, 1994)

The first challenge of a moviemaker is to visually engage the audience. The story, the actors, and the production design may be first rate, but the movie begins its *life* when all of this is recorded on film stock. The spirit, beauty, and detail of a film are found in the images that the cinematographer creates. The initial pleasure of motion pictures comes from well-photographed images.

The **cinematographer**—or the more preferred title, **director of photography (DP)**—is the person in charge of shooting the film. Most camera professionals who work regularly in Hollywood belong to the American Society of Cinematographers (ASC), and are identified by the letters following their names. As players on the creative first-team of filmmaking, cinematographers are chosen for their record of aesthetic taste, solid organizational skills, and ability to translate the director's vision onto film. Cinematographers create visuals—working in a special world of light textures, cameras, lenses, film stock, filters, and spatial composition. Expertise in all of these areas is basic to the job. In addition, the DP must not only firmly understand the thrust of the story and the visual ambiance desired for the film, but also have the ability to capture the acting strengths of the performers through their screen characters. Each DP combines these skills in varying degrees.

BACKGROUND: THE EVOLVING ART OF CINEMATOGRAPHY

"The Alton films we watched together were inspirational in many ways, especially in terms of the quality of light. But they were primarily inspirational because they helped the two of us develop a vocabulary and syntax. By forming a common grammar, we could expand on what we were doing."

Robert Richardson, ASC (*Casino*, 1995)

The movie *Casino* brought together director Martin Scorsese and DP Robert Richardson for the first time. Because Scorsese was unsure of their visual compatibility, he screened several films shot by the great cinematographer John Alton (*T-Men*, 1947) for Richardson. Alton's style was quintessential *film noir*, and as the two filmmakers envisioned shooting this mob film set in Las Vegas, their appreciation of this previous visual master gave them a common starting point.

When movies began, the cameraman controlled the set. Subjects were recorded on film and, logically, the person running the camera was in charge. As filmmaking quickly evolved, the concept of a "film director" took hold, and the "cameraman" became a more specialized craft. Billy Bitzer, D.W. Griffith's great cameraman, is given credit for much of the inventive photography that distinguished that director's work. Their films became primers for all that followed **(7–1)**.

Because many cinematographers in the first half of the twentieth century were permanently employed at various movie studios, the films from these companies took on a rather consistent look. Most cameramen quickly became aware of what each studio wanted and fit their talents to its visual expectations. Each studio eventually developed its trademark look: MGM was elegantly polished; Paramount was softly artful; 20th Century Fox was slick and meticulously framed; Warner Bros. looked raw and hard. A few cinematographers had the talent to advance the art of the movie camera beyond the conventions of the day. One of the pleasures of watching older films is enjoying the variety of photographic styles that evolved from the silent period through the 1950s. The best work of that era was sometimes unpretentious and flawless, but quite often the cinematography was elegantly innovative.

Every craft in film draws on its past, none more than cinematography. Filmmakers borrow freely from movies of the past and present. The camerawork of former times is a steady source of learning and inspiration for those in the field of motion picture photography. The techniques and styles of great cameramen form the body of knowledge on which the art is based, and from which they build. In black-and-white photography, many look back to the intense light contrasts created by the camerawork of such cinematographers as the genius Stanley Cortez (*Night of the Hunter*, 1955); and Russel Metty, ASC in Orson Welles' *Touch of Evil* (1958). Many contemporary American photographers, for instance, give credit to the color work of Vittorio Storaro, ASC in *The Conformist* (1971) as a breakthrough movie in which tonal qualities were elegantly matched to the theme of decadence immersed in tasteful style. But Europeans also looked to Hollywood's master cinematographers. Darius Khondji, ASC says that in preparation for shooting *The Beach* (2000), "I recalled images from American films shot by Conrad Hall, Haskell Wexler, Gordon Willis, and Vilmos Zsig-

7–1   *The Magnificient Ambersons*   The art of cinematography owes much to the cameramen in the first fifty years of filmmaking who painstakingly discovered the wonders of light, the powers of the lens, and the versatility of the motion picture camera. The work of Stanley Cortez, ASC in *The Magnificient Ambersons* (1942) is recognized as ultimate refinement of the exquisite photographic style of his day. In this frame, his bold mastery of light and shadow, the remarkable depth of focus, and his crisp images bring a dreamlike reality to the story. The movie was badly mutilated by the studio during editing and many of his best scenes have not survived.   (Museum of Modern Art)

mond during the Sixties and Seventies. These four cinematographers really changed the look of cinema, and in Europe we regarded their films with awe." The films of these and other premiere cameramen became permanent reference works to study and imitate.

It is important to remember that cinematographers in the past had to work with equipment that, although it was state-of the-art at the time, was limiting and bulky by today's standards. In earlier times, a cameraman had to work with 165-pound cameras and lights that generated an immense amount of heat. Today, the industry works with 45-pound cameras that can be manipulated in countless ways on jibs and dollies of every design, with a huge choice of lenses that instantly alter the image, with much faster film, and with lighting systems that do not overheat the set. The rapid advances in camera technology make it easier to do more dazzling camera work. Whatever techniques are currently used, most professional cinematographers know that they are building on a marvelous heritage of past visionaries.

MEMORABLE CINEMATOGRAPHY

A list of important cinematographers in the earlier part of the century would fill pages. In 1999, *American Cinematographer* magazine polled its knowledgeable readers for their opinion regarding the best-shot movies of all time. The top ten movies and their cinematographers from **1894–1949** follow:

1. *Citizen Kane* (1941)—Gregg Toland, ASC

2. *Gone with the Wind* (1939)—Ernest Haller, ASC and Ray Rennahan, ASC

3. *Sunrise* (1927)—Charles Rosher, ASC and Karl Struss

4. *Metropolis* (1926)—Carl Freund, ASC and Gunther Rittau

5. *The Wizard of Oz* (1939)—Harold Rosson, ASC

6. *The Magnificent Ambersons* (1942)—Stanley Cortez, ASC

7. *Casablanca* (1942)—Arthur Edeson, ASC

8. *The Battleship Potemkin* (1925)—Eduard Tisse

9. *Third Man* (1949)—Robert Krasker, BSC

10. *Birth of a Nation* (1915)—G.W. "Billy" Bitzer

The best ten films between **1950–1997** were rated by *American Cinematographer* as follows:

1. *Lawrence of Arabia* (1962)—Freddie Young, BSC

2. *The Godfather* (1972)—Gordon Willis, ASC

3. *2001: A Space Odyssey* (1968)—Geoffery Unworth, BSC

4. *Days of Heaven* (1978)—Nestor Almendros, ASC

5. *Schindler's List* (1994)—Janusz Kaminski, ASC

6. *Apocalypse Now* (1979)—Vittorio Storaro, ASC, AIC

7. *The Conformist* (1971)—Vittorio Storaro, ASC, AIC

8. *Raging Bull* (1980)—Michael Chapman, ASC

9. *Blade Runner* (1982)—Jordan Cronenweth, ASC

10. *Touch Of Evil* (1958)—Russell Metty, ASC **(7–2)**

7–2 *Touch of Evil* The cinematography of Russell Metty, ASC in *Touch Of Evil* (1958) refined the *film noir* visual style that by the late 1950s was well established. The film, directed and co-written by Orson Welles, contains many of the elements of the filmic attitudes of film noir—sharp contrasts of black and white, a brutally corrupt border town shrouded in shadows, and extreme camera angles to accent its cynical and neurotic characters. In this shot, a retarded motel manager (Dennis Weaver) is threatened by a gang of young thugs. The meticulous and energetic camera work of Metty has continued to influence contemporary cinematographers. (Museum of Modern Art)

WORKING WITH DIRECTORS

"There's no such thing as complete freedom for a cinematographer. You have to do the director's film. There's no such thing as a cinematographer's film."

Vilmos Zsigmond, ASC
(*The Ghost and the Darkness*, 1996)

The job of the **director of photography** starts with extended conferences during the preproduction phase, first with the director, then with the production designer. Ideally, the **DP** will be on hand part-time, 6–8 weeks before shooting, and then have a solid final 2 weeks with a director to select equipment and the crew. Every DP would like to get involved as early as possible in preparing for a film, but movie budgets do not always allow for this. The wages of the DP are considered a "below-the-line" craft item, even though a top-flight cinematographer sometimes makes $20,000 a week. Because of the crush of responsibilities and details that happens on the set, more prep time usually shows up on the screen in the form of more thoughtful and probing cinematography, but today's shorter production schedules make a generous planning period an increasingly rare luxury. Therefore, it is not uncommon for the director and production designer to already have the locations and art designs chosen before the DP comes on board.

Because the visual presentation of the film is at stake, it is essential there be complete understanding of the director's particular intentions for the film. Such a unity of purpose is not easily achieved. Although it might be assumed that the cinematographer's job is narrowly focused on merely translating script ideas into pictures, the work demands a clear and agreed upon storytelling perspective **(7–3)**. Robbie Green-

7–3   *The Mystery of Rampo*   The relationship of the film director and the director of photography is necessarily very close. In a very real sense, the DP must become the eyes of the director, creating visuals that express the director's conception of the film. Typical of the ongoing communication during principle photography, Japanese director Kazuyoshi Okuyama (right) confers with his cinematographer Yasushi Sasakibara on the set of *The Mystery of Rampo* (1995), a visually spectacular fantasy about a popular mystery writer.   (Samuel Goldwyn Company)

berg, ASC (*The Milagro Beanfield War*, 1988) comments, "I've been on films where there is no point of view. You struggle for the entire film trying to find it—just so that there's something in your work that is consistent to the story or helpful to the story. But it's surprising how often it doesn't exist." In the course of the hundreds of choices made during principal photography of a movie, differences in taste and judgment are almost inevitable. Film directors will often team with the same DP for succeeding film projects, an indication of the value they put on having worked out clear channels of communication and a common aesthetic harmony.

From the cinematographer's point of view, there are two kinds of film directors: those who know the movie camera well, and those who do not. "Some directors have their own ideas about staging, lighting, and composition. Others are mainly interested in the actors. You must be able to form a relationship with both types," Sven Nykvist, ASC observes. The first group are those film directors who know exactly what they want photographically and have expertise with both cameras and lighting the set. This ability then becomes a base for deeper communication with the director of photography, one that provides for more refined collaboration. A type of time-saving "shorthand" develops between the two as they move through the stream of visual challenges and agree on a common vision, as it did between Nykvist and director Ingmar Bergman during their many successful film collaborations.

Rather than putting their creative energy into the art of photography, the primary interest of a second group of directors is with the story concept or the performances of the actors. Often, these directors have no training and little interest in the complexities of the camera, and, frankly, rely on their director of photography for the visual concepts and execution. Director/actor Kenneth Branagh and Matthew Leonetti, ASC worked on *Dead Again* (1991) together. At the time, Branagh said honestly, "Communication is especially important to someone like me, because technically I couldn't be more ignorant. . . . I still have trouble talking in any kind of technical language. . . ." Directors of this persuasion can show up quite well if they choose their camera team well.

Therefore, the DP, working with a director with weak fundamental knowledge of camerawork, can be successful if the director easily delegates authority to those people with more expertise. This is not to say that the director must give up final control regarding cinemagraphic decisions. It is the film director, not the cinematographer, who guides the story's progress and must ultimately take charge of what needs to be photographed. Vilmos Zsigmond, ASC has seen the limits of a cinematographer's contribution when extended too far: "If you have a weak director and you take over, the photography is going to be terrific but the film is going to die because there would be nothing there except beautiful images. The images have to follow the story."

Each director's relationship with the cinematographer is unique. It is, after all, the job of the DP to put the director's vision on film. The first problem is getting a clear idea of just what that vision *is*. If the director somehow miscommunicates what he or she wants, it is hard to fault the DP for not getting it on film. Some directors push their DPs to take chances rather than playing it safe. When this trust builds, the risks taken can create exciting photography. Other directors are more conservative, approaching their subject with tested visual conventions and styles of camera work. Sometimes, differences in visual attitude do not surface until everyone is on the set.

At times, serious problems occur with directors regarding differing aesthetics, even with cinematographers of reputation. On the *Chinatown* (1974) set, for example, director Roman Polanski fired his DP Stanley Cortez (*The Magnificent Ambersons,* 1942) and replaced him with John Alonzo (*Harold and Maude,* 1972). The blow-up was triggered when Cortez wanted to shoot Faye Dunaway in a more traditional, old-studio style, with diffusion and classic lighting. Polanski wanted a more natural cinemagraphic approach. In another situation, Academy-Award-winning DP Haskell Wexler (*Who's Afraid of Virginia Woolf,* 1966) was let go after creative differences with director Milos Forman on *One Flew over the Cuckoo's Nest* (1975). The talents of well-intended artists do not always mesh. But when they do, the results can be spectacular. Director Oliver Stone and DP Robert Richardson have worked on films from *Salvador* (1986) to *Nixon* (1995). Stone says, "We know each other like husband and wife. We fight. We disagree. But it doesn't get so emotional that we lose our bond." However the situation works out, the final call belongs to the film director.

The Crew

"This isn't computer graphics, with you locked into a room by yourself."

Stephen Goldblatt, ASC
(*The Pelican Brief,* 1993)

The director of photography chooses a camera crew to work on the movie and has the responsibility of being the steadying force with them. Whereas movie directors may become consumed with working with actors and larger story issues, the director of photography must stay focused on how the story is being told through light, lens, and camera placement. The camera crew goes a long way in determining the standard of expectations on the set by establishing the creative environment of the shoot. Part of the test for a DP becomes one of insuring that the expertise and enthusiasm of the camera crew mesh with his or her own talents (the vast majority of directors of photography doing studio work, however, are men).

The director of photography does not physically operate the camera, the assignments on the shooting set are multitiered **(7–4)**. The breakdown of responsibilities is as follows:

- The **camera operator** is responsible for the hands-on functioning of the camera equipment. This person oversees lining up shots, adjusting lenses, starting and moving the camera. The maintenance and repair of cameras are also part of this job.

- The **first assistant camera operator** is charged with moving the ring of the lens to keep it in continual focus, and for this reason is sometimes called a "focus puller." While doing this, he/she does not look through the camera but relies on measurements previously taken in the rehearsal of the shot. Responsibilities may also include loading the camera, fixing the filters, setting the aperture and other duties.

7–4 *Hud* Crew   The director of photography (DP) needs a crew of many assistants to find and maintain the complexities of getting the right look for a shot. Note that in this production photo of the camera truck from *Hud* (1963), because the shot is so brightly lit from the harsh noonday sun, reflectors are used to soften the stark shadows with light bounced from another direction. The film was shot by the legendary cinematographer James Wong Howe, ASC.   (Photograph by Bradley Smith)

- The **second assistant camera operator** operates the clapperboard and records all the takes and shots. (Traditionally, a clapperboard is used at the start of each take to synchronize picture and sound with the bang of its hinged boards. The sound of the board and written information on it detailing the scene and specific take number assists the editor later. Today, an electronic system is often used.)

- The **gaffer**, as the chief electrician, coordinates the lighting requirements of the DP for the daily schedule. The gaffer is assisted by the **best boy**—the **first assistant electrician**—whose job it is to prepare the lighting equipment for the next set with the help of the **grips** and other electricians.

- The **key grip** works with the DP in planning and executing the arrangement of the subsequent setups, as well as supervising personnel and equipment.

The **second unit crew** is used most often by the director of photography for master shots with available lighting or for necessary *inserts*—the single shot of a billboard along a highway. This crew may be used more extensively when scenes must be shot at a remote location at which the film director chooses not to go. For example, in the much maligned film *Bonfire of the Vanities* (1990), second unit director Eric Schwab gained a small but significant reputation for his spectacular opening shot of a Concorde jetliner landing at a New York airport, taken from the Chrysler building in Manhattan. In *Glory* (1989), the second unit roamed through the action, giving the film a different point of view in the battle scenes by showing essential details of soldiers loading guns, shooting, and falling. Sometimes second units take on a larger creative role in films, especially when they are specialists in underwater, aerial photography, pyrotechnics, or other special effects.

The Daily Routine

"Every picture defines its own look, and that definition begins with the director's intention."

Sven Nykvist, ASC (*Virgin Spring*, 1959)

There is hardly a typical day for a director of photography. Because movies are shot under such a wide variety of conditions, the schedule of a DP is determined by circumstances that sometimes are not easily categorized. *The White Dawn* (1975) was shot by Michael Chapman inside igloos at Baffin Bay; *Shy People* (1987) in the bayous of Louisiana by Chris Menges; and *Straight out of Brooklyn* (1991) in the housing projects by John Rosnell. In most location movies, the DP has to work with what is presented as the basic background of the story and then creatively react to the evolution of unexpected circumstances. For *12 Monkeys* (1995), director Terry Gilliam and DP Roger Pratt, BSC searched out abandoned power plants in Baltimore and Philadelphia to photograph their rotting interiors, often not knowing quite what to expect on the day of the shoot. Although Gilliam had previously relied on storyboards to preplan his day, he moved away from that tactic in this film. "It's interesting to see if you can do things instinctively—to go to a location and see what's there on that day." Of course most movie projects have some portion of their work shot on studio lots, using soundstages for interiors, and permitting the DP to film in a completely controlled situation.

Each director has a particular working rhythm, and the director of photography must develop habits that blend with it. But it works both ways. The DP may be a person who spends an inordinate amount of time getting the lighting just right, and nothing photographically can move ahead during these prolonged setups. Bill Fraker, ASC (*Rosemary's Baby*, 1968) claims, "The one person who runs the set on a production is the cameraman. He's the one who really controls the time: He's the one who can bring you in on schedule or put you over." When "time is money," the pressure on the DP to budget time can be enormous. John Buckley, gaffer for *Titanic* (1997), also felt that responsibility during production, "When we were on top of the ship trying to light something, there were usually hundreds of cast and crew people waiting for each setup." Other unplanned delays caused by irresponsible behavior of an actor or turmoil on the set, for example, can throw hours of camera strategy into confusion. When this happens regularly, the problem causes a disruptive ripple effect throughout the film crew.

The DP tries to get on the set very early in the morning, well before shooting, to walk through the days scheduled setups. If the director uses extensive rehearsals, the DP roughs in camera placements, blocking, and lighting at this time. Work routines have to be established. While working on *Batman Forever* (1995), DP Stephen Goldblatt relates, "Our goal, on the biggest sets we had, was to be shooting by 11 A.M. at the latest. We'd be pretty frustrated if we weren't shooting by 10. That sort of thing involves a lot of people working very late at night, sometimes all night, and on weekends. We didn't have that nightmare feeling of people walking around in porridge, waiting to find out what on earth is going on." The pace of the day's actual shoot is unique to each movie, depending on budget, the physical circumstances, and the drive of the production team.

At the end of the day, the director, director of photography, actors, and others look at the **dailies** (also called **rushes**). These are prints of the previous day's work and are used by the DP to confirm decisions on lighting and aspects of the camera work. Commonly, every department comes to watch the dailies to see that their contribution has turned out as envisioned. Afterward, the DP may go over the setups for the next day with the key grip, gaffer, and camera operator. This routine is repeated during the months of production.

Thinking ahead is always a part of the daily routine. The DP must stay aware of not only what is presently being photographed, but how each shot will link to preceding and subsequent footage. Normally, the issue concerns providing enough film **coverage**—necessary film footage from a variety of angles covering the essential action—of a scene to give editors an array of choices. Although, strictly speaking, one could say that such linkage is the problem of the editor, the DP must give the postproduction people shots that naturally lend themselves to efficient editing. "Half of what a cinematographer does, I think, is work out the cut points—the editing certainly is dictated by how the film is shot," notes Mark Irwin, ASC (*Say It Isn't So*, 2001). In very practical ways, a good DP must have an editor's sensibilities.

Whereas professional still photographers often develop and print their own film, keeping a great deal of control, for practical reasons cinematographers do not easily have that option. To monitor the subtle visual nuances that cinematographers had intended in exposed film, certain ones might follow their prints to the *film processing labs*. Mistakes can happen. For example, although movie industry labs generally are highly efficient, technicians—*color timers*—working there might think that footage that was intentionally shot in low light should be brightened. Most directors of photography, however, simply do not have enough time to shepherd their work through this important stage, and they must trust their film to the expertise of others.

THE CAMERAS

"Motion pictures are nothing but a succession of still pictures. Once you understand that, you can unlock all kinds of mysteries."

Introvision president Tom Naud

The camera is the one essential tool of moviemaking. By rapidly photographing a series of images at the rate of 24 frames per second, the illusion of motion is created when the pictures are finally projected on a screen. The 35mm camera is still preferred for feature film production, although smaller, lighter weight Super 16mm cameras are used at times. The 16mm format has been traditionally more popular with documentary filmmakers.

The basic technology of the motion picture camera has changed little over the years. Refinements are continually being added to cameras, however, in the form of viewfinders, noise and weight reduction, the range of frame speeds, and other features. For instance, a *video assist* camera with monitor is now often attached to a viewfinder, the result being that the director can instantly see what was shot, no longer having to wait for the dailies to judge the quality of what was shot. Another example of innovation is the wide use of *remote camera* operation. In *Other Peoples*

7–5 Bertolucci and Mitchell® Camera
Mitchell® cameras were standard equipment for shooting movies for over fifty years. Although they were extremely heavy, their soundproof design and mechanical reliability made them popular throughout the professional movie world. Today, a variety of camera makes (especially models by Panavision®) have overtaken the older camera on the stages of Hollywood studios. Here, Italian director Bernardo Bertolucci (lower) poses during the shooting of the epic *1900* (1976) with his internationally renowned cinematographer Vittrorio Storaro.
Paramount Pictures)

Money (1991), Haskell Wexler hid the cameras behind some cans in Grand Central Station so the cameras wouldn't get the attention of the crowds there. He then operated them from 200 yards away. Other examples of refined camera technology includes remote control *crash cameras,* which can be installed in a metal Firebox® that survives extreme heat, being hit by speeding cars, or powerful explosives.

Familiarity and success with one camera system naturally builds strong loyalties to certain brands of cameras for most cinematographers. In general, Hollywood production tends to favor Panavision® camera equipment and lenses **(7–5)**, but individual cinematographers like the more portable German Arriflex® models with Zeiss® lenses, the Austrian Moviecam® system, or the Aaton® 35mm hand-held and Super 16mm camera.

Film Stock

"I find that if you change any element in filmmaking, it will show up on the screen in some manner. It may be very subtle, but any approach you make towards making a film different—if you change the equipment, change the film, or change anything—it will show up on the screen."

Bill Butler, ASC (*Jaws,* 1975)

The purely physical appearance of movies is strongly influenced by the nature of the film stock on which it is shot. Any amateur still photographer has a range of film stocks from which to choose, depending on the expected light conditions. This choice is most crucial for the professional cinematographer. Each type of film stock will create a slightly different texture for its images. In turn, the subtle qualities of screen imagery strongly affect the way we experience any movie, that is, how we feel about what we are seeing.

Several points are worth noting regarding film stock. The acetate base of film material is covered with an emulsion of varying degrees of light sensitivity. The nature of its photosensitive elements—the number and size of microscopic particles of silver halides containing visual information—establishes the quality of grain in the film when it is projected. Small grains are activated when exposed to intense light; larger grains capture low light levels. Film stock has greatly improved over the years, becoming more sensitive and thereby allowing subjects to be photographed with less light. Each manufacturer rates its film by several gradations, between **slow film** and **fast film**:

- *Slow film* is often selected for studio shooting on soundstages because of the ability to use and control strong light sources **(7–6)**. The image produced is of *fine grain*, sharply defined and vivid. Because of this, more visual "information" is available in film of this stock. Translated, this means that the purity and denseness of blacks and whites is strongly pronounced.

- *Fast film* is generally used in limited or low light situations. It creates a *very grainy* image with the rough, hazy sparkle that we often associate with the realistic look of a documentary. In terms of color, the rougher grain tends to mute the look of what is photographed, as sharp contrasts are diminished.

Another way of talking about film stock is in terms of its varying degrees of *contrast*. Each shot situation has a special contrast, that is, the relative amount of light and dark. Film is said to be **high contrast** when it is designed to capture shots in which there are sharply defined lines of shadow, with little gradations into gray. **Low-contrast** film reproduces shots in which light tends to be nondirectional and the grays

7–6   *Ed Wood*   Because *Ed Wood* (1995) is a blatant parody of low-budget schlock films of 1950s director Edward D. Woods Jr., Tim Burton, and Stefan Czapsky, ASC wanted to capture the overheated visual style of the period. Slow film—stock that requires more exposure and illumination—was used to simulate the look of films shot cheaply on stages with limited but powerful light sources. Johnny Depp playing Ed Wood performed with the glazed look of dazed optimism and dimwittedness that lingered at the fringes of Hollywood moviemaking during the 1950s.

blend, as in fog **(7–7)**, while film with **normal contrast** is the middle ground, recording light that is directional but diffused, with an easy gradation of whites, grays, and blacks.

The nature of the story influences the choice of film stock. The many gradations of film speed allow the cinematographer a choice of film images, from *coarse* to *satiny*. A cool urbane murder mystery may call for a high-contrast look, filled with strongly defined shadows. A war film might be more convincing if done with fast film, available light, and the frequent use of long lenses to give it a rougher, less-controlled appearance. Sometimes, however, the filmmakers will do the unexpected, with interesting results. *Midnight Clear* (1992), a war film about young soldiers isolated in the snowy French countryside, was shot with very high-definition film stock as well as wide angle lenses, the result being that the soldiers fought in an oddly pristine and sharply colorful landscape. The choices gave the movie a visual beauty that was an intended ironic contrast with the sudden brutality of the battle scenes.

The **gauge** of film stock refers to its width. The larger the film size, the more highly defined the image will appear on the screen. Standard commercial film both in cameras and in theaters is 35 mm. Although 16mm is widely used for a range of filmmaking because it is much less expensive, there is some reluctance to resort to this format in standard commercial films because, although it can be "bumped up" to 35mm in film processing, there is concern over the loss of image quality. The visually admired *Leaving Las Vegas* (1995), however, was shot entirely with 16mm film. In rare

7–7 *Europa Europa* Low contrast shots expand the gray scale, diminishing the strength of the extremes of light and dark. In Agnieszka Holland's *Europa Europa* (1990), based on a true story of a boy's war odyssey between enemy lines, the shot of Marco Hofschneider (right) and Leni Delpy (left) has a large range in the gray scale, with minimal light contrast. The hazy effect is a visual metaphor for the young man's uprooted and confused life. (Orion Classics)

circumstances, an epic film may be shot in 65mm to enhance the richness of the spectacle. The expense of this large film format and the limited number of theaters that have proper projection equipment limit its use. Mikael Solomon, ASC, however, shot *Far and Away* (1992) in this gauge. "Shooting a 65mm film is like comparing a compact laser disc to a vinyl record. You are getting a lot more fidelity out of the image." This may be so, but there is no rush among producers to adopt it.

The Camera Lens

Cinematographers must determine the appropriate lens for each shot. Every size lens has a distinctive quality, each giving special emphasis to some aspect of the envisioned shot. In 35mm, the cinematographer can choose to shoot with various **focal lengths**—the distance between the film and the center of the lens (designated in millimeters) when a distant object comes into critical focus. A *short focal length* takes in a wide area; a *long focal length* narrows the range. Various focal lengths include *wide angle*: 8mm to 29mm; *standard*: 40mm to 50mm; *long:* 85mm to 180mm; and *telephoto:* ranging from 180mm to 2000mm **(7–8a-e)**. Cinematographers and directors have favorite lenses. Martin Scorsese generally rejects long lenses, choosing the wider field of view afforded by the shorter lenses: "I really like working at 32mm and then 24mm. Those lenses are a bit wider, and I like their crispness. Sometimes I work even wider, at 18mm or 10mm." The selection of lenses will strongly influence the visual style of the movie.

7–8a   The Wide-Angle Lens   The wide-angle lens changes the image in interesting ways. This 25mm lens allows an angle of 47.5 degrees and has significant depth of field. A depth of field is the area of satisfactory focus before and behind the primary subject being photographed. The wide-angle lens affords the DP a clear foreground, middle ground, and background in which to arrange characters and objects, and still have them in focus. There is a subtle but important difference between the visual effect, for instance, of a 29mm lens and a 35mm lens. When shooting in a room, a camera with a 35mm lens has the effect of being about a yard closer to the subject. The effect of very wide lenses produces a seeming distortion of reality, in that things closest to the camera appear somewhat outsized, and a person moving from the background forward does so with exaggerated swiftness. (Photograph by Nick Karras)

7–8b   The Standard Lens   A standard lens for a 35mm movie camera ranges from the 40mm lens to the 50mm lens. These size lenses approximate the depth relationships at which a person normally seems to perceive the world. This 50mm lens has a horizontal angle of view—the measurement from the center of the lens to the horizontal limits of the field of action—of about 25 degrees. When a film is shot with a straightforward conventional visual approach, either of these lenses will probably be frequently selected. (Photograph by Nick Karras)

7–8c   A Long Focal Length Lens   A long focal length lens is useful when the primary focus is on a specific object and less concerned with backgrounds and sets. This long focus 100mm lens, for example, has an angle of 12.5 degrees. At 100 yards, for example, longer lenses diminish depth, the effect being that objects on various planes compress and appear to "pile up." A shot down a crowded street makes people look as though they are walking against an invisible tide of resistance. When photographing actors, the lens is very complimentary to faces, softening their contours with a slightly wider image and a small degree of favorable distortion.   (Photograph by Nick Karras)

7–8d Zoom Lenses   Zoom lenses are useful because they have a variety of focal lengths, 25mm to 250mm (a 10:1 ratio) for instance, which can be easily accessed by a button on an electric motor of the camera while shooting (this shot is at 200mm focal length). It creates flexible alternatives for the cinematographer. Zoom shots can move the viewer from a wide angle to a long focus (or the reverse). With a zoom in, the effect draws a selected subject closer by "pulling" the selected area toward the viewer. In doing so, the figure and background are brought closer equally, flattening the planes. The dangers of the zoom shooting is the temptation for overuse, pushing and pulling images for no apparent reason beyond the camera operator's fascination with the technique.   (Photograph by Nick Karras)

7–8e The Telephoto Lens   The telephoto lens greatly foreshortens and blurs the depths between the planes, while keeping the prime subject in clear focus. This 600mm lens, for instance, magnifies images, giving the viewer a sense of "spying" on the subject and providing a voyeuristic sensation of secretly watching things transpire. The lens also seems to slow any movement toward or away from the camera. Its screen image is often associated with documentary filmmaking. In some cases—when recording a raging street battle—it is necessary for the photographer to be at a substantial and discrete physical distance from the subject, yet have a large detailed image. The telephoto lens is the perfect answer.   (Photograph by Nick Karras)

The choice of camera lenses is more than just a dry technical decision, but has to do with the very nature of both the relationship of the camera to the subject during filming and the aesthetic experience in the viewing. For Jane Campion's *Portrait of a Lady* (1996), for example, cinematographer Stuart Dryburgh and the director chose to shoot much of the film with long lenses, mostly Panavision Primo® zooms at 200mm to 400mm lengths. The choice of these lenses was somewhat unusual because many period films set in nineteenth-century England, no matter what the high drama being played out, often want to emphasize the backgrounds, containing glorious estates, lush gardens, and rolling green landscapes. But Campion and Dryburgh wished to focus on the characters. By isolating them within the zoom lens frame, Dryburgh comments, "You only see a very small portion of the background, maybe six-foot square. It becomes sort of a medley of color, texture, light, and shade." The film style gave the movie a desired contemporary attitude, matching Campion's feeling that the issues and emotions in this distant Henry James novel are very relevant today. Mounting the film as a series of pretty pictures featuring the visual delights of England and Italy would miss the point.

Camera Speeds

Because movies are normally shot at 24 frames per second, shooting at a faster or slower rate creates a special effect. When projected at the same rate, filmmakers intentionally shift us out of the normal mode of experiencing the physical world and into a time warp of their creation.

- **Slow motion** on the screen is achieved by running the film *faster* through the camera. Cameras can be "overcranked" to run at, say, 36, 48, or 72 frames per second. The effect varies depending on the subject being photographed, but it often makes high action sequences, or even mundane activity, take on a lyrical quality. Sam Peckinpah and cinematographer Lucien Ballard made violent gun play a dark ballet of death in *The Wild Bunch* (1969) when they caught the action in slow motion. In *Congo* (1995), special effects cinematographer John Fante pushed his camera to over 300 frames per second to record and make realistic the volcanic explosion of a miniature mountain.

- **Fast motion**, less frequently used, comes about by exposing film at a *slower* rate, often 16 to 9 frames per second. (Remember, it is later projected on a screen at the normal 24 fps). The result usually elicits amusement, as people or cars race frantically around the screen. Richard Lester used accelerated motion very effectively at times in *A Hard Day's Night* (1965) for comic purpose as the Beatles attempt to escape their fans. In the feature-length documentary film *Baraka* (1993), Ron Fricke used fast motion most wonderfully, giving us wildly shifting shapes of clouds rushing across the sky, streaming patterns of car traffic, and lights that imprinted the glaring madness of modern city life on the viewer. The result is an experiential film with insight into the frantically robotic way we live on this planet.

LIGHTING

"Photography is the literature of light. The cinematographer is a writer who utilizes light, shadow, tonality, and color, tempered with his experience, sensitivity, intelligence, and emotion to imprint his own style and personality on a given work."

Vittorio Storaro, ASC
(*The Last Emperor*, 1987)

The director of photography spends a great deal of time on the set making decisions about the quality of light in the upcoming shot. With the cost of filming running into the thousands per hour, the responsibility of choosing the right lighting the first time falls on the shoulders of the cinematographer. Lighting the set well is a tricky business. Bill Butler, ASC (*The Conversation*, 1974) says, "It takes twice the effort to make it a little bit better. It doesn't take just a little bit more effort, it takes twice the effort. And it doesn't get twice as good." The effort involves very subtle aesthetic challenges. It is, after all, an exercise in arranging light and shadow, and faint gradations between the two make all the difference.

The nature of light has a direct influence on how the audience will respond to an image. Every movie, and particular scenes within it, calls for particular lighting for its visual ambiance. An ordinary shot of two lovers kissing will have a very different effect if it is done in the sharply contrasted *hard light* of the sun at high noon, rather than the diffused *soft light* with candle fire reflecting off walls of a small room. The latter will have a much more "romantic" feeling. The choice of lighting establishes the ambiance in a shot and directs our attitude toward what we are watching. Light sources are measured by their *quality, direction, designation,* and *intensity*.

Light Quality

"In truth, reality isn't always perfectly balanced. I love to have images a bit over the top—either too light or too dark—because they provide energy and a more 'realistic' dynamic range."

Conrad Hall, ASC (*American Beauty*, 1999)

Light quality goes beyond superficial niceties of style and can touch into the core of a film's thematic meaning. Certain movie stories call for lighting that is realistic and natural; others lend themselves to highly controlled and symbolic illumination. Most cinematographers use *artificial light* in varying degrees to imitate the actual look of natural light **(7–9)**. Adding light is a very subtle art because it works best when the change does not call attention to itself, but significantly enhances the effect of the shot. Certain directors of photography are known as innovators in the use of artificial light, and their approach to lighting the set is very inventive. They assert their vision onto the story and tend to use visual images to blend both the interior worlds of the characters and the objective environment of the story. The thoughts of DP Vittorio Storaro might be representative of this approach: "By lighting half the face and leaving the other half in

7–9   *The Wild Bunch*   Many movies appear to be shot in unmodified light, that is, not enhanced by artificial light. Filmmakers want that realistic perception, especially for scenes shot outdoors. Yet the sun is often the enemy, casting hard shadows that starkly define images rather than gradually blending darks and lights. In this shot by Lucien Ballard, ASC from *The Wild Bunch* (1969), at first glance the horsemen (Ernest Borgnine, William Holden, and others) may seem to be photographed "naturally," in that elements within the frame do not draw undue attention to themselves. Notice, however, that although light from the sun appears to come through the trees, in fact shadows are cast by the legs of the horses, indicating a strong light source directly illuminating the riders from the front. Most movies, wherever they are shot, use some artificial light.   (Warner Bros.)

shadows, I show the unconscious and conscious—a separation, like man and woman, sun and moon, light and shadow." These cinematographers lean toward creating symbolic meaning or intense emotional response with the light values selected.

On the other hand, some cinematographers, because of their personal visual tastes, may insist on *available light* whenever possible **(7–10)**. They believe that whatever the inconvenience caused by the unpredictability of weather and its tendency to change quality abruptly, it is more than made up by the physical truth caught by the camera. Their motto might be: "Every reality has its own natural visual integrity and drama; it's not necessary to 'improve' it through the manipulation of light." While this might be an ideal, no cinematographer working in mainstream movies would adhere literally to the position. Most DPs who favor using available light generally modify this attitude by adding some degree of artificial light, but only from the natural points

7–10 *Close to Eden* The physical beauty of the Russian film *Close to Eden* (1992) is honestly displayed by effective use of **available light.** The film records the life of a sheep and cattle herding family in Mongolia, seemingly the last of a vanishing breed. The message of the film (that mechanized society relentlessly encroaches even in Mongolia) is found in the natural visual poetry and power of its photography. Director Nikita Mikhalkov and cinematographer Villenn Kaluta captured the majestic landscape with minimal use of artificial lighting. (Miramax Films)

where sources would normally occur. For example, if the light on the set of a bedroom could logically come from only one origin (a window), then they would prefer to use that single source with little other enhancement.

Every director of photography is acutely aware of the subtle variances in light quality. For instance, the "magic hour" is a favorite time of day to shoot film. During this delicate period of last light before sunset, the natural color and light intensity blends to give the photographer a richness that is hard to get at any other time of day. The problem for the cinematographer, burdened with the disparate elements of a large crew and cast, is that the time of day is so fleeting. In a scene from *Short Cuts* (1993), Matthew Modine accuses his wife of infidelity in a room illuminated by light at dusk. It was shot in real time, and the gradually darkening room reflected his deteriorating relationship. The visually spectacular *Days of Heaven* (1980) was shot in the summer on the great plains of Western Canada and is universally applauded for visually reverent and sweeping portraits of a sparsely populated land troubled by stirrings of change at a newly mechanized time earlier in this century. Nestor Almendros, ASC faced special problems

> We would prepare and wait all day, then shoot at the time after the sunset. We had twenty minutes before it got dark. We would shoot frantically to make use of this beautiful light. . . . If I shoot 15 minutes before sunset, and continue long after, many types of light occur. Daylight streams in the window, followed by sunset's phases, then near darkness and the artificial light from the street, followed by the sets of artificial light.

His dedication to getting the right lighting to convey the moment is clearly and wonderfully present on the screen. The cinematography of Almendros states the theme of the film more clearly than any character could speak it.

Light Direction

"The first thing I do is look for a light source, assuming it's a scene that warrants source lighting. Or if it isn't, I have to have an imaginary source even if there's no logic to it. I have to find someplace where I can imagine, either on real or surreal terms, there would be illumination."

John Bailey, ASC
(*The Accidental Tourist*, 1988)

Proper placement of lamps to light a shot takes experience. The director of photography, in consultation with the gaffer, works out the arrangement. The dramatic logic of the scene and the visual style of the entire movie will determine the final choices. Certain movies are shot primarily in high-key lighting; others tend toward low key.

- **High-key** lighting is created by placing the **key light**—the strongest source of lighting—right next to the camera. This means that the shadows of the subject are cast directly behind it and are invisible to the lens **(7–11)**. When enhanced with a **fill light**—a softer light designed to diminish whatever shadows are left—the effect is that the person before the camera takes on a radiant appearance, "standing out" in a glowingly cheerful but somewhat unreal looking world. The diffused lighting creates a *slow fall-off*—very little shadow contrast—when illuminating a figure. Certain movie genres have traditionally used high-key lighting. Musicals and comedy films are suited to the fanciful look of unrelieved high-key lighting, visually announcing their pretense and delight.

7–11 *Desire* High-key lighting was especially popular during the "Golden Age" of filmmaking. Most movie stars and their cinematographers loved the complimentary way it disguised facial lines by eliminating shadows. Typical of the satiny manner in which major actors were photographed, the grandly sublime images of Marlene Dietrich and Gary Cooper in *Desire* (1935) were created on film by the much-in-demand cinematographer Charles Lang, ASC. (Paramount Pictures)

7–12   *Monsieur Hire*   **Low-key lighting** is normally used to produce strong dramatic visual moods. Patrice Leconte's *Monsieur Hire* (1990) is a tale of sexual obsession in which a woman (Sandrine Bonnaire) is spied upon by a neighbor. In this shot, a single key light provides the major source of illumination on her body, casting half of it and the rest of the frame into shadow. In common with most films shot in a *film noir* style, the visual implications of the shot tell of their disturbed emotional state. In a sense, the viewer's imagination is left to fill in the blanks.   (Orion Classics)

- **Low-key** lighting is the opposite extreme. When the key light is moved in any direction, deepening shadows progressively take shape **(7–12)**. In this illumination mode, the fill light is much less intense in relationship to the key light, so that the contrast between light and dark increases. When lighting a face, for example, much of its detail will be lost in shadow—called a *fast fall-off*—in its extreme contrast of brightness. If the ratio of key light to fill light is 2:1, the effect is considered high key; if the ratio were increased to 6:1, the result would be low key. Low-key lighting opens the way for a variety of visual moods. Movies shot in the film noir style are its best example, but *horror* films and other high drama movies also play with a range of intense visual styles that low-key lighting can achieve. A high percentage of their central images are shrouded in darkness, leaving much for the viewer to subliminally "fill in."

Most films will work in an illuminated space somewhere between the extremes of high- and low-key lighting. In fact, rigidly sticking to one look can work against the film. Haskell Wexler, ASC (*Matewan*, 1987) has this opinion: "Even a very well done picture that is all low-key has a numbing effect on the audience." In such a situation,

Wexler will "blast" the viewer every once in a while with a high-key scene to relieve the monotony of tone.

Light Designations

"I see a lot of films that are very 'lit.' Because films are now influenced by MTV, you see big shafts of light, extreme backlighting, and that stuff can be nice but is easily overdone. It makes you aware that you are looking at someone trying to make a pretty picture."

Director John Milius
(Flight of the Intruder, 1991)

The placement of light sources is critical to how the dramatic events in a shot will be weighed. The eye is naturally drawn by strategically positioned or unusual lighting within the frame. Set illumination is aided by three basic types of lighting options: kicker lights, back lights, and an eye light. Each one of these produces distinct visual and emotive effects on the subject and surrounding space being photographed.

- **Kicker lights** strike the primary subject from the opposite direction of the key light, for example, from the *side* or the *back* of a woman photographed in a large room. The lighting effect "kicks" out her body from the background, giving a more pronounced three-dimensional aspect to the entire frame image.

- **Back lights** are normally placed *behind* and *above* the subject to outline the figure, another way to make the figure stand out from the background **(7–13)**.

7–13 *Citizen Kane* **Back lighting** in this shot from *Citizen Kane* (1941) of excited reporters in a projection room is a classic example of its use. Contrasted with the documentary visual style of a newsreel preceding it, back lighting in this scene provides a sense of the revelations to come. The men are literally in the dark regarding the word "Rosebud," the last utterance of the dying Charles Foster Kane. Throughout the movie, director of photography Gregg Toland and film director Orson Welles widened the boundaries of orthodox camera technique of the time. (Museum of Modern Art)

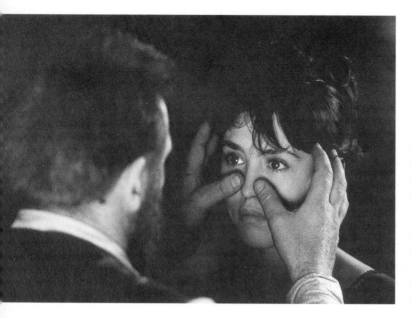

7–14 *Camille Claudel* The **eye light** is a lighting technique of photographers that accents and gives intensity to the eyes. Here our attention is immediately drawn to the eyes of Isabelle Adjani in *Camille Claudel* (1989) in a shot that shows her character's distress as she sinks deeper into her tragic relationship with the French artist Auguste Rodin. The effectiveness of the film moment greatly depends on how well her eyes are set off. (Orion Classics)

At times, when a backlight is used without the key light, the effect presents the subject in silhouette. The light placement is sometimes called a *hair light* because, when used on persons with full hair, the light shines through its strands, producing the glow of a halo.

- The **eye light**, or *catch light*, is a highly focused light placed next to the camera and intended to bring an added glint to the eyes of an actor **(7–14)**. Sven Nykvist, ASC (*Another Woman*, 1988) especially likes it. "The face is a world in itself. I think it is almost my specialty. If you are interested in human beings, you must be interested in faces. I always try to catch light in the actor's eye, because I feel the eyes are the mirror of the soul." Because it reduces shadows, the light minimizes facial wrinkles, seen as important for aging stars.

Light Intensity

"West Coast light is harsher, the sun almost colorless. In New England, you find a gray and green wash. Objects appear saturated and more three-dimensional. The shadows pull the eye behind things. You tend to look more at the background."

Michael Fash, BSC (*Dorothy Day*, 1995)

The control of **light intensity** is another issue for the DP, and it is especially problematic when shooting outdoors. If the sun is the primary light source, the situation is volatile. Nature cares not at all for the needs of the photographer, and acclimating to this great free source of light is a good part of the job. For instance, an intensely dramatic outdoor scene may be written to take place at noon and on the screen last for two minutes. But shooting the scene could take eight hours. Obviously, as the sun moves across the sky, light quality and direction changes, complicated further by passing clouds. To smooth out and compliment the situation, cinematographers use scrims, diffusers, and filters.

- *Scrims* are made of black gauze netting or stainless steel mesh and are placed in front of the light source to soften and reduce the light intensity. Blue gauze scrims are sometimes stretched over windows to moderate light. A butterfly scrim is a large overhang used when shooting outdoors to make light more uniform in quality. Scrims help alleviate the cinematographer's race with the sun.

- *Diffusion materials* are of many types. When a beam field of light is directed at a subject, the image is given a certain "punch." But deep shadows or extreme intensity can also be objectionably hard. Frosted glass or mesh may be put in front of either the camera lens or the light source to soften the edges of the subject photographed. The effect is flattering, especially to older actors.

- *Filters* are *gels* that come in hundreds of shades and are used to filter light for a variety of purposes. Certain filters heighten the contrast values of light and dark by reducing light waves. Other tinted filters lend their hue to the entire image for particular mood effects. Each of the color *gels* will emphasize particular qualities in the image. For instance, a particular light green filter will brighten green leaves while darkening the blue sky. In *Terminator 2* (1991), cinematographer Adam Greenberg, ASC used filters to establish the unworldly look of Arnold Schwarzenegger, "I always lit the Terminator with a cold light to make him look less than human. I used blue and cyan gels on the lights, which was good for Arnold and the story. When I hit Arnold with some very good, strong lights, he looks like a piece of sculpture, he looks incredible." Such decisions set the visual tone for movies.

An entirely new computer-generated dimension has been introduced into the use of filters. It is now possible to first shoot film with a naked lens, then transfer it to a digital format. With computer software that brings a range of color filters that can transform images, the cinematographer can alter the previously filmed images in a multitude of ways. Steven Tiffen, owner of a company that previously made traditional optical filters for the film industry, explains the possibilities: "Cinematographers can create precise split-diffusion filters that will enable them to soften the image of an actress' face and make her look more glamorous without affecting the rest of the frame. They'll be able to make scenes warmer or cooler to establish the mood or augment the story." The computer revolution continues to give new meaning to the work of the cinematographer.

Shooting outdoors at night has always posed its own problems. If the film story puts the action in the darkness of raw nature without the logical possibility of a light source beyond the moon and stars, a way to create credible illumination must be found. One way to beat the problem is to shoot the scene in the daylight while using special red filters and *underexposing*. In *Black Robe* (1991), Peter James, ASC used blue-green filters to get the cold night look of the snowy landscape in Quebec. This *day-for-night* shooting can make the exercise much less expensive than attempting the other lighting possibilities required in actually shooting at night. It is not as hard if the camera does not shoot the sky. When the film is deeply underexposed, the gray shadows become black and the lighter areas look like moonlight.

Night location shooting usually allows for artificial light sources within the context of the story. In turn, decisions must be made regarding the selective intensity of each light source. Depending on the needs of the film, there are a number of bulbs used today, from a 15 watt fluorescent, a 1000 watt incandescent, a 3000 watt xenon, a 10,000 watt Quartz Tungsten-Halogen, to a 24,000 watt metal halide or carbon arc *brute* light sources. A wide variety of lamp designs are available, including freestanding lights to truck-mounted designs. At times, the demands can be logistically overwhelming. For a five-mile chase scene along the Long Beach Freeway in *Terminator 2*, Adam Greenberg spent three full weeks working nights requiring ten generators, ten 100-foot condor cranes, and all the existing cable from every major studio in Hollywood. The effect was a dazzling series of shots from a helicopter as it chases a truck through the darkness, but in the glow of an urban raceway.

AESTHETICS OF THE CAMERA

"Selznick once said, 'There are two kinds of class: first class and no class'. And the same is true with visual taste. You can teach certain principles to people but the application of those principles may not function for them."

Gordon Willis, ASC
(*All the President's Men*, 1976)

Whatever variety of techniques and equipment are used, it is the artistic sensibilities and taste of the cinematographer and director that provides the distinctive vision of the movie. As with all the arts, greatness is measured in terms of the ingenious choices that go into the work. In choosing a film stock, lenses, lighting, filters, camera angles and movement, every director of photography must weigh factors as varied as the *thematic elements* of the film and the *consistency of image*.

Camera and Theme

For a director of photography, the needs of the story must take precedence over every other consideration. The theme of a film is the overriding consideration of the cinematographer when determining the most appropriate photography. In a narrative film, the *theme*—its message or central idea—becomes clear when its plot, visual style, and performances unify.

The director of photography has a strong hand in accomplishing this. First, the script itself will impose some limits. Owen Roizman, ASC (*The Exorcist*, 1973) says flatly, "If it reads well, it's going to play well. If it doesn't read well, it usually doesn't work." It may be true that outstanding camera work, in some instances, has made a weak film more impressive. But the opposite is also true. More than one film has gone awry because of virtuoso attempts by the cinematographer to attract attention, the result being that the film's subtler points are visually overwhelmed.

In preproduction conferencing, a general photographic attitude is laid out for the film. Every movie is shot in small, individual increments, each one presenting a problem and demanding the special attention of the cinematographer. Owen Roizman comments, "Every scene requires a different approach. If a scene will work better by moving the camera a lot, getting across the point of the scene, then it is better to be stylish. And if it is better to just sit back with a wide lens, not to move it and be absolutely static, then that works too."

The camera is the primary tool of storytelling on film, and it can function in several ways. That is, at times the DP will choose camera work that directly tells the story by pushing the action forward in a manner that is visually unambiguous. Action/adventure films typically use the camera to graphically present their rush of events. This often involves spectacular and innovative camera techniques, and whereas the results can be visually thrilling, the primary intention is to drive the viewer forward through the story. For instance, in *Lethal Weapon 3* (1992), Stephen Goldblatt, ASC creates exciting moments on the screen, but he never sacrifices the characters or slows the progress of events to explore the possibilities of mood and ambiance in a scene. The fast action and mix of star personalities are the prime attractions of this type of film, and the viewer is rarely asked to linger on the inherent thematic meaning of an important shot.

In other movies, the quality and style of the cinematography are more inseparable from the meaning of the film. The images so inform the story with their content that one cannot speak of the plot without summoning up visual sequences of the movie. To simply retell what literally *happens* in the film misses the point. In *Cries and Whispers* (1972), the unsparing camera work of Sven Nykvist penetrated to the heart of the tragic relationship of three warring sisters **(7–15)**. The camera not only recorded events, but it leads the viewer to the secret passion within each person's soul. The lingering shots of Agnes (Harriet Anderson), who is dying of cancer, cradled in the arms of the servant girl Anna (Kari Sylwan) carry the somber message of the impenetrable logic of suffering. The subtle choices made by the cinematographer and director Ingmar Bergman blend with the subject matter to create something greater than the parts.

Each movie project challenges its cinematographer to find the visual key that will reveal the full potential of the story. When Aldo Scarvada shot *L'avventura* (1960) for Michelangelo Antonioni, his austere camera work—stretching our sense of time with widescreen deep focus shots that isolated characters in barren surroundings—matched perfectly the existential theme of the film. The shadowy expressionistic photography of Freddie Francis, ASC in *The Elephant Man* (1980) brings back an authentic nineteenth-century Gothic atmosphere so popular in the literature of that period. In *Blue Velvet* (1986), Frederick Elmes, ASC contrasts the drab interiors of worn apartment buildings in a middle American town with splashes of sunlight and primary colors in the exteriors, creating a visual metaphor for a story of decadence and fragile innocence. In *House Of Games* (1987), Juan Ruiz-Anchia, ASC chose studied camera angles and placed the camera at a cool distance to keep the viewer at an odd objectivity of the bizarre characters in the story. Philip Rousselot, ASC framed the figures in *Therese* (1986) from an even greater distance, forcing us to watch the life of this nineteenth-century saint in quiet and formal reverence. In a small but bril-

7-15 *Cries and Whispers* Camerawork by Sven Nykvist for director Ingmar Bergman was consistently noteworthy for its urgent recording of emotions that flood over the face in times of stress. In *Cries and Whispers* (1973), the camera lens relentlessly tracked the actions and reactions of actors Ingrid Thulin (left), Liv Ullmann (right) and Harriet Andersson (not pictured), three sisters struggling with their relationships as one nears death.   (New World Pictures)

liantly shot Canadian feature, *The Adjustor* (1991), Paul Sarossy enhances the strange theme of an insurance man as a modern-day societal healer by continually surprising the viewer with slightly surreal visual compositions in an otherwise commonplace suburban life.

Certain interpretations of film subjects lead to extensive camera movement to capture the spirit of the story. In *Choose Me* (1984), Jan Kiesser, ACS employed prolonged dolly movement and slow panning shots, helping to give this modern story of backdoor relationships its slippery, luxuriant feeling. He used this flowing camera movement to match and comment on the constant flux of disconnected characters, a theme in the film. Dealing with the story of the Sex Pistols in *Sid and Nancy* (1986), Roger Deakins, ASC jumped into the chaos of a drug-dazed love affair with seemingly unconstrained "catch-as-catch-can" photography and grainy film stock. Jean Desegonzac, in *Laws of Gravity* (1991), was able to sustain dramatic continuity even though the extreme duration of the shots and the constant physical movement of characters were formidable obstacles. By encouraging spontaneous responses from the actors and then cleverly capturing their peak dramatic interchanges, he was able to successfully photograph the actions of a desperate group of young people trying to cope with the hard realities of Brooklyn.

Some viewers are impressed most by "pretty" cinematography, but this is a narrow understanding of the purpose of good camera work in a film. Appealing pictures may attract the layman's eye; professionals look for much more. Jan De Bont, ASC (*The

Hunt for Red October, 1990) comments, "The hard part is to light a scene that dramatically supports the story. And that doesn't necessarily mean beautiful images." In *Bugsy* (1991), the most visually memorable shots by DP Alan Daviau may have been the crane shots of the Flamingo Hotel standing out in the vast glowing brown of the Mojave Desert. But by his own admission, the cinematographer's subtle interior work in Bugsy Siegal's dimly lit living room was far more difficult to shoot and make effective. In a similar but even richer mode, Gordon Willis' visual conception of Marlon Brando in the opening scenes of *The Godfather* (1971) sets the entire tone of the story. Don Corleone sits in his dark office shuttered from the afternoon sun, as comfortable as the worn leather furniture, but a treacherous silhouette to everyone in the room. Although a DP will hope to create a steady flow of striking images, good cinematography does not necessarily call attention to itself. Lisa Rinzler, ASC (*Three Seasons,* 1999) notes, "Some of the most beautiful images in movies, still photography, and painting speak in a quiet way. Loud stripes of light can be appropriate, but they are often imposed. Quiet photography is something to work toward and be comfortable with. As a cinematographer you don't have to say, 'O.K., look at me, I did this.' "

Every director of photography strives for visual distinction. That desire, however, cannot be a cause for conflict with the intentions of the film. Nevertheless it is true that the cinematography in film may be more interesting than the story it is trying to tell **(7–16)**. A few examples of cinematography that went well beyond the limited prospects of the basic story make the point: Vittorio Storaro's camera in *One from the*

7–16   *Kafka*   In some cases, the quality of photography in a film outstrips its story. For *Kafka* (1991), a film fantasy about the paranoid mind of the writer Franz Kafka, director Steven Soderbergh and cinematographer Walt Lloyd chose to shoot in black and white, in a style inspired by a Czech photographer of Prague, Josef Sudek. Relying on heavy back lighting, pools of illumination, and studied camera placement, the photographic style attempted to manifest the near-mad interior world of the protagonist. But whereas the cinematography was inspired, the self-conscious script failed to match it.   (Miramax Films)

Heart (1981) captured a dreamy Las Vegas glow on soundstage sets for a story that was intended to be light-hearted but kept sinking; John Seale's photography in *The Hitcher* (1986) gives this sadomasochistic film an odd visual humor; Peter Suschitzky's mock *film noir* vision in *The Public Eye* (1992) is the best thing going on in an otherwise misguided comedy about the mob. In these cases, the enjoyment of the film is often found solely in its visual pleasures.

The great James Wong Howe, ASC (*Hud*, 1963) said it simply, "Do what looks the best." Some stories are lyrical; others are fantastic; and others tell of everyday life—each film calls for a special visual approach. The ultimate "beauty" of a cinematographer's images is in how convincingly the camera tells the story.

Consistency of Image

The look of each film is distinctive and becomes the environment that we accept and live in for a few hours. It is upsetting if, for no apparent reason, there is a shift from one set of visual characteristics to another at seemingly random times within a movie. Uniformity helps to establish and maintain a visual harmony. In terms of lighting, an overriding concern for the director of photography is **matching shots**.

It is relatively easy to make one shot look good, but the challenge for a DP working under the pressures on the set is to make one shot look like a natural outgrowth of the one preceding it—especially when, chances are, they were shot at different times. Because scenes, and shots within scenes, are often shot out of sequence, the challenge is to make the work visually seamless **(7–17)**. Mikael Solomon, ASC notes, "You have to know what to light and how to light it. And what you did six weeks ago, or even six months ago. . . . That's what the job is all about." Much depends on impeccably consistent lighting. That may be doubly hard when separate locations are used but must be masked. *Evita* (1996) was a musical set in Buenos Aires, Argentina, yet part of the film was shot in Budapest, Hungary, as a substitute background. In terms of architecture, the two locations were similar but the natural light of each place was very different: The light in Argentina was white, strong, and harsh; the light in Hungary was blue-green and wintry. Cinematographer Darius Khondji said, "In both places, it was important for us to understand that light was going to be like a character in the film." To achieve consistency, Khondji used a series of filters, diffusion techniques, camera adjustments, and lab work to balance the images so that the viewer is unaware of the shift of locations.

There are times, however, when the opposite effect is sought. For example, it is not usually desirable to mix visual textures within the same film. But in the movie *JFK* (1991), Robert Richardson, ASC shot both color and black and white, in 35mm, 16mm, and Super 8 formats, using fourteen different film stocks. In *Nixon* (1995), he repeated a similar visual style. Each scene had its own unique look, and the linkage of them created a powerful tapestry. The intentions of the filmmakers varied. For example, moving from shooting the comfortable executive offices of the White House in vivid color, Richardson shot grainy black-and-white sequences to record the young Richard Nixon and his Quaker family living during the depression. The radical visual

7–17   *A Man in Uniform*   A primary responsibility for the director of photography in most movies is to produce film images that have consistent physical qualities. This requires lighting, film stock, and lab work that aligns with the nature of story and the taste of the director. Movies such as *A Man in Uniform* (1993) with the look of *film noir*—grim, starkly lit films shot featureless rooms and back alleys—must carry the visual style through each scene. Here, Kevin Tighe, playing a cop, meets up with Tom McCamus, a strangely deluded TV cop who enters the real world of crime.   (IRS Releasing)

disruption transported the viewer to a more stark existence, creating the sense of a past remembered. As the movie went on to bombard viewers with a variety of seemingly disconnected visual qualities, the effect was one of a story being told from many emotional and historical perspectives.

Movies are seldom shot in exactly the same physical conditions and each situation invites a special photographic attitude. Movie locations can vary from the tightly controlled soundstages of a Hollywood studio to a cold winter morning in downtown Cleveland or a steamy night in Cairo. For example, when considering the physical environment of a shoot, the DP determines what film stock and filters will best present the essence of the subject. Eastman Kodak, Fuji, and Agfa sell a wide variety of film stocks, each made for a particular film condition or desired effect. Some types of film stock work better with outdoor natural light; others are designed to pick up grays or skin tones; still others are better suited for poorly illuminated interior scenes, underwater conditions, or sets with fluorescent light. Every DP has an opinion about what particular lenses or lighting conditions captures just the right tonal qualities, given the conditions on the set.

COLOR

"Color adds a new dimension to everything. It brings excitement and joy, makes us aware of the things around us, and helps organize our environment."

Herbet Zettl, Writer
in applied media aesthetics

There is an unmistakable physical pleasure in seeing an unexpected spectrum of colors combine on a screen. Anyone who has shown film slides can attest to how the most common backyard photos can suddenly become vibrant with emerald green trees, an electric blue sky, and bright Hawaiian shirts that went unnoticed before being projected. Images from motion pictures add other dimensions: sound and movement. Directors of photography take advantage of the medium to explore both the aesthetics of color composition and their emotional impact on the drama.

Black-and-white film dominated movies for the first fifty years of the twentieth century. Black-and-white photography has an aesthetic all its own. The many great cinematographers of the past refined their art to extremely high levels in this format, and it is only one's visual unfamiliarity with black-and-white film that could judge it as an inherently reduced experience. Whereas color describes the world in familiar ways, black and white is the medium of mood and suggestion, at times a dreamland filled with silver shimmer. To choose to shoot in black and white is to enter into the cinematographer's personal realm of perception, an unrealistic visual landscape that, paradoxically, can be starkly truthful. Our deepest emotional memories may come to us in harsh contrasts that resemble the factual world of black and white **(7–18)**.

7–18   *American History X*   Certain subject matter cries out for black-and-white photographic rendering. Tony Kaye directed and photographed *American History X* (1998), a bleak story of racial hatred starring Edward Norton. Although black-and-white imagery would seem to be appropriate for such a confrontational theme, Kaye shot the movie with film stock, lighting, and lenses that produced fine satiny photography, going against the aesthetic expectations of such a raw story.   (New Line Cinema)

In many ways, black and white is more difficult to shoot than color. At the very least it presents different problems to the cinematographer. In color, objects in the frame visually separate by their obvious color contrasts—a woman in a green dress against a tan wall—but in black and white the use of light is the essential element that separates and enhances the three dimensional aspects in a picture. The cinematographer concentrates on the *gray scale*—the incremental gradations between black and white—and the expected use of those subtle values in the spectrum creates a sense of depth in a frame.

Despite the potentially diminished popular appeal of black and white in the past forty years, many visually outstanding films have been made in the format, including *Who's Afraid of Virginia Woolf* (1965); *In Cold Blood* (1967); *Paper Moon* (1973); *Raging Bull* (1980); and *Rumble Fish* (1983). Conrad Hall, ASC *(In Cold Blood)* states, "You work harder, as an audience, in black-and-white. I don't think that's a bad spirit to have between the film and the audience." Steven Spielberg chose to shoot *Schindler's List* (1993), a film recounting the horror of the Holocaust, in black and white. The effectiveness of the film's message was greatly enhanced by this aesthetic choice. Even its director of photography, Janusz Kaminski, was moved by its impact, "The newsreel quality of the black-and-white seemed to fade the barriers of time, making the footage feel like an ongoing horror that I was witnessing firsthand."

A Snapshot of Color Development

Although the absence of color is not a "natural" depiction of reality, the technology and economics of color film were slow in making it a practical option. Yet from the start, filmmakers employed various methods to experiment with color. Various tinting procedures were used through the early years to give more life to movies. George Melies' *A Trip to the Moon* (1902) was hand-painted frame by frame. The Technicolor Motion Picture Company was formed in 1915 when a new two-color process was developed and a small number of commercial movies were made in this format. The Hollywood studios of the 1920s showed only sporadic interest in making color an industry-wide standard, the revolution in sound having sapped their financial resources. By the 1930s, three color-separation negative prints became available, so that Walt Disney began to delight viewers with vivid color in animation. By the late 1930s, a few selected feature films, most notably *Gone with the Wind* (1939) and *The Wizard of Oz* (1939), won audiences in record numbers. Still, it was not until the 1950s, as a response to both the challenge of newly arrived black-and-white television in most homes and the continued technical improvements of color film by Eastman Kodak, that the studios responded to the competition and color movies became the standard for quality productions.

The subtleties of color application in movies, however, had yet to be realized. Up to this point, Hollywood had used color primarily to dazzle and overwhelm the viewer in musicals and epics. For many cameramen originally trained in black and white, the same high contrast visual styles also became the controlling aesthetic in color. Cinematographers were challenged to relearn a fundamental part of their trade. As John Bailey, ASC (*Ordinary People*, 1980) observes

> When European cinematographers started going to color, they were using very soft color that was unknown in the Hollywood mainstream at the time. When most Hollywood productions started going to color, most of the cinematographers who were shooting them were old guard who were black-and-white cameramen or else they were the high-key color musical type.

Crosscultural influences in motion pictures have always been lively, and Hollywood learned about the artfulness of movie color from both Japan (with *Gate of Hell*, 1953) and Europe (in such films as *Red Desert*, 1964). By the 1960s, American cinematographers were seriously approaching color, not as a sensational come-on to find new audiences, but as a method to search out and enhance the possibilities of film themes. They learned that color in film presented any number of aesthetic choices for the filmmaker, that color could be more subtly manipulated and used in ways not before explored.

Computers are rapidly changing the manner in which color is captured and manipulated on film. The traditional photochemical techniques done in labs during postproduction are being gradually replaced by digital processing. For *Pleasantville* (1998), the original footage shot by John A. Lindley, ASC was digitized frame by frame, then doctored by a graphics computer to shift from a world of black-and-white to one of color. In the future, this method may become standard for the rendering and enhancement of all color cinematography.

A word about **colorization**—media companies who have bought or inherited the rights to older black-and-white films transform them into color movies because of commercial considerations. The results, aesthetically speaking, are mixed at best. Some television executives claim that the public demands color, and if movie classics are to gain a new audience, they must compete with other color programming on the TV screen. Most film purists, however, strongly object to the practice. The very thought of a colorized version of *Citizen Kane* (1941) is nightmarish to those who appreciate the skill and attention that went into that black-and-white production. The color choices that would be made for Xanadu's grand interiors or Susan Alexandra's operatic wardrobe would prove permanently distracting. Fortunately, the crisis seems to have passed. American Movie Classics, Turner Classic Movies, and others on cable present a host of black-and-white films from the past, and younger audiences are being regularly exposed to classic movies in their original formats.

The Language of Color

In elementary school art classes, we may have learned that the color spectrum can be divided into *warm colors*—red, orange, yellow—and *cool colors*—green, blue, violet. While this observation is generally adequate, it is more complex than that. For example, when yellow has a strong bluish tint, it feels cool; whereas reddish blue tends to be warm. *Complementary colors* lie opposite one another on the color wheel (red and green are complementary); *related colors* lie close to one another on the color wheel (yellow and orange are related).

The mastery of cinematic color is an endless investigation for the photographer. An in-depth consideration of the subject is too complex for this study, but some general principles can be stated. Because the essence of color is light, the spectrum of a rainbow created by a prism signals the range we see. Color is said to have certain attributes:

- **Hue**—The colors of the rainbow spectrum are pure *hues*. (Most colors we see combine light wavelengths and greatly expand the variety of hues.)

- **Brightness**—The amount of light reflected determines its *brightness*, whether the color is perceived as dark or light.

- **Saturation**—This is the strength or intensity of a color. If the color orange were progressively *desaturated* by adding white, the color would ultimately shade into gray. The effect can be realized by *flashing* the film, a process of putting a small amount of light on the film stock just before or just after exposing the negative. Although the effects of flashing are somewhat chancy, such devices as a Panaflasher® allow controlled adjustments to be made.

It is useful to consider the reasons that a DP might choose to desaturate the color in a film. The process is used when the dramatic nature of the story calls for a toning down of images. In *Godfather II* (1974), when cinematographer Gordon Willis presented a memory-faded history of the Corleones in Sicily and Ellis Island at the turn of the century, he used filters, film stock, and lighting to desaturate colors—pale brown, amber, washed-out blue—to give an antique affect and convey a bygone time. Sharp, bright colors often infer a present time frame or mental orientation. When the story moved to the present time at a Lake Tahoe retreat, the color became stronger and more active. When Walt Lloyd, ASC read the script for *Short Cuts* (1993), a story of the everyday people living in everyday chaos, he sensed that the quality of the color should match the theme. "I thought we should see a side of Los Angeles that is not exactly monochromatic, yet drained of its energy and life," he said. Lloyd desaturated the film with impressive results. A prime example of the effective use of desaturated color was the lengthy opening battle scene on Normandy beach in *Saving Private Ryan* (1998). DP Janusz Kaminski, ASC wanted to achieve the stark realism that historical documentary footage of the war showed. Kaminski comments, "The perception of that period is tinted by time—almost as if time is fading away—so I felt the movie needed to be very washed out in terms of color and contrast. The closer the photography was to black and white, the more successful its storytelling would be."

However, some filmmakers choose not to desaturate their film and stay with more vivid color, despite the historical nature of the story. Cinematographer Alan Daviau and director Barry Levinson, for *Avalon* (1990), didn't want to use desaturated sepia tones or heavy diffusion to indicate the earlier period of this century because they felt the technique had become a cliché to indicate the past in this visual manner.

Cinematographers play with color and are acutely aware that color can control the overall tone of a film. Color choices affect how we feel toward the setting and characters in a film. For example, how would color be applied in a waterfront bar frequented by dockworkers, as opposed to a comedy about karaoke clubs in the suburbs? Color selections by the director, production designer, and the cinematographer are critical. Several considerations, unique to color, must be taken into account: color energy, color symbolism, and color composition.

- **Color energy** can be *high* or *low* and is allied to the nature of the hue. In general, warm colors are high-energy colors, cool colors are low energy. A red car in a film looks hot, as does a yellow neon sign and an orange T-shirt. Our eyes are quickly drawn to these high-energy colors that tend to dominate a frame. At the start of *Titanic* (1997), the photographic color treatment scenes on the present day research ship intentionally lacked high energy. Camera operator Jimmy Muro points out, "In that section we were trying to create some fairly blasé tones—a gray, industrial feeling. But when we go back in time, it's like, *Technicolor!* As an audience, we never see the past in anything but black-and-white, but Jim [Cameron] wanted the images to just burst off the screen, dripping with colors." Saturation, together with brightness, is the key to the color energy. *Dick Tracy* (1990) is an example of the extreme of color saturation, with an entire palette of shocking and uncompromised primary hues. Cool colors may also be high energy if they are purely *saturated*. And whereas *Batman* (1989) and *Batman Returns* (1992) would seem to be exercises in the use of cool colors, the films exude high energy because the electric blues and glowing blacks, although at the dark end of the scale, are saturated.

- **Color symbolism** follows the cultural attitudes that associate particular colors with certain emotional or intellectual states. For example, *The Last Emperor* (1987) is a film that covered the entire life of Pu Yi, the last person to sit on the Dragon Throne as emperor of China. Vittorio Storaro, ASC washed the film with color to broadly symbolize the stages of his life.

  > *We worked to build visuals with colors representing the different styles of Pu Yi's life. We started with monochromatic concentration camp sequences. Birth is red; childhood orange, and the conscious adult is yellow. Green represents maturity, blue the intelligence and strength of the forties, indigo the power of the fifties, and violet the end of life and transfer of power to someone else.*

  However, color paradoxes are everywhere. American filmmakers are well aware that the color *black* has a heaviness about it, linking it to death, funerals, mourning; on the other hand, black clothing awakens the viewer to provocative sexuality or a rebellious young society. The swirling *red* lights atop a police car can signal danger or welcome rescue; *green* can be eerie, but is also the color of the renewal of life; *white* is traditionally virginal, but in turn can indicate a diminished or washed out energy. Naturally, the context of the film will determine how color symbolism is to be used and interpreted. When color symbolism is done well, its message tends to unify all of the visual elements in the film.

- **Color composition** refers to the designed harmony, or discordance, that color brings to the individual shot and scene. Just as one might want to coordinate colors when putting together the interior of a home, filmmakers also attempt to use color subtly to create a specific emphasis in a shot. Like the painter, the cinematographer composes the limited dimensions of the surface with colors that visually please and work to complement the theme. In John Dahl's murder mystery *Unforgettable* (1995), muted colors were chosen for the interiors of many rooms. But DP Jeff Jur, ASC felt that although this color palette was appropriate to the noir look of the subject, the lead character, a medical examiner played by Ray Liotta, needed a different visual treatment. Jur comments, "My view of the movie was that, while the Liotta character may live in a dark world, he always believes there's some way for him to find out the truth. So I wanted some part of the frame to have a very bright, overexposed area to suggest that ray of hope." When watching a film, we often register the artistic choices of the filmmakers at a deep reactive level. But mistakes can happen. For example, an otherwise insignificant bright yellow water tower in the background of a shot might control every other color within the frame, so that the attention of the viewer is inadvertently drawn to it at the expense of a more important object in the foreground. Each shot must be analyzed beforehand for its color harmony or intended discordance.

A CASE STUDY: DON'T LOOK NOW

A quick study of color in director/cinematographer Nicolas Roeg's *Don't Look Now* (1973) is instructive. The color *red* is strongly symbolic to the story and leads us emotionally through the film. The movie is set first in England, then in Venice, Italy. The script deals with the tragic death of a young girl and the growing desire of her parents to make a supernatural connection with her. Its basic color scheme of the film emphasizes cool colors—blues, greens, grays; when other colors are presented, they are desaturated to give the film a subdued, natural look. *Bright red*, however, is the exception. It represents an ominous warning of death and possible strange conspiratorial forces of the supernatural behind it.

In the first few shots we see a young girl in a red raincoat running toward a pond. She throws a red striped ball in the water. The camera tilts down to pick up what seems to be the distorted image of the red raincoat in the water. In her home nearby, John (Donald Sutherland), her father, looks at slides through a viewer as he talks to the mother, Laura (Julie Christie). As John looks at a slide of a Venetian church interior, a hooded figure in red can be seen sitting in one of the pews. After he accidentally spills water on the slide, red dye runs from the mysterious figure in a ragged arc. John senses that something is wrong and rushes from the house as the shot cuts to the image of the girl in the red raincoat submerged in the pond. By the time her father pulls her out she is dead. The horror of the red imagery in the quiet green countryside is deeply implanted in the viewer's mind.

As the story moves to Venice, where John is an art restoration consultant, the same shade of red is used very selectively to foreshadow spiritual and physical danger. Two elderly women meet Laura and one of them, a clairvoyant, wins her over to believing that contact with her dead daughter is possible. In the events that follow, the color red is introduced at moments of tension: Two red caps are seen in the foreground at the start of a pan shot that eventually shows a drowned woman being pulled from a canal; a quick flashback of the child in the red raincoat underwater; red ceremonial clothing of a Catholic monsignor; a red votive candle

strategically placed. Finally, John wanders madly along the labyrinth of dark canals in search of his missing wife. In a dark passageway, he comes upon a dwarf figure dressed in the now familiar red hooded clothing. John meets a tragic end. A reprise montage of the prophetic red images is shown, then a funeral barge adorned with red flowers completes the movie.

When outlined in this manner, the color imagery may seem overdone and obvious. But, in fact, the use of red permeates the film at an almost subconscious level. In superior movies, filmmakers approach color with the same sensitivity that a painter brings to a canvas.

SUMMARY

"The audience is insatiable with their visual needs," says Richard Edlund of Boss Films, in what could be a summary of the challenge for cinematographers. Technical advances in the field of visual imagery, as is true in many other aspects of the film industry, are in a constant state of evolution. New technology comes on the market each month—more sensitive film stock; radically designed dollies; smoother camera mechanisms; cooler, more powerful lights; and digital innovations of every kind—giving directors of photography ever more options in their work. Some cinematographers feel threatened by the growing conflicts between the traditional control held by them and the demands for visual effects artists for effects-driven movies. Often changes in the intent of a shot will be made by technicians in a visual effects studio long after an image is photographed. Caleb Deschanel, ASC (*The Haunting,* 1999) observes, "The cinematographer's work is becoming part of a mosaic. The real footage that is actually shot is like brushstrokes. The weight is shifting more to production design and to the editorial and visual effects house."

But apart from finding ways to incorporate the on-rush of new equipment, every cinematographer deals with the same basic situation that early camera operators faced: how to light, frame, and shoot action in ways that give vision to the director's interpretation of the script. It is that focus that demands attention of the men and women who record images and shape the action in the camera lens.

SPOTLIGHT

The Cinematographer: Bill Pope Interview

After having worked for years shooting and directing music videos, Bill Pope has been a director of photography on many feature films: *Darkman* (1990); *Closet Land* (1991); *Army of Darkness* (1992); *Fire in the Sky* (1993); *Blank Check* (1994); *Clueless* (1995); *Bound* (1996); *Gridlock'd* (1997); *Zero Effect* (1999); and *The Matrix* (1999).

Richard Peacock: Before your first credit on *Darkman*, what was your background?

Bill Pope: I went to NYU graduate film school. I graduated in 1977. I did the usual things people do, knocked around, worked as a gaffer, camera assistant. I did every job on the set. I started in New York then moved to L.A.

RP: What do you consider your first big break?

BP: Sometimes you do something that, at the time, you don't know the importance of. My advice is: Take every job, you don't know what will pay off. In my case, the first thing I ever shot were music videos, but they weren't called that in the 70s. The videos were shown on closed-circuit systems in places like Blockbuster. They cost about a thousand dollars to shoot. We'd shoot four in a day. I did a bunch of these, then forgot about it. Then in the early 80s this channel started up called MTV. They started to look for people who shot this stuff before, and I was recommended. So suddenly I wasn't a gaffer anymore, I was a director of photography and I was shooting music videos. I did an enormous number—two or three hundred in the 80s.

RP: What is your most recognized music video?

BP: In '88 I won the MTV award for best cinematography for a black-and-white Sting video called "We'll Be Together Tonight." That was sort of my ticket out. After that I got an agent, and I started doing commercials. Then I started directing a lot of music video. And even though it was a good living and fun to do, it was still the farm league. There was a stigma attached to it.

RP: How then did you move up?

BP: Sam Raimi gave me a call because he was going to make his first studio movie. He was a close friend of the Coen brothers and Sam had asked their cameraman, Barry Sonnefeld, to recommend somebody. Barry and I had gone to film school together. When Sam called he wouldn't take no for an answer. I had tried to turn him down several times. I'd been through that several times, you know, where they want to hire you for a first feature but they want to see your other first feature. But Sam said that he wanted to hire me for *Darkman* based on Barry's word.

RP: Looking back at that film, it had some people in it who have become big stars, Liam Neeson and Frances McDormand.

BP: They were really relatively unknown at the time.

RP: Do individual actors—in your case Tim Roth, Alan Rickman, Alicia Silvertone, Kneau Reeves and others—influence how you actually shoot a film?

BP: Totally. There's the director, the technicians, and the actors—the three of them and I have to do this little dance everyday. It's a push and pull, give and take thing. Every actor is different.

RP: Do you actually have contact with the actors, or does it come through the director?

BP: I have some direct contact, but it's not my job to affect performances, other than general blocking of performances. I don't affect motivation, characterization, or any of those things. My opinion carries an enormous amount of weight because I am the first *viewer* of the movie. I'm looking through the eyepiece, and I see things a little better, because they are looking at a TV monitor. So my perspective is special. But I don't speak to the actors about it, I talk to the director. It's his or her job to use the information or not use it.

RP: At what point do you normally come on a film project? Is it at the same time the director joins on or is it some time later?

BP: Most of my work has been when the director is generating the project. To me those are the most engaging movies. Writer/directors interest me—people who have something to say. I think the movies are better. Or a director who has taken a project and has hired someone else to write it, but who is in it from the inception. So those directors are in it much earlier than I am.

RP: How much time do you spend with a director lining up your strategies for shooting a film?

BP: Generally, I like to sit down with a director and go through the script page by page, and at some point, shot by shot. Some directors don't like to do that. But some directors love the process because we are really making the movie, talking about it shot by shot, performance by performance. A lot of times the director and I act the whole thing out, figuring out just where the camera is going to be. We go to locations and talk. It's the best way to understand things.

RP: How long does this take—a week, a month?

BP: I generally like a month at least. Most productions will budget you a month of preparation. If that's so, I like to take one week of that very early—maybe two or three months before the start of shooting to have a week of conversation with the director so that his or her concept is stuck in my head. Mostly I just listen, so for the next while I'm dreaming along the same line as the director.

RP: Do you and the director ever screen other films in this creative process?

BP: Nearly always. It's impossible to talk to anyone in the movie business without talking about other films—even if it's films you want to *avoid* looking like. Of course, in these days of videotape you don't have to see them on film. But if there's a movie that's really interesting to us, we'll have it screened. You can't tell what they really look like unless you actually screen them. You find yourself a good print and watch it.

RP: When you think about it, is there any definable reason why *you* are chosen to shoot a film? I mean, what do you think is your perceived strength as a cinematographer?

BP: Wow! [laughter] I think most relationships are personal. It's just a matter of spending enough time in this world of movies. It's that happenstance I mentioned earlier—you're working on a movie and some actor introduces you to another director and puts in a good word for you, and maybe that person likes you. Word of mouth has a lot to do with it. And I also consider myself pretty easy to get along with. Of course there are some movies I've made that people in the business like, and I get sent scripts or directors call me up based on my reputation. But it's usually personal.

RP: Is there any cinematographer from the past that you especially admire?

BP: I grew up in the 60s, and the great cinematographers of that period were Raoul Coutard, who shot Godard's movies, Gordon Willis in *The Godfather* and other movies, and the guy who shot *Fat City*—Conrad Hall. In other generations, I've always love Gregg Toland's work, *Citizen Kane*, of course.

RP: How do you see the role of the director of photography on the set?

BP: I firmly believe that the director is in charge. And that actors are to be made to look good. I'm a believer in all the traditional things about motion pictures.

RP: What input do you have in hiring the camera crew—the first and second camera operators, the gaffer, the key grip, or whomever?

BP: The director of photography should have total control, with the possible exception of the director or producer who has had a bad experience with one of these people. I have never encountered that, or even heard of it. I choose the best people I can, but I'm also accountable for them.

RP: Looking at the films you've shot, almost all of them are on the dark side, both in their theme and in their look. Maybe you have an affinity for low-key lighting. [laughter] Is this by chance or is this an aesthetic choice on your part?

BP: It's totally by choice. As I've said, I like movies written by directors or writers with a strong vision, and those films tend to be darker movies. There are exceptions—*Clueless* is a bright sunny movie. I took that movie based on the script and that wonderful lead character. I was just very captured by her. The script had a strong voice to it; it was quite unusual.

RP: What kind of challenges did *Clueless* bring that you hadn't faced before?

BP: Well, comedy is a very difficult thing. What is "funny"? This was a type of movie in which the camera was much less a character than I'm used to doing. I'm used to driving home a point-of-view—the literal point-of-view a camera gives you. But comedy is much quieter; it has much subtler use of the camera. The lighting is also more restrained. My inclination is to always amplify what I am doing. But in that one I had to learn to step back It was fun actually. I liked it a lot.

RP: How closely do you work with the production designer—Eve Cauley on *Bound*, for example—and what does that creative contact entail?

BP: A series of conversations. She and the directors [the Wachowski brothers] had a very clear vision about the color and various formal things in the background—the way people's apartments characterize them. I totally respect them and do everything I can to help them out. Sometimes, they come up with entire color schemes for the movie. Like the use of greens and whites in *Bound*. That was worked out entirely between the director and the production designer. We feed off one another in some ways. Eve came up with the idea of the two women being in this "box" all of the time. It's the standard *noir*-thing of people being trapped in frames. So I would try to work my own composition frames with other frames inside it provided for me by Eve. The walls had frames within frames. You try to keep the characters within them so they can't get out, so they are trapped by their circumstances. Choices come up: Does the use of white at various times suggest purity; when does red come in, and what will that do? It's all rather subconscious, but you have to plan it out.

RP: *Bound* is such a tightly woven story, with seductive images and controlled pacing. Did you have a clear concept of how it was going to look in the end, because it has a very special visual style?

BP: We knew. The Wachowskis were pretty specific about what they wanted, and they are very strong visually. We went through this movie shot by shot, page by page, before we started. It was meant to be a seamless journey throughout. It was not planned to be scenes starting and stopping, but a situation in which you never know where you are. You travel from point A to point Z and you never know how you got there. You just slip in and out of situations. It was their conception, and I think they pulled it off. I don't know what happened with that movie but in my mind it should have received more attention.

RP: I laughed all the way through it. Its humor is a surprise, created by the film's visual precision.

BP: Many people don't get that. The directors had an enormous amount of control. I always appreciate that quality in directors.

RP: *Closet Land* was a very different kind of challenge, I suspect. It's basically done in one room with just two actors—a male inquisitor [Alan Rickman] and a female victim [Madeleine Stowe]. What problems did that hold for you?

BP: The basic one is holding the audience's interest. The prime concern is this: How kinetic do you make it, and how quiet can you make it? With such a simple physical situation, you don't want to become too flamboyant because that will turn off interest, but if you do quiet, you'll never get the audience's interest at all. So that's the tightrope that you walk. I'm not sure that we walked it all that well.

RP: When I've shown it to classes, women respond quite strongly.

BP: They do respond to it. Women have come up to me and said, "Thank you for making that movie." I'm somewhat amazed by that.

RP: Because of the size of the production, did *The Matrix* present you with problems that you had not encountered before?

BP: Because of my experience in other movies—*Darkman*, the second unit and the effects unit on *The Addams Family*—I was more or less used to it. It's just a different way of approaching things. You become much more of an administrator, a person who delegates authority rather that doing it firsthand.

RP: Did you find yourself relating more to the special effects people, say John Gaeta of Manex Visual Effects, than to the directors, the Wachowski brothers?

BP: No, it was all very close. We started by having week-long sessions in Australia where it was eventually shot, walking through warehouses or in hotel rooms, probably a year before the movie started. And it continued while I was living down there three or four months before we began shooting. There was very little hierarchy. Everything moved ahead at the same time—the production designer, the physical effects people, the stunt people, the producers—otherwise production would fall behind and mistakes are made.

RP: Was the situation for you a fairly smooth production?

BP: It was, because the Brothers knew how complicated the project was going to be and took great pains to get everybody into it. They were very methodical about it and very inclusive. If production at the top is very exclusive, if information isn't readily disseminated, people working on the film just start to assume things. And they start running around making mistakes. But props have to be made, locations have to be chosen. The Brothers included everyone in.

RP: *The Matrix* had spectacularly choreographed fight scenes by the Hong Kong filmmaker Wo Ping.

BP: Well, Wo Ping is an experienced director himself, having made seventy films in Hong Kong. He did this as a favor to the Wachowskis. They "wooed" him into it with their enthusiasm, presenting it as a one-time opportunity for him to break into the American market and show his stuff to a new audience.

RP: How did you actually work together?

BP: The Brothers would explain to Wo Ping how they conceived the fights—the two had thought about them very deeply and storyboarded them. Wo Ping and his team then worked out with the actors for a full month on the concept. He would shoot the fights on videotape in empty warehouses with tape and stuff representing the set that were to be built. Then he would show the tapes to the directors. It was an ongoing, back and forth, process of refinement. Finally, on the set, we could then show the crew a segment of the videotape and say, "This is our next shot." The choreography was so complex—it's not your average fight, we couldn't anticipate anything—that if we didn't have this assist, there would have been a tremendous waste of time.

RP: Is your experience with *The Matrix* going to change in any way the nature of the way you work?

BP: Hopefully, it will make me more careful. It's helped me to concentrate harder. It's taught me to push my particular talents farther, because the pay-off is there. I thought—and the Wachowski brothers thought —that we would have no audience whatsoever. We thought we were making it too strange, too dark, too stylized. That the movie would have a minor audience and then disappear. And yet we were willing to do it. The film taught me that if you just put what you really believe on the screen, it will find an audience.

RP: And the movie continues to find its audience worldwide.

BP: True. To go along with that, there are 2 million DVD owners in the U.S., and the first week it sold 1 million copies.

RP: Larry Wachowski has said that you very much like using "black" on the screen. If that's true, what does it mean?

BP: In *The Matrix*, where the powers of darkness play such a large role, and in *Bound*, a *film noir* in which morality is broken into strong darks and lights, I like to reflect the contrast in my photography. Also, compositionally it helps focus the eye if certain areas of the frame are very dark and what you want to see is what is lit. I also find that people will concentrate harder if it's harder to see. My own theory is that it's good to make a shot that almost requires a shot before and after it, so that I compose the scene itself. The picture is contemplative, it leaves something out so that the shot that follows is required. You never give enough information in the shot so that it is complete in itself. It's like a long puzzle.

RP: Is there any film genre that you haven't worked in but you would like to?

BP: I've spent my life doing fringe movies. I hadn't done a mainstream movie, until *The Matrix*. I'd also love to do a musical. My student movie was a musical at NYU. I wrote and directed it. I have a great fondness for musicals. ◀

FILMS TO CONSIDER

The inspiration and expertise that a good director of photography and his or her camera crew adds to the success of a film project is hard to measure precisely, but if brilliant pictures arrive on the screen, you can bet their work was essential in creating it. The following films are but a few of the best:

- *Sunrise* (1929): The exquisite lighting and exploring camera movement of cine-matographers Charles Rosher and Karl Struss make this film the crowning jewel of the silent movie era.

- *Grapes of Wrath* (1939): The plight told in the faces of immigrant farm workers and their families, so well recorded by still photographers of the 1930s, is con-vincingly reproduced with the movie camera by Gregg Toland.

- *Detour* (1946): This underworld "B" movie, shot by Benjamin Kline, helped cre-ate a taste for movies photographed with minimal light, with large portions of the frame inked out to enforce their stark themes.

- *Gate of Hell* (1953): Director Teinosuke Kinugasa and his cameraman Kohei Sugiyama awakened viewers to the discerning use of color symbolism in advanc-ing the theme of a movie, in this case the remorse of a man who accidentally killed a lover.

- *Touch of Evil* (1958): Orson Welles refined the film noir style in this small budget melodrama of a border-town corrupt cop by taking advantage of the masterful vision of DP Russell Metty in using limiting locations to their fullest visual impact.

- *Vertigo* (1958): This eerie story of self-doubt and lost love was shot by Robert Burks, Alfred Hitchcock's DP in his Hollywood days, with a subdued color palette and camera lensing techniques that remain the strength of the film.

- *Red Desert* (1964): The cinematography of Carlo DiPalma in his first film (he later became Woody Allen's primary DP) perfectly captures in pictures the theme of industrial oppression and spiritual despair in this Antonioni movie.

- *The Conformist* (1971): In this Bernardo Bertolucci film about decaying morality in fascist Italy, cinematographer Vittorio Storaro suggests in his use of color composition the deep conflicts that permeate the society in the 1930s.

- *Cries and Whispers* (1972): The camera of Sven Nykvist studies the three con-flicted sisters in typical Ingmar Bergman close-up manner, but it is the bold use of color as a death metaphor that finally distinguishes this film visually.

- *Don't Look Now* (1973): The ominous beauty of the Venice canals has never been shown better than by cinematographer Anthony Richmond in Nicolas Roeg's chilling film of a woman driven by occult beliefs to reach her dead daugh-ter.

- *Godfather II* (1974): Surpassing even Part I for sheer physical beauty, Gordon Willis, ASC takes distinct photographic approaches, with warm colors and softer focus for the extended flashback sequences.

- *Days of Heaven* (1978): The natural beauty of Western plains, often shot in late twilight by cinematographer Nestor Almendros, strongly establishes the distant time frame and melancholy mood of this tragic love triangle.

- *Visions of Light* (1993): Although not a narrative film, this documentary is a must-see film for anyone desiring a short but fulfilling history of developing tech-niques and aesthetics of cinematography.

- *Breaking the Waves* (1996): The versatility of Robby Muller's hand-held camerawork fits perfectly into the spontaneous style of director Lars von Trier for this film about soaring passion and keen grief.

THOUGHT QUESTIONS AND EXERCISES

Watch a film from those listed.

1. In terms of the overall visual appearance of the film, what graphic elements impress you most? How would you characterize the contribution of its photographic style to the achievement of the film?

2. In the spectrum from very grainy to very fine, how would you categorize the film you have watched? In your opinion, what was it about the subject matter of the movie that influenced the choice of film stock? In what ways is it effective?

3. Choose a scene from a film. Take note of the quality of light. How would you describe it: high key, low key? From what direction do the primary light sources originate? What are the aesthetic effects?

4. Does the film tend to rely on more natural available light, or does the filmmaker use greatly enhanced light from electrical sources? How does the choice contribute to the style and content of the film?

5. Does the color in the movie tend toward vivid intensity or a more desaturated look? Why do you think that the choice was made? Pick out a memorable scene in the film and describe the impact of its color scheme.

FURTHER READING

Alton, John. *Painting with Light* (New York: Macmillan, 1962).

American Cinematographer Magazine. 1782 N. Orange Dr., Hollywood, CA 90028.

Carlson, Sylvia E., and Verne Carlson. *Professional Lighting Handbook*, 3rd. ed. (Storeham, MA: Focal Press, 2000).

Clarke, Charles G. *American Cinematography Manual* (Hollywood, CA: ASC Press, 1993).

Deleeuw, Ben. *Digital Cinematography* (Boston, MA: Aprofessional, 1997).

Elkins, David E. *Camera Terms and Concepts* (Storeham, MA: Focal Press, 1993).

Eyman, Scott. *Five American Cinematographers* (Metuchen, NJ: Scarecrow Press, 1987).

Ferncase, Richard K. *Basic Lighting Worktext for Film and Video* (Storeham, MA: Focal Press, 1992).

Malkiewicz, Kris. *Cinematography: A Guide for Filmmakers and Film Teachers* (New York: Simon & Schuster, 1992).

Maltin, Leonard. *The Art of Cinematog-*

raphy: A Survey and Interviews with Five Masters (New York: Dover, 1978).

Ohanian, Thomas A. Digital Filmmaking: The Changing Art and Craft of Making Motion Pictures (Woburn, MA: Butterworth-Heinemann, 1996).

Rogers, Pauline B. More Contemporary Cinematographers (Woburn, MA: Butterworth-Heinemann, 2000).

Schaefer, Dennis, and Larry Salvato, eds. Masters of Light (Berkeley: University of California Press, 1984).

Sterling, Anna Kate. Cinematographers on the Art and Craft of Cinematography (Metuchen, NJ: Scarecrow Press, 1987).

Toulet, Emmanuelle. Birth of the Motion Picture (New York: Abrams, 1995).

Wilson, George. Narration in Light: Studies in Cinematic Point of View (Baltimore: Johns Hopkins University Press, 1986).

Young Freddie. The Work of the Motion Picture Cameraman (New York: Hastings House, 1972).

———. Seventy Light Years (New York: Faber & Faber, 1999).

PART THREE

THE POSTPRODUCTION PHASE

*"My first love is editing. It's what I came out of,
and it's still what I enjoy the most."*
George Lucas, director

The period of *principal photography* described in previous chapters, is marked by the intense creative activity of a director, actors, and a large production crew struggling to find harmony in the midst of chaos. The director engages in momentous consultations with cast and crew, ending with the call for "Action!" The anxiety produced by the situation naturally draws attention to itself. An adoring (or hostile) press and public wait, never far off. Moviemaking is tangibly exciting during principal photography.

When the completed film footage is finally "in the can," the work of moviemaking takes on a very different configuration. In the **postproduction phase**, a curtain seems to close off the activities of the artists and technicians. Much of postproduction is conducted out of sight, so to speak, almost invisibly. Now, instead of a cast and crew of hundreds, the creative decisions rest with a handful of

men and women working in relatively small, efficiently equipped studios. These editors, music composers, and sound designers are given rough footage filled, hopefully, with random pieces of high action, brilliant dialogue, and terrific cinematography. They are expected to methodically make a movie from parts of it. For a while, even the strategies of movie marketing people may be quietly taking shape.

The final three chapters— "The Editor," "Sound Design," and "Marketing and Distribution"—deal with the last stages of filmmaking, a time when all the previous creative activities are brought together and given final form before being presented to the public. It should be remembered that these chapter discussions are designed for the convenience of learning each distinct movie process coherently. In reality, the activities described are not as neatly blocked out as they are presented here. Although film edit-

ing, music composition, sound effects, marketing, and distribution are rightfully considered part of the postproduction phase, many people working in these specialties have been actively engaged in the filmmaking process through the earlier production phases.

Just as a director's job carries through all stages of movie production, the work of actors bridges the shooting phase into **postsyncing** sessions, and most *editors* have become involved when the film is still being shot. During principal photography, many editors are in constant contact with directors as they evaluate the daily footage. Likewise, before postproduction, it is common for *music composers* to already be at work roughing out the basic themes to give the film an emotional foundation. *Sound engineers* are active throughout the shoot, picking up live sound to carry into postproduction. For their own purposes, the *marketing staff* is in touch with the movie through every stage, attempting first to discover and define the specialness of the film, then shaping a media image of it for the public.

The postproduction process has its own set of pressures. Ideally, the postproduction phase should be an exacting progression of carefully laid-out steps. Depending on when the exhibition dates have been scheduled and the economic realities of the project, the period is often a wild rush to completion and release. Situations vary. A relatively short postproduction period would be about three months; some very complex films take over a year. Miracles happen: Director David Lean, with cinematographer Frederick A. Young, shot 31 miles of film for *Lawrence of Arabia* (1962). Just four months later, Anne V. Coates, an editor and member of the American Cinema Editors (A.C.E.), and her team premiered the film with a running time of 3 hours and 42 minutes to triumphant reviews.

Postproduction can be very expensive. Good editors, composers, musicians, and sound teams do not come cheaply, and the process can add greatly to the budget of a film if the movie lags in this final stage. Relative to the shooting stage, however, postproduction is usually much less costly. For a below "average" $26-million-dollar Hollywood production, only about $3 million will be budgeted for postproduction work, half of it going to sound production. With fewer people involved, and with the situation in a more controlled working environment, financial pressure to produce on a rigid schedule is heightened.

The digital revolution is impacting the postproduction phase of filmmaking in most profound ways. Not only is the new technology allowing for faster postproduction work, the industry is having to rediscover the very mechanics of how films are processed in editing, special effects, and sound. Computerized editing and sound equipment have given the filmmakers faster, easier, and technically advanced ways to move through postproduction. Using a digital editing system from *Lightworks*, William Friedkin was able to quickly view the 200,000 feet of film he had shot with 11 cameras of two basketball games for *Blue Chips* (1994).

In addition, the advances in digital hardware and software now allow the industry to preserve films from the past in their best possible state. This is a boon to both the art historian and the economic interests of the entertainment business. With movies being continually recycled through various media, keeping films in mint condition is essential to the industry. Disney's *Snow White and the Seven Dwarfs* (1937), a national film art treasure, was restored digitally by a service company—*Cinesite*—enhancing the film in a way that cleaned the dirt and scratches from the original negative. The company has developed new computerized postproduction techniques, the name of which may herald a new era, "Digital Backlot."

Each film has a tentative release date, and given the eco-nomic realities of the movie competition, a good deal of madness can shower the postproduction phase. The final phase—marketing and distribution—may seem to deal with film in a crass, commercial manner. But because of smart decisions made at this end of the moviemaking process, many excellent films that might otherwise have been ignored by the public in the crush of competing movies have found an audience. Then, too, the industry perception gained by market research and analysis of audience behavior will determine which future movie projects get off the ground and which gather dust on producers' shelves. The reality of this industry is no different from any other: Companies must make a profit to stay in business. Men and women working in movie distribution usually provide a good and necessary service to the creative work of others.

This final phase is critical to a movie. Truly *bad* film projects that come into postproduction are beyond hope. If the script is dumb, if the acting is out of control, if the direction is unfocused, or if the cinematography is less than ordinary, there is little that can be manipulated by others in postproduction to save the project. But *good* material coming into this phase can become *great* in the hands of inspired editors, lab personnel, musicians, and sound designers.

Wonders can be performed by creating rhythms in cutting and impact with sound, awakening the viewer to a full appreciation of every artful contribution.

Postproduction has its own excitement—blending, polishing, and presenting the film to its audience.

CHAPTER 8

THE EDITOR

THE ART OF EDITING

"The problem is that the more successful an editor is, that is to say the more practiced he becomes, the harder it is to recognize how much craft has gone into the achievement."

Jonathan Miller,
from *Images and Understanding*

After each day's shoot, editors piece together film footage for the director to screen and weigh. When the controlled bedlam of principal photography is finally wrapped, thousands of film shots—or more accurately film *takes*—are put in the hands of an editor to, together with the film director and a few assistants, look at, study, and assemble. Isolated in small quarters, this small team must hold in their memory a vast amount of film material. The editors then begin joining together the movie, strip by strip, sometimes frame by frame. The general moviegoing public knows little about the activities of editors. They work in relative isolation. In this postproduction period, their job is to give shape to the artistic contributions of many others.

Movie film is photography with a temporal dimension. That is, every shot has a certain time duration. The editor manipulates strips of film with their sequenced images—cutting them, combining them, and ordering them. Andre Malraux, in *The Psychology of the Cinema*, has claimed that the act of editing introduced filmmaking as *art*, and that it gave film a language. The complex intricacy of the work has produced an entire family of terms unique to editing. That language is quite specialized, describing and defining the unique magnitude of editing. Much of this chapter will explore how editing functions.

Film editing is genuinely creative work. As with all art, the key to editing is selection. The French director Jean-Luc Godard compared it to directing: "One improvises, one invents in front of a moviola just as one does on the set." Ironically, unlike much of the jolting editing seen in Godard's movies, many editors feel that when they do their job well, the result on the screen is almost undetectable. The movie will be a seamless flow of images and sound effortlessly carrying its audience into and through the story. When the shooting has finished, an editor must look at a vast amount of footage. Being thoroughly aware of the director's intentions for each scene—and the overall thrust of the story—is essential to the editor. The array of choices, ways in which various lengths of film can be joined, is almost infinite. Tom Rolf, ACE (*Black Rain*, 1989) comments, "It's like having an enormous picture puzzle—1,000 pieces will make it perfect, but they give you 100,000. It's going through all the pieces, to try to get the best parts." Few in the audience are alert enough to comment on the fine points of editing in a movie, even though each person's moment-to-moment experience is shaped by the choices made in editing.

Editing gives film meaning. Cinematographer/director John Bailey believes that "Editing is where the real work of discovering the movie begins." Without the creative contributions of the editors, the movie would be a string of disconnected bits of visual information, perhaps strikingly brilliant images captured at seemingly random moments and ultimately incoherent. The context of shots—*determined by the interrelationship of what comes before and after*—generates the shifting meanings in a movie. It is the editing process, which selects and links shots together, that creates the context of a film. Editors help establish the order of the shots, blending and juxtaposing visual ideas, creating mosaics of like and contrasting images **(8–1)**.

8–1   *Modern Editing Room*   Movie editing today has taken on a new complexion. The modern editing room tends to resemble an efficient corporate office rather that a legendary cubbyhole of earlier days on studio lots streaming with rivers of filmstrips. With several monitors presenting digitally stored film footage, the editor today has an instant overview of the shot alternatives that can be selected by computer and quickly tested for effectiveness.   (Courtesy of EditDroid®)

THE CENTRAL ROLE OF EDITING

"Films are a series of details—details within details."

Jerry Greenberg, ACE (*Scarface*, 1983)

Although editing is essential to the construction of a narrative film, it was not until 1934, the seventh year of the Academy Awards, that editing was acknowledged as being worthy of the organization's recognition. The original focus of the movie industry was first on its stars, then on its most visible contributors—directors, cinematographers, interior decorators. Despite their exclusion, editing had always been perceived as essential to the filmmaking process. From early in the twentieth century, advancements in editing technique were central to the developing art of cinematic storytelling. With the arrival of *Birth of a Nation* in 1915, D.W. Griffith clearly showed on a grand scale his skill at controlling dramatic rhythms and visual intensity by cutting scenes into small increments of action and reaction. Master shots, medium shots, and close-ups could be mixed to continuously shift perspectives. His camera was no longer obliged to shoot a scene in one extended take, but could break every scene into more controlled shots and actively *build* drama. The *pacing* of cuts became a more sophisticated practice in editing. A peak of dramatic climax was recognized by the acceleration in the number of cuts during those moments. He convinced audiences that the revealing detail of a close-up carried as much dramatic weight as the most grand and sweeping long shot. Other filmmakers not only enjoyed the movies of Griffith, they studied his work closely.

Soviet Editing Experimenters: Kuleshov, Eisentein, Pudovkin, Vertov

"The foundation of film art is editing."

Director V.I. Pudovkin
(*The End of St. Petersburg*, 1927)

This statement introduces Pudovkin's book *Film Technique*. His conviction grew out of his training during the early 1920s, and it reflected a serious theoretical approach to cinema that he maintained throughout his career. Pudovkin and other Soviet directors did not gain their opinions from idle academic speculation, but from exacting experiences in working with film that shaped their analytic orientation toward the medium.

Stemming from the embargo placed on equipment and supplies by Europe and the United States after the Bolshevik revolution of 1917, the Soviet film community after World War I found itself isolated. But by this time, D.W. Griffith's well-crafted movies had made their way to Russia, and their advanced techniques were recognized by Soviet filmmakers. With little raw film stock available and camera equipment in disrepair, fledgling film study groups used what they had—prized prints of Griffith's *Birth of a Nation* and *Intolerance* (1916). Unable to actually shoot films, students analyzed these movies intently, going over them until the underlying technical structures of the photographed material became clear. The students then began to experiment with the films, taking the stock apart and editing them in various orders, all the while observing closely how meanings changed when the structure was altered. Lev

Kuleshov held workshops attended by young Soviet film students. Two of them, Sergei Eisenstein and Vsevolod Pudovkin, would go on to be masters of the new Soviet cinema. Pudovkin tells of the lessons learned from Kuleshov,

> *He maintained that film-art does not begin when the artists act and the various scenes are shot—this is only the preparation of the material. Film art begins from the moment when the director begins to combine and join together the various pieces of film.*

To drive home the point that a shot takes its meaning from the context in which it is placed, Kuleshov conducted the following often retold experiment: He used a close-up shot of the famous actor Mozhukhin, which, by itself, could be called bland and expressionless. He then cut this image into a film, joining it separately with:

1. a shot of a bowl of soup;
2. a shot of a woman in a coffin;
3. a shot of a child playing.

Even though the actor's face was unchanged, viewers interpreted his expression to fit the shot with which it was matched. That is, in the first situation Mozhukhin was seen to be "hungry"; in the second, "sorrowful"; in the third, "fatherly." The *juxtaposition of images* invited the viewer to give significance to an otherwise meaningless expression on the actor's face. The point was driven home that the emotional and intellectual impact of a film grows out of the conscious placement of shots, one to the next. It makes the point that meaning comes from the structure and interrelationship of elements. This simple exercise holds a profoundly elemental lesson for the film editor. As an audience, we *make* sense of movies.

Sergei Eisenstein explored these editing principles in his films, but added significant twists. In his book *Film Form,* he compared shots to cells within an organism. A *synthesis* is created by combining the cells—or even more strongly, by the *collision* of these shots. With his confrontational way of describing a sequence of shots, Eisenstein concluded that "Montage is conflict." (It should be noted here that film students must be alert to the term *montage*: Soviets used it to mean editing with a distinctly *creative edge*; Americans use it to describe *a secession of shots*, often disconnected, that form a poetic impression or passage of time; for the French, it simply means *any cutting of the film*.)

We can see Eisenstein's attitudes about editing clearly explored in the famous sequences of his film *The Battleship Potemkin* (1925). Again and again, shots of opposing content are juxtaposed, and surprising degrees of energy and insight result. In his powerful "Odessa Steps" sequence, the dramatic situation pits czarist army troops against a large unsuspecting crowd who have gathered on a waterfront plaza to cheer on rebellious sailors on a ship off shore. A vast array of shots are chosen and cleverly linked in visual counterpoints to implant the theme that brute cruelty of an entrenched elite is a primary weapon to suppress the working class **(8–2a–p)**. Eisenstein gives viewers a rapid-fire series of cuts which shocks us into seeing—and feeling—the crushing violence of the troops. A partial account of the height of the action in the sequence follows:

a

b

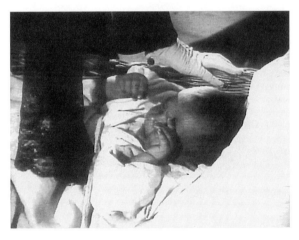

c

d

8–2a-p   *The Battleship Potemkin*   The sequence of shots is a small part of the explosively edited "Odessa Steps" section in Sergei Eisenstein's *The Battleship Potemkin* (1925). A squadron of czarist soldiers suddenly attacks citizens gathered along a waterfront to support a mutiny by oppressed sailors off shore. From the top of a long public stairs, the tragic events in front of the line of march move at a breakneck pace. Eisenstein's style of film cutting was termed **collision editing**. The intent and effect was to visually shock the viewer into new perceptions of an experience by juxtaposing cuts of contrasting image size, movement, or inherent content. The effect also gave the viewer the experience of simultaneity—witnessing this confusing event from the point-of-view of an omniscient observer watching its various elements, as it were, "all-at-once."   (Museum of Modern Art)

e

f

g

h

i

j

k

l

m

n

o

p

a) a long tracking shot of soldiers relentlessly marching down the waterfront steps with fixed bayonets

b) a close-up of the panic and surprise in a woman's face

c) a close shot of her baby crying in a carriage

d) a full shot of the terrified woman in front of the carriage

e) a mid-body shot of the soldiers moving down

f) again, a close-up of the mother screaming

g) a shot of the steps with the soldiers' boots entering the frame

h) a shot of the aiming rifles in profile

i) another angle of the rifles exploding with gunfire

j) a close-up of the woman's face at the moment of being struck by a bullet

k) the teetering wheels of the baby carriage on the dangerous steps

l) a close-up of the woman in the shock of pain

m) a close-up of her hands grasping her belt buckle

n) an extreme long shot of troops on horseback attacking a fleeing mass

o) a close-up of the woman's belt buckle

p) now oozing blood from behind it

The sequence continues at this accelerated pace until the massacre is complete. By showing the physical confrontation of a cruel political establishment with the deeply felt rage of the masses, the message becomes strikingly clear. Eisenstein manipulates time, stretching it by continuously going back to the same (but slightly altered) image again and again, intensifying the emotional response to the sequence. If the very nature of dramatic art is conflict, then for Eisenstein, film is truly on course when this is realized in its most elemental construct: editing.

Both Pudovkin and Dziga Vertov advanced editing theory and technique. Vertov had made experimental newsreel films entitled *Kino-pravda* ("film truth") to present political propaganda charged with visual excitement. In 1929, he released *The Man with the Movie Camera*, a virtual explosion of camera technique and editing styles, including split-screen, superimpositions, dissolves, varying camera speeds, and more. This boldly cut film blasted the audience with the raw kinetic power of cinema. Pudovkin, on the other hand, was a master at linking images dramatically to push forward his narrative films. Rather than the harsh clash of images that attracted Eisenstein and Vertov, Pudovkin, in *Mother* (1926), blended shots to more quietly draw out symbolic meaning and deepen the levels of the story. The difference is at once subtle and profound. Every shot, when cut to another, creates a shift in perception: Whereas Eisenstein's collision approach shocked the viewer into abrupt cognitive realizations, Pudovkin built his images to lead the viewer's *emotional* responses through his movies. The overall contributions of the Soviets awakened other filmmakers to the controlling power of the editing process. They not only made movies, they consciously studied the very nature of cinema. Their approach to filmmaking was both formal and practical, and their special attention to editing suggested a daring inventiveness to others who followed.

BACKGROUND: THE ART OF EDITING EVOLVES

There have been many landmark films that demonstrate especially creative editing. Following are a few singular movies, each one an important step forward in the art of editing.

In France, Abel Gance's *Napoleon* (1927) can be compared to the work of Eisenstein in its pure visual energy. The film used highly innovative camera and editing techniques—mounting a camera on a swinging pendulum to photograph politicians of the right and left as they clamor in a hall and using the film to intercut with a rocking boat at sea carrying Napoleon to the rescue of the country. The technically ambitious movie had not only the visual magnitude of an epic; it successfully focused on the personal life of the mythic general within the story. Later, with the arrival of **sound**, editing became a far more complex craft because, among other concerns, care had to be taken to not only match images but editors had to allow for words spoken off-screen to be integrated into shots. Musicals posed a problem because its sound, recorded live with the pictures, demanded more finessed techniques to blend when being cut in editing. Rene Clair, in the musical comedy *Le Million* (1931), smoothly merged image, movement, and sound into his editing style, giving his movies a disarming naturalness. American editors, at the advent of the grand years of the 1930s musicals, took special note.

Citizen Kane (1941) was a breakthrough film on almost every level, and its editing style was part of the innovation. Although many of the shots were very long in duration and scenes were not dependent on extensive cutting, the broad and elaborate *flashback* structure built into its storyline was challenging to audiences of the time, as the viewer watched a famous man's life unfold from at least six points of view. Robert Wise, later a major director, edited the famous "breakfast table" scene in which Kane and his wife sit opposite each other as the shots dissolve from filmed moments of the shy romantic whimsy of new lovers to the coldness of two older people with almost nothing in common but their privileged station in life.

During the late 1950s in France, Jean-Luc Godard (*Breathless*, 1959) began making films that broke most of the editing "rules." Through the years, editors had developed a working "grammar" for editing, which most movies faithfully followed. Conventional editing practices called for the continuity of action to be seamless. Certain kinds of cutting were frowned upon. For instance, Godard's frequent and flamboyant use of the *jump cut* broke the rules. Editors had, as a matter of aesthetic principle, avoided jump cuts because they jolted the viewer out of the illusion of the smooth flow in the film's action, wrecking spatial continuity, and reminding the audience that they are "only watching a movie." The positive side of the jump cut was that it gave Godard's movies a snappy freshness, as if pushing the action forward at any cost. Godard realized that sophisticated viewers could take in and put together visual information at a much faster rate than most films allowed. Whatever dislocation the viewer experienced was made up for in the excitement his movies generated with their fast pacing.

The editing style of Godard's "New Wave" movies had a distinct influence on other filmmakers. Editor Anne V. Coates acknowledges that after seeing films of Godard she rethought the editing style planned for *Lawrence of Arabia* (1962). Instead

WOMEN AND EDITING

In the early 1920s, Ukrainian-born Esther Shub was commissioned to edit prerevolutionary and foreign films in the Soviet Union. She mastered editing techniques to the point that Ronald Bergin, a Sergei Eisenstein biographer, claims that while young Sergei was still a student finding his way in film, "It was at Shub's cutting table that the mystery of montage was revealed to Eisenstein." A radically new editing style was born. It is worth noting, but it is not entirely clear why, women have been very successful as editors, while other industry crafts have excluded large numbers of them for so long. Even today, female directors of photography, for example, are uncommon on major productions. But the ranks of the Editor's Guild are well numbered with women working regularly in the field.

It could be that women are sought out at this later stage of a project, consciously or not, because they bring a feminine perspective that balances the traditionally heavily male input of the director and crew. Carol Gilligan, in her book *In a Different Voice: Psychological Theory and Women's Development*, writes that women are more detail-oriented and more attuned to human relation-

ships and context than men. These traits, if true, certainly fit the profile for an editor. Anne V. Coates, a leading editor since the 1950s, feels that women bring a different sensibility to human relationships in film: "Every good editor needs to have patience, and I think that's why women are good at it. You also have to be adept at dealing with people, because there are an awful lot of people involved in a project." In *Tunes of Glory* (1959), her editing contributions developed a delicate relationship between an old-school military father (Alec Guinness) and his caring daughter (Susannah York) bent on establishing her independence. Coate's editing of their scenes gave insight into the nuances of a father/daughter relationship. A male editor may have interpreted very differently the fragile nature of their issues, especially those from the daughter's point-of-view. Tom Rolf (*9 1/2 Weeks*, 1986) observes that a woman editor brings something special to a movie: "If you take a picture like *The Accused* to a woman to cut, you'll not find a much different picture, but you'll find a much different substance or texture to it overall. It's a sensitivity to the editor's life experience and values. It's going to be different."

Such opinions are controversial but widely held.

It may simply be that once a few great women editors broke through the sex barrier, others were encouraged to follow. Dede Allen is universally acknowledged as one of the great editors in modern times, an innovator and teacher to many men and women who have come after her. In *Bonnie and Clyde* (1967), *Little Big Man* (1970), *Reds* (1981), *Henry and June* (1990), and *Wonder Boys* (2000), among others, Allen consistently found new ways to bring out a vigor in scenes that seemed organic to the material. Her work in Sidney Lumet's *Dog Day Afternoon* (1975) was an exercise in almost nonstop cutting on movement, giving the film its visual and emotional energy. Some other outstanding female editors in recent times are: Claire Simpson-Crozier (*Platoon*, 1986); Suzanne Baron (*The Tin Drum*, 1979); Eva Gardos (*Barfly*, 1987); Katherine Wenning (*The Bostonians*, 1984); Nena Denevec (*Amadeus*, 1984); Caroline Biggerstaff (*The Stuntman*, 1980); Lisa Day (*Stop Making Sense*, 1984); Sylvia Ingemarsson (*Fanny and Alexander*, 1983); Veronica Haussler (*An Angel at My Table*, 1990); Les-

continued ▶

ley Day (*Mona Lisa*, 1986); Julie Monroe (*Hanging Up*, 2000); Anne Gousaud (*Iron-weed*, 1987); Priscilla Anne Nedd (*Pretty Woman*, 1990); Debra T. Smith (*The Moderns*, 1988); Lynzee Klingman (*Living Out Loud*, 1998); Jacque-line Cambas (*Racing with the Moon*, 1984); Lisa Fruchtman (*Children of a Lesser God*, 1986); Marcia Lucas (*Star Wars*, 1977); Belinda Haas (*Up at the Villa*, 2000); Trudy Ship (*House of Games*, 1987); Mia Goldman (*Choose Me*, 1984); Thelma Schoonmaker (*Casino*, 1995); Simona Paggi (*Life Is Beautiful*, 1998); Jane Kurson (*Beetlejuice*, 1988); Lisa Zeno Churgin (*The Cider House Rules*, 1999); and Carol Littleton (*The Big Chill*, 1983).

In the past 25 years, the art of editing has grown in sophistication. Editors continually scan movies and freely borrow successful techniques. For example, although the car chase through the streets of San Francisco had thrilled viewers in *Bullitt* (1968), when Jerry Greenberg, ACE edited the famous chase scene in *The French Connection* (1972), which scrambled cars under the elevated tracks in New York City, he established a new level for cutting action sequences containing nonstop movement. In another vein, the exquisite slow motion of the cruel fight scenes edited by Thelma Schoonmaker in *Raging Bull* (1980) helped set the movie apart from any other boxing film made before or since. *JFK* (1992) brought new attention to the role of the editor. Indeed, because of its evident and unusual complex visual structure, the movie has been labeled an "editor's picture." An entire team of editors—twelve in all (counting assistants)—used the latest electronic editing equipment to cut 600,000 feet of film in the Super 8, 16mm, 35mm, and 65mm formats, including 20 hours of stock footage. Their work directly accounted for the worldwide success of the movie.

Unlike actors or directors, film editors have no fast lane to success in their profession. The training is a long, arduous process spanning many years, first as an apprentice, then as an assistant editor. Every editor tells stories of gaining facility and confidence very gradually under the guidance of a person with much more experience. Today, for many who want to get into film editing, work in television has become an excellent arena to gain practice and polish.

THE EDITOR/DIRECTOR RELATIONSHIP

"It has to be a creatively alive relationship. You're sitting with that person for months in a dark room with nobody else around, and if you don't get along and have a productive relationship, its going to be a nightmare."

Director Martha Coolidge (*Angie*, 1994)

The first responsibility of the editor is to the director. Their relationship must be close creatively, so that the editor is able to intuit the intention of the director in each scene. For the director's part, he or she should anticipate and provide the range of film coverage needed by the editor. Richard Marks, ACE (*Broadcast News*, 1987) claims, "It's a marriage. Sometimes you make a bad guess and it's a rotten marriage and sometimes it's a glorious one."

Perfect agreement, however, is not necessary. The editor affords a uniquely valuable perspective in the frantic grind of daily film work and should feel free to make independent judgments about the footage coming in. For example, the director and cinematographer may fall in love with a long Steadicam® shot, but in the editing room it may simply not look as good as imagined while shooting it. Or dialogue, which seemed witty at the time of shooting, may sound contrived or unevenly paced on closer inspection by the editor. Directors tend to think in large sweeping concepts. "Editors think in very minimal small steps," notes Jerry Greenberg, ACE (*American History X*, 1998). Both conceptual approaches are important and need to be taken into account.

One of the most important times for the editor with the director is when they watch the dailies together. "You can ask all the questions you want: performance selection, intent of scene, etc. You need to feel in sync with the director to work freely on your own," says Anne Grousaud, ACE (*Ironweed*, 1987). Often, when editors look at the rushes with a director, they let it be known what shots are needed that weren't shot, such as more close-ups to fill in as **reaction shots**. An experienced editor can be a godsend for first-time directors, giving them detailed guidance about how to cover a difficult scene.

Working styles vary with each combination of editor and director. Some editors, especially those of the old school, prided themselves on never letting a director into the editing room when in the actual process of cutting a film. Editor Rudi Fehr (*Key Largo*, 1948) claimed that even the great directors John Huston, Alfred Hitchcock, King Vidor, and Michael Curtiz never came in his editing room. These editors tended to be fiercely independent, and they disliked anyone looking over their shoulders. They cooperated with the director in following every instruction as they screened the rushes, but the editing room was off limits. Some of this had to do with the highly defined compartmentalization of the old studio system.

Most editors today welcome a close contact with their director. Editors are frequently on the set during principal photography or are otherwise available to make sure that the needed shots—clean exits and entrances, for example—will be provided by the director so that the footage will cut together well. Some directors, such as Robert Wise, have training as editors, and therefore feel quite comfortable working with them. Susan E. Morse, ACE has worked closely with Woody Allen, editing most of his films since *Manhattan* (1979). Allen is a continual companion in the editing room, working closely with Morse in the selection of material. Thelma Schoonmaker, ACE edited every Martin Scorsese film from *Raging Bull* (1980) to *Casino* (1995), and their working relationship allows them to intuit each other's needs. "He directs the editing, and he's a great editor," Schoonmaker states. "Ours has always been a very strong collaboration, and I love that: I love having him in the editing room." This sentiment is more common in postproduction today. But in the end, the pressure of a deadline of the movie's release date hastens the editing process and prolonged deliberations are a costly luxury.

Still, many editors now do not believe that they get enough respect. Muary Winetrobe, ACE (*The Boost*, 1988) complains, "Many directors are guilty of saying 'I'm editing my film.' . . . I feel that there are a lot of directors out there who have been reluctant to give credit where credit is due." Certain of the best editors now have written into contracts the same "perks"—special attentions that Hollywood studios can dispense so generously—on a film as the director of photography.

THE SKILLS OF EDITING

"A good editor needs to be aware of the other contributions and heighten them, to bring out the best qualities in performance, art direction, cinematography, or the direction of the film. It's really my job to be the interpreter of other people's work and ultimately rewrite the film using image and sound."

Carol Littleton, ACE (*Grand Canyon*, 1991)

Though the editor must be in tune with the intentions of the director, he or she should also fully understand the contributions of others, especially the director of photography, the actors, and the production designer. Most editors feel a responsibility to present the contributions of these artists and craftspersons in the best possible light. Aside from the overriding mission of telling the story clearly, the work of the editor is to show off the talents of these people.

The art of editing assumes two qualities for those working in the field: 1) the aesthetic flexibility to see the impact of both the most minute editorial choices, and at the same time, the sweep of larger story themes and character development; and 2) technical skills and emotional toughness to successfully carry through the intensity of the process. Although it is hard to make general statements that hold true for all editors, some universal factors present themselves in their work:

- An experienced editor brings to a project an invaluable asset: *an objective eye*. For the editor, the raw footage may suggest different rhythms of movement, moments to cut upon, integration of physical action, and emphasis of human emotion than were originally envisioned by the director or cinematographer.

- Editing is not simply a mechanical procedure that follows a rigid preset plan, but a *dynamic process* involving creative choices and surprises. Character relationships, visual energy, and even story themes can be discovered by the editor during the cutting process, and the results can refocus the final makeup of the film.

- The editor will be faced with *judging and selecting* from many takes of the same basic shot. Although these takes are repetitive, each single take will have slightly different values, due to variations in lighting, camera movement, actor's performances, or other production complications. The selection of one take over another is a major part of the critical sense that an editor develops.

- Editors should have an acutely graphic *visual sense*. Each shot has special physical qualities—of light, color, motion, and line. In assessing the effect of a sequence of shots, it is important not only to analyze the *content* of the film footage—the way the dialog and action push the story forward—but it is also valuable to see how the *form* of succeeding shots visually match (or mismatch). The glint of sunrays off the ocean in a shot may be followed by an extreme close-up of the sun reflecting off eyeglasses, then the shine of oil on a tanned naked stomach. The attraction to the series for the editor may be that each shot pictured the same essential qualities of reflected light. Editing the shots together can add visual reinforcement, for example, of an overriding sense of lethargy in a movie about the idle rich.

- Editors must present coherent *spatial relationships*. Take, for example, the problems faced in editing action between two armies on a battleground. At the start, the editor has only a load of filmstrips containing bits of dramatic motion and reaction. The first job is to orient the viewer to just where the two forces are situated in relation to each other. That may be achieved as simply as choosing shots that show the blue army in the left third of the frame looking right, then cutting to the red army facing left. As observers to the action, we visually understand that they are in physically opposing positions. But keeping spatial relationships clear is seldom so simple. Throughout a narrative film, the editor must carefully map the dramatic territory.

- Editors establish the *rhythm* of a film. Because each shot selected has a particular temporal duration, similar to musical phrasing, editing can take advantage of the aesthetic pleasure found in the pulsation of visual beats. Shot sequences may be cut in short staccato bursts to underline bold action. At the other extreme, the decision can be made to wrap the action in long and languid shots, if they are available, that ease the viewer into the lyrical dimensions of the story. Ultimately, an editor's cutting builds a rhythm. "The creation of rhythm is almost fifty percent of an editor's job," notes Thelma Schoonmaker, ACE (*The Age of Innocence*, 1993). Some editors, much like actors, even refer to finding the number of *beats* in a sequence of film rather than referring to frames. Action within the shot often has perceptible rhythm that imposes itself on the sensitive editor **(8–5)**. The work then is playing with the shot length to sustain and enhance that beat. At other times, editors deliberately create rhythms by cutting material in both predictable and unpredictable patterns.

8–5 *Flirting with Disaster* The editor's skills are especially tested in the comedy movie genre. For movie humor to work, the rhythm of each scene, and timing of each shot within it, demands the best intuitive comic sense of an editor and director. In David O. Russell's *Flirting with Disaster* (1996), Mel (Ben Stiller), having just found out he was adopted, sets out to discover his real biological parents. The search puts him in bizarre and potentially funny situations. A comic highlight (pictured here) happens when Mel mistakenly believes he has found his father (David Patrick Kelly), a borderline psycho. The explosively edited scene gives the moment its hilarity.   (Miramax Films)

- An editor's job entails the smooth *manipulation of time*. Most commonly, the editor *telescopes* time, collapsing it within a few shots. Rather than showing the entire progress of an activity, editors cut to significant moments, letting the viewer "fill in" the rest. The opposite is also true, however. In some scenes, a moment is *expanded*, stretching out action by warping time with cuts that show off the slow power of the visuals. Editors, following the intentions of the director, also create time shifts using *flashbacks* and, less often, *flash forwards*. Inventive editing can change the structure of a film, moving it from having a logical story flow forward to a more convoluted storytelling mode **(8–6)**. For example, when an editor mixes a few frames or an entire sequence showing the moments in the fictional past of the story and places them in the middle of the ongoing narrative, the audience can be led into other levels of character perception and understanding. Other emotional effects can be achieved through the seeming *expansion of time*, in which numerous cuts are made, inserting shots that give fragmented pieces of a moment and extend its dura-

8–6   *Toto Le Heros*   The Belgium film *Toto Le Heros* (1992) directed by Jaco Van Dormeal gives us uncommon insight into the mind of a depressed older man by means of **flashbacks** into his earlier life as an adult and a disturbed child. This shot is from a happy youthful moment with his father (Klaus Schindler) and sister (Sandrine Blanke), both of whom die tragically during his childhood. The flashbacks do more than just point out earlier situations in the man's life. By means of inventive editing, which weave throughout the story, we experience what it was like to see the world through the eyes of a young boy, discovering first-hand the impact of the past on the present in this person's life.   (Triton Pictures)

tion beyond real time. Accelerating the number of shots in a sequence can stretch our sense of time. In the rapid-fire cutting style of *Run Lola Run* (1999), Lola (Franka Potente), after receiving a frantic telephone call, has 20 minutes to save her boyfriend from being killed by disgruntled drug dealers. By feverishly cutting the action and disorienting our sense of a normal time-space continuum, the filmed sequences of Lola's wild 20-minute sprint through city streets becomes a 90-minute film. Director Tom Tykwer says, "You can beat time only in movies. In the movies, there's a miracle quality, the feeling that there is the control of time. It's one of the basic elements why cinema for us is so magic." The final killing scene in *Bonnie and Clyde* (1967), as the two fugitives/lovers struggling to get out of their car were caught in cross fire from a police ambush, is extended not only by slow motion images but also the number of cuts that shocked the viewer by prolonging the reality of their final agony.

The work of editing lies at the center of the moviemaking process. William Reynolds, ACE (*The Turning Point*, 1977) makes the point, "When a director is filming, he's not making a movie, he's making the material from which a movie is going to be made, and it's going to be made in the editing." Editors have long been aware of the quiet power they hold.

The Aims of Editing

"*In* The Day The Earth Stood Still, *the spaceship landed in Washington on the Mall. Bob Wise made a shot in which a figure came out of the machine and stood by the door. It didn't look good, it just looked like some actor in an uncomfortable costume. So I thought, why show it? We had a shot of the crowd reacting to the ship. I cut to the people looking and watching and all of a sudden they gasp, and I cut to the figure just standing there. I simply took the entrance out, so that we didn't see any of the awkwardness of it.*"

William Reynolds, ACE

The essence of editing is contained in the anecdote of William Reynolds. A fantastic event in this 1951 movie became credible within a few frames of film because of certain standard, and clever, editing practices. Instead of showing the continuing action of spacemen walking out of the ship (and not allowing the movie viewers to scrutinize their disguised humanness), the editor cut away to the dramatic impact of the horrified faces of the crowd (clueing the viewers how to respond to what has been seen), then to the visual shock of the creature boldly present. Such techniques are the stock and trade of the editor.

In the broad scope, editing functions in three modes: *cutting to facilitate continuing action; cutting as a thematic statement; cutting for dramatic impact.*

- *Cutting to facilitate continuing action* is inherently important to narrative film. Continuity editing lends itself to storytelling because it lets the viewer observe the great and small details of behavior and events in an abbreviated but realistic form **(8–7a-c)**. For example, it might take eight minutes of *real time* to

a

b

c

8–7a-c *Don't Look Now* This three shot sequence from Nicolas Roeg's *Don't Look Now* (1974), edited by Graeme Clifford, shows **editing for continuity** at its most basic level. A studious art restorer (Donald Sutherland) races past one child to a pond to save his drowning daughter. By cutting on movement, the editor creates quick visual energy. But look carefully at the pictures. Do you think the action was shot with multi-camera coverage of a continuous dash to the water? (Paramount Pictures)

trace the mundane activity of a woman parking her car, locking it, crossing a wide lot, entering a building, waiting for the elevator, following her in and up, exiting, and finally arriving at her plush office. Instead, an editor telescopes time by showing the woman locking her car with the office building in the background, then cutting to her arriving at a 13th floor suite of corporate offices. (*screen time: eight seconds*). The audience gratefully fills in the blanks and accepts the lack of intervening detail. Editors usually seek out ways to present a flow of normal activity most economically.

Richard Halsey, ACE (*Edward Scissorshands*, 1990) has said that he always tries to imagine how he can, "tell the story with the least number of shots." Repeatedly throughout a film, editors are confronted with footage that contains credible activity, but which must be cut down or eliminated because it adds nothing to the advancement of the story.

- *Cutting as a thematic statement* usually involves juxtaposing seemingly disconnected, and perhaps dissimilar, images to achieve deeper insight into the meaning of the film (**8–8a-d**). This often is shown as a *montage*. Typically, this use of montage might have random shots of lovers at play in flower fields, running, touching, and enjoying their freedom. The sequence of segmented action

8–8a-d *All That Jazz* **Cutting for a thematic statement** usually refers to a series of shots which, when they are linked, combine to suggest a particularly relevant meaning that is greater than the parts. The opening of Bob Fosse's *All That Jazz* (1979) is a quick series of shots showing Joe Gideon (Roy Scheider), a driven Broadway director, in his bathroom revving up on drugs to face the day. These shots (and others in the sequence not shown here) are isolated bits of visual information that add up to a rather grim portrait of the man pushing the limits of his stress level.   (20th Century Fox)

a

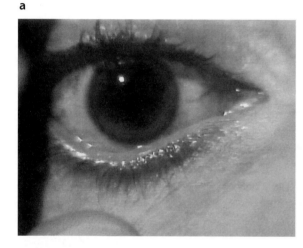

b

c

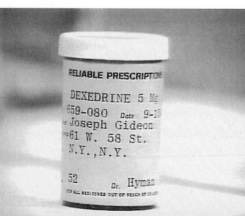

d

makes a statement about who they are and sets the tone of their relationship. Editing in this way sums up the current mood of the scene as the flow of shots washes over the viewer with its sensuality. Montage is also used for other purposes, most importantly to show the passage of time between events or in the development of a relationship.

• *Cutting for dramatic impact* is achieved by using shots in combination to impose a particular emotional or cognitive response. As pointed out in the previous section outlining the contributions of Kuleshov, audience reactions can be easily manipulated by a sequence of edited shots. Consider the series of six shots illustrated here **(8–9a-f)**. The shot selection is typical of how editors can juxtapose shots to suggest a variety of dramatic revelations. Notice how the order of shots can induce attitudes about what we see.

8–9a *Full shot* of a man and woman—seemingly lovers—embrace in an apartment. (With this frame and those following, the duration of each shot would be crucial to the emotional impression and meaning of the sequence.)

8–9b *Close shot* favoring the woman that shows her to be apparently consumed in loving moment.

8–9c *Close shot* favoring the man. He appears to be either uninvolved or oddly distracted. At this point the viewer will attempt to read meaning into the man's expression.

8–9d *Close up* of letter opener (or is it a knife?) on the table. This surprising insert is from an angle congruent with the man's eye direction. The length of this shot is important. If it is a quick cut, its primary effect might be simple shock. But holding on the shot for several seconds would let the full implications of the potential weapon sink in. Whichever choice is made, the inclusion of this shot radically changes our perception of what has gone before this moment, and what might come after.

This simple illustrated six-shot sequence creates dramatic tension. Editing the shots in this manner triggers apprehension. After a rather warm embrace, cutting to the shot of the knife introduces an entirely different dramatic statement. Every movie uses similar techniques to play upon emotions and trigger responses. More than simply pushing the action forward, this type of editing charges the context of a scene with excitement and involves us more deeply in the narrative.

Cutting at this level is quite technical, meticulous, and subtle. Actors talking together in close proximity, but shot separately, must be edited for matching *eyelines,* so that it is clear that they are indeed speaking directly to each other. In a boxing ring,

8–9e *An extreme close up* of the man is pivotal. Again, the duration of the shot would determine its impact. A long intense stair could increase tensions, allowing the viewer to project any number of meanings onto situation. What are some?

8–9f With this *close shot* favoring the woman, the audience now knows much more about the situation than she does. Feelings of apprehension for her are raised in the face of a possible menace. The manner in which the editor cur the sequence provides us with visual information that clearly signals *danger*.

the editor will attempt *rhythmic cuts* on movement to make the action of one shot physically flow into the next. Cutting for *clean exits* and *clean entrances* is essential to the natural progression of action, so that no part of an actor's body is seen before entering the scene and that when leaving, the performer moves completely out of sight.

At other times, the juxtaposition of shots might encourage an ethical judgment. If in a movie an extended shot were to record a very obese person in a garish dress and high heels awkwardly racing down aisles of a colorfully well-stocked grocery store stuffing food into her basket in a "Supermarket Sweepstakes" parody, a viewer might well see the incongruity of the situation as rather *comic*. However, if following this shot, the editor cut to an emaciated young girl sitting alone on a dusty road in Somalia under a hot sun, the response of the viewer would probably change from humor to one of shock, and with it a sense of terrible injustice. If the previous supermarket scene were cut to again, feelings of unfairness would be even more strongly enforced. A moral question would suddenly and naturally arise: Why does one person have such abundance and the other live a deprived existence? Is the first person somehow more deserving? In the first shot, what was witnessed simply as slightly comical behavior would now take on a probing political and ethical message. Editing can be used to draw out vivid thematic statements.

Editing Story Transitions

"The ability to take in information has changed. Take a hypothetical movie 50 years ago. Bogart says to Bacall, 'We'll meet in Paris.' Then they'd cut to an airplane flying. Then dissolve to a picture of the Eiffel Tower. Then a subtitle would say 'Paris, France.' Then they'd cut to a little cafe and the two would be at a table. Now you can skip all that. 'See you in Paris,' cut to an ashtray and you're in a bistro."

Writer Steven E. de Souza (*Die Hard*, 1988)

Editing transitions acceptable to viewers have gradually developed through the years. Experienced moviegoers know their function and meaning when they see them. The style created by these editing decisions not only establishes the rhythm of the film's storytelling, but the entire visual pace of the movie. Included are the following:

- **Straight Cut**. This cut simply abuts one shot with another. In its simplest form, the editor moves sharply from one face to the other as two people converse. When going from one scene to the next, an editor might abruptly place one shot (a woman sitting in a restaurant) next to another (the same woman at home in bed). The viewer is jolted from one place to another and thrust ahead in time. Although in former times this type of cutting was seen to be crude, today it is often preferred for the brisk pace it establishes.

- **Fade Out/Fade In**. Traditionally, an editor can signal the end of a scene by gradually, over a number of frames, taking a shot to blackness. With the help of an optical printer, it may be a quick *fade out* or can be extended for emphasis. At times the screen may remain dark for several seconds, then the process is reversed with a *fade in*. The whole process is usually meant to indicate some passage of time (night to morning; winter to spring; etc.). Editors have played with variations of this storytelling device. To keep the audience slightly off balance, Dede Allen in *Bonnie and Clyde* (1967) used *fade out/cut in* (and a *cut out/fade in*) to charge the film with life. She dubbed it an "energy cut" because of the invigorating visual surprise that the technique elicits. Each editor develops a sense of the duration of the fades, depending on the needs of the film.

- **Blackout Cuts**. For particular effect, a filmmaker may wish to abruptly stop the flow of images and cut to a darkened screen for a few moments, then just as suddenly resume the visuals. The result of this punctuated style can become an integral part of the psychology of a movie's storytelling. In Mike Figgis' *Leaving Las Vegas* (1995), these seemingly random blackout cuts are meant to match the lapses of consciousness of a desperate alcoholic, played by Nicolas Cage. The jolting cuts give the viewer insight into the subjective reality of this erratic and damaged main character.

- **Dissolve**. As one image fades out, another fades in *through* it, for a few moments creating a blend or evolution of color and shape. Depending on the duration and imagery of the dissolve, the effect can be very interesting, even poetic. It may mean a smooth passage of time or the merging of two elements. The dissolve technique is inherently evolutionary—one image "growing out of" the other—and it works well with subjects that make that thematic point.

- **Jump Cut**. As explained earlier, the visual illogic of this type of editing seems to go against the principles of good editing. The sudden displacement of the subjects in the frame can rattle the audience. Films such as Woody Allen's *Husbands and Wives* (1992) may use jump cuts extensively as an offbeat visual device to emphasize the disjointedness of present-day life. A **jump cut** has several variations: 1) when concentrating on a person, it is a sudden cut to a later moment without changing the camera angle; 2) while showing what is seemingly a natural and continuous action, it abruptly cuts out the center film frames; 3) *jump cutting* arbitrarily switches from one time period, action, or place, but uses the same camera angle. Thelma Schoonmaker (*Goodfellas*, 1990) comments: "A lot of jump cutting happens later in the editing process when you decide to pack more energy into a scene by truncating it."

The editing practice of **crosscutting**—cutting to parallel action to show two or more actions happening simultaneously in the context of the story—has structural implications in a movie that go beyond simply matching shots to push forward the film. Crosscutting works best when each separate action has a similar dramatic weight, even though they may not be given equal time on the screen. It is often done to build visual, hence dramatic, tension into a story. Cutting between the damsel in distress and the posse on horseback en route to save her, is an editing formula discovered and used since the early days of moviemaking. *Frequency* (2000) is a time-bending story about a present-day policeman and son (James Caviezel) suddenly getting in touch with his dead father (Dennis Quaid), a firefighter killed in 1969. The heartwarming story connects the two men by means of an old ham radio that traverses time because of some unexplained aurora borealis phenomenon. Although the storyline and events are heavily contrived, the emotional father/son relationship is affecting. The film relies on increasingly rapid crosscutting to pull together the action happening in the two parallel existences, especially in its concluding scenes when a common serial killer threatens them both. The editing of David Rosenbloom accelerates at a very quick pace as their two worlds almost merge at the end.

The same may be said for the **flashback**. This storytelling device has been a staple since the early days of filmmaking. A shot or segment edited into the forward flow of a story to give a visual presence to a past event or emotional reflection. If a few frames of an earlier moment is flashed on the scene, it is usually taken to be the subjective memory of the person we are following at the time. In *Dead Man Walking* (1995), short segments of a brutal murder are strategically placed throughout the film, the effect being a constant reminder of the horror of the crime committed by the death row inmate (Sean Penn), even as our sympathy for his situation grows. Longer flashbacks entailing not just shots but entire sequences are used to give more complete backstories.

The **flashforward** is less common. Flashing to the future has the problem of verisimilitude because, whereas everyone remembers the past, few people claim to see graphically into the future. Still, the editing technique can be powerful in the right circumstance, when used as a premonition of a fated future. In Bob Fosse's *All That Jazz* (1979), Allen Heim continually cut from present time to scenes after the death of the protagonist (Roy Scheider) as he is being chided by his heavenly counselor (Jessica Lange).

The **freeze frame** is yet another option open in the editing process. With the use of an optical printer, the editor can choose a single frame and "hold" on it. The effect visually suspends a moving image in a timeless moment. The final shot of Francois Truffaut's *The 400 Blows* (1959) was a freeze frame of a desperate boy's racing to the sea. It is an inspired final comment on the pathetic life of a misunderstood youth. Ironically, the director had not planned to edit the film this way. "The final freeze frame was an accident. I told Leaud [the actor] to look into the camera. He did, but quickly turned his eyes away. Since I wanted that brief look he gave me the minute before he turned, I had no choice but to hold it: hence the freeze frame." Sometimes great art happens by chance.

Sound overlap is used to connect scenes and create a sense of story flow. Even though separate scenes are supposedly distinct units of action, overlapping sound, often in the form of dialogue, from one shot to the next by moving the track ahead a number of frames, has become popular with editors. This sound-bridge physically and emotionally ties scenes together and that link can set up the viewer for the action in the following shot.

THE AESTHETICS OF EDITING

"With me its all touch and feel. It is all emotion with me. If it demands lots of cuts, then that's what I do, or if the emotion is there in one setup, I'll let it play. The film talks to you, it tells you."

Lou Lombardo, ACE (*The Wild Bunch*, 1969)

Each editor must find the proper dramatic and stylistic attitude for the film. As in all creative pursuits, the combination of both experience and intuition is essential. There is no standard way to edit a movie. Is the movie a languid romance, tense thriller, or a fast and loose caper movie? Whatever practices prevailed during the old studio days have long ago evolved and been refashioned to fit the changing tastes of filmmakers today. Depending on the film footage available, the director, and the personal style of editors themselves, each person's method will be different.

One major element that editors must take into account is instructive. Editors help

8-10   *Seven*   **Diegetic space** is the unseen but imagined "world" beyond the border of the frame. In *Seven* (1995), the filmmakers force the viewers to project onto the image what detective Mills (Brad Pitt) and Lieutenant Somerset (Morgan Freeman) might be encountering. For editors, shots rich with diegetic possiblities lead to any number of options for the selection of the following shot.   (New Line Cinema)

establish and explore diegetic space in a movie. **Diegetic space** relates to the entire physical environment assumed but not shown on the screen. Every frame in a film is, in a sense, exclusive. That is, each shows only a fragment of the total spectrum of a given reality; it cannot show everything. Editors know that what is *not* seen can be as powerful as what is literally put on the screen **(8–10)**. The diegetic space beyond the boundaries of frame is a limitless and often sharply imagined reality. Although a filmmaker may take pains to imply the physical context of a shot, ultimately the viewer fills in the space beyond with imagination. Editors must anticipate this and manipulate film to suggest possibilities. For example, if a uniformed commando is secretly moving through the hallways of a dangerous hi-tech testing facility, the camera may actually show very little of the actual building. From selected shots by the editor showing small pieces of visual information about the layout of the place, the viewer fills in the rest of the implied atmosphere. The editor may stay with close shots of the commando, partial glimpses of complex technology fleetingly seen in the background, but the audience is satisfied that he is moving through a more authentically complete space. An editor must be able to sense just what and how much is necessary to show for the audience to believe the moment. This aesthetic responsibility falls, to a great extent, into the hands of the editor.

Approaching the Material

"You are working on something that is already there, but when you take a sequence or a section of a story and switch it around, put the sunset here instead of there, even with minor things, the whole piece begins to take on a glow. That's the creative part of editing."

Ralph Winters, ACE (*Gaslight*, 1941)

Some editors take a *deductive* approach to their assignment. That is, at first they gain a very keen sense of the script, and then commit to a faithful translation of the story and its characters as originally conceived. Despite being engaged with incoming fragments of the work as the film was being shot, this clear overview provides a strong starting point, allowing the editing team an organizing principle when approaching the massive amount of unedited footage. With a coherent understanding of what the editor is looking for in both small and larger units of the footage, pieces are sought out to complete the puzzle.

Other editors tend to work in a more *inductive* mode. Of course they must know the script, but just as importantly they look at the footage constantly arriving with an eye for discovering what, in fact, is most dramatically successful and visually interesting. Outstanding performances, effective cinematography, or emerging story twists may cause them to suggest editing the film in unexpected ways. Geraldine Peroni, ACE, referring to the approach she took when faced with the huge amount of footage that the movie *Short Cuts* (1993) generated, stated, "I couldn't think about the whole thing at the start; that would have been too overwhelming. I'd just go from scene to scene, trying not to impose a structure but allowing one to evolve. That's the reason we screened and screened and screened: It's like water seeking its own level." This approach would argue that you cannot know what might be built into a scene until you actually see what has been shot.

New technology in editing, described later in detail, has changed the thinking process of some editors. The shift from manually working with film on an older Moviola to instant-access editing at digital workstations has altered the conceptual mode of approaching material for some editors. The meticulous discipline and slower procedure of the older editing systems demanded that the editor focus more inductively on the individual pieces of film that were being sequentially considered. Anne V. Coates, ACE comments: "With film, I always used to say that you cut from the inside out: Now you cut from the outside in. I'm talking about the way you build a scene. I used to build a scene from bits of film, but now all of the footage is in front of you at the same time on several different screens."

Every scene has a beginning, middle, and end, no matter how obscure those elements may be. A standard practice would be to move from the longer *mastershot* and create more intensity by moving to tighter shots. But discovering the heart of a scene in the shots available is more complex than that. Some editors search out what they consider the few very *key shots* in the footage. After finding a shot that infuses a major scene with its essential meaning or visual energy, an editor then uses that shot to anchor the scene, building other cuts around it. For instance, many editors would first seek out the best performance and use it, even in close-up, then arrange other shots

8–11   *Too Beautiful for You*   Bertrand Blier's *Too Beautiful For You* (1990) is a romantic comedy about an astonishingly attractive woman (Carol Bouquet) who is ignored by her unconventional husband (Gerard Depardieu). This seductive image of the wife is the centerpiece shot of a scene in which she attempts to win his affections. In creating each scene, often one especially telling shot will be the starting point for the editor and it will be used as a focal point for other shots to build around.   (Orion Classics Release)

to complement those moments **(8–11)**. Terry Rawlings, ACE (*Alien 3*, 1992) says, "First you choose the takes that you think are great. Then you try to balance them, to keep the movie and actors in character." The editor must find shots that first set up the moments in the scene for which there is some emotional or informational payoff.

The approach of every editor will be modified by the taste and wishes of the director. Certain directors favor a more *realistic* attitude toward their subject, and therefore may want to use takes of a longer duration, uninterrupted by numerous cuts that manipulate audience attention. Other directors want the punch of snappy editing to bring added emphasis to the screen. The editor quickly adjusts to the style of the director. But at times movies are beyond repair. "You can work your tail off and do some of your best work on films from lousy scripts and they still don't come off," says William Reynolds, ACE (*Heaven's Gate*, 1980).

Coverage

The work of an editor is strongly influenced by the **coverage** shot by the director. Heavy coverage of a scene means that it was shot with several cameras, from a variety of distances, with many takes. It is the responsibility of the director to give the editor enough good film footage to have a solid base of options available when constructing scenes. An editor's nightmare is not to have enough of the right footage—good **cutaway shots** of facial reactions or details of the set—to realize the maximum dramatic potential of a scene. To ensure that enough coverage is shot, many directors—especially beginners—want an editor on the set. David Bretherton was the editor on Bob Fosse's *Cabaret* (1972) and described his procedure of getting good coverage in a scene with Liza Minnelli performing on stage in a Berlin nightclub.

Fosse shot Liza Minnelli with five cameras. You had to cut away to something to sustain it. Fosse was so intelligent and well versed, that he gave me all the cutaways. There would be a close-up of a girl or one of the dancers, there was all this coverage. First you cut it normally, the simple graceful way, because I believe that simplicity is the key for most pictures. The dances look dull, you're trying to build up Sally Bowles [Minnelli] and make it more exciting. All of a sudden I would say, "I'll cut on the half beat," and then Fosse says, "That's not enough. That was a good look on that guy with the flash of his head." You'd cut it in. Every cut you make changes another cut. Then all of a sudden this opens up a new way of doing something.

The results are not always so favorable. For instance, although multicamera coverage is desirable because it gives an editor several angles from which to weave the action, the disadvantage (besides being expensive) is that while the lighting may be perfect for one camera, it is not suitable for another. The editor is then stuck with footage with *content* that matches, but the quality of *light* is incompatible. Directors tend toward more heavy coverage today than in the past. The rationale is that any added expense is simply insurance against unforeseen needs in the editing process. But this may simply reflect insecurity on their part. With high stakes riding on each movie project, some directors want to protect themselves by providing all the raw material possible.

Excessive footage can be a mixed blessing. When carried to extremes, it leaves *too* many choices of angles and takes for the editor **(8–12)**. Some movies have gotten buried under the weight of superfluous film footage. The editing nightmare of *Heaven's Gate* (1980) is a prime example. Tom Rolf, one of its editors who spent 17 months dealing with the 1.3 million feet of print, says of the project, "It was so overwhelmingly pretentious. I just knew it didn't have a chance. . . ." More does not necessarily mean better. Often the only result is that a greater number of editors, sometimes five or six, must be assigned to the project. Shooting excessive amounts of film in the hope that the editors will find some quality in the midst of it all is not a good formula for filmmaking. DP Nestor Almendros confirms this point,

With many films in America, I have the impression that they're always cutting for no reason; it's just because they have another shot of it. . . . Then by having all these choices, the editors also chop up the film too much. You have a close-up here and an insert there, a long shot here, an establishing shot there and it becomes too mechanical. It becomes too just a mechanism and it has no personality, the film has no style.

A balance is preferable. Editors and directors who have a history with each other can predict the kind and quality of the coverage that will be used. During her long experience with Martin Scorsese, Thelma Schoonmaker can depend on the relevance of the footage that comes to her: "Marty has a very strong hand in the designing of the

8–12 *Apocalypse Now* *Apocalypse Now* (1979) was a nightmare for its editors. Having shot over a million feet of print, the editors had to find the essential story and its connective tissue. The ending proved to be especially troublesome. Director Francis Ford Coppola wrote several endings that were shot quite differently. In this scene at the end of its mission, the patrol boat of Captain Willard (Martin Sheen) arrives at the primitive outpost of the strange Colonel Kurtz (Marlon Brando). Brando's conception of his role was a mystery to most people involved. The final ambiguous version of the film was conceived in the editing room with the footage of Brando that was available. (United Artists Corp.)

shots. He thinks up all the shots before he gets to the set, like Hitchcock. So I have the great luck to be working with a director who shoots so that the stuff works. More and more, he's stripping down and shooting the essentials that we actually need."

Editing Styles

"There are editors whose thumb print you can see in several movies, even if the directors are different."

Director Renny Harlin (*Deep Blue Sea*, 1999)

The conventional wisdom regarding editing has been that cutting a mainstream film should be done in a manner that does not call attention to it. Ralph Winters, ACE (*Seven Brides for Seven Brothers*, 1954) sums up this approach: "When you sit down to look at a movie you should be able to look at it as one piece of cloth, one piece of film. You shouldn't be conscious of cutting any more than you would a fine underscore."

According to this thinking, the art of editing is effective to the degree that it brings out the richness of its subject. A well-edited film moves the story ahead at a pace and in a style determined by the aesthetics of its director. The editor quietly makes it happen. Karel Reisz, in his classic handbook *The Technique of Film Editing*, had stated, "Harsh, noticeable cuts tend to draw attention to technique and therefore tend to destroy the spectator's illusion of seeing a continuous stream of action." For many editors, any such disruption was a cardinal sin.

But somewhat like the Soviet films of the 1920s, many films today are intentionally edited to jar the viewer awake with startlingly rapid cuts and bizarre juxtapositions of frame content and graphics. The result can be both visually stylish and effectively useful for the intentions of the story. For example, a high-action film usually works well when the pace and surprise in the editing strengthens its grip on the attention of the audience. Fast cuts produce a heightened degree of visual energy and excitement. The fan of the *Lethal Weapon* series can attest to this. But spectacular cuts in themselves do not necessarily equate with great editing. It takes no special talent to randomly bombard the viewer with an extended series of dazzling shots, no matter how momentarily hypnotic the effect. Evan Lottman, ACE (*Sophie's Choice*, 1982) says it simply, "The technique serves the meaning; it doesn't dominate it. . . ." Too often, frantic editing is a cover for a lack of good footage or a well-developed story.

But audiences today have learned to read stories on film much faster than previous generations. Anne V. Coates, ACE notes, "In the old days, you'd laboriously put in a lot of stuff that seemed necessary but probably wasn't. Over time, filmmakers and editors discovered that you could jump the story from here to there without constantly explaining everything to the audience. Gradually, audiences got used to much quicker cutting." With clever editing, a typical three-minute music video can present a montage of poetic images, conveying an entire progression of physical action and complex evolution of mood changes. A 30-second commercial can suggest an intertwined backstory of the characters in it. This kind of visual experience has carried over into feature-length filmmaking.

The hardest editing work often appears as the most subtle. The best editors deftly cut their films in ways that the talent of others—actors, cinematographers, art directors—is shown to the fullest. Exacting attention is demanded of editors to build a series of separate shots into a smooth flow of images that seems to be an inevitable evolution of events. Evan Lottman, ACE asserts that his most difficult editing task, which went almost unnoticed, came at the climax of *Sophie's Choice* (1982) in the moment when Sophie (Meryl Streep) and Stingo (Peter McNichol) are sitting on a bed and she tells him about her first experience of Auschwitz. "I think it's some of my best work in the movie. I'm not sure that people would recognize it as well-edited, but I think it is well-paced and deals with the subtleties of the performances and the emotions." Such films demand that the editor take advantage of every small opportunity to shift the perspective of the audience while sustaining the performance flow of the actor. Carol Littleton, ACE claims it was easier for her to edit *E.T.: The Extra-Terrestrial* (1982) than *Swimming to Cambodia* (1987), a film that would seem quite simple to edit because it was a head-on performance monologue by satirist Spalding Gray. Her problem was that editing options were more limited. By whatever means, an editor must command the attention of the audience for the duration of the film.

The genre of a movie can suggest different styles of editing. Some subject matter has its own stylistic conventions. When going to see a *love story*, we would expect a silkier editing pace than found in a *slap-stick comedy* or a *kick-boxing* film. Editors must gear their work to the current conventions of the genre, at the same time investigating ways to make their material strikingly original.

Action-adventure films, for example, present intense physical conflict in which we pull for one side against the other. They demand that the editor keep clear the general logistics of the story setting as well as each character's physical relationship to the other persons or objects. The editor has to literally hook the audience into watching and clearly understanding *who* is doing *what* to *whom*. Frequent and extensive use of master shots can help by showing the entire context of an action. For example, an extreme long shot tells us where, in graphic physical terms, the bank robber is in relation to the café, the parked police car, and the bank building across the street. But, normally, an editor cannot linger with this shot because master shots do not keep audience's attention for long. Action-adventure films thrive on movement, and this can best be felt in closer shots. Richard Marks, ACE (*Dick Tracy*, 1990) claims that action films are easier than other films to edit because the cuts are normally on movement. "It always gives you the justification to cut and create its own rhythms. There's an internal rhythm to movement. The axiom of action cutting is, never complete an action. Always leave it incomplete so it keeps the forward momentum of the sequence." But because of the number of movements being tracked, the audience can easily become disoriented and lost. Most frequently, the problem of making visually effective high-action drama rests with the manner in which the film director has conceived and filmed fight sequences. Film critic David Denby complains,

> *Can't anyone shoot an action sequence anymore? In* Gladiator, *Ridley Scott thrusts us so close to the combat that all we see is a lot of whirling and thrashing, a sword thrust here and there, a spurt of blood, a limb severed. There's hardly a scene that is cleanly and coherently staged in open space. The violence comes mainly from the editing, in the cheapening use of montage.*

Other genres call for different editing values. *Musicals* rely heavily on the intuitive sense of timing of an editor. David Bretherton (*Cabaret*, 1972) observes, "My basic approach to cutting a musical is, I don't want anyone to see a cut. I don't want them to know that the picture is edited." Editing in musicals tends to be more invisible, whereas *comedy* sometimes benefits from abrupt cuts. Some editors claim that cutting a comedy movie is most perplexing because the *timing* is so difficult to get right. Typically, in a comedy, a funny action or piece of dialogue will be delivered. However the comic punch, and laugh, often happens in the *physical reaction*—an amazed facial expression—to the piece by another character in the skit. Walter Murch, ACE (*Ghost*, 1990) says, "It's all about timing, and the slightest difference between the delay and the look will make a joke fall flat." Predicting when the laughs will come is a hazardous business, especially when one is alone in a dark editing room after ten hours of repeatedly watching the same footage. Live audience feedback during the preview of a comedy is, perhaps, the only true test. The problem is that by that time, it is very difficult to make extensive or meaningful changes.

Editing Performances of Actors

"If you go right for the action and don't set up the relationship, you don't have a picture."

Michael Kahn, ACE (*Empire of the Sun*, 1987)

Despite the engaging action that many films offer, most movies live or die on the strength of the relationships established among the characters. The work of the editor is to reveal those relationships by sculpting scenes in which they appear. Quite often, when two or three characters are in a conversation that may reveal important information about who they are and what they feel, the nature of the situation is inherently visually static. The problem is that, at its worst, the screen can look like an illuminated billboard for "talking heads." The content of actors' dialogue alone cannot carry the scene very well. The task for the editor becomes making the scene dynamic, seducing the viewer to become intensely involved with the characters. A well-edited film usually puts the audience in the middle of the emotional center of a scene.

Editors search out ways to best show the solo performance of an actor or to explore the energy of interchanges between several actors. Some films are shot with large chunks of the continuous performance by an actor, and the editor's job is to stay with those exciting moments when both the actor and the audience is discovering the character. The films of director John Cassavetes are filled with such wonderfully uninterrupted performances. But most directors and editors like to work in smaller increments, piecing together bits of an actor's work that can be then rhythmically shaped.

The **reaction shot** is an indispensable visual device of the editor for capturing the drama of human interchange **(8–13)**. In the jargon of communication theory, the makeup of every verbal interaction includes a *sender* putting out a *message* to a *receiver* who then responds with *feedback*. A movie's reaction shots are that feedback. In many cases, this shot is a purely nonverbal visual response. During principal photography, the director will have shot a great number of **cutaways**—the takes of the actors' faces expressing a range of feelings. This footage is extremely valuable to the editor in that it not only expands the possibilities for heightened drama but also can cover jump cuts and other problems.

In a disaster/survival movie, for example, when Actor A (in a close-up) tells a wounded Actor B that she has decided to leave the crash site of their airplane alone to find help, the editor has the option of cutting away to a reaction shot of Actor B at several points in the monologue. Actually, a shot of Actor B could precede the speech, establishing his state of mind. But the editor could also cut away at two or three key moments during Actor A's desperate speech to watch the changing emotional reactions of Actor B to her words. Or an editor might use just one reaction shot of Actor B, but extend it for a substantial section of Actor A's monologue so that we

8–13   *Dancing at Lughnasa*   For the editor, the **reaction shot** is an indispensable piece of film that tells us how the shot preceding it is to be interpreted. In *Dancing at Lughnasa* (1998), three sheltered Irish sisters (Meryl Streep, Brid Brennan, and Sophie Thompson) react to the sight of their unconventional brother Jack, just returned from Africa where he was a missionary. Study the expressions. What are the women silently saying about Jack's arrival?   (Sony Pictures Classics)

see how the spoken words of the actor off-screen are continuously impacting the mental state of Actor B, as reflected on his face.

Considering this further, when a moment is presented in which one actor poses an important question to another, editor Tom Rolf will often choose to cut to the reaction cut to capture ". . . how they are trying to formulate their answer in their face or dialogue. I find it much more interesting." The audience reads the reaction of the person receiving the message to get clues about where the dramatic direction of the scene is going and how they themselves should react. Director Mike Leigh (*Naked*, 1993) makes the point,

> *What somebody is saying is part of what they're doing, part of how they're being, and not only that, but how the other person is reacting is equally important. What's interesting to me, what interests me in life, is life itself. I am saying this to you now, but what's going on while you're listening? And that is a subject. Therefore, you can't cut automatically on dialogue. Because the event is very complex actually.*

For example, the dramatic impact of the outstanding film *The Remains of the Day* (1993) to a great extent hinges on the emotionally curbed *reaction shots* of the culturally repressed butler, played so forcefully by Anthony Hopkins. Throughout the film, he is unable to articulate his deep feelings for a coworker (Emma Thompson), and the tragedy of his life centers on this arrested ability to communicate.

When two people play off each other in such scenes, a cause/effect relationship builds. Editors use this to find and create a rhythm of shots. Richard Marks, ACE (*Broadcast News*, 1987) notes, "In dramatic cutting you have to create your own rhythms—how long you stay on a character, how much of a beat you give a character before you cut to someone else, who you play on camera, and who you play off." A scene with an intense argument might mean using staccato shots to drive home the fury of the exchange; a romantic scene might be languid with intermittent long takes between the lovers; a tension-filled crisis could be cut with syncopated rhythms to set the viewer on edge. The movie *Glengarry Glen Ross* (1992) is taken from a stage play about the hellish pressure of high-powered sales, and it relies heavily on the explosive dialogue delivered by its small cast of established actors. Even though the story is well written and performed, its editor, Howard Smith, faced the problem of keeping the film visually active in the confines of its limited sets and weighty dialogue. His daring editing in several important scenes, most pronounced in exchanges between Alan Arkin and Ed Harris, gave the movie a charged atmosphere. In one scene, as these two men sit at a bar planning a robbery of their own realty company, unusually rapid cutting of their changing expressions gave an otherwise conspiratorial conversation a goofiness that lightened, for the moment, an otherwise dark movie.

Editors can modulate performances of actors. They have the unique power to select a snippet of an intriguing glance, a coy smile, or a few well-delivered lines from the many takes of an actor. "Hopefully, when you screen the dailies, you react to something—a glance between two actors that came out of nowhere—where something magic happens," Geraldine Peroni, ACE observes. "If you're lucky, you have something like that in every scene that you focus on." Some editors look for idiosyncratic acting moments in scenes that are otherwise predictable. Sometimes it takes extreme measures. When Tom Rolf was told to make the character played by Mickey Rourke in *9 1/2 Weeks* (1986) more appealing, he searched the existing takes for expressions that would soften him. Finding none in the regular footage, Rolf discovered some moments after the director "Cut," when Rourke thought he was finished and smiled in relief. This editor used the frames as reaction shots to show another side of the film character.

In certain movies, reaction shots relieve the filmmaker of the need to otherwise detail story information that is hard to get across visually. For example, *Searching for Bobby Fischer* (1993) is a plunge into the competitive world of chess as experienced by a young boy. The director Steven Zaillian and DP Conrad Hall faced a dilemma: It must be assumed that the primary activity of the film—the rules of the game of chess—is unfamiliar to a high percentage of the average movie audience. Literally showing the board strategies would be visually uninteresting and meaningless to most people. But the movie kept the viewer physically attentive through its extensive number of reaction shots by the boy (Max Pomerac), his father (Joe Montegna), and his two teachers (Ben Kingsley and Laurence Fishburne), all of them responding to the unseen tension developing on a chess board. Cinematographer Conrad Hall comments, "I would watch a person's eyes until I thought the result of a move was about to happen, then I would move before the eyes went to it; on the way to the piece, the hand would overtake my move and grab the piece." A reaction shot would often be edited in following such camera work, giving the audience a favorable or negative signal for how to respond.

In general, the overriding problem for editors is finding consistency in the various takes, so that the characters in the film are coherent and whole. What may be an uneven performance can be smoothed over. Performances can also be improved, and actors can look their very best with the help of an editor. Some editors see this as part of their mission. Anne Grousaud, ACE (*Ironweed*, 1987) comments,

> *Our job as editors is to protect actors. If someone is really bad, I don't think you can ever make him or her good. But if someone is mediocre, you can make that person good. A performance can be cleaned up from the best bits of different takes. Sometimes it's a tremendous amount of work . . . like a lacemaker.*

Editors must also be in touch with the intentions of the actors in specific scenes. Jerry Greenberg, ACE states that it is important for the editor to recognize "what the actor is trying to do beyond what he or she is asked to do," and take some risks along with them. Actors love to take chances in their roles and an editor should not automatically subdue the performance for the sake of editing consistency. For instance, when acting has strong improvisational brilliance, it should not be broken up with cuts, even though the shot may seem too sustained. Such cutting can diffuse the build-up of energy on the screen by breaking the visual concentration of the audience. On the other hand, Dede Allen cut out one of Paul Newman's most impassioned speeches from *The Hustler* (1961). (He later claimed it cost him the Academy Award). "It didn't move the story," Allen flatly explained.

EDITING MOVEMENT

"Try pulling your eyes off movement—you can't do it."

Ralph Winters, ACE (*The Great Race*, 1965)

Movies are not still photography, and although any single frame can be isolated for study, motion pictures are alive with *movement*. The study of movement has to do with vectors. In its original sense, a **vector** is a physical substance having magnitude and direction. In the aesthetics of cinema, *a vector is a directional force*, usually associated with the movement of objects that carry our eyes with its thrust. The movie screen is continually being shaped and reshaped by the movement of elements within it. Knowing the theory of how vectors work is important to the editor wishing to lead the viewer both physically and emotionally through the intended purpose of a series of shots.

The editor can use movement to charge the movie with energy. Early filmmakers quickly realized the compelling optical fascination of a posse on horseback chasing bandits at full tilt, or the delight in seeing cars speed down city streets. Filmmakers soon came to realize movement—*any* movement—has the uncanny ability to alert and control our visual awareness. The viewer's eye is drawn to any movement, large or small on the screen—the hand of a seductress slowly brushing hair back from her face, a boy diving off a ledge into a river below, a hit-man quietly feeling his suit pocket for a cigarette lighter. The *path* of such movement, sudden or slowly paced, has a directional sweep—a vector **(8–14a-b)**.

8–14a-b *Run Lola Run* Motion pictures love motion. The German film *Run Lola Run* (1999) is a sensational exercise in kinetic intensity. Lola (Franka Potente) must get big money to her boyfriend by 12 o'clock—20 minutes away—or he will die at the hands of drug dealers. Director Tom Twyker and editor Mathilde Bonnefoy construct Lola's frantic rush through the streets with precision cutting on movement, using the anticipated directional force of her running—the vector—to energize the screen. (Sony Pictures Classics)

a

b

A line of movement has a force that not only captures the eye, but also causes the viewer to project its continuing direction. The perceived direction of movement creates something like the physical force that builds before a wave. For example, when a massive truck roars down a highway in an extreme long shot and it edges closer to the boundary of the frame, the audience is caught up in the hypnotic lure of the vector of the shot. The shot seems to contain an almost tangible energy.

The viewer is constantly scanning the screen to take in the evolving information presented there. The shifts are continual—as subtle and flowing as human body movement can be or as abrupt and physically disturbing as one car ramming another, jolting us awake with its force. We absorb the total complexion of movement within the frame, its configuration of elements in relation to one another, and quickly process that information. This happens as much on an emotional level as on an intellectual one. Editors work with this visual energy.

Over the years, each editor develops a way of working through the problems of visual storytelling. Some of the techniques come from the cumulative knowledge of the craft, others from the unique taste of the individual editor. Every editor has a personal bag of tricks, ways of cutting a film that secretly smooth over transitions or fix our attention. For retention, the eye needs three to four frames of film footage. If a quick shot is wanted for a startling visual effect, an editor must know these limits. A few pieces of common editing wisdom follow:

- Find the shot that is most interesting in the scene and do not cut away from it until it is fully exploited. The shot may be of a particular performance or an action, but if it has a hold of the viewer, do not give it up.

- In the same vein, don't be afraid to use takes of long duration, when playing them out still manages to hold the viewer's attention. Long takes have their own internal tensions and the manipulation of cutting away often defuses the dramatic build-up within the shot.

- Some directors and editors do not like to break up the continuity of a single action. They routinely cut only *after* the completion of an action, intent on finishing the motion, no matter how simple. Therefore, a person getting in a cab will be done in a continuous take until the door is closed, rather than breaking down the action into two or three shots.

- Conversely, other editors will habitually cut in the *middle* of a physical action, seldom letting an action shot go on until its natural completion. Typically, if the shot were of a baseball player throwing a ball, the cut to another angle would be at the beginning of the follow-through. This technique gives the action a "kick" of added energy and works smoothly if the succeeding shots continue the vector—the direction of movement.

- Editors know that they literally control the viewer's eye location and movement. The viewer follows the tail of a movement, compulsively drawn along its direction. This allows editors to "cheat" when succeeding shots do not

8–15 *Matewan* Creating and capturing the forcefulness of movement is a challenge for the editor. In this shot from *Matewan* (1987), a film about the injustices in West Virginia coalmines of the 1920s, a striker (James Earl Jones) races to escape and hop on a train. Imagine some possibilities for an editor if the following coverage were available: 1) a long shot tracking with Jones, his arm outstretched; 2) a close shot of the hands of Jones and the train man; 3) a medium shot from behind Jones moving at the same speed; 4) a moving vehicle shot of Jones legs churning along; 5) a close-up of Jones face sweating and breathing heavily. How could you combine the shots to intensify the chase? (October Films)

match perfectly. The eye is invariably captured by movement, making almost everything else in the frame irrelevant for that visual moment **(8–15)**.

EDITING ENDINGS

Editing the final scenes of a movie is especially tough. Depending on what is presented and how it is done, the meaning and impact of the entire movie can hang on the visual nuances within the last few scenes. Alan Heim (*All That Jazz*, 1979) says, "It's murder to put an ending on a film and make it seem comfortable. Either it's very predictable or it seems to come out of nowhere." Generally, endings should grow out of the thematic logic of the story, but at the same time the final scenes should have a turn of emotion or insight that makes the movie memorable. The last response of an audience to the ending can determine its interpretation of the film as a whole **(8–16)**.

8-16   *The Englishman Who Went Up a Hill but Came Down a Mountain*   Ending a film is always a delicate matter for the editor. This final selection of cuts can leave the audience delighted, satisfied, thoughtful, or muddled. Often the very last shot choice will be a summary emotional or philosophic statement of everything that has come before. In *The Englishman Who Went Up a Hill but Came Down a Mountain* (1995), the characters played by Hugh Grant and Tara Fitzgerald resolve their differences in a well-tested film manner, a final kiss that provides a suitably happy ending.   (Miramax Films)

Evan Lottman, ACE and two other editors on William Friedkin's *The Exorcist* (1973) completely restructured its ending on their own. The original ending, after the excruciating ordeal of exorcising a devil, had the detective (Lee J. Cobb) asking a priest (Jason Miller) to go to a movie with him. This calm ending would have the effect of having the two men putting closure on the calamitous events and getting on with their lives. Lottman remembers, "We moved the final scenes around to the end with the priest looking down the fatal stairway, and up at the boarded up window in the house." This ending sets off a very different response. Is the threat from evil spirits *really* over? The new ending kept alive the possibility that the horrific supernatural events were subdued, but not over. Friedkin had not planned it in this way, but went along with the altered ending. Fortunately, it was also a natural opening for the movie sequels that followed.

The editing of movie endings is continually fretted over by both filmmakers and critics. Concluding *Thelma & Louise* (1991) with a freeze-frame of the two women sailing through the sky to their certain death was a suitably dark and poignant ending for a story of two women caught in a harsh, male-dominated cultural system they understood but could not control. Instead of leaving the audience with the thoughtful messages inherent in such a visually powerful ending, however, the director and the editor provided the story with a up-beat reprise. Rather than staying with the emotional impact of their mad race over the cliff, an edited sequence gave the viewer flashes of the women at happy moments from earlier parts of the film. The final tone of the movie suddenly switched to an energized and oddly light-

8–17 *The 400 Blows* The **freeze frame** can be a very effective means of ending a movie, emphasizing a memorable image and the emotions contained in it. The appearance of a static picture is a surprising and sometimes impressive departure from the norm. In Francois Truffaut's *The 400 Blows* (1959), a young boy (Jean-Pierre Leaud) is driven to rebellion by a confining society. The last shot is of the boy in freeze frame facing an uncertain future on an empty, windswept beach. The figure of the lost boy sums up the youthful confusion and despair prevalent throughout the film. The rock star Beck has said that this shot inspired the idea for his music video "Devil's Haircut." (Fox Lorber)

hearted sentiment, sending audiences from the theater smiling. It could be argued that editing in this arbitrary story conclusion sacrificed dramatic integrity for the sake of purely commercial considerations. The filmmakers would argue that the movie was about female camaraderie, and the ending underlined this more positive theme **(8–17)**.

Editors are not mechanics. Although their skills demand an efficient command of a very specialized technology, their aesthetic sensibilities are their most highly valued assets. Good decisions made at an editing console regarding the movie's theme, action, and performances are invaluable in the many stages of postproduction editing. An experienced editor can save money, a director's sanity, and sometimes even a movie.

THE WORK OF EDITING

"The job requires enormous meticulousness. You want someone who is obsessive about detail, about completing things and following through on ideas. There's nothing vague about editing. It's the most specific job there is, other than writing. You're making a conscious decision every time you cut the film."

Director Lawrence Kasdan
(*Grand Canyon*, 1991)

By the time movies end up in their final **release print**, they are usually ten or eleven reels long (each reel being about 900 feet) and come in at 100 to 110 minutes long. But to arrive in this final condensed version, editors have had to wade through ten times that amount of footage. Good organization is the key. In the editing room, the procedure and sense of order for every editing team is different. The traditional editing room was a cramped place equipped with film viewers, rewinds, splicers, and trim racks and bins to save potentially useful portions of takes. Today, the equipment varies. The three primary methods of editing film are with the classic Moviola®, the reliable *flat-bed* editor, and the latest *computer technology*. The computer has effectively taken over.

⭐ TRADITIONAL EDITING TOOLS

A **film viewer** is the key instrument of editing, and a few editors working in motion pictures still have a passionate loyalty to a very old fashioned one. The **Moviola®** had been the standard tool in Hollywood for many years, and this old upright motor-driven machine, while looking like an antique, was cherished by many editors. The beauty of the machine was its simplicity. A person using it had immediate physical control over its variable speeds, as one would an old sewing machine. This equipment demanded that the editors physically handle the film, and this tactile feature wed the person to the image and sound being cut. Some editors claim that the extended time needed to work on a Moviola® became part of a necessary rhythm of the creative process. Dede Allen, ACE puts it simply, "With a Moviola®, you're very close to film." Most editors working with them prefer two such machines: one with the shot they want to cut away from, the other what they want to cut to.

Flat-bed editing decks—the most popular being the **Kem®** and **Steenbeck®**—are much faster because many reels—up to four separate rolls of film—can be activated at once. The machines are very useful for quickly viewing various segments of sound and picture tracks at once. For instance, when working on a musical, dance footage usually gives the editor many choices, and these can be presented in a way that makes the options of combining shots more instantly graphic. The machine is also faster than a Moviola®, allowing the editor to find a scene or take more quickly. Even though some editors resisted actually editing on a Kem®, most major editors had them available to at least locate footage.

Computer Editing

"The digital editing revolution is probably the biggest technical development in film-making since the arc lamps went out."

Jeremy Kasten, ACE (*The Lovemaster*, 1997)

The advent of electronic editing has stirred immense changes in the nature of an editor's work. Editing technique is now defined differently: linear editing vs. nonlinear editing. The nature of the new computer

technology has transformed the basic approach of the studios. Postproduction facilities have moved on to the *nonlinear* advantages of the new electronic systems. Editors have discarded the limited *linear* mode of the Moviola® system that ordered information sequentially with its retrieval limited by the same time-consuming process.

Working with the new editing systems can be compared to a writer using a word processor instead of a typewriter. The easy access to stored information makes all the difference. Once an editor becomes comfortable with the formidable equipment, using digital editing is relatively simple and very fast. This access speed is its distinguishing feature, allowing the editor random access to material. An editor can jump immediately to any point in the film material. Because the system is nonlinear, an editor can freely insert and pull out what's needed from frames of a take, then move them around quickly and at will. Dailies, as well as the editor's versions of the cuts, can be put on video. An editor is then able to use the material as a complete reference file, moving through the images at high speed to compare performances, angles, and picture quality.

The application of computers and digital editing equipment had a rocky and slow evolution in the film industry. The reasons were twofold:

First, any of the best and most established editors were quite comfortable with older equipment and work procedures. To those not coming from a background in computer technology, the new equipment was at best intimidating, at its worst, downright brain numbing. There was almost a cultural resistance to it. Another drawback is that the facile access to the film in electronic editing may actually discourage an editor from becoming as intimate with the content of the film. When one is forced to go through the laborious task of physically handling the film with a Moviola®, editors report that a personal bond with the material evolves. Whereas *The Sheltering Sky* (1990) was the first to use laser disc editing systems, its director Bernardo Bertolucci and editor Gabriella Cristiani used a flat-bed Steenbeck® for fine work. Bertolucci remarked, "I missed the smell, the touch, the vibration of the film." This sentiment is being heard less today. Editors coming from television backgrounds are more friendly to electronic systems, and many postproduction video facilities are equipped with the technology.

Second, for many years the promise of electronic editing was not matched with the flawless equipment needed for the precise needs of the craft. Pushed by George Lucas and others during the 1980s, electronic editing was slow to catch hold because of high costs, breakdowns, and the lack of an accepted industrywide standard. Every new technology is expensive, cranky, and needs a breaking-in period. For instance, digital and videodisc systems are accurate, but film is shot at 24 frames per second and videotape speed is 30 fps. This was a major problem in the translation when something was shot on film, transferred to video for editing, then back to film for the actual cut. For the editor, exact frame accuracy is essential, and in the beginning the systems could only come very close.

Editing environments have also rapidly changed. Producer/director George Lucas began as an editor and has always taken a healthy interest in the special physical needs of the editor. At his Skywalker Ranch north of San Francisco, Lucas has created a state-of-the-art editing facility. "Creative people need an environment that's conducive to being creative and thinking well. It may be possible to create in small, cramped spaces but, the truth is, it doesn't come out the same." Although his ideal rural setting is not common in the industry, editing facilities have been streamlined to accommodate new technologies.

Time Schedules

"Everything on the shoot is just material. A motion picture is basically made in the editing room, and it's not wise to shortcut this process."

Director Michael Mann (*The Insider*, 1999)

Ideally, editors want to frequent the set during production in order to be in touch with the creative attitudes of the director, cinematographer, and actors. During the shoot, editors are called upon to cut short segments of film to give the director the feel for how the action is working or the actors look. Directors indicate the takes they favor, and these are molded to the desired rhythm of the film. When principal photography is finished, a **rough cut** of the footage—the primitive version following the general story line put together without fine cutting—is sometimes possible even within a week or two.

Time management is essential to the editor because of the pressures applied by the movie release schedule. In the early 1960s, a 39-week postproduction period was normal, but as tightened budgets became a reality, 20 weeks later became more common. Ten weeks to three months is generally felt to be an adequate editing period for many films. Today, the bargaining skills of the director will try to increase those limits. Quite naturally, every film has its unique postproduction history, and some films have had greatly extended postproduction periods. *Reds* (1981) was the largest editorial project ever undertaken, involving 64 people involved in postproduction for six- and seven-day weeks over 19 months. *Apocalypse Now* (1979) had a first cut that was 7½ hours long, and one of its editors, Richard Marks, worked on the film for two years and ten months. The producers of *Who Framed Roger Rabbit?* (1988) even wrote a special postproduction handbook to guide their teams of editors and animators through the complex system of communication, entailing 300 animators in England needing the dialogue, and special effects tracks being created in the United States before the drawings could be done.

When editors have the luxury of sufficient time to thoroughly study the footage, they can take more creative chances. David Ray, ACE (*The Handmaid's Tale,* 1990) states, "A lot of what an editor does is experimental—we try things. Which is one thing we have over directors of cinematography—they can't try things, they have to get it right the first time." But with the high cost of filmmaking (on borrowed money accruing interest), there is great pressure to get the movies out even faster. Many varied commercial interests depend on exact deadlines being met. For example, elaborate promotional tie-ins—television advertising and personal appearances, a simultaneous book publication, gift store paraphernalia—are often synchronized many months ahead to match the film opening. On top of this, many producers re-edit until the last minute in an attempt to win larger audiences.

The editors feel the crunch. The studio rush to release tends to flatten out the uniqueness of an editor's creativity. Carol Littleton, ACE (*Grand Canyon,* 1991) claims, "It's giving us more homogeneous movies. You end up with a film with few surprises, no originality." The result of hasty work may not always be clearly evident to the viewer, who can never know the choices that were bypassed, but audiences often sense that something is missing in movies that have been raced to the screen. 20th Century Fox pressed director Renny Harlin and editors Robert A. Ferretti and Stuart Baird to complete *Die Hard 2* (1990), a film with a $50 million budget, with only eight weeks of postproduction work. Harlin comments, "After the first preview, Barry Diller [then Fox chairman] said to me, 'There's a real good movie *somewhere* in there.' I thought so too. It always haunted me that, with enough time to distance myself from the material and try different things, I could have done more." In another case, *Patriot Games* (1992) had the ten weeks allotted to shape the director's cut reduced to three weeks. The studio moved its release date up to Memorial Day from the Fourth of July, resulting in the brunt of the pressure being felt by the editors of this $42 million movie. Its editor, Neil Travis, points out the need for a certain minimal duration for this exhausting activity: "There is a certain amount of time, a gestation period, where you see your mistakes." It is not unheard of that editors are pushed to work 18-hour days during the final weeks of postproduction. Flawed movies are almost inevitable when postproduction periods are badly curtailed.

Budget-conscious studios love the idea of electronic editing because it promises to cut down the cost of postproduction with its speed and facility. Currently there are two ways in which digital systems work: *hard drive* and *optical disks*. The new electronic technology—Avid®, Lightworks®, CMX6000®, EditDroid®, Harry®, DaVinci®, Montage®, and more—have been incorporated into editing to various degrees. Used in films beginning with *Full Metal Jacket* (1987) to almost every major current film, this newest technology has established itself as state-of-the-art. *The Sheltering Sky* (1990) was the first film to use laser-disc editing. The director and editors of the film watched the rushes, then transferred what they wanted to keep onto laser-disc—without the hassle of the fast forward or rewind of standard editing. Just punch in a shot number, and it's *there!*

Nonlinear editing systems have become so sophisticated that what was normally postproduction work has become, for some filmmakers, a production tool. The speed and efficiency of some new editing systems have encouraged editors to put together rough cuts during the shoot so that each day the director can determine whether the camera coverage was complete. For *Cutthroat Island* (1995), editor Dan Moore was able to almost immediately show director Renny Harlin digitized footage "shortly after we'd finished a scene. Sometimes I'd be able to get in a second version as well." Because the film was being shot in places remote from traditional film centers, such as Malta and Thailand, the portable nature of the editing system was a great asset. But traditionalists miss the spirit that is generated when screening the dailies on film as a group. Editor Esther Russell says, "Now you're more likely to make tapes and send them to the producer, the director, and the DP separately, which I think is a shame."

Paradoxically, at the workstations, the new systems have encouraged more *team* editing. Some people think this allows for more creative input. With the increased amount of footage being shot in films such as *JFK* (1991), the need for more help is evident. One of its editors, Joe Hutshing, comments: "It's good to have the extra feedback of the team." However not everyone is enthusiastic about this outcome. Editing may have simply found another way to get tangled. Editor Thelma Schoonmaker points out, "They're putting three to six editors on a picture, and problems can arise from lack of a single style . . . even though Lightworks® increases the speed of physical editing, it still takes time to get the film right. The rhythm, structure, and pacing—you can't get that by waving a magic wand of digital editing." Another problem is that producers, studio executives, and others with some clout are now tempted to get into the editing act. Because the technology is so quickly accessed, everyone, even to the last minute of release, has an opinion of how the film could look different and be improved. Debra Neil (*Fried Green Tomatoes,* 1991) thinks that the situation is ripe for abuse, "It makes the job of editor more political."

Stages of Cutting

"There can be 5,000 people working on a film but basically it comes down to your hands."

Tom Rolf, ACE (*Sneakers*, 1992)

Editing is physically demanding. Because of the inevitable rush in postproduction schedules, it can mean working 12-hour days, 6 days a week. Confined to small, darkened rooms and their eyes taxed by staring at small screens, editors are in continual danger of emotional and physical burnout. Added to this, editors as a group feel that their contribution is undervalued both by the public and even within the industry. Tina Hersh, ACE (*Gremlins*, 1984) says, "I think its more ignorance than maliciousness. Many of them really don't understand what we do." But like most persons in essential creative posts, editors are paid well: union scale is $1,700 a week with the best making up to $10,000 a week. The Motion Pictures Editors Guild protects their interests, and the American Cinema Editors (ACE), an honorary group, gives them deserving prestige.

The ideal team for many film editors usually consists of a first and second assistant, and an apprentice. Every member is important. Each assistant must anticipate the needs of the editor and develop a rhythm of working. Because of the close quarters and the long hours, the relationships can become very intense. Most film editors want to get involved in as many aspects of the project as possible: sound, music editing, dubbing. This information gives them a greater command of the choices to be made. But time allotment is always a factor, and an editor's talents can be spread too thin. The typical procedure an editing team faces for bringing a film through the postproduction stage would follow these lines:

- A scene is shot on 35mm negative film. The sound for the scene is recorded on ¼-inch magnetic tape.

- The film director tells a camera assistant which **takes** have been selected to be printed. Every frame of footage has a *key number* on the edge that identifies it. In addition, the **script supervisor** has kept a record of each camera setup and this is given to the editor.

- The lab develops the negative film and stores it, making a positive print of the selected takes. Likewise, the ¼-inch audiotape is transferred to sprocketed magnetic stock.

- The two materials are sent after each day's shoot to the editor. This process takes place over a 24- hour period for the duration of the shooting. These are called the **dailies** or rushes. Having been coded, they are viewed regularly by the director, editor, actors, cinematographer, and anyone else invited to the viewing room.

In shaping the final structure of a movie, editors take the process through several cutting stages. The film becomes progressively refined as it moves along **(8–18)**. Richard Marks, ACE (*Pennies from Heaven,* 1981) explains that "cutting a film is an ongoing process where you are really trying to distill the essence of the idea behind the script." Working with various combinations of standard editing equipment, the editors normally take about twelve weeks to put together the film. The major versions are the editor's cut, the director's cut, and the final cut.

The **editor's cut** *(or assembly cut)* is a first general construction that gives a graphic idea of how the film will be laid out. The editor's first cut is considered reasonable if it is about 15 percent longer than the perceived *final cut.* This cut includes all the scenes and dialogue that were shot. It is sometimes called the "European cut" because the shots usually play very long, allowing the director the chance to see expanded editing alternatives. Although it is necessarily overly long, many editors are intent on making it look as good as possible. But even before this cut, editors begin sharpening the film as the takes are coming in during the shooting. Michael Kahn, ACE (*Empire of the Sun,* 1987) explains, "Many editors want the director to give them a free hand in the first cut and not get extremely specific in their choices. The way to do that is to strike while it's hot, get back to the director a day or two after the scene is shot. . . . Most of the refining is done before the director and I look at the first cut."

Editors know that directors are most likely to go along with cutting decisions that are presented with a polished look. Perhaps because of this, complaints are heard that some editors put too much refinement into their first cut, adding music and extra sound to convince the director of the value of their version. For instance, an editor may arbitrarily put in *scratch music* or *temp track music*—existing music that is laid over

Digital Offline Editing

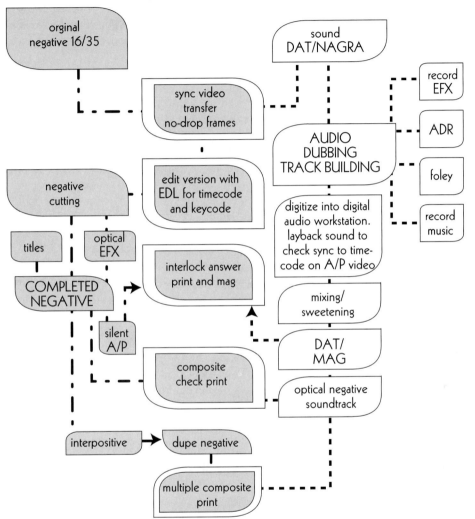

8–18 *Digital Offline Editing* The stages of the editing process are formidable and complex. The EDL, the edit decision list, is the chronological record of editorial decisions, each stored in computer memory. When a shot is modified, both versions stay on the list. As each phase of sound and visual image merge technology and art toward a final composite print, the process of editing completes the postproduction stage.

the cuts to enhance the viewing experience. Sometimes it works wonderfully, as when Lou Lombardo put in the music of Leonard Cohen over *McCabe & Mrs. Miller* (1971) just to facilitate the ending. The director Robert Altman kept the music and it became an integral part of the final film. Certain temp tracks have been very popular with editors over the years, including Randy Newman's score for *The Natural* (1984), Dave Grusin's music for *The Firm* (1993), and Ennio Morricone's theme in *The Mission* (1986). Naturally, music composers for film generally hate the practice because when people get used to seeing the film with certain music, nothing else seems right. Most editors refuse to overdo their cut with this kind of attention, trusting the director to see the worth of their work unadorned.

The **director's cut** (or *rough cut*) is then put together, with fine cutting, sound effects, music, and dubbing added at this time. Legally, by way of terms guaranteed by the Director's Guild of America, the director has ten weeks to deliver to the studio the director's cut, although pressure to bend agreement is common. This cut is the edited version that the director would like to reach the theaters. In the now well-known situation of Ridley Scott's *Blade Runner* (1982), because the original final cut of the movie ran into some unenthusiastic audience response when it was previewed, the investment sources forced some radical changes on the film. A **voice-over** was introduced to lead the viewer through the dark futuristic story, and an upbeat ending replaced an ambiguous one. But the unique ambiance of the film was diminished. The movie did poorly at the box office. In the following years, it was rediscovered by new audiences on video, and gained a reputation as a stylish classic. Rumors persisted, however, about the brilliance of the original director's cut. In a very rare occurrence, ten years later, Warner Bros. funded Scott to reedit his film, adding trims and original music not even included in the first release. This version is now in distribution. In preparing the director's cut, fine-tuning of the film can become obsessive. Terry Rawlings, ACE (*Alien 3*, 1992) observes, "You never want to stop cutting, but you finally get to the point where you're not making the picture better, you're just making it different."

The **final cut** (or *fine cut*) has several meanings. For the editor, it usually means the last edited cut of the film before it goes to the sound editors for a sound mix. For the producers, the term refers to the composite print combining image and sound ultimately approved by the producers and the studio. As such, it may or may not be the same as the director's cut. A very few privileged directors can demand and get the final say on the final cut. Warner Bros. former co-chairman Terry Semel, commenting on the commanding position of the late director Stanley Kubrick, observes, "When Stanley showed you the movie —his cut—that was the finished movie. There are just a handful of directors that can do that. Steven Spielberg is one. Clint Eastwood is another. It's because they've proven over the years that one cut is all that's necessary." But horror stories of fights abound between studios and directors: directors claiming that their artistic vision is being compromised by distant money managers at the studio; studios complaining that their marketing experience tells them to change (usually shorten) the movie, and that the director's ego is getting in the way of good business sense. Because the studio pays the bills, it usually wins. But the results can be disastrous. Martin Scorsese's *New York, New York* (1977) was originally 3½-hours long, and from all accounts, worked extremely well. The studio would not release the film at that length, however, with the result that the two-hour version was stripped of its connective tissue, and the viewer could not understand the characters in any depth. Sergio Leone took eleven months shooting *Once Upon a Time in Amer-*

ica (1984), but when the 228-minute length was cut to 147, the film was reduced to unexplained violent acts that took on unwanted comic dimensions.

Conversely, a longer film does not necessarily make a better film. Directors can lose sight of the film's original intentions and indulge in personal reverie. When a director's judgment goes bad, the only real checks on it are those of the producer. The feelings of Maury Winetrobe, ACE (*Taps*, 1981) are shared by many: "There hasn't been a film that I didn't think could have gone out at least 10 or 15 minutes shorter. . . . You have to look at the overall picture and see if there is dead wood. If it's holding up the story or whatever you are trying to say, definitely it has to go. Being human, directors, writers, and editors fall in love with certain sequences they think are vital to the picture. Whoever has the last word usually wins."

The final workprint is sent to the *negative cutter*. This person (or team) creates exact dupes of this approved workprint from a master print of the pristine original negative. All **release prints**—those thousands of reels that are distributed to theaters around the world—have gone through this process.

SUMMARY

New technology has changed the way editors handle their daily work routines. The time is quickly coming when everything shot and recorded will continue to be stored on laser disc, digitized, and easily random-accessed. Although handcrafted films put together on Moviolas® will always have nostalgic adherents, the speed and efficiency of the developing technology in these days of skyrocketing production costs makes nonlinear editing an inevitable step forward.

But the concern of some people is not with the technology of editing but with its changing aesthetics. The accelerated pace of storytelling is changing the tastes of movie audiences. Rapid cutting jettisions images across movie screens, creating kinetic sensations more and more devoid of story context and meaning. Subtlety in the art of editing is being lost. Editor Dede Allen comments,

> I worry if we're raising enough people in a generation who are able to sit and look at a scene play out without getting bored if it doesn't change every two seconds. We talk an awful lot about cutting, we talk very little about lousing something up by cutting just to make it move faster. I'm afraid that's the very thing I helped promulgate, through directors I've worked with who like that energy. It may come back to haunt us, because our attention spans are so short. In the old days, everyone played more slowly, and people were more patient. Now people are being hired because they're hot, they're flashy.

And yet despite the new methods of an editor's electronic wizardry or whatever styles of cutting evolve in the future, the essence of editing will remain the same. Editors will continue to make their choices based on the values of the director, the personal taste of the individual editor, and the traditional practices that have evolved in the art of editing. And, as in the past, the best work of an editor will usually go unnoticed.

SPOTLIGHT

The Editor: Carol Littleton Interview

Carol Littleton was a French literature and music major in college, winning a Fulbright scholarship. Her career as an editor spans over twenty years, her credits including: *Legacy* (1975); *Body Heat* (1981); an Academy-Award nomination for *E.T.: The Extra-Terrestrial* (1981); *The Big Chill* (1983); *Places in the Heart* (1984); *Silverado* (1985); *Brighton Beach Memoirs* (1986); *Swimming to Cambodia* (1987); *The Accidental Tourist* (1988); *White Palace* (1990); *Grand Canyon* (1991); *Benny & Joon* (1993); *Wyatt Earp* (1994); *Diabolique* (1996); *Magic Hour* (1997); and *Mumford* (1999). She is vice-president of the West Coast Film Editors' Guild.

Richard Peacock: When and how did you discover film editing?

Carol Littleton: I was not a film student. I had a scholarship and I found myself studying in Paris. This was in 1963–64. It happened to be at the height of the French "new wave." I had a drama teacher who was very enamored of film at the time. He encouraged all of us to go to the cinema and see the archival films and the experimental work being done. There I fell in with a group of film students. That's when I discovered that the French see *montage* as important as *mis-en-scène* and direction. The filmmakers had a rather heady way of cutting that we see in Godard's films. I became aware of what film editing was and I thought, "That could be very interesting." When I came back to the States to continue my studies, I was very attracted to the idea of film but had no thought of working in it. But then I moved to Los Angeles to be with a young fella who is now my husband, John Bailey, the cinematographer. He was in graduate school at USC, at which point I fell in with all his friends, and I started doing odd jobs on their student movies. I then gravitated toward the cutting room. One of the first entry-level jobs I had was for a strange little company that did sound transfer for dailies and for a couple of Hollywood sound effects editors. I was organizing their libraries and one of the guys suggested that I start breaking down shots and cutting units together. Before I knew it, I was an apprentice. I just learned editing on the job. Once I was in the cutting room I realized that it was the part of filmmaking that definitely attracted me.

RP: As an editor, at what point in the production schedule do you get involved?

CL: I work on a lot of films that are done by writer/directors. If you consider editing to be the final rewrite, what I'm doing is more closely related to writing than anything else. So I get involved by the time of rehearsals, if not before. I might come on anywhere between two weeks before principal photography and four months prior.

RP: How important is it that you not only know the director's intentions, but that you also have an independent read on the subject matter itself? Do you go to the original novel or the first script in your personal research?

CL: It's very worthwhile to go back to the source, whether it be a novel or a play. You have to keep your finger on the original material. That also goes for a script that has gone through a number of rewrites. I'll sometimes go back to the first draft. Sometimes you refer as much to the original material as you do to the current script, because it's not unusual to lose the focus.

RP: Losing your way in a film must be a problem at times. How do you keep in balance the micro and macro aspects of editing—the minute details vs. the big picture?

CL: It's one of the big problems in film editing. I try to step back and look at the overall picture. You can get so absorbed in the tiny details of editing that you can forget the larger issues of structure or simply whether the narrative is working. I like to put myself on a schedule, so that we look at the film every week or so, without starting and stopping—just looking at it on a big screen at least every ten days. It helps you keep a fresh point of view. You also realize that film is very plastic. It's very much like a piece of clay. A little change can have a ripple effect three scenes later.

RP: It would seem that the work of editing can be approached as a *deductive* activity—one in which the editor has a very clear idea of the intention of the director in a scene or sequence and the job is to piece together the footage that achieves this end. Or the process can be an *inductive* activity—one in which the editor discovers the special dynamic of the scene while becoming enmeshed in the film at hand. Have you had situations where one or the other was primary?

CL: The process of editing is a little bit of both. Sometimes you're patient with the process and let the film instruct you. You don't impose a personal bias on the material and work within the context of the film that was shot. In addition to what you have stated, it's also a process of accretion. Many times added detail can enhance an idea that may have not been very sharply made in the writing or direction. So you have to be aware of *all* the tools you have to tell a story. For example, right now I'm working on *Magic Hour* (the working title) directed and co-written (with Richard Russo) by Robert Benton. We're at the point now that we're experimenting with the structure—dropping scenes, moving things around, changing the sequence of events, rethinking the dynamic within the scenes—really rewriting in the cutting. Obviously when you do that you use as many devices as film affords—sound effects, music, opticals, you name it. The goal is to find out what really works in the film and what doesn't. So we are going through some very reductive versions

RP: to see where the bare bones are. And then we'll start adding things back as the story will permit us.

RP: When the film is being shot, does the director ever ask you for input, for example, in matters of coverage?

CL: Sure. I'm in the Hollywood system so editors start right from the beginning. For example on a previous film with Benton—*Places in the Heart*—we reviewed what I had cut every Saturday or Sunday. In the case of Benton, I was on the set a lot. He didn't need me, he just wanted me there. Sometimes it works that way, sometimes not. As quickly as the film can be processed and printed in the lab, it's digitized and I start cutting. I'm usually two days behind camera.

RP: Do you look at older films dealing in the same genre when you approach a new project?

CL: Absolutely. For instance if the cinematographer has a film that he thinks is particularly pertinent stylistically, or the producers have an idea of what they want, or the director has a film that inspired him, especially if it's a genre picture, or I have something for them to see. We all look at those things together.

RP: You've worked with Lawrence Kasden on several films—*Body Heat, The Big Chill, Silverado, The Accidental Tourist, Grand Canyon, Wyatt Earp,* and *Mumford.* What kind of shorthand between a director and editor develops in that kind of relationship?

CL: Certainly with Larry, I understand his aesthetic. He doesn't have to say much, all he has to do at this point is twitch. He's very economical—he may have an actor shoot six takes of a particular image size, and print only two or three of them. Even if he prints all of them, I can see the evolution from take one to take six. I immediately know what he's working toward. I know the subtleties of his direction—the writing, performance, or camera areas that he feels are particularly strong or weak. He's pretty specific about it and speaks with brevity and clarity.

RP: Describe a bad day for an editor.

CL: [laughter] A bad day for an editor is when you're needed in five places at once. A very bad day is when you hear that the release date of the film has been moved up a month. I might get off on a tangent here but let me. You know, studios are run now by their marketing departments. Regardless of how I might feel about something, if it looks like there is a better slot for a film on September 1st rather than October 30th, they'll do it. Then it becomes my problem. It's happened on two or three movies I've worked on. Directors contractually are supposed to have ten weeks for their cut, but many times because of the scheduling they end up with as little as three weeks with it.

RP: Digital editing has come on strong in the recent past, replacing the traditional Moviola® or Kem®. How has the transition affected you?

CL: It happened very quickly in the industry. Very quickly. The changeover took less than two years for us to convert to digital editing. The wave crashed and it crashed big. I have some misgivings about it. Digital editing is a wonderful tool, but it has been misunderstood by producers. They think it's going to make things shorter and you'll have less to do. Unfortunately it generates *more* work, more personnel, costs three times as much as cutting on film, and although at times you can edit more quickly, sometimes you can't. So it requires educating a lot of people about what is realistic and what is totally unrealistic.

RP: The reduced time schedule encouraged by digital editing must affect your creativity.

CL: It does. There used to be a process in editing with film that people understood—it was a standardized procedure. There was a lot of faith in what editing could do. Director and editor and educated producers would know what could be done in the editing process. We could try odd and strange things to create breakthroughs because we got to know the film so well. But that takes time. You have to have time for this rewriting because it takes a great deal of thought. When the schedule is very short, you can only put pieces together and *hope* that you're making a good movie. It doesn't afford the time one needs to ponder, to change, to experiment, to stretch the material, and to mine it. Lack of these elements cheat the process. Unfortunately, the breakthrough now often comes two weeks after the movie has been released!

RP: Do you see the situation evolving?

CL: We're going to level out very soon. Hollywood takes all kinds of innovations and just absorbs them. Back in the 60s, new smaller portable cameras with crystal sync were introduced. Then lab processes were changed and every thing, whether you needed it or not, was polarized. Later Steadicam® came on the scene, and it was used excessively. So digital editing is the new toy, and in two or three years we'll probably look back and say "That film was cut when they first got this new gadget and they were playing with fun stuff."

RP: When you are working on a film with one or several well-known actors, how does the politics of "star power" play into your decisions in editing?

CL: It comes in inevitably because stars have tremendous salaries and they are going to sell the film eventually. It changes the way you think about the movie. I can't say it's so crass that someone comes in my room and says, "We paid this guy millions and I want to see his mug in every scene. So if he's not in the scene, cut it out." No, it's never a "cut to the money" kind of thing. But it has altered the way Hollywood movies are done, period!

RP: What does a typical day look like in the midst of editing a film?

CL: A typical day is a long day. During production, I start early in the morning and finish in the evening after dailies—it can be a 14- to 16-hour day. The work is a continual process of cutting new scenes and revising old ones. We don't shoot in sequence so if groups of scenes are available to me—I may have seen scene 103 then I get 101, then 102, then 99, then a month later scene 100. So now I have a block. And it is a process of seeing new material and revising old stuff. As head of my department, I have to make sure the flow is going on from the production to the lab and back to us, with the added steps of going to telecining and digitizing. On Hollywood films we have two projects: the *digital* project and the *film* project. Both have to be organized by the assistants, but I'm responsible for them. In that regard, I like assistants who are versed in film and digital, and who can be equally conversant in both. I also want assistants who see themselves as future editors—people with critical and analytical minds about story. And I do have two fabulous assistants on this movie.

RP: What genre or style of film causes the most problems for you?

CL: Every film I've done has been challenging because they're all different. But in an odd way, I feel that film noir is the most difficult. In this genre, there has to be an element of suspense, and you have to find ways of creating that. Filmically there are certain visual and stylistic demands as well as very economical characterizations. Many times it ends up that you may have three different pictures that work, but they don't work together. The romance may be good, the suspense may work, and stylistically the film may look impressive, but when all of them are put together, the movie doesn't happen. Film noir is a reductive kind of filmmaking. And in today's filmmaking climate, a director or studio thinks that the amperage, either decibels or visuals in chase sequences, is what makes suspense. They think that the way to instill extra drama is to make it faster. On the contrary, it may not be that at all. But film noir juggles other elements. Preceding us today, the sound engineers at the studio had been working on John Woe's *Face Off*. When our footage came on, they hadn't lowered the sound levels and it took us a minute to realize that something wasn't right. We were getting sound-blasted; our film was much more subtle.

RP: Are you aware beforehand of how music will be used to underscore a scene when you are editing it?

CL: I always work with temp tracks. When I start a film, I always gather a lot of music that I feel will be useful as temporary tracks. I usually work with two music tracks, concert music and cues from other scores, and I find that it really helps in discovering emotional qualities in the scene. Even if I never show the scene with that music, it's very instructive to me. But many times I do show it with temp music. For instance, in the movie I'm now working on, the main character is being played by Paul Newman. It's a very melancholy character who has had a very tragic past, as we discover through the course of the film. But he doesn't dwell on it and moves on, a kind of modern hero. In using music that matched his mood, the score just became a leaden weight. Music has to be somewhat contrapuntal to the emotional life of the main character. So by cutting temp tracks I discovered a lot about the style of the film. I'm sure it will be helpful when the composer joins the process. It certainly gives me insight, and that's what I care about during editing.

RP: Multiple camera coverage would seem to give the editor more choices. Does it work that way?

CL: Interesting. I think that scenes done with a single camera—excluding big explosion situations that you can only do once—is a better way of working because then every angle is lit and composed properly, and therefore is useable. Many times when you are doing dialogue scenes with multiple cameras, there's usually a throwaway angle. It doesn't work—there's a shadow here and something else there. Timewise, you have to set up three cameras, clear three mic lines, clear three eye-lines, and hope that all three angles can cut to each other. It's a false economy and a false notion. Why not just do it with one camera?

RP: Have you ever suggested creating a flashback that wasn't in the script?

CL: [laughter] I've done the opposite, where there was a flashback for ten minutes and I suggested we drop it. I nearly had my head chopped off for that, but it wasn't in the finished movie. I think that flashbacks are used as a device for storytelling when they can't think of any other way of doing it. I don't like it.

RP: It would seem that an editor must be especially sensitive to the dynamics of human relationships, at least as aware as writers, actors, and directors. Do you find this to be true?

CL: This is where I think that women are particularly helpful in the editing process. For generations, many things have been denied to women. As a result, we've become very good observers. If we were blocked from participating, we had to become game players on another level. I think that the psychological web that surrounds human experience interests women a great deal. I think that some of those discoveries are ones that may not even interest some men. In working on film, that keen sense of observation is very important. Performances convey the truth of human experience. I think we're pretty good interpreters of it.

RP: Describe a moment of pleasure in the editing process.

CL: It's always fun when you have a serendipitous notion, or even make a mistake, and it comes out brilliantly. And that happens all the time when you open yourself up to doing wacky things. You start moving things around and before you know it, a chanceful moment becomes a major idea that you can build on. A good example was in *Swimming to Cambodia*. We had access to just three minutes of footage from Roland Joffe's *The Killing Fields* to use in this picture—the moments when the helicopters were hovering over the Saigon embassy evacuating the Americans, and the Vietnamese who had supported us were left behind scrambling and reaching out. Jonathan Demme, the director, and I were stuck and couldn't decide how to use it. We decided to just plop it in different places and see where it worked best. The cuts found their home, and it all looked planned. There's a moment when Spaulding Grey says "O.K. bye-bye, O.K. bye-bye," as if he were a small Vietnamese child or woman, and at that moment we cut to those big Huey transport helicopters going *schump-schump*, and the sound of that massive war effort "O.K. bye-bye" was powerful. It was devastating—the saddest moments in the movie.

RP: When you finally see the movie released, are there sections where you can say, "That's purely my work"?

CL: I truly believe that the best kind of editing is collaborative. Two minds are better than one, and that's usually the director and editor. It's the best way to discover what is in the material. It's not about being powerful. It's not about I did this and you did that, keeping the score card. The editor does have a tremendous influence, but it's largely input. But within that context, you're right—there are moments when you have an idea and it just stays. Sometimes when I first cut a scene, it never changes. There are two scenes like that in this movie, *Magic Hour*. As of yet, they have not changed one frame. However it's not necessarily that I cut it well, it's that it was written strongly, acted beautifully, and the day they shot it everything just came together. ◀

FILMS TO CONSIDER

The following films are noteworthy for how they were assembled, the quality of their editing:

- *The Battleship Potemkin* (1925): The editing in every sequence of this revolutionary film by Sergei Eisenstein is worthy of close study, as it has remained a virtual primer for beginning movie editors.

- *The General* (1925): Impeccable timing is essential to good comedy, and Buster Keaton's visual jokes in this silent film of a rogue soldier who becomes a hero rely as much on his uncanny editing as on his acting skills.

- *Napolean* (1927): In a silent era that demanded that stories be told primarily with pictures, director Able Gance used every editing technique known at the time to perfection—crosscutting, split screen, superimpositions, cutting for rhythm, and more.

- *The Man with the Movie Camera* (1929): Although the film is a documentary, this unique work by the Russian Dziga Vertov, with its rapid interweaving and juxtaposing of staged and spontaneous moments, is an editing exercise worth watching.

- *The Seven Samurai* (1954): The action during the ending battle is a superbly edited sequence, a model for anyone wishing to analyze how the logistics of opposing forces in the heat of fighting can be kept in spatial perspective as they become more enmeshed.

- *Wild Strawberries* (1957): Ingmar Bergman's film of a doctor haunted by youthful fears opened new doors for filmmakers to give psychotic depth to characters by his effective use of flashbacks infused with Freudian symbolism.

- *Breathless* (1959): Breakneck speed of screening cinematic information, aided by shaky camera work and rough jump cuts, became a trademark style of French New Wave director Jean Luc-Godard and his many admirers that followed.

- *8 1/2* (1963): The seemingly disconnected way in which this autobiographical film by Federico Felinni was cut is at first confusing, but the result is that the sense of fixed events moving linearly is replaced by an awareness of all-at-once-ness.

- *Bonnie and Clyde* (1967): Film editor Dede Allen established herself as a top creative player in this comic book story of cops and robbers with cutting that was at once seductively sly and bluntly shocking.

- *The Wild Bunch* (1969): The pace and style of editing high-action films accelerated into a new dimension, especially during the vengeful shoot-out sequences edited by Lou Lombardo with director Sam Peckenpah.

- *The French Connection* (1972): The famous car chase, edited by Jerry Greenberg, under elevated tracks through the streets of New York is still unsurpassed for its pure energy and tension.

- *All That Jazz* (1979): Editing dance sequences is always a challenge for the editor, but this film edited by Alan Heim, with flash forwards as well as flashbacks, had to meet the criteria of a master, director/choreographer Bob Fosse.

- *Choose Me* (1984): The clever editing by Mia Goldman in this film about city dreamers followed several parallel stories and yet appeared seamless as action pushed the story forward.

- *Landscape in the Mist* (1988): Director Theo Angelopoulis tells the story, in both realistic and allegorical modes that call for varied cutting styles, of two children on the road alone in search of their father.

THOUGHT QUESTIONS AND EXERCISES

Watch a film from those listed.

1. Watch one film in its entirety while staying generally aware of its editing. What can you say about the pace and rhythm of the film? Did the style of editing complement the theme of the film? Cite some examples.

2. Did the editing submerge itself into the flow of the story, or did the editing call attention to itself with an intentional collision of images? Was the editing appropriate to the nature of the story and its genre?

3. With a VCR, analyze a short scene that contains intricate movement of its subjects (for example, a fight scene or a car chase). Watch the segment closely, breaking the scene into its separate shots. Make note of the exact point at which the filmmaker chose to cut from one movement to the next. Describe your findings.

4. Again with a VCR, select a scene in which two people are conversing. Take note of the cutting technique used in the back-and-forth verbal exchange. Does the camera favor one person over the other? Within the context of the story, do the editor's decisions work well?

5. The editing at the end of a film can be crucial to its lasting meaning. Watch the last five shots of the film. Describe the content and duration of them. In your opinion, what did the editor and director intend for the ending with these choices?

FURTHER READING:

Bayes, Steve. *The Avid Handbook* (Boston: Focal Press, 1998).

Bergin, Ronald. *Sergei Eisenstein: A Life in Conflict* (Woodstock, NY: The Overlook Press, 1999).

Bouzereau, Laurent. *The Cutting Room Floor* (New York: Carol Publishing Group, 1994).

Browne, Steven E. *Nonlinear Editing Basics: Electronic Film and Video Editing* (Boston: Focal Press, 1998).

Case, Dominic. *Film Technology in Postproduction* (Boston: Focal Press, 1997).

Dmytryk, Edward. *On Film Editing* (Boston: Focal Press, 1984).

Hollyn, Norman. *The Film Editing Room Handbook,* 3rd ed. (Los Angeles: Lone Eagle, 1998).

Kuleshov, Lev. *Kuleshov on Film* (Berkeley: University of California Press, 1974).

Leemann, Sergio. *Robert Wise on His Film: From Editing Room to Director's Chair* (Los Angeles: Silman-James Press, 1995).

Leyda, Jay. *Kino: A History of Russian and Soviet Film,* rev. ed. (Princeton, NJ: Princeton University Press, 1983).

LoBrutto, Vincent. *Selected Takes: Film Editors on Editing* (New York: Praeger, 1991).

Murch, Walter. *In the Blink of an Eye: A Perspective on Film Editing* (Boston: Silman-James Press, 1995).

Ohanian, Thomas. *Digital Nonlinear Editing* (Boston: Focal Press, 1998).

Oldham, Gabriella. *First Cut: Conversations with Film Editors* (Berkeley: University of California Press, 1995).

ON: Production & Postproduction Magazine. 5700 Wilshire Blvd., Suite 120, Los Angeles, CA 90036.

POST Magazine. 25 Willowdale Ave., Port Washington, NY 11050.

Reisz, Karel. *The Technique of Film Editing,* 2nd ed. (New York: Butterworth-Heinemann, 1998).

Rubin, Michael. *Nonlinear: A Guide to Electronic Film and Video Editing,* 2nd ed. (Gainesville, FL: Triad, 1992).

Solomon, Tony. *Avid Digital Editing Room Handbook* (Los Angeles: Silman-James Press, 1999).

Stafford, Roy. *Nonlinear Editing and Visual Literacy* (London: British Film Institute, 1995).

Watson, Rupert. *Editing Avid's Media Composer* (Storeham, MA: Focal Press, 1999).

SOUND DESIGN

THE NATURE OF SOUND IN FILM

"Cinematic sound is that which does not simply add to, but multiplies, two or three times, the effect of the image."

Film Director Akira Kurosawa

Because the visual elements of a motion picture are so overwhelming, viewers often take the kind and quality of film sound for granted. The actor's voices, sounds detailing any action in the visual background, and even music laid over a scene provide a natural adjunct to the events on the screen. We unconsciously accept whatever audio elements go along with the pictures because there is hardly the awareness to do otherwise. Moviemakers use a variation of a magician's psychology: gain the attention of the audience with compelling visual action, but shape and enhance the illusion with subtle audio play.

As Kurosawa suggests, the effect of sound added to the cinematic image produces an affective force that is difficult to quantify. Anyone who has muted a movie on TV knows this: Unless they are designed for silent presentation, images stripped of sound lose their power. One is left with what seems to be pictures senselessly mutating and disconnected shots relentlessly appearing on the screen. Some short movies or segments of longer narratives are specifically designed for their pure visual poetry, and the appearance of silent images can be quite astonishing. But for films made without that intention, the full viewing experience is not only diminished but also easily lost.

As with all the other elements in filmmaking, creating sound is a highly skilled mix of art and craft. A good sound track is the result of exacting effort on the part of numerous people in the sound department. Every scene, every shot, every frame of a film must be evaluated to see how the image might be strengthened when wedded to particular sounds. Sound services movies in two fundamental ways:

- Sound anchors the audience in the *physical realities* of the dramatic action: the clink of stoneware dishes being washed in a kitchen sink or the cold metallic sound of a key turning in the door lock of a darkened house. It complements and explains the picture, reinforcing the existence of whatever is apparent on the screen. Each scene in a movie is alive with both the ambient background resonance common to everyday life as well as particular sounds coming from the graphically identified action. Almost every element seen on the screen has the potential of emanating a unique sound, from the light buzz of fluorescent lights in an office to the guttural roar of a diesel truck tearing down a desert highway.

- With the addition of sound to image, the manipulation of the viewer's *emotional response* is achieved. Sound insinuates itself to our feeling level: sometimes with shocking abruptness, at other times imperceptibly. In a sense, film sound takes advantage of us, touching directly and deeply into the unconscious. A sentimental music track laid over a shot of a forlorn child standing by a gravesite can rather easily move an audience to tears, or the continuous roar on a sound track of jet engines launching aircraft from a carrier into the sky will exhilarate us. Director Philip Noyce (*Newsfront*, 1978) says, "Atmosphere or sense of place is often created more strongly for the audience by the sound track than by the images. Sound goes directly from the ear to the heart. Images go from the eye, then are decoded by the brain. Sound is the most piercing and direct emotional connection you can have with your audience." At other times, sound—whether from *sound effects* or *music*—will provide a counterpoint to the image, seemingly disconnected from it but nevertheless making a provocative comment.

In short, film sound brings the screen alive. The strategies for applying sound to film are intricate and exacting. "Putting sound on film is probably the most collaborative part of making a movie, and it's one of the most elaborate team efforts you will ever experience," says supervising sound editor Gloria Borders (*Bram Stoker's Dracula*, 1992). In common with other movie crafts, persons working with sound function within set parameters and in relatively fixed time frames.

BACKGROUND: THE CHANGING TECHNOLOGY OF FILM SOUND

"Music is fully 50 percent of the movie. And I'll believe that till the day I die."

Producer Howard Koch (*Casablanca*, 1942)

Motion pictures have always been inspired by sound, because even silent films were never *really* silent. The harmonium, a type of organ, was the first instrument used to accompany film. It was used with the Lumiere films in London in 1896. By 1908, the first film score was purposely composed for the French film *The Assasination of Duke De Guise*. In 1909, the Edison Company in the United States started providing musical suggestions to accompany the showing of its films. Filmmakers and exhibitors quickly realized that music in the theater could partially mask the sound of noisy projectors, but more importantly, could prompt desired emotional responses from the audience.

The sounds used to accompany silent films included almost anything: musical bells installed in various locations throughout the theater, phonograph recordings, piano and drum accompaniment, phonographs electrically synchronized with the film images, sound effects machines, live narrators amplifying the highlights of the story, lone violinists, organists, brass bands, choir boys, opera singers, actors talking from behind the screen, even audience sing-a-longs. By the 1920s, great theaters employed full orchestras; many others installed huge organs; small movie houses had special sound effect and music machines—the sounds on these machines ranged from applause to babies crying to the sound of a kiss. Books were published that suggested music (sinister, heroic, cataclysmic, etc.) to accompany certain kinds of films. Very important silent films had scores written especially for them.

Because sound often was not synchronized with the images, audiences often complained about the sound as a distraction. Much of the music did nothing to aid audiences in understanding the film. It was not until 1926, over twenty years after movies became popular entertainment, that an acceptable sound system was adopted by the industry. Warner Bros. selected the *Vitaphone* system—a method of mechanically synchronizing sound recorded on disks with the images shown by movie projectors—from a number of other sound reproduction technologies being developed. With *Don Juan* (1926), the first movie with a synchronized score, and then with the movie *The Jazz Singer* (1927) adding a few scenes of the synchronized voice of Al Jolson singing and speaking, the sound revolution began **(9–1)**.

9–1   Location Sound Recording Truck   Moviemakers in early days of sound wanted to record live sound on location. Special mobile units were designed to efficiently carry complex sound equipment to any location. The quickly evolving technology allowed production companies to break away from the sound stages of studio lots to a variety of more realistic settings. The situation is a forerunner of the later job designation known as the **production sound mixer.**   (Academy of Motion Picture Arts & Sciences)

In 1929, a new technology was introduced: the "double system sound." This **sound-on-film** method converted sound waves into electrical impulses and then put that information on film, later to be made into sound again by a light beam in the projector. By 1930 all studios in the United States had converted to this system. This new mode of making and presenting movies caused a profound revolution throughout the industry, though not all of it positive. Music was regularly used indiscriminately to fill up the background soundtrack. With sound being recorded live, microphones had to be hidden at critical locations on the set with the actors encamped close by. The clarity of the actor's voice, rightfully, became the primary concern. For a time, cameras were encased in stationary soundproof booths so that the clamor of their motors would not be picked up by the microphones. To the dismay of directors, the sound engineers suddenly began to dominate the movie set. This awkward filming process on the set at first inhibited the finely tuned skills that directors and actors had acquired in the silent era.

Moviemakers, however, adapted quickly. During the 1930s they found that sound could be handled separately from the picture, therefore music and sound effects could be manipulated in any number of ways in postproduction. The early audio advances by director Rouben Mamoulian in *Applause* (1929), a dated, but intriguing early melodrama about a burlesque dancer and her religious daughter, were important. In this movie, much of it set in the streets of New York City, the director recorded the dialogue of actors taken from two microphones and mixed them on the final soundtrack. This advanced the practice of recording several tracks separately to be mixed into a single track later. Newly invented directional microphones and boom devices were developed to suit a variety of sound needs. Filmmakers realized that a film could have its music "sketched in," then be given full orchestration at a later date rather than performed live. All of this freed up the camera to move again, telling its story with visual emphasis.

Since then, the best directors have been acutely aware of how, when sound is creatively applied to their movies, the experience of visual images is magnified. It is no accident that a key to the dramatic mastery of Alfred Hitchcock lay in his use of sound. In telling production notes that he wrote after viewing a rough cut of a sequence in *Psycho* (1960) that has Marion (Janet Leigh) fleeing town with stolen money and heading toward her unfortunate destination at the Bates Motel, Hitchcock gives the following detailed instructions for dubbing sound effects:

> *When we reach the night sequence, exaggerate passing car noises when headlights show in her eyes. Make sure that the passing car noises are fairly loud, so that we get the contrast of silence when she is found by the roadside in the morning. . . . Just before the rain starts there should be rumble thunder, not too violent, but enough to herald the coming rain. Once the rain starts, there should be a progression of falling rain sound and slow range of the sound of passing trucks. . . . Naturally, the windshield wipers should be heard all through the moments she turns them on. . . . The rain sounds must be very strong, so that when the rain stops, we should be strongly aware of silence and odd dripping noises that follow.*

Every movie presents similar creative challenges involving sound for the director and the sound design team. Since the advent of sound technology, the level of expertise in a whole range of sound specialties has pushed filmmakers beyond anything imagined at the rude beginnings of simply wishing to record the actor's voice.

THE USES OF SOUND IN MOVIES

Sound design for film efforts break naturally into three distinct areas:

- **The Spoken Word.** Since we need to hear the words of actors not only for advancing the story, but also simply to enjoy special nuances of a performance, basic clarity of dialogue is essential. The primary responsibility for attaining good sound is in the hands of the **production sound recordist** and **location sound mixer.** They are on the set when the film is shot. Later, the **ADR** (automatic dialogue replacement) **supervisor** works with actors in postproduction dubbing. A **dialogue editor** ensures that the tracks are of the highest quality.

- **Music.** The music score—whether original or borrowed from already published recordings—can be considered an independent element in filmmaking. Although the score may be initially inspired in conversations with the producers and the director in the film's initial stages, the **composer** in a private creative environment puts down the music scheme for the film. The track is normally begun and added to the film after principal photography, grafted to the shots and scenes in the postproduction stage by the **music editor** and **conductor**.

- **Sound Effects**. All sounds whose source is not voice or music fall under the title of *sound effects*. These sounds are either recorded live or created on separate tracks. The **effects editor** records the sounds, and with the help of the **Foley artist** and **Foley mixer**, lays down an array of background sounds for each shot. Sound effects establish the texture of film, whether it is an intimate love story featuring the seemingly simple incidental sounds of urban apartment living or the boom of cannons and clash of metal on a medieval battlefield.

Each of these sound elements has its special problems and techniques for their resolution. Finding the right sound expression requires very different skills, and the production time frames in which they are most active vary.

The person with overall responsibility for creating and effecting the aural elements in movies is often called the **sound designer**, a title that appears to have been coined for Walter Murch with his work on *Apocalypse Now* (1979). The designation of sound designer became popular in the early 1980s when moviemakers and exhibitors finally became convinced—because of the new artistic possibilities stemming from state-of-the-art sound technology—that a single person was needed to oversee the complex strategies of the sound track. This element of filmmaking not only requires technical excellence, but also has become an exciting field of creative possibilities. The sound

✦ THE PROPERTIES OF SOUND

Despite the elusive nature of sound, scholars and technicians working in the field are forever trying to give exact definitions to the properties of sound and its perceived qualities. Although sound can be measured accurately with instruments, because sound is not tangible the ways to describe its qualities are rather poetic. There are certain accepted characteristics of any sound:

- **Attack and Decay** are special terms alluding to the way sounds begin and end. The attack of a sound may be sudden and brittle, or gradual and gentle. The decay of a sound may fade slowly or end abruptly.

- **Timbre** refers to tone and color qualities. Sounds may be harsh, guttural, whooshie, brassy, strident, warm, etc. Certain musical instruments produce distinctive timbre. For instance, the clarinet gives a reedy sound, perhaps appropriate to accentuate the plaintiveness of a movie scene.

- **Pitch** indicates the lowness or highness of sound. Low sounds are used to move an audience at levels of deep feeling, subtly registering warmth, growing determination, or possibly fear. High sounds are usually more playful, but they can also be terrifyingly shrill.

- **Rhythm** describes the recurrence of regular or irregular patterns of sound, most often associated with music. The occurrence of strong or weak beats establishes rhythms ranging from simple to complex. In a film, for example, steady and forceful sound rhythms might be used to accent a suspense film. On the other hand, a more complicated and erratic beat might trigger the desired anxiety from a scene even more.

- **Tempo** relates to the rapidity of sound patterns. Sound tracks with slow tempos can be languid and reassuring; fast tempos tend to put the audience at the edge of the seat. A

movie might employ a slow sound tempo in a scene of a man fishing by a pond on a warm July day, unless the filmmaker would want to associate a more energized comment on the visual image by using an upbeat tempo.

- **Volume** registers the loudness or softness of sound. Some high-action films intentionally overpower the audience with the volume of their sound tracks, whereas a love story may soothe with more muted volume. Volume is measured in decibels. At the low end, humans first discern sound at about 20 decibels (the sound of fingers brushing cloth). Dialog in movies registers about 85 decibels, ten points higher than normal conversation. Sound tracks played at levels over 120 decibels for sustained periods risk damage to the ears.

designer manages the invention of a sound track that blends *dialogue, music,* and *sound effects* into a unified whole.

Although not every film designates one person as the sound designer—often the responsibility falls to a **supervising sound editor**—approaching a movie in terms of its sound design is common today. While people work independently on these separate tracks, the supervising sound editor oversees their coordination. It is a complex task, given the conflicting sound needs of some films. Wylie Stateman, supervising sound editor for *JFK* (1991), defines his work: "I consider myself a designer, a map-maker really. I lay things out on paper, orchestrate sound effects and dialogue, then experiment with ideas." During postproduction, a **studio sound recordist** monitors the play back and mix-down sessions at the sound studio. In the end, the **re-recording sound mixer** takes all three of the sound elements and assembles them by blending the tracks in ways that add maximum impact for the film at hand.

THE SPOKEN WORD

The nature and range of the tonal qualities of actors during their dialogue often provide the first hints of the physical or psychological context surrounding the characters. These qualities offer clues that provoke our reactions. The quality of the reproduced voice expresses a variety of information.

- **Character**. Normally when watching a film, we do not get a totally accurate read of the personality of the character until he or she speaks. Voice textures can range from warm, thin, and breathy, to crisp, rich, and booming. Marlon Brando in *A Streetcar Named Desire* (1951), playing a brutish husband threatened by his sister-in-law, surprised the audience when he assumed a slurred, high-pitched voice to express his rage; the fragile southern drawl of Laura Dern in *Rambling Rose* (1991) indicates her sensitivity and dreaminess; the thick, whiskey-smudged voice of Al Pacino in *Scent of a Woman* (1992) strongly points to the backstory of his character. Getting the desired acoustical effect is essential, so that every nuance of voice inflection and diction registers clearly with the audience. In the self-conscious voiceover technique employed to open *Manhattan* (1979), Woody Allen displays his character's narcissism, self-importance, and delusions of grandeur through voice texture. As the narrator attempts to describe Manhattan, he voices his words so quickly that they merge into one another and create a sputtering that tells us of his neurotic anxiety.

- **Location.** The quality of the pitch, volume, and resonance of a voice will tell an audience much about the atmosphere in which the scene takes place. For example, in a suspenseful movie, the muffled pitch of two huddled persons whispering in a dark closet reinforces the tension of the dramatic moment. The claustrophobic dimensions of the space need not be shown because the quality of timbre heard in their voices tells us of their fear of the intruder in the outer hallway. In a similar vein, the voice reverberations of two lawyers (John Travolta and Robert Duvall) talking in the marbled halls of a courthouse in *A Civil Action* (1998) lets us know the size of the location without having to see space in a long shot.

- **Dramatic Weight**. The sound quality of voice introduces the level of a film's *dramatic intensity*. The icy tone of a lover shutting off a relationship, the whispered warning of a prison guard to an inmate, the confident tempo of a father

9–2 *Notorious*   Cary Grant and Ingrid Bergman were masters of the nuances of voice control and delivery, such as this one from a scene in Alfred Hitchcock's *Notorious* (1946). American agent Devlin discovers that Alicia, a counterspy, has been drugged and is being held captive. The rich sound quality of their voices, recorded by sound technicians John E. Tribby and Terry Kellum, creates the sense of intimacy between two lovers. Their whispered words have a texture that is at once caring, urgent, and sexual. Hitchcock could engage viewers in private dramatic exchanges to an almost embarrassing degree.   (RKO Picutres)

giving advice to his son, or the lilting, warm greeting of an Irish bartender tell us much about the dramatic exchange. The rise and fall of the dramatic tension are indicated in the pitch and volume of voice quality **(9–2)**. In *The Sixth Sense* (1999), the clipped but breathy sound of Haley Joel Osment's young voice carries the dread he represses after his repeated visions of dead people. The considerable suspense permeating the movie hinges on the intense moments when he verbally reveals his emotional state to others. The texture and phrasing of the actor's voice carry the weight of a scene.

Once again, however, content and technology are never too far removed from one another when discussing the role of sound in cinema. Much depends on the acoustical characteristics of the environment in which the voices are recorded. The science of acoustics defines spaces in terms of their *reverberations*—the multiple sound reflec-

MICROPHONES AND SOUND

When sound was first recorded in 1927, the noise of the camera mechanism could be picked up by the microphones used to record voices. Because of **mic** sensitivity, cameras were confined in soundproof booths. By the early 1930s, directional microphones and improved camera housing eliminated the problem. For a sound recordist, selecting a specific mic is as complex a choice as camera lensing is to the cinematographer. In general, microphones fall into two categories: *omnidirectional* and *unidirectional*.

- **Omnidirectional microphones** were used when sound first came to film, and this type is still widely employed. Its distinguishing quality is that sound is picked up from all directions. Remember, rarely is a person in an environment with absolutely dead silence. *Ambient* sounds—normal background sounds that might include the soft whir of an air conditioner, faint traffic noises, or the buzz of florescent lights—usually fill the void. Thus, giving the voice a full background ambiance places the actor in a natural, rounded-out sound environment. The negative side of omnidirectional mics is that they do not discriminate among sounds, and the sound recordist cannot easily control what is being picked up. Unwanted background noise may be recorded.

- **Unidirectional microphones** were introduced during the 1940s, and many versions have since been developed to suit the increasingly sophisticated demands of the industry. Because they focus specifically on the voice of the actor, these microphones solve the problem of undesirable ambient noise. These mics, especially very sensitive condenser types, pick up the intensive qualities of the voice to the exclusion of all other sound. On the negative side, an actor may sound isolated in the forced and somewhat artificial intimacy of its sound quality. Unidirectional mics must also be very accurately placed or else even the movement of an actor's head away from its narrow pick-up pattern will be a problem.

The vast majority of scenes in films are recorded with a microphone affixed to a fishpole or boom just over the actor and out of the camera range, controlled by the **boom operator**. The sound perspectives roughly match the camera distances, since the mic is closer to the subject on tight shots and backs away on longer ones. There are alternatives.

- The **shotgun microphone** is likened to a telephoto lens in that it compresses the distance between the background and foreground. This may or may not be desirable. If persons are conversing in the foreground with heavy car traffic in the background, the loudness of both will be roughly equal, resulting in voice discrimination problems.

- **Lavaliere microphones** are designed to be worn on an actor's body in either a wireless or "hard-wire" version. They are usually highly sensitive omnidirectional mics, but because they are placed so close to the mouth, the background is downplayed. One common problem for the sound recordist is the exaggerated noise of clothing as the actor moves.

tions. **Direct sound**—one speaker talking right at a listener at close range—does not bounce off any other surface. Its resonance suggests intimacy. In the extreme, words spoken on an open field have zero reverberation. However, most sound does reflect off walls, ceilings, and floors in various degrees and speeds. For the sound recordist, these environments range from *very lively* to *dead*, depending on the quality of reverberations caused by the nature of the construction materials and their configurations. For example, sound echoing in a church has a long *decay* time, less so in a tiled bathroom. A voice in a carpeted and draped living room has much less reverberation and almost none in the interior of an enclosed automobile. Each recording situation carries with it potential sound characteristics to dramatically impact the story. The sound quality fills in significant story elements.

Looping Sessions

Live voice recording is a most delicate element of filmmaking because so much of the impact of a drama depends on the absolute clarity and desired texture of the actor's voice. These exacting standards are often missed for any number of technical reasons when the film is initially shot. Because the live voice recording during the shoot is often faulty, the original actors must perform their work again in the postproduction phase. Dialogue can be fixed later in **looping sessions**—also called **automatic dialogue replacement** or more commonly **ADR**—in a *dubbing studio* after the film has been shot. The **ADR supervisor** programs the sessions, working with the director to accomplish what is needed. An actor, in front of his or her projected image, restates dialogue to the exact lip movements. It is time-consuming and exacting work, calling for the actor to recreate the original emotional intensity and pacing of the scene. Many actors (although their contracts commit them to ADR) dislike these artificial and very time-consuming sessions. New digital systems, with their ability to break sound into bits of electronic information, ease the way by electronically matching the sounds to the original lip movements.

Some scenes are shot **M.O.S.**—"mit out sound"—a playful imitation of native German directors who came to Hollywood in the 1930s. It refers to movie sequences shot with the dialogue and sound applied later. In Europe (especially in Italy), entire films are produced M.O.S. Because perfect microphone placement takes up valuable production time, it is far easier to relegate the problems of sound to the dubbing stage. A common criticism of these films is that the voices of the actors often sound detached from the physical environments. But even in Hollywood films, outdoor scenes shot at a distance involving actors speaking are almost always shot M.O.S. For example, two lovers talking as they walk on a beach would be shot M.O.S., with their voices dubbed in later. It is really impossible to try to balance the irregular sounds of the wind and ocean waves with the exact voice textures expected in such a scene **(9–3)**.

Replacing the singing voice of an actor postsynchronously with a talented professional singer has been a standard practice over the years in films. Musicals usually

9–3   *Kangaroo*   It is almost impossible to record premium quality sound of dialogue in certain locations because of the relentless or unpredictable nature of background interference. This beach scene in *Kangaroo* (1985) had to be re-recorded in a looping session with actors Judy Davis and Colin Friels saying their lines, with wind and waves laid in later on separate tracks.   (Cineplex Odeon Films)

demand an excellence of voice quality beyond the reach of ordinary actors. The most famous singing dubs were those by the talented Marni Nixon who substituted for Deborah Kerr (*The King & I*, 1956), Natalie Wood (*West Side Story*, 1961), Audrey Hepburn (*My Fair Lady*, 1964), and for many other less talented voices. Many of the great musicals of the past, such as *South Pacific* (1958), had some of their stars lip-synching someone else's music.

A common use of the dubbing stage is putting a **voiceover** on images of the movie. This narrative style is not uncommon in a film that emphasizes its "storytelling" quality. An actor, the voice detached from the action going on in pictures, usually speaks in measured phrases, giving insight into what we are seeing. The original version of *Blade Runner* (1982) used an extensive voiceover of Harrison Ford to explain his motivations. In a variation, William Holden in *Sunset Boulevard* (1950) shows up dead in the first scene and the rest of the film is an extended flashback with his character in a voiceover giving ironic perspective on his life for the previous six months.

MUSIC

"When you look at film history—the golden days, as they are called—it was the writer, the director, and the composer who were the three primary creators of the film. In many cases, some scores were written on the composer's reading of the script. That's where some of the greatest themes have emanated."

Jay Chattaway, president of the Society of Composers and Lyricists

Movies invite music. When music is applied to the rapid succession of moving pictures, a magical transformation takes place, and the screen becomes charged with feeling. The music composer can shape our attitude about whatever we are watching—from the subtle few notes of music as a woman reads a love letter, to a complex and exhilarating score as a sailing ship leaves port on a dangerous voyage.

Background: Evolving Variations in Film Scores

The advent of sound in the late 1920s had a profound effect on the attitude of the studios toward film music. Almost overnight, the production studios rather than the exhibitors became responsible for the composition and quality of the music score. The major studios set up "Music Departments," with a **music director** in charge, in the same highly structured division of labor that marked their other filmmaking units.

In the early days of silent movies, most film music had been a brash, mood-setting device suggested by filmmakers to broadly approximate the action on the screen. Later, silent film experimented with music composed especially for it. For example, the noted German composer Edmund Meisel wrote original scores for Sergei Eisenstein's *The Battleship Potemkin* (1925). His music became an integral part of the movie experience, reinforcing the images with massive percussion at every turn. Eisenstein writes, "So it was *Potemkin* at this point that stylistically broke away from the limits of the 'silent film with musical illustrations' into a new sphere—into *sound-film*, where true models of this art-form live in a unity of fused musical and visual images, *composing the work with a united audio-visual image.*" Eisenstein and Meisel attempted to make music organic to the nature of the action, rather than "off-stage" music wishfully joined to pictures.

Naturally, "musicals" became the rage. To draw in crowds, theater marquees boldly announced *"They Sing!!!"* At first, Broadway musical reviews such as the Ziegfield Follies, with their lines of glamorous dancing women and continuous song, were a ready source for quick adaptation to the screen, as exemplified in *Glorifying the American Girl* (1930). The *musical*—a film whose primary intention is to feature a series of songs and instrumental pieces wrapped into a lightly dramatic setting—soon became a standard and very popular genre. Conventions of the musical became fixed, as songs became the building blocks of a film. The story was spun around its music, depending on melody, lyrics, and dance for its dramatic turning points. Composers were tempted to apply operatic attitudes to film, filling them with highly emotional music that directly mirrored the imagery on the screen. If a particular song was especially good, it was put over the titles, and would be repeated in various instrumental arrangements. Within the boundaries of the genre, many outstanding Hollywood musicals were made, and indeed, the age was musically golden.

As major studios set up "Music Departments," with a music director in charge, musicals became a dominant genre and boom box office. The musical—a film whose primary intention is to feature a series of songs and instrumental pieces wrapped into a lightly dramatic setting—caught the imagination of a public mired in the depression of the 1930s. Conventions of the musical became fixed, as songs became the building blocks of a film. The musical in America continued to be popular during the post–World War II era, following the pattern initiated and epitomized by the movies of Fred Astaire and Ginger Rogers. The Astaire-Rogers paradigm had set up a tension between debonair sexuality and formal propriety, but their films usually resolved the two attitudes through the graceful zest of their music and dance. The result was that audiences were eager to find delight in their light-hearted stuffiness. Postwar Gene Kelly musicals shifted the public's taste. His naturally athletic dance style expressed a boyish romantic drive that reflected a more engaging small town democratic spirit, just right for a nation back from battles overseas. In the 1950s, musicals fully matured with the sure directorial touch of Stanley Donen in *Seven Brides for Seven Brothers* (1954), *Funny Face* (1957), and *Damn Yankees* (1958); and the romantic genius of Vincente Minnelli in *An American in Paris* (1951), *The Band Wagon* (1953), and *Gigi* (1958).

Because filmmakers waited so long for onscreen music to be a viable possibility, early film music filled up the background in nearly every movie, simply because it was possible. The most sought-after movie composer of the 1930s, Max Steiner, who composed music for 147 films in his career, declared, "Every character should have a theme." For movies with smaller budgets, music was recycled in bits and pieces from previous films. By the middle 1930s, Hollywood was inviting major classical composers to write for film, although surprisingly few responded. From today's perspective, many of the films from the 1930s, 1940s, and 1950s seem overorchestrated: too grand and greatly overstated. The worst offenders were the religious epics, such as Cecile B. DeMille's' *The Sign of the Cross* (1932). Their heavy-handed musical scores superimposed current religious piety onto biblical stories, the effect being grand ethereal music themes rooted more in the fantasies of studio conference rooms than in the traditions of Near Eastern deserts **(9–4)**.

Despite these trends, some outstanding movie music evolved. A significant musical breakthrough—music that accented and expanded the action of a film—came with the work of the Russian composer Seigei Prokofiev in his highly detailed score for Eisenstein's *Alexander Nevsky* (1938). Although composer Arthur Bliss had written a very successful independent track for the British futuristic film *Things to Come* (1935), Prokofiev was a world-renown musician who created music precisely for the images in the film. *Alexander Nevsky* deals with the invasion of Russia by Teutonic armies. An example of Prokofiev's masterful fusion of sound and image takes place in the "Battle on the Ice" sequence in which gothic chants underline each thrust of the drama of battle. To enhance the collision of the two forces, microphone distortion

9–4 *Alexander Nevsky* Renowned composer Sergei Prokofiev provided a startling and relentless music score to Sergei Eisenstein's patriotic Soviet film *Alexander Nevsky* (1938). For once in a movie, the power of the image was matched by the energy of the music, frame by frame. Although the film proved to be a textbook wedding of picture and sound, as the film wears on, the paralleling of the music and picture tends to become slavish. (Kino International)

exaggerated certain instrumental sounds. In an uncommon show of directorial respect for the work of a composer, Eisentein at times cut some scenes to *match* the music that had been written for the film.

Orson Welles continued this practice in certain scenes with the music of Bernard Herrmann in *Citizen Kane* (1941). The movie is noteworthy in every area of cinematic invention, and its use of music is no exception. Herrmann had come with Welles from New York having done scores for Welles' famous radio dramas and readily applied many of the techniques that worked so well to film. For example, Herrmann used snappy music transitions, common in radio drama, to indicate a quick bridge in time between scenes. The effect of these musical passages is that the dramatic action is continually pushed forward. The inventive variations on the theme music, from light strings to ragtime and polkas, are a constant comment on Kane's changing fortunes.

In 1944, David Raksin composed the haunting theme song for *Laura*, starring Gene Tierney and Dana Andrews in a romantic murder mystery **(9–5)**. The film is basically *monothematic*, that is, the movie used variations on a single theme that were sustained throughout to define the hauntingly beautiful woman. The song was so closely wedded to the ghost of the woman's character that even a few strains of it made the audience feel her presence. Although its complex harmonies were not a popular formula for music of the day, the song became the first of its kind to become a hit record independent of the film. Later, other film music would follow this path, most notably Dimitri Tiomkin's "Do Not Forsake Me Oh My Darlin" from *High Noon* (1952), which became its musical emblem. The enormous success of this music alerted filmmakers that such songs were a real source of revenue as single releases. Since that time, studios have retained the rights to their music and many have actively entered the music industry.

Although this brief history of movie music is not meant to be comprehensive, the work of certain composers in this period should be mentioned. The great American composer Aaron Copeland did sensitive scoring for *The Heiress* (1949). The plaintive and heroic music of Hugo Friedhofer in *The Best Years of Our Lives* (1946) helped it to win an Academy Award. Miklos Rozsa used an unusual musical instrument, the *theremin*, to create very eerie effects in *Spellbound* (1945). In the same vein, the odd and unrelieved *zither* instrumentation of Anton Karas established various moods for *The Third Man* (1949). By the 1950s, jazz themes were introduced, a seemingly radical departure from the traditional use of music in film, first by Alex North in *A Streetcar Named Desire* (1951), and later by Elmer Bernstein in *The Man with the Golden*

9–5   *Laura*   In the 1940s, music directors began to experiment with music that emotionally stretched the movie audience in new ways. Composer David Raksin's theme for *Laura* (1944), with Dana Andrews and Gene Tierney, both complemented and greatly intensified the melancholy mood of the story and its cinematography. Upon seeing the film, it is almost impossible to disassociate the image of the mysterious Tierney character from the haunting musical score.   (20th Century Fox)

9–6 *Strictly Ballroom* Although its heyday was in Hollywood's Golden Age, the dance/musical has not died. Given its relatively low budget, Australian Baz Luhrmann's *Strictly Ballroom* (1992), with Paul Mercurio and Tara Morice, was a surprisingly polished work in its exhilarating blend of music and dance. (Miramax Films)

Arm (1956). In 1959, a new Latin music was introduced to a worldwide audience with the Bossa Nova rhythms of Antonio Carlos Jobim and Luiz Bonfa played by Bole Sete over backgrounds of Rio's Festival in *Black Orpheus* (1959).

The style of musical genre evolved through the years, just as the public's taste for rhythms, instrumentation, harmonies, and lyrics have changed. The fairytale quality of romantic musicals in this earlier era began to clash with harder realities of the radical cultural changes in the 1960s **(9–6)**.

More Recent Trends

"Music is really the defining line of a society: where it is emotionally, where it is economically, where it is racially. If you just take the music and throw away all the news, throw all the analysis away, you would be able to put your finger pretty easily on the pulse of this society."

Producer George Jackson
(*New Jack City*, 1991)

Today's movies blend contemporary music with strong or realistic story conflicts. Musicals in the last two decades tend to be stories that shape their sound track from the music situation that they chronicle. Because the performers and settings are immersed in a music environment, the industry now labels them "music-driven." *Saturday Night Fever* (1977); *Grease* (1978); *The Rose* (1979); *Purple Rain* (1984); *Dirty Dancing* (1987); *The Doors* (1991); *The Commitments* (1991); *Mr. Holland's Opus* (1996); *Shine* (1996); *Selena* (1997); *Topsy-Turvy* (1999); and many other films stressed music, but within a solid dramatic context. Disney's attempt at reviving an older style song-and-dance musical with *Newsies* (1992) failed, whereas *The Bodyguard* (1992), a hybrid romantic-thriller/musical featuring Whitney Houston in musical performances, and Tina Turner's dark musical biography *What's Love Got to Do with It?* (1993) had explosive music tracks and seemed to strike the right chord. *Evita* (1996) with Madonna was a "wall-to-wall" musical, successfully adapted from the stage. Woody Allen and composer Dick Hyam's parody of the classic musical *Everyone Says I Love You* (1996) was a brave attempt to prove that, yes, we can all sing.

Music in movies today is not created to simply add dramatic emphasis or momentary delight. Frankly stated, there is too much potential for money to be made on a sound track that both magnifies the film for which it was written and that can stand on its own as an exciting music CD. In fact, the very concept and viability of a film may hinge on the type of music and performers chosen for it. This is certainly true for movies designated as *musicals*, but it is also increasingly true for many films that produce either a complete music track or selected songs to transform the story into a stirring and distinctive screen experience.

Movie music tracks both reflect and determine general musical tastes **(9–7)**. Elvis Presley had done a number of cheaply produced films that did little but extend the popularity of his music. The Beatles and their new music stormed the screen in the sharply-made *A Hard Day's Night* (1964). Simon and Garfunkel provided a perfect music ambiance for *The Graduate* (1967), and two years later the compilation music track of *Easy Rider* (1969) helped define a generation to itself. The music of *Saturday Night Fever* in the 1970s launched the worldwide "disco" trend, extending to clothing

9–7   *Sid & Nancy*   The life and death of Sid Vicious (Gary Oldman) of the Sex Pistols was the subject of Alex Cox's *Sid & Nancy* (1986). Like many contemporary films with music background stories, the film gives a realistically dire look at not only the unleashed musical talent of a popular underground star but also the social and psychological factors that shape it.   (Samuel Goldwyn)

and even nightclub design. The movie was a hit, but revenue from its record sales topped even great box office figures.

Music tracks from movies found a receptive audience in the 1990s. The music track of *Boyz 'n the Hood* (1991) sold 1 million copies; the album from *The Commitments* (1991) over 2 million; the single by Bryan Adams, "(Everything I Do) I Do For You," from *Robin Hood* (1991) sold over 10 million copies; both the album and Whitney Houston's single "I Will Always Love You" from *The Bodyguard* (1992) became two of the fastest-selling records in history; and her title song from *Waiting to Exhale* (1995) entered the music charts at number one, a first for a song from a film. At one point in 1992, nine of the top 200 albums were film scores, including the award-winning music of Alan Menken and Howard Ashman in *Beauty and the Beast* (1991) and *Aladdin* (1992). The amazing box office success of *Titanic* (1998) carried over to an equally impressive showing for James Horner's musical score. He and lyricist Will Jennings composed the hit song "My Heart Will Go On" sung over the final credits by Celine Dion, included in the *Titanic* album that became the best-selling film score ever.

The success of an album sometimes is independent from the acceptance of the movie. The soundtracks of *Until the End of the World* (1991), *Sliver* (1993), *Last Action Hero* (1993) , and *Set It Off* (1996) sold well, despite the box office disappointment of the films. Jerry Goldsmith's electrifying score for *The Final Conflict* (1981) (the last of the *Omen* series) ultimately gained more attention than the film. An album by major recording artists who were simply *inspired by* the film *Dead Man Walking* (1995), but not included in the movie, found a large audience. Successful film music is not limited to pop culture. In the 1940s, *A Song to Remember* (1945) generated a huge new interest in the piano music of Frederic Chopin; *Amadeus* (1984) brought Mozart to a generation not known for its classical tastes; and *Hilary and Jackie* (1998) presented the exceptional cello work of the British musical genius Jackie DuPre. Filmmakers have good reason to pay special attention to film music **(9–8)**.

9–8 *Singles* Music scores have provided huge additional revenues for movie producers and artists. For example, *Singles* (1992), starring Bridget Fonda and Matt Dillon, was only a mild box office success, but the CD from its soundtrack was a hit. Music director Paul Westerberg mixed original music by himself, Alice In Chains, Pearl Jam, and others, combining it with prerecorded music by Soundgarden, Jimi Hendrix, and Chris Cornell.
(Warner Bros)

CONTEMPORAY COMPOSERS

Just as actors are type-cast, some composers also become known for their special aptitudes in film music. Most people writing music score are very versatile and invite a variety of movie themes. But certain composers are recognized mostly for their high-powered scores suited for action films, among them: Harold Faltermeyer (*Top Gun*, 1986); Michael Kamen (*Lethal Weapon I & II*, 1987 and 1989); Elliot Goldenthal (*Batman Forever*, 1995); Graeme Revell (*The Craft*, 1996); Randy Edelman (*Daylight*, 1996); James Newton Howard (*Dante's Peak*, 1997); and Jerry Goldsmith (*The Edge*, 1997).

Others tend toward more august or grandly romantic music: Maurice Jarre (*Ghost*, 1990); Ennio Morricone (*Cinema Paradiso*, 1988); John Barry (*Dances with Wolves*,

1990); Henry Mancini (*Victor/Victoria*, 1982); Marvin Hamlish (*Sophie's Choice*, 1982); Rachel Portman (*The Cider House Rules*, 1999); George Fenton (*Shadowlands*, 1993); John Williams (*Angela's Ashes*, 1999); Elmer Bernstein (*The Age of Innocence*, 1993); Stephen Warbeck (*Shakespeare in Love*, 1998); and Gabriel Yared (*The Talented Mr. Ripley*, 1999).

Working at times in distinctively offbeat modes are composers such as Tangerine Dream (*Legend*, 1985); Eric Serra (*Subway*, 1985); Mark Isham (*Trouble in Mind*,1986); Joe Delia (*The Funeral*, 1996); Howard Shore (*High Fidelity*, 2000); Phillip Glass (*The Truman Story*, 1998); and Thomas Newman (*American Beauty*, 1999).

Many movie composers first established their own reputations in the record industry

as jazz or rock performers, including Quincy Jones (*The Color Purple*, 1985); Herbie Hancock (*Round Midnight*, 1986); Randy Newman (*Pleasantville*, 1998); Branford Marsalis (*Mo' Better Blues*, 1990); Stanley Clarke (*Dangerous Ground*, 1997); Ry Cooder (*The Buena Vista Social Club*, 1999); Miles Davis (*Siesta*, 1987); Larry Carlton (*Against All Odds*, 1984); and Dave Grusin (*Random Hearts*, 1999).

Certain composers become linked to specific directors, working with them on a series of films: Nino Rota with director Federico Fellini; Bernard Herrmann and Alfred Hitchcock; Danny Elfman and Tim Burton; Angelo Badalamenti and David Lynch; Dick Hyman and Woody Allen; Carter Burwell and the Coen brothers; Mark Isham and Alan Rudolph; Bill Lee and Spike Lee.

THE STAGES OF MUSIC PRODUCTION FOR FILM

"The greatest music score of all time is not going to make a bad movie into a good picture. It can't do it. It can make a picture look better than it is, fool you into thinking it's really a classy picture."

Composer Randy Newman (*Toy Story 2*, 1999)

In common with other elements of the filmmaking, the clear understanding of how the music process works is best approached in terms of what happens during preproduction, principal photography, and postproduction. Each phase has special demands made for the music track. During these times, the collaborative efforts of the director and music composer will depend on the personal styles and work habits of both. Certain composers and directors find that, although they appreciate the demands of each other's art, they can do little creatively together until the film is in the final stage. Other individuals are much closer, providing give-and-take regarding the nature of how the music will influence the visuals.

Preproduction Choices. The first issue faced is, as always, the proposed budget. If the movie is "music-driven," a **music supervisor** is hired to determine the quality of talent, the number of songs needed, recording and orchestral fees, etc. The possibility of a sound track album is always considered, but questions abound. Is the recording artist also the star in the film? If so, who controls the album revenue? Is the music to be *prerecorded* or *original*?

- **Prerecorded music** has the advantage of instant familiarity, as in the inspired choice of Bob Seeger's music for *Risky Business* (1983). The audience may find the combination of music they know well set in the context of a movie narrative to be pleasurably inventive. But choosing the right preexisting music isn't necessarily easier or any less expensive. Depending on the number of songs and the way they are used, license fees for existing music can skyrocket the cost of a film. Elliot Lurie, VP for music at 20th Century Fox, says, "I'll bet it was more expensive to license all the existing records in *Goodfellas* than to score a film with a ninety piece orchestra." Often, film directors are not acutely attuned to current popular musical taste, and the music supervisor is in a strong position to shape the music track. Joachim Holbeck for the "chapter breaks" in *Breaking the Waves* (1996) put in familiar music by classic rock artists over static images of watery landscapes. The effect was surprisingly contemplative. Music supervisor Danny Bramson comments, "I'll literally program the director's world, starting in preproduction through the actual shoot, making him tapes to hear to and from the set and in the dressing room and trailers. Not too many of them are listening to rock radio." Older music and their artists can be given a new life in the exposure movies provides. Vintage music can also take on a new life in another way. In *Blue Velvet* (1986), director David Lynch revises Bobby Vinton's 1963 sugar sweet tune "Blue Velvet" for his character, Dorothy (Isabella Rossellini). Dorothy's rendition of "Blue Velvet" is sultry. In her nightclub lounge act, the song becomes a melancholy and sadomasochistic reflection of the world in which she is trapped. She fragments the song, sings it deeply and slowly, and she whispers her desire for blue velvet over her bare shoulder. In the audience, Frank (Dennis Hopper) gazes upon her while sadistically fondling a piece of blue velvet fabric he has cut from her robe. By giving the song a context loaded with danger, Lynch invests it with a newer and darker meaning.

- **Original music** requires hiring a **composer** with a thorough understanding of the needs of the project, and the ultimate hiring of a full complement of musicians for recording sessions. Hopefully, the music will be dynamic, inspired by the dramatic energy of the film and expressive of that spirit. It may be as exotically soaring as the score by Ryuichi Sakomoto and David Byrne for *The Last Emperor* (1987), as perfectly integrated as Ennio Morricone's music in *The Mis-*

sion (1986), or Gabriel Yared's haunting compositions in *The English Patient* (1996), and as contemporary as the varied track composed by Jimmy Jam and Terry Lewis for *Mo' Money* (1992). Some particular songs become hit singles, such as "Because You Loved Me" by Celine Dion from *Up Close and Personal* (1996); "Gangsta's Paradise" by Coolie in *Dangerous Minds* (1995); or "Sittin in My Room" by Brandy for *Waiting to Exhale* (1996). Filmmakers are well aware that the right movie can launch a special piece of music to independent success.

Most composers seek out a wide variety of musical challenges and welcome working on different types of movies. In a single year (1996), composer Hans Zimmer received credits for six major films in very different genres: the military special-effects feature, *Broken Arrow*; a children's tale, *Muppet Treasure Island*; a star-laden prison thriller, *The Rock*; the madman-on-the-loose thriller, *The Fan*; a subtle period romance, *The Whole Wide World*; and an angelic fantasy in urban setting in *The Preacher's Wife*. Each of the films called for a contrasting set of musical considerations. Composers are often drawn to work on a film because of its special subject. James Horner (*Titanic*, 1997) is one of the most sought after and highest paid composers in movies, but he wrote the score for *The Spitfire Grill* (1996) for a fraction of his fee because of his attraction to the humanistic theme of this small independent film.

Inspiration During Principal Photography. The **composer** usually comes on board about four weeks before the end of principal photography when it becomes clear just what the director has put on film **(9–9)**. Each director works differently

9–9   John Williams   John Williams is one of the most distinguished composers in film. Nominated for scores of Academy Awards since 1967, Williams has composed music for over 80 movies since the early 1960s, but is perhaps best known for his music in George Lucas' entire *Star Wars* series, for his work in several Steven Spielberg productions, including *Indiana Jones* (1984); *Schindler's List* (1993); *Jurassic Park* (1993); *Saving Private Ryan* (1998); and *The Patriot* (2000).   (PBS)

with composers and music at this point. David Lynch, for example, tells his frequent composer Angelo Badalamenti what mood he hopes to create in each scene, and music is written with that in mind. To further help him when shooting the scene, Lynch has the music piped into his earphones as he directs the action. At times, he will have the director of photography listen to the same music when shooting, "Because when they're panning the camera, I can say 'slow' or 'fast,' and it's all relative. But if they're listening to that music, they turn those wheels just perfect. It just gives you that added thing to nail down the mood."

After watching the dailies several times, the composer will get a sense for the type of music needed. Some composers prefer getting involved at this point rather than earlier. Composer Randy Edelman (*Dragonheart*, 1996) explains, "What the filmmaker creates may be very different from the concept on the page. You have to *see* the dog in *Beethoven*, the dragon in *Dragonheart,* or Jim Carrey in *The Mask*. You have to *see* Daniel Day-Lewis running through the woods in *The Last of the Mohicans* looking a certain way and conveying a certain feeling before you can capture it properly in music." By this time, a song must be readied for inclusion in the trailer of the film, as well as any other marketing vehicles, such as radio or television spots. As budget pressures increase, the time frames for delivering the music shorten. A constant lament of composers is the tight schedule allotted for writing the score.

At rare times, music is recorded entirely live at the time of shooting and then edited without a note changed. For *Kansas City* (1996), a film attempting to capture a special time in the 1930s when jazz greats were first discovering both their music and one another, director Robert Altman chose to film the performances of the musicians entirely live. By filming the musical segments in a nightspot with three cameras, he was able to successfully record the spontaneous solo improvisations of saxophonists Joshua Redman, Craig Handy, and other musicians in a manner that, in Altman's estimation, would have been impossible to recreate in postproduction sessions. In typical fashion, Altman took a chance bypassing the safer path of most filmmakers, but he comments, "Most directors or producers have to take advice from technical people. And the technical people want everything done the easy way."

Postproduction Performance. The most intense work begins at the stage when shooting ends. The composer, assisted by the **music editor**, closely studies the movie, one reel at a time. A rule of thumb: About *one-half* of an American movie will have *some* kind of music (European films usually have far less). At first, composers will normally concentrate on thematic music, creating melodies that can be identified in the first few notes so that strains can be used throughout the movie.

Music serves a multitude of purposes in movies. Because it can function with bold force or a feathery touch, the job becomes not only finding the right music to suit the story, but finding the specific moments in the action at which music should be interjected. Paradoxically, the question also becomes when *not* to use music. With the producer and other major decision makers, the composer defines the various moods desired for significant moments in the film. The composer, with the music editor, scans the footage on the screen to find every instance when music may help out the movie. They look for the exact point in the scenes where the music will begin and end—a process called **spotting**.

A most natural place to introduce music, for instance, is at a cut to an important shot, a dramatic shift in the dialogue, the beginning of a movement, or at the start of new scene. This visual shift of attention helps mask the introduction of the music, allowing for its more subtle and effective influence. The opposite is also true. Music is often introduced before the end of a scene to mask a following cut. These points in the film are given a **cue**, and the exact duration is recorded with a stopwatch. Some passages are long, allowing for fully developed musical themes, others so short that only a few bars are needed. This information becomes their working blueprint. With it, the music editor has written a **breakdown** of all the action so that the composer has a ready time-coded guide sheet. The tempo of the music is controlled by the action in the scene. At times, the relationship of the music and the cutting is not immediately clear to the director. Director Walter Hill explains his method: "Sometimes I'll edit things that don't seem to make a lot of sense at the moment, but I'm leaving room for the kind of music I want. Then when I put the music in, it does make sense."

The **scoring session** is often done in a recording studio with a conductor, music, and cue sheets at hand, while watching the film footage projected on a large screen, and with musicians present **(9–10)**. Some composers choose not to conduct the

9–10   Hans Zimmer   Hans Zimmer is one of a group of frequently sought out music composers for movies of high action and adventure, such as *The Red Line* (1998); *MI: I-2* (2000); and *Hannibal* (2001). Part of his talent is his ability to write music that successfully matches and intensifies the accelerating visual images of the film as they unfold. Seen here in a studio recording suite, Zimmer has been nominated for several Oscars, winning with his score for *The Lion King* (1994).

orchestra, preferring instead to study the performance from the control booth. James Newton Howard (*The Vertical Limit*, 2000) comments: "Things that sound good to me out on the podium sometimes sound terrible in the booth. I can talk to the director and address his concerns better in the booth." Usually, in the control booth are engineers, the orchestration, the music editor, the film producers and director, sometimes the film editor, and the *contractor*—the person who actually hires most of the musicians.

Composers may choose working with a **click track**, a digital metronome locked to the picture to sync the music. Music, after all, is a series of rhythmic beats, and the composer must attempt to find the moments when musical emphasis underscores critical visual action—that exact instant when the lips of lovers kiss. In scoring sessions, some composers choose a method known as **free timing**. The projected filmstrip has a diagonal marking called a "streamer" gradually running on, pointing toward a moment of dramatic importance at which a musical downbeat can be made. This allows composers more freedom to put personal emphasis into the melding of image and music. In the extreme, some music attempts to tightly mimic significant movements on the screen at every turn, usually for a comic affect. The style has been labeled **mickey mousing** because of its original widespread use in cartoons.

The makeup of the groups of musicians and the selection of instruments can vary greatly. In Hollywood, about 1,000 musicians form the nucleus of the Recording Musicians Association, with about half of them working regularly on film scores. Cost is always a factor. Union rules state that only five minutes of useable music can be recorded per hour. Large budget films can have orchestras ranging from 30 to 90 members, but there are a limited number of recording studios that can handle those numbers. Los Angeles, London, and Munich are the primary sites for film recording, although Prague and Budapest offer excellent and less expensive facilities and musicians.

An ever-evolving array of *synthesizers* has revolutionized film music recording, due to their sound flexibility, inventive potential, and low cost. The big sound of synthesized music can create a complex sound track that blurs the line between sound effects and music. Producers of low-budget films love them because of the polished sound tracks now possible for a very low price. In fact, young filmmaker Robert Rodriguez parodies the role of the synthesizer in the music world and in cinema in *El Mariachi* (1993). In this film, a young mariachi travels throughout Mexico looking for a place to settle and to entertain his people in the traditional way. Like his father and his grandfather before him, he travels alone with his guitar. Upon arriving in a new town and seeking employment, a bartender is quick to demonstrate why he has no need of a traditional mariachi. The bartender has hired one man with a synthesizer that simulates an entire mariachi band. Rodriguez comments on the fact that musicians and composers working with a wide variety of equipment and computer software at their fingertips can now experiment with seemingly infinite combinations of sounds, many quite foreign to traditional musical instruments. Composer David Foster (*The Bodyguard*, 1992), about his digital multi-track tape machine, says, "I can't imagine working without it." Paradoxically, the vast range of musical choices and their easy reconfiguration by this new technology can become its own problem. William

Goldstein (*Shocker*, 1989) notes, "Because there are so many possibilities, it can slow you down." Oddly, the employment of full orchestras is making a comeback. "You can never truly re-create the wonderful sound of a big orchestra with synthesizers," declares Bill Varney, VP of sound operations at Universal Studios.

By the end of postproduction, firm decisions can be made about the independent commercialization of any film music, as a single or an album. Ideally, a *music video* with some of the score interwoven with compelling images from the footage will be put together to promote the film. Timely coordination of this complicated process is essential.

The Application of Film Music

"Part of the trick is keeping it sort of simple; you have to give the impression of not that much music playing when there's really a lot."

Composer James Horner (*Titanic*, 1997)

Film music is seductive. Music in movies is broadly defined as *melodic sounds of any length that add some degree of emotional effect to the screen image.* At times a score can be bold and demand attention. However, while watching a film, we are often quite unaware that music is being performed. Music used in movies divides into two of the following general categories:

- **Source Music.** Simply, this is music that is recognized as having a source of *realistic origin* located within the context of the story **(9–11)**. Most obviously,

9–11   *Smooth Talk*   Finding ways to introduce music into a scene can be resolved rather naturally at times by relying on **source music**. In Joyce Chopra's *Smooth Talk* (1985), a jukebox is used to create a realistic music environment while adding an emotional dimension to the encounter of the two characters. Directors often search out different sources—street musicians, car radios, boom boxes—from which music might logically originate and enhance a scene.   (International Spectra)

when an actor breaks out into song, it is source music. But more commonly, a character might turn on a car radio to fill the background as she drives through the rolling countryside, or a couple might casually pass a street performer playing a guitar as they head to a restaurant. We can logically identify its source. In the Canadian film *I've Heard the Mermaids Singing* (1987), filmmaker Patricia Rozema has her lead character place her favorite album on the turntable, letting Delibes' "Lakme" permeate the onscreen room as well as the audience theater. The voices in "Lakme" impeccably signify the sound of mermaids singing, a sound the lead character identifies with as fuel for her soul. Using music in this way allows the director to keep the film within a realistic mode, while at the same time naturally adding melodic flavor to the scenes.

- **Underscoring.** This is the music in movies that comes from nowhere. That is, the music has no recognizable screen source in the narrative, but is used to add emotional meaning in a shot, a scene, or the entire film **(9–12)**. In most films, partial melodies or strains from musical instruments are constantly laid over shots to influence the impact of a visual. Although an extremely orthodox, realistic director might shun this as emotional manipulation of the audience, underscoring with music is a traditional and fundamental element in the art of cinema. The moody and introspective Hans Zimmer score for the war story *The Thin Red Line* (1998) covered battle scenes as well as the lulls between the fighting, creating for the audience not only a heightened sense of the surrealistic nature of battle but also the personal anguish of soldiers

9–12 *My Father's Glory* Musical **underscoring** is a common method used by filmmakers to lead the audience toward a desired emotional attitude regarding the action on the screen. Considering this scene with two delinquent boys on a sun-filled day from Yves Robert's *My Father's Glory* (1991)—a tender story of youth remembered—what kind of music and instrumentation would you use to underscore the scene? What viewer attitude toward the film moment would you hope to elicit with your choice? (Orion Classics)

engaged in it. Audiences have learned that music is used for the purposes of effective drama, but they remain vulnerable to its manipulative uses.

Much film music is intentionally unannounced, softly coloring a shot or scene before fading out. The audience may be moved to deeper feelings, yet beyond the logic of the literal drama on the screen, be unaware of exactly why that is so. It should be remembered that when conceiving film music, consideration should not be limited to the tightly structured and nicely encased songs associated with music on record albums.

AESTHETICS OF FILM MUSIC

"Music in film must not just add emphasis but must give more body and depth to the story, to the characters, to the language that the director has chosen. It must, therefore, say all that the dialogue, images, effects, etc., cannot say."

Composer Ennio Morricone
(*The Legend of 1900*, 1999)

Both underscoring and source music are used in a wide variety of ways to enhance films. Audiences have come to intuitively understand the subtle codes governing the methods and tastes of film music. Through the years, the following musical conventions have evolved:

Introduce and Conclude Films. Music, either a single song or a rhythmic instrumental treatment, played over the titles of a film can establish the emotional energy for the story to build upon. The credits or opening shots are "free time" for the composer, in the sense that music can be boldly laid over the pictures with the primary intention of grabbing the attention of the audience. Henry Mancini's catchy tune over the credits of *The Pink Panther* (1964) presented clever musical phrasing that then became associated with its entire series of six sequels. The opening sequence of *Much Ado about Nothing* (1993), composed by Patrick Doyle, is an extremely dynamic wedding of music and image, creating the charged energy that carries through the rest of the film. Bruce Springsteen's "Streets of Philadelphia" introduces the audience to feelings of urban melancholy in the movie *Philadelphia* (1993). At the conclusion of *The Crying Game* (1992), Lyle Lovett's version of "Stand By Your Man" not only ends this provocative film on an upbeat note, but both resolves and extends the irony presented in the final screen images of one friend visiting the other in prison. The beginning and end of a film are commonly assigned as spaces to showcase music.

Enhance Thematic Resonance of Stories. Finding the perfect theme song for a movie is a major challenge for the composer. Apart from the evident financial rewards as a separate recording, theme music that both captures the essence of a film and can stand on its own is a valuable asset. Great theme music not only merges with a story, but also transforms a movie into a larger experience. We come out of the theater with it intricately associated with the screen story. "Lara's Theme" by Maurice Jarre will

9–13 *Doctor Zhivago*   A single theme song is often used in many musical arrangements to intensify the film's central emotional or spiritual statement. For the sweeping Russian epic *Doctor Zhivago* (1965), with Omar Sharif and Julie Christie pictured here, the film producers were so taken with composer Maurice Jarre's "Lara's Theme" that they discarded much of Jarre's other music written for the film and applied this theme with a heavy hand. This single piece of music was used so extensively throughout the long film that some critics complained that it became somewhat cloying. Jarre's heralded screen composition work spans from *Lawrence of Arabia* (1962) to *The Taste of Sunshine* (1999).   (Photograph by Bradley Smith)

forever be connected to *Doctor Zhivago* (1965) **(9–13)**; Paul Simon's "Mrs. Robinson" from *The Graduate* (1967) is as important to the success of the movie as any other element that went into it; Fred Neil's theme for *Midnight Cowboy* (1969), sung by Harry Nilson, summed up the wandering spirit of the film. Renowned music can take on various colorings with creative musical arranging, as in the multiple renditions by Michael Kamen of the Latin swing-era classic "Brazil" in Terry Gilliam's film of the same name. This fine but unlikely song was rediscovered in an array of tempos and instrumental variations throughout the spectacular visual fantasies of the film.

The type of music and its placement within the film must bend to the thematic needs of the story and its images. Therefore screen action is served by music, not vice versa. Some composers seem to use movies to show off their music selections, with secondary regard as to whether the choices strengthen the movie as a whole. Composer Hans Zimmer (*Rain Man*, 1988) claims, "There's nothing worse than going to see a film and suddenly the score belts you over the head and rips you out of whatever the emotion of the film is, and you can't watch it any more because you're listening to the music."

If the music is very special, it becomes hard not to let it dictate visual editing. But as a rule, the choice of music should grow out of the perceived theme of the movie. Director Spike Lee (*Do the Right Thing*, 1989) complains of the approach of many studios: "They go to *Billboard* Magazine and see who the top 10 groups are. They get the 10 top producers and the 10 top songwriters and they get 10 songs and spend a bundle of money and hope they get a hit. But the music is not organic. It has nothing to do with the movie." When music is deftly applied, its rhythms dance smoothly within a film—sometimes taking the lead; more often following the momentum of the screen images. Lee opens *Do the Right Thing* with a mellow horn solo that suddenly slips into the jarring sounds of "Fight the Power." "Fight the Power" provides the film with thematic strength as well as dissonant juxtaposition to the tranquil opening horn music.

Establish Time Period or Provide Setting.   Music styles are as dated as clothing fashions. A song can quickly tell the general time frame of a story. Music supervisor Steve Tyrell comments: "The music in *Forrest Gump* had to establish a time period or you didn't know where you were." In *The Man in the Moon* (1991), with the thickly romantic lyrics of "Loving You" covering the opening credits against a splendid full moon, eventually transposes to the thin sound of a cheap record player on a screened-in porch of an idyllic rural farmhouse, we know that the movie is set in the 1950s. When a film shows a high-school hop with kids dancing the "twist," as in *Cry Baby* (1990), the music selected by Patrick Williams pinpointed the period as the early 1960s. A very different musical mood was needed for the pastoral setting of *A River Runs Through It* (1992). The Scottish melodies by composer Mark Isham reflected a simpler time early in the century and afforded a gently appropriate background for the many scenes of boys' fly casting in the streams of Montana. The sounds and pictures merged perfectly to confirm the time period. Although the camera gives us the physical details, music anchors the atmosphere with the textures of its audio information.

Set General Mood and Pace.   An audience will align its emotional cadence and temper to the kind of music underscoring a film. Most composers consciously attempt to make audible the mood that the pictures and drama suggest **(9–14)**. The soaring music of John Barry washes over the sweeping landscapes of Western Australia in *Walkabout* (1971), transforming the isolated countryside, for us, into a mystically primitive journey of two lost youths. The shots of inner city street life in *Street Smart* (1987) could have been approached by a composer in any number of ways: rap music, ominous electronic sounds, a slow blues guitar, discordant passages, etc. But because the legendary Miles Davis was chosen as the film's composer, the jazz track featured his cacophonous yet rhythmic trumpet work, which hovered between musically describing the urban chaos and capturing the cool style of the uptown streetwise. In an opposite mode, the odd syncopation of composer Nino Rota conjures exotic images of endless street carnivals, and they created a playfully ironic underscoring for Federico Fellini's best movies, including *La Strada* (1954), *La Dolce Vita* (1960), *8 1/2* (1963), *Amarcord* (1974), and others. The wonder of Fellini's trademark style owes much to the enchanting musical scores of Rota. Francis Ford Coppola used Rota's talents as a composer for Italian rhythms in all three of his *Godfather* movies.

9–14 *Paris, Texas* The slide guitar compositions of Ry Cooder have been incorporated into many movies with Western settings. The slow and slippery rhythms that are part of the Southwestern musical heritage seem to reflect the emptiness of its small towns and the vast landscapes of that region. Much of the affective laconic mood of director Wim Wenders in *Paris, Texas* (1984) (with Harry Dean Stanton) was due to Cooder's evocative sound track. (20th Century Fox)

Build Leitmotif. Composers attempt to associate leading characters—or important events, locations, and even ideas—with specific music. This is a **leitmotif,** a musical idea common in the opera and translated as "leading motive." This musical device establishes an easy shortcut to the emotions of the audience. In *Blue Velvet* (1986), set in the quiet town of Lumberton, evil people lurk. Sandy (Laura Dern) and Jeff (Kyle MacLachlan) discover their attraction for each other while investigating a spiraling series of cruel situations that engulf their world. Laura becomes the one beacon of goodness and hope in his life. To underline her salutary image, during an early scene in which they sit in a parked car telling of possible horrors surrounding them, the sound of a nearby church organ builds to become an inspiring (but slightly mocking) musical underscoring as Sandy affirms the essential goodness of the world. A transcendent blend of organ and angelic voices is unconsciously established in the mind of the audience as "Sandy's Theme." Composer Angelo Badalamenti expands on this music when Sandy is presented in all her shining blond purity at crucial moments in the film to lift Jeff's disillusioned and compromised heart. Only a few chords of the theme are needed to indicate a positive turning point in their disconnected relationship. By the end of the movie, when the two embrace while dancing, the now-familiar theme music automatically brings back feelings of tenderness and optimism. As an audience, the music tells us exactly how to feel toward Sandy's saving presence in Jeff's life. Music has led us through their relationship and conditioned our emotional responses at every turn. Director David Lynch drolly plays with archetypes of good and evil, as the religious overtones of "Sandy's Theme" both reassure us and make us question whether, in the end, all's right with the world.

Comment on Internal States of Characters. As the camera concentrates on a character, music often gives us an external interpretation of his or her inner attitudes. Because film requires that we read characters quickly and accurately, music is a deft way to discover many unspoken thoughts and feelings. When a shot pans across a police line-up and rests on the composed face on the end, if a few intensely menacing notes of music are played over the image, we can safely guess that the submerged mental state of this person is something to be dealt with. Likewise, if a mother opens the door to the nursery to find the baby safely snuggled in, and this is accompanied with the tunes of a music box, we are reassured for the moment that all is calm in Mom's world. In *Scent of a Woman* (1992), Al Pacino's gruff military character is contrasted with his surprisingly high spirit when he dances to tango music with a young woman. Thereafter, musical traces of the tango are played to signal moments of growing optimism in this character's struggle with depression. Another aspect of the use of role identification is through the music bluntly assigned to the characters. In *Batman Forever* (1995), composer Elliot Goldenthal wrote music for the Riddler that was maniacal and kinetic; for Batman, music that was heroic but had darker Wagnerian elements; for Two-Face, a negative hissing sound. All of the characters interacted within a larger musical setting created by Goldenthal, "I just thought of Gotham City as this jazzy, alive, bustling place."

Emphasize Narrative. Although composers can effectively juxtapose the tone and tempo of music with the visual content for special plot needs, in general music works best when it *parallels* some significant element in the scene. If two veteran soldiers come together in a high-spirited reunion at a bar, music could be expected to complement the energy of the meeting and perhaps carry it even further. If the meeting is intended to show the soldier's initial enthusiasm, but then slowly bring out tragic memories of lost buddies, the music *underscoring*—or the *source music* coming from the jukebox—should match the dramatic content of the scene. Music that does not in some way parallel the emotional content on the screen risks confusing or unduly upsetting the audience.

Although music adds a degree of ambiance to any visual, it is sometimes unnecessary and even detrimental. A wise motto: "If alone the dialogue in a scene can carry its dramatic impact, let it be." Moreover, if a scene is not acted well or has other inherent problems, music will not cover up its shortcomings. On the contrary, music will simply draw more attention to it. Composer Jerry Goldsmith (*Basic Instinct*, 1992) has clear opinions on this: "My preference is that music be used as sparingly as possible. I feel that if there is a constant use of music, or too much music, it will eventually vitiate the needed moments. The music becomes a white background. It's a little like living in an area that has a high degree of density of traffic noises. Your ear eventually tunes out those frequencies." Indeed, simply letting the natural sounds in a scene control its aural needs can give a movie a needed realistic base. Composer James Horner makes the point, "On *Apollo 13*, I wanted to give the impression of no music at all. I wanted it more documentary-like." He felt that the images were the strength of the film and its message.

Underline Specific Action. A basic way music works is to mark significant activity. Despite whatever imaginative cinematography has been done to capture the many important moments in a film—a woman walking down apartment steps after saying goodbye to her relationship, two cowboys fighting it out in a barroom, or a child home alone searching through the kitchen cupboards—music infuses an emotional attitude into a scene, joining feelings of sadness, tension, or humor to the physical action. In Hitchcock's *Psycho* (1960), an overhead camera shot pictured Martin Balsam reaching the top of the stairs in the gothic Bates house when he was suddenly attacked by a shrouded figure with a long knife. Composer Bernard Herrmann, with an effect he called "black and white sound," interjected the screech of stridently icy strings insuring a completely terrified response from the audience. In spotting a film, composers pay special attention to such moments as ripe opportunities for emotional underlining.

Create Dissonance and Surprise. Just as separate shots can be intentionally edited to appear disjointed for purposes of irony or shock, so too with music and image. We "expect" certain images to be matched with comparable music. Dark city streets would seem to call for contemporary urban music or eerie electronic sounds. But in the cautionary movie from Anthony Burgess' novel, Stanley Kubrick's *A Clockwork Orange* (1971) gives us the booming classical music of Beethoven seemingly in conflict with the film's decaying hi-tech images set sometime in the near future **(9–15)**. The result, how-

9–15   *A Clockwork Orange*   In *A Clockwork Orange* (1971), music director Wendy Carlos and director Stanley Kubrick chose to underscore the futuristic film with a daring music track that combined the music of Beethoven and a few modern composers, juxtaposing them against the cruelly antiseptic visual imagery in the film. The effect was intentionally disconcerting in its chilling and darkly comic message about the near future.   (Warner Bros.)

ever, is that the juxtaposition opens the possibility of many interpretations of the movie's theme. The clash of aesthetic values can give fresh insight into a future time in which traditional artistic taste is usurped by a startling and very frightening neofascist culture. However the seeming juxtaposition may also be seen as a natural connection between the cult of bullies in the film and music that ennobles and venerates their power. Music/visual juxtapositions, fortunately, are also done with a more humorous intent. However, in the low-budget movie *Zebrahead* (1992), source music from the radio of an open jeep continually puts out an overly loud wall of sound that seriously distracted from otherwise interesting visual detail on the screen.

Bridge Shots and Scenes. Film music is used for very practical, even structural, filmmaking reasons. When devoid of music, the desired flow of film images can appear as a string of jagged cuts. However, when appropriate music covers the shots, the result is a smooth series of pictures that seem easily linked by a unifying theme. The bridge that music creates ties shots or scenes that otherwise might seem disconnected. For example, the underscored amorous mood music in a scene with two lovers embracing in a small apartment late one night may *cover over*, giving the sequence a sense of continuity, into the next morning with a scene of them in front of the building parting for work. Composer/performer Ry Cooder (*The End of Violence*, 1997) uses his signature languid slide guitar sound to ease the visuals from one place to the next. "It works because it cuts and moves in a nonlinear way. And you can do it in different ways, so it's got this sort of stretch." Music also links up a *montage* of shots, as when it is laid over a series of seemingly random images, making them a unified visual experience. Another standard music technique employs light, energetic "traveling music" as background for trains, planes, and cars to more quickly and enjoyably get from here to there.

Experimentation. Because music is not usually a film's central focus but is used to support the images and the story, composers have a free hand in some respects. Due to the very different compositional requirements of movies, creating music can test a composer's range of talent in a variety of uncommon areas. For example, film composers can combine unlikely instrumental sounds, imitate the tempo of the kinetics on the screen, attempt to translate the psychological underpinnings of the characters with harsh musical dissonance, play with primitive or irregular rhythms, or create sensuous tone poems of various lengths. Michael Nyman, an experimental English composer and performing musician with a cult following in Europe, had never been invited to the United States to play. But his score for Jane Campion's *The Piano* (1993) brought him international attention by allowing his music to become the emotional expression of the mute lead character played by Holly Hunter. It is true, in one sense, that film music is only as good as its contribution to the goals of the story. But whereas music might not initially be accepted if it were first heard apart from the movie, once audiences favorably associate the music with a film, they often go on to respond to the music independently, and quite favorably. Composer Leonard Rosenman (*Star Trek IV*, 1986) observes, "I have personally had the experience of hearing musically unenlightened people comment positively and glowingly on a 'dissonant'

AN EXTENDED MUSIC APPLICATION

In Kenneth Branagh's *Henry V* (1989), a single piece of music, composerd by Patrick Doyle and orchestrated by Lawrence Ashmore, runs *uninterrupted* for over four minutes: The situation is the aftermath of the battle on the devastated fields of Agincourt. The English have beaten the French, but at great human cost. The first three minutes and 45 seconds of music covers a single long tracking shot that starts with a close-up of a single soldier, his lonely voice invoking a religious song of deliverance. As the camera pulls away, King Henry comes into view carrying a dead comrade over his shoulder. The shot follows the King across the wreckage of the battlefield, and as he walks, the single voice becomes a small echoing chorus whose sound thickens until it is joined by strings. Fuller harmonies then shift the piece into another key, horns joining to give the music a triumphant aspect. A female chorus blends in, giving the music an even richer dimension. The voices soon drop out while a full string section carries on the spirit, until the full chorus rejoins to give the muddied but wiser warrior King a heroic posture. In the final twenty seconds of the music, the screen makes its first cut to a medium shot of the exhausted King, the soaring music heralding the raw survival of the man and his tattered army. With that, the music bridges a cut to a later time when, in the calm splendor of the French court, Henry and Charles meet to settle terms of the peace.

score after seeing the film. I have played these same people records of the score without telling them that it came from the film they had previously seen. Their reaction ranged from lukewarm to positive rejection. . . ." Composers as varied as George Fenton (*The Madness of King George*, 1994); Danny Elfman (*Dead Presidents*, 1995); Eric Clapton (*The Hit*, 1985); Anne Dudley (*The Crying Game*, 1992); Brian Eno (*Dune*, 1984); and many others have used the film medium to explore the frontiers of musical composition for audiences otherwise unavailable to them.

SOUND EFFECTS

"Adding that one simple sound which gives the scene a subtle emotional impact without the audience being aware of the manipulation—that's where the challenge lies."

Sound mixer Richard Beggs
(*Godfather III*, 1990)

Sound effects refer to all those sounds in a movie that do not relate to either dialogue or music. In addition, sound effects include any nonmusical sounds superimposed on the film to bring about emotional response. The word "texture," as it relates to film sound, is appropriate. Although not tangible, sound effects are literally woven into films, intertwining layer upon layer on various tracks. Over the years, work in this field has become increasingly complex and sophisticated, with state-of-the-art sound equipment for *encoding* (with advanced recording technology) and *decoding* (with new speaker systems) pushing sound farther than earlier technicians could have hoped for. Filmmakers have become more aware of the audio powers of movies, relearning the lesson that inspired sound effects establish the essential emotional impact of the film experience. This is the work of sound technicians, sometimes as many as thirty or forty assigned to a production. If the mix is good, the final sound track will seem to be one complete multicolored audio quilt.

Every assigned sound effects team is aware of the following considerations as they approach their job: 1) Many film scripts have their special effects very explicitly indicated, especially those in which directors have had a hand in writing; 2) Some sound effects may be added as the film is put together, in cleaning and looping scenes during the editing phase; 3) Most commonly, sound effects are laid in during postproduction when the background *source-sound* is cleaned out of films shot on location.

The Sound Effects Team

The **sound designer** (or **supervising sound editor**) manages the entire process of sound application. The position requires more than simply technical excellence, demanding also a creative ability to effectively manipulate a spectrum of aural effects. The actual hands-on work of sound effects is done by separate units of sound personnel, each with their trade specialties. The sound crew is divided into three general working units, headed by:

- The **location sound mixer** is the chief technician in charge of all sound recorded live at the actual film site, on location, or on the studio set. Whenever possible, Hollywood filmmakers attempt to record the performance of actors with live sound as their work is being staged for the camera. Carl Warner, production sound recordist, claims, "Really good production sound mixers should generally be able to get at least 90 percent of the production sound on a feature film clean enough when no ADR is required." Because the spontaneous live rendering of a scene is often by far the best, it is important to get as clear a recording as possible at the time the actors are being photographed. Capturing with clarity the full texture of voices when actually shooting a movie is not an easy matter. There is a constant temptation to ignore acquiring fine quality production sound when shooting a film, trusting that everything can be made right in a postproduction recording studio. "There is a myth that most sound is done later. That is mostly true for heavy-duty science fiction movies. You can get actors to do lines again, but you will never get that emotion from being there," says sound mixer Russel Williams (*Mo Money*, 1992). A different recording process backs up the job of capturing sound on the first take. The **production sound recordist** picks up *wild sound*—sounds coming from a jet engine or a crashing glass that are not synched to the picture but which may be useful later as background. Over 85 percent of the sound in *Apocalypse Now* (1979) was applied in postproduction. The location sound teams struggle to do their jobs. Sound mixer Jeff Wexler observes, "There's not much glory in sound because this is a visual medium. Location sound is almost the first thing to go in a difficult production situation.

Many directors are prone to say 'let's lose the sound' if the light is fading and they want to make a shot in a hurry." Despite best efforts of the production sound team, live sound sometimes takes a back seat to urgent photographic problems and other time-consuming considerations on the shooting set.

- **Postproduction sound teams** create, record, and mix the sound effects, music, and spoken word. The **effects editor** heads a group that produces the wealth of incidental sounds that fill a movie—the muffled hum of the motor inside a cruising Mercedes, the sound of sheets as lovers turn in bed, dogs barking outside in the night. Sound crews take great pride in their resourcefulness. In his career, sound designer Ben Burtt (*Star Wars*, 1977) has used many unlikely techniques to gain his effects: to provide the sound of Luke Skywalker's landspeeder as it displaced air, the steady roar of traffic on a freeway was recorded through a vacuum cleaner tube. Skip Lievsay (*The Silence of the Lambs*, 1991) broke down each of the sound elements—chainsaws, metal crashing against metal, the low roar of a motorcycle—then imitated them on a Synclavier® computer synthesizer. For *Independence Day* (1996) a unique sound had to be created for the introduction of the invading aliens. Sound designer Sandy Gendler said, "It reminded me of the flying monkeys from *The Wizard of Oz* and we went with that idea. We took baboon screams, processed them, added a jet engine, processed it, sped it up, and added some wind buffets." For those effects editors who are less inventive, cannot afford it, or are simply in a rush to finish the track, commercial **sound libraries** have thousands of prerecorded sounds for almost any circumstance. Producer Tom Mount (*Bull Durham*, 1988) observes, "There are very few good sound effects editors. There are a handful that are great and they're hugely sought after." Another part of the effects process is called **Foley** (named after the innovative sandman, Ed Foley, employed at Universal in the 1940s), the building of the hundreds of small sounds that give movies their special sense of intimacy. A **Foley artist**, with eyes riveted to the screen in a specially outfitted sound studio, matches the visuals with appropriate sounds. Often that means replacing the sound of footsteps in hard packed snow or the high heels on a marble floor. It could be that heavy breathing is enhanced or, by using **handprops**, unseen keys jangle in a pocket. For *Hook* (1991), the sound of Tinkerbell's wings became a problem, solved by the combination of bike wheels, a bird feeder, and harmony bells. The **Foley mixer** puts each sound on a separate track and modulates it as the shot progresses. Foley artist John Roesh (*Who Framed Roger Rabbit*, 1988) describes the precision expected, "In this business close isn't good enough—we need to get it exactly right because there's no such thing as close enough."

- **Re-recording sound mixers** fine-tune the many tracks into the film's final sound mix. The **studio sound recordist** does the physical work of mixing down and playing back the tracks in studio sessions. Since the 1970s, the situation has become much more complex. Now the sound recordist must link 4 or 8 or 48 or 100 tracks of audio material with the help of computers. Others, sound engineers, sound technicians, and sound assistants, work in concert as a

★ BUILDING SOUND

In *The Hunt for Red October* (1990), underwater sounds were essential to the visual drama of the film. Much of its effectiveness was built with the underwater sounds that intensify the cat and mouse game going on between Russian and American subs. Great effort went into the research and pursuit of unique sound. Sound technicians Celia Hall and George Waters went on a two-day cruise on a nuclear submarine to find the right sound effects. The team sought them out everywhere: They recorded the sound in the sub when it blew its ballast's; at 150 feet deep off Catalina Island they picked up the sound atmosphere of a tanker five miles away. Then at Disneyland they recorded the stressful groans of the steel structures created by the rides; they discovered that motorboat engines passing underwater are a good match for the sound of an unleashed torpedo, and they were able to use hundreds of "ping" sounds created by a harmonizer to give the eerie sonarlike sound that so effectively built excitement in the submarine chases.

team and make up the rest of this specialized group. Being the last chance to significantly alter and perfect what will arrive in theaters, the entire process is often closely monitored by the film director and lead producers.

Meanings in Sound

"What I do is take a look at the show without any sound at all except dialogue in order to see what kind of movie it is and where the strengths are, then I focus on what kind of film I have reel by reel and decide what kind of sound might enhance it."

Effects editor Bob Grieve
(*Pacific Heights*, 1990)

The sound effects team has surprising latitude in applying aural impact to shots and scenes in a film. Their meticulous scrutiny of a movie, with the single focus of finding points in the action to enrich the sound track, makes their work akin to that of other artists in the final stages of a composition. They may give special attention to refine the detail or apply broad accents to heighten general appearance. Such fine-tuning can make all the difference. Sound effects separate into two basic categories: denotative sound and connotative sound.

- **Denotative sound.** The term refers to those sounds that have a literal referent in the movie, that is, a sound that points to and emphasizes the physical object from which it originates. In a movie, the sound effects fill out the truth of the moment when we not only *see* dishes being washed in a sink, computer lights blinking in a spaceship, or keys turning in an automobile ignition, but also at the same time *hear* the sounds that match them. The pictures come alive

9–16 *Salaam Bombay!* In *Salaam Bombay!* (1988), the young street boy Krishna (Shafiq Syed) saves his drug-addicted and suicidal friend Chillum (Raghubir Yadav) from a train that races by. The moment is underlined by the denotative high-pitched screeching of the train's whistle and the metallic clap of the railroad cars on the tracks. Although the high-pitched sound underlines the desperation of the moment, commenting on the lonely chaos of their lives, it is primarily used to ground the viewer in reality. (Cinecom Pictures)

(9–16). *Denotative sound* has a second use, more subtle but very effective. This sound points to things that are unseen because they are off-screen. In the make-believe of movies, the sound designers remind us that the world does not end at the edges of the screen, that we are watching only a selected piece of a larger reality. Therefore in a movie about a stand-up comic, the laughter heard off-screen needs no immediate visual reference, we *know* it comes from the crowd before which the comedienne is performing. Off-screen denotative sound indicates the complete context of a scene.

• **Connotative sound.** Certain sounds carry with them not only their literal meaning, but are also associated with strong emotional feelings. These sounds are used to call forth desired responses. For example, an old movie standard (still used regularly) is a distant wailing police siren heard as two people in an inner city apartment talk about the imminent relationship crisis in their lives. You can bet that this subliminal warning is meant to signal a troublesome dramatic turn in the story, often totally unrelated to any law enforcement unit that will be introduced later in the scene. This sound not only subliminally alerts us to the danger surrounding daily contemporary life, but also signals a general dangerous emotional situation within the story. Therefore, in *Grand Canyon* (1991), a humanistic movie about some stark truths of modern city life, a constant groaning flutter of unseen police helicopters imposes itself on everyday life in central city neighborhoods. A guttural mechanical flutter was used not only to indicate the presence of the helicopters, but also to give the feeling of the constant pressure and paranoia of living in urban Los Angeles. **Hyperreal sound**—the blatant exaggeration of a familiar sound for its emotional effect—is frequently used to increase tension. Hitchcock's *The Birds* (1963), is a classic example. The frightening screeches of the attacking birds become ear-splitting and incessant, the sound finally not needing the on-screen images of birds to strike terror. The sounds in both movies become symbolic aural reminders of the danger hovering in contemporary daily life **(9–17)**.

Some connotative sound is **nonobjective**, that is, it does not directly relate to an object on or off the screen, but rather is intended to conjure emotions and reinforce

9–17   *Das Boot*   Connotative sound suggests new meanings or reinforces emotional moments in a movie. The recrafted soundtrack for the 1997 re-release of *Das Boot* (1981) is a classic example of the connotative use of sound. Much of the 207 minutes of the film is spent in the confined quarters of a hunting and hunted World War II German submarine. The intensity of the crew's existence is largely told through metallic echoes, leaking water pipes, the steady hum of engines, the ping-ping of ultrasound detection devices, underwater explosions from unseen depth charges, broken steam ducts, and unnerving silences. When we associate what we hear—the unrelenting cacophony of machinery—with the confining imagery on the screen, the tension produced is as gripping as any action ever recorded in movies.   (Sony Pictures Classics)

the impact of the dramatic purpose of the scene. Coming from a background in radio, Orson Welles was a pioneer in this area: In *Citizen Kane* (1941), Susan Alexander (Dorothy Comingore) stands among frantic stagehands at her opera house debut performance, the cacophony of many unidentified sounds reflecting the controlled hysteria in the singer's soul. This is one of many scenes in the film of which soundman James G. Stewart has said

> *Welles simply freed sound. In that day and age if you did something unrealistic in the middle of a scene, most producers would say, "What's that?. . . What's going on there?" Welles didn't believe in this. He believed that anything you could do to heighten the drama of a scene was worth doing.*

Today, the electronic sounds of various generations of synthesizers are regularly used to invoke deep feelings of fear, tension, excitement, etc. The versatility of the synthesizer has given composers and sound engineers new landscapes of sound to explore. The Synclavier®, an electronic editing system with instant random access and a collection of sound tracks, was first developed in the music recording business. Any number of combinations of desired sound can be laid out without harming the quality of the original mix. Editors can play with combinations of sound endlessly.

The Application of Sound Effects

Sound effects engage the audience by making the pictures emotionally convincing in the following manner:

Sound to Highlight Action. In the first great movie car chase—*Bullitt* (1968)—*seeing* one car chasing another through the streets of San Francisco is fun. But *hearing* the distinctive roar of each engine, the shifting of gears, the burn of the tires landing after being airborne, the slam of car springs, and the rush of air displacement made the chase real and put its audience at the edge of their seats. In the time since *Bullitt*, the genre of action/adventure has relied on convincing louder-than-life sound effects that punch up the action on the screen and rivet audiences by bringing elements vibrantly alive. Sound mixers often take great liberties with some scenes, jacking up the volume and pitch of the sounds and enriching their timbre. A very strong sound track can sensually overwhelm the viewer, the effect being that the good visuals become spectacular ones.

Sound as Ambiance. Every shot is filled with physical information, much of it having an environment of corresponding sound. In a busy corporate office scene, for example, sound effects engineers would attempt to imitate its ambient foreground and background sounds: the noise from computer keys busily at work; the low hum of conversation punctuated by slightly more distinguishable voices and a laugh; footsteps on a tiled floor, signifying workers moving from desk to desk; the movement of bodies shifting on cloth-covered chairs. Sometimes an invented off-screen sound is strangely perfect in lending atmosphere. Sound designer Bob Grieve tells this story:

9–18   *Patti Rocks*   For this shot from *Patti Rocks* (1987) with Chris Mulkey and John Jenkins, imagine that you are a sound engineer whose job it is to apply ambient sound—those subtle and detailed background sound effects put onto a track to give a movie the audile textures of unadorned reality. Study the photo. What ambient sounds might be both expected and appropriate?   (FILMDALLAS Pictures)

"There was a scene in *Grand Canyon* where Kevin Kline and Mary McDonnell are having a conversation in a washroom about the baby she found and what they were going to do about it. For some reason I decided to put on Rainbird sprinklers out the window to give it some texture. I can't explain why I did it, but it worked." It may be that the fresh swish of water being sprayed over a lawn gives the familiar and comforting sense of summer, a reassuring sound at a time of decision. An innovative audio track can combine with the picture to enhance the movie experience beyond the sum of the two parts **(9–18)**.

Sound Effects to Bridge Shots and Scenes.   Again, just as music is used as a *bridge*, sound effects often create a *segue*, linking one shot to another. The sound of the crashing surf in one shot, for example, may abruptly become the hiss of jet engines in the next. In a variation, the disturbing noise of heavy traffic may come up as a person stands in a normally quiet sunny field, but the sound is an **audio lead-in** to the next shot—a crowded freeway. Some directors choose to make scene transitions with sound rather than depending solely on the visual cut.

Sound to Evoke Emotions. Just as music registers deep within us, drawing up predictable feelings, so too with sound effects. Sounds in the context of certain situations are associated with feelings that are shared by most people. In a horror film, certain sounds conjure fearful reactions—the metallic scrape of a knife being unsheathed, heavy footsteps beyond a door, the gurgle of water in a bathtub drain. Once a sound is linked with a visual image, it can be used again in a film to summon the original response. Director Fred Schepisi comments on the film *Plenty* (1985): "The sound of parachutes opening at the beginning I use again all through the film, when people are opening tablecloths and curtains, because it brings back a certain feeling." Just as a musical *leitmotif* can repeatedly suggest a desired emotion, repeated sounds bring with them plot associations. Sometimes characters are given a *signature sound* to reinforce their identification with a particular attitude. In *The Silence of the Lambs* (1991), Dr. Hannibal Lecter is given growling animal sounds mixed with human screaming. In *Robin Hood: The Prince of Thieves* (1991), the magnified sound of the arrow became the hero's signature, as it were. (Because the arrow had to be regularly heard over the din of battle, it took forty sound people using twenty combinations of "whoosh" sounds to get it right.) The flaring picture/sound image was used as a gripping emblem of the quick justice that could be administered by Robin Hood.

Paradoxically, the *absence of sound*—perfect silence—can be a powerful emotional statement. For *Three Kings* (1999), an offbeat war drama, co-supervising sound editor Bruce Fortune explains the varied use of sound in the film: "This picture isn't about explosions and flying bullets. That's not to say there isn't a fair amount of that sort of action—there is. But those moments stand out all the more when they're juxtaposed with silence. That's the effect we were going for. We were trying to bring out the emotional components in the script—what is was like not only to be in a fire-fight, but also what it feels like right after." Filmmakers too often mistakenly overload the screen with unnecessary sound simply because it seems to thicken the visual environment with auditory textures. But what is true of all art also applies to the use of sound—sometimes less is more.

THE FINAL MIX

"The final mixer can really make or break the movie. The sound editors work hard to put all those little bits and pieces in, and they want somebody who will be able to play them. If the mixer doesn't have the patience to look for them all, then all the work is thrown away."

Director Renny Harlin (*Abominable*, 2000)

The final mix of the entire sound track is a delicate and grueling affair. The sessions take place in a mixing studio, ideally outfitted with state-of-the-art mixing consoles with over seventy inputs and fifteen output channels, projection equipment and a screen, and superior sound speakers. In the studio, three *sound mixers*—one each for dialogue, music, and sound effects—work at console stations, an activity called "riding the board." They assemble and mix their various tracks into one

INNOVATIONS IN SOUND RECORDING AND THEATER SOUND SYSTEMS

1940s: Magnetic tape is introduced because of its better fidelity for recording. As tape technology later developed, 4-track, 1-inch tape advanced to a 16-track on ¼-inch tape format.

1960s: The compact and lightweight **Nagra® tape recorder** comes on the market. It features a highly efficient machine equipped with "crystal-sync"; can control the operation of both the camera and the recorder. This recorder allowed filmmakers extreme freedom to shoot in almost any location and get first-rate sound with ease.

1970s: The **Dolby® sound system** is invented. It reduced background noise by compressing the sound range while recording, then selectively increased the amplification of soft recorded sound to mask the noise which the system inherited. In stereo, four separate sound tracks are generated from two optical channels.

1980s: George Lucas and his chief sound engineer, Tomlinson Holman, developed advanced **THX® sound systems** as a way to enhance the movie experience. Lucas started the Theater Alignment Program (TAP) in 1983 to help exhibitors upgrade their venues to match the superior quality of sound produced at the studios. Theaters that qualify and pass a yearly inspection are certified to use the **THX** logo. The **THX** group also made recommendations for the projection systems and general maintenance of movie houses. These standards were adopted in 1989 by the National Alliance of Theater Owners (NATO) **(9–19)**.

1990s: Cinema Digital Sound ® (CDS), followed by Sony's **SDDS®, Digital Theater Systems (DTS)®,** and Dolby's **SR-D®** digital sound systems now compete in presenting state-of-the-art sound in theaters and strive to become the industry standard. Digital sound is a process that converts sound to numbers, then stores them in some form of computer memory. When reproduced and presented in theaters, in effect, it is only one generation removed from the original.

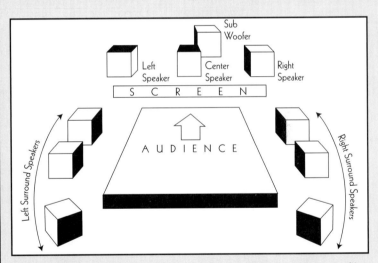

9–19   State-of-the-Art Sound Systems   A major improvement in film exhibition over the past 25 years has been in the area of advanced sound delivery systems. State-of-the-art sound systems in theaters are necessary to deliver the quality of sound produced by the high audio standards used by sound technicians during a movie's final mix. Typically, a ten-speaker auditorium configured to surround the movie audience is considered the optimal to fully appreciate the excellence of modern film sound technology.

balanced sound unit under the supervision of the **re-recording sound mixer.** Because *dialogue* is of prime importance, this mixer often doubles as the person in charge of the sessions. The nature of the mixing work requires cutting down on the material given them. Until this time the three tracks have been separate, and the job becomes one of blending them into a seamless whole. A *work print* is brought to the studio and projected during the mixing sessions. *Cue sheets* tell the points on the sound tracks at which sounds are recorded. The team of mixers will mix the tracks in terms of volume, balance, and voice pitch, synching them to the projected film. At times new sounds may be added if it appears needed.

The process is highly exacting and very time consuming, as the sound and projection machines are continually backed up and sent forward to fine tune the mix. Weaker elements in the sound tracks are strengthened. This final mix, in most cases, is the last opportunity for the filmmakers to tinker with the movie, and there is a temptation to fuss endlessly. The process can take a month, but triple that time is not unheard of. The producers and the director are usually present during much or all of these studio sessions, being aware that this stage is crucial to the success of all the creative effort that has gone before it. Sound editor Skip Lievsay describes the tension: "Almost without exception the most difficult part is the final mix, not because of the work but because of the personalities involved. You're on the line, and everything you know is on the line."

When the work of the *re-recording sound mixer* and *sound designer* have satisfied the group of filmmakers in control of the project, the movie is finally ready to be printed. The momentous job of making a movie is complete.

SUMMARY

"The perception of sound is necessarily bound up with the perception of image; the two are apprehended together, though sound is often perceived through or in terms of the image and, as a result, requires a 'secondary' status."

John Belton, writer in film technology and aesthetics

Sound brings film alive, giving it the breath of passion. The steady flow of purely silent visual images on a screen has an eerie, unworldly quality. But the sensuous *whisper* of Bess (Emily Watson) in a wanton telephone call to her husband (Stellan Skarsgard) at sea in *Breaking the Waves* (1996) tells of her sexual urgency in a way that could never be conveyed with pictures alone. The *music* of Mahler in *Death in Venice* (1971), underscoring the futility of the aging intellectual Gustav (Dirk Bogarde) and his pursuit of pure beauty in the person of young Tadzio (Bjorn Andresen) during one summer in a disease-ravaged Venice, produces the bittersweet emotions that distinguish the film. In *Fargo* (1996), the subtle *sound effects* of blowing wind and crunching footsteps in brittle snow helps create the audio textures that give the frozen northern locations such convincing character.

Sound came to film years after the power of visual imagery of movies had been explored and refined. This may have added to the perceived "secondary" status of sound. In the silent era, music was separately and uniquely applied each time the movie was shown. This somewhat chanceful, if important, circumstance certainly became part of the lore of early motion picture exhibition. After sound was put on film, audiences welcomed it and quickly adjusted to its new uses. It was perhaps natural that the primary attention of moviegoers was focused on the quality of its visual images, rather than the excellence of its sound track. Sound in film brings with it a different psychology. The visual image in film is a continuously conscious element. Sound—whether it be voice quality, underscored music, or sound effects—is very often unconsciously received. Of course this very factor affords sound its surprising effectiveness in movies.

Advances in sound technology encoding—more specialized microphones, digital recording equipment, etc.—are at the stage of being matched by increasingly elaborate sound systems in theaters to decode the signals. Highly trained staffs working in state-of-the-art sound engineering facilities have set exacting standards in the competitive field of sound creation and enhancement. The result has been that sound quality in film is both expected and openly enjoyed by a moviegoing public ever more sensitive to the pleasure of *listening*.

SPOTLIGHT

The Composer: Mark Isham Interview

Mark Isham has been composing for film since 1983. He was a successful trumpet player before changing his professional direction. Isham's career is strongly linked to a particular director, Alan Rudolph. Their collaboration covers *Trouble in Mind* (1985); *Made in Heaven* (1987); *The Moderns* (1988); *Love at Large* (1990); *Mortal Thoughts* (1991); *Mrs. Parker and the Vicious Circle* (1994); *Afterglow* (1997); and *Breakfast of Champions* (1999). Among other notable movies are *Mrs. Soffel* (1994); *Reversal of Fortune* (1990); *Losing Isiah* (1994); *Quiz Show* (1995); *The Gingerbread Man* (1997); *Blade*, (1998); *October Sky* (1999); and *Imposter* (2000).

Richard Peacock: What was your first big break in composing for film?

Mark Isham: It was *Never Cry Wolf* for Carroll Ballard. I never got to the bottom of exactly how it happened, but Carroll heard some music I had written. I really had no aspirations about being in the film business. I didn't know much about it. I was a fan of film but I really never considered writing music for it. Anyway, this music fell into his hands and he was at a rather desperate point in making the film. He said, "That's what I've been looking for." He'd already tossed out two scores. Disney had just come to him and said, "Just get John Williams, we'll pay for him. Just get it done." Ballad said "No, he's never done this before but I'm hiring this guy." It's a real credit to Carroll's tenacity that he got them to agree. To this day it's rather remarkable. I'm sure the reason was that using me gave them unbelievable savings.

RP: When do you like getting involved with a film project?

MI: To a certain degree, early on—so I have time for ideas to percolate. Even if I'm not writing, I'm thinking about the film. The traditional idea of film composing was that your palette was a symphony orchestra, and you wrote in the neo-romantic popular style—so that you wrote a *theme* that was appropriate. What's interesting in the last 20 or 30 years—well, maybe it started with *The Third Man*—is that we're in a wide-open field. There's no set way that a film should be scored. I think any genre music, whether it be free jazz or rap or any musical genre, is capable of scoring a film. It depends on whether you're good enough at manipulating that genre.

RP: Do you have any method of composing?

MI: My first thing is to look at the film and get a feel for it so that I can pick a genre. I score films very differently. I come from a jazz background *and* a classical background. But I also spent a number of years playing in rock bands so I understand the breadth of music available in this part of the twentieth century. I think the first decision is this: What is the musical environment for this film? Is there more than one? Is there a whole side of the film that is heavy rock, but when it goes romantic, can we go to an orchestra, and will the film still make sense?

RP: Do you start watching the film with the rushes, or at a more finished stage?

MI: It varies. I think that most directors like to have an assembly. Their main concern is this, "Is my film *working*?" They don't like anybody seeing it till it works. So most directors out of self-preservation will wait and say, "I don't want you to get confused, to misunderstand it. I want you to see it when it's communicating what I intend."

RP: How much contact do you have with the director during the creative process?

MI: The director is the main terminal I work with. So I really insist that that relationship be constant—as much as once a day when we're into the whole thing. And certainly when I've written things, I demo all my themes. Given the time, I will demo every *cue* in the film. I'll have the director come to my home studio and listen and watch—and basically sign off. So that by the time we spend any large sums of money on recording anything, directors know what they're getting and approve it.

RP: If you're using prerecorded music, who chooses it?

MI: I have been brought in on songs and source music. I've also been excluded from it. I would say that more often these days the composer is left out of that. There are many types of prerecorded music. If it's just a source thing with no song impact, then I can be brought into that. It really depends on the whole relationship the composer has with the producers and director. There is obviously a lot of interest in having big pop songs in film. When that idea is being worked, there's so many elements other than "Does it musically make sense?" More often the questions are these: "Does it *financially* make sense?

Does the schedule make sense? Will the artist have this song recorded in time? Will the record be released at the right time? Will the video be done?" Blah, blah, blah. Whatever considerations I might have from an artistic point of view are really lower on the list.

RP: What is the hardest part of underscoring for you?

MI: The hardest part—what I devoted the most attention to, because it's what a lot of people *don't* recognize—is the ability to actually duplicate a director's and/or a producer's and/or studio executive's point-of-view. What is really needed and wanted by them. I mean, I think that for someone who is a pro-fessional musician, dealing with the music is something that comes naturally and easily. It isn't really that hard, compared with working in a group dynamic environment. There you've got major personalities with big opinions about how things should be. You're trying to translate the verbal description of things into musical language. That is hard. Because you'll have somebody say such abstract things as "It's just got to be more *green!*" And you have got to figure out what that *means*. Does that mean that A minor chord should be a major chord? Does he hate English horns, is that what he means? Because non-musicians will end up talking in words that are very significant for them and describing what they feel, but what's the translation here? Do I delete the English horn or do I start all over again? I've had dramatic differences like that, where I'll say to myself, "My god, I'm going to have to write this whole thing all over! I've completely missed it." Then I'll tell them, "Let me play it for you this way," and I'll take the drums out. And they'll say "Oh, that's perfect!"

RP: Are you the initiator in spotting the film?

MI: That's collaborative. Most directors who have really done their homework and have seriously thought through their film will have a pretty good idea of how to spot things. They'll always look for your input, but I find that the most intelligent, creative directors know where they're going, and they're usually right. They'll have made the really big decisions like what style or genre of music will work best, and that's one of the reasons they've picked you, because you're supposedly good at a particular type of score. And if a direc-tor knows little about music, the best of them will say "Here's an area that I know almost nothing about, what do you think?"

RP: Do you orchestrate your own music?

MI: Not directly. I make the overall decisions—strings, brass, winds, things like that—but I work on a computer so I get it down to groups like that. And then I hand it over to an orchestrator who decides what the third clarinet and the fourth bassoon will play.

RP: How much is the shaping of an album a factor in selecting the music for a film?

MI: I try to factor that in. In the early days it was all I could do to get the score done and keep the director happy. Then as my skills improved, I thought,

"How can I do that, plus make a strong album?" I just try to work those things into the creative process. I may quickly sketch out a 3 1/2-minute version of this music instead of a 45-second version—because I know it is an incredibly strong theme, but we only hear it for a short time. Then at the end of the day, we record the longer version so that we have it. You just plan those situations into your schedule.

RP: Who or what were some of your influences in music?

MI: None of my influences were really film composers, because when I was studying music it wasn't my goal to become a film composer. I was actually very interested in Baroque music because I'm a trumpet player. But by the time I'd gotten into high school, I discovered jazz—Miles Davis, not only as a trumpet player but as a musical conceptualist. I sort of came into music backwards because it wasn't till my 20s that I said, "Oh ya, pop music isn't so bad! There are actually some interesting people working in it." Later, the fusion motion—especially Weather Report—brought global music and improvisation together. For me, it showed that music has no boundaries. You could put an African rhythm section in with a string quartet. This served me very well as a film composer, the feeling that there are no restrictions. Brian Eno became a very big influence for me. He took a lot of those twentieth-century compositional ideas and made them work for the everyman, as it were—not just for papers published by French art magazines. Eno is doing music that is sold and appreciated by large numbers of people. You know, I always thought that John Cage wrote better *about* music than he wrote music. And yet someone like Eno comes along and takes Cage's ideas and applies them to popular music, and it's really exciting.

RP: How has the work of a composer in Hollywood changed since you first got involved?

MI: Unfortunately, one of the things that has really changed is the amount of time you have. It seems to shrink every year. Most production schedules get more and more truncated. A lot of it is because of this computer technology. The production executives immediately say, "Well, they've got computers, they can handle it."

RP: Is there any kind of subject matter in movies that you are especially drawn to?

MI: I used to feel comfortable doing only more esoteric films. When I first started, I definitely thought that I had a very specific style of music and that I could only write in that one area, and therefore the film had to match that or I couldn't score it. But over fifteen years, just out of keeping myself from being bored, I guess, I've wanted to keep expanding and exploring and learning new things. So I started changing my attitude toward film music. Now I feel very comfortable doing pretty much any kind of film. I don't have any particular considerations about film genre. Oh, straight comedies are still the ones that I think, "Well, how can I do that?" Slapstick or very broad stroke comedy, that's an area I'm a little more nervous about. Comedy music is tough. Because if you find a director who says, "I want funny music," you're sunk. I think the best comedy movies are the ones that when the music is taken out of the film, the music is actually straight. It's the juxtaposition against the particular scene that brings out the comedic element. I've done some comedies and that's the way that I've handled them.

RP: Such as *Miami Rhapsody*?

MI: Yes, and there is the perfect example. Because if you take that music away from the film, it's just great swingin' early '60s style big band jazz. And yet you put the music in that situation, and it really accentuates the whole comedic thrust.

RP: Is there a movie you've done that is a special favorite?

MI: *Romeo Is Bleeding* is still a favorite of mine, even though the film is a bit bizarre. Certainly not everyone's taste. But it was an opportunity to write in a jazz style, which is closest to the one that I personally like to perform. It's very rare for a film to support that. I wrote for me—I'm the featured player on the film. We had no money, but we still managed to get pretty dramatic music on tape.

RP: I love your score for *Trouble in Mind*. I have the tape and often play it when I write.

MI: That's one with similar characteristics. It's unique and there are a lot of improvisational elements on it. A world of it's own. Those two films are my favorites. With them I found a brand new musical environment, and it really works to sustain those films. It all hooks up.

RP: What is the most satisfying part of your work, let's say, at the end of the day?

MI: Dustin Hoffman said it best at the Golden Globe awards. It's the same for me. The playback is fine, the premiere is fun, and it's nice to hear the track loud on the big speakers. But ultimately, it's the times when you solve that special problem creatively—that moment when you *get it!* As Stravinsky said, "When you find that note." That's why I keep doing it—I want to find the new notes that work. ◀

FILMS TO CONSIDER

Dialogue, music, and sound effects are continually at work in making the movie experience a richer one. The following are some films that, when attention is given to their sound tracks, are quite outstanding.

- *The Third Man* (1949): Composer Anton Karas wrote and performed, with his zither music variations that gave background to almost every scene, the musical equivalent for the cultural strangeness and political intrigue of postwar Vienna.

- *Singin' in the Rain* (1952): This is not only a great song-and-dance movie, the story also shows, in a most entertaining way, the impact of the sound revolution on silent film artists and technicians.

- *Black Orpheus* (1959): A tragic love story set in Rio during Carnival, vigorously accented by Brazilian jazz greats Luis Bonfa and Antonio Carlos Jobim, setting off a worldwide introduction to their sublime style of Latin music.

- *A Hard Day's Night* (1964): The hit sound track of this first Beatles movie ushered in a new era for film music, one that began to put music in film not only for its relevant dramatic purposes but also for its independent commercial value.

- *Juliet of the Spirits* (1965): The surrealistic elements in this Fellini film about a woman's jealousy are counterbalanced by Nina Rota's carefree music score that spreads throughout the movie.

- *Blow Up* (1965): Even though the film about murder in mod London is filled with striking Antonioni images, the simple sound of leaves whipped by the wind over shots of a tree-lined park introduces much of the tension generated by the movie.

- *Death in Venice* (1971): The choice of Gustav Mahler's 3rd and 5th Symphonies as themes to emote the melancholy of the aging artist's sense of unattainable beauty is an example of *underscoring* at its most effective.

- *A Clockwork Orange* (1971): When Stanley Kubrick juxtaposed the classical music of Beethoven with the "ultraviolence" of a futuristic street gang, the result was that their brutal acts took on a coldly distant and even flip aspect.

- *Walkabout* (1971): Composer John Barry created soaring spiritual theme music to transform the desperate wandering of two white youths and an aborigine boy in Australia's Outback into a journey of primal beauty.

- *The Conversation* (1974): In this cautionary movie, a surveillance expert (Gene Hackman) uses his obsession with recording sound by means of high-tech devices to invade the lives of unsuspecting designated enemies.

- *Blue Velvet* (1986): Complementing a moody score by Angelo Badalamenti, sound designer Alan Splet and mixer Mark Berger created levels of sound effects that gave this troubling film added depths of emotion.

- *Trouble in Mind* (1986): The film noir mood of this off-beat story of an ex-cop finding his way in Rain City was kept dark and chancy with the incessant rhythms of composer Mark Isham and a disquieting theme song by Marianne Faithful.

- *Much Ado about Nothing* (1993): In this hearty Shakespearean screen adaptation, the opening sequence of a triumphant band of horsemen returning from war gets off to a rousing start thanks to the buoyant musical score of Patrick Doyle.

- *Sweet and Lowdown* (1999): The style of 1930s jazz innovator Django Reinhardt is imitated by music director Dick Hyman (and Sean Penn's flawless finger movement) to set the stage for Woody Allen's satire about the world's second best guitarist.

THOUGHT QUESTIONS AND EXERCISES

Watch a film from those listed.

1. Watch an entire film, paying close attention to the general sound quality. What is your assessment of its sound design? Was the sound application especially distinctive in any one area? Give an example.

2. Does the original music composed for the film fit its theme? In what manner does it enhance (or detract) from the film? Would a different musical score be more effective?

3. Are there points in the film at which prerecorded music is used? For what purpose and with what effect was the music used at that point in the film? Turn off the sound on your set and watch a scene. If possible, play a piece of music that you think appropriate over the silent section. What new emotional meaning is realized?

4. Underscoring adds emotional coloring to a scene or shot. Choose a segment of a film and describe the exact moment when music is introduced. What dramatic meaning did it add to the images? When and why did the scoring end?

5. Choose a significant scene, one without underscoring. List every primary and incidental sound that you can discern in the background of the scene.

FURTHER READING

Alten, Stanley, R. *Audio in Media,* 3rd. ed. (Belmont, CA: Wadsworth, 1990).

Altman, Rick. *The American Film Musical* (Bloomington: Indiana University Press, 1987).

———— [ed.]. *Sound Theory, Sound Practice* (New York: Routledge, 1992).

Bazelon, Irwin. *Knowing the Score: Notes on Film Music* (New York: Van Nostrand Reinhold, 1975).

Brown, Royal S. *Overtones and Undertones: Reading Film Music* (Berkeley:

University of California Press, 1994).

Bruce, Graham. *Bernard Herrmann: Film Music and Film Narrative* (University Micro Films International, 1984).

Burt, George. *The Art of Film Music* (Boston: Northeastern University Press, 1994).

Eyman, Scott. *The Speed of Sound: Hollywood and the Talkie Revolution 1926–1930* (New York: Simon & Schuster, 1997).

Feuer, Jane. *The Hollywood Musical* (Bloomington: Indiana University Press, 1982).

Gorbman, Claudia. *Unheard Melodies: Narrative Film Music* (Bloomington: Indiana University Press, 1987).

Hagen, Earl. *Advanced Techniques for Film Scoring* (Los Angeles: Alfred Publishing, 1990).

Kalinak, Kathryn. *Settling the Score: Music and the Classical Hollywood Film* (Madison: University of Wisconsin Press, 1992).

Karlin, Fred. *Listening to Movies: The Film Lover's Guide to Film Music* (New York: Schermer Books, 1994).

Lack, Russell. *Twenty-Four Frames Under: A Buried History of Film Music* (London: Quartet Books, 1997).

Nesbett, Alec. *The Studio Sound,* 6th ed. (Boston: Focal Press, 1995).

Palmer, Christopher. *The Composer in Hollywood* (New York: Marion Boyars, 1990).

Prendergast, Roy M. *Film Music: A Neglected Art*, 2nd ed. (New York: W.W. Norton, 1992).

Schelle, Michael. *Score: Interviews with Film Composers* (Los Angeles: Silman-James Press, 1998).

Thomas, Tony. *The Art and Craft of Movie Music* (Burbank, CA: Riverwood Press, 1991).

———. *Music for Movies* (Los Angeles: Silman-James Press, 1997).

Weis, Elizabeth, and John Belton, eds. *Film Sound: Theory and Practice* (New York: Columbia University Press, 1985).

Zarza, Tony. *Audio Design: Sound Recording Techniques for Film and Video* (Upper Saddle River, NJ: Prentice Hall, 1991).

CHAPTER 10

MARKETING AND DISTRIBUTION

FINDING THE AUDIENCE

"This whole business is a crapshoot. The bottom line is that you don't know until it opens."

Michael Fleming, editor at *Variety*

The business side of the moviemaking process clearly emerges when a film is released for distribution. Some academics would argue that the business of selling movies is unrelated to the loftier considerations of the aesthetics of cinema art. The strategies for the marketing and distribution of a film are often dismissed by critics as simple commercial maneuvering—an unholy mix of internecine financial dealings and blatant media hype. That opinion has some value. After all, movies are made in Hollywood. But economic success in this final stage—by successfully distributing films and then convincing people to *see* them—ensures that moviemaking can survive for the benefit of everyone connected to a movie project: the financial backers, the skilled technicians in the industry, and its artists.

In truth, a complete study of the process of moviemaking should not bypass this final stage. In the terms of *communication theory*, the cycle of exchange is incomplete if a message (the movie) is without a receiver (the theater audience). It is with this final element—the public's reception of the movie—that filmmakers are rewarded for their creativity with both recognition and money. The continued vitality of the movie industry is directly linked to both of these. Poor critical response, pallid public resonance, and a weak box office will send a movie into quick, if perhaps temporary, obscurity. What is more, the ripple effect of either a successful or a failed movie could determine the way in which the film business approaches similar movie themes and stars in the future. For example, if a high-budget Western with major stars, a good script, and high production values turns out to be a box-office flop, good business sense might well warn against the idea of another major Western in the near future. Other Western movies in development might be held back or abandoned; future movie scripts with themes of the old West would not likely be pursued. The opposite is, of course, also true: A surprise studio hit about "female bonding" will send others scurrying to find similar magic ingredients. The box-office responses tell the nature and style of this industry's mainstream art.

KUBRICK'S INVOLVEMENT IN MARKETING HIS LAST MOVIE

Most directors would prefer to not see their influence end at the termination of the final cut. Michael Herr, cowriter of Stanley Kubrick's *Full Metal Jacket* (1987) writes of the director: "He loved the biz, the action he observed day and night from his bridge; all those actors and directors and projects, all the dumb energy endlessly turning over in the studios and the PR that came with each new product; he loved being a part of it from his amazing remove, and in terms of being a player, he didn't see himself as better or worse, higher or lower, than any of them, all of them in play together, playing toward commerce and art, big expensive art and works of art for the cash register or, as I've sometimes thought in his case, art films with blockbuster pretensions."

A common but often incorrect assumption is that after making a movie, the director gives up control or even interest in how the film is advertised, marketed, and released. The much-honored and reclusive director Stanley Kubrick most certainly did not believe that carefully designing and monitoring almost every aspect of the theatrical release of *Eyes Wide Shut* (1999) was beneath his status as an artist. Although he died shortly after the completion of the film, Warner Bros. followed a highly detailed marketing strategy laid out by Kubrick. Because of the controversial sexual nature of this high profile movie, Kubrick knew that he had to devise an especially enticing marketing campaign, one that both peaked the interest of a large audience and yet held back essential information about the film. As an example, despite opening the film on over 2,500 screens, the film was not shown to critics until the last moment. The film had been shot over a period of 15 months with superstars Tom Cruise and Nicole Kidman, yet almost no explicit information was released, even in media press kits normally filled with tales of the shooting of a movie. Kubrick himself specified what length and frequency TV commercials should run. Every detail of the photographic image of Cruise and Kidman physically relating to each other on film posters was dictated by Kubrick. In terms of the studio's expectations, *Eyes Wide Shut* achieved mild box office success **(10–1)**.

10–1 *Eyes Wide Shut* The distribution and marketing of motion pictures is an expensively hazardous business at best. *Eyes Wide Shut* (1999) was a famous director's final film (Stanley Kubrick), had two most popular lead actors (Tom Cruise and Nicole Kidman), contained sexy subject matter, and opened with immense free media coverage. Yet the film was a disappointment for Warner Bros. at the box office. Weak reviews and unenthusiastic word-of-mouth quickly dampened the hype that had preceded it. The final judgment of the film's critical and financial worth will probably be told sometime in the future. (Warner Bros.)

PATTERNS OF MOVIE DISTRIBUTION

The key to the success of any large-scale business that makes a salable product is found in its method of **distribution**—the system of contracting, transporting, and merchandising goods. The movie industry is no different. Unless movies are made easily available to their potential audience, their financial and artistic worth is unrealized. The distribution process for film is a complex, multilayered series of steps that engage people from a broad spectrum of interests. These include men and women from studio sales departments, advertising agencies, theater chains, marketing research companies, public relations agencies, entertainment law firms, and media acquisition interests. A host of support services, including the producers of **trailers** and poster materials, print reproducing companies, transportation systems, and many others work together. The networking that goes into the promotion and distribution of motion pictures is a hazardous maze, and, for either a major movie studio or an independent releasing company, surviving in it requires experience, uncanny instincts, and some good fortune (Table 10–1).

The process of film distribution to exhibitors is very complex and filled with detailed revenue compensation variables. Some very high-profile movies go through a bidding operation to competing theater chains with specific amounts of money and fixed film runs guaranteed. The terms of most films, however, are usually negotiated by the releasing company and the theaters, typically with 90 percent of the box office receipts—minus the house operating expenses—going to the distributor, with that figure tapering to a 35 percent minimum in succeeding weeks. Over the years, con-

TABLE 10–1 TOP GROSSING MOVIES YEARLY (U.S. BOX OFFICE FIGURES IN MILLIONS)

1999	Star Wars	430.4
1998	Armageddon	201.5
1997	Titanic	600.8
1996	Independence Day	306.0
1995	Toy Story	191.7
1994	Forrest Gump	329.6
1993	Jurrasic Park	365.8
1992	Aladdin	217.3
1991	Terminator 2	204.4
1990	Home Alone	285.0
1989	Batman	251.1
1988	Rain Man	167.7
1987	3 Men and a Baby	167.7
1986	Top Gun	176.7
1985	Back to the Future	210.6
1984	Beverly Hills Cop	234.7

troversies over percentages often have caused the exhibitor/distributor relationship to be adversarial, but, in fact, both parties recognize that it is in their best interest that each side stays financially healthy.

Studio backing affords the media clout necessary for success in today's market. In 1999, the average production and distribution cost of a movie in wide release was about $70 million, with over $17 million of it spent on media marketing expenses. Each studio has its own marketing strategies, but for most larger companies, television (including network TV, spot TV, cable-TV networks, and syndicated TV) commands most advertising revenue by far—well over 70 percent—with newspaper ads taking in about 20 percent. Some big-budget films can exceed $30 million in marketing alone.

Typically, a major movie will open on a Friday nationwide with huge advertising campaigns and frenzied public relations coverage. Of media coverage, Marc Shmuger, marketing chief at Sony Pictures, observes, "How a film does its opening weekend is treated like late-breaking news. People have an insatiable appetite to know who's on top. Everyone wants to be part of the winning team." Often, by Saturday morning and certainly by Monday, studio executives can usually predict if the film is a *hit*. If the figures add up, they will be on the phone devising strategies on how to build even more momentum. If not, they will start thinking immediately about ways to cut their losses. Ad agency head Tony Seininger reflects the thinking of the business when he says, "Everything focuses on the first weekend. The more successful the movie is, the higher the marketing budget." (Table 10–2)

It must be remembered when we speak of movies being released to theaters in the United States and Canada that these are a small percentage of the films actually made throughout the world each year. During a typical year, over 3,500 films are produced around the world. Almost every country with a vital economy makes films. But the vast majority of films made each year will never be distributed to North American theaters. The record shows that American movies dominate about 70 percent of the world market, and in 1998 the major studios took in 55 percent of their global revenue total from the international market. Movies, in fact, have become the United States' second biggest export.

This extraordinary American marketing situation has nothing to do with the worthiness of foreign films as art. Many of the movies produced around the world are cinematically outstanding in content and execution, but because of the weak economic projections by American distribution companies, the films were simply not chosen for release in the United States. Unlike the rest of the world, this country has no mass-market audience for dubbed or subtitled films. Only a small number of foreign films are picked up by domestic distributors each year. This selection process for international films might seem capricious or arbitrary and, in some cases, it is. On the other hand, releasing companies are most often right in believing that the majority of them would never find a significant audience here. For example, of the over 800 films made in India each year, very few would hold any popular interest in the United States because of the extreme cultural differences, limited and redundant themes, and unfamiliar production values. The high cost of successful movie distribution prohibits frequent mistakes in judgment.

TABLE 10–2 TOP 10 MOVIES BOX OFFICE (WITH DOLLARS ADJUSTED FOR INFLATION; APPROXIMATE DOMESTIC FIGURES IN MILLIONS)

1939	Gone with the Wind	919.8
1977	Star Wars	798.0
1965	The Sound of Music	638.0
1997	Titanic	600.8
1982	E.T.	600.7
1956	The Ten Commandments	586.9
1975	Jaws	573.8
1965	Doctor Zhivago	542.5
1967	The Jungle Book	485.3
1937	Snow White	476.3

THE MAJOR DISTRIBUTORS: MAINLINE HOLLYWOOD

The big name movie studios of old Hollywood—taking into account the tangled and bewildering changes in ownership—are still, for the most part, the major distributors of film today. Although the emphasis of the old studio production system has changed from the heydays of the 1930s and 1940s, today's restructured major studios inherited the traditional methods of developing and marketing movies, as well as negotiating with the national and international exhibitors. The business of movies has always been based on networking among groups or individuals with entrenched financial interests. Studios have had a history of being at the center of commerce in film.

In the golden era of studio filmmaking, each major studio produced about one film a week. Today, the top studios distribute between fifteen and twenty-five films a year. Many of these films will be entirely financed and produced within a studio; others will be produced by independent companies and partially financed by a studio; some movies will be **negative pick-ups**—completed films looking for wide scale distribution. An increasingly popular practice is for a large studio to join with another in sharing the cost (and risk) of a big-budget film, as 20th Century Fox and Paramount did for *Titanic* (1997). There is no set pattern; the history of each film project has its own unique set of circumstances.

A significant number of films, 100 or so each year, are released by "independent" distribution companies such as *Artisan* or *Lions Gate,* which "pick up" films they believe to be of special interest in some way. These movies are often outside the mainstream of popular taste for the average American moviegoer and usually have to struggle to find exhibition locations. Many of the films are from foreign countries, some are feature-length documentaries, others are films with unique stories or unusual styles made by smaller or independent American production companies. Their marketing budgets are by nature very limited, and the strategy relies on good word-of-mouth and

TABLE 10–3 TOP 10 U.S. DISTRIBUTORS (1999)

THE HOLLYWOOD STUDIOS	NUMBER OF FILMS RELEASED	AVERAGE PER FILM (IN MILLIONS)	TOTAL MOVIE REVENUE	TOTAL FOR ADVERTISING
Buena Vist	21	$57.15	$1,200.24	$297.0
Warner Bros.	21	62.16	1,095.28	278.8
Universal	19	49.66	943.45	269.0
Paramount	15	59.07	886.04	248.1
20th Century Fox	15	51.47	772.04	162.5
Sony	27	25.65	692.63	239.9
DreamWorks	7	55.84	390.90	99.0
New Line/Fine Line	19	18.05	324.92	99.2
MGM	12	26.60	319.23	99.1
Miramax/ Dimension	32	6.87	219.91	107.5

solid reviews. The eternal hope is that one such film will get great press, trigger the fancy of some latent taste for the movie idea or appearance, and catch fire.

There is no doubt, however, that a small number of film distributors control the vast majority of the movie business. These *majors* dominate over 90 percent of the domestic market. The ultimate stakes—which include domestic and foreign release, videocassette sales, commercial TV rights, and product "tie-ins"—are high. The major studios do a yearly retail business of about $20 billion worldwide in a growing market. Distribution fees going to the studios are commonly pegged at about 30 percent of domestic and up to 45 percent for overseas revenues. This money is used to cover the studio overhead, maintain the distribution network, and create a financial base for further movie investment. Advertising, prints, and other marketing costs are made *in addition* to the fee. Even though questionable accounting practices of the large studios have been a traditional source of complaints and lawsuits, most filmmakers want to be under the banner of these film distributors because they represent the surest chance for large financial rewards. But the movie business is tough. Many ambitious companies over the years, such as Orion, DeLaurentis, and Imagine, have failed to compete in this arena. But newer companies such as Gramercy Pictures have found success, being bought from PolyGram by USA Networks, which also acquired October Films from Universal. The maneuvering in Hollywood's entertainment industry never stops.

Despite the expertise and experience of the large studios, marketing any single film is forever a new and perilous test. Costs of advertising and distributing a film are beginning to rival the expense of production (Table 10–3). In 1998, the average cost of marketing a movie was $25.3 million. Every decision at this final stage has the potential of either making the movie a success or sinking it. Although some would like to treat the movie business like any other, both the nature of the product and the volatility of customer tastes are special. Confident predictions quickly turn sour. After George Lucas zoomed to the top with the *Star Wars* series and *Indiana Jones* (1984), he washed out with *Howard the Duck* (1986), a film that cost $50 million and returned only $10 million. *Cutthroat Island* (1995), costing more than $100 million to produce, was a major financial disaster. Every new season brings in a film that dashes the dreams of its producers and damages the careers of the studio executives who gave the project the green light.

As much as possible, the major studios attempt to protect and advance their investments by structuring their marketing process in a number of ways. The following sections outline the primary functions of the distribution arm of a typical major studio, which commonly includes four promotional departments: *marketing research, advertising and media, publicity,* and *sales.*

MARKETING RESEARCH

Every business wants information about its customers. An entire satellite industry has grown up to provide this data. *Demographics, psychographics,* and *target audiences,* terms borrowed from Madison Avenue advertising research, have found their way into the jargon of Hollywood. Certainly, the movie industry wants to know just who is going to the theater and what they like. With the skyrocketing cost of making movies, studios have given a great deal of attention toward researching the multiple profiles of their various audiences. Recently, the MPAA reported that 28 percent of Americans go to the movies once a month. In the past, young people—ages 13 through 25—held the key, and they are still important. This group averaged about 12 admissions a year, from a peak year in 1983 when they accounted for 55 percent of the tickets sold. But that number has declined significantly. More recent figures show that this age group's percentage has dropped to 37 percent, with the 25–50 age group surpassing them in movie attendance. The size of the over forty moviegoing public has doubled over the last decade. This shift becomes an important puzzle for the movie business, and questions arise. What kind of movies have the most appeal, and to which of the audiences? What types of films attract more than one age group? Chris Pula, head of marketing at New Line, tells of the merchandising strategy on *Dumb and Dumber* (1995): "We spent like fiends against boys 12 to 24. Then when it caught on, we broadened our focus." In addition, there are about 35 million retired people in this country, many with time and money to spend on movies. Are any films being made aimed at their tastes? These are U.S. figures, what about international trends? What are the demographics of the important market of videotape rentals? Are these trends temporary or permanent?

Defining preferences of movie audiences is a problem worth solving. As a first step, market research has found that moviegoers choose a film in one or more of the following ways:

- **Advertising and Publicity.** An effective advertising campaign, as it will do for any product, puts a film on the map. Getting the word out in print and the electronic media, as well as with **trailers** ("Coming Attractions"), insures public recognition. In addition, there are myriad ways for a movie to gain attention. Publicity departments and public relations companies assigned to a film are dedicated to gaining free media attention and can saturate the print and electronic media with information about the film and its featured players.

- **Resonance of the Perceived Story**. Certain movies ring a bell with large segments of the public. Regardless of how we hear about a film, when our expectations of its content or style mesh perfectly with what we want to see, the movie takes on a life of its own **(10–2)**. Unusual movie themes—even ones that at first appear to be silly or dumb—if they are marketed well practically *draw* people in. Film industry advertising has traditionally, very often successfully, emphasized and promoted the promise of sexual stimulation in both its movie stories and stars. But an exact understanding or prediction of what excites the imagination of the general public often eludes the most experienced in the movie establishment. What accounts for the box office success of the quirky story of *Fargo* (1996) and the failure of the much-publicized, action-drenched *Judge Dredd* (1995)?

- **The Production Values.** The quality and cost of a film will usually be strongly emphasized in the way a movie is presented in advertisements and publicity. Most people are enamored by *high-concept* movies—films with contemporary themes, extravagant action, and a big name cast. Big studio productions, and the media exposure that accompanies them, can give such films a "must-see" aura. Long before they came out, mass audiences had seen the

10–2 *Indecent Proposal* Although movie critics can bury some films, others survive and even flourish in the face of negative press. *Indecent Proposal* (1993), the story of a millionaire (Robert Redford) who pays a young married woman (Demi Moore) for an intimate night with him, received generally bad reviews. Yet the film went on to be one of the biggest movies of the year at the box office. When a story resonates with the general public in some deeply felt ways, critics normally have little influence over their opinions. (Paramount Pictures)

startling and intriguing images of *The Lost World: Jurassic Park* (1997), *Saving Private Ryan* (1998), and *Mission Impossible 2* (2000), and waited expectantly to see the movies.

- **Recommendation of Critics**. Just as we learn about fashion and fads through the mass media, so too do magazine, newspaper, and TV critics help shape attitudes that influence general movie taste. Although the exact nature of their ultimate audience impact raises some questions, if a mainline Hollywood film receives unanimous rave media reviews, big crowds will normally follow. Although some films with bloated budgets are rightfully, even severely, panned by reviewers, certain movies prove to be bulletproof. *Wild Wild West* (1999) was given mixed or negative reviews by the vast majority of film critics, but the movie went on to score well at the box office, living up to industry predictions. An offbeat film with a good story but a small advertising budget often times cannot be saved no matter how well the critics treat it, regardless of its superior qualities.

- **Word of Mouth.** Getting a positive movie review in person from someone whose opinion we trust is the strongest endorsement a movie can have. "In our business, the one thing you can't buy is word of mouth," says Tom Sherak, VP of marketing and distribution at 20th Century Fox. Although the process can be slow, when a movie generates a good report from people who have seen it, a wave of interest can steadily build. New Line's very successful *Seven* (1995) was a very dark movie with high-profile stars—Morgan Freeman and Brad Pitt—not normally associated with such films. Chris Pula, who was in charge of marketing, felt that if the audience had wrong expectations, "It would've completely handicapped our word of mouth." Although the advertising budget was substantial, the strategy was to obscure the glamour of the stars and emphasize the mystery, relying on a positive audience response to the story to spread. The grapevine is still a lively medium.

  Word-of-mouth momentum has taken on a new dimension with the media's fascination for quickly announcing the top revenue grossing film of the weekend. Major newspapers, network television, and syndicated shows such as *Entertainment Tonight* incorporate the joys and disappointments of studios regarding box office figures into their daily gossip about the industry. Moviegoers, fascinated by statistical wars between rival movies in distribution, see these figures as an endorsement for a film just released, and a strong opening will bring a lemming-like response. "It's become like an addiction," comments Sherak.

Predictions based on consumer loyalty to particular actors are chancy. Superstars have instant recognition but filmmakers have long ago learned that putting them in the wrong movie can be disastrous—Jack Nicholson, Sylvester Stallone, and Arnold Schwarzenegger have had their share of flops. With the exception of Disney, the logos of major studios no longer inspire confidence as they did in earlier times.

Market researchers have tried to pin down the cultural climate of the society in order to create marketing strategies. *Impulse buying*, in fact, accounts for most of the moviegoing decisions. Research says that over one half of the public decides to see a film on the same day they attend. Is there a genuine trend toward family-oriented values? Just what kind and degree of violent action triggers audience interest? Is the subject of dying and death a valid basis for romantic stories, or are such stories simply depressing? How explicitly sexual should themes be in a relationship movie? The answers are hard to firmly fix. But once a movie becomes a hit, a **sequel** will surely follow. This happens because, quite simply, the original film clearly revealed popular tastes.

Previews

Studios regularly screen their films before selected theater audiences in advance of their general release. The primary source for audience reaction to movies is the National Research Group (NRG), an independent market research company employed by almost all the studios to gather and analyze audience responses to particular movies. NRG tests movie ideas, trailers, print advertising, and titles, in addition to registering viewer's comments about upcoming movies after special screenings. There are two primary ways in which this test marketing works.

1) Production Previews.   A movie may be previewed long before its release date so that the producers can get a practical gauge on how the **cut**—the latest edited version—plays to a live audience. In the months of shooting and postproduction, those who have worked closely with the project can lose perspective. Showing the film to an audience on a studio-lot theater can give a skewed viewpoint because attitudes are naturally sympathetic to the filmmaking community. A theater is picked in a "good preview city" (San Diego, Sacramento, and Seattle are favorites), so that production executives and marketing heads may observe and question the audience. With this information, the filmmakers go back into the project with ideas for fine-tuning it. The process is especially useful for comedy films. If there was no laughter in the theater, it is a pretty clear sign that something needs to be fixed.

The process can backfire. Paramount's *The Temp* (1993)—a movie about a fill-in secretary creating havoc at a cookie factory—was previewed by a test audience who thought that the ending was too cruel. Less than a month before its scheduled opening, and after a frantic series of conflicting rewrites, a decision was made by committee. The studio reshot and substituted another ending, and the result was an even less crowd-pleasing climax. The movie was both an artistic and financial disaster. A studio production member commented later, "No one person should be blamed for what happened. The ending is the result of a collaborative effort on the part of the filmmakers, the test audiences, and the studio. The studio system, for better or worse, operates by collaboration." On the other hand, after director Steven Soderbergh recognized that the audience at a screening reacted very negatively to a seven-minute shot in *Out of Sight* (1999), he wisely cut out the bravura camerawork that took the audience out of the film. Sometimes, second guessing works.

2) Marketing Previews.   A film preview at one or more theaters may be arranged before its scheduled play-date in hopes of not only attaching added excitement to a

10–3   *The Cable Guy*   For the high-profile movie *The Cable Guy* (1996), the publicity department at Sony had an especially difficult task. The **marketing previews** showed strong audience dissatisfaction. Because the film starred the very popular comic actor Jim Carrey, many people had thought that the movie would build on the comic goodwill he had won in his pervious films. But the movie had a very dark, even cruel, edge to it that defied easy description. Although the film was not strictly a financial failure, the anticipated box office revenues by the studio were well short of its expectations.
(Columbia Pictures)

film, thereby creating a strong *word-of-mouth* campaign, but also determining the advertising and release strategies for the film. "It's a way of separating yourself from the pack," says producer Scott Rudin. *The First Wives Club* (1996) had very successful sneak previews in 1,100 theaters nationwide, had its official debut the following weekend, and broke the all-time box-office record for movies released in September.

The process becomes baffling, especially if a film with high expectations gets disappointing reviews from the preview audience **(10–3)**. This happened with Martin Scorsese's *Goodfellas* (1990), when people after preview showings complained about its level of violence and extreme length. But by the time it was released, the intact movie had gained great press from the critics. Exit-interviews of audiences suddenly changed, following the lead of the critics in praising the film, and the movie went on to a very successful run. Normally, films that do not play well and have no hope of being helped with last minute tinkering are routed for a *fast play-off* before the bad word spreads.

BACKGROUND OF THE RATING SYSTEM

"I'd like to think that the industry is motivated by conscience or some sense of morality. But the fact is, if you make R-rated movies, you exclude a large part of the audience."

An anonymous studio executive

A motion picture code was first established in 1922 in response to a series of sex and drug scandals that dominated newspaper headlines of the country. Fearful of popular reactions and governmental regulations, the Motion Picture Producers and Distributors of America (MPPDA) was established under Will Hays, a former postmaster general, to monitor moviemaking. The Hays Office continued through the 1920s, but became capriciously zealous under successor Joseph Breen in 1933. For the next twenty years the Breen Office, with its ethical standards mirroring the more conservative moral attitudes of the Catholic Church, controlled the limits of taste for the entire movie industry, scrutinizing every line of every script that was produced by the major studios.

This restrictive cultural tone prevailed in the Production Code Administration (PCA), without whose seal a film could not be released. Plot lines that depicted crime and criminals in a realistic manner or stories that explored human relationships in their sexual dimension were banned, except when the violators were duly punished by the last act. Scenes with "lustful kissing" or suggestive dancing were exorcised, even

10–4   *Midnight Cowboy*   The definition of what is morally acceptable continuously fluctuates in our society. Despite being rated X, John Schlesinger's *Midnight Cowboy* (1969) won an Academy Award and both Jon Voight and Dustin Hoffman were nominated for one. By today's standards, the same film would get no stronger than an "R" rating. Because of the radical social and ethical changes happening in the late 1960s, movies began to reflect the rapid transformations seeping into every level of the American culture.   (United Artists)

⭐ THE CURRENT RATING CLASSIFICATIONS

- **G** rating is for general audiences, indicating the movie contains nothing that would be "patently offensive to parents whose young children might view the film." Sexual content is not present, but mild violence is acceptable.

- **PG** rating is for themes that parents may find unsuitable for children under 17. There should be no drug use, no "cumulative violence" or explicit sex, but brief nudity is allowed.

- **PG-13** rating was added in 1984 to cover those films that had some sexually explicit language and a degree of violence that might be disturbing for anyone under 13. It is a poorly defined area, a catch-all for sexuality and violence that is not deemed too strong for the early teen years.

- **R** rating contains nudity or lovemaking, hard language, drug abuse, or ongoing violence of a graphic nature. Persons under 17 cannot attend without being with a parent or guardian.

- **NC-17** rating was created in 1990 to cover movies with explicit sexuality or very graphic violence, some of which would have been labeled **X** under the previous guidelines. The MPAA takes no stand on the legal ramifications of the content of these films, leaving that to the courts.

- **NR** indicates that the film is not rated. It is not imperative that a filmmaker submit a movie to the rating board, however the NR label seems to set the film apart into release limbo land.

In 1998, for example, in round numbers profiling the 662 movie releases judged, **G** rated films held 6%; **PG** 11%; **PG-13** 17%; **R** 65%; **NC-17** 1%.

The actual rating board, named the *Classification and Rating Administration*, is made up of twelve men and women drawn from a cross-section of racial and employment backgrounds but all of them residing in Los Angeles. Their names are kept secret to protect them from pressure from both the movie industry and other interested groups. Filmmakers never come into contact with board members, but may express their concerns through a MPAA executive. Producers who are unhappy with the initial rating of their films, after reading the board rationale, usually resubmit them with editing that brings them into line and satisfies the members.

between married couples; a long list of words, including such expressions as "gawd," "hell," and "nuts" were not allowed. These codes were not only tolerated by the studios but quite rigidly enforced.

By the mid-1950s, cultural tastes were changing, strict moral attitudes regarding sex became more relaxed, and movies began to reflect the real world in which most people lived. Finally in 1968, the MPAA (Motion Picture Association of America) established the first rating system, one based on perceived viewer maturity **(10–4)**. The stated purpose of the self-imposed rating system is to give "advance information to enable parents to make judgments on a movie they want their children to see or not see."

Today, an essential part of marketing a movie is determined by the **rating** that it receives. In the United States, large segments of the movie audience can be encour-

10–5 *There's Something about Mary*   As his girlfriend's parents (Keith David and Markie Post) watch with contempt and horror in the bathroom, an emergency rescue squad responds to Ted's (Ben Stiller) dilemma—having his "family jewels" caught in his zipper. The comedy movie *There's Something about Mary* (1998) pushed back the sexual boundaries of what mainline studios present in an "R" rated film. The U.S. movie audience heartily accepted it, making the film the surprise box office hit of 1998.   (20th Century Fox)

aged, warned, stimulated, or banned by the rating assigned to a movie. Significantly, different marketing strategies for a film come into play with this designation.

The rating system appears to have been useful. Polls show that the majority of parents refer to the ratings when judging a film. But the value and effects of the ratings go well beyond those intentions. The system, in a purely informational way, tells all moviegoers the level of explicitness they can expect for their money. Film producers target certain markets when they send the cut of their movie to the *MPAA* for review and a rating. It is the industry's method of shaping the limits of popular taste, an important step when selling such a volatile product as movies.

At one time, studios deliberately sought out R ratings for many movies, reasoning that the designation would draw patrons who wanted films with more risqué or graphic experiences unavailable on network television **(10–5)**. Now the expanded interests of the industry, with the huge **tie-in** and **home video** businesses surrounding movie production, can more often best be exploited with films rated lower than R-rating. The studios today take a much more market-oriented approach and regularly demand that film come in as PG-13 or PG, opening the films to a larger share of the market. Research analysts have shown that PG-13 and softer rated films are three times more likely to make $100 million than R rated films.

The old X rating originally assigned to some mainstream films was usurped by the porno industry to give its films a racy recognition. Film producers are not required to submit their films to the rating board for classification, but labeling a movie NR seriously limits distribution possibilities in this country. Writer/director James Toback (*Two Girls and a Guy,* 1998) is one of many filmmakers who has run into the problem: "They can say and do whatever they want, because they can always respond with, 'Fine, then don't get rated—no one is forcing you to get a rating,' knowing that you can't get your movie shown in 25 percent of the theaters in the country and you can't advertise. So it's *de facto* censorship."

Cultural values and biases in the United States have continued to randomly skew how the NC-17 and other ratings are applied. The NC-17 rating has not worked as the code designers had planned. Rather than creating a category in which serious filmmakers could explore adult themes freely, major studios have backed away from this rating because of restrictions banning the showing of such films by certain theater chains and leaseholders of theater property. The situation for NC-17, however, is in a state of flux because of the relative box office and videocassette success of MGM's *Showgirls* (1995) here and overseas, despite getting terrible critical reviews. The film broke many barriers both in its wide distribution pattern and the media's acceptance of its advertising.

Over the years, the movie industry has tried to take the pulse of the public, at times lagging behind changing standards of contemporary taste, at other times stretching the boundaries. In 1953, *The Moon Is Blue* was condemned by the Production Code for using the word "virgin," and yet by 1969 the X rated *Midnight Cowboy* won an Academy Award for best picture. In 1993, Phillip Noyce's *Sliver* was first given an NC-17 rating because of its voyeuristic sexual content, until over 100 cuts were made to bring it an R rating. Frankly sexual scenes, whether in a rape situation or in a loving encounter, are given the same weight and regularly assigned an R rating, with more explicit sex of any kind getting NC-17. In addition, some have complained of built-in sexist attitudes, and that frontal nudity of women, for example, is acceptable in many films, whereas rare frontal nudity for men will usually mean a more restrictive rating. Director Antonia Bird found that her film *Priest* (1994), a well-told story about a young cleric struggling with his homosexual leanings, had to be severely cut from its European version to get an R rating in the United States. As a Britisher, Bird observed, "We don't think violence is acceptable—but we think sex is great. You guys like violence and hate sex." This statement perhaps oversimplifies the issue, but does voice an often-heard complaint.

The issues of sex and violence in film continue to cause controversy. Although the two issues are often linked together, some ethical scholars argue that the two are very separate discussions. Explicit sex is consistently regarded more seriously than explicit violence by the MPAA board (the reverse is true in Europe). In a convoluted manner, frequently the values of this society are ultimately reflected in the MPAA rating system. Violence in films has been a cause of public concern recently **(10–6)**. In films rated PG-13 and higher, the level of unrelenting graphic violence grows more intense. Since the 1970s, realism in films has been popular, and more artfully convincing renditions of violence have taken on a competitive edge among filmmakers. The darkly blunt atmosphere of Martin Scorsese's *Taxi Driver* (1976) evolved into the high-powered cruelty of Quentin Tarantino's *Reservoir Dogs* (1992) or the nonstop gratuitous violence of John Woo's *Hard Target* (1992) or Brian Helgeland's *Payback* (1999).

"Slasher films," for example, are now a separate genre, and these movies have become most profitable when the frequency and explicitness of gore matches the inventiveness of its presentation. The dramatic story need for conflict has been translated into deadly and unsparing combat and worse. Responding to the relentless excesses of Joel Schumacher's *8MM* (1999), studio story analyst Katherine Fugate writes, "The onslaught of images, abuse, hurtful words, and misogyny finally lead me to reduce my weekly pay by declaring 'no more serial killers' to the studio. By eliminating the genre alone, my workload lessened noticeably. At least I'm able to sleep better at night without the constant reminder that the majority of men [writing] want me spread-eagled, beaten, dead, raped, drugged, or vivisected."

10–6   *The Fight Club*   Excessive violence in movies has been a center of controversy for parents, government, and the movie business. Box office revenues from movies with violent action generally have flourished and the movie industry is reluctant to tamper with success. But studies linking the apparent sanctioning of extreme graphic cruelty and gore with an imitative audience mind set are disturbing. *The Fight Club* (1999), with Brad Pitt (pictured here) and Edward Norton, tested the limits of what violent activity could be shown within the R rating.   (20th Century Fox)

French filmmaker Bertrand Tavernier tells that violence as it is presented in movies currently is used without a moral motive or consequence. He distinguishes between films that show violence as an aberration and those that use it as mere spectacle. *The Wild Bunch* (1968) was a breakthrough movie in terms of its graphic depiction of violent death. Tavernier comments:

> *It's a film that was considered too violent when it came out. But there is a lot of attention from Peckinpah on the effects of violence: a kid, a woman being wounded, somebody crying, a child frightened. It's not only a matter of violence, it's a mater of the result—of the reverse shot. Now in many films you don't have the reverse shot on people who are submitted to violence. In one John Woo film, a woman is thrown from a plane. OK, its an incredibly beautiful shot. Exciting. But where is the effect of her death? Where is the body of the woman? Raoul Walsh or Sam Peckinpah would have a shot to show it's a woman who was killed. Now there is a lack of reaction shots. Violence has become just another special effect.*

Violence must be "excessive and sadistic" before a rating stronger than an R is given. Because of a gradual increase in the tolerance of these norms, it seems that the board itself has become desensitized from overexposure. The rating policy quite regularly appears to consider the *amount*, rather than the *context* of violence, as more important. There is also an unfounded assumption that violence shown to those under the age of thirteen is more harmful than those in their early teens. But studies have shown that regular exposure of both groups to this kind of violence desensitizes them toward reports of brutality, and fosters in young people deep-seated anxiety, resulting in compulsive, disturbing thoughts and nightmares. Copycat mayhem raises legitimate concern for those persons aware of the power of movies to influence antisocial behavior. Most producers have learned the game of what the MPAA board will allow for a rating, and they play within those vague guidelines. In future years, the rating system, for what it is worth, will continue to evolve with the taste and tolerance of the public.

ADVERTISING AND THE MEDIA

"There's no dearth of ways of getting a message across to the public. Everywhere you turn, some advertiser is trying to get your attention, whether it's the top of a taxi or the back of the bus or the stall of a bathroom."

Marc Shmuger, VP of marketing
at Sony Pictures

The **advertising** unit of a studio arranges for the creation of ads in newspapers, magazines, billboards, radio, and television. To do this, they must first decide what is distinctive about the movie, so that it can be promoted in the artwork and copy. When done right, great advertising anchors the marketing image of a movie in the minds of the public. The **media unit** then lays out the actual strategy for purchasing the space. To help with this, outside advertising agencies sometimes are enlisted, with the studios giving advice and approval as a client.

The movie industry spends almost $2 billion a year domestically in advertising. Since the 1970s, television advertising has become the preferred media buy for most major releases. In 1998, over $1 billion was spent on television alone. Karen Hermelin, a VP of marketing at New Line Cinema, claims that, "70 percent to 80 percent of opening-weekend decisions are made based on what people saw on TV the night before or that week." The beauty of television advertising is that audiences for particular movies can be targeted based on their TV viewing habits. Movies geared to male-oriented audiences favor advertising on such programs as "NFL Monday Night Football" or "NYPD Blue"; female-oriented films choose "Friends" or "Ally McBeal"; movies with youthful themes advertise on "Beverly Hills 90210," "The X-Files," or "Saturday Night Live"; very high-profile movies that cross-over demographic lines might use "The Simpsons" or "ER." Whatever the current season's programming line-ups offer, movie marketers are alert to audience taste in entertainment. Hermelin goes on, "The great thing about TV is that you can match the programs sensibility to the movie's sensibility." Television advertising expenditures also go to Cable TV Networks, Syndicated TV, and Spot TV—short commercials not aligned with a particular show and targeted to specific demographic, geographic, and psychographic audiences. Radio advertising is a small but constant media outlet in the advertising picture. The Internet has now entered into the mix and is being explored by all parties. Studios report that Web sites for *Titanic* (1997) and *Armageddon* (1998) drew millions of "hits." The cost commitment for all of this, however, is very high and therefore very dangerous if it fails.

Print advertising, especially in newspapers, has traditionally been important for movies. Apart from major newspapers—*The New York Times* and *The Los Angeles Times*—in media centers that are used as advertising showcases for the arrival of movies, newspapers are important as usefully splashy means for movie listings. Magazine advertising has the advantage of delivering highly targeted audiences. *Premiere* and *Entertainment Weekly*, for example, have a built-in readership interested in movies. The "city" magazines and newspapers of every metropolitan area offer the right readership profile for a movie industry that likes to be seen as the trendsetter of cultural tastes. In addition to these, outdoor advertising can be selectively effective with movies with quick visual identification.

From the 1920s, movie posters, called **one sheets,** have been the icons of the business. Some posters have survived as genuine art; others as supremely clever promotional work **(10–7)**. For example, in the past thirty years, Tony Seiniger has been a major designer of posters for a score of very successful films, including *Jaws* (1975); *One Flew Over the Cuckoo's Nest* (1975); *Born on the Fourth of July* (1989); *Total Recall* (1990); and others. For *Alien* (1980), to promote its weird futuristic suspense, he created a single egg cracking with light, with the great line "In Space No One Can Hear You Scream." *Home Alone* (1990) was teamed with the telling copy "A Family Comedy Without A Family." A tendency in film posters is to seasonally copy styles that have proved successful for leading movies in the genre. It may become current, for example, to feature the stars' faces in profile if a leading film has made money with that format.

10–7 *Citizen Kane* Movie **print advertising** materials are an art form unto themselves. Most ad campaigns are meticulously planned and executed. But some are unintentionally strange or comical. The uncertainty and confusion that RKO had about their extremely controversial film *Citizen Kane* (1941) can be seen in their ad campaign. The lead *"It's Terrific"* seems to be throw-away filler. The poster misses the film's darker investigation into the life of an incredibly wealthy and controversial man, instead presenting an unrecognizable Orson Welles in an oddly heroic stance. The image is one better suited to *Gone with the Wind* than the figure of a driven and haunted Charles Foster Kane. (RKO)

Certain films present a problem for advertisers. Orion Pictures found that to be true with *Dances with Wolves* (1990). Because they thought young audiences would be turned off if they perceived it as a Western, its advertising pitched the film as an action movie to that target group. At the same time, it was billed as rich in the suppressed heritage of our history to the older population. The approach worked, bringing in a surprisingly diverse audience. Other films, such as *Hudson Hawk* (1991) (an out-of-control caper movie with pretensions toward musical comedy), prove impossible to conceptualize in ads, and the productions fail at the box office. Some years ago, *Family Business* (1989) starring Sean Connery, Dustin Hoffman, and Matthew Broderick appeared to be a sure hit on the face of it. But the cast failed to generate the right chemistry. When the studio tried to sell it only on the strength of its cast, with the generic adjectives "Terrific," "Wonderful," and "Brilliant," the public got no sense of the film's content. There is no advertising that can save a bad film.

With the **Annual Key Art Awards** given out each year, the movie industry recognizes excellence in the creation and design of movie advertising materials. The best creative marketing work is honored in the areas of outdoor advertising, theatrical trailers, print ads, TV commercials, video packaging, lobby displays, and other media. Movies afford artists in every medium a rich and almost unlimited resource to express their interpretive talents.

Trailers

> *"A bad trailer can hurt much more than a good trailer can help. When I see a bad trailer, you'll never get me back, no matter how many TV ad buys you make. As a moviegoer, I've made up my mind. You just can't recover from that."*
>
> Joe Roth, Film producer

Most theaters show ten to fifteen minutes of pre-show material, including four or five **trailers**, spots hailing concession stand delights and the *THX* sound system, admonitions for silence, and the theater chain logo. Trailers—also called "previews of coming attractions," or simply "previews" by most moviegoers—are the most powerful sales tool for future movies. The cost for producing a trailer usually falls in the $75,000 to $200,000 range. These two-minute shorts have an ideal chance to win over a captive and already receptive audience when shown in theaters. Normally, trailers must be ready six to ten weeks before the film opens. This abbreviated presentation of the film is crucial to its future success. If, because of the trailer, the audience is not intrigued by the film, the studio has no one to blame but itself. It is, after all, a capsule form showing what the film-makers think is appealing about their movie.

Distilling the story on the screen has some risks. More recently, producers in their anxiety to insure that the audience "gets" the message of their movie have tended to tell the entire plot in digest form. Going to see the actual film may seem redundant. But with the high cost of tickets and the competition for leisure time activities, audiences have become inclined to want no doubts left about the outcome of the entertainment they seek. Filmmakers can also misrepresent the tone of a film. An early trailer of *Boyz 'n the Hood* (1991) presented the film simply as a violent story about gangs in a south central neighborhood of Los Angeles, rather than a tragic story of a heroic young man struggling with real issues in his daily life. For *Rising Sun* (1993) with Wesley Snipes and Sean Connery, a film in danger of being labeled either a "buddy-buddy" movie or a Japan-bashing piece, 20th Century Fox tested thirteen different trailers from several companies before settling on one that presented the film as a crosscultural thriller.

Teaser trailers—often only the titles and a dramatic voiceover—announce big-budget films six months or more ahead of their release dates. In one famous instance, the teaser trailer influenced the actual movie. The teaser for *Robin Hood: Prince of Thieves* (1991) created the unique imagery of an arrow whizzing toward a tree and splitting another arrow. The impact on test audiences was so effective that director Kevin Reynolds incorporated it into the released version of the movie. A much-praised teaser was done for *Twister* (1996), in which neither the cast nor the special effects image of the twister was ever shown. What audiences did see was the view of a darkened sky from behind the wheel of a truck with a tire suddenly flying at it and smashing the windshield. Even more important is what the audience heard—a booming soundtrack with over 300 sound effects that enveloped them.

Distilling the essential theme of a movie and then translating it into a two-minute compelling visual summary is a small but crucially important art in itself. Produced by about ten boutique companies that service the studios and independents, the selection of material, the pacing, the compressing of the action (called **upcutting**) can rivet us to the screen. It is not uncommon to hear the complaint that the previews were better than the featured movie. A great trailer will bring back its audience. The Australian film *Crocodile Dundee* (1986) won expected attendance with the kicker at the end of its trailer as actor Paul Hogan exclaims, "You call that a knife?... *This* is a knife!"

Publicity

The publicity department at a studio focuses it efforts on creating a positive "buzz" around its movies **(10–8)**. The term refers to those charged expectations fueled by feverish rumors that circulate during production through the release dates of a film. This media climate does not happen by chance, rather it is an orchestrated mix of subtle press influence and blatant hype. Each film is assigned a *unit publicist* to meet the daily demands of the media and public. A *stills photographer* shoots the performers in action and behind the scenes throughout the production. *Press kits*, both printed and on video, are made as promotional tools for newspapers and television spots. The attractive thing for the studios about such publicity is that, compared to advertising, it is relatively inexpensive.

10–8   *Dead Presidents*   Finding the audience for a particular film is challenging, especially when the intent of the movie's producers is to widen its appeal and go beyond its normal demographic market. *Dead Presidents* (1995) was such a film. Its story recounts the tragic plight of a group of African-American men who grow up in a ghetto, go to Vietnam, and come back to desperation and a life of crime. Buena Vista Pictures was successful in marketing it as a **crossover film,** that is, one that bridges cultural gaps and draws in a wider range of people than normally comes to films with an all black cast.   (Buena Vista Pictures)

★ MOVIE TITLES

The first contact we have with a film is its title. A good title should give some sense of the theme, tweak one's curiosity, and be easily repeated. A bad title can hurt a film. "There's no way to exaggerate how important a movie title can be. We're surrounded by so much cultural clutter that you're halfway home if you can find a title that helps you distinguish your product and connect it with a specific image or sell-phrase," says producer Joe Roth.

Because many movies come from books or plays, their titles simply reflect the original source. But others are composed strictly with the movie audience in mind. Movie titles come in all sizes and connotations: complete sentences (*Don't Be a Menace to South Central while Drinking Your Juice in the Hood*, 1995); prepositional phrases (*About Last Night*, 1986); gerunds (*Raising Arizona*, 1987); inseparable pairs (*Tender Mercies*,

1983); personal names (*Shirley Valentine*, 1989); exotic name places (*Casablanca*, 1942); traffic signs (*U-Turn*, 1997); even bland adjectives (*Big*, 1988). Some titles are provocative (*Scent of a Woman*, 1992); menacing (*Hollywood Chainsaw Hookers*, 1988); enigmatic (*If*, 1968); inexplicable (*To Wong Foo*, 1995); accurately descriptive (*Clueless*, 1995); or, when released in England, mistakenly comical (*Free Willy*, 1993). Producer Mel Brooks laments, "The biggest mistake I made was calling the film *Life Stinks*. I assumed that America understood irony, since it's an ironic title. I was wrong." For this and whatever other reasons, the MGM film died quickly. For a variety of reasons, some titles just do not work. What did Jack Nicholson's *The Two Jakes* (1990) say about its being a sequel to the convoluted tale of treachery in *Chinatown* (1974)? The newer title seems better suited for a comedy.

Studios register their properties and titles with the MPAA (Motion Picture Association of America), a system that allows each studio to retain control over 250 titles (and because the largest studios have many affiliated production units, they hold thousands of title rights). Disputes sometimes arise over the use of movie titles. When two movies appear during the same season with common words or similar sounding titles, the issue is arbitrated by the MPAA. For example, when a Meg Ryan romantic comedy entitled *Paris Match* was to be released shortly after Billy Crystal's *Forget Paris* (1995) of the same genre, arbiters sided with the latter film noting that the similarities could be confusing to the public. Ryan's film title was changed to *French Kiss* (1995). Issues are often resolved when studios simply buy or trade rights to titles held by other companies.

Some publicity departments are able to *spin* the theme of a movie to become a current cultural issue. For example, *Thelma and Louise* (1991) (a Warner Bros. production) was presented as a movie that makes a statement about women's culturally repressed rage toward men, and therefore newsworthy enough to give it a cover story in *Time* magazine (a Time/Warner publication). To be successful, another Warner Bros. film, *Malcolm X* (1992), was seen to need a "crossover" audience—the white moviegoing public going to see a controversial black hero—and therefore studio publicity sent study guides to history teachers in 100 top markets. They also hired a Black advertising company to create a public relations campaign to influence opinion leaders in the African-American media. At the same time, Warner Books republished his autobiography after 30 years, and it became a best seller.

There was a time when the movie industry used media—magazines and newspapers, mostly—to parade its stars and latest hits, relying on them for favorable stories and pictures. It is still true today, but now the situation is a two-way street. With the expansion in media possibilities, entertainment producers in every medium need the movie industry to provide the content of *their* work. With the proliferation of entertainment programs giving inside scoops on upcoming films, late night talk shows competing to get the hottest stars, magazines dependent on images of the movie elite to satisfy the taste of film fans, newspapers feeding gossip about the movie community, tabloid television sensationalizing the gossip, and books being published simultaneously with the release dates of movies, it is not always clear who is using whom. The relationship of movies to the other media has become neatly symbiotic.

Tie-ins

"The film isn't so much an end in itself as a way for the company to get into the Godzilla business."

John Calley, President of Sony, which produced *Godzilla* (1998)

Today a select group of high profile movies bring with them images that can be merchandised far beyond a theater auditorium. The ultimate value of such movies, and the justification for their budget, often hinges on how the concept of the films can be translated into product lines to be licensed to toy, clothing, and food corporations. For the industry, the financial rewards are enormous. Movie and TV licensing average between $6 billion and $8 billion a year, more than the annual box office income for films, about $5 billion yearly. The standard royalty fees to studios are from 7 percent to 10 percent.

For an individual film to make a strong impact, a number of elements have to combine. Primarily, a film must become an **event movie,** with its archetypal characters being dynamic enough to approach not-so-lofty mythic levels. In a rare circumstance in which studios have given up financial control, *Star Wars* (1977) creator George Lucas negotiated with 20th Century Fox for his eventual sole ownership of merchandising rights to movie allied products. To date, this has meant about $4 billion in licensing fees. Paramount's *Star Trek* movies and TV series challenge that figure. The largest tie-in market to date, however, may go to the dinosaur imagery licensed by the producers of *Jurassic Park* (1993). Thousands of product licenses were contracted worldwide, with the revenues still being counted at Universal Studios.

The products spinning out from these films fill catalogs: *Batman Returns* (1992) issued 120 licenses for products such as breakfast cereal, yo-yos, pajamas, computer games, and T-shirts; *Home Alone II* (1992) opened just in time for Christmas, with replicas of Macaulay Culkin's "Talkboy" tape recorder; *Bram Stoker's Dracula* (1992) inspired a high fashion line; *Malcolm X* (1992) licensed the "X" for a variety of 160 products, and with the help of endorsements from Michael Jordan and director Spike

10–9   *Toy Story*   Tie-ins are today a major consideration for studios when entering into a film project featuring images or merchandise that can be popularly marketed. The licensing of products spinning out of these films has become an independent source of immense revenue in the movie industry. Characters created by the computer graphic company Pixar for *Toy Story* (1995) and *Toy Story II* (1999) show up on plastic cups and children's wear around the world. Buzz Lightyear, therefore, is not only entertaining on the screen but also has a long shelf-life in toy stores. With its theme parks as their marketing foundation, the Walt Disney Company has long been considered the leader in this field.   (The Walt Disney Company)

Lee, a store in Los Angeles was opened to exclusively merchandise "X" clothing. The Walt Disney Company (Buena Vista Films), however, leads the way. *The Little Mermaid* (1989) has become the second most licensed image, next to Mickey Mouse, for Disney, with *Pocahontas* (1995) and *Hercules* (1997) not far behind. But the ultimate Disney merchandising coup may go to its promotion of *Toy Story* (1995) **(10–9)**. This highly successful animated feature is filled with images of toys and games—Mr. Potato Head, Slinky Dog, Woody, Buzz Lightyear, Erector sets, Battleship—many of which have been on the market for years. Commercial tie-ins with Coca Cola, Burger King, Frito Lay, and others reproduced these images endlessly, all to the benefit of Disney Studios licensing. Not to be outdone, Lucasfilm's *Star Wars—Episode I: The Phantom Menace* (1999) franchised its tie-ins for this film and its two sequels to Hasbro toys for $600 million, along with collectible cans for Pepsico and an array of games and glasses for Taco Bell, KFC, and Pizza Hut.

Disney and Warner Bros. also have their own retail chain stores to sell and advertise their movie logos on merchandise. Hollywood is firmly planted in cyberspace and sells its products via various pages on the World Wide Web. All of the major studios have sites available on the Internet where they promote not only their latest releases but sell their logos on everything from T-shirts to toys. Smaller distribution companies, such as Alliance Communications, find the democratic nature of the Web gives them a fairer network to present their products.

In another attractive commercial vein, **product placement** in movies is a lucrative sideline. In the past, Disney Studios sent out a letter soliciting companies to put their products—autos, beer, detergent bottles, etc.—into their films: $20,000 for it to be seen; $40,000 for an actor to mention it; $60,000 for an actor to use it. Almost nothing one sees in a film today arrives there by chance. In the movie business, everything is for sale.

THE SELLING OF MOVIES

The sales division of a large studio gets involved with the movie in the preproduction stage when the size and climate of the project is being determined. With the heavy investment made in most studio productions, a firm sales plan must be envisioned as early as possible. One crucial area to be projected is the **release pattern** for any given movie.

- **Limited Release.** Studios take on a few films each year that must be handled with special care **(10–10)**. Often, these quality films have controversial or unconventional subject matter or have familiar themes that have been given an unusual production treatment. In any case, the studio may decide to open the film in the major media centers of Los Angeles, Toronto, and New York, considered sophisticated movie cities, so that influential audiences and reviewers can generate a whirl of interest, sending it on to wider distribution.

- **Slow Release.** In a variation of the previous pattern, studios will slowly release certain films in which they have confidence, but which they recognize still need careful handling. This may mean opening in perhaps 200–500 selected theaters and building on the good will of the movie. Costs can be kept down while waiting for the film to catch on. As the momentum builds, the sales office stays alert, pushing the film to a *wide release* at just the right time.

- **Wide Release.** With a maximum advertising blitz, many films open on more than 3,000 American and Canadian screens on the same day. This is very expensive: The cost of a single 35mm print runs about $1,200; a 70mm print up to $10,000. A saturation release can work both for potential blockbusters, by overwhelming the public with the media presence of the films, and for the potential box-office flop, by getting people into theaters for a fast monetary return before grim reviews and bad word-of-mouth response sinks in.

10–10   *American Beauty*   Because *American Beauty* (1999) (with Kevin Spacey and Annette Bening) did not fit into an easily recognized film genre, its studio wisely decided to open the movie in a very **limited release** pattern—just sixteen screens nationwide— thereby depending on positive word of mouth to ignite the campaign. The marketing strategy worked perfectly. The stylish dark comedy about American suburban frustrations quickly caught on with audiences, and in two weeks the movie release expanded to over 400 screens, then to 1,500. When planning works so well, the industry marvels, applauds, and, in this case, rewards the film with Oscars.   (Dream-Works Pictures)

A major studio will maintain a central sales office in Los Angeles, as well as regional sales offices throughout the United States and Canada, with sales staffs and bookers to closely monitor its film rentals in every city. Although the opening weekend is crucial to a movie's box-office success, the second week is also very telling. Normally, films will experience a 20 percent to 35 percent "fall-off" in attendance from the first week. This is considered acceptable. A fall-off of only 10 percent would indicate that the film had "legs"—the stuff to sustain a long theatrical run—and more money might be found to accelerate and fine-tune the ad campaign; a 50 percent decline in the second week says the movie is fast dying and advertising budgets are cut back accordingly.

The Movie Calendar

"We're working in an environment that is more cluttered and competitive than ever. And it's not just the peak times of summer and Christmas. There are no slow weekends anymore."

Gerry Rich, Head of MGM marketing

In this last stage, nothing is more important to a major studio movie than its **release date**. The very content of many motion pictures is shaped for the seasons of the year. With decades of marketing experience, Hollywood has molded its movies to conveniently match with school vacations, the weather, and national holidays. The studios incessantly jockey for a starting position. Films that claim blockbuster status stake out their dates first; lesser movies use these as referent points and finesse themselves around them, avoiding head-to-head confrontation, if possible. Traditionally, Fridays open a movie run, although Wednesdays sometimes are used to get a jump on other films.

- **The Summer Season.** Mid-May to mid-September. Summertime holds the greatest promise for the movie industry as people have more leisure time to spend on entertainment. Emotionally, summer is associated with vacations and carefree fun. Apart from an occasional specially promoted serious movie with a strong pre-sold audience, the studios emphasize light and fun-filled movies, while avoiding controversial or heavy themes. Studios bring out their very big-budget, hi-tech films early in the summer season in hopes that large crowds will carry these movies for many months during this long period. 20th Century Fox executive Tom Sherak says, "In the summer, people have a fluffy, fun-in-the-sun attitude. In the fall, you can aim a little higher."

- **The Fall Season.** Mid-September to mid-November. Studios use autumn to bring out more literate and complex stories. A back-to-school spirit seems to encourage people to get serious and, in turn, watch these more challenging films. Movies drawn from thoughtful books or successful plays commonly open during this season. These films are often designated by their studio as "important"—that is, designed for Oscar nominations—and releasing them later in the year allows the films to be fresh and newly established in the mind of the public.

- **The Christmas Season**. Mid-November to early January. Christmas is the second biggest movie season, and although it is shorter than the summer, it has several advantages. The general mood is festive and outgoing. It is a hearty season for big event movies inviting family attendance, and many releases are directly aimed at that lucrative audience. Some weightier films are inevitably wedged in to qualify for industry honors announced early in the following year. If a movie of quality genuinely connects with the public, it can string out its run into January's Golden Globe Awards and various critic and guild citations, then into February with its Academy Award nominations. With luck, this may boost the film through the next two months because of the surrounding free publicity generated by March's Oscar ceremony.

- **The Winter Season**. January until the week before Easter. Winter in the northern climates tends to give homebound television and movie cassette rentals an entertainment advantage, so this season is used by studios to experiment with films that are thematically difficult or just quirky. Because few really top films are released at the first of the year, movies with outstanding and risk-taking individual performances can find an audience, although, unfortunately, it is probable that they will be only dimly remembered by the time awards are given out the following year.

- **The Easter Season**. Easter to mid-May. This was the industry's slowest season, but not lately. Some new movies can take advantage of the limited but upbeat holiday to register strongly at the box-office. The releases, reflecting the spring season, tend toward broad comedy, high adventure, and romance. But studios normally will hold off their most important movies until the summer film season, just around the corner **(10–11)**.

10–11   *When Harry Met Sally*   Choosing the best season, and even the exact date within it, has become an essential part of the selling strategy of a movie. As proscribed by Hollywood studio sales, certain movie themes, genres, or even styles, are better suited for one season over another for a variety of reasons. Consider *When Harry Met Sally* (1989), an offbeat and well-produced romantic comedy with Meg Ryan and Billy Crystal. In which season would you recommend opening the film? Which particular date of the season? In what type of a release pattern? What are the pros and cons of your decision?   (Columbia Pictures)

★ VIDEOCASSETTE, LASER DISC, DVD, AND COMMERCIAL TELEVISION

The combination of videocassette, laser disc, cable, and television outlets in need of product has generated an enormous amount of moviemaking. "Unquestionably, ancillary revenues are behind the increase in the number of films being made," says Marc Merry of AMC theaters. Currently, 70 percent of American households have VCRs, a growing source of customers for home movie viewing. This *ancillary market* is fed by about 28,000 video specialty outlets in the United States and many more worldwide. It is quite common that films accrue one-third of their profits from videocassette sales, in some cases, much more. In 1991, Disney's *Fantasia* (1940) brought in an estimated $350 million in retail video sales alone (it was a financial failure when first released in 1940); *The Rescuers Down Under* (1990) did only $14 million in theaters, but $65 million on tape. Movies that are family-oriented entertainment—*Babe, Toy Story 2, Nutty Professor II: The Klumps*—traditionally head the list of videocassette sales and rentals, a market that now brings in about $10 billion annually. "The VCR revolution has built a totally new audience in the home, more than doubling the

size of the movie audience," claims Jack Valenti, president of the Motion Picture Association of America.

Many films bypass theatrical release and go *directly to video*. Generally, these are of two kinds: 1) those films that, when finished, are deemed unmarketable to theaters for any number of reasons—weak production values, undistinguished stories, lack of star power, miscalculated distribution opportunities—and therefore rather than waste money on futile theatrical promotion, the movies are routed directly to the video market; or 2) some very low-budget film entrepreneurs make films for a few hundred thousand dollars with hard action, an intriguing title, eye-catching box, and perhaps a recognizable ex-TV actor, intending from the start to go straight to video release. In a limited way, the rewards can be worth the effort. Raedon Entertainment is a company that regularly puts out films for videocassette release with $200,000 budgets. Its president, Dennis Donovan, says "It's not art, man, it's commerce." New Horizon's *Attack of the 60 Foot Centerfold* (1995) speaks eloquently to this remark.

Laser technology for movies is a much more advanced for-

mat than tape, with random access, a crisp picture, and better freeze frames. Laser Discs were slow to catch on because of the quick success of VCRs in the 1980s, but a segment of the public began to demand more refined viewing quality. Film titles on laser disc became available at a cost comparable to videocassettes. The newer DVD (which stands for nothing, despite the claim it is an acronym for "digital versatile disc") technology promises to usurp both the laser disc and videocassette markets to become the standard format in future home video sales. DVD has many features that make it superior, including: a huge disc storage capacity, a studio-quality horizontal video resolution of nearly 500 lines, the capability to display multiple aspect ratios (the standard 4:3 or the letterbox 16:9), and 5.1-channel Dolby Digital Surround sound. Just as the CD format quickly displaced vinyl in the recording industry, hardware manufacturers and software suppliers (often the same company) are primed to revolutionize home viewing with extraordinary visual and sound quality.

Cable and network television is an ongoing customer of the movie industry. HBO, Showtime, and the networks

continued ▶

not only compete in presenting TV premieres of first line films, but they also produce films for their own purposes. A quality production can add respect and prestige to the entire lineup of shows for a cable company. With the proliferation of channels available through cable and worldwide satellite broadcasting, a constant need for program content has made the vast libraries of movies, new and old, a ready source of entertainment. Many movies are butchered for their TV appearances (as well as in-flight airline showings) to conform to the various time constraints and censorship tastes of those in charge. Today, the potential of continuing revenue for a movie on TV never ends.

The Internet holds the most excitement for independent filmmakers working in both feature-length formats and shorts. The personal computer is a flexible screening site capable of catering to the eclectic movie tastes of a vast audience. Some net sites such as pay-per-view *SightSound.com* download standard independent movies to hard drives. The Internet, more significantly, has provided an invigorating new cyberspace for short films. For the past fifty years, viable commercial distribution of short films was almost impossible, yet many noted filmmakers started by creating minor masterpieces in that format. Internet sites, such as *Atom.com* and *Switch2.net*, now make available to Web browsers a huge library of short films from around the world, generating new life into a previously neglected art form. Tom Guard, director of the award-winning short film *Inside Out* (2000), makes the point: "The internet will challenge filmmakers to explore new areas. It will definitely have an influence on the way films are made."

Opening dates are essential to meet once they have been fixed. Keeping time commitments is part of the code for an industry that interlocks so closely. Francis Coppola complained heartily that his Christmas opening for *Godfather 3* (1990) was forcing hasty and therefore error-prone postproduction work. He was pressed to open on schedule, Christmas Day, because it would have otherwise ruined the media blitz—magazine articles, TV ad spots, and celebrity bookings, etc.—that need considerable lead time to mesh. The resulting film, true to form, looked as though it suffered from the pressure of the opening date deadline. James Cameron faced a similar dilemma with *Titanic* (1997), which had originally been scheduled for a lucrative July 2 opening before the popular summer holiday weekend. The $200 million movie had staked out the prime date months in advance, and theaters had cleared their calendars for the film. But time-consuming technical difficulties related to visual effects made it impossible to keep this commitment. Nothing is simple in the movie industry. Rather than move the film's opening to a less desirable time later in the summer, 20th Century Fox and Paramount Pictures studios, co-owners of the movie, opted to delay the release until December 19 in the middle of an already solidly booked Christmas season. By not opening on time in July, it is reported that the interest charge alone cost the producers an additional $10 million. The net result, however, only seemed to prolong the public's anticipation for the film and records were set when *Titanic* was finally released.

Box office success on the first weekend—Friday through Sunday—is deemed essential in the high stakes world of movie distribution. The obsessive focus on being number one pushes studios to fever-pitch levels of anxiety. Entertainment lawyer Tom Hansen wryly notes, "You've got a project that takes two or three years, the work of hundreds of people, and the expenditure of millions of dollars, and it seems to boil down to what happens in the first weekend. That makes people so nervous, so unhappy, so tortured." Media outlets stand in wait for the figures. A company named Entertainment Data collects the numbers, and another firm, Exhibitor Relations, distributes them to a judgmental public.

THE FUTURE OF MOTION PICTURE DELIVERY SYSTEMS

At present, film distribution is a clumsy business. Thousands of individual prints must first be made, then delivered to theaters in every corner of the United States and the world. The process is costly and full of problems. Distributors are forced into expensive guesses as to how many prints to strike. If a widely distributed movie fails after the first week, the company is stuck with an excess of relatively valueless reels of film. Release schedules are often pushed to the limits with prints being physically rushed to exhibitors at the last minute. Any breakdown in the system can mean an empty screen. Film prints are often damaged with scratches after several showings, diminishing the viewing experience. In addition, popular movies are regularly stolen, copied, and then black marketed in remote locations or copied to video for sale. The "pirating" of movies, especially in developing countries, has been a constant source of financial loss in the industry.

New technology promises to reconstruct the entire movie delivery system. In the future, movies will be transmitted to local theaters from a central computer distribution point. Movies can be scanned into a telecine machine and digitized, and then the compressed video is transmitted through fiber-optic phone lines, decompressed, and projected onto screens with a high definition projector. Conventional 35mm film routinely delivers over 10,000 lumens of light output, with 1,500 lines of resolution and a 200: 1 contrast ratio. Current electronic projectors are capable of giving less than two-thirds the visual quality. Although this screen image does not match that of a fresh 35mm print projected in the traditional manner, many industry people feel its quality is as good as the average print, which has been projected several times and has suffered some small deterioration. And the technology will improve. Some serious problems must be hurdled, however. About 34,000 screens in the United States and some 50,000 overseas would have to be converted to the new electronic technology, at a cost of around $90,000 per screen. What party would pick up the cost of the changeover is being debated. Ed DiGuilio, director of R&D at Cinema Products, says, "Electronic technologies won't wipe out film instantly—film will continue for another 20 years after electronic projection is considered viable." The film community is taking the question seriously and the Technical Council of the Motion Picture-Television Industry, a body of senior production executives and technicians, is now studying the ability of digital technologies to deliver a picture equal to the best 35mm film image to theaters.

In addition, technology is available to download movies directly from broadband

Internet connections into home computers and domestic television sets. A major drawback to this personal type of film distribution is the complex rights of film ownership and the scramble of media giants to control the means of access. And the theft by computer hackers pirating downloaded movies is a vital concern in the industry. The speed at which digital visual information can be anonymously stolen and then reproduced presents a whole new set of problems for makers of movies. The potential revenues from such a radically new mode of distribution are immense, sending the traditionally conservative suppliers of movies into both fearful and greedy expectations.

A new electronic delivery system may solve some problems, but it also raises new, and perhaps troubling, possibilities for the art of cinema. If movies could be easily controlled from a central source, several versions of a film—some with undesirable language or action cut out for certain communities—could be made available with relative ease. Bob Stewart, project manager for PacBell video services, enthuses, "A studio could have 10 or 15 different endings and the audience could vote when they come in on which one they want to see. Majority rules." It is, however, an extension of this distorted democratic credo that sends chills down the spine of most artists.

OVERSEAS MARKETS: THE GLOBALIZATION OF AMERICAN FILM

"The foreign market used to be an afterthought. In short order it has become a forethought."

Ted Shugre, Sony Pictures executive

A random check for any week of film attendance at international sites in *Variety* will usually show that eight out of the top ten films in Tokyo, Stockholm, London, Paris, Sydney, and other capitals are American produced. Increasingly, movies are being seen as a primary export commodity. Whereas in 1980 the industry income from overseas markets was 30 percent of its profits, today over one-half of the revenue comes from outside the United States. As theaters continue to be opened in other countries (Germany still has only about 4,000 screens, Japan 2,000, Australia 900; with ticket prices in Europe ranging from a high in Geneva of around $10 to less than $1 in Hungary), it is predicted that by the end of the century, studios will be making 75 percent of their revenues from abroad. Although recently the *multiplex theater*—a building with more than six screens—has become a North American standard, movies in most countries are still seen in single screen theater. However, the industry estimates that 20,000 multiplex screens will be built worldwide by the year 2006. At one time, Europe and other important markets used to have to wait months before films opened in their countries; now movies are released almost simultaneously in major cities to capitalize on media attention, which reaches everywhere at once. Although the domestic market for film seems to have limits, the massive populations of China, India, Indonesia, and Russia are ripe for Western movie entertainment if it is strategically planned.

The movie tastes of the worldwide market are now given serious consideration in deciding the content, the stars, and the budgets of films produced by Hollywood. The major movie studios will not consider making a large budget film unless it has strong overseas potential. Important producers have always aimed their film toward the largest possible audience, but today's market realities have redefined the demographics to include international dimensions **(10–12)**. Films with hi-tech action and heavy violence, strongly erotic themes, for instance, are sure-fire hits in most overseas markets. *Die Hard with a Vengeance* (1995) had a solid domestic gross of $100 million, but the foreign box office topped $250 million. *Godzilla* (1998) was a success in North America with $138 million in receipts, but internationally the film pulled in $239 million. The critically panned *Striptease* (1996) collected a respectable $33 million here but a surprising $80 million abroad. Even the regional romance *The Bridges of Madison County* (1995) made $105 million in foreign markets, compared to $75 million at home. Broad physical comedy sells well in other countries, but not as easily. *Dumb and Dumber* (1994) grossed $127 million domestically, $10 million more than it brought

10–12 *The Matrix* As well as *The Matrix* (1999) did in terms of domestic revenue, the film did even better internationally. It is not unusual for American films, especially those in the action/adventure genre, to make more money overseas. This futuristic action/thriller had all of the elements deemed necessary for success abroad—minimal dialogue, visuals that carry the story, and engrossingly effective special effects. In this series of frames, Neo (Keanu Reeves) battles agent Smith (Hugo Weaving). (Warner Bros.)

in overseas. Still, entertainment tastes are changing in these markets. "The rule used to be that comedy didn't travel well," says Disney executive Joe Roth, "now, what's a hit here is a hit there."

There is understandable cultural resistance elsewhere to the "Americanization" of the mass media, including movies. By custom, American films in Germany, Italy, Spain, and all of France (aside from Paris) are dubbed in their languages; in other countries, films are subtitled. Some cultures feel that their traditional moral and aesthetic attitudes are threatened or overrun by the volume of media entertainment coming from production facilities and distribution points in the United States. Free trade between countries, such as conceived in the GATT agreement, may work well with products made to be

TABLE 10–4 TOP 15 U.S. MOVIES IN OVERSEAS REVENUES
1. *Titanic* (1997)
2. *Jurassic Park* (1993)
3. *Independence Day* (1996)
4. *The Lion King* (1994)
5. *Star Wars: Episode I* (1999)
6. *The Lost World: Jurassic Park* (1997)
7. *Forrest Gump* (1994)
8. *Armageddon* (1998)
9. *Men in Black* (1997)
10. *Star Wars* (1977)
11. *Terminator 2: Judgment Day* (1991)
12. *E.T.: The Extra-Terrestrial* (1982)
13. *Ghost* (1990)
14. *Indiana Jones and the Last Crusade* (1989)
15. *The Bodyguard* (1992)

physically used or consumed, but movies are by their nature steeped in certain cultural values and assumptions. National pride comes into play. When in France, for example, 70 percent of the screens are dominated by American movies, many people there feel invaded and overwhelmed. Jacques Le Glou, an independent film exporter, complains that France is the proud heir to over 100 years of cinema history and wants to hold on to those unique roots, "European production is essentially a cinema of reflection. American cinema is one of distraction." This may be a faulty simplification but it is one shared by many, in some form or another (Table 10–4).

AMERICAN INDEPENDENT PRODUCERS AND DISTRIBUTORS

"The most important thing when a filmmaker says he is an independent is that somebody cannot beat him to a pulp and force him to make a film that the financier wants made."

Lindsay Law, President
Fox Searchlight Pictures

Going back to 1919, many superior movies have been by filmmakers who chose the freedom of independent production and distribution. With the founding of United Artists by Charles Chaplin, D.W. Griffith, Mary Pickford, and Douglas Fairbanks, a movie company was formed with hopes of bypassing both the weighty decision-making process of other studios, which they felt hampered creative freedom, and, more importantly, attempted to cut out the economic "middleman" function of established studios, which they believed unfairly controlled film distribution. In the 1930s, David O. Selznick, under the banner of Selznick International Pictures, produced and had distributed a few select films, which he had personally supervised every step of the way. Although *Gone with the*

10–13 *The Secret of Roan Inish* Good critical reviews and the positive word of mouth that usually follow are necessary for commercial success of smaller **independent filmmakers**. With tight advertising budgets, these filmmakers must rely on any free publicity and any other media attention that they can get. John Sayles, for example, is a filmmaker who for decades has been fiercely independent. His *The Secret of Roan Inish* (1994), a well-crafted movie of Irish fables, had a modest but loyal audience that was successfully reached within the limited resources of its distributor. (First Look Pictures Releasing)

Wind (1939), the greatest blockbuster of all time, was distributed by MGM, Selznick's reputation as an independent filmmaker was a badge of courage in a time when a few big studios dominated the system. Likewise, Sam Goldwyn carefully chose his projects, such as *Wuthering Heights* (1939), and his name over a film was synonymous with quality.

Typically, a well-produced American independent film is a labor of love. Many times the filmmakers have a vision that cannot be fully realized by going through the studio system. Independent producers work successfully on the fringe of the mainstream system. Independent producer Edward Pressman, for example, has shown an eclectic taste in film projects, including *Badlands* (1973), *Wall Street* (1987), *Reversal of Fortune* (1990), and *American Psycho* (2000). He has continued to successfully find financial backing for his films because of his uncanny sense for producing popular films of artistic quality. For many others, the funding for their project was rejected by the majors at some point in early development, leaving the filmmakers to seek out alternate money sources and eventually line up with independent distributors. For still others, their films have uncommon concepts that on the face of them hold no interest for major studios, so they pursue other production paths from the very start. The result is that the best of American independent movies are free of formulas, take creative risks, and have artistic integrity. But it is also true that most of them are hastily put together and of little lasting merit. Films like *Bad Girls from Mars* (1990) do not end up in festivals. This then is not a blanket endorsement for the courage of independent filmmakers **(10–13)**.

Giving independent filmmaking a concise and definitive description is hard. Many attempts at a definition explain the process in relation to the experience of working in mainline Hollywood. "An independent movie is a movie with a strong point of view," says producer Lawrence Bender (*Reservoir Dogs*, 1992). "The filmmakers are supported so that they can get their point of view across—as opposed to the 'studio' film, where you have a group of people figuring out what the film should be." Just as great literature presents the unique universe of its author, the mission of some independent moviemakers is to put together an uncompromising film statement, free from the demands of studio oversight and uncluttered by cross-purposes. Brad Krevoy, formerly at Orion Pictures, expands on the idea: "Some of these studios with their hordes of executives going through every page of a script and telling the director or producer to do this, do that, do this, are the antithesis of a pure independent who basically executes his or her particular vision." In a more unhampered environment, a spectrum of unconventional styles and bold themes can be tested. Because their budgets are not so frightening, good independent films usually have a steady confidence about them. Director Mike Figgis (*Leaving Las Vegas*, 1995) has struggled under the big studio system and has chosen the route of an independent filmmaker, "The bigger the budget and the bigger the crew, the slower the process becomes and the harder it is to be spontaneous."

What independents do not have is a large advertising and publicity budget to give them greater exposure. Most struggle for attention. It should be remembered that the vast majority of the films released worldwide are from independent producers. A major problem for some independent distributors continues to be the lack of national electronic media support. Most people get their information from TV and unless attention is paid in some form by that medium, an independent film will struggle. In the past, a common strategy was often repeated. If a film has won a festival prize, the distributor would try to build interest with whatever publicity could be generated. Typically, a small film would open in Los Angeles and New York in hope of receiving good reviews that might help carry the film further. But today, even for a limited release, the total opening costs can easily range up to a half million dollars. Unlike a major release that can establish itself on the first weekend of its release, independents must build an audience with word of mouth quickly, over three to four weeks in an art-house theater, with the danger of being bumped by another struggling film. In the past sometimes things worked out famously, as when Hemdale opened Oliver Stone's *Platoon* (1986) in just two theaters and then watched its reputation sweep the country.

Although today's independent distributors are in the same business as the major studios, traditionally they have faced much different funding, marketing, product, and audience configurations. Whereas the majors deal in the high-powered international world of corporate giants and mass audiences, these smaller film-releasing companies work on a more limited playing field with films thematically and stylistically different. Independent distributors deliver film to that significantly sizable movie audience that wants to see films that break away from the formula-driven offerings of the majors. It is a venturesome business, with few guideposts to insure how to proceed. Film distribution involves a sophisticated network of industry connections. Because the successful release of a film is so expensive, companies must be very selective in acquiring their films and cautious in their marketing campaigns. Until recently, most independent film distributors were under-financed and therefore their life spans were tenuous.

No matter how many independent and foreign films are released each year, they only exist for the viewer if they can be seen. Of the approximately 34,000 commercial movie screens in North America, only about 500 screens regularly program "art house" movies. There are about 50 theaters with repertory policies and 150 sites at universities, museums, and film societies. An influx of high-profile independent films in recent years has created a limited resurgence in exhibition chains that are willing to invest in opening new theaters and refurbishing older sites. The largest art house chain, Landmark Theaters, will soon have 170 screens nationwide; Reading Cinemas has launched its Angelika theaters, and Robert Redford has teamed with General Cinema theaters to open 70 screens in 15 cities under his Sundance logo. Cities such as Seattle and Minneapolis have been centers for supporting independent films and the trend is spreading to other metropolitan areas **(10–14)**.

An independent distributing company may come upon a film in any number of ways, and although some of the larger companies themselves will finance and produce three or four movies each year, **film festivals** are the primary way in which movies are discovered. Currently, there are at least 325 film festivals and market expositions staged worldwide each year. Most film festivals are put on to promote civic pride and commerce, but the Sundance, Toronto, and Cannes festivals, as well

10–14 *Being John Malkovich* Finding the audience for a film that defies established genres is a special challenge for distributors. *Being John Malkovich* (1999) was a shaggy story about the real-life celebrity John Malkovich playing himself (pictured here being sexually assaulted by Catherine Keener). The film by Spike Jonze is a Chinese box of ideas and realities, with characters moving in and out of each other at will. Word of mouth was a key to its success, even though it is questionable how people could convey the plot adequately. (USA Films)

✳ THE CHANGING FACE OF INDEPENDENT FILM COMPANIES

"What distinguishes the mini-majors from the studios is their focus. They have the flexibility to make decisions quickly."

Amir Malin, President of Artisan Entertainment

There is disagreement as to what "independent" means today. Indeed, the label "mini-major" is now given to the biggest of these companies. At one time an independent distributor was a company with shaky funding in desperate search for an oddly engaging film to cleverly release that might just catch on and bring in a healthy return. There are still many small companies that fit that definition. "Distributors must go big or go small, the middle is dangerous," says independent film producer Jonathan Dana. But today even the small have gotten bigger or have been absorbed by the bigger players. The term "independent" producer/distributor may be as much an aesthetic attitude toward filmmaking as it is a definition of a company's movie industry ties. These distributors choose movies that fall into three general categories: *American independent films, international films,* and *nonfiction films.*

In 1993, Disney started a trend when it bought the highly successful independent distributor Miramax (*Il Postino,* 1995; *Trainspotting,* 1996; *Shakespeare in Love,* 1998; *Daddy and Them,* 2000) and their film library. Although Miramax retains its managerial autonomy, the realigned company now has a huge financial base that is not common for most independents. In 1999, this opportunistic movie company signed a co-production agreement with MGM for eight films. Miramax commonly handles over twenty films a year, as many as a major studio, occasionally producing its own projects with budgets exceeding $20 million. Its success has fostered a spin-off division, Dimension Films (*The Faculty,* 1998). New Line/Fine Line Features (*Shine,* 1996; *Austin Powers,* 1997; *Fifteen Minutes,* 2000) is now owned by Time Warner/Turner. MGM bought out Metromedia that owned Orion Classics (*Jeffrey,* 1995), and it now operates Goldwyn Films and United Artists International.

Most of the major studio/distributors now have a division or affiliate that specializes in smaller budget films. Sony Pictures Classics (*City of the Lost Children,* 1995; *Shanghai Triad,* 1995; *Broken English,* 1997) is a division of the larger parent Sony Studios. Twentieth Century Fox formed Fox Searchlight Pictures (*The Brothers Mcmillan,* 1995; *Stealing Beauty,* 1996; *Paradise Road,* 1997) to acquire nonmainstream films. PolyGram Filmed Entertainment, Gramercy Pictures (*Dead Man Walking,* 1995; *Fargo,* 1996; *Portrait of a Lady,* 1996) and the successful independent October Films (*Breaking the Waves,* 1996; *Secrets & Lies,* 1996; *Three Seasons,* 1999) were bought by USA Networks.

Smaller independents are still active and successful: Strand Releasing (*All the Vermeers in New York,* 1990); First Look (*Alegria,* 2000); Trimark (*Stalingrad,* 1995); New Yorker Films (*A Mongolian Tale,* 1997); Alliance Independent Films (*The Sweet Hereafter,* 1997); Northern Arts (*Drunks,* 1997); Castle Hill (*End of Summer,* 1997); Artisan (*Requiem for a Dream,* 2000); and others—release from three to ten films a year, carefully guiding them through the phases of promotion.

as the American Film Market (AFM) in Los Angeles, are the most important events at which new movies are screened, with filmmakers and distributors from around the world coming together in hopes of securing lucrative arrangements for their projects. Karlovy Vary, Seattle, Telluride, New York, Rotterdam, Chicago, Berlin, Edinburgh, San Sabastian, Venice, AFI Los Angeles, Istanbul, and others are popular film gatherings, but are mainly used to show off film rather than provide markets for their sale to distributors. The key to the success of an independent is the smart selection of **pickups**. A typical example of this was when Miramax Films paid $50,000 for the North American rights to a small Danish film, *Twist and Shout* (1986), which then grossed $1.5 million at the box office and sold 20,000 videotapes. Today, the bidding is more substantial. In 1996, Miramax paid $10 million to acquire the rights to the independently produced *Sling Blade*, a film that went on to gain not only a financial windfall but also critical acclaim.

A number of factors influence what films are bought. A first choice is an **auteur film,** one by a famous director. This was truer in the 1960s when a few dominant names were universally recognized as superior directors. However this no longer guarantees that a film will be picked up. Films by world renown directors—Michelangelo Antonioni (*Identification of a Woman,* 1982); Theo Angelopoulis (*The Beekeeper,* 1986); Krzysztof Kielowski (*Dialogue,* 1988); Federico Fellini (*The Voice of the Moon,* 1990); and Roman Polanski (*Bitter Moon,* 1991)—were stalled by U.S. distributors for a variety of reasons. The problems in acquiring such films by an independent are now more complex. Certain films only have their domestic rights for sale, and it is not profitable to the distributor if the video and overseas ancillary rights are not available. Video rights are especially important in that some independent films find a much wider audience in that format.

As in other industries, independents aim their films at a *target audience*, that is, that fraction of the public who want to see films made with the artistic integrity of the director, writer, and actors in tact. The hope is that somehow these films will also click with the mainstream audience. With the critical recognition of such films as *Howard's End* (1992); *Like Water for Chocolate* (1992); *The Crying Game* (1992); *The Piano* (1993); *Pulp Fiction* (1994); *The Usual Suspects* (1995); *The English Patient* (1996); *The Apostle* (1997); *Elizabeth* (1998); and *The Golden Bowl* (2000), more independent films are finding a larger audience. Harvey Weinstein, co-chairman of Miramax Films, says, "I think what we are seeing is that independent films might not be called art films someday. They might just be called movies." Actually, art movie houses have had a small renaissance in this country, as the moviegoing public seeks out unique film entertainment. But more importantly, the reconfiguration of theaters, with multiplexes offering six or eight screens, has encouraged exhibitors to devote one of the screens to more specialized movie productions.

In pure numbers, the independents are strong. In 1998, as an example, the majority of the 327 films theatrically released in the United States were produced by independents. In any single year, many such films stand out. A resurgence of interest could be said to have started with the recognition won by the film *sex, lies, and videotape* (1989). Since then, many stars who can command very high salaries in major studio films opt to work for scale (and a percentage) in independent films of their choice.

THE BLAIR WITCH PROJECT PHENOMENON

The successful distribution and marketing of an independently produced film is almost always a problem. Often the subject matter appeals to what is perceived to be a "niche" audience and the money to advertise and market the movie is simply lacking. The case of *The Blair Witch Project* (1999), however, is a storybook of clever marketing decisions and a triumphant financial outcome **(10–15)**.

Haxan Films, an Orlando Florida group of young filmmakers, shot the film for $30,000. Before finishing it, some footage was shown on the Bravo network, and viewers were directed to the filmmaker's Web site. The buzz started. Another $320,000 was eventually spent for sound and color correction and a 35mm blowup print, as well as $100,000 for other finishing costs. The total cost of production, therefore, was about $450,000.

Artisan Entertainment acquired the film for distribution for $1.1 million after having seen it screened at the Sundance Film Festival. By choosing to spread the word about the film through the Internet and other creative channels of free advertising, Artisan built a groundswell of interest among younger people across the country. Then, rather than opening the movie immediately in a wide-release pattern, the distributor released the film at only 27 screens. Theaters were jammed and word of mouth fired up. For the second week, they put the film on 1,100 screens—still not a wide-release. Amir Malin of Artisan pointed out, "Nothing is better than knowing a film is sold out. Everybody wants to see it." By the fourth week the film was on 2,100 screens. More prints could be made by this time, and the advertising budget could also reflect the popularity of the movie. Artisan Entertainment costs for print and advertising were estimated to be $25 million.

Compared to the estimated revenues, the total costs were minuscule. It is thought that

10–15 *The Blair Witch Project* *The Blair Witch Project* (1999) defied the conventional wisdom of Hollywood. The movie was a resounding financial success, despite its low-budget (initially, $35,000) and intentionally awkward production values. Ironically, the blatant amateurishness of the production was an asset, catching much of the audience off-guard and shocking them awake. Lost deep in the woods, the "director" (Heather Donahue) turns the camera on herself for a moment of unexpected truth.   (Artisan Entertainment)

continued ▶

> *The Blair Witch Project* will gross $150 million in North America, $50 million overseas, $66 million in home video and DVD sales, $35 million for broadcast and cable rights, $4 million in pay-per-view receipts, and another $7 mil- | lion for licensing and merchandising its image. The estimated total—$312 million—is a number that high-profile Hollywood films fifty times more expensive would admire. The film may have the effect of reorienting the consciousness | of the traditional studio management, not only toward the message that American independent films deliver, but also the nature of effective marketing and distribution for any movie.

Obviously, having a star boosts the chances of an independent by greatly enhancing box-office prospects. In the past few years, films with modest budgets have been fortunate to sign Bruce Willis (*Pulp Fiction*, 1994); Diane Keaton (*Marvin's Room*, 1996); Woody Harrelson (*Welcome to Sarajevo*, 1997); Peter Fonda (*Ulee's Gold*, 1997); Nick Nolte (*Affliction*, 1998); and the star-studded casts in Robert Altman's *The Player* (1992) and *Short Cuts* (1993). The annual "Spirit Awards" are given to the best independent films, domestic and foreign, in March of each year.

International Films

> *"In France, the box office, yes, it's important, but it does not mean everything. Because we are making more middle budget films, we are allowed to do films that are not so popular."*
>
> **Actress Catherine Deneuve**

The successful distribution of international films in the United States has had a mixed history. During the turbulent movie culture of the McCarthy era of the 1950s, the sudden rash of outstanding imported films won over substantial audiences across the nation. The *art movie house* designation gave a new dimension to theaters, and they opened in every large city. These places—usually small theaters destined for extinction—catered to emerging movie tastes. Sophisticated audiences were curious to see films from countries with different moral values and styles of art. What Americans discovered were films of unusual depth, spectacular cinematography and editing, offbeat themes, and much more explicit sex. This popularity continued through the 1960s: Five of the top ten grossing foreign films date from this period—*I Am Curious Yellow* (1968); *La Dolce Vita* (1961); *Z* (1969); *A Man and a Woman* (1966); and *8 1/2* (1963).

The phenomenon waned in the 1970s as Hollywood incorporated many of the themes and directorial styles of foreign films, with the big advantage of having no subtitles. During the 1980s both American and international films struggled with defining their direction, but certainly moviegoers worldwide have been conditioned to the high-powered non-stop energy of American films. The personal, humanistic stories of directors from other countries often were simply overlooked by the American public.

A second wave of interest in international films seems to have opened new markets. A new generation is showing an appreciation for non-American cultures in the 1990s, touching into all of the arts and fashion. The media-connected world is becoming less "foreign." Movies produced in Britain, Ireland, Australia, and Canada readily gained acceptance because of their common language and the easy exchange of English-speaking actors. Movies such as *A Room with a View* (1985); *My Left Foot* (1989); *Flirting* (1990); *Life Is Sweet* (1991); *Riff-Raff* (1991); *Enchanted April* (1991); *The Commitments* (1991); *Howard's End* (1992); *The Crying Game* (1992); *Strictly Ballroom* (1992); *Proof* (1992); *The Piano* (1993); *Orlando* (1993); *Naked* (1993); *Muriel's Wedding* (1994); *Once Were Warriors* (1995); *Trainspotting* (1996); *Topsy-Turvy* (1999); and others had extensive exposure.

Selected foreign language films have found new audiences, depending on the chemistry of their subject matter, media exposure, and fortunate timing. Academy Award and other festival nominations help these films find an audience. Some recent movies have claimed strong critical success and a loyal following, such as *Best Intentions* (Sweden, 1992); *Toto Le Hero* (Belgium, 1991); *Burnt by the Sun* (Russia, 1995); *Raise the Red Lantern* (China, 1991); *Indochine* (France, 1991); *All about My Mother* (Spain, 1999); *The Double Life of Veronique* (Poland, 1991); *Leolo* (Quebec, Canada, 1992); *The White Balloon* (Iran, 1995); *Breaking the Waves* (Denmark, 1996); *Strawberries and Chocolate* (Cuba, 1995); *Bandit Queen* (India, 1995); *Stalingrad* (Germany, 1996); *The Postman* (Italy, 1995); *Central Station* (Brazil, 1998); *Gohatto* (Japan, 2000); and others. With a growing Hispanic population, *Like Water for Chocolate* (Mexico, 1992) became the highest grossing foreign language film in the history of American theater exhibition until it was surpassed by Italy's *Life Is Beautiful* (1998) **(10–16)**.

Despite the fact that people have gained a taste for more diverse movie fare, the future of international film distribution looks less than hopeful. Although there is an

10–16   *Life Is Beautiful*   *Life Is Beautiful* (1998) by director/actor/writer Roberto Benigni is a good example of the creative control exercised by many international filmmakers and the success that can follow. The story set in Fascist Italy during World War II is a unique hybrid of comedy and tragedy. The unlikely theme of a man attempting to create a humorous safe harbor for his son in a death camp won many awards and captured the attention of a large portion of the American movie audience, making the film the highest grossing **foreign language movie** release in history.   (Miramax Films)

increasing interest in foreign films on college campuses and film societies, the commercial box office gross for such movies is less than 1 percent of the entire theater business in North America. Given that small figure, nearly 75 percent of the revenue is earned in the four metropolitan areas of New York City, Toronto, Los Angeles, and Montreal. Much of the remaining market can be found in Chicago, Boston, Seattle, Minneapolis, and San Francisco. Eamonn Bowles of Miramax Films interprets the climate of the times this way: "People used to go to foreign films for a more personal vision, more sophisticated outlooks and less cookie-cutter, formulaic filmmaking. The rise in the American independent has sort of serviced that need without making people have to read subtitles." Unfortunately for most people, going to see a foreign film on a large theater screen is becoming a rare and exotic experience.

Nonfiction Films

"The penalty for realism is that it is about reality and has to bother forever not about being 'beautiful' but about being right."

Documentarian John Grierson

The third category of films that independent distributors handle is **nonfiction films,** more popularly called **documentaries.** The documentary has very rich traditions. Most men and women drawn to it do so with a genuine sense of vocation. Filmmakers working in this mode have a passion that consumes them, sometimes to the point of putting themselves in life-threatening situations. The dedication and integrity of great nonfiction films comes through in every creative decision that a documentarian makes.

To the uninformed, nonfiction films would appear to offer little range of individual expression for a director. Quite the opposite is true. Although the primary intent of many documentaries is the presentation of unvarnished truth, its methods are even more diverse than the fiction film director. At every stage of moviemaking, the nonfiction directors face different sets of challenges than their counterparts making fiction narrative movies. Clarity of presentation is the first virtue. Although photographic style is important, the explanation of the film's subject is primary in nonfiction. Whereas a director of fiction narratives going into a project has defined story expectations, the documentary director is usually quite free to *discover* the focus and style of the film as the subject being studied reveals itself. One technique of documentary films, named **cinema vérité**—literally "camera truth"—was an interview style, first used in Jean Rouch's *Chronicle of a Summer* (1960), in which the filmmaker freely questioned a subject in a manner that elicited spontaneous and naked honesty.

Cultural and political turmoil of any time period invited a style of filmmaking labeled in the United States **direct cinema.** The prime focus of these nonfiction directors was capturing reality rather than staging it. Stephen Lighthill (*Berkeley in the Sixties,* 1993) explains, "In a documentary, you can't intrude and alter reality. You can't restage a shot if you miss it. The documentary gets its sense of authenticity by just being there and building drama out of small human moments. There's a tremendous

10–17   *Deadly Currents*   The **documentary film** *Deadly Currents* (1991) by Simcha Jacobovici is a prime example of the dedication of nonfiction filmmakers to fairness and honesty. Plunging his film team into the complex struggles of the daily reality of the Israeli and Palestinian people, the result is a first-hand account of the cultural differences and long-standing turmoil that affects the heart of both intertwined societies.   (Alliance)

power in truth." Therefore, the effective organization of the film crew is essential. For many nonfiction films, tight scripting is impossible because of the unknowns inherent in the nature of delivering the subject. On-site shooting is often more loosely planned, always open to opportunities to present themselves.

Although most nonfiction filmmakers do not usually set out to make films beautiful looking for their own sake; the best of these movies meld their images and ideas in such a way as to make them enormously attractive. They appeal to those people who are stimulated by watching films that attempt to capture "the real thing" **(10–17)**. Still, nonfiction films are a hard sell to American theater audiences. They must fight the general idea that documentaries are those didactic pieces of dry film that substitute teachers in high school use to fill up the hour. At best, documentaries are seen by many people as a worthy activity, but more suitable for public television. While it is true that many excellent nonfiction films thankfully are seen on TV, most notably Ken Burns' superlative series *The Civil War* on PBS, many of the best documentaries—*Hoop Dreams* (1994) being a prime example—need and deserve the scope of a large theater screen to have the full impact.

THE CONTEMPORARY DOCUMENTARY

A new spirit has won over numerous distributors in the last twenty-five years. A quick glimpse at the range of subject matter opened and explicated by filmmakers working in nonfiction is instructive. Any listing of outstanding documentaries in the past few years must be arbitrary because the field is so filled with films of genuine accomplishment. The following are just a few directors and their films—among the many—that stand out:

- Richard Schmiechen's *The Times of Harvey Milk* (1983)—a film that looks at the hate that drove one man to coldly murder a popular gay San Francisco politician.
- *George Stevens: A Filmmaker's Journey* (1984)—a loving summary of the highly talented Hollywood director's life by his son George Stevens, Jr.
- *Shoah* (1986)—Claude Lanzman's unrelenting 9-1/2 hour document of varied eyewitness responses to the horror of the holocaust experience by survivors and participants.
- Errol Morris's *The Thin Blue Line* (1988)—a partly dramatized examination of a

murder conviction that was so thorough in its findings that the convicted man was released from jail on the strength of the film.

- Michael Moore's widely distributed *Roger & Me* (1989)—a devastatingly funny and sadly discouraging look at the cold business practices of General Motors in Flint, Michigan.
- The stunning film footage of outer space found in the NASA vaults by Al Reinhart in *For All Mankind* (1989).
- The drug ravaged life of jazz great Chet Baker in *Lets Get Lost* (1989) by Bruce Weber.
- Barbara Kopple's *American Dream* (1989) looks hard at the state of union workers in their fight for survival during a strike against a meat packing giant.
- *Paris Is Burning* (1990)—an inside account of a New York City fringe crowd that thrives on "voguing" and drag balls by Jennie Livingston and Barry Swimmer.
- Eleanor Coppola's *Hearts of Darkness: A Filmmaker's Apocalypse* (1991)—an unusually blunt and painful record of the making of her husband's *Apocalypse Now*.

- Barbara Trent and David Kasper investigate the political decisions that were behind the U.S. involvement in Panama with *The Panama Deception* (1992).
- Mark Achbar and Peter Wintonick give the linguist and media critic Noam Chomsky an effective platform to voice his thinking about media control in *Manufacturing Consent* (1992).
- A detailed history of important but lesser known activists in the civil right's movement are honored by Connie Field and Marilyn Mulford's *Freedom on My Mind* (1994).
- Gene Bach's *A Great Day in Harlem* (1995) researched a rare photographic session in the 1950s that brought together an all-star cast of Black musicians.
- *Theremin: An Electronic Odyssey* (1995) traces the unbelievable career of a genius inventor who was tragically caught among the unrelated worlds of politics, science, and music.
- Beth and George Gage's *Fire on the Mountain* (1995)—an unabashedly inspiring story of the heroic lives of the men who formed the 10th Mountain

continued ▶

Division during World War II and their surprising impact on the culture afterward.

- Leon Gast's *When We Were Kings* (1996), capturing the electric personalities and strange politics surrounding the 1974 heavyweight championship fight in Zaire between Muhammad Ali and George Foreman.
- *The Last Days* (1998) by James Moll, a very personal remembrance of the Holocaust by five survivors.
- *Speaking in Strings* (1999) directed by Paola di Florio reveals the fabulous musical talent of violinist Nadja Salerno-Sonnenberg, and more, her completely honest and passionate attitude toward life.
- Michael Apted's series of documentaries that has followed the lives of a group of young Britons of varied economic classes from age seven, the last installment being *42UP* (1999).
- *Cinema Vérité: The Defining Moment* (2000) by Peter Wintonick and the Canadian National Film Board is a comprehensive review of the documentary filmmakers who gave new definition to nonfiction film in the last half of the twentieth century.
- Frederick Wiseman, the most consistently productive documentarian of the twentieth century, lovingly tells the story of ordinary working people in his four-hour film *Belfast, Maine* (2000).

These nonfiction films, and hundreds more, form a body of work from which high standards of excellence are derived.

Funding projects is a universal problem for the nonfiction film. Budgets are normally very tight, challenging the director to be continuously cost conscious. Yet their dedication usually overrides the many financial and logistical problems that inevitably come up. An organization—the International Documentary Association—promotes the causes of documentary filmmakers within and out of the entertainment industry. But for those caught in the obsession of this form of movies, what keeps them going is usually very personal. Bill Coutrie, producer of one of the few truly great environmental films, *Earth and the American Dream* (1995), says, "I used to have a burning desire to make dramatic films in Hollywood, and that's not quite the same as it was. The notion of getting rich and famous, that's sort of fallen away." David Douglas, maker of *Fires of Kuwait* (1993) for IMAX screens says it another way, "Documentaries don't make much money, but they can say things of lasting value." A growing segment of the film audience has awakened to the vitality and satisfactions found in nonfiction movies.

The distinguishing feature of nonfiction filmmakers is their commitment to ethical principles. Whereas it is common for a narrative film to claim that it is based on a true story of someone's life, and then go on to bend or ignore the facts to suit its dramatic purpose, nonfiction films are held to the very high principles of good journalism. Documentary filmmakers continually struggle with issues involving fairness, honesty, and objectivity. In an age of deteriorating ethical standards in journalism, most glaringly exemplified in the psuedo-documentary work of tabloid television, the serious nonfiction filmmaker tries to retain the integrity of the documentary tradition. In his brilliant documentary *Crumb* (1994), director Terry Zwigoff painstakingly chronicled the eccentricities and art of the iconoclastic underground artist and friend Robert Crumb. The result is a film portrait that is both disturbing and exhilarating. The complexity of the man's life, however, was only captured with the unrelenting dedication of the filmmaker.

The nonfiction filmmaker must forever deal with questions of professional ethics while keeping in mind that whatever is finally produced must be genuinely interesting to an audience. In working out a code, each person must weigh his or her biases toward the subject matter. The director's personal conclusions are inevitably reflected in a film.

CRITICAL RESPONSES

"I learn more from critics who honestly criticize my pictures than from those who are devout."

Swedish director Ingmar Bergman

We are all movie critics. Leaving the theater, a significant commitment of time has been made watching a movie and the experience calls for a response. Typical conversation about the movie might sound like this: "I loved Billy Bob Thornton as the weird brother, totally believable!"; "I couldn't get into the love relationship, no chemistry."; "What did you think about that lame ending?" Movies offer such a wealth of intellectual and sensual information that it may seem hard to determine where to start the discussion. Although watching a movie can move us into confronting intense emotions, an especially effective film often takes some period of time to digest. Of course, sometimes the worth of a film is simply stated in terms of the ticket price—"It was O.K., but I wouldn't recommend paying $7.50 to see it!" Certain movie critics in the mass media also work at this basic level of verbal economy.

Many people have a difficult time with movie critics. On the one hand we rely on them to give clues on what to see next weekend—a helpful service. If a movie reviewer's critical position matches our experience, we are not only agreeing with the opinions of the critic, but also drawn to feel a connection with an invisible body of contemporary taste. There is a subtle comfort in feeling that our aesthetic instincts are confirmed by the spokespersons of the larger culture. We share more elite perceptions. On the other hand, when a film does not at all resemble what we were expecting, based on a critic's commentary, our quick response takes on a righteous tone—"What qualifies that guy as an expert on movies?"

The question is in some ways valid. Good criticism is found in the mix of a critic's film experience, insight, and facility with language. The recognition of elements in a movie previously unnoticed or appreciated affords a high level of intellectual satisfaction. This is not always readily apparent when reading or hearing an isolated movie piece, but trust can grow with repeated encounters. Truly insightful criticism—in any of the arts—is a pleasure to consider.

Film studios and distributors also have mixed feelings about the critics in the media. Positive reviews provide the great gift of free publicity, important to both independent and major studio productions. The hope of distribution companies is to build momentum in their advertising with splashy quotes from the "rave" reviews of critics—"*THRILLING, MAJESTIC, AND AWE-INSPIRING*"; "*HILARIOUS FROM START TO FINISH*"; "*TWO THUMBS UP!*" "*5 STARS!*" Always leery of a negative buzz put on their latest movie, studio publicity departments frequently set up plush junkets for media movie critics to New York or their Los Angeles studios for special screenings a week or two in advance of openings, complete with interview access to the stars and weighty *press kits* giving press-ready biographical material on the making of the film.

There is, however, a question about the ultimate impact of positive or negative reviews of a film at the box office. Some industry observers discount any serious reaction from the general public to what print or even television reviewers think about a movie. The critics hated *Home Alone 2* (1992), an unimaginative sequel to the simple yet quick-witted original, but the second film became a huge financial success. On the other hand, most critics rated *The Player* (1992)—an extensive in-joke about Hollywood industry types—in the top ten films of its year, yet the general public almost ignored the movie. A classic example of a critical turnaround is found in the release of Arthur Penn's *Bonnie and Clyde* (1967). The tragicomedy of two young gangsters (Faye Dunaway and Warren Beatty) was a radical departure in style and tone from other films of the day, and Warner Bros. was at a loss about how to market the film. It showed at the Montreal Film Expo to enthusiastic audiences, but the influential *New York Times* film critic Bowsley Crowther hated the film and gave the movie a scathing review. That response seemed to set up a negative predisposition in other critics, leading the distributor to open the film without fanfare. Joe Morgenstern, a film critic for *Newsweek* magazine, wrote a dismissive piece on the film. But then an odd thing happened. After having been prematurely pulled from distribution in the United States (the film was an immediate hit in Europe), audiences here were stirred by a strong word-of-mouth reaction. Morgenstern, on a second viewing of the movie, completely reversed his opinion and, in an unprecedented act, wrote another review that praised the film. *Bonnie and Clyde* went on to garner ten Oscar nominations.

Although it is impossible to say with certainty how critics affect the success of movies, the following principles seem to hold true:

- Great reviews can send a good movie over the top.
- Bad press will sink a film of borderline quality.
- A series of strong reviews of a small or special niche film will awaken those persons loyal to film art, giving a movie enough survival time to find its audience.
- Poor reviews will have little negative affect on a major movie that is backed by a powerful advertising and publicity campaign, if its basic story somehow resonates deeply with the current temperament of the general moviegoing public.

The case of Barry Levenson's *Diner* (1982), a movie that introduced Steve Guttenburg, Mickey Rourke, Daniel Stern, Kevin Bacon, Ellen Barkin, and others in featured roles, is a further illustration of the unpredictable fate of movies. Because of poor test screenings, MGM was set to shelve this small, affecting film. However, its producer was able to induce Pauline Kael, at the time the most influential movie critic in the country, to privately screen the film. She loved the movie, promised MGM that she would give it a praising review in *The New Yorker*, and rightly predicted other critics would follow her lead. The film opened and touched a surprisingly large audience, launching the careers of many artists connected to the film.

Certainly, filmmakers vie for the awards given by the critical establishment. Yearly honors in multiple categories are given out by the *National Society of Film Critics, New York Film Critics Circle*, the *National Board of Review*, the *Los Angeles Film Critics Association*, and the *Hollywood Foreign Press Association (Golden Globes)*. The publicity generated from the awards of these organizations is immediately translated into advertising copy for the film or actor.

Critics writing seriously about film as both an art form and a cultural phenomenon have a smaller, more selective audience. Persons interested in film at this more academic level are interested in the very nature of motion picture art, how it functions technically, and the cultural milieu in which it exists. This level of film criticism demands a certain fluency in what has been called the *cinematic capability*, and asks more thoughtful questions:

- In what ways is the theme of the film reflective of the political culture in which it took place?
- How did the lead actor interpret his or her character, and how did this tilt the direction of the story?
- What cinematic influences from the past are evident in the movie in question?
- How does the film mirror the social mores or sexual climate of the period in which it was produced?
- What choices did the cinematographer make to supply the right visual correlative for the film's subject?

Approaching the film experience in these or similar terms calls for a higher degree of thought, attention, and cinematic insight.

Reporting about Film in the Media

"The marketing overpowers the critics."

Brian Grazer, co-chairman of Imagine Films

The style and content of every writer will be strongly influenced by his or her perceived audience. This is especially true for the film critic. Because movie patronage has such a wide demographic profile, it is nearly impossible for any single film critic to effectively reach the entire audience, or even substantial portions of it. Although it is futile to determine exactly what person any one critic is influencing, the mass media can provide target audience profiles of groups needed to be reached, and by what means. Network television obviously has a much larger and more diverse audience than, for example, *Cineaste* or *Film Quarterly* magazines. Therefore a journalist working in any medium, of necessity, will discuss movies with different assumptions of audience interest, knowledge, and taste. It might be useful, then, to categorize film writers by the media formats in which they work.

Television and Radio. The mass audience of television tends to inhibit criticism of genuine intellectual substance. The same guidelines that rule most of TV and radio—the bottom line appeal to the lowest common denominator in the audience—also influence film criticism coming through both media. Apart from the entertainment shows, such as the E! Channel, that are blatant showcases for movie promotion, the bulk of movie reviews on TV are on the quip-filled network morning shows with Gene Shalit or Joel Siegel. At the low end of this type of criticism, for example, an ex-weatherman might enthusiastically gives "5 stars" to the latest high-budget release that he assumes his audience is anticipating and that he would do nothing to disillusion. Lower yet are the "blurbmeisters"—reviewers like Jim Ferguson of Preview Channel, a self-promoting movie service, Jeff Craig of "Sixty Second Preview," and Paul Wunder of WBAI Radio. Studio marketing people curry favor and regularly select snappy one-liners or exploding adjectives from self-promoting pieces of such "critics," the payoff to these reviewers being that their names and affiliations are headlined in movie ads. "I can get all kinds of bad reviews and still cut myself a 30-second television spot that makes it look good. . . . *'Splendid!' 'Magnificent'* whatever. We are a sound bite culture," says Terry Press, Head of Marketing at DreamWorks. This cheerleading posture—*"A Must-See Movie!" "Riveting From The Start!!" "HOT, HOT, HOT!!!"*—services both the needs of desperate movie marketers and the questionable careers of otherwise anonymous reviewers. Occasionally, this effusiveness is replaced with the blunt critical dismissal of a film when it strays from well-tested and accepted formulas. In effect, the job of popular media then becomes one of reassuring viewers with conventional wisdom—that what they already suspected about the movie is right—and to reassure them that the film in question has no value, and therefore that they rest securely tonight at home in front of the set.

At the high end, film critics on television such as the thoughtful historical commentary on The Movie Channel and American Movie Classics, or the shows of Roger Ebert and the late Gene Siskel, provided a good short format for provocative film discussion. The syndicated "Siskel & Ebert" show set a tone and style that some others have attempted to copy. One advantage that TV has over the other media is its use of movie clips. A studio would often rush a new print to Chicago so that its movie will get an early review on their very influential TV program. When done smartly, these visual excerpts are effective for underlining a critical commentary. But many TV stations have dropped their local film critics. Ebert complains, "Now TV is totally dominated by celebrity profiles and puff pieces—'Are they on drugs? What are they wearing? Have they had plastic surgery? But not 'Is the movie any good?'"

Radio has solid potential for serious film commentary. The medium is not as time-pressured as TV, and its "narrowcasting" methods allow for more specialized film criticism specifically aimed at target audiences. Audio selections from a movie work quite well in conveying the drama of a critical scene. The best example is National Public Radio with critic Stephen Schiff, a solid source of good film journalism.

Newspapers. Some newspapers' movie reviewers are susceptible to problems similar to popular TV commentators: A primary concern of many print critics is discovering the taste of their readers and giving them back what they want to hear. Working from studio publicity handouts, some of these writers simply retell movie plots, adding a few personal superlatives. However, the better critics on newspaper staffs match writers in any other media. Their work demands that they watch and review several films a week, and the frequency of deadlines creates pressure to write with accuracy and fresh insight each time out. The cumulative moviegoing experience of these critics gives them a formidable background in the art.

Newspaper critics in cities where the film and allied entertainment industries are concentrated have the most visibility, with their opinions sought out and quoted by many other sources. Over the years, such critics as Janet Maslin and Vincent Canby (*The New York Times*), Andrew Sarris (*New York Observer*), Carrie Rickey (*Philadelphia Inquirer*), Gary Arnold (*The Washington Times*), John Hartl (*Seattle Times*), Kevin Thomas and Kenneth Turan (*Los Angeles Times*), and Michael Wilmington (*Chicago Tribune*) and others have consistently produced solid bodies of work. Although these and other writers are primarily found in newspapers, they also frequently write for magazines and produce books on film. Discovering a newspaper critic who aligns with your taste is a great practical help in wending through the many films released each week.

Magazines. The depth of writing about film in magazines varies greatly. James Agee, writing for *Time* and *The Nation* during the 1940s and 1950s, was the first great American magazine film critic. His impressionistic style showed a dedication to exploring how film affected sensitive audiences. "It is my business to conduct one end of a conversation, as an amateur critic among amateur critics. And I will be of use and of interest only so far as my amateur judgment is sound, stimulating or illuminating," he once said. By positioning himself as an "amateur," he placed himself squarely in the general film audience and would report on how films touched the human spirit. Pauline Kael, writing for *The New Yorker* from 1967 until 1991, advanced and popularized film criticism, influencing in some way every other person working in the field. Until her time, movie criticism was a rather undistinguished job, even though Agee, Otis Ferguson, and Manny Farber in articles and books had already established a high standard for modern film criticism. The key to Kael's success was, simply put, that she was blatantly passionate about movies and that she was a most engaging writer. At the height of her power, everyone in the movie business (many very grudgingly) paid attention to her reviews. A strongly favorable reference to an actor's work in her article matched almost any award that might be given. Other magazines such as *Rolling Stone* (Peter Travers), *Newsweek* (David Anson), *Playboy* (Bruce Williamson), *New Republic* (Stanley Kauffmann), *The New Yorker* (David Denby and Anthony Lane), and *Time* (Richard Corliss and Richard Schickel) have regular film critics with respected reputations.

General circulation entertainment magazines such as *Entertainment Weekly*, *Premiere*, and *Movieline* feature writing that reports on the gossip and glitz of movies, as well as the internecine maneuvers of the business. These are modern-day versions of the "fan magazines" from the early days. David Anson of *Newsweek* cynically remarks: "Magazines are in bed with the movies. They want to sell tickets; we want to sell magazines." Coming from a different perspective, *Variety* and *The Hollywood*

Reporter are not only indispensable movie trade periodicals, but their film reviews, especially those by Todd McCarthy in *Variety*, are written in a refreshingly straight-forward manner, with critical acknowledgments to all of the movie crafts. Other peri-odicals are targeted toward particular technical interests. *American Cinematographer* focuses on the details of lighting and shooting current films; *Cinefantastique* is designed for devotees of horror, fantasy, and science fiction; *Cinefix* details the emerging world of special effects.

Longer and more scholarly film criticism, such as the writing done in the past by Stephen Farber, David A. Cook, Peter Wollen, Molly Haskell, Mary Ann Doane, Parker Tyler, John Simon, Jane Feuer, Dwight Macdonald, David Thomson, Vernon Young, David Bordwell, Kristin Thompson, and many others, are found in literary magazines and specialized film periodicals such as *Commentary*, *Film Comment*, *Film Culture*, *Sight and Sound*, *Quarterly Review of Film Studies*, *Cinema Journal*, and oth-ers. Because they are not as concerned about rushing to print with the most current reviews, these studies are of a broader scope and are often written with a more aca-demic tone. The beauty of film magazines is that they indulge their readers.

The Internet.   The speed and accessibility of the Internet has afforded a vast, if ill defined, audience with personal Web sites created by a host of self-appointed film critics. Often the sources that the Internet writer relies upon are able to scoop the established print critics with information containing inside gossip from a movie set or an unauthorized previewing of a new film. The quality of insightful writing ranges from critical essays that are startlingly well-informed and filled with keen perceptions to eccentric vanity pieces that are, at best, blandly voguish. The movie industry, how-ever, cannot ignore the potential of these new critics for creating a positive or nega-tive buzz about an upcoming film, given the unpredictable nature of the electronic media's influence. A studio publicity woman has remarked: "The Internet can be a marketing tool, but it can also be a marketing hurdle."

SUMMARY

The commercial end of moviemaking—the advertising and distribution of film—is often considered by its critics to be unworthy of serious discussion when studying cinema. Sales strategies and practices seem to have little to do with the creativity of the true artists of film—the actors, director, and allied technical talent. For some, the whole subject of movie promotion smacks of media hype and base commercialism.

Yet stories abound of genuinely worthy films that have gone unseen and unappre-ciated because of the flawed policies of the releasing company's marketing plans and distribution policy. The reality of the entire moviemaking process is this: Before the creative arts in the film can be communicated, appreciated, and enjoyed, necessary information about the film must be presented through the media, which gains atten-tion and entices the audience. Every filmmaker—foreign, independent, or main-stream—is more than thankful when the engines of the industry do their work well in this crucial phase. Good marketing and distribution of a movie not only rightfully links the film to its potential audience, but the financial success of a movie is the surest way of enhancing the opportunity for the filmmakers to carry on their work in succeeding movie projects.

Common to all the arts, the aesthetic response of film critics and cinema scholars to movies is a natural reaction. The effect of varying forms of film criticism on movie distribution is complex but can have immediate economic effects. The media having the quickest avenues to the public—television, radio, newspapers—obviously have the most clear cut impact. Most of the marketing money is spent promoting films through these conduits. Another level of movie analysis is done in film-oriented magazines that call attention and give weight to high-profile movies and background pieces on industry. Still other periodicals—academic publications giving insight into the nature, art, and history of cinema—can build, explain, or harm reputations of particular films and filmmakers.

Serious moviemakers care about all levels of critical response, from the viewer commenting while leaving the theater to the scholar writing for publication. For the many people connected to the production of a movie, this is their vocation. The economic realities of motion pictures drive the business, the technical capabilities provide the methods, but it is the art of moviemaking that infuses its spirit. It is the passion for excellence that inspires the best filmmakers to go beyond the limits of what is expected and brings to us into darkened theaters their dream to share on silvery screens.

SPOTLIGHT

The Film Critic: Peter Travers Interview

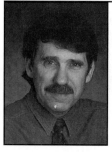

Peter Travers is one of the most influential film critics in the entertainment industry. He joined *Rolling Stone* in 1989 as a senior features editor and is best known for his regular "Movies" column in that magazine. Mr. Travers also co-hosts a regular film review feature segment on CNN's "Showbiz Today." In addition, he is the editor of the *Rolling Stone Film Reader* and a contributor to several books, including *Love and Hisses*.

Richard Peacock: In your formative years, was there any single film experience that woke you up to seeing movies in a different or more profound way?

Peter Travers: *Vertigo*. I guess that I was 13 or 14 years old when I first saw it. I had gone to the movies regularly. I wasn't a movie fanatic but I went every two or three weeks. That movie just stopped me cold. I didn't understand it. I wanted desperately to understand it. No one in my age group would talk to me about it. My parents just said they didn't think *Vertigo* was up to the standard of Alfred Hitchcock. I was always looking for people who would give into my demands of discussing it or seeing it. I remember looking for material on Hitchcock to unlock the mystery of the film. This year has been a particularly good time for me with the revival of the film. It remains my favorite movie because it made me see the value of movie criticism. I would find a critic or book that had an answer or a clue to the mystery. And even if people didn't give me the answer, they would lead me somewhere else.

RP: Who were some of the critics?

PT: The best critic I ever found on *Vertigo* was the British critic Robin Wood. Reading him was a pleasure since his review was so detailed and expansive. Having been brought up around New York City, that was the first time I became aware that critics didn't just write for newspapers and give out star ratings. It was the equivalent in those days to thumbs up or down. Most criticism of *Vertigo* at the time was that it was a disappointing movie—"You found out who did it long before the movie was over!" But it was that aspect of the film that plays with the confusion between illusion and reality that hooked me, and I'm still hooked.

RP: When and where did you actually get started writing film criticism?

PT: I did it as soon as I could, which was in high school. I basically lied to my local newspaper in Westchester County and told them I was in college—that I was specializing in movies. They would let me write very short pieces. I used to run around finding out ways to either write about movies or talk to people who were involved in the movies. Since I was near New York, I was occasionally able to finagle such things.

RP: Then what was the point in your life when you first began to define yourself as a "film critic."

PT: After *Vertigo*, I kept journals. If I saw a movie that affected me, I would write about it. I was always interested in English and literature classes in school, so I would always be jotting down my thoughts about films. I also tried to find a place to watch special films again and again. This was before the videocassette revolution, so I'd come down to the Museum of Modern Art and try to get a screening of something. I think that when I started keeping those journals, my fate was sealed.

RP: Now you write for *Rolling Stone* magazine. When writing your critical reviews, how much does the consideration of its readership profile influence your writing?

PT: This may seem strange but I'm rather obstinate about not letting that influence me. There have been times when I've reviewed films like *Sense and Sensibility,* and people in the research department would say, "Why are you doing that? Do you think anybody cares?" Well, it's my little crusade that they *should* care. If there is some quality in the movie that I think is worth their attention, I write about it. I've worked for a fair number of places and freelanced at different magazines and newspapers. *Rolling Stone* hits a predominately 18- to 34-year-old male audience, almost 65 percent men and many attending college. The readers respond more fully and more contentiously to what I write here than any other publication where I've worked. They care. And they're not limited to the genres that the media assigns to them.

RP: When you were learning your trade, what other critics or other writers—you've already mentioned Robin Wood—influenced your work?

PT: James Agee, for sure. I think that anyone who does this job is aware of Pauline Kael, though I wouldn't call myself a "Paulette," a person who tries to write in her style. Also Andrew Sarris hit me pretty hard with the *auteur theory*. When I was in film school, they were the two gods. Then as I started working, I was invited to join societies like the New York Film Critics and National Society of Film Critics and got to actually know those people. And they were diametrically opposed to one another. Kael thought auteurism was completely insane. I thought it was a fascinating way of looking at movies, without ever believing in it totally. Nobody could convince me that Hitchcock's *Topaz* was up to his *Vertigo*, or that every director's new movie had to be better because it developed his themes. But that theory alerted me to look for themes, and I find the approach valid even to this day. Look at Clint Eastwood's *Absolute Power*. If you come to that movie as just another movie, it might seem disappointing—it's a little slow moving. But if you look at it in the context of Eastwood's best films, you see a lot of the themes he's been dealing with being worked out in the thriller genre. I think this perspective enriches the experience of seeing the movie.

RP: You say that you belong to various societies of critics. Is there much personal or professional exchange that goes on?

PT: Critics usually don't talk to each other about movies. They may have little cliques but typically when we come out of a movie, we get in an elevator and there's complete silence. A month later you might have this chat over coffee somewhere. But normally it's just not done. I remember at one of the voting meetings of the New York Film Critics, when Pauline Kael was still doing it, you would take a piece of paper and write down your first choice and then the votes were added up as we all sat silently in a room. I remember my disappointment when I first joined this august group that nobody ever talked. We sat there and the chairman tallied the votes, no names were read aloud. When Kael was there she would insist that each critic verbally state his or her choice. That provocation was really important. One time Steve Martin was up for best actor for *All of Me*, a comedy, in the face of others playing more traditional dramatic roles. She stopped the group and said, "We never consider how hard physical comedy is, how it is a lost art," and went on to give an impassioned speech. On the next vote Martin won. That was influence, but I don't think it was a negative one. She was performing the role of a provocateur within that society of critics.

RP: Very simply, what makes a good film critic?

PT: Tops on my list are enthusiasm and passion for the subject. And by that I don't mean being a mindless movie buff. I mean that you should be genuinely engaged by the medium and have a feeling for its history. I know too many people doing this for a living who seem to hate it, who feel that nothing in it is worthwhile. Or that what was worthwhile ended 25 years ago and that there's nothing to see anymore. I was at the Sundance Film Festival recently and there was a panel of under-30 filmmakers. The question of a Hitchcock or Scorsese influence came up and one filmmaker said, "I don't give a damn! I don't even know who they are. I just need to make my movie the way I'm going to make it!" Well, I understand that position coming from a filmmaker, but I don't understand it in a film critic. We really need to know that field and try to bring that experience to the party.

RP: Yes, you can feel a sourness in some movie critics. I think that Pauline Kael got some of that near the end of her career.

PT: I think that she started to feel that the people she first championed weren't performing up to her standards. She had a tendency to turn against some of the people who she had once helped to make, such as Scorsese and Brian DePalma.

RP: Do you keep up with more academic writing about cinema—the *deconstructionist* school of thought, etc.?

PT: I do, just as I keep up with what some of my colleagues are writing. I talk to Stanley Kaufmann and Andrew Sarris and other teacher/critics like David Sterritt from a more academic angle. I find that level of conversation very enriching. The worst thing you can do in reviews is be stuck just relating movie plots and saying, "I give it a big thumbs up."

RP: The critics have always been important for movie distribution companies, but nowadays critics seem to have risen to new heights of importance in relation to the success or failure of a movie. Do you agree?

PT: No. I don't believe that at all. If you are talking about mainstream Hollywood movies, critics have no influence at all unless as a group we say, "If you go to see *Showgirls* for any reason other than its high camp value, you're crazy." I think that the only place where critics make a difference is with smaller movies, independent films that might fall between the cracks. But I also think that it's a very good place for critics to have influence.

RP: Are you aware when you write that if you give a positive review, you will be widely quoted?

PT: You can get yourself locked into circumlocutions to avoid it. I watched John Simon trying not to be quoted by saying things like, "He gave a not uninteresting performance." I work at a magazine that uses a star system for music reviews. I've always fought the star system for movies. It's a shorthand that stops people from reading, "Oh, he gave it 2 1/2 stars so that's that." I don't like grading movies. My opinion is the least important aspect of what I'm offering. What's crucial is my argument—why I believe what I believe. There are some critics, however, who think you should never give an opinion, that film should only be discussed in abstract ways. I don't agree with that either.

RP: Does whole movie marketing affect you in any way?

PT: As far as being quoted, I don't want to play that game. If I think a movie is good, I'll say it and that's my equivalent of a super rating. Then I'll go on to what I think is the crux of a good review. Most people look at ads and just see a jumble of names and adjectives. I once wrote a year-end essay in *Rolling Stone* about the whole process of "the blurb world." I talked about the worst example of what happened to me. It was a big movie—*Indecent Proposal* with Robert Redford and Demi Moore. I had called it "sexist propaganda" and I said that it was "shamelessly packaged as a date night hit." The blurb in the paper the next day announced, "A DATE NIGHT HIT!" I protested, and we had our legal department write a letter, but I found out that legally there is not much you can do about it. The studio eventually stopped it when they went to their next ad. Now there's a whole substratum of people dedicated to writing blurbs and nothing else. I don't know who they are or where they work. I just see these titles behind their names. They're completely off the deep end.

RP: Is there some element in a movie that especially excites you when it's done well?

PT: Good screenplays truly excite me. It's an odd thing to say in a world in which everything is image. One of the things that I like about Quentin Tarantino in *Reservoir Dogs* and *Pulp Fiction*—even though there are people who don't like the violence in them—is that they are extremely well written. They're solidly constructed, have humor, and are written in an original style. Tarantino's influence is literary, especially the novels of Elmore Leonard, and people speak in huge gobs of dialogue. Yet if you stopped someone on the street and told them that those films had more dialogue than violence, they probably would disagree.

RP: It's great to go to a movie and see a good screenplay at work through the images.

PT: Right. Maybe it's that we're approaching the summer season and I'm seeing nothing but action/adventure movies in which they seem to have given up on the idea of good writing. Some people might say that I'm writing for a younger audience so why should I keep referring to Billy Wilder and *Double Indemnity* if I'm reviewing *The Usual Suspects*. Well, today people can have access to classic films at the drop of a hat at any video store. It gives them a truer touchstone in the *film noir* category. They've been given a chance to compare and contrast. They should take it.

RP: If you had to choose one decade in movie history to label as "golden," which would it be?

PT: I know that the popular thing to say is the 70s, and I think that it was the *last* golden one. But I have a tremendous affection for the 50s. I know it's an unpopular choice but I think right from the beginning when Joe Mankiewicz wrote and directed *All About Eve*, so much was accomplished in that decade.

As a screenplay, Douglas Sirk's *Written on the Wind*, released in 1956, is insane, a total melodrama, yet Sirk is telling a whole different story through his German expressionist images. Director Nick Ray opened the decade with *In a Lonely Place*, a movie that is right up there with the best of *film noir*. It's a movie about movies. The cynical screenwriter, played by Humphrey Bogart, is someone Ray knows from the inside. The 50s is a striking decade and one that hasn't been given it's due. Think of John Ford's *The Searchers*; Orson Welles's *Touch of Evil*; John Houston's *The Asphalt Jungle*; Alexander McKenzie's *Sweet Smell of Success*; Stanley Kubrick's *Paths of Glory*; Howard Hawk's *Rio Bravo*; Billy Wilder's *Sunset Boulevard* and *Some Like It Hot*. These were peak years for Hitchcock with *Strangers on a Train, Rear Window, North by Northwest*, and of course *Vertigo*. Hollywood produced three of the finest musicals in *Singin' in the Rain, The Band Wagon*, and George Cukor's *A Star Is Born*. And there were great foreign-language films from Truffaut, Bergman, Fellini, Max Ophuls, and others.

RP: Professionally, what is your typical work week like?

PT: Hell. I'm on a deadline structure, so I'm seeing between six to ten movies a week. Then I am deciding which of those to review for a publication that comes out every two weeks in which I review five or six at the most. Then I have to decide which movie to write a longer lead review. Before this I was at *People* magazine where I would have to write reviews in condensed forms. That's why *Rolling Stone* was so attractive to me. I can write 4,000 words on a single movie if I like. It's a privilege when I can do that on a movie like Robert Altman's *Short Cuts*, with it's great screenplay from the short stories of an author, Robert Carver, whom I greatly admire. The work became something else when it became a movie—a fascinating collaboration of the two. If you were asked to write about that in 500 words, you couldn't begin to do it justice.

RP: Do you have a particular process—even ritual—that you go through in writing a review? Do you set it aside, for example, for a day before rereading it and submitting it?

PT: I think that one of the reasons we critics don't talk to each other after a screening is that we haven't formulated an opinion yet. I have to live with it. I take a train to work and I love to hold a newspaper, faze out on what I'm reading, and just reflect on the movie I saw. It's not the notes I take on a movie because at the time I'm just jotting down ideas. But in the days after, what comes into my head—the rebuilding of the movie—may not be exactly what I saw on the screen, but how it affected me. That's what I owe the reader. That, and the sense of history about film and any other arts a film relates to. There are some who say you should not write about how you were personally affected. I take the other position. When film is the art form it aspires to be, and so infrequently is, I always want to walk around the block afterwards and drink in the experience. Maybe I'm intemperate about it, but

I get really enthusiastic. Just as I get very disappointed when a movie does not come through, given the talent involved.

RP: What's the hardest part of your work?

PT: Writing itself is a sweet torture. The hardest review is writing about a film that you really admire. You want to do the movie justice without gushing like those reviewers who praise everything because they need access for their radio or television shows. The put-down is the easiest thing to do. It's so easy to be a smart ass. There are those critics who feel that to like something is a sign of weakness. So it becomes like a bullfight, with the writer collecting ears and showing superiority over the medium being reviewed. Both positions are unworthy.

RP: Given that, what position should the film critic take?

PT: I want to articulate this very strongly and correctly. Criticism was important to me growing up because I was looking for that special voice to share the experience of a movie with me. Not a voice to tell me what to think, but one to help me think. A good critic is a teacher who provides historical perspective and artistic touchstones that broaden horizons. Too often, though, reviewers narrow those horizons. They make a quick judgment, whether a movie is good or bad, and end it there. Movie criticism as *Gong Show* doesn't inform either the reader or filmmaker. After reading a good review, a filmmaker should believe his or her work has been grappled with, that there has been a match. Other critics trade the gong for the pulpit. They show off and pontificate. Look how smart I am, they seem to say, referring to films they saw at festivals that the reader has no access to. They don't feel the need to explain their terms to provide a context or even an opinion. I don't believe that's responsible criticism. Those "serious" critics are so appalled by the Hollywood product that they forget that this is what the public sees. What they should be doing is using Hollywood movies to bring the reader to the next step. If readers are responding to a big-budget thriller such as *Ransom* with Mel Gibson, why not use that interest to guide them to something better like the independently produced *Fargo*, and point out the improvements in characterization, humor, and style. When readers learn to trust your expertise and instincts, a dialogue develops that frees readers to absorb what they learn and form their own opinion. It works the same way in teaching.

RP: If you were to change a couple things in the American movie industry today, what would they be?

PT: What I would change is Hollywood's fear of doing anything new. Back in the 50s, the Zanucks, the Warners, the Harry Cohns and other studio chiefs were monsters, but those executives also wanted to make good movies. They were embarrassed in front of one another if they only turned out junk. That's gone. So all we have now are executives who say that we've got to remake last year's hit. The studios don't seem to want to do anything new.

RP: On the other side, what is good about the current state of cinema today?

PT: It is a good time for independent movies. They are being recognized as a viable alternative to the junk that is out there. Does it mean that we're going to see a lot more of them? I don't know. But people in the industry are seeing a market there. Harvey and Bob Weinstein at Miramax use every marketing trick in the books to promote some truly good movies. Take *The English Patient* and *Sling Blade,* for example. What needs to be changed is the attitude that says a movie that costs $5 million and earns $25 million is a failure. It isn't. That's a comfortable profit. You maintained your artistic integrity. Isn't that enough? When will the greed stop? Why should every movie make $100 million to be considered a hit? The independents should have a place to grow, and Hollywood should have a place for its *Star Wars* and other spectacles. It shouldn't have to be one or the other. I just wish that the studios would take chances more, like the world of independent film does.

RP: I take it then you still enjoy going to movies?

PT: I still do, every time. I may come out disappointed, but I always go in thinking, "This is going to be an adventure!" The fun comes in the search—I'm still trying to find out what *Vertigo* really means. ◀

FILMS TO CONSIDER

Broadening one's preferences in movies is similar to expanding one's choice in food. To acquire a taste, you first have to sample what's on the dish. However, you can't order what's not on the menu, and, unfortunately, many of the best films are not easily available. But with a little searching about, almost any movie can be found. Here's a starter, fifteen films that are a few favorites of this critic:

- *Woman in the Dunes* (1964): The special ability of cinema to confine the viewer in the world of the filmmaker's imagination is best experienced in Hiroshi Teshigahara's severe yet sensual movie about woman and man trapped in a sandpit.

- *The Umbrellas of Cherbourg* (1964): In this engrossing one-of-a-kind movie, all of the dialogue sung (with lyrics by Jacques Demy and a jazz score by Michel LeGrand) as two lovers wend their way through their disrupted lives to regain their lost romance.

- *Repulsion* (1965): Roman Polanski's spare but erupting style of storytelling works with special force in this plunge into the distorting mind of a beautiful young woman (Catherine Deneuve) during a few days alone in an apartment.

- *Fat City* (1972): John Huston's gritty film about down and out boxers in Stockton, California, is a perfectly realized production that combined great performances by Jeff Bridges, Susan Tyrrell, and Stacey Keach with the subdued visual style of Conrad Hall, ASC.

- *Aguirre: The Wrath of God* (1972): Fiction meets reality in this Werner Herzog film about the madness that ensues as a band of Spanish conquistadors led by an increasingly insane leader (Klaus Kinski) makes their way down the Amazon.

- *Stavisky* (1974): The lure of comfortable decadence is the basis for this stylishly mounted film by Alain Resnais about a financial wizard and conman (Jean-Paul Belmondo) whose corrupting power finally brought down the government in 1930s France.

- *Bye Bye Brazil* (1980): Director Carlos Diegues's movie, seen through the experiences of unlikely characters roaming rural Brazil with a small carnival, gives us the high spirits and grim reality of lives lived with bright dreams and simple needs.

- *Man Facing the Southeast* (1986): When a mysterious man arrives at an Argentinean asylum claiming to be an extraterrestrial, he quietly asserts himself into the consciousness of everyone who surrounds him with what seems to be supernatural powers.

- *The Unbearable Lightness of Being* (1988): The Milan Kundera reality-based novel growing out of the tragedy of Prague 1968 is superbly translated to the screen by Philip Kaufman, dramatizing the tensions between political idealism and the carefree sexual existence of the major characters.

- *Daughters of the Dust* (1991): The rich narrative of director Julie Dash about female decendents of slaves living on the Sea Islands of Georgia is a quiet movie of remembered hardship and jubilant bonding as they contemplate a move to the mainland.

- *Bandit Queen* (1994): This harrowing story is based on the experiences of an Indian woman sold into marriage at age 11 but who discovered her strength as an outlaw leader of anti-government bandits and who, amazingly, effected real political change.

- *Safe* (1995): The opaque attitude of director Todd Haynes toward the plight of a woman (Julianne Moore) who becomes increasingly convinced that her illness is caused by the vagaries of pollution is subtly delivered in the airless world of lifelessly staged scenes.

- *Antonia's Line* (1995): Told by director Marleen Gorris in a long and telling flashback, no life has been better summed up and understood on film than that of Antonia, a nonconformist living in a tight Dutch community, on the day she has chosen to die.

- *L'america* (1996): That a narrative film can best convey the plight and hope of the human condition is powerfully shown in this film about Albanian men and woman seeking to emigrate from the wasteland left after the fall of communism in 1991.

- *West Beiruit* (1999): The incremental changes that war brings to the lives of normal people is told with poignancy and humor through the experiences of a irrepressible teenage Lebanese boy living with his family in the divided city of Beiruit.

THOUGHT QUESTIONS AND EXERCISES

Watch a film from those listed.

1. Watch a film. Apart from the fact that it might be in a foreign language, define the differences between this movie and the average Hollywood film shown at local multiscreen theaters. What about the nature of the film prevented it from gaining a larger American audience? Speculate at length.

2. Choose a film. If the film were about to be released this year, and putting yourself in charge of its distribution, list the methods you would use to successfully maximize the film's viewership. What season on the movie calendar, for example, would you choose for its release date? How would you get the word out on the film?

3. If you were making a *trailer* for the film, what about the movie would you emphasize? Make up a short storyboard listing the moments from the film that you include. What are the key images that would present the essence of the movie?

4. Look up three reviews of the same movie. Which critic most closely reflects your attitude to the film? From which review did you gain the most insights? In a purely literary sense, which critic is the best writer and most enjoyable to read? After the experience of reading these reviews, have you altered your opinion of the film?

5. Write a review of the film in a popular style that might be suited for inclusion in a daily newspaper. Take into consideration the nature of your audience. Give the review a headline.

FURTHER READING

Agee, James. *Agee on Film: Criticism and Comment on the Movies* (New York: Modern Library, 2000).

Andrew, J. Dudley. *The Major Film Theories: An Introduction* (New York: Oxford University Press, 1976).

Arnheim, Rudolf. *Film Essays and Criticism* (Madison: University of Wisconsin Press, 1997).

Austin, Bruce A. *Immediate Seating: A Look at Movie Audiences* (Belmont, CA: Wadsworth, 1988).

Barnouw, Erik. *Documentary: A History of the Non-Fiction Film* (New York: Oxford University Press, 1993).

Bordwell, David. *Making Meaning: Inference and Rhetoric in the Interpretation of Cinema* (Cambridge, MA: Harvard University Press, 1989).

Bywater, Tim, and Thomas Sobchack. *Film Criticism: Major Critical Approaches to Narrative Film* (New York: Longman, 1989).

Corrigan, Timothy. *A Short Guide to Writing about Film* (New York: Longman, 1998).

Doherty, Thomas. *Pre-Code Hollywood: Sex, Immorality, and Insurrection in American Cinema, 1930–1934* (New York: Columbia University Press, 1999).

Film Comment Magazine. 70 Lincoln Center Plaza, New York, NY 10023.

Henderson, Brian, and Ann M. Martin, ed. *Film Quarterly: Forty Years, A Selection* (Berkeley: University of California Press, 1999).

Hill, John. *American Cinema and Hollywood: Critical Approaches* (New York: Oxford University Press, 2000).

The Hollywood Reporter Magazine. P.O. Box 480800, Los Angeles, CA 90048.

Kael, Pauline. *Movie Love: Complete Reviews 1988–1991* (New York: Plume, 1991).

Levy, Emanuel. *Cinema of Outsiders: The Rise of American Independent Film* (New York: New York University Press, 1999).

Mast, Gerald, and Marshall Cohen, ed. *Film Theory and Criticism,* 3rd ed. (New York: Oxford, 1985).

Murray, Edward. *Nine American Film Critics* (New York: Frederick Unger, 1975).

Puttnam, David. *Movies & Money* (New York: Vintage Books, 1999).

Silverman, Kaja. *The Subject is Semiotics* (New York: Oxford, 1983).

Squire, Jason E., ed. *The Movie Business,* 2nd ed. (New York: Simon & Schuster, 1992).

Variety Magazine. P.O. Box 6400, Torrance, CA 90504.

STUDENT WRITING

Peter Rainer makes a good point. In film criticism there are few utterly right or absolutely wrong judgments. Your job as a film critic is one of leading the reader through the film experience as you have perceived it. In doing so, you first have the responsibility to make the reader genuinely interested in your point-of-view. This demands clear writing in which you first lay the groundwork for an approach to the film, then you explain in detail the reasons for the position you are taking. If this is done in good prose style, your paper is on its way to being successful.

Every teacher has a particular approach for writing assignments in cinema studies. Some teachers prefer research papers on cultural, historical, or aesthetic themes; others prefer shorter film reviews that demand more personal responses. Therefore it is hard to generalize about what kind of writing could be required. However, if you are in the dark about how to start, you might consider the following suggestions.

At times during the semester, you may be called upon to write at some length about one or more films. Surprisingly, students are often at a loss when it comes to putting something on paper, even though they know movies well and enjoy them. Old viewing habits can block the facility to analyze closely what is on the screen and to form conclusions in writing. Movies, after all, race by at 24 frames per second. A common complaint put to film teachers is: "I liked the movie but what do you want me to write?" It is tempting for the teacher to respond that, look, in all probability it took hundreds of very talented men and women about eighteen months of concentrated work to produce the movie in question. Surely such a creative effort on the part of the filmmakers can generate a 500- to 1,000-word response, either as positive criticism or a negative analysis.

But as we have learned, movies can be elusive. It is sometimes hard to get a firm starting point from which to write about them. If so, try this simple method. Ask yourself the question:

"How does the movie *work*?!"

When a comedy *works*, it makes us laugh. When a horror film *works*, we are terrified. When a romance *works*, we are filled with desire and affection. If the film worked for you, why did it? Was the *film direction* especially masterful? Did the *theme* have a special resonance for you and the audience? Did the *camerawork* give the film a special graphic imprint? Was the *acting* pivotal in bringing the story to life? Did the *story structure* afford the film a conflict that made sense? How did *music* or *sound effects* enhance the film? Which *production values* came together for the film to achieve its goal? These and many similar questions give specific insight into how an aesthetically successful movie *works*.

On the other hand, when a movie *doesn't work*—the science fiction film that is dull and indecipherable—the same artistic and technical areas can be analyzed. In many ways, bad movies are even more interesting to investigate. Because of the complexity of moviemaking, many things can and do go wrong. Other films may be a tangle of conflicting elements—*misdirected actors doing heroic jobs with a weak script in well-photographed locations that arrived on the screen with mangled editing and a delightful sound track.* It takes a practiced eye to sort it all out.

A LIST OF PROBES

Use one or two of the following statements to trigger your writing. Stay with the ideas and explore them at some length in an essay.

1. Identify the *theme* of the movie. In what ways was the theme revealed in the story structure, characterization, and visual imagery of the film?

2. In what way is the *theme* relevant to the audience for which the film was intended? Is the message realistic or idealistic? Did the theme have a twist that gave it an unusual energy? Specifically, how was that brought out?

3. Was the introduction of the *characters, setting,* and *time frame* especially effective? Exactly how did the director choose to tell the audience the *back story* in the first few scenes of the film? Was this setup both credible and strong enough to carry us into the rest of the story?

4. What was the *central conflict* of the story? Exactly when in the story did the conflict become clear, and under what conditions? Was the conflict unexpected, or did it naturally grow out of the story established up to that point?

5. *Story conflicts* have a way of compounding through the middle of a movie, testing the director's skill at sustaining interest. How does the energy of the conflict build? Is it effective, or does our interest wane? Explain this in detail.

6. What is the nature of the *conflict*? Are the antagonistic forces in the story primarily external or internal? If internal, how do the director and actor show the depth of the problem? In what ways does the particular conflict have more universal implications?

7. In dealing with the conflict of the story, was the *motivation* of the protagonist believable? What *exactly* pushed the person into the series of actions that followed? What new motivations, if any, were introduced along the way?

8. Great *casting* brings together actors who mesh opposing personalities in ways that rivet our attention. Was the casting effective in this film? What attributes did each of the major actors bring to crucial scenes that charged the movie with needed energy and won us over? Analyze a single scene in detail.

9. What unique qualities of the *actor* playing the protagonist in the film makes him or her especially suited for the role? Define the personal qualities and acting style that makes this person suitable to play the character in the story. Was anything lacking in the performance?

10. The production design of a film establishes its *look*. Did this production design illuminate the intention of the film? In what way do the sets establish the style of the film? What does the interior design of the protagonist's living arrangement say about the person?

11. *Color* helps create mood. What basic color patterns were chosen for the film? Describe in some detail the three primary sets of the film in terms of color and design. What effect do the color choices have on our attitude toward the subject of key scenes?

12. The location of the camera gives us our physical relationship to the subject. Choose on important scene, and describe the *camera placement* and *movement*. Were the choices made by the director and cinematographer effective?

13. Great pictures can make a great movie. What was special about the *cinematography* in this film? Did the cinematographer choose any particular stylistic approach to the subject matter that you can identify?

14. Although the work of an editor is elusive, are there scenes in the film in which good *editing* clearly helped achieve its intended impact? Describe the scene shot by shot, explaining the particular effect of the editor's choices.

15. Was the *music* in the film appropriate to its theme? In what sequence did the music especially interpret the screen action? Could the music have been lengthened, shortened, been louder or softer to the advantage of the drama? Be specific.

16. If the film had *special effects,* did they add to the credibility and excitement of the action, or were they a distraction, shifting the focus to the tricks of the craft? What unique sensual element did they bring to the movie?

17. Good *sound effects* can add dramatic tension. Can you identify places at which the choices of the sound engineers made the film stronger? Choose an important scene and detail the sound in it.

18. Was the *ending* of the film a logical conclusion to the story, given the motivations of the characters and their situation? Did the ending feel manipulated in a way that diminished the film experience? Explain your sense of this in detail.

19. Did the movie achieve what it set out to do? Define its *intentions* as closely as

you can, and explain the particular ways by which the director and producers realized their goal.

20. When the movie opened at theaters, what was its reception? If it met with a solid public response, to what do you attribute it? What was the *marketing strategy* for the movie? Check into the total dynamic of its release pattern. If the film was largely ignored, what happened?

SOME WRITING HINTS

Every writer is free to develop his or her own style. However, based on years of having read thousands of submissions, I am moved to make the following suggestions for those students wanting a fair and even sympathetic response from an instructor:

- Do not simply retell the plot of a movie. The point of your writing should be an insightful interpretation of the film, not just the fact that you could slavishly list the sequence of events in it.

- Be concrete. When writing about your attitude toward a movie, describe in detail an actual sequence, scene, or shot that graphically illustrates your point.

- It is fine to make general statements—"Ethan Hawke is great in the part." or "Alicia Silverstone shines."—but follow such claims with *specific examples* of *why* you came to that conclusion. Just *what is it* that brings out his or her performance in this film?

- Focus on only two or three aspects of the film and *get into them*. In a short paper, you cannot cover everything of importance in a movie without quickly becoming superficial.

- It is acceptable to write about a past personal experience that a film may have triggered, but watch out! It comes down to a matter of degree. Whereas your subjective response to a film is valid and useful when clearly and very briefly stated, the basic intent of the paper is an elucidation of the film, and not a jumping off point for prolonged autobiographical reminiscences.

- Don't slip into using jargon. It may be tempting to write about "chick flicks" when a part of the general media uses such terms regularly, but this level of language does not come through well in a student paper.

- Don't fault a film for simply being original. We are often oblivious to the fact that most mainline movies follow a rather rigid and predictable formula of story development. It is a narrative method that becomes expected. Therefore, when a film breaks into a fresh way of telling its story, some viewers become automatically uneasy.

- Use the word *boring* very sparingly when being negatively critical of a film. For some students, the word is a catchall expression. It seems to say that good films are only those in which nonstop action keeps them visually and emotionally buzzing. Certain films *are* genuinely boring, but many more just develop at a sly pace that is unfamiliar. With patience, a viewer can slow to the different rhythm of various film styles. If you use the term, explain in detail your reasons for that judgment.

- Don't complain about subtitles in foreign films. There is no better alternative, except to simply limit oneself to English-speaking movies. Most people would be embarrassed to announce that they only ate "American" food, to the exclusion of French, Italian, or Japanese cuisine. Yet some otherwise sophisticated people are not hesitant to express their ethnocentricity regarding film viewing.

- Have patience. Remember, the essence of the experience of drama demands that the audience "suspend disbelief." As an extension of this idea, it is important to initially "give" the filmmaker his or her *subject*. That is, every story needs some space to develop its dramatic landscape, the shape and style of its ideas. Sometimes the mix of a theme and visual technique will not click until deep into the film.

- If you like a film, *do not* conveniently assign it 4 Stars **** (and if you don't like a film, don't give it an exploding hand grenade). Although we all like to see ourselves as at least equal to our local film critic, it is best to leave such quick rating systems to those truly in need of them.

For a brief but complete text for student writing, see *A Short Guide to Writing about Film,* 3rd edition by Timothy Corrigan, New York: Longman, 1997.

SAMPLE OF A STUDENT PAPER

There are many approaches to writing about a movie. The following "500 word" review is included here to give you just *one* kind of model to use when writing a short film review.

MISERY

Stephen King's work has often been brought to the screen, sometimes very successfully, as in *The Shining* and *Stand By Me*, sometimes grossly in films such as *Creepshow II*. But director Rob Reiner provides a perfectly perverse and ironic sense to King's novel in his adaptation of *Misery*. The story could have been treated as a chance to exploit a willing audience with overheated ghoulish action, but the precise control by Reiner of the story turns, and the superior performances of Kathy Bates and James Caan, establishes the movie as a minor classic.

The plot is wickedly simple. Paul Sheldon (Caan), a popular romance writer of cheap novels, is finishing yet another book. In the opening scene, he sits in front of his typewriter writing his last line, which he punctuates with "The End." He knows that he's a hack writer and is satisfied, popping a bottle of champagne and having a smoke. He puts the manuscript in his beatup briefcase and heads out. It becomes clear that Sheldon has isolated himself in a rustic cabin in the mountains, the perfect writer's retreat. But when he heads down the mountain in a snowstorm, his car skids off the road and crashes. Pinned in the wreckage, Sheldon's leg is smashed.

Luckily, he is saved. Unfortunately, it is by the wrong person, ironically his "number one fan." Annie Wilkes (Kathy Bates) is an eccentric nurse living in this rural area, a woman who is obsessively in love with Sheldon's whole book series. His writing features a character named Misery Chastain who has finally died. What follows is a long nightmare for Sheldon. Recuperating in the nurse's secluded home, Sheldon gradually realizes that he is being held prisoner to this woman's bizarre controlling desires. Annie demands that he write a new book bringing Misery back to life. To get her way, she rattles on in love/hate testaments, until she smashes his legs and imprisons him to finalize her demands.

James Caan is perfect in the role of the worn-out writer of pulp fiction. Although looking slightly haggard, he still can call upon a deep raw strength that marked his earlier work. His character needs it all to survive this mess he finds himself in. Caan also adds a needed comic touch to the character. He has always had a malicious twinkle around his eyes, but he can also give you that blank, amazed look of a straight man, so necessary for comedies about relationships. Kathy Bates has found a defining role in her characterization of the nurse. Always fun to watch, the scizhoid nature of the nurse gives Bates the chance to play a wide range of twisted sides—the saccharine sweet helpmate, the no-nonsense bully, the rage of a madwoman. In the future, she will be associated with this part.

Rob Reiner has made the black comedy suitably tight. Movies shot mainly within a limited setting—in this case, a few rooms of a small house—must rely on a combination of strong performances, thoughtful camera placement, and perfectly appropriate lighting. On the one hand we must experience the claustrophobia that Sheldon feels; on the other, the movie must continue to move forward. Reiner drew out of the actors their finest performances, and he should be given that credit. The right blend of humor and horror is one too rarely achieved in movies of this kind. *Misery* captures us, and keeps us locked in from start to finish.

THE SCENE STRUCTURE OF A MOVIE: FATAL ATTRACTION

The hit movie *Fatal Attraction* (1987) was controversial when first released, triggering a new round of confrontation for some men and women in the arena of sexual politics. Interest was heightened when it was learned that two separate endings for the film had been written and shot. But whatever position one takes on the content, from the viewpoint of screenplay structure, *Fatal Attraction* is a finely sequenced and dramatically sound model.

As previously pointed out in Chapter 2, the primary unit of development for the screenwriter is the *scene*. In the initial stages of structuring a screenplay, it is a common practice for writers to outline their movie by reducing scenes to their basic dramatic action. Often, the information about each scene is put on separate cards so that the writer can easily rearrange the story sequence. It is instructive to analyze in detail the *52 scenes* that screenwriter James Dearden and director Adrian Lyne used as building blocks for the telling of this tightly scripted work.

ACT I

The screenwriter sets up his story by stepping into the lives of an ideal couple, Dan and Beth, and by giving us a close-up look at their family, friends, activities, plans for the future, and a disturbing new relationship with a woman, Alex. Revealed are some human frailties that will be the beginning of Dan's undoing by the end of Act I.

1. The credits come over an **establishing shot**. Camera pans the New York City skyline at twilight, zeroing into a high-rise apartment window.

2. In a modestly upscale apartment, Dan (Michael Douglas), Beth (Anne Archer), and their six-year-old-child Ellen (Ellen Hamilton Latzen) are introduced as a happy, if harried, family. Dan seems to be a professional, and with Beth, in a rush to go out for an author reception.

3. At the author's party, the smart social milieu of New York publishing is presented. Dan's lawyer friend Jimmy (Stuart Pankin) is rebuffed by a wild-haired Alex (Glen Close) when he flirts with her. However, at the bar later in the film's *inciting incident*, Alex introduces herself to Dan. They show a submerged interest in each other.

4. At home in the bedroom and still enlivened, Dan has hopes for sexual intimacy with Beth. But first the dog's nightly walk, then an awakened Ellen climbs in bed with Beth, ending the evening's possibilities.

5. In the apartment lobby and on the street, Dan sees his wife and child off as they go to see Beth's parents in the country for the weekend.

6. At a rare Saturday staff meeting, we find out that Dan is a book publisher's lawyer and that Alex is a new editor. There is electricity between them as they exchange glances.

7. In a short scene in the rain after the meeting, Dan and Alex are both stuck without a cab. They hastily decide to make the best of it and have a drink together in a nearby restaurant.

8. The restaurant scene is pivotal. During it, a seemingly casual conversation leads to coyly seductive exchanges controlled by Alex. A very willing Dan is drawn in. An understanding is reached. They both appear to agree on the sexual narrow limits of the evening's affair.

9. In the kitchen of Alex's apartment, the two make love with abandon. The scene dissolves to a later hour with them exhausted in bed. Suddenly, Alex announces that the night's not over.

10. Still the same evening, Alex and Dan dance in a frantic music scene at a chic city nightclub.

11. Finishing off the night, they enter Alex's apartment building, a converted warehouse in a meat packing area of town. On the freight elevator, Alex takes the lead initiating more uninhibited lovemaking. Dan is out of his league.

12. After an early morning departure, back at his apartment in the morning and feeling guilty, he gets a call from Beth at her mother's house. She will be staying for another night to look at a house that she has heard is for sale. Just as Dan hangs up, Alex calls with an invitation to play more. After a half-hearted resistance, Dan says O.K.

13. In Central Park, Alex, Dan, and his dog run exuberantly. Suddenly, Dan falls and playfully pretends to have died of exhaustion. Alex is strangely unamused and gravely says her father died of a heart attack, only to deny it a moment later with a cruel smirk.

14. With "Madame Butterfly" in the background, they make dinner in her apartment later. The scene is intimate until Alex asks direct questions about Dan's marital situation, which embarrasses him, creating a distance.

15. After making love in her bedroom that evening, Dan gets up to leave. A verbal argument ensues, which escalates into a surprisingly ugly scene in which Alex accuses Dan of just using her. He leaves the room in confusion and anger. In

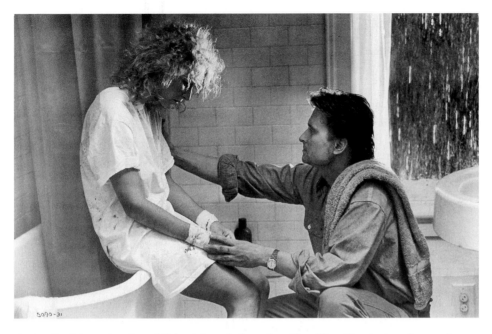

A–1 *Fatal Attraction* Dan (Michael Douglas) soothes Alex (Glen Close) after she cuts her wrists in despair at the end of Act I. (Paramount Pictures)

the kitchen a short time later, a despondent Alex apologizes, but while the two embrace, the camera reveals her wrists *slashed*! In panic, Dan rushes to bandage the wounds. Later, the scene finally slides into a quieter moment when he speaks on the phone to his wife, as Alex rests in bed. This is much, much more than Dan ever bargained for **(A–1)**.

16. In the morning, we witness a caring goodbye between the wounded Alex and sobered Dan.

ACT II

The conflict of the story, at this point, has been clearly established. The protagonist, Dan, had thought the understanding with Alex was for a one-night sexual lark. He now realizes that he seriously misread her personality, that she is out of control, and that his involvement with her has forced on him a dimension of unexpected responsibility. As much as he would like to, he cannot just walk away from the situation. Act II will explore the results of this conflict.

17. Back in his apartment on Monday morning, Dan tries to cover his tracks by making the place look lived-in.

18. In a very short scene, we see Dan at his office early, plunging into work.

19. At his apartment that evening, Dan thankfully indulges in a newfound appreciation for the security of the family circle. Beth is excited about the dream house she found, and Dan guiltily jumps at the chance of driving to the country to see it the next day.

20. At the idyllic country house, the couple roams the empty rooms and finds them perfect.

21. Perhaps a week later, as Dan enters his outer office, Alex is waiting for him. After apologizing for her behavior, she asks him to forgive and forget. Dan says yes but remains cool, rejecting her invitation to see "Madame Butterfly" in two weeks. He is feeling the pressure.

22. Crosscutting, we see Dan, Beth, and their friends Jimmy and his wife Hildy, laughingly engaged in the All-American sport of bowling. Meanwhile Alex sits alone on the floor of her apartment flipping a light switch in dazed depression.

23. At his office, a call from Alex awaits him. Dan has no patience for any more of this and shuts her off.

24. Later, at home, an erotic moment is caught as Dan, with loving desire, watches Beth in lingerie put on her make-up.

25. At a small dinner party, Dan celebrates his possible elevation in the law firm. The phone rings. Immediately Dan is alerted, undermining the joy of the moment. Beth answers but the caller is silent. *[Throughout the film, the telephone is a major instrument of tension and intrusion.]*

26. As Beth and Dan sleep in bed at 2 A.M., the phone rings. The scene cuts to Alex awake with bristling frustration pacing her apartment and demanding that Dan meet with her tomorrow. Pretending that it is a business call, Dan complies.

27. In an important subway scene, Alex announces that she is pregnant! The information stops Dan cold. He recovers and says that he will help with an abortion. But to his amazement Alex says that she wants the child and that she hopes he will want to be part of the process. Although there is some suggestion that she might not be telling the truth, the idea of being locked into the fate of this woman's life is clearly abhorrent to him. The way out is not at all clear.

28. In a very short scene of just two shots, at home Dan sits at his desk alone with his secret dilemma, listening to Beth innocently read to their child in the next room.

29. Dan watches Alex leave her apartment, then lets himself into it. He frantically looks for anything that will give a clue to who this woman really is. In her desk, Dan is further confirmed in what he suspects of her growing madness when he finds an obituary notice of her father. He is not still alive; he *did* die of a heart attack.

30. In a law library, for the first time Dan confides in someone else—Jimmy. Asking for advice, the other lawyer holds out little hope that the problem can be easily solved.

31. As she lies in self-isolation on her bed, Alex finds out that Dan's telephone number has been changed, and she screams an obscenity.

32. As Dan enters his apartment, he is shocked to find Alex talking to Beth! **(A–2)** The pretext for Alex being there is that she is inquiring into the sale of the place. The tension-filled scene ends with Beth innocently giving their new telephone number to a self-satisfied Alex.

33. In angry desperation, Dan shows up at Alex's apartment. But Alex matches his anger, and as an argument ensues, she claims that Dan is morally responsible for the situation. Threats are exchanged and Dan, in a quick fit of rage, slams Alex against a wall before leaving.

34. It's "moving day" at the new house. Dan finds welcome relief when the phone rings and it is simply a friend calling.

35. On the phone from his office, Dan tells Beth that he has bought Ellen the much-desired white bunny rabbit on his desk. He leaves with it.

36. In a multilevel parking garage, Dan rides the elevator. We spot Alex observing him, then darting between cars. When Dan reaches his car, it is covered with steaming acid. The violence has taken a decidedly insane turn.

37. In a rented car, Dan drives home. The scene crosscuts between Dan listening to a tape of Alex's rambling love/hate monologue, and Alex herself following him in a car.

A–2 *Fatal Attraction*   In Act II, Alex makes a surprise visit to the apartment of Dan and his wife Beth (Ann Archer).   (Paramount Pictures)

38. At home finally, Dan goes into the house. Alex parks and crosses the lawn in the dark to a picture window revealing what appears to be an ideal family sitting in the glow of a fireplace with the new bunny. Alex is overwhelmed with revulsion, to the point of becoming physically ill in the bushes.

39. Later in his attic office, Dan is driven to listen to the rest of Alex's tape. His concentration is broken in a playfully scary shot of Beth surprising him.

40. At a local police station, Dan, pretending to represent a client, asks advice of a lieutenant on how to cope with one person stalking another. "Catch the person in the act" is the answer from the cop.

41. Ellen, first in the backyard looking at the rabbit, then at her grandparents, is seen as a bright and sensitive child. Dan hugs her tightly, an anchor of meaning in his chaotic life.

42. As the family walks through the house upon returning, something is terribly wrong. A pot steams on the stove. Ellen rushes to the hutch in the backyard, as Beth opens the lid to find the dead rabbit boiling in water!

ACT III

In working out the primary conflict of the story, Dan's decision to keep his liaison with Alex a secret from Beth created intense pressure in the second act, allowing the screenwriter to create a series of events that turned up the heat. At this turning point, Alex has dared to literally enter Dan's home, a final transgression. The third act recomplicates the plot, as Dan's life is radically changed when he faces the full consequences of his mistaken actions and then resolves the issues of the story with its powerful ending.

43. As a traumatized Ellen lies awake, in the living room Dan finally decides things have gone too far and it's time to come clean. He gives a stunned Beth an outline of the situation. When he tells her that Alex is pregnant, Beth explodes with hurt and anger, her shouting only silenced by their crying child in the doorway.

44. Later, with bags hastily packed, Dan passes his daughter's room crushed by the humiliation he has brought on. In the living room Dan calls Alex to announce that he has told Beth everything. Beth takes the phone to say that if Alex does another thing to her family, she will kill her.

45. Some days later, Ellen gets a call from her estranged father as Beth plays the piano. Life is joyless.

46. Beth arrives to pick up Ellen at school and is told that someone has already taken her. In sheer panic, Beth combs the streets of her town in the car. Intercut with this scene are shots of Alex and a trusting Ellen in an amusement park as they board a roller coaster. The pace of the crosscutting intensifies, as the rush of emotions accelerates for everyone. Distracted, Beth

smashes violently into another car. In a weird calm, Alex lets Ellen out at her driveway.

47. At the hospital, Dan hits bottom. Filled with self-contempt, he comes to see his damaged, bedridden wife. A hint of forgiveness comes over her face and reconciliation may be possible.

48. Dan races through traffic. Something has snapped. When he arrives at Alex's place he bursts in and attacks her with a fury of blows. Alex is fighting for her life, and in a lull, suddenly attacks Dan with a knife. When he finds himself choking her, he comes to his senses and slowly backs out of the place.

49. At the police station, a totally shaken Dan honestly reports the threats to his family. The weary lieutenant recommends calm and routinely says he will look into it.

50. Back home in the calm of Ellen's bedroom, Dan assures his daughter that the world is right again, and he won't be going away.

51. As the steam rises from hot water in the tub, a wounded Beth slowly prepares for a bath. In the bedroom, Dan checks in with the police by phone. He then tenderly brings more towels to his wife. Parallel action builds tension in this complex scene. Downstairs, Dan locks up and puts on water to boil. Beth continues to pamper herself until the image of a crazed Alex appears in the doorway with a knife. Alex mumbles her distorted reality to Beth as she wields the knife, then she attacks. The screams are temporarily blocked out by the whistle of a tea kettle in the kitchen, but Dan then races to Beth's aid **(A–3)**. He fights off Alex, finally choking her underwater. In a double ending unworthy of the movie, Alex almost supernaturally recovers, only to be finished off by Beth's pistol.

A–3 *Fatal Attraction* During the violent climax in Act III, Dan is attacked by Alex and ends her threat. (Paramount Pictures)

52. In the front of the house the police leave, Dan moves inside to embrace Beth. A close-up of a family portrait suggests that things may get back to normal.

THE END

In terms of screenplay structure, this outline *is* the movie. Granted, in this form the movie is still a 52-scene story skeleton. In preproduction, scenes could easily be added, taken out, or shifted around in varying sequences. Each of these scenes, of course, must come alive as it is filled out with dialogue, with the production values created by the craft teams, and with subtle character interpretations by the actors. But with this tight blueprint of action, not only Adrian Lyne but a good number of other directors could begin to make a superior film.

When writing the script and planning the shoot, first the writer then the director had to decide whether these scenes would adequately tell their story. The structural qualities of the *Fatal Attraction* script are found in its blend of complex emotional layering, which continually raises the stakes of the conflict, and the physical action in the movie, which matches this building intensity. In viewing the film, one senses the rightness in the choices made by the filmmakers in every phase of the production. When considering any film, the first place to look for its strength or weakness is screenplay structure.

GLOSSARY

Italics indicate cross references to other glossary terms.

Above-the-line-costs.   Those expenses which are negotiated by individual contracts, usually covering the producer group, screenwriter and story rights, actors, film director, and director of photography.

ADR.   Automatic dialogue replacement is the postproduction process by which actors lip-sync their voices to their projected image.

Aerial shot.   Refers to the camera being positioned at a high angle above the ground, usually fixed to a crane or helicopter.

Ambient sound.   The general sounds, no matter how faint, that fill the background of the primary recorded sounds.

Anamorphic lens.   A special camera lens that compresses (or expands) the horizontal aspect of its subject, leaving the vertical intact. When the image is projected on a screen, a comparable lens expands it.

Answer print.   A term used loosely to refer to a print returned to the filmmakers with both sound and all optical effects.

Arc lamp.   An older-style light generating an intense whiteness caused by an electrical current moving between two carbon rods.

Art director.   In older films, this designation was given to the person now referred to as the *production designer.* However, the title still

exists with the responsibilities specialized into heading the art department.

ASC (*American Society of Cinematographers*).   Members of the guild usually identify themselves with the letters after their name.

Aspect ratio.   The image ratio relating width to height. The standard Academy ratio is [1.33: 1]; the wide screen ratio is [1.85: 1]; the anamorphic ratio is [2.35: 1]; the 70mm ratio is [2.2: 1].

Auteur theory.   A critical approach to film that emphasizes the essential role of the director as the author of the work, with his or her presence imprinted in every aesthetic choice.

Beat.   A term used by actors, musicians, and editors to indicate the rhythmic stress and pause inherent in the flow of their work.

Below-the-line-cost.   A film budget designation for the expenses of all production activities, including camera supplies, set construction, film processing, and fixed salaries of the crew. Not included are any negotiated contracts of the performers and major technical staff (see *Above-the-line-costs*).

Best boy.   The first assistant (male or female) to the key electrician (or *gaffer*).

Bi-pack.   The method of putting two strips of film in contact through a camera, projector, or printing process.

Blocking a scene. The process of arranging the active elements of a shot, including their choreographed movements, in relation to the camera.

Blue-screen. A process by which objects are photographed against a special blue background in white light. After a series of laboratory printings, a *traveling matte* is achieved, the effect being that different foreground and background images are combined in a single *composite*.

Boom microphone. In order to pick up voices of actors or other elements moving on the set, a microphone is suspended from a pole out of camera range.

Cinema vérité. A French term used to describe an unadorned approach to filmmaking, in which the "truth" of the moment is the primary consideration. Associated with the attitude and visual texture of the documentary, the primary impact of films shot in this style is their sense of immediacy.

Close shot (CS). When its subject is a human body, a shot that includes shoulders and head.

Close-up (CU). When the subject is a person, a shot that fills the frame with only the face. If the shot is of an object, the term indicates its narrow field of view for the purpose of intensifying the object's dramatic value.

Composite. Two or more separately photographed images combined on a single print.

Continuity. During principal photography, a person is designated to keep a detailed record of each shot for the purpose of continuity. When used in relation to editing, the method of cutting that visually leads the viewer to accept the flow of edited images as a natural sequence of action by matching movement and dialogue.

Contrast ratio. The relative difference between light and dark surfaces of an image. An image with sharp distinctions between the two is said to be **high contrast;** an image with a wide spectrum of gray gradation is called **low contrast.**

Coverage. The footage shot by the director with the intention of capturing the dramatic action of a scene in its fullness. Without adequate coverage, an editor's work is impaired.

Cover shot. A shot that clearly shows the entire desired situation and ensures that the recorded footage will not lose any significant dramatic elements. Also called a *master shot.*

Crane shot. A shot taken from a camera mounted on a crane. Because of its elevated angle and mobility, the shot gives a dynamic overview of its subject.

Cross-cutting. The editing technique of selecting shots, cutting back and forth between actions taking place at two or more locations. This usually implies that the events are happening simultaneously, creating a sense of parallel action.

Cutaway. A shot inserted into the continuing flow of action that calls attention to itself for dramatic or informational impact.

Dailies. Prints of the previous day's shoot that are quickly assembled to give the filmmakers continuous feedback on the progress of the work. Because of this, they are also called **rushes**.

Day-for-night. A method of filtering or exposing a shot so that subjects photographed in daylight appear to be taken at night.

Depth of field. That space before and behind the focus plane that through a lens appears to be sharply defined.

DGA. *Directors Guild of America.*

Dialogue replacement. Also called *looping* or **dubbing**, it refers to the process of putting good sound quality dialogue on film not achieved when the original footage was being shot. These post-synchronization recording sessions are common in filmmaking.

Director's cut. The edited version of the completed film approved by the film director. This may not be the same as the *release print* version controlled by the producers.

Dissolve. The superimposition of a *fade-out* and a *fade-in.* The blending effect makes a smooth, poetic transition that can be a comment on the nature of the subjects photographed.

Dolby sound.   A patented process of noise reduction that reduces the hiss on sound tracks. The company has evolved through many generations of the technology.

Dolly shot.   A free moving shot that is achieved by fixing a camera on a specially designed cart, or dolly. The advantage of the shot is its fluid freedom as the camera moves through space.

Establishing shot.   Normally an *extreme long shot* used to orient the viewer to the larger geography or dimensions of a setting, giving what follows a physical context.

Executive producer.   A film credit usually reserved for the person who was most strongly influential in arranging funding for a film project. Normally this person does not have a hands-on role in the production.

Expressionism.   Derived from a turn-of-the-twentieth-century art movement, this cinematic style stresses the inner psychological states of the characters through the use of exaggerated mood lighting and unusual camera placement and movement.

Extra-diegetic sound.   A sound that is not physically associated with what is presented on the screen, but which may emotionally comment on the action.

Extreme close-up (ECU).   A very tight shot of a detail, often of a part of the human body, which fills the screen when shown.

Extreme long shot (ELS).   A shot that places its primary subject, in its broad field of view, at a great distance from the camera.

Eye-level shot.   A shot that is taken from an angle parallel to the ground at a height of a person's eyes being photographed. Films shot in a realistic mode would tend to use this shot because it is the "normal" perspective from which we experience our world.

Fade.   When light is withdrawn slowly from a shot, becoming a black field, this transitional shot is called a **fade-out.** When light comes up from a black field to reveal an image, it is a **fade-in.** The style of transition usually implies a significant passage of time.

Fast motion.   When camera speed exposes film at fewer than the common 24 fps, its projection at that standard frame rate will create the effect of fast motion on the screen. The speeded movement can be quite humorous.

Fill light.   Secondary lighting added to a subject for the purpose of reducing and softening the shadows caused by the primary light source.

Film Noir.   A visual style of film, most notably urban thrillers in the 1940s and 1950s, that made graphic the tough, uncompromising realities of contemporary life. Characterized by extremely *low-key lighting*, resulting in strong dark/light contrasts, the term translates as "black film."

Final cut.   The completed version of a movie ready for a negative to be made, and prints to be struck and released.

First cut.   An early cut of footage deemed appropriate to be shown to producers and others, giving a fair consideration of how the *final cut* might be expected to play.

Flashback/Flashforward.   An editorial time shift that interrupts the normal sequence of present-time story telling. The **flashback** may be a shot or an entire sequence, giving historical or emotional background to the characters. A **flashforward** is less frequently used, but is most often employed to indicate psychic insights into the future.

Focal length.   When the lens is focused on an object at infinity, the focal length is the distance from the film plane to its optical center bringing the object into sharp definition.

Foley.   The addition of sounds to duplicate sounds not picked up in the original shooting of the film. A **Foley artist** in a special studio applies sounds while watching projected images. Typically, footsteps across a floor are put in in this manner.

Fps (frames per second).   The rate of speed that film passes through a camera or projector, the modern standard being 24 fps.

Freeze frame.   An image that appears unchanged on the screen because it is repeated on the print. The technique is used to visually underline some aspect of what is presented.

Front projection.   By reflecting footage onto a background screen with a beam-combiner (a semireflecting mirror) between the camera and the subject, the primary subject can appear to be placed in front on almost any environment. Front projection gives a brighter projected image than *rear projection*.

Full shot (FS).   A shot that shows the human figure from head to feet, with some part of the background to give context.

Gaffer.   A term for the chief electrician on a movie set.

Genre.   In regard to movies, the term refers to a recognized category of film defined by its subject matter or common cinematic treatment. Labeling movies by genre is useful in the film industry because it has established a ready reference tool for the public to identify types of movie content. For example, the Western was a favorite genre during the 1950s.

Grain.   Refers to the size of the metallic silver crystals within a frame. **Fine grain** film has smaller crystals; **coarse grain** film has larger. A filmmaker must decide on the type of film stock that best suits the intended look of the movie.

Grip.   A general purpose stagehand assigned to many of the more physical tasks on the set.

Gross.   The total amount of money taken in by a movie before deducting the production and distribution expenses.

High-angle shot.   A shot taken by a camera located above its subject tilted down toward it.

High-key lighting.   A lighting arrangement that fills a set with very bright illumination from the *key light,* and when enhanced with *fill light,* the effect is an image with almost no shadows. This type of lighting has been traditional in musicals and comedies.

Hue.   A color gradation of the spectrum.

Insert.   An independent shot cut into a scene, usually intended to give specific information and influencing the action surrounding it.

Intercutting.   In its broadest use, a process of editing that interweaves segments from separate scenes to indicate a dramatic association.

It also refers to the process of selecting individual shots to be inserted in a master shot.

Iris.   A transitional style of ending or starting a scene by using a contracting or expanding circular mask. The method was popular in the silent era.

Key.   The term is used in many contexts in film production, designating either a primary supervisory person (e.g., a **key grip**), or a principal piece of equipment (e.g., a **key light**, which is the light that creates the basic illuminating look of a set).

Leitmotif.   A method of associating a musical piece with a character or other element, that then recurs throughout the movie at significant moments, triggering a desired emotional response.

Line producer.   The person who oversees all day-to-day elements of the production during the shoot. The responsibilities include being a personal link between the main producers and the director.

Lip-sync.   The exact matching of the dialogue track with the lip movements on the screen.

Live sound.   The sound tracks recorded during the shooting of a film (rather than created in postproduction), also called **production sound**.

Long lens.   The term usually designates any 35mm movie camera lens with a focal length greater than 50mm. The visual effect flattens space and diminishes perceived distances.

Long shot (LS).   A shot that makes its primary subject appear less than half the size if the vertical dimension of the frame. If a human figure, it is seen in full within the context of an ample background.

Looping.   The activity of synching dialogue by an actor in a rerecording session, matching a new reading while watching the existing images on a projection screen. Also referred to as **dubbing**.

Low-angle shot.   A shot that is taken from a camera tilted up toward its subject.

Low-key lighting.   Because the set is dimly illuminated with low light except for generally one strong source, the visual effect is one of deep shadows and some bright surfaces. This creates what is termed high contrast ratio.

Magnetic sound track. A filmstrip having magnetized iron-oxide stripes. Although this format creates better reproduction, it is usually reserved for special films presented on 70mm prints. Because *optical sound tracks* are less expensive and theater projectors are universally equipped to accommodate the format, magnetic sound tracks for normal movie exhibition are rare.

Mask. A specially designed piece of material placed in front of a camera that blocks out part of the subject. Later, another image can be added to the black area to create a *composite image.*

Master shot. Usually a long shot taking in a prolonged action. The intention is to cover the scene with a single basic shot, into which other shots may be introduced to enhance more specific visual drama.

Match cut. An editing technique that links two pieces of related action, resulting in a single smooth flow of imagery.

Matte shot. The use of a flat black matte (or mask) to cancel light out of a portion of the frame. A *composite* image is then created, combining seamlessly two separate shots onto one. The technique is one of the oldest in the special effects repertoire, and it is still used effectively.

Mechanical special effects. Any special effect that is created by the implementation of a mechanical device. Everything from fog machines to the gadgetry in a science fiction film is included in mechanicals.

Medium shot (MS). When the subject of this shot is a human body, its field of view will include the knees or waist ranging to the head.

Miniature. A small-scale replica of a set or object. The design and photography of these models is done by special effects units.

Mise-en-scène. A French term, literally "placing into a scene," borrowed from the stage, which in film refers to the physical arrangement and staging of people and objects within the frame.

Mix down. Any mixing of sound tracks which reduce their number.

Montage. For American films, the word is used to describe a series of cuts superimposed on one another, usually with a visually poetic effect. Europeans use the term to refer to standard editing. The early Soviet filmmakers applied it to a specific dynamic style of abrupt editing.

M.O.S. Film shot without sound.

MPAA (The Motion Picture Association of America). Among other activities, the organization provides the rating board that evaluates movies and assigns a code designation.

Narrative film. A film that tells a story, normally used to describe a fictional movie.

Negative. The word is used for exposed film stock whose black-and-white values are reversed. The original edited negative is preserved so that final prints can be made from it.

Nitrate film. Films from the first half of the twentieth century were made of the highly flammable cellulose nitrate stock. When well stored, the stock retained its excellent original values.

Nonfiction film. An inclusive term to distinguish the subject matter from fiction film. Nonfiction dramatizes factual rather than situations. It is often used interchangeably with the term "documentary film."

Normal lens. A lens with a focal length of 40mm to 50mm, roughly imitating the perspective of "normal" eyes.

Optical printer. To achieve numerous optical effects such as dissolves and fades, as well as special film exposures, a special printer is used, interlocking a camera and projector. On raw stock, each frame is rephotographed. By changing lenses, film speeds, and light, any number of visual effects can be realized.

Optical sound track. The common method of putting sound on film today, achieved by various densities of light passing through a beam photographed on film to a photoelectric cell in the projector.

Outtake. Those edited pieces of film that are not included in the final cut of the film.

Pan shot. A shot that is made from a camera pivoting horizontally from a fixed axis, usually a tripod.

Persistence of vision. The split second after-image retained by the eye when a single moving picture frame is brightly projected on a screen. The effect allows for the illusion of continuous motion.

Pixel. A small particle of color and brightness on a video or computer screen. Screens with a strong density of pixels have a more sharply defined resolution.

Principal photography. The phase of production during which the major cinematography is completed. It is the shooting period between preproduction and postproduction.

Process cinematography. Any camera work shot with the aid of *blue screen, rear* or *front projection,* or other technical help.

Producer. The person or group in charge of the film project from its beginnings. The prime responsibility of the producer is to obtain funding for the film and hire people to be associated with it. The title is generic and has many dimensions, depending on the film project.

Production designer. Formerly called the *art director,* this person, together with the director, creates the physical look of the film in terms of its sets. Also oversees the coordination of the costumes, color design, and other visual elements.

Realism. A visual and dramatic approach to film that presents an unvarnished world. Its subjects are often depicted as living in a unadorned world with the harsher aspects of life presented frankly. The camera choices reinforce the raw look and message of the film. Realism is not a fixed style, but has various stylistic shadings to fit the movie.

Rear projection. The projection of an image onto a translucent screen from behind the main subject. The effect places the subject in front of any desired environment. Typically, the view through the back window of a car in a movie was rear projection.

Release print. The print that has been approved for distribution in theaters.

Reverse shot. A shot that reverses the field of view from the previous shot. When photographing a conversation, alternating shots usually are taken from angles that roughly approximate the previous ones.

Rough cut. Sometimes called the *director's cut,* this is a version of the film achieved by the editor and the director which approximates the final version, but without interference from the studio or producers.

Scene. Although it can entail only a single shot, a scene is normally a series of shots presenting a unified piece of dramatic action in one location. Most scenes contain some sort of dramatic arc.

Segue. A visual or sound transition from one scene to the next.

Semiology. The formal study of signs and their systems. In cinema, the terminology of the approach is seen as especially necessary because of the unique way film communicates.

Sequence. Usually used as the designation for a series of scenes that have some unifying element. The term can be helpful in pointing out a section of a film.

Set dressing. The placement of all of the specific details on a set—furniture, lamp fixtures, dishes, etc.

Setup. The coordination of the camera and lighting with the action of a scene before shooting. The setup is a time consuming operation requiring much planning between the film director and the director of photography.

Shooting script. The final screenplay set to be shot, with detailed shot selection.

Short lens. Any lens with less than 25mm focal length.

Shot. The basic photographed unit in movies, one continuously exposed piece of film. The word is at times used interchangeably with *take.* A take is any one of several photographed versions of the same shot, some of which will be discarded.

Slow motion.   A visual effect achieved in the camera or with an optical printer that is achieved by producing a greater number of frames per second than the projection rate (24 fps).

Sound design.   A term now used to describe a comprehensive and integrated approach taken toward film sound, including all elements of sound effects, dialogue, and music.

Sound editor.   The person who edits either the sound effects track or the music track.

Special effects (SPFX).   A inclusive term that refers to any *optical, mechanical,* or *digital* effects that are not part of normal shooting procedures and that demand special expertise.

Steadicam®.   A patented camera support system that facilitates smooth and flexible movement of a camera through space by a single camera operator with relative ease.

Storyboard.   A series of drawings by an artist to help filmmakers inexpensively visualize possible shot compositions, dramatic action, and camera movement, similar to a comic strip.

Straight cut.   A cut free from any optical manipulation, simply one shot affixed to the following.

Swish pan.   A very rapid pan shot that creates blurred images. Often used as a transitional device or to reflect the psychological reality of a character.

Sync.   Short for *synchronization*. A **sync track** is sound recorded precisely with the picture.

Take.   As a verb, the act of shooting a single *shot*. As a noun, the result of it. Directors will require many takes of an action or dramatic performance, searching for the best version for inclusion in the *rough cut*.

Telephoto lens.   A very long lens, usually one with a focal length greater than 200mm, that has the effect of flattening out the planes in the frame while bringing in more closely the primary subject.

Tilt shot.   A shot obtained when the camera records while moving in a vertical direction from a fixed axis.

Tracking shot.   Not unlike a *dolly shot* in effect, but the camera is mounted on a wheeled platform designed to move on tracks. The tracks are laid down, often over an uneven surface, to make the movement as smooth and predictable as possible.

Transitional device.   Any optical method such as a *wipe* or *fade* that moves the visual action of the story from one scene to the next.

Traveling matte.   A sophisticated process whereby separate images are matted together forming a *composite* picture. This version of the matte process allows for movement in one or both of the images, thus achieving a sense of a singular reality, despite the elements being originally photographed separately.

Two-shot.   A shot composition that takes in two principal players.

Voiceover (VO).   The stylistic device of putting a narrator's voice over the pictures. The monologue is often used in a classic storytelling mode, or to reveal the inner thought of a character.

Wide-angle lens.   A lens with a focal lens of less than 20mm, resulting in a distorted depth relationship and exaggerated image.

Wild track.   A track produced by the production sound recorder, which is not in *sync* with the pictures but that may be useful in some other phase of the *sound design*.

Wipe.   A moving horizontal cut (most often) which brings on one shot as the other is removed.

Workprint.   The working copy of the film footage that the editor uses while putting the *final cut* version together.

Zoom lens.   A lens with a variable focal length allowing a continuous and smooth magnification effect. Because of its easy adjustment to suit rapidly changing conditions, it is a favored lens of documentarians engaged in photography requiring a safe distance from their subject.

INDEX

Numbers in **bold** are illustrations.